# DESIGNING GOVERNMENT

# Designing Government

## From Instruments to Governance

Edited by

PEARL ELIADIS,
MARGARET M. HILL,
AND MICHAEL HOWLETT

McGill-Queen's University Press
Montreal & Kingston · London · Ithaca

© McGill-Queen's University Press 2005
ISBN 0-7735-2844-X (cloth)
ISBN 0-7735-2845-8 (paper)

Legal deposit first quarter 2005
Bibliothèque nationale du Québec

Printed in Canada on acid-free paper that is 100% ancient forest free (100% post-consumer recycled), processed chlorine free.

McGill-Queen's University Press acknowledges the support of the Policy Research Initiative in the publication of this book, as well as the support of the Canada Council for the Arts for our publishing program. We also acknowledge the financial support of the Government of Canada through the Book Publishing Industry Development Program (BPIDP) for our publishing activities.

**Library and Archives Canada Cataloguing in Publication**

Designing government: from instruments to governance / edited by Pearl Eliadis, Margaret M. Hill and Michael Howlett

Includes bibliographical references.
ISBN 0-7735-2844-X (bound). – ISBN 0-7735-2845-8 (pbk.)

1. Public administration. 2. Political planning. I. Eliadis, F., Pearl
II. Hill, Margaret M., 1964– III. Howlett, Michael, 1955–

JF1525.P6D48 2005          351
C2004-905641-7

This book was typeset by Dynagram Inc. in 10/12 Sabon.

# Contents

# Contributors

HANS TH.A. BRESSERS is professor of Policy Studies and Environmental Policy at the University of Twente in the Netherlands and Scientific Director of the Center for Clean Technology and Environmental Policy of that university. He is also an independent scientific member of the Commission on Sustainable Development of the Dutch Social-Economic Council (SER). He has published over two hundred articles, chapters, reports, papers and books (both in Dutch and in English) on policy instruments, implementation, evaluation and policy networks, mostly in reference to environmental policies

PEARL ELIADIS is a lawyer and Chief Knowledge Officer at The J.W. McConnell Family Foundation (Montreal). Before that, she was Senior Research Director of the Policy Research Initiative (Privy Council Office) and Director, Policy and Education at the Ontario Human Rights Commission. Her research interests include governance and human rights and development, including four UN missions in Rwanda. She co-edited *International Human Rights Law: Theory and Practice* (1992) with Irwin Cotler, and has edited and authored numerous reports and articles.

NEIL GUNNINGHAM is a lawyer and interdisciplinary social scientist who specialises in safety, health and environmental regulation. He currently holds Professorial Research appointments in the Regulatory Institutions Network, Research School of Social Sciences, and in the

School of Resources, Environment and Society, at the ANU. His books include *Leaders and Laggards: Next Generation Environment Regulation* (with Sinclair, 2002), *Shades of Green: Business, Regulation and Environment* (with Kagan and Thornton, 2003), and *Smart Regulation: Designing Environmental Policy,* (with Grabosky, 1998).

MARGARET M. HILL is Director, Research and Analysis, at Infrastructure Canada. She has worked at the Privy Council Office and Environment Canada, and was formerly a lecturer in comparative public policy and public administration at the University of Exeter (U.K.) and visiting professor at the School of Public Administration, Carleton University, Ottawa. She has authored several books, articles and reports on government regulation, the tools of government and environment policy in North America. The views she expresses in this volume are her own and do not necessarily reflect those of Infrastructure Canada or the Government of Canada.

JOHN HOORNBEEK earned his Ph.D. from the University of Pittsburgh in 2004. He has more than 20 years experience working on policy-related issues in public sector settings, and has published research in peer-reviewed public policy journals. His past work experience includes assignments with the U.S. Environmental Protection Agency, the U.S. Congress, the State of Wisconsin, and now the National Environmental Services Center (NESC) at West Virginia University. The views he expresses do not necessarily reflect the views of his current or past employers.

MICHAEL HOWLETT is Burnaby Mountain Chair in the Department of Political Science at Simon Fraser University, and specializes in public policy analysis, Canadian political economy, and Canadian resource and environmental policy. Professor Howlett is co-author of *Studying Public Policy (2003 & 1995), In* Search of Sustainability (2001), *The Political Economy of Canada* (1999 & 1992) and *Canadian Natural Resource and Environmental Policy* (1997 & 2005). He has edited several books, and his articles have been published in numerous professional journals in Canada, the United States, Europe, Brazil, New Zealand and Australia.

PIERRE ISSALYS has taught administrative law, social security law, legislative science and legal theory at the Faculty of Law at Université Laval since 1978. His publications include *Unemployment Insurance Benefits* (with G. Watkins, 1977), *L'action gouvernementale* (with D. Lemieux, 2nd ed. 2002), *Loi et règlement* (with P. Garant, 1980) and *Répartir les normes* (2001), as well as contributions to several collected works (*e.g. Aux frontières du juridique,*1993; *L'amour des lois,* 1996). He is currently writing a *Précis de science législative,* and is researching issues related to "government by contract" and public participation.

BRIDGET HUTTER is Peacock Chair of Risk Management at the London School of Economics and Co-Director of the Centre for Analysis of Risk and Regulation (CARR). Her research interests span sociology of regulation and risk management; the regulation of economic life with particular reference to regulatory enforcement and corporate responses to regulation, and the social control of organisations. She is the author of numerous publications on regulation and is currently examining recent trends in regulating risk in economic life and in the corporate regulation of risk. She is also the Editor of the British Journal of Sociology.

RÉJEAN LANDRY is professor at the Department of Management of the Faculty of Business at Laval University (Quebec City). He is a Chair on Knowledge Transfer and Innovation (funded by the Canadian Health Services Research Foundation and the Canadian Institute of Health Research) and has been a Fellow of the Royal Society of Canada since 1999. He has published extensively on public policies, innovation and knowledge transfer. Dr. Landry is also the head the Réseau du Réseau Innovation Network (RIN)

RODERICK MACDONALD is F.R. Scott Professor of Constitutional and Public Law at McGill University, where he was Dean of Law (1984–1989). He chaired the Task Force on Access to Justice for the Ministère de la justice du Québec (1989–1991), served as Director of the Law and Society Programme of the Canadian Institute for Advanced Research (1989–1994), participated in the Ontario Civil Justice Review (1995), and was founding President of the Law Commission of Canada (1997–2000). He was elected to the Royal Society of Canada in 1996, and was named a Fellow of the Pierre Trudeau Foundation in 2004.

LAURENCE J. O'TOOLE, JR. is Robert T. and Margaret Hughes Golembiewski Professor of Public Administration and head of the Department of Public Administration and Policy, School of Public and International Affairs, University of Georgia, USA. He is also appointed Professor of Comparative Sustainability Policy Studies in the Faculty of Twente University, The Netherlands, where he works in the Center of Clean Technology and Environmental Policy. He has published extensively on public policy, policy implementation and public management, particularly in complex institutional settings.

B. GUY PETERS is Maurice Falk Professor American Politics at the University of Pittsburgh. He also holds the position of Professor II at the University of Bodo (Norway) and Senior Research Fellow at the Institute of Public Management of the Catholic University of Leuven (Belgium). Among his recent publications are *The Handbook of Public Administration* (co-edited with Jon Pierre), *The Quest for Control: Politicization of Public Administration* (co-edited with Jon Pierre), and *Institutional Theory in Political Science*, 2nd edition.

MICHAEL J. PRINCE is Lansdowne Professor of Social Policy at the University of Victoria. From 1997 to 2005 he served as Associate Dean and as Dean of the Faculty of Human and Social Development. Areas of research interest in Canadian social policy include federalism, pension reform and retirement, public budgeting and disability studies. His article in *Changing the Rules: Canadian Regulatory Regimes Institutions* (co-edited with B. Doern, M. Hill and R. Schultz) (U of T Press 1999) introduced the concept of "civic regulation" to the instrument choice literature in Canada.

SEAN REHAAG is a doctoral candidate at the University of Toronto's Faculty of Law. His academic interests relate primarily to migration law. His ongoing doctoral work focuses on the interaction between multiple overlapping state and extra-state legal frameworks that aim to regulate the movement of persons across state borders.

ARTHUR RINGELING is professor of Public Administration at Erasmus University Rotterdam (The Netherlands). His inaugural lecture was on the subject of government tools or instruments (*De instrumenten van het beleid, Alphen aan den Rijn*, 1983), a subject that has influenced much of his work, and which underscores the features of governmental tools beyond "instrumental" factors, extending to political, administrative, societal, cultural, philosophical, and juridical aspects. He has authored or edited fifteen books and more than 100 articles and reports on public policy, evaluation and public administration.

STEPHEN J. TOOPE is President of the Pierre Elliott Trudeau Foundation. On leave from the Faculty of Law, McGill University, where he has worked since 1987, and of which is a former Dean, Professor Toope's scholarly interests cover the full range of public international law. His current research focuses upon the bases of legal obligation in international society. Prof. Toope served as a law clerk to the Rt. Hon. Brian Dickson, Chief Justice of Canada. Professor Toope has served as board chair and member of various organizations promoting human rights and international development.

MICHAEL J. TREBILCOCK, is University Professor and Professor of Law at the University of Toronto. In 1987 he was elected a Fellow of the Royal Society of Canada and was awarded the Owen Prize in 1989 by the Foundation for Legal Research for his book, *The Common Law of Restraint of Trade*. He serves as Director of the Law and Economics Programme at the University of Toronto. In 1999, Professor Trebilcock received an Honorary Doctorate in Laws from McGill University and was awarded the Canada Council Molson Prize in the Humanities and Social Sciences. In the same year he was elected an Honorary Foreign Fellow of the American Academy of Arts and Sciences. In 2003, he received an Honorary Doctorate in Law from the Law Society of Upper Canada.

FRÉDÉRIC VARONE is professor of Political Science at the Catholic University of Louvain (Belgium) and co-director of the *Association universitaire de recherche sur l'action publique*. He specializes in comparative policy analysis, program evaluation and public service reform. Professor Varone's 1998 book, *Le choix des instruments des politiques publiques,* was published in Berne by Paul Haupt, and his numerous articles include "Les instruments de la politique énergétique: analyse comparée du Canada et des Etats-Unis", Canadian J. Political Science, XXXIV (1): 3–28, March 2001 and "Energy Efficiency: The Challenges of Policy Design", Energy Policy, 29 (8): 615–629, June 2001).

KERNAGHAN WEBB is an Adjunct Research Professor with the Carleton School of Public Policy and Administration, and the Department of Law, a Sessional Adjunct at Queen's University's School of Policy Studies, an Honorary Lecturer at the University of Dundee's Centre of Energy, Petroleum and Mineral Law and Policy, and Senior Legal Policy Advisor and Chief of Research with the Canadian Office of Consumer Affairs. Dr. Webb has written and published extensively on regulatory and compliance issues, voluntary codes and interest groups.

# DESIGNING GOVERNMENT

# Introduction

PEARL ELIADIS, MARGARET M. HILL,
AND MICHAEL HOWLETT[1]

In 1982 the Economic Council of Canada published the seminal study *The Choice of Governing Instrument*, by Michael Trebilcock, Robert Prichard, Douglas Hartle, and Donald Dewees.[2] This study captured the essence of earlier groundbreaking insights by distinguished scholars such as Harold Lasswell, Murray Edelman, Theodore Lowi, and Lester Salamon into the actions of governments.[3] It provided a concise conceptual touchstone for further investigations into the nature of government action and played an important role, in Canada and elsewhere, both in catalyzing the development of what is now generally called the "instrument-choice" perspective on public policy and administration and in helping to sensitize policy practitioners to the merits and demerits of different forms of public action.

The year 2002 marked the twentieth anniversary of the publication of *The Choice of Governing Instrument,* and the idea for the present volume, *Designing Government: From Instruments to Governance,* had its origins in a casual observation about the significance of this milestone for Canadian public-policy studies. As often happens, subsequent conversations between the co-editors about how the instrument-choice perspective has shaped the understanding of public policy and administration over the last two decades led to a research project that culminated in a conference and this book.

From its early phases, the project was championed by the federal government's Policy Research Initiative (PRI), using the twentieth anniversary of *The Choice of Governing Instrument* in an appropriately instrumental way: to bring together some of the original contributors to the instrument-choice perspective, along with a second generation of scholars and practitioners influenced by their work. PRI and Justice Canada (Quebec Regional Office) co-hosted an international conference in Montreal in September 2002 to assess and reflect upon both the contributions and the limitations of the instrument-choice perspective in relation to the theory and practice of public policy and administration.

Building on the conference results, the present volume offers both a retrospective and a forward-looking approach to what Margaret Hill – in her chapter, "Tools as Art" – calls the "expressive content" of instrument choice. The volume seeks to trace the evolution of the instrument-choice perspective and the insights it offers scholars and policy practitioners, as well as its influence on a wide swath of writing in many countries in public policy and public administration, political science, economics, and increasingly, public law. The chapters in the collection address a number of current issues related to the instrument-choice approach. Most significantly, taken together, they argue for the need to link systematically, and in an integrated, multidisciplinary way, instrument choice with governance and the broader contemporary challenges of designing government.

## CURRENT ISSUES IN INSTRUMENT-CHOICE THEORY

The development of an instrument-choice perspective is relatively well documented: At its core, it is rooted in a commitment to understanding policy formulation and implementation, as well as the policy-making process itself, by focusing on instruments of government action rather than on policies and programs. By "instruments" we mean the range of instruments spanning law and regulation, subsidies and grants, organization and privatization, and information dissemination and taxation. The proposition that "some forms of public action are more likely to address successfully certain public problems or social issues than others" lies at the heart of how governments approach choices about instruments.[4] Indeed, governments have struggled for years to evaluate which instruments are more likely to achieve their ends, and studies of their choices have aimed both at helping to set out the parameters of the choices to be made and at improving the chances of success.

Early, or first-generation, studies in the instrument-choice tradition tended to focus on the relative merits of individual instruments, with the majority of writing emanating from the fields of political science and economics. The focus was on substantive instruments – that is, those instruments that seek to effect changes in how governments address public issues or deliver services, including classic command-and-control regulation, public enterprises, and subsidies, to name a few. In Canada a critical step in the evolution of the instrument-choice perspective was the 1982 study *The Choice of Governing Instrument,* mentioned above. As noted, the study built on earlier work but arguably offered a more developed and sophisticated conceptual foundation.

The next generation of studies on the instrument-choice approach, as Michael Howlett describes it in his chapter, is located in the larger literature on governance, as indeed it must be – that is, in the recognition that governments achieve public purposes by "steering" diverse, complex networks of public and private actors, institutions, ideas, and policy instruments. This reflects important changes in the tools available to governments and in government predilections for their use, changes that are discussed in a great number of important recent academic writings, including Lester Salamon's 2002 opus *Tools of Government.* As Salamon has expressed it, governance has moved – or is moving – from reliance on vertical, or hierarchically based, instruments to network-based regulation and the adoption of new indirect tools of government.

This relationship between instruments and governance is an important fulcrum for the present collection. While several chapters employ varying definitions of governance, framing the concept slightly differently, several common themes emerge. These themes in turn point to the still-emerging next generation of instrument choices. Kernaghan Webb, for instance, addresses the intersection of instruments and governance in his chapter, "Sustainable Governance in the Twenty-First Century: Moving beyond Instrument Choice." He adopts a view of governance as "the sum of the many ways individuals and institutions, public and private, manage their common affairs" and assesses the types of instruments now available to governments in the implementation of their plans and programs. Bridget Hutter describes the move from government to governance in her chapter, "Risk and Regulation," as embracing "a broad mix of state and nonstate sources of regulation and the use of various instruments that combine incentives and sanctions and that appeal to varying deterrence and social-responsibility motivations among the regulated."

As both these authors and the other contributors to this volume attest, it is impossible to think analytically or sensibly about governance without also thinking about the tools or instruments that make it a practical reality. The reverse is true as well, in that the emerging focus of instrument choice is not so much the typologies or narrow inquires into efficiency or technical effectiveness that characterized "first-generation" thinking but rather a perspective that helps us to understand how to best "steer" complex networks of actors toward a form of governance that is both sustainable and legitimate.

The emphasis on legitimacy is a recurring theme in the chapters comprising this book, a theme that straddles the relationship between the integrity of policy design and instrument choice, on the one hand, and the shift to a governance focus, on the other.

## INSTRUMENT CHOICE FROM A PRACTITIONER'S PERSPECTIVE

One of the early steps in the development of this volume was the research conference "Instrument Choice in Global Democracies," organized by the federal government's Policy Research Initiative and the Quebec Regional Office of Justice Canada. More than one hundred scholars and senior government officials convened at the Faculty of Law, McGill University, in the early autumn of 2002. A general consensus emerged on a number of key issues related to the current "state of the art" in the instrument-choice field. It was agreed that:

1 Solely economic perspectives provide an inadequate basis for instrument choices, which should be primarily a function of governance criteria rather than only (or even primarily) determined by cost, technical effectiveness, or economic efficiency
2 All instruments, particularly those designed and implemented outside of the legislative process, have important repercussions for the legitimacy and accountability of public action
3 The legitimacy of particular choices is bound up with political, legal, ethical, programmatic, social, and economic factors that operate across both domestic and global dimensions
4 The debate must move from the level of individual instrument choice to that of instrument mixes, thus recognizing that instruments are context-sensitive and rarely, if ever, designed or implemented in isolation
5 Governance strategies and frameworks are needed to ensure both legitimacy and optimality in instrument-mix design and implementation.

In addition to these issues, participants highlighted the need for the next generation of work on instrument choice to investigate further the implication of the push for greater implementation of instruments beyond the usual suspects – that is, beyond regulations, taxation, and spending. As Pierre Issalys and many other contributors to this book note, over the past two decades there has been a virtual explosion in the knowledge of, and types of, instruments and instrument mixes used by governments, which has implications for accountability, legitimacy, and other facets of governance. So far these implications have not captured the attention they deserve from scholars or policy makers.

For many countries within the Organization for Economic Cooperation and Development (OECD), the practitioner's interest in evaluating instruments is relatively recent. Despite the wide range of earlier theoretical work, there has been a flurry of activity, especially in the last two decades, aimed at improving the knowledge framework for evaluating instruments and at providing better knowledge about how they contribute to government performance overall.

Nonetheless, knowledge about how instruments perform relative to each other, especially in different governance contexts, is generally still limited. Public servants complain that they are ill-equipped to assess the relative merits of instrument choices and that more knowledge is needed, especially with respect to the effectiveness of "innovative" instruments and instrument mixes such as voluntary codes, partnerships, and co-regulatory instruments. Basic research questions remain unanswered, including which instruments are most likely to work, either singly or in combination, and how instruments interact both with public and private actors and institutions and with past policy choices. More basically, the focus on evaluation and efficiency across different, separate instruments may – paradoxically – diminish the value of the fundamental objective of good instrument choices: good governance.[5]

For example, alternative service-delivery instruments such as contracting-out (or "managing-out") were favourites of the New Public Management era because they encouraged competition and were said to decrease the role and size of direct government, supporting the popular principle that governments should "steer, not row." However, steering may be entirely inappropriate in some circumstances: The literature is full of examples where rowing would have been a better option. Instrument failures may occur when potential negative consequences – such as loss of legitimacy or unintended or unexpected spillovers to other sectors and policy areas – are overlooked in the rush to develop cost-efficient alternatives or effective policy strategies.

At its worst, the abandonment of rowing in favour of steering can damage the policy objectives that policy makers set out to achieve. For example, health and safety were casualties in Ontario's 2000 Walkerton tragedy.[6] The 2004 Canadian "ad-scam" scandals offer another example: There was a loud and sustained outcry in Canada, especially in the media, following the release of a report by the Auditor General of Canada that alleged the frittering away of tens of millions of dollars through contracts to various advertising companies and strategy firms in exchange for poorly documented services. These services were in aid of the ultimately successful federal campaign for Canadian unity at the time of the 1995 Quebec referendum on secession from Canada. In terms of the themes of this volume, it is noteworthy that the proclaimed "effectiveness" of the federal government's advertising campaign did not carry a good deal of weight with the public and resulted in the loss of public support following a perceived loss of legitimacy.

Another feature of the current environment is the attempt to "grow" the number of useful new policy instruments and tools in order to move away from "command-and-control" instruments, notably regulation. This is part of the view that regulations are inherently problematic, expensive, and burdensome. Although this concern has been the primary driver of inquiry into instrument choice in the Federal Government of Canada, to take one example, little is actually known about whether these views are correct. There is a great deal of literature on "traditional" instruments, such as regulations, spending, and taxation, but very little on their relative effectiveness and even less on their effectiveness in relation to innovative instruments and instrument mixes.

One criticism resulting from the explosion of new instruments is the lack of information about their effectiveness and the consequent loss of transparency – and thus loss of public accountability – associated with "network" governance structures, with related concerns about erosion of the rule of law. Stepan Wood, for example, a Canadian legal scholar writing about voluntary standards and environmental policy, observes that technical standards can usurp public accountability and possibly the public interest by ousting broader policy debate. As Wood has argued:

[T]he technologies of contemporary state environmental regulation embody, to a significant extent, the same managerialist tendencies ... to obscure the stakes, struggles, and repressions of environmental politics, relying heavily on technical expertise, detailed, mundane, repetitive techniques of measurement, monitoring, calculation, assessment, inspection, and so on, and relying increasingly on private-market dynamics. While EMSs [environmental management systems] are a particularly clear example of these tendencies, state environmental regulation shares the same characteristics to a significant degree.

Viewed as governmental technologies, then, EMSs and standardization render environmental management a matter of technical expertise, organizational routine, and market preference, contributing to the expulsion of a set of environmental and economic issues from the political domain.[7]

In his chapter, Neil Gunningham addresses this classic instrument-choice conundrum through the lens of standard setting and the environment, characterizing the diversification of instruments, especially voluntary ones, as "regulatory reconfiguration" rather than as a "retreat of the regulatory state." A related strategy is seen in the context of risk-based regulation by Bridget Hutter in her chapter, "Risk and Regulation." She points out that in the UK, among other examples, there has been increased attention to this form of regulation as a strategy to ensure both public accountability and regulatory flexibility.

But many writers in the collection, including Michael Howlett, Neil Gunningham, Hans Bressers and Laurence O'Toole, and Réjean Landry and Frédéric Varone, are especially interested in understanding relative performance, especially that of the newer instruments that rely on nongovernmental actors. Thus studies have begun to focus on understanding the shift from what Arthur Ringeling in his chapter terms "vertical instruments" (command and control being the classic example) to "horizontal instruments" (partnerships and coordinated national planning, for example) as well as on the drivers and contexts of instrument choices, as distinct from the features and effectiveness of individual instruments. This is reflected in countries such as Canada by attempts to deploy horizontal instruments as substitutes for traditional (and presumptively resource-intensive) vertical ones. But evaluative knowledge about how other, newer instruments perform individually, let alone in relation to or in combination with each other, is limited, as such evaluation has only recently been tackled on a large scale in North America.

The governance implications of new rapidly proliferating instruments and sources of governance (or networked governance) include a move away from politically accountable institutions, such as legislatures, and toward these new sites of governance, with the potential for a loss of legitimacy, transparency, and accountability.[8] The hidden side of government has generated demands for more transparent government action through "reregulation," or as some have put it, "regulatory shifts." In Canada, for example, there have been extensive efforts within various policy frameworks to ensure the legitimacy and accountability of legislative tools, including regulatory impact-analysis statements and tightly structured mechanisms designed to guarantee accountability and compliance with constitutional rights and freedoms. However, because the rapidly proliferating group of other, innovative instruments has no legislative basis, it has not been subject to the same criteria. Indeed, the Federal Government of Canada does not even keep an inventory of such instruments, although attempts have been made to develop a typology.

Another feature of the emerging focus on governance is the growing awareness that instrument choices cannot be reduced to a matching of economic means and ends. One strategy for addressing this concern is to look directly at the components of good governance, including not only legitimacy, but also other aspects, such as "sustainability."

This last topic is addressed by Kernaghan Webb in his chapter. He points out that environmental policy has been especially prolific in generating industry-led standards and other voluntary instruments, especially in the area of environmental management. Several important advantages are said to flow from these alternative instruments. Both federal and provincial Canadian governments want the benefit of industry expertise and also want industry participants to be more involved in the development of rules to control industry practices through consultation processes and working groups. There is a belief that industry-led approaches will create greater industry buy-in and that pressure from customers and shareholders will support greater compliance than would a government-imposed regime. Self-regulatory approaches may also reduce compliance and enforcement costs for government. To be "sustainable," instrument-based innovations must, as detailed in a series of criteria, or standards, proposed by Webb (chapter 10):

- Work particularly well against a backdrop of conventional governance institutions, rule instruments, and processes
- Recognize the value of having multiple centres of authority and responsibility address the same policy context
- Frequently include both policy-development and policy-implementation elements
- Often harness (or attempt to harness) citizen, consumer, community, nongovernmental-organization (NGO), and industry energies to address a particular policy problem (not just fear of government-imposed legal liability)
- Explicitly acknowledge the value of multiactor collaborations, particularly those that cross the boundaries between public, private, and third sectors
- Work under the assumption that a certain amount of rivalrous institutional, rule-instrument, and process friction is valuable as a check-and-balance mechanism and as a means to stimulate creative tension among initiatives and actors.

Notably, cost benefits, efficiency, and effectiveness, the main concerns of "first-generation" instrument theorists, do not make this list, at least not among the "high-level" set of instrument-choice criteria.

## THE CANADIAN EXPERIENCE

While this volume contains contributions from a number of OECD countries, Canada's experience in the area of instrument choice provides an illustration of how the instrument-choice perspective has evolved. As Margaret Hill observes, "the study and practice of public policy and administration have not been conducted with sufficient attention to history," at least not in Canada, where the instrument-choice perspective has had unique resonance for both scholars and policy makers for whom understanding and explaining the policy process and improving governance are essential.

Over the years, the principal driver of instrument-choice study in Canada, particularly in the federal government, has been deregulation. In the 1970s and early 1980s, growing inflation and a reduced capacity for sustained growth generated concern among Canadian governments about whether laws and regulations could successfully address these phenomena and whether they had led to a web of counterproductive hyper-regulation. (Of course, as Bridget Hutter notes in her chapter, this development was not unique to Canada.) There was skepticism about the value of these traditional regulatory mechanisms and increasing interest in the search for alternatives.

The Economic Council of Canada commissioned several studies in the mid-1970s to assess the impact of the regulatory environment. One of them, *The Choice of Governing Instrument,* was primarily concerned both with testing the "axiomatic principle" that instruments are chosen for their technical or instrumental efficiency and with developing alternatives to this principle. The authors rejected the efficiency principle and, in its place, proposed an alternative hypothesis of what has become known as "politically rational instrument choice." While some of the forecasts made by the authors have not been borne out by experience, *The Choice of Governing Instrument* nonetheless had an important historical impact by explicitly locating the exercise of choice not in technical efficiency but in rational choice.

By the 1980s several significant reforms in OECD countries sought to step up deregulation and to encourage the identification and increased use of other instruments. However, as late as 1992, Canada's Sub-Committee on Regulation and Competitiveness of the Standing Committee on Finance observed a clear preference for regulations over nonlegislative tools of government. Several initiatives took place during the 1990s to expand the range and use of other instruments and to force policy makers to think in a more inclusive way about how governments choose instruments. These initiatives are too numerous to set out in detail here but are well described in the OECD's 2002 *Review of Regulatory Reform in Canada*.[9] Nonetheless, two observations are relevant to the present volume's purposes. First, these initiatives resulted in attempts to move from regulation-based instruments to other kinds of instruments. Second, policy makers quite reasonably responded to these attempts by seeking information about what these other instruments are, how well they work, and how risky they are likely to be. However, the literature dealt only sparingly with quantitative data arising from qualitative comparisons of the rise and use of particular forms of instrument-specific aspects of risk and governance.

One result of the push for alternatives to legislative tools was an effort, at least at the federal level, to try to use horizontal instruments (partnerships and other forms of participatory governance) in lieu of vertical tools (especially law-based ones). This was no doubt inspired, at least in part, by the OECD's exhortations about the positive effects of alternatives to regulation, including a reduction in regulatory and resource burdens on government, increased likelihood of compliance if industry has participated in developing the standards, and improved flexibility in coping with technological, cultural, and behavioural changes among regulated entities. The OECD further notes that these aspects may be especially useful in dealing with issues that have international/extraterritorial dimensions, in which case diversity among the regulated entities is greater.

The push to consider alternatives to regulation-based instruments is now a standard feature of Canadian regulatory reform policies. According to the OECD's 2002 report, Canada has made positive strides by decreasing "regulatory inflation" and by improving transparency and accountability through the publication of regulatory impact-analysis statements. However, there is little evidence that these developments have resulted in less complexity or improved compliance. It is just as likely that there has been a shift from legislative to nonlegislative rules and that the costs and complexity now lie elsewhere. There is also an important difference between a requirement to consider alternatives to legislative tools and the assumption that these alternatives are inherently superior – a proposition for which there is a great deal of theoretical support but little authoritative evidence.

The result in Canada has been an oppositional, "either-or" relationship between law-based and other instruments. The impact of setting up choices in this binary way has been a bifurcation of knowledge streams. A great deal of procedural and inventory information is available about legislative instruments (for instance, about regulatory impact analysis, about how many statutes and regulations there are, about the precise steps one must go through with respect to a regulatory matter, etc.), but little has been done to manage or document cross-cutting knowledge about how other kinds of instruments perform, how they are being used, or even the extent of their use, outside of sporadic and partial inventories or narrow project-based evaluative exercises.

The push to consider alternatives to regulations was reinforced most recently in Canada with the federal government's establishment of the External Advisory Committee on Smart Regulation. The committee was set up in 2003 "to develop a regulatory strategy for the 21st century" and to "recommend areas where government needs to redesign its regulatory approach to create and maintain a Canadian advantage."[10] The history of its development is worth mentioning. Immediately before the creation of the advisory committee, the Public Policy Forum, a leading Canadian policy think-tank, had called in a national newspaper for a "smart-regulation" initiative that would "rescind ... hundreds, and perhaps thousands, of regulations ... Smart regulation would ... open the door to the possible use of voluntary codes of conduct and self-regulation."[11] This vision epitomizes the near-messianic belief in Canada that the elimination of regulations (in the narrow sense) is the desired policy goal and that this will necessarily lead to an improved regulatory environment for business and citizens. The only added nuance from the Forum seemed to be that the ensuing improved regulatory environment would be populated by new, "smart" tools, developed and enforced by business or by other elements of society.

It is positive that the advisory committee's final report, released in September 2004, suggests both an inventory and an improved knowledge base for new instruments, as well as emphasizing sustainable development. The report also makes sensible suggestions about getting rid of rules that create competitive disadvantages in minor commercial matters (such as cheese content in certain snack foods). Otherwise, however, many of the old chestnuts of regulatory reform in Canada are repeated: the objective of reducing the "burden" of regulations on business (no evidence is provided, but the committee helpfully suggests that this would be a fruitful avenue of future research); the importance of markets; and a focus on "efficiency" and "effectiveness," with an emphasis on "protection." More troubling, attention to the rule of law, compliance with international law, and accountability to Parliament in relation to nonlegislative instruments (at least, those that are outside the purview of tribunals or similar adjudicative bodies) are barely mentioned in the committee's report.[13] It is both ironic and disappointing that, two decades after the first serious analysis of regulation and the other instruments of government in Canada (see Hill's chapter in this volume), the end result of the task force's work is a report that falls short. It fails to reflect the increased sophistication of the theory and practice of regulation compared to the 1970s and 1980s as well as the many lessons learned across the OECD world over the past decade or so about the fundamental connections between regulation and the other instruments of government with governance. In short, while the report purports to set out a regulatory strategy for the twenty-first century, it is hampered by its own preoccupation with the knowledge base of the latter decades of the twentieth century.

Although deregulation and "smart-regulation" initiatives had led to awareness in Canada of the need to generate innovative knowledge about instruments, they have not yet led to a cross-cutting framework of evaluative knowledge. In short, systematic and comparative evaluations of instruments in Canada have been isolated and underfunded in the federal government, let alone among provincial governments, where studies and reports on the subject are nonexistent.

## STRUCTURE OF *DESIGNING GOVERNMENT*

As Dwight Waldo famously reminded us, the history of public administration and the ideas and leaders that have been part and parcel of this history are too often overlooked.[13] This volume seeks to make a small contribution to filling this gap through a retrospective and forward-looking reexamination of the value of the instrument-choice perspective as an analytically and practically useful way of thinking about government action.

At the same time, the collection casts new light on how the instrument-choice perspective has itself matured and, in particular, on how it has in equal measure forced and allowed scholars and policy makers to reconsider the nature of the choice process. This development in turn has broadened their original preoccupations with single instruments, turning their attention to instrument mixes and, most important, to the broader questions about governance, such as globalization of the policy process, legitimacy, risk management, and the dynamics of policy and program reform.

The chapters in this collection explore a number of interrelated themes. First and foremost, all consciously recognize the inadequacy of solely economic perspectives on policy design and implementation. Together the chapters conceptualize instrument choice as having intrinsically intertwined political, legal, ethical, programmatic, socially constructed, and economic dimensions. Various chapters also point to the new or at least revised motivations and principal questions driving the instrument-choice perspective.

One such theme is that in their design and implementation, instruments are context-sensitive and profoundly tied to governance, both domestic and international. Different policy tools invoke different governance regimes; thus diverse ideas, institutions, and policy actors, including non-governmental actors, are now all key elements in the dynamics of instrument choice, as are new genres of domestic and international instruments that continue to gain importance for policy makers around the globe. As a result, as B. Guy Peters emphasizes in this volume's conclusion, there is a pressing need to refine even further our understanding of both the interconnections between different tools and their regimes and the nature of the public problems they address and help to shape.

The book is divided into three parts. Part 1 addresses the "Origins and Evolution of the Tools Approach" from three vantage points. The first chapter, by Margaret Hill, examines the origins of the tools approach in Canada since the 1980s and the empirical situation on the ground for Canadian policy makers. Michael Howlett's contribution in chapter 2 widens the perspective by tracing the evolution of instrument-choice literature. He starts with an overview and inventory of policy tools, noting the existence of both the traditional "substantive" instruments governments use to affect the production and distribution of goods and services in society as well as those "procedural" instruments designed to affect policy processes. He also sets the groundwork for chapters appearing later in this volume by revealing the relationship of instruments to institutional styles and policy contexts. Finally, Michael Trebilcock – one of the authors of *The Choice of Governing Instrument* – provides a retrospective on the seminal 1982 study in chapter 3. He revisits his earlier work and places the issue of the choice of government instrument in the context of larger issues relating to policy change and stability.

Part 2 more closely examines the linkages between policy and instruments. Focused on "Form and Function: The Tools Approach to Policy Design," this part begins with an examination of the relationship between policy tools and policy problems. In chapter 4, B. Guy Peters and John Hoornbeeck examine what it is about specific social conditions that predispose policy makers to address certain kinds of "problems" using particular kinds of "solutions." So far this facet of instrument choice has been underexamined. The authors argue that the changeable and context-specific lens created by institutional and political cultures is often the driving force behind policy makers' choices of instruments. These macro-level examinations are complemented by the discussion presented in chapter 5 by Réjean Landry and Frédéric Varone, who examine the micro-level elements of the choices that are made to adopt particular instruments.

In chapter 6, Hans Bressers and Laurence O'Toole look at instrument mixes through the lens of policy-network analysis. They develop a set of hypotheses related to the interrelationships of policy instruments and policy actors, and they see a shift in governance from command-and-control strategies (notably legislative solutions) to "network-management" arrangements. Echoing the hypotheses of many of the contributors to this volume, they argue that these arrangements have the potential to improve policy making through citizen engagement by increasing the involvement of nongovernmental organizations and citizens in policy implementation and by improving transparency.

It is interesting to compare this structural theory of how to improve policy making (with its attendant consequences for policy design) with the more normative approach adopted by Pierre Issalys in chapter 7. Issalys points out in his provocative contribution that the primary role of legal-policy studies is to assess instruments from the perspective of legitimacy, or justification, by looking not so much at efficiency or effectiveness but at the rule of law and at political accountability and fairness, to name a few. Legitimacy thus becomes a guidepost for policy makers, as opposed to a constraint, as well as an important benchmark in the assessment of whether particular instruments actually improve governance.

Issalys's work is echoed by later contributions in part 3 of the book, especially by Roderick Macdonald and by Stephen Toope and Sean Rehaag, who present law as uniquely well placed to assure the justification and coherence of instrument choices by emphasizing the *institutional* context within which behaviours take place, with particular regard for the relationships between government, individuals, civil society, and markets as key channels for policy interventions. From this perspective, Pierre Issalys cites the work of Pierre Lascoumes, who views law "less as a constraint than as a resource," or "as a system of potentialities from which are deployed specific activities for the mobilization of rules."[14] Indeed, as the chapter by Toope and Rehaag suggests, state-centred perspectives on policy making, and consequently on the effectiveness and legitimacy of instrument choices, must instead be benchmarked against the burgeoning standards created by regional, intergovernmental, and international agreements and mechanisms. Legitimacy flows not only from domestic adherence to the rule of law, but also from the new rules imposed by globalization. Whether defined as the "end of geography" or as the rapid transborder integration of institutions and networks, globalization has a profound influence on instrument choice. Toope and Rehaag observe the growing influence of international and regional forces on instrument choices that are made in the national sphere. Echoing Issalys's work, they point to legitimacy in relation to the increasingly dense web of external sources of norms: continental policy approaches, international covenants and protocols, and trade agreements and other bilateral and multilateral instruments, to name a few. Governments are called on to harmonize (or at least to conciliate) internal instruments with international or regional agreements, such as trade agreements and human-rights covenants. Hence there is pressure on instruments to incorporate and reflect external norms or to adhere to framework regulations that ensure legal and policy coherence.

Arthur Ringeling's contribution in chapter 8 is an interesting example of how the process described by Issalys comes full circle to reflect political realities – a point made in 1982 in *The Choice of Governing Instrument* that Ringeling examines afresh with a governance twist in the European context. Ringeling notes that the relationship between government and other sectors is being reconstituted through numerous configurations and that all instrument choices are inherently governance-based, political choices.

Part 3 of the book, "From Instruments to Governance," is focused on the realm where instrument choice and governance intersect. The chapters in this part address an area of growing interest and a central theme of the research in this project, namely research on instrument mixes and their relationship to governance. The challenge for today's policy makers is to design effective governance strategies with respect to a huge range of policy tools, many of which are relatively new additions to the toolkit. In short, while the instrument-choice perspective as developed in the years after the publication of The *Choice of Governing Instrument* focused heavily on the regulatory sphere of government, it is incumbent now more than ever that it systematically venture into the terrain of governance and governance strategies. As the chapters in part 3 demonstrate, this is both the promise and the challenge for instrument-based policy design in the years ahead.

As the "instruments," or "tools," metaphor suggests, policy making is assessed as an instance of instrumental, or means-ends, logic: A tool is selected to fit the job at hand. In chapter 9, "The Swiss Army Knife of Governance," Roderick Macdonald critically examines this perspective by using the analogy of the multifaceted and flexible Swiss Army Knife. Since certain basic tools can be adapted to an infinity of uses, an abstract analysis of policy tools or instruments actually tells one very little about the nature of the exercise in which policy makers are engaged. The instrument-choice perspective is thus in danger of becoming a myopic attempt to abstract tools from the complex legal, social, and political contexts that created them.

Chapter 10 picks up a second yet related central subtheme in the area of governance, namely sustainability, and its relationship to the vitality and viability of systems of instruments and innovation. In this chapter, Kernaghan Webb provides a framework for assessing the wide range of potentially appropriate instruments that could be combined in a policy mix. He notes that instrument mixes tend to form "ecologies" that can sometimes ossify but that can also create the opportunity for a diversity of options that encourage innovation and greater flexibility in public policy. Although diversity may be perceived as negative in that it leads to overly complex rules (or too many rules), it can also offer a wider range of options that increase the adaptive capacity of our legal systems and of our social and economic structures.

In chapter 12, Bridget Hutter looks at the nature of risk and the manner in which instrument choices can be embedded in general strategies of risk management. Indeed, appropriate instrument choices have been explicitly linked to the potential for reduced litigation, a perspective that has attracted considerable interest in Canada among legal officials. As Hutter notes, however, while reducing risk is clearly an important policy-design objective, the research shows that institutional styles of risk management actually play a larger role in adverse outcomes than do "real" risks. In other words, how a particular institution has historically perceived and managed risk can be a better predictor of outcomes than an examination of the risk itself.

Institutional styles have had another consequence: The domination of an economics focus, especially in the regulation of commercial industries, has fostered a lopsided body of research and knowledge about instrument choice. In chapter 11, "Welfare State to Social Union: Shifting Choices of Governing Instruments, Intervention Rationales, and Governance Rules in Canadian Social Policy," Michael Prince builds on his earlier work to remind us of the oft-forgotten "other half" of the instrument-choice equation, namely the evolution of social-policy regulation in Canada.

Part 3 ends with Neil Gunningham's chapter on "Reconfiguring Environmental Regulation." Expanding on his earlier work in this area, Gunningham discusses the diversification of policy instruments designed to engage rather than deter regulatory targets. He deploys five analytical lenses through which to understand the new governance: reflexive regulation, regulatory pluralism, environmental partnerships, civil regulation, and participatory governance and "ecological modernization" (or the "green gold" hypothesis). Gunningham essentially updates the traditional economists' perspective, which regards market forces and government regulation (in its broad sense) as important means of changing behaviour through the provision of incentives.

In the conclusion, each of these themes is pulled together by B. Guy Peters, who outlines a future research inventory for policy-instrument studies. There has been progress in understanding the nature of instruments and their importance to the policy-formulation process, both for academics and for practitioners, as the genesis of this book demonstrates. If the instruments approach is to reach its potential, some of the key issues raised herein – globalization, multiple sites of governance, policy styles, and instrument mixes – will have to be addressed as part of the instrument-choice equation. Coping with the real, and increasing, complexity of policy poses fundamental challenges to legitimacy and good governance, raising questions about their relationship to our social and legal structures in an increasingly complex and interconnected world.

# PART ONE
# The Origins and Evolution of the Tools Approach

# 1

# Tools as Art:
# Observations on the Choice
# of Governing Instrument

MARGARET M. HILL

Tools are what make us human and allow us to build civilization; they make work possible, they make ideas possible.[1]

What makes a great painting great or a great piece of sculpture great? As students of art appreciate, "all study [of art], whether critical or historical, logically begins with the work of art itself" (Taylor 1981, ix). What makes the work great is its elegant mixture of *subject matter* and *expressive content* (ibid., 51).

Greatness is judged in many ways. A work of art may be considered great because it has "wow" power for visitors to a gallery. It may achieve the status of greatness because it has a profound, long-lasting impact on those who have "learned to look," or because it uniquely captures a time, an event, or an idea, or because it compels the viewer – or a society more generally – to think, to contemplate, or to do. Greatness is sometimes recognized only with the passage of time.

This chapter is about policy tools as art. It focuses on the seminal study *The Choice of Governing Instrument* by Michael Trebilcock, Robert Prichard, Douglas Hartle, and Donald Dewees. To borrow Taylor's terms, the immediate objective is to examine the subject matter of the study in order to set the context for the remainder of the volume's examination of the instrument-choice perspective. In addition, the chapter examines the expressive content of *The Choice of Governing Instrument*: that is, its contribution to the study of public policy and impact on administration and public-policy making.

The second objective is driven by a firm belief that, in Canada at least, the study and practice of public policy and administration have not been conducted with sufficient attention to history. With a few notable exceptions, the leading books, studies, and individuals who have shaped the trajectories of the discipline and indeed of public policy over time have not been adequately consulted. Each generation of scholars and policy makers can point to its touchstones. For those who did graduate studies in Canada in the 1980s, for instance, one of the principal touchstones was the Macdonald Royal Commission and the famous rainbow of colour-coded research studies that seemed to fill miles of shelves in university libraries across the country. At the same time, however, these touchstones have not been subject to systematic analysis, and we know very little about how and why some books, studies, and individuals have more impact on the development of the field than others and about why – and whether – this knowledge gap matters.[2]

This chapter is intended to make a modest contribution to filling the gap. The first section provides essential background on *The Choice of Governing Instrument*. The second presents the basic argument developed therein by Trebilcock and his colleagues. The final section examines the contribution and impact of their work.

## BACKGROUND

In February 1978 the prime minister of Canada and his provincial counterparts met at one of their early first ministers' meetings to discuss the state of the Canadian economy. To the surprise of many participants and sherpas involved in the meeting, the afternoon communiqué from first ministers indicated their agreement that "the whole matter of economic regulation at all levels of government should be referred to the Economic Council [of Canada] for recommendations for action, in consultation with the provinces and the private sector." Thus was born the Economic Council of Canada's Regulation Reference.

The terms of reference for the council's study were conveyed to the chairman, Dr Sylvia Ostry, by Prime Minister Pierre Trudeau in a July 1978 letter. The prime minister requested that the council "undertake a number of studies of specific areas of government regulation which appear to be having a particularly substantial economic impact on the Canadian economy." As he noted, there were growing concerns that increased government regulation was having serious adverse impacts on the performance of Canada's firms and industries and on the macroeconomy. The council was requested to complete an interim report by the end of 1979 and a final report by the end of 1980. The final report was to provide practical guidelines for improving the process of government regulation in Canada.

The Economic Council of Canada had been set up in 1973. Under the federal Economic Council Act, the council was mandated to examine and provide advice on key economic and social goals for Canada (e.g., full employment, a high rate of economic growth, and an equitable distribution of rising incomes) and on the challenges of achieving them simultaneously and consistently in the medium term. Section 10 of the Act allowed for the federal government to refer issues to the council for study, as it did in the case of the Regulation Reference.

As suggested in the prime minister's July 1978 letter, Dr Ostry submitted a preliminary report on the Regulation Reference to the meeting of first ministers in November 1978. The preliminary report outlined the research agenda for the Reference as well as initial plans for consultations. A director of research, W.T. Stanbury, was named. In addition, a list was developed of the almost one hundred consultants, mainly academics, to be engaged in the Reference's various research activities. The list included D.N. Dewees, D.G. Hartle, J.R.S. Prichard, and M.J. Trebilcock, all of the University of Toronto.

### THE CHOICE OF GOVERNING INSTRUMENT

Published in 1982, the study undertaken by Trebilcock, Prichard, Hartle, and Dewees was titled *The Choice of Governing Instrument*. The aim of the study was to investigate the pressure to regulate and, in particular, "the tendency in the policy-making process to adopt new regulations uncritically and to maintain existing ones long after they have outlived their usefulness" (Economic Council of Canada 1979, 5).

The study went beyond a simple investigation, however. Indeed, to address the issue of the pressure to regulate, the authors elaborated a fairly refined framework for analysis based on three key pillars. The cornerstone of the framework was the notion that regulation is only one of many tools – such as expenditures, taxation, and exhortation – that governments can use to exercise influence over the economy and society. Here, they built on the earlier pioneering insights of Hood (1986), Salamon (1981), and others who argued for a focus on the tools of government action rather than on government programs or policies, as was the conventional approach.

For Trebilcock et al., regulation and the other tools in the toolboxes of governments were not all created equal, necessitating choice. Indeed, they contended that the tools are, in principle, both substitutable and complementary; thus, once government has settled on its objectives, it can – indeed, must – choose the most appropriate tools for achieving them.

The second pillar in the analytical framework developed by Trebilcock et al. was the idea that the choice of governing instrument is motivated by self-interest. By this, they meant that the self-interested motivations of the actors involved in the choice process – that is, their political rationality – determine the choice of governing instrument. They noted that while choice may be an efficiency issue in part, political rationality is the primary factor in choosing between substitutable instruments.[3] In this they echoed the seminal work of Wildavsky (1964), Downs (1967), and Stigler (1971) on the economics of politics and public policy and on the use of economic principles to predict the behaviour of bureaus and bureaucrats, now commonly referred to as public-choice theory.

Finally, Trebilcock et al. conceived of the choice of governing instrument as deriving from courses of action rationally pursued by different political actors. The choice process, for them, comprised a series of intersecting games involving three key players: politicians, bureaucrats, and interest groups. Explanation for the choice of instrument was accordingly sought in the interactions of these actors, in the quantity and quality of information available to them, in the formal and informal rules under which they operate, and of course, in the goals they pursue, mainly as self-maximizing individuals.

Trebilcock and his colleagues focused their analysis on the political game. They argued that the self-interest of politicians in reelection is one of the leading factors explaining the pressure to regulate in Canada. While untested, their study did imply that the games made up of bureaucrats and interest groups and their respective (undefined) self-interests are not insignificant.

Given the nature of the Regulation Reference, it was not at all surprising that Trebilcock and his colleagues' principal interest was in regulation as a policy instrument. They drew a number of important conclusions. They argued, for instance, that many inherent features of regulation, such as its perceived low cost, accounted for the heavy use of regulation in Canada compared to in other countries and made it a – if not *the* – most favoured instrument of government.

Trebilcock et al. also contended that the choice of mode for regulation – that is government by ministerial department or government by independent agency – can be explained with reference to the interests of politicians in being reelected. They speculated, for example, that politicians consider the departmental mode to be more responsive to political will and therefore turn to it when they anticipate having to make constant marginal adjustments in regulatory policy or even when the main policy objectives for regulation have been settled but the costs to be incurred in making sure regulatory officials maximize the appropriate objectives are calculated to be low relative to the agency mode.

Trebilcock et al. implicitly pointed in their work to a strategy for regulatory reform. On the one hand, the toolbox framework suggested that reducing the regulatory burden is partly a matter of choosing a nonregulatory instrument and creating the appropriate incentives and disincentives to achieve this outcome. At the same time, the authors' analysis confirmed that simply reducing the number of regulations on the books of governments across Canada was not a meaningful strategy for reform; fewer regulations did not equal a reduced regulatory burden.

## CONTRIBUTION AND IMPACT

The chapter now turns to examining the expressive content of Trebilcock et al.'s pioneering work and its ideas about the tools of government, or roughly, what is now commonly termed the instrument-choice perspective. The contribution and impact of *The Choice of Governing Instrument* has been significant in at least three ways: (1) It provided the basis for a more mature instrument-choice perspective on government regulation; (2) it played an important role in raising the bar for analysis of public policy; and (3) it planted the seeds for subsequent work by scholars and practitioners.

The challenges of mapping the impacts of ideas and individuals, let alone assessing them, are well known. This is especially true in the study of public policy and administration, where significant scholarly effort has rightly been devoted in recent years to investigating the ideational basis of policy making, with varying degrees of success.[4]

A series of key yet deceptively simple questions can, however, be used to guide the analysis in this chapter: How do we conceptualize impact or influence; what has impact; when and how does the impact or influence happen; how do we measure it; who is subject to the impact or influence and why; and what are the implications?[5]

Moreover, Wilson's classic 1981 piece on the role of intellectuals in public policy helps to crystallize the approach further. Wilson argued that the impact of "policy intellectuals" is greatest when three conditions are met: (1) There is theorizing; (2) there is objective study based on actual experience; and (3) there is receptiveness in the political system. The analysis that follows suggests that Wilson's hypothesis may be equally applicable to the domain of scholarship, not just to public policy, and that the contribution and impact of the instrument-choice perspective as reflected in *The Choice of Governing Instrument* had an almost unique resonance with both scholars and policy makers despite their different methods for acquiring and using knowledge.[6]

## The Instrument-Choice Perspective on Government Regulation

Undoubtedly, and not in any way a surprise, one of the principal areas where *The Choice of Governing Instrument* has had an impressive and long-standing impact is in the study of government regulation. The instrument-choice perspective on government regulation – which emerged as a result of and alongside the general theory of instrument choice reflected in *The Choice of Governing Instrument* – has been described as one of the dominant approaches in the study of government regulation in Canada and the United States (Hill 1997).[7]

The various ways in which Trebilcock and his colleagues applied their concept of instrument choice to regulation and the pressures to regulate have already been described. Their focus on regulation resonated with more general concerns that were being expressed in other quarters about the rise of the regulatory state in Canada and the negative impacts of too much regulation on the state of Canada's economy and on principles of political accountability.[8]

It is important to note, however, that while the instrument-choice perspective did allow scholars and practitioners to think about regulation in a new, dynamic, and (in principle) expressly comparative way, it did have several important weaknesses. Even twenty years after *The Choice of Governing Instrument*, empirical analysis inspired by the perspective has been limited for the most part to the question of why politicians choose regulation. The interests that regulation can serve for other policy actors, such as regulatory officials, other bureaucrats, and private-sector organizations and individuals, have been virtually ignored. The latter approach suggests treating the choice of regulation as a communitywide policy exercise rather than restricting it to a closed shop of elected representatives.[9]

Another advantage of extending the instrument-choice theory of regulation beyond politicians is that it encourages us to question the decidedly secondary importance Trebilcock et al. assign to technical efficiency. For some actors, considerations besides political rationality may be relevant, such as their familiarity with regulatory administration or their prestige in the regulatory process. Moreover, after an extended period of regulatory reform, deregulation, and now regulatory management, we may be in a position to legitimately question instrument-choice theory's downplaying of technical efficiency. The evidence may be that the calculus of instrument choice puts a premium on achieving efficiency and effectiveness rather than on other sorts of rationality in some circumstances.[10]

Another important weakness in the way the instrument-choice perspective on regulation has developed over the past twenty years is especially ironic. For the most part, the perspective has generally looked only at regulation, not at regulation in relation to other tools of government. As later chapters in this collection emphasize, this is something that must be systematically addressed if the full potential of the insights offered by the instrument-choice perspective is to be realized. The single-instrument focus – rather than a fully comparative, cross-instrument, mixed-instrument one – is especially lamentable because it has afflicted the study and practice not only of regulation, but also of most of the other tools.

## Concepts and Theorizing

Perhaps the most important contribution of *The Choice of Governing Instrument* was to provide an elegant and concise conceptual touchstone for further investigations into the nature of government action. In the wake of behaviouralist-inspired efforts to make the study and practice of public policy and administration more science than art, Trebilcock and his colleagues' work offered welcome added theoretical rigour and an explicit analytical framework through which to examine government policy and decision making.

Equally significant, this analytical framework presented a far more nuanced understanding of the nature of government itself. In some ways reminiscent of Allison's *Essence of Decision* (1972), Trebilcock and his colleagues looked internally at government and its functions. The analytical framework they used to explain the choice of policy instrument presented government and the policy process not as a monolithic entity but as a panoply of actors, instruments, and motivations. This was something again that had clear resonance for practitioners: It captured the reality of their world.

Trebilcock et al. drilled down into government and cast new light on the policy process in another critical way as well. It was fundamental to their perspective that there were multiple policy actors. While politicians exercised key influence on the choice of governing instrument, so too did other actors, specifically the bureaucracy and interest groups. While, as noted earlier, this aspect of their analysis was particularly underdeveloped, it intrigued many. It arguably set the stage, too, for later more serious and nuanced looks by Coleman and Skogstad (1990) and others at the networks and communities that are part of the policy process.

At the same time, *The Choice of Governing Instrument* was one of the first studies to outline a system-based perspective on the policy process and especially on government regulation. Previously, the basic contours or elements of the Canadian regulatory state were fairly well known.[11] What had been missing was an integrated perspective, one that privileged not just regulatory institutions and the issues they raised, but also the relationships between them. In many cases, these relationships were founded more on the dynamics of political economy than on the machinery of government. The *Choice of Governing Instrument* made this explicit.

As Greenberg et al. (1977) contend, a principal weakness in the development of theories of public policy has been the lack of attention paid to the dependent variable. In the terms of Trebilcock and his colleagues, this is the choice of instrument itself. Clearly, this is one of the most developed parts of their analytical framework and of their analysis in *The Choice of Governing Instrument*. What is significantly less clear, however, is the nature of the connection they see between the choice of instrument and the nature of the policy problem being addressed through this choice. As Peters argues elsewhere in this volume, this part of the dynamics of instrument choice is one of the key areas where further theorizing and conceptualization are required.

### A Catalyst

Twenty years on, there is no question that the instrument-choice perspective as reflected in *The Choice of Governing Instrument* has staying power. The more important point, however, is that it has had staying power because it has played a critical role in catalyzing subsequent research and policy practices. Sometimes this role has been achieved not so much in a positive way as through the crystallization of critiques and of alternative and complementary perspectives on government and public administration.

The *regulatory-regime* concept developed by Doern and his colleagues is an excellent example.[12] These scholars position their regime concept as responding to the fact that the policy-instrument perspective on regulation "does not solve the practical analytical problems that arise when real situations are studied or when regulators talk about what they are actually doing" (Doern and Wilks 1997, 5). For them, a regulatory regime is "an interacting set of organizations, statutes, ideas, interests, or processes" with "some inner core of shared norms, features, or characteristics." They contend that, in contrast to how they are portrayed by proponents of the instrument-choice perspective on regulation, regulatory regimes and institutions are much more than aggregates of individual preferences.[13]

In addition, like Trebilcock et al., Doern and his colleagues are interested in questions about the nature of regulatory institutions and processes and, especially, about the drivers of regulatory change. They, too, offer what could be called a systems-based perspective, this time in sectors, in horizontal framework regulation, in government's approach to managing regulation, and at the international level. For them, however, a more disaggregated, more refined notion of key interests drives regulation and regulatory change. Their analysis highlights the influence of party politics, business, consumers, and ideas themselves and points to their convergence and collision, at the intra- and interregime levels, as the principal source of changes in regulation.

Similarly, the instrument-choice perspective is central to regulatory management and to the other practices that governments at the federal and provincial levels in Canada and elsewhere have adopted to improve the exercise of their regulatory functions.[14] Regulatory management is distinct from deregulation and regulatory reform. Its underlying premise is that regulation is a distinct instrument of government within a larger toolbox of policy instruments. There are two problems with regulation in this scenario: (1) its aggregate negative effects for individuals, firms, society, and the economy; and (2) the challenge of finding the right mix of regulation and nonregulatory instruments in order to improve the effectiveness with which public-policy problems are addressed. In both regards, this is significantly different from the problem of regulation seen through the lens of deregulation or regulatory reform.

Canada's experience with regulatory management suggests, in turn, that the prescriptions are similarly different. In the case of regulatory management, the emphasis is placed on introducing more flexibility and responsiveness into regulation, using alternatives to regulation, developing new instruments that mix regulatory and nonregulatory features, and designing performance measures for regulation. The logic is that regulation, like the other tools of government, can be used more or less effectively and can be managed, much like spending and taxation.

The impacts of the instrument-choice perspective have also extended to areas beyond the exercise of the regulatory functions of government. In the late 1990s and early 2000s, for instance, the point of departure for the programs of work launched by two challenge teams at the deputy-minister level – one focused on regulatory reform and the other on law making and governance – was that "governments pursue policy objectives through a variety of means ... and that these policy instruments, as they are known, have been undergoing an important shift in the last decade, not just in Canada but throughout the OECD" (Treasury Board Secretariat of Canada 1998, 1).[15] The ensuing work was important for at least two reasons. First, it catalyzed efforts to refine and, where possible, bring a greater degree of coherence to the various analytical frameworks used in the federal government[16] to inform the matching of instruments and policy problems at the

Treasury Board Secretariat and in-line departments such as Environment Canada and Justice Canada. Second, one of the key conclusions to come from the deputy ministers' activities was that reforming the law-making process – or making instrument choices *writ large* "smarter" – takes place in, is influenced by, and influences the broader context of governance, whether this entails the relationship between public and private actors, principles of accountability, or the institutions of Parliament and public administration.[17]

### CONCLUSION

This chapter has examined the subject matter and expressive content of the pioneering study by Trebilcock, Prichard, Hartle, and Dewees on *The Choice of Governing Instrument*. The central argument has been that over the course of the past twenty years, the study has made a leading contribution to the evolution of the instrument-choice perspective on government regulation and to refining the concepts and theories that are relied upon by scholars and practitioners to understand and explain the policy process. Equally important, the study has created a creative tension that has generated both alternative and complementary perspectives on governmesnt and public administration.

   In closing, the chapter confirms the value to be gained from bringing a greater degree of historical consciousness to the study of policy instruments. In short, by looking to the past, we can contribute to charting a creative and meaningful course for future research that will help scholars and policy makers alike to better realize the full potential of the instrument-choice perspective.

# 2

# What Is a Policy Instrument?
# Tools, Mixes, and
# Implementation Styles

## MICHAEL HOWLETT

INTRODUCTION: "FIRST-"
AND "SECOND-GENERATION" THINKING
ON POLICY INSTRUMENTS

Policy instruments are techniques of governance that, one way or another, involve the utilization of state authority or its conscious limitation. They fall not only within the domain of political science, but also, since they often affect the behaviour of individuals in society as they go about their daily tasks, within the realm of economics. Not surprisingly, therefore, the study of policy instruments has long been characterized by the existence of two virtually independent streams of literature. There is the study of policy instruments undertaken by economists and that undertaken by political scientists, and the two approaches differ substantially.[1]

Both sets of investigators, however, have often been guilty of oversimplifying instrument use and selection in their early works. "First-generation" economists studying the tools of government, for example, were concerned largely with the study of business-government relations and with the effects of state regulation and economic policy formation on business efficiency. Although internecine debates between neoclassical and welfare economists over the concept were sharp, first-generation instrument-choice economists concentrated their efforts on identifying the "market failures" that would "justify" government "intervention" in market exchange.[2]

First-generation political scientists rejected the deductive approach to instrument choice put forward by economists, preferring to develop their theories inductively from the empirical record of actual government decision-making processes. Welfare models were viewed as basing rationales for policy-instrument choice on the discussion of what governments ought to do rather than on empirical investigations into what they actually do. Political scientists, as a result, never simply assumed that policy makers chose governing instruments in order to fine-tune the economy but attributed a political rationale to instrument selection.[3] Although it was acknowledged that, in some circumstances, governments might well choose particular instruments based on their technical efficiency and theoretical appropriateness, it was argued this was likely to occur only in very specific circumstances, such as when economists controlled the decision-making process and had a relatively free hand in doing so – for example, in areas such as fiscal and monetary policy.[4]

First-generation studies of policy instruments conducted by political scientists thus tended to be motivated precisely by the desire to understand what economists simply assumed: the rationale for policy-instrument choice. Public-policy makers were not generally thought to be driven by questions of theoretical purity – especially when, as is the case with economic theory, the theory is contested – but rather by a more overt political calculus of electoral or ideological cost and benefit.[5]

Both these currents in early, first-generation work led to simplistic, cleaver-like recommendations for tool selection and promoted a Manichean view of instrument options. This was especially true for economists, as most neoclassical accounts consider many governing instruments to be inherently inefficient, distorting production and consumption decisions in the marketplace. As a result, many proponents of this view would restrict governments to the direct provision of pure public goods through government departments and agencies.[6] Although the recommendations of political scientists were less sure, they, too, tended to caution against the use of "too much" government authority and expressed a definite preference for the use of "less coercive" instruments.[7] Both these kinds of early instrument analyses had two problems. First, they tended to focus on single instrument choices and promoted a misleading view of the technical nature of instrument choices. Second, they tended to portray instrument choices in stark, "good vs evil" terms, embracing "good" pro-market choices and rejecting "evil" nonmarket ones.[8]

Not all early studies shared these characteristics, of course, and some presented more complex and nuanced models and analyses.[9] Building on the base of case studies and insights developed in these works, "second-generation" students of instrument choice have attempted to address the issues of both the influence of policy context and the nature of instrument mixes in their work.[10] Promising new work on instruments has attempted to apply different models of economic thinking to the evaluation of instrument choices – such as transaction costs[11] – and to assess the question of the potential to develop optimal policy-instrument designs.[12] This work emphasizes the need to overcome one by-product of first-generation thinking about policy instruments and instrument choices: a disjuncture between the complexity of administrative practice and the simplicity of instrument analysis. That is, while students of instrument choices have focused on decisions to adopt individual instruments, administrative practice usually involves the use of multiple tools or "policy-instrument mixes." As a consequence, the nature of these mixes, or "governance strategies," has remained until recently understudied and less well understood than are choices to select specific types of instruments.[13]

Both theorists and practitioners need to move beyond simple, dichotomous zero-sum notions of instrument alternatives. Dichotomous sets of policy alternatives (like market vs state) and metaphors (like carrots vs sticks) lend themselves to blunt thinking about instruments and their modalities. Administrators and politicians need to expand the menu of government choice both to include substantive and procedural instruments and a wider range of options of each and to understand the important context-based nature of instrument choices. Scholars need more empirical analysis in order to test their models and provide better advice to governments about the process of tool selection and how to better match the tool to the job at hand. This chapter illustrates the origins of the deficiencies of simple models of instrument choice and suggests that, ultimately, both scholars and practitioners are interested in the same thing: designing and adopting optimal "mixes" of instruments in complex decision-making and implementation contexts. Toward this end, the chapter introduces and develops the idea of an "implementation style" as a stable, predictable preference for a particular policy mix.

## DEFINING AND CLASSIFYING POLICY INSTRUMENTS

Most policy objectives can, in theory, be accomplished by a number of instruments; in other words, most instruments are to some degree "substitutable." Thus, in theory, a government seeking to promote health care for the population, for example, could leave it entirely to the family to provide health services, with the competence and availability of family members determining who gets how much and at what cost. Or the government might go to the other extreme and provide health services through its own administrative agency, paid for directly out of its general tax revenues, leaving no room for the market or other private organizations. In between the two extremes lie a range of other instruments, including exhorting the population to keep healthy, subsidizing those who are poor, and regulating doctors and hospitals – which could, in theory, equally well address health-care issues.[14]

In most cases, however, in practice policy makers use a mix of instruments in seeking to achieve their desired ends. This raises the questions of (1) why specific mixes exist at present in different issue areas and (2) whether and to what extent the instruments that comprise a mix are counterproductive or complementary. Expressed in a manner more germane to this volume, the question is: What are the constraints and impediments blocking optimal instrument use in the design and implementation of governance strategies?

Many of the later chapters in this book address the issue of instrument mixes and broach subjects such as their design and whether criteria like optimality and suboptimality can be addressed in the types of combinations of instruments that larger governance strategies entail. This chapter has a more modest goal in addressing the nature of the "toolbox" from which both individual tools and instrument mixes are selected. It does so by examining many of the classification schemes put forward by scholars in the field, arriving at a primary designation of policy tools as either "substantive" (designed to alter the mix of goods and services provided and available in society) or "procedural" (primarily intended to alter policy processes rather than substance, per se). As a contribution toward the analysis of policy mixes, it also notes how procedural and substantive instruments tend to be used together and outlines the basic "implementation styles" that result from typical combinations of these instruments.

## BASIC TAXONOMIES OF POLICY INSTRUMENTS

Early students of policy making tended to have very flexible notions of the multiple means by which governments can affect, or give effect to, policy.[15] In his path-breaking early works on public-policy making, for example, Harold Lasswell conceived the main instruments of politics as involving, among other things, the manipulation of symbols, signs, and icons. Lasswell noted the extent to which governments could affect each stage of the policy process through such manipulations and argued that a principal task of the policy sciences must be to understand the nuances of these actions and their effects.[16]

By the early 1980s, at the urging of Lester Salamon and others, attention began to be focused on more precisely categorizing policy instruments in order to better analyze the reasons for their use.[17] Careful examination of instruments and instrument choices, it was argued, would not only lead to considerable insight into the factors driving the policy process and the characterization of long-term patterns of public-policy making, but also allow practitioners more readily to draw lessons from the experiences of others with the use of particular techniques in specific circumstances.[18]

In the post-Salamon era, studies of instrument choice tended to look at instances of single-instrument selection and, on the basis of such cases, to discern the general reasons why governments would choose one category of instrument over another. These studies, heavily influenced by economists, tended to focus on what I have termed "substantive" instruments – that is, those (such as classical command-and-control regulation, public enterprises, and subsidies) that more or less directly affect the type, quantity, price, or other characteristics of goods and services being produced in society, either by the public or private sector.[19]

The emphasis upon the systematic study of policy instruments in the 1970s and 1980s quickly generated a large volume of academic literature that was immediately applied in the design of new, substantive policy initiatives in areas such as pollution prevention and professional regulation.[20] Studies in Canada and elsewhere generated useful taxonomies[21] and shed light on significant subjects, such as the reasons behind shifts in patterns of instrument choices associated with the waves of privatization and deregulation that characterized the period.[22]

Much less attention was paid by analysts of this period to the systematic analysis of their procedural counterparts, even though early students of the policy sciences had always been interested in policy processes and in the manner in which governments design and manipulate these processes to achieve their ends. In these early works, "policy instruments" had often been defined broadly in order to include a wider range of tools, or techniques, of governance than in the post-Salamon era. By 2000, however, this neglect had been noted, prompting the emergence of systematic treatments of procedural instruments,[23] such that knowledge of both types of instruments, their effects, and the reasons they are chosen is now very much up-to-date.

## CLASSIFYING SUBSTANTIVE INSTRUMENTS

In the case of substantive policy instruments – i.e., those instruments intended to directly affect the nature, types, quantities, and distribution

Table 2.1
A taxonomy of substantive policy instruments

| Objective | Principal governing resource used | | | |
|---|---|---|---|---|
| | Nodality | Authority | Treasure | Organization |
| Alter social-actor behaviour | Advice Training | Regulation User charges Licences | Grants Loans Tax expenditures | Bureaucratic administration Public enterprises |
| Monitor social-actor behaviour | Reporting Registration | Census taking Consultants | Polling Police reporting | Record keeping Surveys |

Source: Adapted from Christopher Hood, *The Tools of Government* (Chatham, NJ: Chatham House, 1986), 124–5.

of the goods and services provided in society – a great deal of conceptual progress has occurred over the past two decades.[24] Taxonomies, for example, have been provided by many authors, one of the most well-known having been developed by Christopher Hood.[25] In Hood's scheme, instruments are grouped together according to (1) whether they rely on the use of "nodality" (or information), authority, treasure, or the organizational resources of government for their effectiveness and (2) whether the instrument is designed to effect a change in a policy environment or to detect changes in it. A typical taxonomy of substantive policy instruments based on Hood's schema is presented in Table 2.1.

## Classifying Procedural Instruments

Procedural policy instruments, as noted above, have been studied less systematically than substantive ones, although many studies of individual-tool use exist.[26] The works of Bressers and Klok,[27] Schneider and Ingram,[28] and others[29] have identified a large number of typical procedural policy instruments. These include education, training, institution creation, the selective provision of information, formal evaluations, hearings, and institutional reform.[30] Research into the tools and mechanisms used in intergovernmental regulatory design by Canadian analysts and others has also identified several other such instruments, including "treaties" and a variety of "political agreements" that can affect target-group recognition of government intentions and vice versa.[31] Other research, again much of it Canadian, into interest-group behaviour and activities has highlighted the existence of tools related to group creation and ma-

Table 2.2
A resource-based taxonomy of procedural policy instruments

| | *Principal governing resource used* | | | |
|---|---|---|---|---|
| *Objective* | *Nodality* | *Authority* | *Treasure* | *Organization* |
| Promote social networks | Education Information provision Focus groups | Labelling Treaties and political agreements Advisory group creation | Interest-group creation Intervenor and research funding | Institutional reform Judicial review Conferences |
| Restrict social networks | Propaganda Information suppression | Banning groups and associations Denial of access | Eliminating funding | Administrative delay and obfuscation |

*Source:* Adapted from Michael Howlett, "Managing the 'Hollow State': Procedural Policy Instruments and Modern Governance," *Canadian Public Administration* 43, no. 4 (2000): 412–31.

nipulation, including the role played by private or public sector patrons in aiding the formation and activities of such groups.[32] Still other specialized research into aspects of contemporary policy making has highlighted the use of techniques such as the provision of research funding for, and access to, investigative hearings and tribunals.[33]

Hood's taxonomy of substantive instruments can be modified to help make sense out of this disparate (and partial) inventory. That is, classifying procedural instruments in accordance with the type of "governing resource" on which they rely generates a useful preliminary taxonomy (see Table 2.2).[34] While most researchers have focused on the manner in which these instruments have been used to enhance participation and policy-relevant knowledge, it should be emphasized that procedural tools can also be used to negatively affect interest groups' and other actors' behaviour. For example, information-based procedural instruments facilitate both the provision of information and its suppression as well as the release of both misleading and accurate information. Deception, obfuscation, and other forms of administrative delay are, similarly, all forms of authority-based procedural instruments.[35] Hence drawing a distinction between "positive" and "negative" uses of governing resources in terms of whether they encourage or discourage actor participation in policy processes is a useful aspect of the preliminary classification of such instruments.

As was the case with substantive instruments, this taxonomy is useful in so far as it highlights the different basic resources used by different types of instruments, thereby allowing a virtually unlimited number of instruments to be placed in a limited number of general categories.

## THE RATIONALE FOR INSTRUMENT USE: MARKET AND SUBSYSTEM MANIPULATION

Classifying the basic types of policy instruments and their permutations accomplished one of the main goals of students of policy instruments in the post-Salamon era. However, simply describing the nature of the instruments available to policy makers is only the first step toward providing better advice to those same policy makers about which instruments to choose in which circumstances. That is, the aim of the exercise was not only better description, but better prescription. To accomplish this, it was necessary to elevate the discussion from taxonomies to the analysis of the reasons for tool adoption, or what is usually referred to in the literature as "the rationale for instrument choice."

Toward this end, many analysts proposed various schemes that purported to establish the relationship existing between different instruments or categories of instruments and the successful attainment of government objectives.[36] Howlett and Ramesh, for example, developed a spectrum of substantive instruments based on Hood's taxonomy. They focused on the level of direct state involvement in the provision of goods and services as the chief criterion for distinguishing between categories of "effector" instruments.[37] This placed "voluntary" instruments requiring minimal state involvement at one end of a continuum, with state-based instruments (such as public enterprises) falling at the opposite end. Between the two poles lie a wide range of "mixed" instruments involving varying levels of state and private provision of goods and services (see Figure 2.1).

Much the same can be done for procedural instruments. That is, as Dutch scholars such as Klijn, Kickert, Koppenjan, and especially, de Bruijn and ten Heuvelhof have argued, procedural policy instruments can be thought of as involving the manipulation not of economic exchange relationships, as is the case with substantive tools, but of the links and nodes of the network relationships existing among actors involved in policy making.[38] Construed in this way, procedural instruments can be seen to be used to manipulate the number or nature of actors arrayed in the policy subsystems that policy makers face, each category of instrument using a specific resource in order to manipulate an aspect of a policy subsystem or network.

As de Bruijn and ten Heuvelhof have pointed out, a wide range of activities are possible in network manipulation, ranging from limited

Figure 2.1
A spectrum of substantive policy instruments

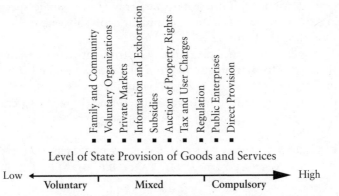

Level of State Provision of Goods and Services

Low ◄─────────────────────────────► High
　　Voluntary　　　Mixed　　　Compulsory

*Source:* M. Howlett and M. Ramesh, *Studying Public Policy: Policy Cycles and Policy Subsystems* (Toronto: Oxford University Press, 1995).

Figure 2.2
A Spectrum of procedural policy instruments

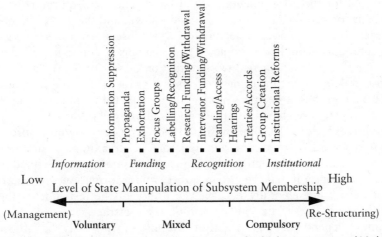

*Information*　　*Funding*　　*Recognition*　　*Institutional*

Low　　　　　　　　　　　　　　　　　　High
Level of State Manipulation of Subsystem Membership

(Management)　　　　　　　　　　　　(Re-Structuring)
　　Voluntary　　　Mixed　　　Compulsory

*Source:* Michael Howlett, "Managing the 'Hollow State': Procedural Policy Instruments and Modern Governance," *Canadian Public Administration* 43, no. 4 (2000): 412-31.

"network management" to more fundamental "subsystem restructuring."[39] Incorporating this distinction allows the procedural policy instruments found in Table 2.2 to be arrayed in a single spectrum according to the level of state manipulation of subsystem membership and activities (see Figure 2.2).

In this spectrum, procedural policy instruments can be seen to range from limited information suppression or release designed to mildly affect subsystem behaviour through "voluntaristic" responses from targeted actors to group or institutional reforms designed to completely restructure existing subsystems by compulsory means.[40]

## THE VARIABLES AFFECTING INSTRUMENT CHOICE: STATE CAPACITY AND TARGET COMPLEXITY

It is still only a start, however, to say that a variety of instrument choices exists that can alter patterns of goods-and-services delivery or policy interactions and that these choices differ in terms of the extent of state involvement in them. Rather, what is needed is the identification of a limited set of factors or variables that can be said to influence instrument choices in specific directions.

In a perfect world, there would be little trouble choosing the appropriate tool for the governmental task at hand. That is, if all the costs and benefits of a tool were context-free and known, and the goals of a policy clear and unambiguous, a decision on which instrument to use in a given circumstance would be a simple maximizing one, and mistakes would not be made. However, in real-world situations, as information difficulties arise in determining instrument effects and as the clarity and precision of goals diminishes, it becomes more and more likely that policy means and ends will be mismatched and that policy failures will occur.

Moreover, it has become more and more apparent to many observers that the kind of precision required for such maximizing instrument choices will never be achieved, not just because of poorly defined, ambiguous, decision-making circumstances and information asymmetries, but more fundamentally because the utility of the instruments themselves, and hence the calculation of their attractiveness, is heavily context-dependent. That is, although instruments may be, in some technical or theoretical sense, "substitutable" in so far as any one instrument could achieve any end – albeit at differing levels of cost – in practice they differ in a number of ways, making the choice of instrument a complex matter.

Salamon and Lund, for example, suggested that different instruments involve varying degrees of effectiveness, efficiency, equity, legitimacy, and partisan support that affect their appropriateness for a particular situation.[41] Thus some instruments are more effective in carrying out a policy in some contexts than others. Efficiency, for example, in terms of low levels of financial and personnel costs, may be an important consideration in climates of budgetary restraint but is a less significant aspect in free-spending times. Legitimacy is another critical aspect of instrument use that varies with context.[42] The ability of an instrument to attract the support of the population in general and, particularly, of those directly involved in policy making in the issue area or subsystem involved must also be taken into account. A relatively heavy-handed approach to regulation of the financial dealings of industry, for example, may be anathema in normal times in many sectors, but in the wake of bank failures and corporate scandals, it may find sudden popularity among both the public and the policy elite.

Abstract notions of efficiency and effectiveness may also become less important criteria in some contexts, such as wartime, when government departments or public enterprises may be preferred tool choices simply because they remain under direct government control[43] or because administrators may be more familiar with their use and risks.[44] Moreover, cultural norms and institutional or political arrangements may accord greater legitimacy to some instruments than others. Thus it is possible that in liberal democracies, citizens and policy makers desiring high levels of individual autonomy and responsibility may prefer instruments that are less coercive than other equally or perhaps more effective or efficient alternatives that do not promote these qualities. Such societies can be expected, for example, to prefer voluntary and mixed instruments to compulsory instruments on philosophical or ideological grounds.[45] Moreover, instruments have varying distributional effects, so policy makers in such societies may need to select instruments that are, or at least appear to be, equitable. Tax incentives, for example, are inherently inequitable because they offer no benefit to those (the poor) without taxable income. Their use, therefore, will vary to the extent that (1) societies are bifurcated along socio-economic, or class, lines and (2) individuals are aware of their advantageous and pernicious consequences.

In addition to these "external" contexts, there are "internal" constraints on instrument choices that must be considered. While instrument choice is clearly not a simple technical exercise and must take into account aspects of the social, political, and economic contexts of instrument selection, it is also the case that the internal configuration of instrument mixes alters the calculus of instrument choice in significant ways. Some instruments may work well with others – as is the case with "self-regulation" set within a regulatory compliance framework[46] – while other combinations may not, such as, notably, independently developed subsidies and regulation.[47]

Both these "internal" and "external" contexts of instrument behaviour and selection must be taken into account in efforts to theorize optimality in the design of those policy mixes that comprise government's "governance strategies."[48] Unfortunately, however, this complexity is often not recognized, and instrument choices are still often viewed through an ideological or conceptual lens that reduces choices to a "one size fits all" motif or, more commonly, to a struggle between "good and evil" in which an existing range of instrument uses is condemned and the merits of some alternative single instrument are trumpeted as the embodiment of all that is good in the world. The unfortunate consequence of such simplistic approaches, if adopted, is usually that the instrument – be it state-driven public enterprises in the case of socialist and developing countries in the first two-thirds of the twentieth century or the virtues of privatization, deregulation, and markets in the last third – is wielded less like the scalpel of a careful surgeon working on the body politic than like the butcher's cleaver, with little respect for the tissue of the patient falling under the knife.

## UNDERSTANDING INSTRUMENT MIXES: IMPLEMENTATION STYLES AS GOVERNANCE STRATEGIES

The foregoing comprises what is well known about instruments. As was pointed out above, most governments do not use single instruments to address problems but usually adopt a variety of tools to accomplish their ends. While these mixes can become quite complex – either by design or by accident of history – it is worth noting that although seemingly faced with a large choice of possible instruments in creating their strategies, governments often repeatedly choose from a much more limited set of options. That is, there is a distinct tendency for governments to develop an "implementation style" in various sectors and to stick with this style for quite some time.

And it is interesting to note in this regard that an implementation style is usually composed of a combination, or mix, of substantive and procedural instruments, at minimum two. Hence, for example, the well-known implementation style found in many US policy sectors, dubbed "adversarial legalism" by Robert Kagan,[49] is composed of a preferred substantive instrument (regulation) and a characteristic procedural one (judicial review) based on widespread, easily accessible legal procedures.[50]

This observation allows us to recast the question of the "rationale of instrument choice" as "why are particular mixes, or styles, adopted by governments?" In answering this question, it is instructive to look at the

Table 2.3
A model of substantive-instrument choice

| Level of state capacity | Level of policy-subsystem complexity | |
| --- | --- | --- |
| | High | Low |
| High | Market or subsidy instruments | Direct-provision instruments |
| Low | Regulatory or information instruments | Voluntary, community, or family-based instruments |

Source: Adapted from M. Howlett and M. Ramesh, Studying Public Policy: Policy Cycles and Policy Subsystems (Toronto: Oxford University Press, 1995).

factors identified by first-generation scholars with respect to substantive- and procedural-instrument use. In the case of substantive instruments, most students of instrument choices have focused on two interlinked sets of independent variables: (1) the organizational ability, or capacity, of states to affect societal actors and (2) policy subsystem complexity, or the number and types of actors that governments must affect in designing and implementing their programs and policies.[51] That is, the type of instruments chosen depends on the intersection of state capacity and the complexity of the networks of social actors that states wish to influence. Howlett and Ramesh, for example, show how these two variables, and their expected relationship to each other, can be used to generate a simple model containing a set of hypotheses regarding substantive instrument choices (see Table 2.3).

This model shows, for example, how subsidy or market instruments should be used – indeed, can be used effectively – only when a high level of state capacity and a complex policy subsystem exist, as is the case, for instance, with most competitive economic situations faced by modern states. By comparison, if a state faces a complex network, or subsystem, but has only limited capacity, it will tend to utilize regulatory or information-based instruments. Direct provision and public enterprises are likely to be used only when a state has high capacity but faces a relatively simple social or policy environment characterized by few actors and a small number of significant interorganizational relationships. Finally, when state capacity is low and the policy environment is not very complex, reliance on voluntary instruments can be effective, as was the case historically in many areas of social and health policy.[52]

This kind of model does not delve into the fine gradations of instrument use within each general category nor into the specific contexts of individual decisions that can result in errors being made in instrument choices. However, the model suggests that although substantive instrument choices are complex, general patterns of such choices can nevertheless be discerned and explained on the basis of the presence or absence of a small number of factors or variables.

While more empirical research is required to help test and construct such a theory with respect to the less well-studied procedural instruments, the existing evidence does suggest that a government's desire to alter a policy process is intimately tied to the extent to which existing processes and procedures are considered credible, or *legitimate*, by policy actors.[53] As is well known, democratic states require the attainment of a minimum level of societal consensus supporting their actions. When a serious loss of legitimacy or trust occurs, the subject of political conflict often shifts from the actual substantive content of government actions toward a critique of the processes by which these actions are determined.[54] This can occur either at the macro (or system-wide) level or at the meso (or sectoral) level, but in either case, governments resort to the use of procedural instruments as a means of altering network configurations in order to construct or regain legitimacy.

In addition, a second key variable of procedural instruments, as with substantive instruments, is the nature of the network or subsystem being manipulated.[55] For example, as May and his colleagues have noted in the case of intergovernmental program design, governments have attempted to build cooperation and commitment among the multiple actors involved in areas such as environmental regulation in Australia and the United States, in addition to prescribing penalties or utilizing incentives, primarily because of the risk to future activities that conflict could bring.[56] And, as Bridget Hutter has noted in the case of European Union program design, the precision and accuracy of targeting appears to have been more significant than, for example, cost or administrative simplicity to policy makers in designing governance.[57]

This discussion suggests two key variables that can capture important aspects of choosing procedural policy instruments: (1) the extent of existing sectoral delegitimation, which directly affects the extent of subsystem manipulation appropriate for the task of relegitimation; and (2) the extent of systemic delegitimation, which affects the capacity of governments to use existing networks to continue policy deliberations.[58] On this basis, a model of procedural-instrument choice can be set out, analogous to that previously developed for substantive instruments (see Table 2.4).

In this model, one would expect governments faced with both sectoral and transsectoral systemic-legitimation problems to utilize "compulsory" procedural instruments such as government reorganization in or-

Table 2.4
A model of procedural-instrument choice

| Level of sectoral delegitimation | Level of systemic delegitimation | |
| --- | --- | --- |
| | High | Low |
| High | Institutional manipulation | Funding manipulation |
| Low | Recognition manipulation | Information manipulation |

Source: Michael Howlett, "Managing the 'Hollow State': Procedural Policy Instruments and Modern Governance," *Canadian Public Administration* 43, no. 4 (2000): 412–31.

der to restructure policy networks, essentially reconstructing legitimacy and trust anew.[59] Governments facing low levels of both sectoral and systemic delegitimation would be expected to favour the use of more modest "voluntary" instruments, such as information manipulation through the release or withholding of documents, since only minor network manipulation is required to legitimate existing policy processes.[60] In between would be found cases where sectoral distrust and discontent are high but systemic delegitimation low, meaning that government funds can be used to relegitimate policy processes through, for example, the infusion of cash to create or selectively support specific interest groups.[61] Finally, where systemic delegitimation is high but sectoral delegitimacy is low, governments can recognize new actors or reorganize old ones through authoritative means, such as the establishment of specialized quasi-independent advisory committees and inquiries that serve to distance sectoral policy processes from overall systemic-legitimation concerns.[62]

## THE CONCEPT OF AN IMPLEMENTATION STYLE

As discussed above, second-generation instrument-choice analyses take their place in a larger literature about the transition from a more hands-on, interventionist style of government to "governing at a distance," the notion of "governance," and the widely employed metaphor of governments achieving public purposes by "steering" complex networks of public and private actors rather than directing an expensive and possibly ineffective bureaucracy.[63] Moving from a focus on single instruments, second-generation analysis looks instead at complementarities and conflicts within instrument mixes and adopts a much more flexible and less ideological approach to instrument use. For second-generation scholars, a key question is not so much "why do policy makers utilize a certain instrument?" – as it was for their first-generation counterparts – but "why is a particular combination of procedural and substantive instruments utilized in a specific sector?"

Second-generation scholars have emphasized the need to design appropriate instrument mixes and have come to focus on a small number of key precepts that embody the "scalpel" approach to instrument use:

1  The importance of designing policies that employ a mix of policy instruments carefully chosen to create positive interactions with each other and to respond to particular, context-dependent features of the policy sector
2  The importance of considering the full range of policy instruments when designing the mix rather than assuming that a choice must be made between regulation and markets[64]
3  In the context of continuing pressures on governments to do more with less, the importance of suggesting the increased use of incentive-based instruments, various forms of self-regulation by industry, and policies that can employ commercial and noncommercial third parties to achieve compliance, such as suppliers, customers, and a growing cast of auditors and certifiers
4  The importance of the search for new network-appropriate procedural policy instruments to meet the challenges of governance, of particular importance being "next-generation" policy instruments, such as information instruments, and various techniques of network management, such as the use of advisory committees and public consultations.[65]

The analysis of both substantive- and procedural-instrument choices presented above suggests that the choice of both types of policy instruments is shaped by the preferences of state decision makers and the nature of the constraints within which they operate.[66] For example, states must have a high level of administrative capacity in order to utilize authority, treasure, and organization-based instruments in situations where they wish to affect significant numbers of recalcitrant policy targets. When a state has few of these resources, it tends to utilize instruments like incentives or propaganda or to rely on existing voluntary, community, or family-based instruments.[67] Similarly, a key feature identified by students of procedural-instrument choice is the government's capacity to manipulate policy-subsystem membership and activities.[68] Implemented to retain the political trust or legitimacy required for substantive policy instruments to be effective, procedural policy-instrument choices are

Table 2.5
A model of basic implementation styles

| Severity of state constraints (resources and legitimacy) | Nature of the policy target (exchange and policy actors) | |
| --- | --- | --- |
| | Large | Small |
| High | Institutionalized voluntarism: | Regulatory corporatism: |
| | exhortation-based manipulation of market actors and institutionalization of policy networks | regulation of market actors and financial manipulation of interest-articulation systems |
| | (e.g., "next-generation," "steering" models of state behaviour in health care; promotion of "compliance" cultures) | (e.g., "corporatist"-style economic-planning models in industrial policy making) |
| Low | Directed subsidization: | Public provision with oversight: |
| | extensive use of financial instruments to influence market actors, coupled with the use of authority to preferentially recognize network actors | use of governmental-organization (personnel and structural) resources to provide goods and services, combined with manipulation of network actors through information release and distribution |
| | (e.g., models promoting industrial development in new high-tech sectors: biotechnology, aquaculture, internet, etc.) | (e.g., wartime production, rationing, and mobilization models) |

Source: Adapted from M. Howlett and M. Ramesh, *Studying Public Policy: Policy Cycles and Policy Subsystems* (Toronto: Oxford University Press, 1995).

also affected by the size of the policy target. For example, whether a government faces sectoral delegitimation or widespread systemic delegitimation affects the choices made between, say, creating a sectoral advisory committee or using funding to enhance the overall interest-articulation system found in society.[69]

Putting these two types of instruments and variables together leads to the model of ideal typical implementation styles found in Table 2.5. In this model, context is crucial and instrument preferences are linked to relatively long-term aspects of the policy-making context. Since the

factors that affect styles – such as state capacities and the nature of societal targets – are relatively long-lasting, this helps to explain why implementation styles can be expected to change infrequently and to
become a quasi-permanent feature of the policy landscape.

An emphasis on long-standing patterns of instrument choices does
not mean, of course, that choices are inevitable or immutable or that
substantial shifts in implementation styles do not occur. Such shifts can
happen as the nature of the constraints that governments face changes
or if governments decide to broaden or narrow their focus on specific
policy targets. Assessing how likely it is for existing implementation
styles to change, therefore, is an important question for policy designers and students of instrument choices.

Certainly, shifts in fundamental implementation styles have occurred
in many governments over the past century due to the influences of activities like colonization and decolonization, war, and other events that
have wrought changes to the organizational capacities of states and
their societies. Even in governments less affected by such dramatic
events, such as those in North America, implementation styles have
moved from, for example, a preference for directed subsidization in the
nineteenth century to the regulatory corporatism associated with the
progressive movement in the 1920s and 1930s.[70]

It is also certainly the case in Europe and North America, and
elsewhere, that contemporary governance currently takes place
within a very different context from that of past decades. Government capacity in terms of human and organizational resources
remains high by historical standards, but the autonomy of governments – that is, their ability independently to affect change – has
been eroded by such factors as the growth of powerful international
actors and systems of exchange.[71] Moreover, at the domestic level,
modern societies have developed increasingly complex networks of
interorganizational actors whose coordination and management are
increasingly problematic.[72]

In responding to, and attempting to lead, these changes, governments in Europe and North America have encountered difficulties in
using existing implementation styles to achieve their preferred policy
outcomes.[73] In order to retain effective service delivery and legitimate
their actions as the size of the targets they wish to influence has
increased, administrators have experimented with a variety of new
substantive instruments, such as advertising, auctions, private-public
partnerships, and elaborate tax-incentive schemes, as well as with
many new procedural techniques, such as stakeholder participation,
and various other forms of "collaborative government."[74] In these

circumstances many governments have turned away from earlier styles, such as "regulatory corporatism" and "public provision with oversight," and toward either "institutionalized voluntarism" or "directed subsidization" depending on the configuration of resources and legitimacy they have encountered in specific sectors.[75]

CONCLUSION:
THE NEED FOR NUANCE AND PRECISION
IN POLICY-INSTRUMENT ANALYSIS
AND PRACTICE

The study of policy instruments over the past twenty years has generated many insights into instrument use, insights that have helped academics to better understand policy processes and have enabled practitioners in Canada and elsewhere to design better policies.[76] However, in the process of developing the taxonomies and models of instrument choice, many investigators at first focused almost exclusively on the specific set of substantive instruments that governments use to alter the distribution of goods and services in society. Because of this intense focus on "substantive" tools, sight was lost of the need, identified by earlier students of public-policy tools, to take both the substance and process of policy making into account when conducting instrument analyses and designing governance strategies.

This shortcoming has become a major problem in attempting to find solutions, methods, and tools to deal with contemporary policy issues and has led to the development of "second-generation" instrument theorists determined to understand the complexity of multiple instrument mixes.[77] As a result of their work, at the present time, the basic contours of both procedural and substantive policy instruments are well known, as are the basic rationales for their use and the factors that have led to their selection. Understanding the use of "bundles," or "portfolios," of instruments rather than of single tools is a crucial step in designing effective governance strategies,[78] and the concept of an "implementation style" developed by second-generation thinkers is a useful one in beginning to assess these questions.

Innovative and effective policy design requires that the parameters of instrument choice be well understood, both to reduce the risk of policy failure and to enhance the probability of policy success.[79] There is a need to expand the menu of instrument choices and to appreciate the nuances and complexities of quasi-permanent implementation styles and the effects they have on instrument choices. This is especially the case given that new governance arrangements are needed in many sectors now that

increased governmental and societal use of capacity-enhancing information technologies, coupled with the increasing sophistication of networks
of citizens and clients, has allowed for greater experimentation with non-
traditional means of policy implementation.[80]

# 3

# The Choice of Governing Instrument: A Retrospective

MICHAEL J. TREBILCOCK

## INTRODUCTION

In our 1982 study, *The Choice of Governing Instrument*, undertaken for the Economic Council of Canada's Regulatory Reference, I and three colleagues (the late Douglas Hartle, Robert Prichard, and Donald Dewees) sought to demonstrate that the policy objectives of government are often radically at variance with the normative prescriptions of welfare economics – according to which state intervention should be limited to correcting for pronounced and reasonably well-defined categories of market failures, such as those deriving from monopolies, externalities, insufficient access to public goods, and imperfect information – and will in fact extend to any number of other objectives, including both principled and perverse redistributive objectives. We argued, too, that even a more modest claim made by some economists is fundamentally misconceived: the contention that, whatever the policy objectives of government (efficiency, redistribution, communitarianism, etc.), it is rational for government to pursue these ends or objectives by the most efficient (i.e., least costly) means.[1] This notion suffers as practical policy advice in part because of an infinite regress between means and ends, whereby stated ends simply become means to some other, more ultimate end – a regress that can only be arrested by assuming that whatever politicians' ultimate ends in espousing given policies, a necessary condition for promoting these policies is achieving political office. As well, the choice of means is almost never a valuationally neutral exercise but entails making trade-offs between various desired policy objectives that different means or instruments impact on in different ways. In this study, we sought to exemplify the explanatory power of the public-choice framework by surveying a wide range of policies and policy proposals in the fields of public inquiries; taxation, expenditures, and debt management; public enterprise; and regulation.

A central message that we sought to convey in our study is that rarely in politics is there a policy vacuum waiting to be filled pending advice from well-informed economists (or other social scientists), nor are existing policies that deviate from the prescriptions of welfare economics usually simply reflections of political ignorance or stupidity that are likely to be corrected once these same economists (or social scientists) point out to politicians the folly of their ways. Rather, the prevailing policies represent some form of political equilibrium reflecting the premise that the various classes of participants in collective decision-making processes (politicians, bureaucrats, regulators, interest groups, the media, and voters) should not be viewed as involved in the common and selfless pursuit of some agreed set of public-interest goals; instead, collective or government decision making should be viewed as a kind of implicit market involving intricate sets of exchanges between and among self-interested actors.[2] That is, actors will be similarly self-interested whether they are acting in economic or political markets. Thus, for example, to attain or retain political office, politicians will find it rational to fashion policies that exploit various political asymmetries: between marginal voters (uncommitted voters in swing ridings) and inframarginal voters; between well-informed and ill-informed voters; and between concentrated and diffuse interest groups facing differential political-mobilization costs (collective-action problems). Moreover, because of short electoral cycles, they will favour policies with immediate and visible benefits that defer costs to later time periods or render them less visible (e.g., by moving them off-budget). Bureaucrats will be motivated to promote policies that maximize their power, pay, and prestige. Regulators will seek a quiet life by coming to accommodations with the interests they are supposed to be regulating and perhaps also by enhancing their prospects of employment in the regulated industry after their tenure as regulators (the "capture" theory of regulation). The media, in order to maximize readership or viewing audiences, thereby enhancing advertising revenues, will trivialize complex policy issues, sensationalize mishaps unreflective of systemic policy failures, and turn over issues at a rapid rate with minimal investigative follow-up in order to cater to readers' and viewers' limited attention spans (rational ignorance).

In the conclusion to our 1982 study, we noted that Prime Minister Trudeau, in his terms of reference to the Economic Council, posed the question: "Are there superior regulatory alternatives ... available for obtaining the objectives of regulation?" In the framework that we proposed, one is forced to recognize the fundamentally political and non-technocratic nature of this question. "This implies that if one wishes to change policies in a significant and lasting way, it is necessary to change some extremely fundamental dimensions of the political system. In particular, changes in the rules and incentives that constitute the political system would seem to be required. The policy outcomes are unlikely to be altered until the structure and processes that generate them are also altered."[3] We were critical in our study of the failure of the Economic Council to acknowledge the essentially political nature of the enterprise on which it was asked to embark in its Regulation Reference:

It may well be that addressing political reform in this way was outside the Economic Council's terms of reference and perhaps its competency. It is easy to sympathize with the reluctance of the Council, as an economic advisory body, to embark upon such an exercise. Because the fundamental question that the Council was asked to answer is not an economic question at all, but a political question – asking how we can achieve superior regulation is equivalent to asking how we can achieve a better system of politics – the question cannot be answered solely from an economic perspective. That the Council may have been asked a question that it cannot answer (perhaps designedly so) cannot be an excuse for naïveté on its part. Failure at least to acknowledge emphatically the essential identity of issues of regulatory and political reform runs the serious risk of having the Council's extensive work on regulation contribute unwittingly to a public delusion (perhaps politically expedient) that a great deal in the way of significant regulatory reform can be accomplished without major reforms of our political institutions and processes. If the latter are not on the public agenda at this time, it may well be that the Council cannot hope to have done more than address its attention to quite modest, micro, regulatory reforms designed simply to redress particular instances of unintended perversities, irritations, and frictions in the regulatory process. Reducing delays, duplication, and paperwork may not be exalted goals; but they are probably all we are left with if major political reforms lie outside our collective will or capacity.[4]

In this chapter, with the benefit of two decades of hindsight, I want to self-critically evaluate the framework of analysis that I and my co-authors developed in our 1982 study and the relatively gloomy prognosis we offered of the prospects for serious policy reform in the absence of fundamental political reform.[5]

Upon reflection, I believe that public-choice theory generally, or at least the version of it that we advanced in our 1982 study, despite its

powerful, salutary, and indispensable insights into collective decision
making, suffers from several important shortcomings as an explanatory
framework for analyzing the process of public-policy making. First, the
theory's adoption of welfare economics and the associated but relatively circumscribed taxonomy of market failures as its normative reference point and its commitment to efficiency (defined as maximizing
the value of the social product or social surplus) as its objective function, with the implication that policies that cannot be justified within
this framework are by default to be explained as self-interested rent
seeking by various participants in the collective decision-making
process, obscures the importance of a range of noneconomic and nonself-interested values that commonly motivate various participants in
collective decision-making processes, including notions of distributive
justice, corrective justice, due process, communitarianism, racial and
gender equality, and so on. Second, I believe that the public-choice
framework, while properly treating institutions as endogenous to the
framework, nevertheless discounts unduly the long-run, independent
impact of incremental changes to institutional design and modus operandi on subsequent policy outcomes.[6] Third, public-choice theory does
not provide a well-developed, dynamic account of what sorts of forces
disrupt existing political equilibria and lead over time (often relatively
short periods of time) to nonincremental policy changes.

None of these reservations, serious as they are, is intended to deni-
grate the important contributions that public-choice theory has made
and can make both to understanding existing policy outcomes and the
public-policy decision-making process that generated them and to understanding the likely impact of changes to various features of this process. Rather, my intention is to argue a somewhat more hopeful view of
the policy-making process than that advanced in 1982 and to claim
that the vicelike grip of the iron triangle of special interests, politicians,
and bureaucrats/regulators (and, I would add, the media) is not as un-
yielding as we contended, while at the same time acknowledging that
no single positive theory of the process of public-policy making has
broad explanatory power, remitting us unfortunately (for analytical
purposes) to a less deterministic, more multistranded, and admittedly
more messy complex of variables that, in terms of future analytical
challenges, we have barely begun to work into a comprehensive positive theory of public decision making.

In a recent superb review of theories of regulation, Steven Croley
identifies at least four distinct constellations of positive theories of regulation: the public-choice theory, the neopluralist theory, the public-
interest theory, and the civic-republican theory. He summarizes these
theories as follows:

Very briefly, the public choice theory challenges the idea that agencies' work-products genuinely respond to market failures. The public choice account holds, much to the contrary, that agencies deliver regulatory benefits to well-organized political interest groups, which profit at the expense of the general, unorganized public. The neopluralist theory also takes organized interest groups to be central to understanding regulation. On the neopluralist view, however, many interest groups with opposing interests compete for favourable regulation, and that competition is less lopsided than the public choice view contemplates. Because the result of interest-group competition often crudely reflects general interests, the neopluralist theory is less critical of the regulatory state than is the public choice theory. Like the neopluralist view, the public interest theory is also ambivalent toward regulatory outcomes. Whereas the neopluralist focuses on interest-group competition, however, the public interest theorist concentrates on the general public's ability to monitor regulatory decision makers. Where regulatory decision makers operate under conditions of significant public scrutiny, the public interest theory holds that regulatory outcomes tend to reflect general interest. Where, on the other hand, the relevant decision makers operate without any oversight, they tend to delivery regulatory benefits to well-organized interest groups at the public's expense. Finally, the civic republican theory provides a picture of regulation rather different from all three of its counterparts. According to it, agency decisions, at least potentially, embody the polity's judgments about how competing regulatory values such as highway safety versus traveler convenience, for example, are to be balanced. On this view, regulation provides occasion for collective deliberation about regulatory means and ends.[7]

Croley concludes that:

The present state of scholarly thinking on regulation, taken alone, teaches surprisingly little. Close scrutiny reveals that available theories are conceptually incomplete, to varying degrees empirically unsubstantiated, and normatively question-begging. What is more, none is ambiguously superior to every other. While some are certainly more developed than others, each trades on supposition.[8]

This chapter, in reviewing the potential for public-policy changes in any context, attempts to situate itself between two very different traditions in economic scholarship. The first tradition – a welfare-economics perspective – purports to demonstrate (often empirically) that in many, even most, areas of public-policy making we have adopted policies that are not welfare maximizing. The economic literature is replete with studies that purport to show that existing policies on, for example, environmental and health-and-safety regulation,

price-and-entry controls, trade restrictions, agricultural supply-
management schemes, and tax-and-expenditure programs reduce net
social welfare and leave us well within the production-possibility, or
Pareto, frontier. The implication of these studies seems to be that these
welfare-reducing policy choices reflect either stupidity or venality on
the part of policy makers. Once the true facts are revealed, it appears
to be assumed that stupidity will give way to enlightenment and that
venality (capture of policy makers by rent-seeking special-interest
groups) will be repulsed by an informed and aroused public. In many
respects, this perspective's assumption that all that is needed for better
policy is better information or ideas reflects a naive view of the policy-
making process given the resistance of many polices to change despite
recurrent criticism from welfare economists.

The second tradition – an austere public-choice perspective – views
existing policy choices as reflecting a stable political equilibrium
among affected interests, politicians, bureaucrats, and regulators and
assumes that no more economically efficient policy outcome is politically achievable.[9] According to this view, welfare economists are
mostly engaged in wishful thinking and utopianism – we are already
doing the best we can in a world not populated by angels. This view
also seems naive and is excessively pessimistic in attributing decisive
influence to special interests and "iron triangles" on the prospects for
policy improvements, as evidenced by numerous instances of significant policy change surrounding us.

This chapter offers a third view of the policy-making process – more
optimistic than the public-choice perspective and less optimistic than
the welfare-economics perspective – in suggesting that particular
constellations of ideas, interests, and institutions under certain conditions are capable of generating significant policy changes and
improvements.

## POLICY STABILITY AND CHANGE

### Policy Stability

Over the past two decades or so, as governments throughout the industrialized and developing world have wrestled with escalating deficit
and debt levels, oil price shocks in the early and late 1970s, global recessions in the mid-1970s and early and late 1980s, intensifying international competition from newly industrializing countries and some
developing countries, and increasingly mobile capital, pressures have
mounted to cut public expenditures and to take seriously policy inno-

vations that enable governments to do less or to do the same for less. The disintegration of centrally planned, authoritarian regimes in central and eastern Europe beginning in the late 1980s and the general movement in these countries and many developing countries toward more market-oriented economic policies and more democratically oriented political regimes have been regarded by some commentators as evidence for the final triumph of economic and political liberalism.[10] In sharp contrast to this triumphalist view, many commentators on the left see many of these developments as entailing or portending the gutting of the welfare state, rising levels of income inequality and economic insecurity, and a conspiracy by international economic and political elites to debase and disempower civil society through the emergence and privileging of some new form of global robber-baron capitalism.[11]

Both these cataclysmic views of the changing role of the state over the past two decades or so and projections of its role as we enter the next millennium are belied by the facts. As Geddes remarks in another context: "Political scientists [and other social scientists] spend much of their time explaining events that have not finished happening."[12] This tendency to overinterpretation of the facts on both the left and the right is revealed by a cursory examination of some basic statistical indicators of the evolving role of the state, at least in developed economies. In a survey of the world economy in its issue of 20 September 1997, the *Economist* magazine provides a compendious synopsis of some of these indicators, from which the following tables and figures are taken. For example, with respect to government spending as a percentage of gross domestic product (GDP) in most countries within the Organization for Economic Cooperation and Development (OECD), the following table depicts a large and inexorable increase over time, including during recent periods.

As the *Economist* sardonically noted in its 1997 survey:

True there are exceptions. Sweden, where in 1993 the government's share of the economy had been 71%, has since repudiated its social-welfare model and cut public spending savagely, to just 65% of national income last year. Or look at the extraordinary transformation in Britain. In 1980, when Margaret Thatcher began wielding her Conservative axe, public spending accounted for 43% of the economy. After nearly 20 years of ruthless cuts, radical dismantling of the welfare state and hard-faced suppression of public-sector unions, the state's share has shriveled to just 42%. Sickened in the end by this remorseless brutality, the British electorate earlier this year swept Labour back into power with a landslide majority.

Table 3.1
Government spending as a percentage of gross domestic product, 1870–1996

| | 1870 | 1913 | 1920 | 1937 | 1960 | 1980 | 1990 | 1996 |
|---|---|---|---|---|---|---|---|---|
| Austria | – | – | 14.7 | 15.2 | 35.7 | 48.1 | 48.6 | 51.7 |
| Belgium | – | – | – | 21.8 | 30.3 | 58.6 | 54.8 | 54.3 |
| Canada | – | – | 13.3 | 18.6 | 28.6 | 38.8 | 46.0 | 44.7 |
| France | 12.6 | 17.0 | 27.6 | 29.0 | 34.6 | 46.1 | 49.8 | 54.5 |
| Germany | 10.0 | 14.8 | 25.0 | 42.4 | 32.4 | 47.9 | 45.1 | 49.0 |
| Italy | 11.9 | 11.1 | 22.5 | 24.5 | 30.1 | 41.9 | 53.2 | 52.9 |
| Japan | 8.8 | 8.3 | 14.8 | 25.4 | 17.5 | 32.0 | 31.7 | 36.2 |
| Netherlands | 9.1 | 9.0 | 13.5 | 19.0 | 33.7 | 55.2 | 54.0 | 49.9 |
| Norway | 3.7 | 8.3 | 13.7 | – | 29.9 | 37.5 | 53.8 | 45.5 |
| Spain | – | 8.3 | 9.3 | 18.4 | 18.8 | 32.2 | 42.0 | 43.3 |
| Sweden | 5.7 | 6.3 | 8.1 | 10.4 | 31.0 | 60.1 | 59.1 | 64.7 |
| Switzerland | – | 2.7 | 4.6 | 6.1 | 17.2 | 32.8 | 33.5 | 37.6 |
| Britain | 9.4 | 12.7 | 26.2 | 30.0 | 32.2 | 43.0 | 39.9 | 41.9 |
| United States | 3.9 | 1.8 | 7.0 | 8.6 | 27.0 | 31.8 | 33.3 | 33.3 |
| AVERAGE | 8.3 | 9.1 | 15.4 | 18.3* | 28.5 | 43.3 | 46.1 | 47.1 |
| Australia | – | – | – | – | 21.2 | 31.6 | 34.7 | 36.6 |
| Ireland | – | – | – | – | 28.0 | 48.9 | 41.2 | 37.6 |
| New Zealand | – | – | – | – | 26.9 | 38.1 | 41.3 | 47.1 |
| AVERAGE | – | – | – | – | 25.4 | 39.5 | 39.1 | 40.4 |
| TOTAL AVERAGE | 8.3 | 9.1 | 15.4 | 20.7 | 27.9 | 42.6 | 44.8 | 45.9 |

Source: International Monetary Fund (IMF)
* Average without Germany, Japan, and Spain undergoing war or war preparations at this time

Government expenditures fall into four broad categories:

1 government consumption, measured by what the state, as a supplier of services, spends on wages and other inputs
2 public investments
3 transfers and subsidies
4 interest on the national debt

For the industrial countries as a group, between 1960 and 1990 public spending as a proportion of national income fell in only one of these categories: public investments (e.g., on infrastructure). Of the other categories, interest on the national debt has grown most

Figure 3.1
Taxing times: General government current receipts, % of GDP

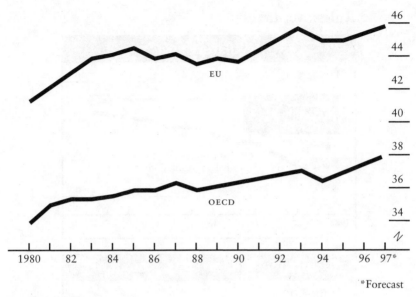

*Forecast

*Source:* OECD

quickly. The next fastest growing category, and by far the largest, was transfers and subsidies, which include income support benefits for the unemployed, the disabled, and single parents and above all pensions. Transfers and subsidies are followed by government consumption – that is, spending on services such as defence, law and order, education, and health.

Unsurprisingly, these increases in government expenditures have been accompanied by increasing levels of government taxation, measured as a percentage of GDP (Figure 3.1).

Tax and expenditure instruments are, of course, not the only instruments of government intervention. Regulation is the other major form of intervention. The *Economist* magazine of 27 July 1996 notes, in referring to US studies, that the costs of complying with US federal regulations has risen to 47 per cent of the federal budget from nearly 40 per cent in 1988. One study estimates that in 1995, federal regulations cost the average American household $7,000 – more than the average income-tax bill, which was $6,000 per household. The growth in regulation in the US is depicted in the figures 3.2 and 3.3.

Figure 3.2
Growth in regulation

## Rules over taxes

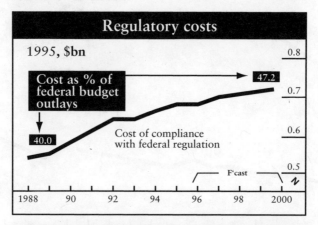

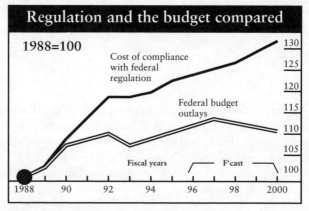

*Source:* Thomas Hopkins, Rochester Institute of Technology; OMB

The distribution of regulatory costs in the US across classes of activities is depicted in figure 3.3, which reveals a significant decline in price-and-entry controls and a proportionately greater increase in environmental and health-and-safety regulation and paper work (less economic regulation, more social regulation).

A study of the costs of regulation in Canada[13] similarly finds an increase in the scale of regulatory interventions by governments in Canada measured in various ways. This growth is captured in table 3.2.

Table 3.2
Cost to Canadians of regulatory compliance, 1973/74–1995/96 (in constant dollars)

| Year | Economy-wide costs | Cost per household* |
|---|---|---|
| 1973/74 | $58 billion | $10,282 |
| 1987 | $78.7 billion | $11,856 |
| 1993/94 | $85.7 billion | $11,929 |
| 1995/96 | $83.4 billion | $11,272 |

Source: The Fraser Institute
* Defined as a family of four

Figure 3.3
Distribution of regulatory cost, %

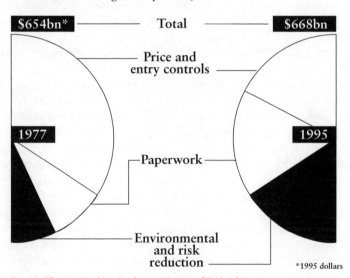

## Earth, air, paper and water
Distribution of regulatory costs, %

Source: Thomas Hopkins, Rochester Institute of Technology

Some commentators have argued that the growth of social regulation and the durability of the welfare state are due to the efficiency of government as a risk manager unhindered by the imperfections or incompleteness of private-insurance and risk-management mechanisms.[14]

## Policy Change

A natural reaction to these aggregate statistics on trends in government expenditures, taxes, and regulation is that both the triumphalists on the right (the economic liberals) and the doomsayers on the left (the communitarians) are engaging in extreme forms of rhetorical hyperbole. In fact, for the most part, for OECD countries over the past two decades or so, it has been "politics as usual," with most policy alterations having comprised only minor or incremental changes in response to prevailing political and economic pressures. But such a reaction would seem to entail a radical disconnection from politics as experienced by citizens in their day-to-day lives in many or most of these countries over this period. Indeed, in my view, the trends in the broad economic aggregates sketched above obscure important shifts in public policy in particular contexts, without at the same time reflecting any sweeping ideological reconceptualization of the relationship between state and market. A number of areas of public policy illustrate this view.[15]

*First,* privatization of state-owned enterprises over the past fifteen years has been an important phenomenon in many OECD countries (setting aside privatization programs in former command economies). For example, the UK has privatized state-owned enterprises (or aspects of them) in telecommunications, natural gas, ship building, electricity, coal mining, railways, and automobile manufacturing and has sold off public rental-housing units to tenants. In Canada a number of state-owned enterprises have been privatized, including most prominently Air Canada (the state-owned airline), Petro Canada (the state-owned vertically integrated oil company), and Canadian National (the state-owned railway). Many other OECD countries and developing countries have also engaged in significant privatizations.[16] *Second,* governments have increasingly engaged various private actors (for-profit or non-profit organizations) both in the delivery of public services through contracting-out, public-private partnerships, and similar mechanisms and in standard setting, monitoring, and enforcement – "third party government" in the words of Lester Salamon.[17] *Third,* economic deregulation with respect to price-and-entry controls has occurred in many OECD countries in the areas of telecommunications, airlines, railways, trucking, oil, natural gas, electricity, and financial services.[18] *Fourth*, in many countries as economic regulation has been contracting, social regulation (health, safety, environmental, and antidiscrimination regulation) has been expanding. *Fifth*, OECD countries and many other countries have been participants in important continuing initiatives in international forums – including the Uruguay Round of negotiations involving nations party to the General Agreement on Tariffs and Trade (GATT) and the World Trade Organization (WTO); the North American Free Trade Agreement (NAFTA); the European Union (EU); and other regional arrangements – to further liberalize both trade in goods and services and foreign direct investment, with tariffs and other border restrictions now, in most cases, having been reduced to negligible levels. *Sixth*, important initiatives have been undertaken in many OECD countries to reform their tax systems by lowering the nominal rates applied to corporate and individual tax payers, reducing the number of tax brackets, and broadening the tax base by eliminating many tax expenditures or concessions, thus reducing the distorting effect of taxes on economic activities. In addition, a number of countries (other than the US) have increased their reliance on consumption taxes relative to income taxes, again reducing tax-induced distortions in savings and investment decisions. *Seventh*, while government expenditures on social services such as health, education, unemployment insurance, welfare assistance, and public pensions may not have significantly declined (and, indeed, have often increased), containing rates of growth in these sectors has forced many governments to embark on policy or institutional changes in these contexts that many citizens find unsettling or even threatening.

Thus, while it may be tempting to subscribe to a "politics as usual" thesis in response to the trends in economic aggregates noted above, this thesis in my view obscures and overlooks important policy changes that have occurred and are occurring at a disaggregated level in many developed and developing countries throughout the world. Thus a more nuanced and contextual exploration is required in order to explain, as a positive matter, why these changes have occurred or are occurring.

### ALTERNATIVE POSITIVE EXPLANATIONS FOR PATTERNS OF POLICY STABILITY AND CHANGE

In this section of the chapter, I review alternative positive explanations for the patterns of policy stability and policy change described above.[19]

### The Illusion of Nonincremental Change

While, as noted above, some commentators have taken the view that a sea change in the form and extent of government intervention has not occurred and that those changes that have occurred are minor and incremental in nature (a kind of "smoke and mirrors" thesis), I do not accept that all the policy changes that have occurred in OECD countries in the past two decades or so can be dismissed as mere tinkering at the margins. As a consequence of privatization and deregulation, the structure and operation of the telecommunications, airlines, rail, trucking, energy, and financial-services industries are profoundly different today in many countries from their structure and operation twenty years ago. Thus the claim that there is really nothing to be explained is not persuasive.

### Ideology

I am skeptical of the claim that those policy changes that have occurred reflect a fundamental ideological shift to the right throughout the world, with publics and policy makers seeking a fundamental readjustment in the relationship between state and market. First, such a view is contradicted by the trends in economic aggregates described above. Second, while it is true that some privatization and deregulatory policies were initiated by conservative administrations, such as Margaret Thatcher's administration in the UK and Ronald Reagan's administration in the US, many deregulatory initiatives actually occurred prior to these administrations – both trucking and airline deregulation in the US were personal causes of Senator Edward Kennedy, a pariah of the American right, and were promoted by Jimmy Carter's Democratic administration. Moreover, in recent years in many OECD countries, we have witnessed the election of centrist or left-of-centre governments that have nevertheless retained and often expanded the privatization and regulatory reform initiatives of predecessor governments of a different ideological orientation. Third, continuing concerns registered by citizens in Canada and many other countries over governmental commitments to high-quality and widely accessible health-care services, public education, and regulation of environmental quality and health-and-safety risks are scarcely consistent with an espousal of a new and widespread belief in minimal, nonactivist government.

### Interests

According to the public-choice view of the policy-making process, the iron triangle of self-interested politicians, bureaucrats/regulators, and rent-seeking special-interest groups (and the media) would seem to be largely impervious to policy change. Indeed, one explanation for the trends in economic aggregates as sketched in the first part of this chapter is that they are consistent with the predictions of public-choice theory. This view is in fact subscribed to by the *Economist* ("the enigma of acquiescence") in the same survey from which these aggregate data are drawn. The *Economist* argues that in the simplest case of a two-party system, both parties will compete to attract the support of the median voter, who occupies the electorally crucial middle ground. The *Economist* claims that this hypothesis is borne out by studies in many countries showing that it is the better-off who benefit disproportionately from most social programs, leading to the idea of "middle-class capture." In addition, the *Economist* also draws on interest-group theory in explaining these general trends, particularly the disproportionate influence of concentrated interest groups relative to diffuse interest groups.

This explanation for the pattern of policy stability and policy change described in the first part of the chapter is puzzling in several respects. First, to the extent that politicians adopt policies that serve the interests of median voters (presumably the majority of voters in most cases), it is difficult to view this as a form of political market failure (at least in the absence of information failures); rather, it suggests majoritarian forms of democracy working at their best. In fact, Donald Wittman argues in a provocative book, *The Myth of Democratic Failure*,[20] that US democratic processes, most of the time, in fact work this way and deliver efficient (i.e., welfare-enhancing) policies. Indeed, public-choice theory does not have a well-developed theory of the political rate of exchange between the political resources of concentrated interest groups (lobbying resources, campaign contributions) and the resources of citizens (votes), which the former largely lack.

The second and somewhat contradictory strand of the *Economist's* claim (i.e., the disproportionate influence of concentrated interest groups in the political process) raises similar puzzles. The trend toward economic deregulation (including trade liberalization) and privatization and the introduction of competition into hitherto monopolized sectors have in most cases generated substantial benefits for consumers,[21] but consumers are the quintessential example of diffuse interests, which in these contexts seem to have triumphed over concentrated, incumbent producer interests, contrary to the predictions of public-choice theory.[22] Similarly, the dramatic growth in environmental, health-and-safety, and other forms of social regulation in recent years again appears to reflect the triumph of consumer, environmental, worker, and related racial and gender interests over concentrated producer interests.

## Technology

It is widely claimed that rates of technological innovation have dramatically increased in recent years, particularly with respect to information and communications technologies, and that these new technologies have undermined traditional assumptions about the boundaries of markets and the nature of industry structures. From a political perspective, technological innovation may upset existing political equilibria that have sustained traditional regulatory policies by introducing new participants or potential participants on the supply side of these markets, often through reductions in economies of scale and scope, and by stimulating new configurations of customers on the demand side seeking access to these new services. This is most clearly true in the telecommunications sector and may also be true to a lesser extent in the financial-services sector, where new information and communication technologies have tended to undermine both national regulatory boundaries and boundaries between different classes of purveyors of financial services by changing economies of scale and scope in the provision of bundles of financial services through given distribution channels. However, technological explanations of shifts in policy seem to have much less relevance to sectors such as airlines, railways, trucking, natural gas, and (with some qualifications) electricity, where technological innovations have been modest. Thus technological change does not offer a broad-gauge explanation for the policy changes noted earlier in this chapter.

## Ideas

While it is obviously self-interested for academics to seek to assign substantial weight to the influence of ideas in the policy-making process as the motivation for major policy changes, self-interest or self-aggrandizement does not in itself disqualify this explanation.

According to an oft-cited claim by John Maynard Keynes, "Soon or late, it is ideas, not vested interests, which are dangerous for good or evil."[23] While not denying the importance of self-interest in the political process, Steven Kelman argues that the economist's (public-choice) view of the political process dramatically underestimates the role of what he calls "public spirit" or "civic virtue," or simply nonself-interested ideas, in the political process.[24] He invokes many examples to substantiate this view, such as the enactment of extensive consumer-protection and environmental legislation in the 1960s and early 1970s in the US and many other countries over the protestations and resistance of concentrated and entrenched interests as well as deregulation, privatization, and tax reform in the late 1970s and 1980s in the US and many other countries, again over the protestations of many powerful and deeply entrenched interests. Indeed, the so-called paradox of voting – why so many citizens choose to vote in national elections at some cost to themselves and with minimal chance of influencing the outcome – suggests a powerful notion of civic virtue at work. In this respect, ideas or values that are likely to be influential will extend well beyond maximizing the total social surplus and correcting for market failures in a welfare-economics framework and are likely to include notions of distributive justice, corrective justice, communitarianism, gender and racial equality, due process, and so forth. Attempts to reductively equate civic commitments to these ideas or values with direct or indirect pursuit of self-interest are often quite unpersuasive. For example, that the majority of citizens in most industrialized countries favour various forms of social safety nets, such as social assistance and unemployment insurance, when many of them face a very remote probability of ever having to resort to these systems, cannot easily be explained in quasi-Marxist terms as an attempt by a well-endowed majority to negate the possibility of civil insurrection by an impoverished minority that might threaten the formers' endowments. This seems intuitively a completely unpersuasive explanation of why most citizens are committed to some notion of distributive justice, even if they do not perceive themselves as likely to be direct material beneficiaries of these policies.

Thus, in Kelman's view, politics is to an important extent as much about what are thought to be ideas (good or, it should be added, bad) as about what are thought to be salient political interests. In other words, persuasion has important currency in the political process in a reciprocal sense: Voters, interest groups, scholars, and policy commentators may persuade politicians, bureaucrats, and regulators of the virtues of a position or idea; similarly, political leaders, bureaucrats, and regulators may persuade interest groups and voters of the virtues of an idea (a form of the civic-republican view of government). Given that entrepreneurs in private markets engage in a ceaseless process of innovation and attempt to persuade consumers of the virtues of their innovations, which necessarily assumes that preferences are not innate and immutable, it seems equally plausible that preferences are not fixed and immutable in the political process. It is an odd irony that political economists, who stress the dynamic qualities of private markets and forces of innovation as well as entry into new markets by means of breaking down entrenched market positions (the "perennial gale of creative destruction," in Joseph Schumpeter's famous words),[25] are inclined to view the political process in such static terms and the role for policy innovations and policy entrepreneurs as so limited. The salience of ideas in the political process is underscored by a simple and commonplace observation: It is rare for interest groups to articulate their claims in political discourse in nakedly self-interested terms – "we are shamelessly seeking to feed at the public trough." Rather, their self-interest will be typically rationalized in a value or policy objective that engages the values but not the interests of other political constituents whose support is required for the adoption of the policy in question.

Notwithstanding the attractions of these arguments about the salience of ideas in the policy-making process, it needs to be noted that many of the ideas that underpin the policy changes noted earlier in this chapter have enjoyed wide currency, at least among economists, that long predates these policy changes (e.g., trade liberalization). Moreover, their implementation has been uneven from one country to the next, from one sector to the next, and in terms of pace of implementation. Thus it is obvious that ideas cannot be abstracted from particular political and historical contexts. Nor can "political market failures" of the kind emphasized by public-choice theory be discounted in many contexts. In particular, ideas need a congenial political context if they are to take root. In this respect, it might be argued that with the recessions (following the oil-price shocks) in many OECD countries in the mid-1970s and early and late 1980s, declining rates of productivity growth, stagnant or falling real incomes, stagflation (high rates of inflation and high rates of unemployment), and rising budgetary deficits and debt burdens that reduced governments' "free cash flow" to underwrite interventionist policies, publics and politicians in many industrialized countries became increasingly disaffected with Keynesian demand-side economic stimulation or stabilization policies. Thus they were increasingly open to other ideas, particularly to the supply-side ideas that largely motivate the privatization and economic deregulation trends described earlier in this chapter – that is, the preference for unshackling constraints and providing incentives for increased competition, new-market entry, new investment, and increased rates of innovation on the supply side in many industries whose economic performance came to be regarded as disappointing.[26] Yet exceptions to these trends, such as agricultural protectionism and the relatively undisciplined nature of social regulation, particularly the limited roles of incentive-oriented regulatory instruments and of rigorous cost-benefit analysis of regulatory impacts, suggest important limits to the political receptiveness to economic ideas.[27] In other words, ideas without supportive and salient political interests are doomed to political oblivion. Thus an appropriate conjuncture of both ideas and political context is required if ideas are to be an important agent of change, implying a need to integrate the role of ideas into a public-choice framework in a more dynamic theory of the policy-making process.

## Institutions

While ideas and interests are important determinants of public-policy outcomes, they must be mediated through institutions in order to be translated into public policy. Much recent literature, especially in the political sciences, emphasizes the importance of the choice and design of state institutions as an independent variable in determining policy outcomes (the so-called "new institutionalism").[28] Weaver and Rockman identify three tiers of institutional variables that may determine which institutions matter and how they may affect governmental performance: (1) the distinction between parliamentary systems and the US congressional system of checks and balances; (2) features, such as the electoral rules and norms, leading to the formation of different types of government (e.g., alternating single-party majorities, durable single-party dominance, or multiparty coalitions) that focus on variations within parliamentary and presidential systems; and (3) other institutional factors, such as federalism, bicameralism, and judicial review.

In the Canadian context, Michael Atkinson argues, the organization and character of political institutions play a critical role in determining policy outcomes.[29] However, the study of political institutions cannot take place in isolation from the study of ideas and interests. Institutions do not suddenly appear fully formed; they have to be invented. Clearly, the organization and character of institutions reflect both competing economic and social forces that struggle to embed their interests in these institutions and ideas about appropriate arrangements for governance. However, once institutions are adopted, they tend to exert an independent influence on which interests and ideas in particular policy domains are privileged or marginalized in subsequent public-policy decisions. According to Carolyn Tuohy: "For some 'new institutionalists,' state institutions assume a privileged role in the explanation of policy outputs. They represent a 'crystallization' of the effects of economic factors, ideas and interests; and they constitute the primary vehicle through which these factors are brought to bear on policy, but they also generate ideas and interests through a process of institutional evolution over time."[30]

Croley argues, in a US context, that the nature of the administrative process adopted by regulatory agencies may profoundly affect regulatory decision making.[31] Changes in ideas about the nature of the regulatory process and the administrative state, particularly the case for transparent and participatory public hearings and consultations and reasoned public decisions – in effect, an expanded notion of administrative due process – have created opportunities for hitherto excluded or marginalized classes of participants to influence regulatory policy making. In a Canadian context, this is most clearly evident in the case of changes in telecommunications policy, which have largely been spearheaded by the Canadian Radio-Television and Telecommunications Commission (CRTC) through a series of extensive and widely participatory public hearings, rather than by government fiat. Expanded notions of administrative due process have also been evident in environmental assessment processes and in the proceedings of various commissions of inquiry into public-policy concerns. However, while such an explanation of policy changes is persuasive in some contexts, in others it seems to have limited or little relevance. Many of the policy changes described earlier in this chapter were not the product of extensive public hearings or consultations but were in fact the result of government fiats arrived at following relatively conventional political processes. Thus, once again, we do not have a broad-gauge explanation for these policy changes.

## The Internationalization of Markets

Another explanation for major privatization and deregulatory policy shifts in recent years in many countries is the internationalization of markets in goods, services, and capital (in part explained by innovations in information and communications technologies). This phenomenon changes the politics surrounding domestic regulatory policy making in a variety of important ways. First, in both traded-goods and service sectors, if one or more of a country's major trading partners have adopted policies that substantially enhance the efficiency and innovative potential of a sector, counterpart sectors in the first country may have little option but to emulate these policies if they are not to lose international competitiveness on either the import or export sides. Second, users of the outputs of these industries as inputs for their own industries will increasingly demand that they not be handicapped in international competition by being denied access to inputs on terms as favourable as those afforded their international competitors. Third, to the extent that consumers are able credibly to threaten to exit or by-pass domestic suppliers – clearly a factor in telecommunications, rail, airlines, and trucking deregulation in many countries – the ability to sustain a restrictive domestic regulatory regime may be undermined.[32] With the liberalization of international capital markets and fewer restraints on personal mobility, the ability of the most mobile factors of production – financial capital and specialized human capital – to threaten exit to more congenial jurisdictions is likely to place increasing pressures on domestic governments to adopt policies that converge with those in these other jurisdictions.

In itself, this explanation does not of course account for why some countries chose to be first movers in making these changes; such an account may largely require resort to some of the other explanations reviewed above. However, even here one cannot dismiss from first-movers' motivations the desire to gain a comparative advantage in international trade and investment. Even if this were not the initial motivation, having gone through the wrenching changes that restructuring entails, and in particular having reduced entry barriers to formerly regulated monopoly domains, providing in many cases access by foreign suppliers and investors to these markets, domestic firms not unnaturally then demand some form of reciprocal access to other countries' markets, where they can exploit their newly acquired comparative advantage. This demand for reciprocity has been very much in evidence in recent WTO agreements on financial services and basic telecommunications. Arguably, it also explains the beginnings of the process of liberalization of the agricultural sector – long viewed as the most impregnable bastion of protectionism – as reflected in the Uruguay Round's agreement on agriculture. Even with respect to environmental and health-and-safety regulations, "excessively" stringent standards by importing countries and "excessively" lax standards by exporting countries have increasingly come to be viewed as nontariff barriers to trade and have become the subject of international efforts at harmonization, especially as tariffs and other border measures have diminished in significance due to trade liberalization.[33]

By moving regulatory policy making from a purely domestic political domain to an international domain, new foreign political constituencies become, in effect, influential participants in the domestic policy-making process. Moreover, at an international level, negotiations often involve a different set of political dynamics from those that typically prevail in domestic-policy settings, particularly the potential for trading off concessions across functionally disparate areas of policy making through elaborate log-rolling exercises – a possibility that rarely presents itself in as marked a form in domestic policy making, where many of the policy changes reviewed earlier in this chapter have been debated and resolved on a largely stand-alone basis. However, it needs to be acknowledged that conventional public-choice theory does not offer a robust explanation for the dramatic extent of international trade liberalization that has occurred in recent decades. Public-choice scholars such as Anthony Downs and Mancur Olson[34] viewed trade protectionism as the classic case of concentrated producer interests triumphing over diffuse consumer interests – which is manifestly at variance with much of the postwar experience.[35] Put more concretely, public-choice theorists can tell a convincing story of why the US auto industry was protected for many years from Japanese competition. But they offer much less convincing explanations for why this protection was eventually terminated.

## CONCLUSIONS

I have endeavoured to show the inherent merits and limits of each of the explanations for the reform phenomena that comprise the focus of this chapter. That most factors have a partial explanatory value, and that none seems in itself adequate as an explanation of all aspects of the phenomena, suggests that positive analyses of the policy-making process should pay increased attention to synergies, or dynamic interactions, between and among various discrete factors or forces in the policy process.

It is important to emphasize that most of the explanations reviewed above can probably be reconciled with a refined version of the public-choice framework that we advanced in *The Choice of Governing Instrument* in that technological innovation and the internationalization of markets have changed the political calculus by introducing new constellations of interests into the policy-making process. The striking exception is the influence of ideas on the policy-making process – for academics, surely a serious shortcoming – although even here explaining when and where ideas become influential in the policy-making process requires some conjuncture with other factors, including supportive and influential interests. In this respect, in our own defence, I would note only that we concluded *The Choice of Governing Instrument* with the following paragraph:

It is important to realize that by influencing voter knowledge and understanding, and hence voter decisions, the insights of economic research (and social science research generally) can be brought to bear on the ultimate decision-making process. Indeed, these effects of new information may be much more effective than the provision of direct information to bureaucrats and politicians. When few voters are aware of it, the latter can often ignore new information when it does not suit their convenience. Politicians cannot, however, easily ignore voters armed with relevant information. One might wonder why so much research is written and published with little if any attention being paid to the dissemination of the results generally. So many economists write – when not writing to one another – as though their task were to advise the prince rather than the public.

In sum, a picture of the policy-making process emerges that is much less rigid, static, and deterministic than that which characterized the public-choice framework that I and my colleagues advanced twenty years ago – a picture that suggests major new analytical challenges in developing a more comprehensive and dynamic positive theory of the policy-making process.

# PART TWO
# Form and Function: The Tools Approach to Policy Design

# 4

# The Problem of Policy Problems

B. GUY PETERS AND
JOHN A. HOORNBEEK

Policy design involves developing models of causation, instrumentation, and evaluation (Linder and Peters 1984, 1989; Ringeling ch. 8 herein) and then finding ways of linking these three models. As the literature on policy design has developed, the principal emphasis has been on the nature of policy instruments, or "tools," and on the political process of linking instruments and policy evaluations. By contrast, the literature linking problems and tools has been less well developed. While the long-term goals of such an effort should be to catalogue differing kinds of problems and to link them logically and empirically with appropriate forms of policy instruments, the objective here is more modest. It involves developing an analytical framework for understanding relevant variations in problems and offering some early thoughts on tying problem characteristics to policy tools. The idea, therefore, is to establish a starting point that may be developed further in subsequent work. Throughout the chapter, examples of policy problems are highlighted, and these examples draw disproportionately from the field of environmental policy. This area of policy making is an appropriate focus because of the changing nature of environmental policy problems and because of the active efforts made over the last two decades to implement alternative environmental policy instruments.

## POLICY INSTRUMENTS AND DESIGN:
## A BRIEF REVIEW OF THE LITERATURE

Although a great deal of research still needs to be done in the areas of instruments and evaluation, there is a substantial extant body of knowledge. For example, the tools literature has progressed from its roots in implementation (Hood 1986; Salamon and Lund 1989; Bardach 1980), through critiques of these models based on ideas of autopoesis and self-referentiality (Ringeling and van Nispen 1998; in 't Veld 1991), and then through some reformulation of the tools approach taking into account the critiques of these more traditional approaches to instruments (Peters and van Nispen 1998). There is at present a further round of development in the implementation approach to instrument theories taking into account the changes that have been occurring in the environment of public policies as well as an improved understanding of the interactions of the various tools in the delivery of services (Salamon 2000). Similarly, in their discussion of policy design, Ingram and Schneider (1997) have pointed to the need for would-be designers to take into account the nature of the populations addressed by instruments, rather than just examining the nature of the instruments in isolation. Timmermans et al. (1998) also place the study of policy instruments within a broad design context, focusing especially on the institutional context and the roles of actors involved in the process of designing.

The instruments literature has also done a rather effective job of cataloguing some of the characteristics of policy instruments. The political nature of instruments has been contrasted with their more utilitarian nature in the delivery of policies (Peters 2000). The value biases embedded in each type of instrument have been identified and discussed. The pervasive impact of national political cultures on the choice of tools also has been demonstrated (Howlett 1991; Trebilcock ch. 3 herein), helping to identify biases in the manner in which tools are selected. This finding, in turn, highlights the emphasis in this growing body of literature on the *conscious* selection of instruments, as opposed to their selection on the basis merely of custom, familiarity, and institutional inertia (Linder and Peters 1998, 1990).[1]

The tools literature has made substantial progress in characterizing the modes of government intervention in the economy and society, and the notion of policy design has become a standard component of the general literature on public policy. What has been less well developed in the available literature, however, is an analytic understanding of the policy problems that are being "solved" through the employment of these instruments. Even if we are now capable of understanding more thoroughly the characteristics of policy instruments, this knowledge might be of relatively little utility (practically or even theoretically) if we do not understand the situations into which *they are used* to implement public policies. The intention of producing desired programmatic results through well-chosen instruments might be unfulfilled if there is no appropriate linkage with the problems being addressed. Therefore, this chapter begins to explore more fully the nature of policy problems. The *ultimate* end is to understand both the nature of problems and how they may be matched with particular instruments and particular forms of evaluation to round out more fully a model of policy design.

Here, the most fundamental point, therefore, is that the contingent relationship argued to exist between problems and instruments is crucial to the enterprise of policy design. In a more recent discussion of the instruments literature (Linder and Peters 1998), the answers that some respondents gave to a survey investigation concerning policy instruments are described as "contingentist." These respondents argued that the real answer to any question about which instrument to select for a problem was that "It depends." They argued that there was no single instrument that should be selected for all situations and that there is a need to select carefully on the basis of the particular problem being addressed (see also Bagchus 1998). The contingentists were not, however, given the opportunity to develop their own ideas about the factors on which tools choice should depend; we shall begin some of that inquiry in this chapter.

The present inquiry concerning policy problems more implicitly makes the same statement about contingent relationships. If we understood completely the characteristics of the range of available tools, there still would not be an algorithm for mapping tools into problems; the answer about the circumstances in which to employ each tool is always, fundamentally, "It depends." For the purposes of this chapter, perhaps the most necessary characteristic of a policy design is its ability to utilize private- as well as public-sector instruments in the delivery of a given policy and through this mixture to begin to address the collective nature of both problems and instruments. Therefore, we need to consider carefully what makes the nature of policy problems more amenable to interventions using mixtures of both public- and private-sector actors. Relatively few answers to these basic questions of contingent relationships between problems and instruments will be provided here; rather the attempt is to develop the correct questions that would then guide one in the selection of instruments and to conduct a preliminary exploration of these questions in relation to the changing nature of environmental and water-pollution problems in the United States.

## THE CHANGING NATURE
## OF ENVIRONMENTAL PROBLEMS

While the need to match problems and policy instruments exists in all policy areas, it is now particularly apparent in environmental policy. In the United States, for example, the last thirty years have brought both substantial progress in addressing environmental concerns and a substantial redefinition of the problems that environmental policies must address. Indeed, in recent years, scholars (Kettl 1999; Ringquist 1993) and practitioners (Alm 1992) alike have called attention to a "new generation" of environmental problems and the need to address these problems through an expanding array of policy instruments. However, beyond general calls for greater use of nonregulatory policy instruments, little effort has been made to determine the most important characteristics of environmental-policy problems and their appropriate relationships to policy instruments.

Definitions of the changing nature of the problems that environmental policies must address have varied, but most of them focus on the recognition that the current generation of problems stem from many diffuse sources and involve pollutant mixes that are often invisible to the eye – a contrast to the "older" generation of problems, which were characterized by relatively obvious and well-defined pollution sources. To a significant degree, therefore, the distinction between "old-" and "new-generation" problems is mirrored by the commonly used distinction between point sources of pollution and nonpoint sources of pollution.

Several words of elaboration are appropriate here, however. Just over thirty years ago in the United States, both the environmental movement and environmental policy making were characterized by efforts to address obvious sources of pollution stemming from an industrialized economy. Industrial smokestacks bellowed air pollution from factories, and untreated sewage and industrial-wastewater pollution flowed from defined outfalls attached to municipal sewage systems and manufacturing processes. The haze and soot from air-polluting manufacturing processes were obvious in many industrialized cities, and the negative impacts of point-source water pollution were dramatized in the late in 1960s when the Cuyahoga River in Ohio caught fire. The perceived failure of the states to address these problems led to national command-and-control regulatory strategies that sought to control these obvious sources of pollution. The earliest and most obvious of these command-and-control approaches emerged in the Clean Air Act of 1970 and in the national water-pollution permit program authorized by the Clean Water Act of 1972.

While these "traditional" regulatory policy instruments have been successful in addressing many obvious sources of pollution, the ambitious goals of these two regulatory acts remain unfulfilled. Approximately 40 per cent of the waters in the United States do not meet established water-quality standards, and many urban areas face continuing problems in attaining air-quality standards on a regular and consistent basis. The problems now, however, are of a somewhat different character than the problems of the early 1970s. The US Environmental Protection Agency (EPA) has estimated that over 50 per cent of current water-quality problems are due at least in part to nonpoint sources, such as runoff from farms, fields, and forests. Air pollution also remains a problem at least in part because advances in air-pollution control efforts and technologies are being counterbalanced by continuing increases in automobile use. There are new pollutants of concern as well, as conventional pollutants such as organic materials in water and particulate matter in air are being supplemented by concerns over both an ever-increasing array of toxic substances and interactive effects among pollutants. Some of these interactive effects – such as "greenhouse" effects stemming from carbon dioxide emissions and acid rain stemming from sulphur dioxide emissions – are even leading some scholars to suggest that there is also a "third" generation of problems that have not only diffuse sources and invisible pollutants, but also regional, or even global, effects (Ringquist 1993).

The common mantra among contemporary scholars and practitioners of environmental policy is that this new generation of problems is most appropriately addressed by a new set of decentralized, and often nonregulatory, policy instruments. While these "new" policy instruments come in many forms, they can be grouped into at least three broad categories. The first category relates to information and education and includes technical-assistance efforts, social-marketing efforts, and labelling efforts of varying kinds – "sermons" in one categorization of instruments. A second category is market-based and includes measures such as pollution fees and taxes (bottle deposits, etc.) and the tradable permitting schemes currently being implemented under the Clean Air Act. A final set of instruments relates to policy-making processes and the increasing efforts in the US to replicate (almost?) more corporatist forms of stakeholder involvement in the policy-making process itself. In the US these efforts have been carried out under the banners of both Republican and Democratic administrations, with changes in faces and terminology masking a fundamental similarity in approach. In the late 1980s under Republican administrations, we saw negotiated rule making and cross-media teams (e.g., clusters) seeking to address wide-ranging problems. In the 1990s under a Democratic administration, these efforts were continued with new names ("sectors" replaced "clusters," for example) and were also supplemented by statutorily required consultation processes (the 1996 Safe Drinking Water Amendments, for example).

A common thread among these approaches is an increasing reliance on nongovernmental organizations and private-sector incentives and processes to achieve public-sector goals. And, in this respect, these changes in the forms of environmental-policy instruments that are being utilized are mirroring larger trends in the development and uti-lization of policy instruments generally (Salamon 2002). In US envi-ronmental policy, the role of federal bureaucrats is increasingly to "facilitate" as well as regulate. As scholars in Europe have phrased it, we are all moving toward the enabling state as opposed to the controlling state.

What is missing in this picture is a clear and definable rationale for exactly why the "new" environmental problems require policy instru-ments that are different from the command-and-control instruments used to address the old environmental problems. Indeed, the reality is that while we are seeing increased use of informational, economic, and policy-process instruments, traditional command-and-control regula-tion remains a (if not *the*) central ground upon which many of these new instruments are built. And, once again, environmental policy is not unusual in this regard. Across the range of public policies in the United States, and elsewhere, there is a need both to define key characteristics of policy problems and to begin to understand their relationship to pol-icy design and the selection and implementation of appropriate policy instruments. Using the changing nature of environmental problems as the principal example, the remainder of this chapter will take some first steps in defining these questions more clearly, with the full expectation that revisions in the questions themselves will need to be made in subsequent work.

POLICY PROBLEMS

Defining policy problems in a way that can be effective for policy de-sign appears to be a two-step process. The first stage in the process is to define what the problem is about; is it a problem of agriculture, envi-ronment, or whatever? This can be a difficult question politically and even empirically, and it is often a crucial question for the ultimate reso-lution of the issue and for the type of response from government. For example, is the problem of how to fertilize midwestern US farmland properly a question of agricultural productivity or of environmental protection, or both? Depending on how this question is answered, dif-ferent organizations in government will be given greater or lesser roles in resolving the problem, and different modalities of involvement will be invoked. Further, if a "wrong" definition of the problem is adopted, it may mean that the ultimate "solution" to the problem will be de-layed. Another confounding characteristic of this stage of defining the policy problem is that the most important problems are becoming less clearly defined. For example, conventional economic problems are now being converted into problems of "competitiveness" that involve not only finance but also environmental, labour, and education issues.

The second stage of the process of analysis is to develop a set of dimensions that can be used to better characterize the problem. Although it is important (at least in practical terms) to link a problem with an agency or ministry and to assign a functional name to the problem, this process may not provide an adequate understanding of the problem for policy-design purposes. Rather, a more analytic understanding of the problem is necessary if one is to understand that the problems defined as being within the control of one ministry or another may, in fact, be very different. In this context, simply concentrating on the nominal title of government agencies and ministries may deceive rather than enlighten. Therefore, a good deal of this chapter is concerned with a preliminary discussion of characteristics that appear useful for describing problems and for linking them with instruments.

### Stage One: What is the Problem?

The existing literature on the social construction of policy problems and on policy framing has done a useful service in pointing to the politics involved in problem definition (Rochefort and Cobb 1994). In the first instance, we have seen how important the minimal capacity to name a problem is for even recognizing its existence and thus for being able to begin to address the problem through the public sector. Problems of spousal abuse and child abuse, for example, had to be conceptualized as such before they could be taken into the political arena for some form of resolution (Nelson 1984). Until there is a label that can be attached to an issue, it is difficult to feed the issue into the political process for any sort of resolution or even discussion; indeed, without this label, the question is not yet really an issue.

The agenda-setting literature in political science (Cobb and Elder 1983; Baumgartner and Jones 1993; Kingdon 1994) also is closely connected with this constructivist mode of argument about issues and problems. Again, there is an assumption that policy problems must be recognized and identified in order to be usable within the political process. The agendas literature tends to argue that problems (or opportunities) present themselves rather independently, although there is ample room for the role of the policy entrepreneur in the process. This entrepreneur will identify and process the issues so that they can proceed onto some active agenda within the political system. Further, the agenda-setting literature tends to focus somewhat more on the organizational basis of politics and on the roles that these structures play in sorting and advocating items for an agenda. Any definition of an issue will advantage some organizations rather than others, making this a potential locus for bureaucratic politics. As Petracca (1992, 4) argues: "how an issue is defined or redefined, as the case may be, influences: (1) the type of politicking which will ensue around it; (2) its chances of reaching the agenda of particular political institution; and (3) the chances of a policy outcome favorable to advocates of the issue." In short, problem definition will set the stage for the final determination of the policy and is therefore crucial for shaping the final resolution of "the problem."

Schon and Rein (1994) have extended this argument somewhat with their discussion of "policy framing." They argue that perhaps the most crucial stage of the policy process is the juncture at which the issue is "framed," or defined, in political terms. This framing defines who the participants will be, who the winners and losers may be, what the range of conflict may be, and a whole range of other components of the debate over the issue.[2] Once framed, the issue is difficult to reframe in the policy debate, with the consequence that initial choices have an enduring impact in the political process. This having been said, reframing is actually one of the mechanisms for resolving the (seemingly) intractable policy problems that Schon and Rein develop (see also Hisschemoller and Hoppe 1995).[3]

The agendas and framing literatures go some distance in the identification of policy problems as a crucial aspect of the *political* process but do not do a great deal in explaining how to deal with issues in the policy process per se. That is, once the issue has arrived on the agenda and must be dealt with, how will decision makers process it, and how do they then move into the mode of designing government interventions to correct the real and/or perceived defect in society or the economy. The psychological and sociological elements of the problem may have been well defined, but this information does not necessarily enable governments to make good public-policy decisions about how to solve the problem that has been constructed. Indeed, the social construction of the problem, which is crucial for its inclusion on the political agenda, may mask more than it reveals about the underlying problem.

### Stage 2: Framing the Problem for Solution

We will now focus on the second stage of the process of defining the problems that governments are addressing. This is the stage in which the problem, having been identified, comes to be understood in a manner that will prepare it for solution. This stage in the policy process has subjective and political elements, as did the first stage, but at this stage there is arguably a larger objective component to the issue. Further, because the problem will have been defined in a manner that tends to assign it to a particular organization within the public sector, this organization will itself have to differentiate the issue beyond the simple functional label that has been attached to it. It will, in short, have to develop and design policy instruments to address the problem.

We will be arguing here that the labelling of a policy problem as being "health"-related, "environmental," "agricultural," or whatever tends to mask a good deal of the complexity contained within the problem and ultimately may limit the capacity of the public sector to solve the problem. Labelling the problem in this particular way indicates an assumption within the political process that the policy organization in question will bring a defined set of tools to bear on the problem that will simplify the problem of policy choice. On the contrary, this labelling tends to ignore the high level of variance within policy areas. While much of the literature in political science and public policy tends to define environmental policy as social-regulatory policy (May 2002), the reality is that – to an increasing degree – the applicability of the social-regulatory label depends on the policy subfield being addressed. In water-pollution control, for example, point-source discharges are dealt with differently than nonpoint-source water-pollution runoff; point sources are dealt with in direct regulatory fashion and nonpoint sources are generally not – at least at the federal level in the US. Thus, even if organizations within a particular government department might like to address all their problems in a particular way, the reality is that they cannot and do not (no matter how hard they may try!).

The basic point here is that the names emblazoned on government buildings are an inadequate guide for the complications involved in the policies that they administer and the problems that they confront.[4] Therefore, as we begin to conceptualize the numerous factors that might be utilized to define problems, we need to think about a broad range of variables, rather than confining our attention to the familiar labels of policy areas and government departments. The labels certainly are very useful at the first stage, as the means of linking problems and organizations, but they quickly lose this utility once the second stage of designing policies is reached.

For the second stage a more variable-based approach appears to be required, an approach that forces the consideration of a number of factors in the single definition of a problem. This inherent eclecticism may appear to be a shotgun approach to a highly complex question, and to some extent it is. Still, the level of theoretical and practical guidance available in addressing policy problems does not appear to permit more than this wide-open attack on the issue at the initial stages. Therefore, the remainder of this chapter will contain a discussion of categories of variables that might be included in a classification of policy problems. We will conclude with some (extremely preliminary) ideas about how to link these variables with the instruments that may be used to implement any programs designed to *resolve* problems.

The above having been said, several extant schemes provide some beginning to the analysis of policy problems. In particular, the Thompson and Tuden (1959) scheme and that developed by Charles Perrow (1970), both of which serve to characterize decision making in organizations, may actually be useful places at which to begin thinking about characterizing policy problems. Both schemes are concerned with the nature of the knowledge that decision makers have about the questions they are facing as well as with the degree of agreement on preferences for the outcomes of the process. In one scheme (Thompson and Tuden), the argument is based on the degree of agreement on the causation of the phenomenon in question combined with the degree of agreement about goals. In the other, problems are characterized in terms more of uncertainty, such that designs of processes (as well as designs of the policies themselves) must consider the degree of robustness required. Still another approach is offered by Gormley (1986), focusing on the complexity and salience of the problems addressed and on their influence of the politics associated with crafting policy solutions.

All of these existing schemes highlight the interaction of aspects of the environment of policy designing, but as interesting as these schemes are, they may understate the complexity of this context and also take into account far too few variables (at least for such a preliminary stage of the investigation). These schemes offer insights into some of the intricacies of problem definition but address only part of the nature of the problems that need to be explored. Therefore, we will continue to opt for a more open-ended enumeration of the attributes of policy problems in the hope of even overspecifying their nature so that some future reduction of these attributes can simplify the problem for both the analyst and the practical policy maker.

## CHARACTERISTICS OF POLICY PROBLEMS

As we begin here to examine policy problems, we are concerned not with developing a taxonomy of problems themselves but rather with developing a set of variables that can characterize the problems.[5] The analytic task, then, is to think about what the problem really is and about what factors determine the applicability of one tool or another. The attributes of problems that should be considered in such an analysis are both objective and subjective; they are both "natural" and socially constructed; and they are both mutable and immutable. The outcome of our enumeration provides a start, but only a start. Indeed, as we begin to make even a partial catalogue of the attributes, we find that each of the variables appears to have subvariables that define it, making the problem increasingly complex. We outline here a total of seven potential variables relating to policy problems, some of which may be related to one another and others of which possess "subattributes" that are subject to differing interpretations in relation to policy-instrument selection. The first three variables discussed clearly relate to the problems themselves and appear as though they may influence the selection of those policy instruments that focus more on process than on substance. The second set of variables relates more to the nexus or connection between problem characteristics and instrument choice, and these variables tend to be somewhat more substantive in their implications.

Rochefort and Cobb (1994) proposed a set of attributes of issues when discussing agenda setting that are not too dissimilar from a list that might be developed for characterizing policy problems. This list was: causality, severity, incidence, proximity, novelty, crisis, and the availability of solutions. Another characteristic, the problematic nature of the population, seems more relevant to agenda setting per se than to objective policy. Nevertheless, some of the problem attributes discussed below raise some of the same concerns about the need to bring the nature of the population into the mix of problem characteristics.

### Solubility

The first, and perhaps most basic, issue to be addressed in looking at policy problems is whether they can be "solved." This is no simple question given both the number of problems that are addressed by government and the difficulty of some of those problems.[6] Further, we are aware that the political realities of policy making require the advocate of a "solution" to act as if his or her program were indeed *the* answer to the problem if for no other reason than that failure to do so would almost certainly ensure that the program would not be adopted. We can imagine the limited success of a program advocate who begins by arguing that his or her policy proposal may or may not really solve the problem but is worth trying anyway. The political reality is that programs and instruments have to be oversold simply to have any realistic opportunity for adoption. This is true even though, for many of the issues confronting government, there is far from any clear idea about either cause or solution (Nelson 1978).

What we are referring to here is whether a problem can be argued to have a finite and definable solution or whether it is likely to appear again and again on the agenda of government. At one level some procedural issues in government (e.g., budget decisions about how much to spend) return to the agenda on an annual, or even more frequent, basis. On a more substantive level, however, some issues appear to return frequently for adjustment and for reconsideration. The absence of durable solutions for some problems implies that they will be chronic questions to be "solved" again and again and thus really not solved at all (see Silberman 1994). The implication here is that problems of this kind may be best addressed through policy instruments that allow sufficient flexibility to revise and adapt specific solutions relatively easily on an ongoing basis. We should note, however, that the absence of durability in a particular set of solutions may be a function either of the politics surrounding the issue or of the more programmatic nature of the issue.[7] Even if a problem has a simple programmatic solution (the technology for abortion, for example, is relatively simple and well known), political considerations may not permit the issue to rest.

Is there any way to predict a priori whether a problem is likely to be acute or chronic? As with much of the rest of this discussion, this kind of analysis is necessarily at a preliminary stage; however, several other variables appear to be useful in making such a prediction. One would be the degree of dissension on values in the policy area and the degree to which the issue touches on fundamental moral and political values. This is clearly true for certain obviously moral issues (Tatalovich and Daynes 1997) that are reconsidered regularly for political reasons (e.g., abortion), but certain environmental issues may also have strong moral overtones that lead to their being the subjects of continuing debate and discussion. In American environmental policy, the "rights" of individuals to use their property as they see fit carries moral connotations that are stronger than the rights of large corporate entities to produce products as they wish (Epstein 1985; at the extreme, see Eagle 1996). Thus, in this sense, the morals of the audience targeted by a policy may have implications that affect the degree to which the problem may be subject to a durable solution, and this susceptibility to policy change may in turn influence the choice of appropriate policy instruments.

Policy durability may also be affected by variables that are more programmatic in nature. Many poverty programs, for example, have been argued "not to work" or to have required excessive expenditures for the benefits produced. In such a case as poverty, it is difficult to separate the political from the programmatic reasons for a problem's becoming chronic, but at least the justification for its reconsideration is phrased in programmatic terms. In either case, however, the fundamental ideological contests taking place in *this* policy area appear to give rise to almost constant tinkering with the programs or perhaps to frequent threats of their termination.

One example of programmatic instability in environmental policy may be the Superfund Program in the US. In this case, there is a relatively widespread recognition that existing policies may be too legalistic to be (cost) effective, and the relatively slow rate at which superfund sites have been cleaned up clearly supports the argument that existing policy instruments will need to be changed if substantial further progress in reaching solutions is to be made. Here, the seeds for policy succession appear to be sown within the program itself rather than in the moral connotations of the problem being addressed. At the same time, however, both this arguably inappropriate application of the current instruments for many years and the slow and very expensive progress in addressing abandoned toxic waste dumps in the US attest to the importance of appropriate policy instrument choice in the first place (e.g., interests can congeal around unsatisfactory solutions as well as satisfactory ones). Despite this arguably unhealthy level of policy durability, in this case the question of changing policy-instrument selection is probably one of "when" rather than "if." In other words, programs that do not "work well" have built-in reasons for policy instability – even if it takes some time for that instability to manifest itself.

Another aspect of the chronic nature of a problem may be the availability of a technology that can indeed "solve" the problem once and for all. Take, for example, the problem of children who are not immunized against all the basic childhood diseases. On the one hand, while there can be financial questions about this issue, there is a simple technology and there is a basic agreement that children should be immunized against a range of serious diseases.[8] On the other hand, public programs designed to eradicate poverty, or even those designed to educate students, may be much less certain about the methodology to be used or about the real effectiveness of the methodology that has customarily been employed. Likewise, when governments take it upon themselves to "eradicate" drug use they enter an area of behaviour with numerous possible causes and also numerous possible remedies, none of which has been fully verified.

In environmental policy, a similar example can be found in efforts to treat "conventional" vs "toxic" water pollutants. While it has been clear for many years that excessive organic materials in water can be treated through aeration and microbial action in "conventional" activated-sludge wastewater-treatment plants, solutions for "toxic" pollutants are often less clear. Based upon findings that wastewater discharges are lethal to living organisms, the US EPA's policies have called for "toxicity reduction evaluations." Although these evaluations are important, there has been uncertainty about the means by which they should be conducted, and their results can be unclear. They are, in effect, a process-based solution to problems that have uncertain technological and substantive foundations.

Chronic problems are also those that are heavily dependent upon external factors, especially upon external factors that are themselves highly variable. The economy is an obvious case of a chronic policy problem. Even when governments believed that they could manage the economy successfully, they did not act as if they could do so with a single dose of Keynesian, or monetarist, or supply-side medicine. Rather, there was almost constant adjustment of these policy instruments to correspond to changes in economic performance.[9]

One interesting way of coping with problems that are insoluble, or that are perceived to be insoluble, is to rely more on procedure than on substance. While procedures rarely solve problems other than those arising from procedural issues, they can be a means of forcing the regular and thorough reconsideration of a policy problem and hence allow for some systematic adjustment. At the extreme, the weekly meetings of the Federal Reserve Board are a procedural device that ensures the regular reconsideration of monetary policy and of economic policy more generally. At less of an extreme, the requirement for regular review of the Social Security Program addresses a problem that was once considered solved but is now much less of a given in American policy (Wildavsky 1998).

### Complexity

The second attribute of policy problems to be examined is their complexity. This term is used in several ways in the policy literature (see Dunn 1994) and is likewise used here. Initially, we must distinguish political complexity from programmatic complexity[10] and, subsequently, differentiate between at least two forms of programmatic complexity.

*Political complexity* refers to the number of political interests and actors involved in the problem and hence to the degree of difficulty in negotiating agreements among the parties involved. One of the characteristics of policy making in the contemporary environment is the difficulty in restraining such involvement, which in turn increases the difficulty in reaching solutions (Gray 1998). Or as Charles O. Jones (1982, 67) has put it with respect to the United States, "iron triangles have become big sloppy hexagons." It is not necessarily the case that this form of political complexity induces policy failure – the Scandinavian countries appear capable of governing effectively even with a wide range of interests involved (Olsen 1987). Still, the involvement of a wider range of interests does increase the load on the political system's decision-making apparatus and may complicate discussions and resolutions of issues related to policy instruments.

*Programmatic complexity* refers to several aspects of a policy problem. One would be its technical content. Problems vary markedly in the extent to which the average citizen in the street is capable of understanding the issues and, more important, capable of intervening effectively in the decision-making process. Most citizens feel perfectly capable of discussing the education of their children or zoning for their neighbourhoods (even though there are experts in these fields as well) but feel much less confident discussing complex technical issues associated with global warming, acid rain, or toxic water pollution. Further, the real knowledge bases in the latter areas are, other things being equal, more demanding than in the former areas.

Another way to think of complexity is in terms of multiple causation. As noted already, we have conceptualized the policy design process as the marrying of models of causation, instrumentation, and evaluation (Linder and Peters 1984). The difficulty is that for many public problems, there are competing models of causation and hence competing experts. In water-pollution control, for example, there has been a historic tendency for civil and environmental engineers to conceptualize environmental problems as largely technological in nature. This kind of conceptual model dominated the early establishment of technology-based treatment controls in the United States, for example. Over the last two decades, however, this technological perspective has been increasingly challenged by biologists and toxicologists who have conceived of environmental problems as problems of behaviour and ecological balance, with the result that there has been a move toward more prevention-oriented policy solutions. The questions have moved, therefore, from how to treat wastes of various kinds toward how to make behavioural and production decisions that produce less waste in the first place.

What emerges from this discussion of complexity is the notion that complexity is a multifaceted concept that yields differing implications for policy design and instrument choice depending on the forms of complexity that are evident in any particular policy-problem situation. When complexity is conceived of in political terms, it appears that policy-design efforts should enable processes that are: (1) flexible enough to respond to varying interests; (2) understood by everyone involved; and (3) defined in terms of specific processes for overcoming stalemate and disagreement. These processes, it seems, may incorporate both public and private sectors in the formulation and implementation phases of the policy process while reserving authoritative mechanisms for public-sector intervention when such mechanisms are necessary to overcome stalemate and/or inaction.

It can also be argued that programmatic complexity that assumes a highly technical form should be inversely correlated with political complexity. That is, as problems become more technical, and hence more dominated by experts and information, it becomes more difficult for other groups of actors (e.g., interest groups) to intervene effectively in the policy process. Of course, there has been significant growth in expertise among the groups opposed to the dominant directions of policy in industrialized democracies – notably environmentalists and other social movements that can now muster a wealth of technical information. Based at least in part on these successes, advocates of deliberative democracy are attempting to open up decision making, even when there are apparently high technical hurdles to be jumped (Elster 1998). Furthermore, governments are themselves developing policy tools that enable counterexpertise to be applied during the policy process, such as the hiring of paid public intervenors in regulatory hearings (Gormley 1986). Even so, it is necessary to recognize that high levels of technical content can create obstacles to widespread participation and that the scope of political conflict often can be minimized by placing greater emphasis on expertise in making decisions and in defining the relevant issues in technical rather than distributive terms.

Finally, when problem complexity is viewed in terms of competing models of causation, it is necessary to recognize that the policy instruments chosen are likely to depend on the model(s) of causation that are viewed as predominant. In practical terms, this may mean that policy-instrument choice will vary over time as differing conceptions of the causal processes underlying specific problems gain and lose support. We see this dynamic in water-pollution control, for example, as older technology-based conceptions of water-pollution problems have given way to more process-oriented approaches, such as watershed-protection activities that are directed toward changing the behaviours of those affecting water quality within particular geographically defined watersheds. The result here (and likely elsewhere as well) is a layering of policy instruments "on top of one another" as instruments conceived under previously accepted models of causality are supplemented with new instruments based on more recent conceptions of problem causation. The end result here, of course, is not the selection of one policy instrument over another, but rather an increasingly complex admixture of policy instruments built on the foundations of changing conceptual understandings of the causal processes underlying the problems in question.

## The Question of Scale

A third attribute of problems that is worth considering here is the scale of the question confronting government. That is, what is the magnitude of the problem, and what are the range of effects that it produces? Phrased somewhat differently, can the problem be disaggregated into smaller components, or is it of such a nature that it requires either a comprehensive solution or no solution at all. Further, is the problem amenable to digesting large levels of input at once, or is it more incremental and cumulative in nature? Some examples may help to clarify the nature of the term "scale" as applied to policy problems.

This term first came to be used by Paul Schulman (1980). He argued that some policy problems were inherently large-scale and therefore required an "all or nothing" approach to solving them. The principal example given was the space program. It would have done NASA little or no good to get a man halfway to the moon; the project was such that partial solutions were, in essence, failures. As a less extreme example, it would do the Army Corps of Engineers little or no good to build half a dam over a river; they have to complete the task or not start in the first place if they are to be successful, and economical, in their use of scarce resources. An even less extreme example in environmental policy may be the "third-generation" problem of global warming, in which small reductions in greenhouse-gas emissions may do little to address the problem, absent a more complete and comprehensive effort. In short, these large-scale problems cannot be readily disaggregated, although reductions in greenhouse-gas emissions may appropriately take place in phases, *but probably require major interventions to be resolved.*

Antithetical examples might be the "war on cancer," the proposed "war on AIDS," or even the nonpoint sources of pollution discussed above. While these problems are of substantial concern to those affected by them, they appear to be susceptible to disaggregation into smaller-scale issues (Rushefsky 1986; Rettig 1977; Perrow 1990). As a result, the appropriate method of policy attack appears to be incremental – that is, based on the accumulation of scientific evidence, careful medical trials, trial and error, and the like. Any attempt to introduce short bursts of very high-level resources into the policy area could lead to "choking" on the resources (Hogwood and Peters 1985) and *potentially* to little real contribution to the resolution of the underlying policy problems. These problems are very amenable to disaggregation, with individual scientists, engineers, and policy makers able to make their own contributions to the resolution (relatively) independently of the actions of others.

Perhaps more than any other aspect of policy problems the issue of scale can be misunderstood and can lead to inefficient and ineffective use of resources. When a problem is identified, there is always a desire to apply the "war" metaphor and to create the moral equivalent of war. In some instances, this may be appropriate. Poverty entails a sufficiently complex (see above) and intertwined set of problems that the only way to address it is through "war." Indeed, the failure of the "war on poverty" may be the result of a failure to apply the metaphor with enough zeal and over a sufficiently long period of time rather than the result of the war metaphor's inadequacy in this particular case. This also points out the extent to which this particular attribute of policy problems, like all others, is at least in part a consequence of framing and political construction (Schon and Rein 1994).

We turn now to a second set of problem attributes – ones that move beyond mere characterization of problems and make more conscious attempts to explicate the relationships between problems and instrument choice. To some extent all the attributes of problems we have presented here are related to instrument choice, but the second set of attributes should be seen as more proximate to this crucial choice in the implementation process.

## Divisibility

The fourth attribute of policy problems to be discussed here is their "divisibility." We noted above that some small-scale problems can be disaggregated, but here we are talking more about the nature of the goods required to "solve" the problems. In a sense, we are referring to the classic economic concern over market failures and most specifically to the classic economic distinction between public goods and private goods (Buchanan 1987). Similarly, James Q. Wilson (1980) has constructed a typology of policies based largely upon the extent to which benefits and costs are concentrated or diffuse, a distinction somewhat akin to economists' conceptions of "jointness" among goods.

The Wilson typology is intended to explain the politics of policy, but the basic idea involved is also applicable to more substantive issues about policy problems. This basic idea is that problems that entail collective action and produce diffuse benefits may be more difficult to solve than those problems for which the benefits are more immediate and more appropriable by individuals. The reasons for this increased difficulty are fundamentally political and relate to generating and maintaining support for policies that yield only indirect benefits to particular constituencies. In politics, however, the nature of the goods being produced may not be as firmly established as economists tend to believe, such that a fundamental question for the political entrepreneur advocating government action to address a problem requiring the development of public goods is how to construct the issue in a manner suggesting that the goods more divisible than in actuality and hence of greater benefit to particular constituencies.[11]

One drawback to this form of analysis is that it appears to lead to problems being solved that are not problems per se but rather opportunities for public action that may confer disproportionate benefits on only one segment of society. That is, if a small group is able to mobilize support for a policy idea that will confer benefits on them while diffusing the costs of these benefits widely, the political imbalance is likely to swing in the direction of government adopting the policy. This process – in many cases – becomes somewhat analogous to Lowi's distributive politics (Lowi 1972), in which the preferred policy instrument is direct or indirect government subsidies for the development of policies that are at least justified by language consistent with the concept of public goods. This style of policy making has been very evident in making tax policy as well as when providing certain types of supports for business, public works, and agriculture (Bonser, McGregor, and Oster 1996). In some ways the real questions that arise in these cases are why more programs like this are not created in the public sector and why programs like this are ever terminated (Mucciaroni 1990).

So what are the implications of these public-goods-related problems for the selection of policy instruments? The first and clearest implication is that they appear to require government interventions in some form if the collective-action problems that give rise to them are to be overcome. What is far less clear, however, is whether any particular form of intervention is preferable to another. As indicated above, the subsidies can take many forms: direct provision of government services (e.g., roads), tax benefits (e.g., credits and deductions), grant subsidies to nongovernmental organizations or lower levels of government (e.g., grants for wastewater-treatment works), and creating government sanctioned monopolies (electric utilities, etc.). While each of these forms of subsidy appears to carry some relatively obvious advantages and disadvantages in terms of both efficiency and accountability, more analytical work is required in order to determine more specifically how these differing forms of government action can be best applied to differing kinds of problems.

### Monetarization

This awkward term is intended to capture the question of whether the policy problem being considered is phrased in monetary or nonmonetary terms – that is, whether in principle money can be utilized to solve, or at least ameliorate, the problems identified. While monies can be, and are, used as discussed above to address "indivisible" problems associated with collective goods, the concept here is broader and also includes problems that are divisible. For example, it is clear that some *divisible* problems, such as the danger of poverty after retirement from employment or health risks associated with lead piping in low-income households, can be (and have been) addressed successfully simply by using money. Other problems, such as civil rights, gender equality, or even reducing automobile use, may not be as amenable to being addressed simply by spending money. Rather, these problems may require that other forms of government action, and perhaps broad societal changes, be implemented. The policy questions here are whether the difficulties identified can be addressed successfully through financial instruments and, if not, what sort of other interventions can be used to address the issues.

As is the case with the divisibility question noted above, the idea of monetarization directly raises a question about the nature of the instruments that can be employed effectively to address an issue, but the importance of the variables in defining a policy problem may extend beyond this factor. The question here is also about the capacity of government to confer status on groups, or to control certain undesirable behaviours through education or other means, or to cope with the increasing range of issues that appear to be defined as public problems.[12] Money as a fungible resource makes the interventions of government apparently easier, but it may make the choices too easy. That is, given the general theme of this chapter, there is a temptation to throw money at problems in the hope that they will go away. Further, although conferring status, rights, and other nonmonetary benefits on members of society is in part a role of the public sector, it is perhaps primarily a task for the private sector. If the general public is opposed to granting these rights, the state will not have the capacity to enforce legislation that confers these benefits on members of society nor to adjudicate all the cases that may arise from these rights. Moreover, to the extent that the problems addressed suggest a need for further educational or socialization efforts, it is clear that these efforts will require involvement from nongovernmental sectors of society in order to be successful.

## Scope of Activity

Another potential variable of concern in understanding differences among policy problems and the appropriate instruments of government to address them relates to the scope of activity or behaviours that contribute to the creation of the problem. In general, where the numbers of people, activities, or organizations involved with a problem are defined and relatively small, the likelihood that direct *regulatory* intervention by governmental bodies will be successful is increased. By contrast, public-sector action can become quite difficult and resource-intensive in cases where many very different forms of activity must be controlled or changed and where government chooses to seek the resolution of a problem through direct regulation.

Most fundamentally, this concern with the scope of the problem relates to the capacity of government. When government regulation is applied to relatively small numbers of similar activities, it has a reasonable chance of success. However, when the activities to be controlled and/or altered are numerous and highly differentiated, the capacity of government to deal with them is likely to be strained, and this strain is likely to make nonregulatory solutions more desirable by comparison. For example, ensuring the safety of nuclear-energy facilities appears to be amenable to successful regulation (although successful and effective regulation is certainly not guaranteed!). There are only so many nuclear-energy facilities to be regulated, and they pose at least somewhat similar risks and concerns. By contrast, it would be far more difficult to regulate directly the manner in which people cook their food in an effort to reduce the potential emission of particulate matter into the air because, in this case, there are hundreds of thousands of mealtime activities to be regulated each day that may take many different forms (charcoal grills, gas stoves, electric stoves, wood stoves, etc.). An effort to accomplish this kind of regulation would significantly tax the capabilities of any government that sought to carry it out. Consequently, it would probably be appropriate to explore other approaches to addressing this problem.

In cases where direct government regulation is infeasible or prohibitively expensive, other policy instruments need to be explored. One approach would be to apply regulatory solutions to different (although related) sets of activities. Using the example above, we might apply regulations to the manufacture of cooking stoves and grills requiring that appliances used for cooking remove particulate matter prior to emission into the air. This kind of regulation would be applied to a smaller number of regulated entities and might require the installation of similar technologies in each case. This, in fact, is somewhat like the rationale behind the Corporate Average Fuel Economy (CAFE) standards used in the United States to reduce air emissions from automobiles (although the limits of this approach are now becoming more apparent, as the number of vehicle miles driven continues to contribute to air-pollution problems in some areas). Another approach would be to move toward nonregulatory mechanisms, such as economic incentives or educational efforts. In these cases, for example, taxes might be applied to cooking appliances based on the extent to which they include devices for minimizing particulate emissions, or educational programs for users of cooking appliances might help people to understand which cooking appliances are environmentally friendly or may provide guidance on how to avoid cooking on days in which particulate matter in the air is of concern.

The point here is that the relationship between policy problems and instrument selection is related to the capacity of governments to carry out differing activities. In general, direct regulation requires significant resources for standard setting, monitoring, and enforcement, and sufficient resources are likely to be available only in those cases where the numbers and types of activities regulated are reasonably limited. Where these conditions are not met, alternative policy instruments should perhaps be considered. In environmental policy, these alternatives may include economic instruments designed to make polluting activities more expensive and educational activities that enable consumers and the public to make environmentally friendly decisions – in other words, sticks and sermons.

## Interdependencies

Policy problems also vary in the extent to which they are confined, or confinable, to a single policy domain. At this point we come full circle to return to thinking about the impact of those ministry names on government buildings. Some problems facing government clearly correspond to the domains of a single building; for example, providing social-insurance pensions in the United States falls within the domain of the Department of Health and Human Services (actually now the independent Social Security Administration). Other policy problems – such as controlling the nonpoint-source water pollution that flows into rivers, lakes, and streams following heavy rains – require the involvement and coordination of a number of departments, agencies, and even levels of government.

The degree of interdependence characterizing any particular problem will influence both the capacity of government to solve the problem as well as the range of appropriate policy instruments. The political requirements of forming and coordinating coalitions across a range of organizations means that more interdependent problems are likely to be more difficult to resolve. Further, it may mean that organizations are less likely to be able to solve such problems through existing processes. In addition, if the problems are large-scale, there is a danger that a number of different organizations will attempt to parcel out components among themselves, thereby reducing the overall effectiveness of the interventions.[13] These problems then become a domestic analogue of the "joint-decision trap" that Fritz Scharpf (1988) discussed in reference to international politics, with decisions perhaps being made that satisfy only the lowest common denominator.

The other rather obvious point here is that interdependent policies are more subject to debates over framing and thus may be more contentious. Some of this contention over policies may represent sincere intellectual differences of opinion about how the problem should be defined, while another part may be a function of attempts to utilize the problem to acquire more budgetary and personnel resources for each department advocating an alternative "frame" for the issue. The need to mobilize political support for programs will also tend to push the definition of programs toward those using instruments that are more likely to deliver private benefits. Likewise, there is a strong political push to ignore identifying the interconnections of policies when possible given that such involvement of multiple actors makes the program less easy for departments to capture.

It appears that over time the degree to which problems can be confined to a single domain has diminished. Agricultural price supports, for example, might at one time have been the concern solely of a department of agriculture, but as these commodities become more linked to international trade, these supports become the concern of departments of foreign affairs, international trade, and the like.[14] Agriculture policy also now entails numerous, often rancorous, involvements with environmental-policy organizations in and out of government. Similarly, educational policy now has a major impact on international competitiveness; thus education ministries must coordinate more with departments of labour, trade and industry, and international affairs if they are to do their jobs effectively.

The overall point here is that the instruments required to address policy problems that have foundations in and implications for many governmental units are likely to be more difficult and controversial to select and implement than those required to address policy problems that are clearly within the jurisdiction of a single organization of government. Instrument choice, in this context, can become quite politicized and complex as competing organizations incorporate arguments about appropriate instruments into larger arguments about how to frame the problem and whether the problem is best addressed by one agency or another. The end results in these situations may often be policy-instrument choices that grow incrementally and in a haphazard fashion out of bureaucratic turf battles rather than out of clear-headed analyses of the policy problems being addressed.

PUTTING THE PIECES TOGETHER:
THE CASE OF WATER-POLLUTION POLICY
IN THE US

We have so far discussed the foregoing seven attributes of policy problems separately, but of course in reality they do not occur in this way and thus must be considered simultaneously when making policy choices. Each policy problem could be characterized by these seven attributes as well as by a host of others. Therefore, in beginning to think about contingent relationships, we need to think about the multiattribute problem and how to cope with variable attributes simultaneously (see, among others, Poulton 1994). To provide a starting point for this kind of effort, we will now look at the example of water-pollution policy in the United States in order to gain a sense of how we might apply a consideration of these variable attributes to particular problems (see also Gunningham ch. 14 herein). The focus here is on both point- and nonpoint sources of water pollution and on the similarities and differences between the problem characteristics that prevail in each case.

Beginning with the first three attributes, it is clear that both point- and nonpoint-source problems are *soluble* to at least some degree. However, this is probably more true of point-source water-pollution problems than of nonpoint-source problems. Point-source water-pollution problems are often soluble through the construction of treatment works that reduce pollutant concentrations in wastewater or through developing industrial-process changes that eliminate pollutants at the source. Once constructed, appropriate treatment works can be quite effective in reducing pollutant concentrations, although the temptation may be to assume that these problems are solved when the treatment works are installed and to forget about the ongoing maintenance and management that are necessary to keep them operating properly. This problem of ongoing maintenance and attention exists to an even greater degree in the nonpoint-source water-pollution case because treatment mechanisms such as buffer zones and increased vegetation may be affected by weather and climate, thus potentially inhibiting their effectiveness over time. Nonpoint-source water-pollution problems also provide additional challenges to finding durable solutions because they tend to rely more heavily on ongoing behavioural changes (environmentally friendly agriculture and forestry practices, etc.) than may be the case with point-source water pollution.

Both point- and nonpoint-source water-pollution problems are somewhat *complex*, but they exhibit this broad characteristic in different ways. Nonpoint-source water-pollution control is quite complex *politically* – more so than point-source water-pollution control – because of the many policy actors that contribute to nonpoint-source water pollution. These nonpoint-source actors include farmers, foresters, construction companies, individual gardeners, local policy makers who control land-use decisions, and others. By contrast, the number of political actors involved in point-source water-pollution control is somewhat more limited, as they primarily include companies discharging wastewater and municipally sponsored bodies that operate local sewage systems. With regard to *technical* complexity, we also see differences. While solutions to nonpoint-source water-pollution problems may often be relatively simple (growing more vegetation, establishing buffer zones, discontinuing use of a problem fertilizer or pesticide, etc.), establishing that specific nonpoint sources of water pollution actually affect water quality can be a tremendously complicated task from a technical point of view. By contrast, the problems created by point sources of water pollution may be quite obvious, while the means to reduce point-source pollution loads can vary from simple and well-established treatments to rather complicated technical efforts.

Nonpoint-source water pollution is also relatively complex from the viewpoint of *causal processes*. Nonpoint-source water-pollution problems have many causes, each of which may result from differing processes (for example, inattentive management, individual behaviours, inadequate treatment processes, etc.). Policy solutions must therefore address a wide range of causal factors if they are to be effective. Point-source water-pollution problems, by contrast, benefit from the fact that they tend to emanate from clearly defined pipes and conveyances, with the result that they often rely on established technology-based treatment models to reduce pollutant loads. Consequently, while concepts of causation may vary to some degree, the general causal presumption underlying point-source water-pollution problems has been that the problem consists of collecting wastewaters and ensuring that they are processed through appropriately constructed treatment works. No similar presumption is readily available for nonpoint sources of pollution. Thus, as a result of their rather defined sources, point-source problems have a well-established causal foundation for the implementation of controls that does not appear to exist to the same degree for nonpoint sources of pollution.

Water-pollution problems also vary with regard to their *scale* and susceptibility to disaggregation. In general, point-source water-pollution problems appear to be moderate in terms of their scale and susceptibility to disaggregation. While the construction of any particular set of treatment works is a major project that yields benefits only upon full completion, one can certainly envision schemes for prioritization that would allow one to prioritize point-source problems and to tackle them one by one on a stepwise basis. By contrast, nonpoint-source water-pollution problems do appear to be subject to disaggregation in many cases because they may frequently involve relatively low-cost and geographically disperse changes in behaviours and processes. And in this regard, they can probably be viewed as smaller in scale than point-source problems since large capital investments are less frequently needed to implement appropriate nonpoint-source water-pollution controls.

We now to turn to a brief comparison of point- and nonpoint-source water-pollution problems in relation to the four attributes discussed above relating to problem-instrument interconnections: *divisibility, monetarization, scope,* and *interdependence.* While water quality is a public good in the sense that all may enjoy its benefits, it is generally *divisible* regardless of whether the major threats relate to point or nonpoint sources of pollution. Both individuals and organizations use and pollute water independently; therefore, the problems to be addressed appear to be divisible, as they are based on efforts to address particular pollution sources. Both problems are also subject to *monetarization* in the sense that financial investments are potentially useful approaches to reducing point- and nonpoint-source water pollution. However, because of the substantial behavioural basis for causation in the case of nonpoint-source problems, one might argue that financial investments may be a less complete solution to nonpoint-source problems than to point-source problems.

Other differences between point and nonpoint sources relate to the *scope* of the activities that lead to water pollution and their levels of interdependence with other policy problems. While particular types of municipal and industrial point sources of water pollution do differ across the United States, they share a common reliance on pipes and conveyances (as noted above in relation to the complexity of causation) that may facilitate efficiency by bringing a single set of regulatory controls to bear on a large number of polluting activities. Nonpoint-source water-polluting activities, however, arguably vary to a greater degree and may therefore require more complicated, and generally less efficient, regulatory schemes. While these varying polluting activities may share a tie to rainfall, this tie does not appear to be as susceptible to the creation of relatively uniform solutions as are the pipes and conveyances involved in point-source problems. As a result, any comprehensive and centralized policy solution to nonpoint-source problems may tend to tax public-sector capabilities. Finally, while there are interdependencies involved in both point- and nonpoint-source water-pollution problems, these *interdependencies* are probably greater in the case of nonpoint-source water-pollution problems than in the case of point-source water-pollution problems. For example, while point-source problems are clearly matters of environmental protection, nonpoint-source water-pollution problems are also highly related to problems of agricultural productivity, forestry productivity, and local zoning and land-use patterns. The causal chain addressed by the regulation of nonpoint-source pollution is therefore more multifaceted than that characterizing point-source problems.

To summarize, then, in a direct comparison of broad groups of point- and nonpoint-source water-pollution problems, we see that they have both similar and dissimilar attributes. We also see that the variable attributes themselves may be interrelated when they are applied to specific problems (note, for example, the likely importance of defined sources in the form of pipes and conveyances when discussing both theories of causation and the scope of activities to be regulated for point-source problems). In general, however, nonpoint-source problems appear to be more complex both politically and in terms of the applicable processes for determining causes than do point-source problems. Maintaining durable solutions to nonpoint-source problems may also require slightly more vigilance. By contrast, the technical complexity of implementing point-source water-pollution controls is probably equal to or greater than that of implementing nonpoint-source controls. Point-source problems may also be of larger scale, meaning that they may be less susceptible to disaggregation than nonpoint-source water-pollution problems. In addition, both point- and nonpoint-source water-pollution problems appear to be divisible and subject to monetarization to some degree, although they appear to differ to a significant degree with respect to scope and interdependence. Nonpoint sources appear to cover a wider scope of polluting activities than point sources and also appear to be subject to a higher degree of interdependence.

We could continue to elaborate these points through further examples, but we would still have just that: a series of examples. The point here is that problems do vary according to the attributes we have outlined, even within the functional area of water-pollution control – a functional policy area that has often been dealt with in undifferentiated fashion. The fundamental analytic question is how to cope with multiattribute problems and the varying forms these problems may take in particular circumstances – a common problem in the policy sciences. One way to cope with the number of factors involved would be a weighting scheme, arguing that some of these attributes are more significant for predicting the nature of the problem than are others. This approach might itself be contingent, with different weightings dependent upon either political or analytical factors. Another possible approach to decision making is lexicography, with one attribute or another being defined as primary. Based on this ranking, a first allocation of problems into broad groups could be achieved, followed by another round of analysis to determine some strong order of importance based on theoretical or practical criteria. As with the other methods of choice, however, if policy makers had sufficient knowledge to establish such rankings, choosing instruments would not be such a difficult task in the first place.

## SUMMARY

This discussion of seven characteristics of policy problems is but an inadequate beginning to an interesting, and we believe important, extension of the current literature both on policy design and on policy instruments as the most well-established component of this literature. The discussion also provides some beginning steps toward providing a systematic foundation for changes that are now taking place in the area of water-pollution control in the US. These first steps suggest that the current move toward decentralized and nonregulatory policy instruments in nonpoint-source water-pollution control may find grounding in the political and causal complexity of the problems involved, in their broad scope, and in their significant policy interdependence. However, what these very preliminary insights do more conclusively is force some consideration of policy problems faced by government in terms of basic attributes that influence how they must be approached by would-be policy formulators. The presence of these multiple attributes of problems also requires additional thinking about how to compile and perhaps weight the multiple attributes that will characterize any given problem. As noted, taking into account the attributes of problems requires going well outside the usual approaches to organizing policy expertise (e.g., on the basis of functional policy areas) and thus necessitates more analytic thinking.

Addressing the underlying characteristics of problems is, we argue, most important for the selection of policy instruments for intervention. This chapter has focused on the nature of the problems themselves and thus has only begun to discuss directly the contingent relationships between instruments and these problems. However, this relationship does exist. For example, based upon several of the attributes discussed above, it is clear that "treasure"-based tools, to use one of Hood's categories (1986), are more appropriate for some problems than for others. Likewise, the "chronic" problems we have identified may be more amenable to being addressed by instruments relying more heavily on "organization" (another of Hood's categories) than on instruments that have a less enduring nature. Again we could provide further examples, but the basic point here is that we have begun to use these categories to define problems in a manner linking them with instruments – an exercise that will bear fruit in the future.

# 5

# The Choice of Policy Instruments: Confronting the Deductive and the Interactive Approaches

RÉJEAN LANDRY AND FRÉDÉRIC VARONE

## INTRODUCTION

Studies on policy instruments usually assume that transformation of the scope, scale, and forms of government intervention triggers either the emergence of new instruments or different choices of instruments (Salamon 2002). This chapter attempts to extend this argument by laying stress on changes in the policy environment – more specifically on changes in the problems needing resolution, in the variety of contexts, and in the diversity of actors' abilities, attitudes, motivations, and reasons for resisting changes in behaviour – that prevent the derivation of one permanent best-policy instrument that is valid for each and every problem (thus the need to avoid the "best instrument of the year" syndrome). To give a concrete dimension to the chapter, we will develop the argument in discussing the case of innovation policies. In this respect, such an approach departs from most studies on policy instruments, which are organized around the study of specific policy instruments (grants, vouchers, tax expenditures, etc.), as is well exemplified by Salamon (2002).

The chapter is organized into four parts. We begin with a discussion of the theoretical issues within policy sciences surrounding the choice of policy instruments, or "tools." In the subsequent section, we review the literature to make explicit those elements at the heart of a deductive theory on policy-tool choice. Then we attempt to develop additional propositions and theoretical predictions while contrasting the rational, deductive approach with the interactive approach. This part of the chapter introduces the case of innovation policies and their associated policy instruments to show how important it is to take into account the specificities of the problems to be resolved by public policies. Finally, we turn our attention to the major results of the chapter and discuss the need for accountability and evaluation in future research and policy making.

## THE CHOICE OF POLICY INSTRUMENTS AS A RESEARCH QUESTION

Policy-instrument choice as an important issue within political science is not new (Salamon 1981, 262). The trailblazing studies by Lowi (1966, 1972) highlighted the theoretical implications of analyzing the means of government interventions. However, it is worth pointing out that Canadian scholars gave the subject a significant degree of sustained attention and completed some of the most substantial research on the tools of government intervention (Woodside 1986). Doern and Wilson (1974) and Simeon (1976) pointed out the necessity of identifying the discretionary instruments that governments use to achieve their goals, the scope of their action, and the distribution of the costs and benefits that result. Salamon (1981), Trebilcock et al. (1982), Hood (1984), Atkinson and Chandler (1983), Howard and Stanbury (1984), and Baxter-Moore (1987) contributed to a systematic discussion of policy instruments and the reasons they are chosen.

The study of policy instruments has enjoyed resurgence among students in the field of policy design. Linder and Peters (1989, 1990), Schneider and Ingram (1990), and Elmore (1987) have proposed using policy-tool choice as a starting point for building a theory of the process and results of public-policy formulation. Bryson and Smith Ring (1990) offer another perspective by discussing the potential contribution of transaction-cost theory to policy-intervention analysis, while Bennett and Howlett (1992), May (1992), and Howlett and Ramesh (1993, 1995) suggest reinterpreting the theories of policy change and policy learning from a perspective of policy-instrument choice. And, more recently, Bemelans-Videc et al. (1998), Peters and van Nispen (1998), Varone (1998), and Salamon (2002) have edited four books that aim at offering policy students state-of-the-art information in the study of policy-instrument choice and evaluation.

## A RECONSTRUCTION OF THE DEDUCTIVE THEORY ON THE CHOICE OF POLICY INSTRUMENTS

In this chapter, we consider a policy instrument, or tool, as the means of intervention by which governments attempt to induce individuals and groups to make decisions and take actions compatible with public policies (Schneider and Ingram 1990, 527). The generic term for these instruments (also referred to as policy tools or governing instruments) captures the myriad techniques that both political and administrative actors use to put their plans into action (Howlett 1991, 2).

Two major deficiencies characterize the present state of research on the choice of policy tools. First, the literature proposes hypotheses in an ad hoc and nonoperational manner. Second, empirical studies are rare, and the comparability of their results is limited. Despite an abundance of partial approaches, there is no research program allowing systematic testing of their explanatory and predictive capacities. By adopting Lakatos's epistemological perspective (1970), we stress the need to develop cumulative knowledge of policy-tool choice. It is imperative to get to the core of the theory, which is why we propose a deductive process that clarifies the explicit and implicit propositions of research on which previous studies are based.

*Proposition 1: There is a limited variety of instruments available to meet public policy objectives. The instruments can be distinguished in terms of four valuation criteria: resource intensiveness, targeting, political risk, and financial and ideological constraints.*

Early studies treated policy instruments used by governments in a quasi-nominal manner. From a strictly nominal perspective, the theoretical repertoire of available instruments is limited only by the imagination of policy actors and policy students (e.g., Kirshen et al. 1964). Later, a more analytical approach was adopted in order to better understand the variety of policy tools available. This process culminated in the development of the concept of a "basic tool kit" of government action (Hood 1984). Experts matched several criteria to further develop the typologies of policy tools included in the tool kit. Criteria were chosen on the basis of research interest and hypotheses elaborated to explain and predict the choice of instruments (Doern and Phidd 1992, 110). Table 5.1 illustrates the logical correspondence between the types of criteria and the various typologies of instruments.

Other typologies are proposed in some of the English-language literature (Dahl and Lindblom 1953; Trebilcock et al. 1982; Howard and Stanbury 1984; Baxter-Moore 1987; Salamon 1989; Weimer and Vining 1992; Howlett and Ramesh 1995; Vedung 1998) and also by members of the German school (Kaufmann and Rosewitz 1983; Koenig and Dose 1993). Today none of these typologies appears to be universally accepted or even dominant.

Table 5.1
Divergences between policy-instrument typologies

| Policy-instrument typologies | Hood (1984) | Doern and Phidd (1992) | McDonnell and Elmore (1987) | Schneider and Ingram (1990) |
|---|---|---|---|---|
| Approach | Resource-based | Continuum | Resource-based | Continuum |
| Classification criteria | Basic resources of government | Degree of legitimate coercion | Expected effect of government action | Behavioural characteristics |
| Generic classes | 1 Nodality<br>2 Authority<br>3 Treasure<br>4 Organization (Hood distinguishes further between detectors and effectors) | 1 Self-regulation (private behaviour)<br>2 Exhortation<br>3 Expenditure<br>4 Regulation (including taxation)<br>5 Public ownership | 1 Mandates<br>2 Inducements<br>3 Capacity building<br>4 System changing | 1 Authority<br>2 Incentives<br>3 Capacity<br>4 Symbolic and hortatory<br>5 Learning |

However, policy-design advocates criticize this classifying approach. Linder and Peters (1990, 107–8) underline two major problems. First, the categories are so large that it is unclear that they are not mutually exclusive and that variance between categories is more important than within the same category. Second, the definition of categories sometimes appears as an end in itself. In many cases, authors have neglected to formulate any explicit propositions on how to incorporate their typologies into the theoretical realm of the choice of policy instruments.

The identification of the limits inherent to the construction of abstract typologies sparked the development of a second process aimed at specifying the fundamental attributes or valuation criteria of policy instruments. More recent typologies are based on criteria by which political and administrative actors evaluate and choose policy tools. Unlike the earlier classification approach, which only dealt with one-dimensional similarities or differences between policy instruments, this approach allows multidimensional comparisons. It proposes a theoretical perspective that aims to clarify the criteria of public-policy design. Table 5.2 illustrates the convergence of policy-tool attributes developed by authors whose theoretical orientations are markedly different.

Even prior to the emergence of this literature, Majone (1976) and Kingdon (1984) had already pointed out the importance of these at-

Table 5.2
Convergence of valuation criteria for policy instruments

| Policy-instrument attributes | Sabatier and Pelkey (1987) | Salamon (1989) | Linder and Peters (1989) | Trebilcock (1994) |
|---|---|---|---|---|
| Theoretical approach | Advocacy-coalition framework | Policy implementation Public management | Policy design | Public choice |
| Valuation criteria | 1 Economic resources 2 Political costs 3 Economic costs 4 Efficacy | 1 Efficiency 2 Political support 3 Administrative feasibility and equity 4 Supply and targeting effectiveness | 1 Resource-intensiveness 2 Political risk 3 Financial and ideological 4 Targeting | 1 Efficiency 2 Political considerations 3 Distributional considerations |

tributes, or valuation criteria, in highlighting the diversity of instruments and the reasons for their choice. The landmark article by Linder and Peters (1989) offers a complete review of the available literature on policy-instrument attributes and puts their influence on policy design into a theoretical perspective.

In short, the proposition regarding the limited variety of policy instruments means that instruments can be differentiated according to four fundamental attributes, or evaluation criteria: (1) resource intensiveness, defined in terms of operating costs; (2) targeting, defined in terms of how precisely and selectively policy instruments target recipients of potential benefits and costs; (3) political risk, defined in terms of public visibility and potential impacts on voters; and (4) constraints on state intervention, defined in terms of ideological and financial constraints on the respective roles of government and the private market. Supporters of proposition 1 assume that the choice of policy instruments is independent from the attributes of the problems and from the context in which actors operate. This is a serious shortcoming if one aims to use policy instruments to solve concrete problems.

*Proposition 2: From a technical point of view, policy instruments can be substituted to attain the same public-policy objective.*

The theory of policy-tool choice assumes that alternative instruments (e.g., regulatory laws of emissions, incentives based on negotiable permits) can be employed to achieve the same political objectives (e.g., a reduction in atmospheric pollution). From a purely logical and technical point of view, policy tools appear to be perfectly interchangeable.

The strength of this second postulate is relativized within the area of policy science itself. Howlett (1991) notes that typologies based on government resources highlight differences between policy tools and implicitly suggests that they are not readily interchangeable. To resolve a policy problem within a defined context, one particular instrument will prove to be technically superior to the others. In contrast, approaching policy tools from the angle of a continuum focuses attention on their similarities. These typologies formalize differences of degree, not of nature, and suggest perfect technical substitutability of policy instruments.

We have discussed the implications of the technical substitutability of policy tools – even in its partial version – for a positive approach to the choice of policy instruments. The supporters of technical substitutability do not usually take into account the influence of policy problems on instrument choice. As we will later suggest in addressing the question of innovation in the manufacturing industries, a predictive and explanatory model dealing with policy-tool choice must examine both the rationality and institutional context of the actors involved in making the choice.

*Proposition 3: From a political point of view, policy instruments cannot be substituted to achieve the same public-policy objectives because each instrument generates its own separate political economy.*

Although different policy tools technically allow government actors to achieve the same political objective, they cannot be substituted from a political point of view. All instruments are inextricably linked to resources, bureaucrats, target groups, and specific institutional procedures. Alternative policy tools thus involve distinct models of intervention and policy processes (Atkinson and Chandler 1983, 12). Salamon (1981, 264; 1989, 8; 2002, ch. 1) argues that each policy tool generates its own political economy and constitutes a quasi-independent system of action in and of itself.

Implementation research demonstrates that policy execution is not just a linear mechanical operation, but instead initiates a social process of conflict resolution and negotiation during which the actors involved defend their particular interests. Consequently, the results of policy implementation are, and will remain, difficult to predict. Moreover, evaluations of implemented policies teach several lessons about the distribution of costs and benefits of alternative policy tools and about the public visibility of outcomes. They also stress that not all instruments are as effective or efficient in resolving the same policy problem.

Empirical evidence has led a majority of authors to accept the idea of separate political economies for each policy tool. They focus on one or another of the multiple modalities of instrument operation from their respective theoretical perspectives (see Salamon 2002, chs 2–16, for illustrations). Salamon (1981, 1989) has examined the structure of policy-tool implementation. He notes that instruments differentiate themselves by the degree of centralism and automatism involved in their implementation. Schneider and Ingram (1990) look at the political economy of policy tools in terms of their impact on designated target groups. They suggest that the instruments vary according to the nature of the behavioural changes they induce and the degree of participation and policy co-production they require. Finally, Trebilcock (1982) and Howard and Stanbury (1984) apply the hypotheses of public choice to formalize the (re)distributive effects of policy tools. They argue that instruments are characterized by different degrees of cost and benefit concentration and by the visibility of this (re)distribution among groups. In sum, the four attributes, or valuation criteria, dealt with in the first postulate allow us adequately to define the principal facets of the political economy of all the instruments.

Choosing between policy tools that are perfectly interchangeable from a technical point of view means choosing between their different political economies. While our two first propositions define the range of instruments theoretically available to resolve policy problems and indicate that a choice is possible, the third proposition lays stress on the political essence of policy-tool design.

In short, proposition 3 rejects the economic thesis according to which policy-instrument selection is a neutral process intended solely to minimize the social costs of government intervention once public-policy objectives are decided upon (Trebilcock 1982). Again, the supporters of this proposition do not usually explicitly take into account the variety of contexts in which policy actors choose instruments. However, the supporters of this proposition acknowledge that the choice and implementation of policy instruments initiate social processes. We suggest that in such contexts, the choice of policy instruments can be more appropriately described using an interactive than a deductive approach because the vision and understanding of the experts have shifted from a rational, deductive understanding to an interactive understanding of innovation.

*Proposition 4: Those who help choose policy instruments take into account previously chosen instruments and other public policies.*

It is unrealistic to assume that policy design, and particularly the choice of policy instruments, begins in a vacuum. As Rose and Davies have pointed out, "Policy-makers are heirs before they are choosers" (1994, 1), and the inherited policy, or program, (at time t-1) directly influences the (re)design of the policy (at time t). They nonetheless explicitly reject strict historical determinism. Rose and Davies therefore note that to achieve the same objectives as previously, decision makers can either keep the same instruments – "that is maintain routine" – or change them through "instrumental adaptation" (1994, 39–43). From this perspective, explaining instrument choice consists of explaining either why the status quo has been maintained or why there is instrumental (re)design.

The concept of policy inheritance focuses attention on the diachronic evolution in instrument choice within the same policy or program. The theory of policy learning enlarges this perspective in two ways. First, it attributes a more active role to policy makers. Second, it analyses the transfer of instruments between different policies and different countries. Bennett and Howlett (1992) interpret changes in instrument choice as resulting from collective learning processes. As for the related concept of "lesson drawing," their theory assumes that actors within a policy network assess policy and draw lessons about the efficacy of the instruments that have already been used. If actors are unsatisfied with these instruments, they search for alternate instruments that have been successfully employed elsewhere. They then determine whether it is technically and politically feasible to adapt these instruments to their particular situations. If this is the case, they then put the instruments to use in dealing with the issues their policies are intended to resolve (Rose 1993).

Proceeding to a meta-evaluation of the theories that propose a causal link between policy changes and policy learning, Howlett and Ramesh (1993) conclude that each of the main authors using this approach "explicitly acknowledges the significance of policy instruments in the process of policy learning as each has suggested that, for the most part, in normal times policy learning is in effect learning about instruments" (1993, 14–15). Many advocates of policy (re)design also subscribe to this theoretical perspective – hence the concept of "policy learning" proposed by May (1992) or that of "design borrowing" suggested by Schneider and Ingram (1988). Weimer (1993) likewise refers to a conscious process of evaluating and transferring policy instruments through time and space.

Besides suggesting new explanatory variables for the choice of instruments (policy inheritance, policy learning), this fourth proposition also carries methodological implications. Indeed, it is impossible to test or falsify a theory of policy-instrument choice without knowing precisely which instruments have already been employed. In conclusion, this proposition advocates always explaining, testing, and empirically predicting the choice of policy instruments as part of the redesigning process within the appropriate contexts. The impact of context can refer to either institutions or to problems. We will now turn our attention to these factors.

*Proposition 5: The choice of policy instruments depends on the institutional context of the actors involved.*

There are two conflicting views regarding the influence of the institutional context of the actors on the choice of policy instruments. On the one hand, the strongest version of the rational-choice theory claims that institutions influence neither the individual preferences of the political and administrative actors involved nor the collective choice of instruments (Sproule-Jones 1996; Landry 1996). On the other hand, the theoretical perspective of sociological and historical neoinstitutionalism (Hall and Taylor 1996) argues that institutions constrain the behaviour of the actors involved in public-policy design in two different ways. First, participants do not evaluate policy-tool valuation criteria in an abstract manner but in terms of the concrete contexts in which they will be applied. For example, the value of the "resource-intensiveness" attribute, and the way it distributes costs between groups, varies depending on whether the implementation structure is centralized or decentralized, consensual or nonconsensual, and so on. Therefore, the choice of a policy tool depends on how institutions shape the way actors evaluate their political economy (Majone 1976, 603). Second, the neoinstitutional paradigm postulates that institutions influence actor preferences and behaviour. It suggests that participants weigh the valuation criteria and resolve policy-tool trade-offs in terms of the values promoted by the institutions in which they operate. Likewise, Linder and Peters (1989) assume that the institutional context framing the work of policy makers influences instrument choice at the national, regional, and micro-organizational level. They stress, however, that this link is not linear but mediated by the cognitive perceptions of the participants.

According to Atkinson and Nigol (1989, 115–16), this fifth proposition carries three implications for the theory of policy-tool choice. First, instrument (re)design is never an isolated choice; it is always linked to a historical process. This is a point that will be addressed more specifically later. Second, the values and preferences of the participants choosing the instruments are defined as endogenous variables. Understanding their true influence on the choice of policy tools requires that one make a precise diagnostic of the problems to be resolved, as the example of instruments aimed at promoting innovation will show. Finally, the organizational characteristics of institutions determine their capacities to adapt to the evolution and changes in the problems to be resolved when policy instruments are being chosen. It is therefore essential to examine institutional objectives, resources, and standard operating procedures.

Adopting a neoinstitutional perspective on policy design, in which actors' rational choices are partially structured by beliefs and institutional norms and rules, we argued that institutions could be interpreted as contexts for the choice of instruments (Timmermans et al. 1998). The rationality of participants in the design process is not only rationally bounded, but also bound to an institutional context. In this sense, proposition 5 refers to the concept of "reasonable rationality" (Norgaard 1996) and suggests that each designer is confronted with a dilemma: On the one hand, neglecting institutions may lead to unviable instruments that cannot be successfully advocated and implemented; on the other hand, designing in perfect conformity with existing institutions may drastically reduce the scope of instrument choices as well as the possibility of developing solutions contributing efficiently to induce changes in behaviour likely to solve problems such as those related to the deficit of innovation in the manufacturing industries. However, the supporters of proposition 5 do not pay enough attention to the concrete attributes of the problems to be resolved, as we will now see with the case of innovation policy and its associated policy instruments.

## CONFRONTING THE DEDUCTIVE AND THE INTERACTIVE APPROACHES

Our reconstruction of the deductive approach to the choice of policy instruments can be summed up as follows: Although the various policy instruments can be substituted, the choice of policy instruments is constrained by valuation criteria, previously chosen instruments, and the institutional context of the actors involved. We will now consider how the choices of policy instruments differ depending on whether the deductive or the interactive approach is adopted.

*Proposition 6: The choice of policy instruments depends on the social construction of the attributes of the policy problems to be solved, as illustrated by the case of innovation.*

Studies on policy instruments usually take into account the impact of the institutional contexts of policy problems but not the impact of their attributes. To illustrate in concrete terms the impact of the attributes characterizing the problems encountered in policy-instrument choice, it is useful to examine a problem that has evolved significantly over a ten- or fifteen-year period. The case of innovation in the manufacturing sector is appropriate for two reasons: (1) The issue of innovation has evolved very significantly over the last decade, and (2) it is a type of policy for which governments have a significant margin for action with respect to the types of instruments on which they can rely.

### Diagnostic of the Policy Problem: What Are the Driving Forces of Innovation?

Despite a large body of empirical literature on the determinants of innovation, there is not yet a consensus regarding the categories of factors that explain innovation. Until a few years ago, studies on innovation as well as on policy makers implicitly assumed that innovation was the result of events initiated by isolated entrepreneurs or isolated inventors. The renewed vision and understanding of innovation lay stress on four categories of ideas:

1 Innovations do not result from discrete events but primarily through problem-solving processes (Dosi 1982).
2 Innovations are determined not only by factors internal to firms, but also by interactive processes involving relationships between firms and the different actors of their environments (Kline and Rosenberg 1986).
3 Innovations are determined not only by an additional productivity of operations, but also by a systemic productivity of relations (Foray 1998, 2000a; Lengrand and Chatrie 1999) generating diversified learning processes: learning-by-using, learning-by-doing, learning-by-sharing (Lundvall 1985; Malerba 1992). Learning may arise from internal or from external sources of knowledge (Dogson 1991). External learning refers to the absorption capacity of firms (Cohen and Levinthal 1990).
4 Innovations are determined not only by isolated learning, but also by social processes of exchange of knowledge that generate an innovative system (Johnson 1995; Lundvall 1992; Acs 2000; Braczyk et al. 1999; Cooke et al. 2000; de la Mothe and Paquet 1998; Edquist 1997; Edquist and Hommen 1999; Holbrook and Wolfe 2000; Landry and Amara 1998; Niosi 1993), a "système social d'innovation" (Amable et al. 1997; de la Mothe 2000), a "milieu innovateur" (Maillat 1995; Storper 1997), or an innovation cluster (Porter 1999, 2000).

These new conceptualizations of innovation have led to revisions in innovation theories. Traditional theoretical and empirical studies focused on firm-specific determinants: research and development (R&D), use of advanced technologies, firm size, and so on. Over time, studies based on firm-specific determinants have added an increasingly larger variety of determinants external to firms, especially with respect to external sources of information used by firms to develop or improve their products or manufacturing processes. The progressive inclusion of information and knowledge into our understanding of innovation carries tremendous implications for the market failures for which compensation is needed through government interventions and for the choice of policy instruments.

The policy-analysis literature has paid considerable attention to the social construction of policy problems and how the framing of issues influences the policy-making process (e.g., Rochefort and Cobb 1994; Schön and Rein 1994). Thus how the attributes of a collective problem are defined must be understood as an integral part of the designing process. It might influence who participates, which administrative unit is in charge, which societal actors might be mobilized, and thus what the final policy design might look like.

### Diagnostic of the Contexts in which Actors Operate: What Are the Implications Deriving from the Diversity of Actors' or Firms' Abilities to Innovate?

The implicit assumption of national – even provincial/regional – innovation policies is that the target group for such policies is made up of homogeneous firms and actors. In other words, these policies assume that firms are all alike regarding resources, organizational culture, and abilities to shape their environment. Furthermore, these policies tend to assume that differences between manufacturing sectors and regions are so small that they do not justify the use of different policy instruments. Studies on innovation – not studies on policy instruments – show that manufacturing firms operate with resources, culture, and abilities that vary tremendously according to the number of employees, industrial sectors, and regions where they are located. For instance, compared to large firms, small and medium firms operate with:

- a more limited resource base
- a different organizational culture with respect to ownership and management
- a more informal and uncodified set of innovation practices
- a lower ability to shape their environment
- a lower internal capacity to access and absorb information and knowledge from external sources

The wide variety of contexts in which firms operate suggests that it is not possible to develop national or provincial innovation policies based on the search for the "best" policy instrument. However, this does not imply that national or provincial/regional policies are deemed to be inefficient; it only means that such policies and their associated policy instruments have to be customized in order to take into account the variety of the situations in which the firms and other actors supporting the firms operate. In short, the variety of contexts in which actors operate means that devising and choosing efficient policy instruments is less easy in practice than it frequently appears to be in the deductive approach to the choice of policy instruments.

### Diagnostic of the Market Failures Calling for Government Interventions

The point of departure of innovation policies is the acknowledgment that innovation in manufacturing firms is a good thing and that there is a justification for government interventions in order to foster more of it in firms (Nauwelaers and Wintjes 2000). However, the justifications for innovation-policy interventions have changed in parallel with changes in our understanding of the innovation process.

Innovation policies implemented in response to technical events initiated by isolated firms are justified by three market failures. First, it is argued that the indivisibility of R&D and innovation activities necessitates fixed costs and levels of investments that cannot be supported by the private sector alone. Therefore, governments are justified in compensating the private sector by using two instruments: subsidies and tax incentives. The second argument is related to the fact that firms are not able to appropriate the totality of the benefits resulting from their investments in R&D and innovation activities. In some cases, the amount of public benefits that is intangible and cannot be commercialized is greater than the amount of private benefits. These types of failures call for the use of subsidies, tax incentives, and patents (to protect private investments). The third market failure derives from the uncertainty pertaining to R&D and innovation activities. As it becomes more difficult to estimate the technical results and the returns of private investments, firms are induced to decrease their R&D and innovation activities. Thus governments are justified in using policy tools likely to decrease the level of uncertainty of R&D and innovation activities undertaken by private firms. This type of failure is usually compensated through tax incentives. Until recently, experts assumed that these three types of market failures represented the only failures calling for government compensation.

However, in a context where it is assumed that innovation is determined not only by isolated learning, but also by social processes of knowledge exchange, knowledge-generating systems, innovative systems, networks, clusters, and so forth, market failures are not limited to a lack of financial incentives; they are primarily related to the lack of skills as regards acquisition and absorption of information and knowledge. Three market failures can be identified in matters of skills deficits. The first is related to the lack of information about opportunities provided by new or advanced technologies. The second derives from the lack of skills regarding the use of new or advanced technologies. And the third concerns the potential for innovation also to be lower than socially desired due to the absence of the appropriate institutions for training, brokering, and exchange of knowledge. These three failures are aggravated by the importance of the tacit, informal, uncodified, and disembodied aspects of the knowledge required to develop successful innovations. This category of market failures calls for government interventions fostering interactions, networking, and brokering of knowledge in order to improve the acquisition and absorptive skills of the private firms. Likewise, the variety of contexts in which firms operate regarding skills, regions, and size also calls for recourse to policy instruments promoting interactions and exchange of knowledge.

## IMPLICATIONS FOR THE CHOICE OF POLICY INSTRUMENTS

Changes in our understanding of the innovation process, in the market failures to be compensated, and in the implications resulting from the variety of contexts in which manufacturing firms operate carry significant implications regarding the basic dimensions of policy instruments used to foster innovation. As indicated in Table 5.3, the unit of analysis in innovation policy has evolved from the program or agency to the distinctive instruments used to implement the innovation policies. And ongoing initiatives in a number of European countries as well as in Canada suggest that policies to support innovation increasingly tend to be implemented not directly by government agencies but through intermediary organizations. These intermediary organizations sign contracts with government agencies mandating them to implement policies to support networking and learning. A large number of regional organizations promoting economic development, innovation, and technology transfers in Europe and in Canada are currently implementing government policies based on mandates handed to them by government agencies. Until very recently, the traditional role of officials in government

Table 5.3
Contrasting dimensions between traditional and new innovation policy instruments

| Dimensions of policy instruments: | Deductive approach to the choice of policy instruments (traditional innovation policies: innovation as an isolated technical event) | Interactive approach to the choice of policy instruments (new innovation policies: innovation as a social process of knowledge exchange) |
|---|---|---|
| Market failures | Government interventions are justified by the lack of inputs preventing innovation in individual firms | Government interventions are justified by the lack of skills preventing innovation in groups of firms operating in particular industries or regions |
| Unit of analysis | Programs promoting innovation | Tools promoting exchange of knowledge and improvement of skills |
| Structures implementing government interventions | Programs implemented by hierarchical government agencies | Programs implemented by nonprofit organizations operating like networks |
| Government actors implementing government interventions | Programs implemented by reactive government agents | Programs implemented by proactive government agents |
| Control of resources and decisions | Resources and decisions are under the control of government agencies | Resources and decisions are under the control of the members of networks |
| Targets of government interventions | Government agencies attempt to improve inputs of firms targeted by policies | Government agencies attempt to improve skills of firms targeted by policies |
| Actors targeted by policies | Individual firms | Groups of firms operating in particular industries or regions |
| Government failures | Information asymmetry: Firms have more information than government agencies on the inputs required for innovation. | Information asymmetry: Firms have more information than government agencies on the skills required for innovation. |

agencies was to wait passively to be contacted by the clients of the programs they were responsible for implementing. Nowadays, through forums like the Canada Economic Development Agency's Strategic Regional Initiatives Program, officials are expected to take a highly proactive role in getting players in the industry or region where they are working to actively cooperate.

The traditional policies of support to innovation that tended to target individual manufacturing firms based on a philosophy of support-

Table 5.4
Classification of policy instruments to support innovation and innovative environments

| Target level of instruments | Forms and focus of policy instruments | |
|---|---|---|
| | *Reactive instruments allocating inputs* | *Proactive instruments focused on learning skills* |
| Firm-oriented (isolated firms) | Type A policy instruments target businesses by emphasizing production inputs:<br>• traditional instruments<br>• examples: subsidized training, recruitment, R&D | Type B policy instruments support businesses by promoting the development of innovative abilities:<br>• proactive instruments<br>• examples: coaching of businesses, innovative centres, strategic intelligence |
| Region-oriented or industry-oriented (interactions between agents) | Type C policy instruments look to the regional environment by supporting production inputs:<br>• instruments foster cooperation<br>• examples: planned R&D alliances, university-industry R&D projects, collective technology transfer centres | Type D policy instruments look to the regional environment by supporting the development of innovative ability:<br>• instruments foster innovation<br>• examples: proactive knowledge brokers, support to clusters, networks, regional-development plans<br>• instruments underused |

*Source:* Adapted from Claire Nauwelaers and René Wintjes 2000.

ing production inputs have been eclipsed by more recent policies that now target the industrial or regional environment based on a philosophy of supporting innovative ability.

Table 5.4 very schematically summarizes the picture that Claire Nauwelaers and René Wintjes (2000) ended up with in their assessment of forty programs to support innovation introduced in eleven European regions. The results of their assessment suggest that government policies should be custom-made to respond to the wide variety of starting situations. Although the table's type A instruments might be considered more traditional and its type D instruments more innovative, one should not conclude that type D instruments are better or more efficient than the type A, B, or C instruments. There is a need for recourse to instruments appropriate to the specificities of the market failures and problems to be resolved. The real challenge is to devise the appropriate portfolio of instruments meeting the variety of needs and problems faced by the manufacturing firms, industries, or regions. In any specific situation, there will be a need for a mix of types A, B, C, and D instruments. For instance, individual firms need to accumulate production inputs (type A instruments) as a necessary step to being able to benefit efficiently from types B, C, and D instruments. The type B instruments are useful when there is a low concentration of innovative firms in a given industry or region. As for the type C instruments, they are useful for fostering knowledge sharing among businesses in one industry or region. However, to efficiently benefit from type C instruments, a firm must, as a necessary condition, have accumulated the required inputs (type A instruments) and the appropriate learning skills (type B instruments). Finally, the type D instruments may only be introduced following the successful use of the types A, B, and C instruments. To still further complicate the picture, differences in the resources and learning skills of regions and industries justify customized mixes of policy instruments. To be efficient, policy instruments need to be adapted to the context of the problems to be resolved. "One-size-fits-all" policy instruments cannot work efficiently. However, it does not mean that no generalizations can be derived regarding the efficiency of the various policy instruments. As has been suggested above, generalizations can be derived regarding categories of problems (allocation of inputs or learning skills) and targets (individual firms or industry/region).

*Proposition 7: The choice of instruments is limited by the bounded rationality and opportunism of participants. This choice always represents a satisfactory, as opposed to optimal, solution.*

Regardless of the approach, but especially for the interactive approach, the choice of policy instruments rests on two critical behavioural assumptions: bound rationality and opportunism. In assuming that policy makers maximize welfare in a subjective manner, we also assume that they mix the four valuation criteria (resource intensiveness, targeting, political risk, and financial and ideological constraints) in a variety of ways. Furthermore, in assuming that they attempt to anticipate the uncertain consequences of their instrument choices as best they can, we make the de facto presumption that their cognitive competence is limited. We can subsequently deduce that policy makers do not seek to maximize their interests regarding the four valuation criteria but rather attempt to obtain satisfying trade-offs from among the four valuation-criteria categories.

Opportunism is induced by the fact that policy instruments are never comprehensive, for they never exhaust all the decision-making possibilities. Although they facilitate decision making by defining the boundaries of acceptable behaviour, policy instruments always carry with them a certain degree of ambiguity. In the context of the interactive approach to problem solving, it is impossible to design comprehensive ex ante policy instruments. This point is important because incomplete policy instruments create room for opportunism – that is, an incentive to use them to satisfy individual self-interest. A certain number of participants in the policy process can be expected to exploit this vacuum for their own advantage. This possibility is much higher in the case of new instruments based on interactions between actors and on enhancement of skills than it is in the case of the more traditional instruments based on increases of tangible production inputs.

These two behavioural assumptions have important implications for policy design. In a decision-making context where policy instruments are inevitably incomplete due to bound rationality and where incomplete policy instruments create incentives for opportunism, individuals are likely to invest their resources in the development and maintenance of policy instruments that simultaneously minimize the recourse to cognitive competence and the occurrence of opportunism.

*Proposition 8: Policy instruments are defined in terms of transactions having four dimensions (asset specificity, measurability, uncertainty, and frequency) that raise four types of problems (redeployability, adverse selection and moral hazard, manipulation, and paralysis) for those involved in their selection. Choosing an instrument consists of minimizing the occurrence of such problems.*

Developing or changing policy instruments involves the transfer of resources from certain groups of individuals to other groups of individuals. To this extent, the policy problems addressed by instruments can be dimensionalized as typical transactions in terms of asset specificity, measurability, uncertainty, and frequency (Williamson 1975, 1985; Milgrom and Roberts 1992; Bryson and Smith Ring 1990).

Recourse to policy instruments may depend on prior investments made in physical assets, human assets, site assets, and dedicated assets. The notion of assets can be interpreted in terms of redeployability of resources. Hence prior investments in assets are considered specific to the extent that their redeployment in alternative policy instruments is considered difficult and costly by policy makers. As is well illustrated by the types A, B, C, and D policy instruments (Table 5.4) that can be used to foster innovation, specific assets have a low degree of substitutability. At the same time, it is important to note that different assets invested in a given policy instrument do not necessarily have the same degree of substitutability: Some may have a low degree of specificity that makes them easy to redeploy, whereas others may have a high degree of specificity that makes them difficult to redeploy. Participants who either control or benefit from investments in highly specific assets have greater negotiating leverage in redesigning policy instruments. However, this advantage does not induce them to support redesign of policy instruments that are socially optimal.

Furthermore, policy-instrument design involves the transfer of resources between policy makers, policy implementers, and policy target groups. From the participants' standpoint, it is less important to know the exact nature of the assets brought to the policy process than to have some knowledge regarding their measurability. Assets used to design policy instruments can be considered easily measurable when they possess two intrinsic characteristics: a unit of measurement and a number of units. When they are difficult to measure, problems of adverse selection and moral hazard are likely to occur. Adverse selection refers to situations where well-informed participants in the policy process deal with participants possessing less information than themselves as the result of the preexisting distribution of information. In these circumstances, participants are induced to behave opportunistically. And opportunistic behaviour is made easier when the chosen policy instruments involve exchange of knowledge and development of skills (type D, the pure case of the interactive approach) rather than the provision of tangible production inputs (type A, the pure case of the deductive approach). As for moral hazards, they occur when the assets contributed by some policy participants cannot be easily measured by others, thus increasing the likelihood of some participants behaving opportunistically. Again, instruments dealing with intangible factors like exchange of knowledge and enhancement of learning skills generate potentially higher incentives to behave opportunistically than instruments dealing with tangible input production factors.

Uncertainty is an analytical dimension used to qualify the nature of the context surrounding policy-instrument design. Instrument choice is influenced by the more-or-less frequent changes in the nature, quantity, and price of the assets required for the use of policy instruments. These changes may result from the evolution of the problems well illustrated by the case of innovation policies and their associated instruments or from changes in the external environments of the actors. To simplify, we can distinguish two extreme cases: highly uncertain environments and highly certain environments. Uncertainty is likely to influence policy-instrument choice by inducing participants in the policy process to manipulate perceptions regarding the impact of policy-instrument alternatives on the four valuation criteria. Manipulation of perceptions is likely whenever it can be expected to enhance participants' interests. It would seem easier to manipulate perceptions in contexts where policy instruments deal with exchange of knowledge and learning skills than in cases where they deal with tangible input factors.

The last important analytical dimension is frequency. Whenever the functioning of a policy instrument requires frequent adjustments and modifications to the combination of assets used, policy makers and other participants involved in instrument choice are induced to develop rules and routines facilitating instrument redesign. Conversely, when repeated adjustments are not required, participants have no incentive to develop rules facilitating low-cost adaptations (vis-à-vis the four valuation criteria). In these low-frequency decision-making contexts, policy participants tend to support the status quo. The result is problems of paralysis. This type of problem is less likely to occur when actors base the choice of policy instruments on the interactive approach – in which case, they then tend to make frequent adjustments and modifications to policy instruments – than when policy instruments are based on a rational, deductive approach and the provision of tangible production inputs.

Let us assume a policy-making context where policy participants consider the costs and benefits resulting from changes to the status quo (situation of redesign). Incentives to depart from the status quo will depend on the structure of the policy-design process, which is the product of a combination of two categories of factors: incentives created by (1) the four dimensions and problems (proposition 8) that are generated by (2) the four valuation criteria (proposition 1). If we imagine a context in which assets required for policy-instrument use are nonspecific, adjustments in resource allocations occur very frequently, assets required by instruments are easily measured, and uncertainty is low, then constraints on the valuation criteria are minimal and the choice of policy instruments is easy because there is a high degree of substitution from among the instruments of the tool box. However, if we imagine a context of highly specific assets, infrequent adjustments, difficulty of measurement, and high uncertainty, then the choice of policy instruments is complicated by the presence of four problems that can occur either in isolation or in combination (see Table 5.5).

From a theoretical standpoint, the absence of problems raises trivial issues, whereas the presence of problems produces challenges of varying degrees of difficulty. Moreover, to explain policy-instrument choice, it is necessary to take into account the problems characterizing the structure of the situation and to identify the incentives that each category of participants in the policy-design process may have to minimize in response to the occurrence of these problems.

## TOWARD RESEARCH HYPOTHESES

In policy-design contexts like these, but especially in contexts surrounding the interactive approach, the choices made by policy

Table 5.5
Analytical dimensions and problems occurring in the (re) design of policy tools

| Analytical dimensions of policy tools | Problems that may occur as the result of policy-tool choice |
|---|---|
| Asset specificity (degree of substitutability) | Problems of redeployability |
| Asset measurability (unit of measurement and number of units) | Problems of adverse selection and moral hazard |
| Contextual uncertainty (policy problem and external disturbances) | Problems of manipulation |
| Frequency of adjustment (modifications to the asset combination) | Problems of paralysis |

participants do not ensure the selection of optimally efficient policy instruments. On the contrary, policy participants who seek to maximize their own interests will tend to select policy instruments that enable them to capture rents irrespective of optimally efficient choices. To better understand why participants in the policy-design process are induced to behave opportunistically, let us consider three categories of participants: policy makers (elected representatives), policy implementers, and policy target groups. According to the traditional propositions of the rational-choice theory, policy makers seek flexibility because of their reelection calculus, which includes policy responsiveness. Bureaucrats seek to maximize the financial resources and the managerial-discretion powers of their agencies. Target groups seek to minimize the costs or to maximize the benefits deriving from changes in policies.

The nature of the assets required to put policy instruments to use will determine the choices of the participants. Policy makers involved in redesigning policy instruments tend to avoid selecting policy tools requiring highly specific assets because they are difficult to redeploy. Instead, they will seek policy tools based on easily redeployable assets. However, policy implementers and policy target groups have opposite interests: They tend to favour policy tools based on highly specific assets because this increases the cost of redeploying assets for use on alternative policy instruments that do not correspond to their particular interests. For instance, one can easily predict that intermediary organizations mandated to implement innovation policies based on instruments fostering interactions between actors will develop vested interests that accumulate over time and become increasingly difficult to question.

Policy tools are not chosen on the basis of optimization calculus but on the basis of a comparative examination of the constraints facing participants involved in the policy-design process. Balancing the constraints imposed by each valuation criterion generates trade-offs. Despite the context of bound rationality, we assume that the participants in the policy process are able to assess the contribution of different policy tools in relation to each valuation criterion. This proposition is justified by the fact that policy participants can act on information accumulated from past policy-design experiences. By taking the four valuation criteria into account, participants involved in the policy-design process are able to identify potential problems and to select policy tools that minimize their occurrence. Based on this argument, we can predict that (1) policy makers will tend to avoid selecting policy tools based on highly specific assets because such assets are less easily redeployable on other tools that could be more likely to maximize votes; (2) policy implementers will tend to prefer policy instruments based on highly specific assets because this degree of specificity is more likely to protect the financial resources at their disposal and the managerial discretion of their agencies; and (3) policy target groups will tend to prefer policy instruments based on highly specific assets because this degree of specificity is more likely to minimize the costs and to maximize the benefits that might derive from changes in the choice of policy instruments. Hence, in the case of the new innovation policies, the intermediary organizations mandated to implement policies based on the interactive approach will tend to develop highly specific assets regarding networks, networking skills, and learning skills that officials in government agencies have no opportunities to develop.

Uncertainty is another factor influencing the choice of policy tools. It encourages policy participants to manipulate perceptions of the impact of alternative policy tools on the four valuation criteria. The extent to which policy participants are induced to manipulate perceptions concerning policy-tool costs and benefits is partly shaped by the degree of uncertainty and partly by their roles in the policy-design process. The more frequent the changes in the nature, quantity, and price of the assets that policy instruments require, the greater the incentive to manipulate perceptions about the cost-benefit appraisals of the other participants involved in the policy process. Certain participants can therefore be expected to try artificially to increase the benefits perceived by participants who oppose their choice of policy tools, while at the same time artificially reducing the costs perceived by those who support their preferred policy tools. As a result, we can predict that (1) policy makers, policy implementers, and policy target groups will tend to artificially increase the perceived benefits or artificially reduce the perceived costs of policy tools whenever policy tools are based on assets that are subjected to frequent changes; (2) policy implementers will tend to avoid choosing policy tools based on assets whose nature, quantity, and price change frequently because such assets are less likely to protect the level of financial resources of their agencies and their managerial discretion; and (3) policy target groups will tend to avoid policy tools based on assets whose nature, quantity, and price change frequently because such tools are less likely to minimize costs or maximize benefits deriving from changes in policies. The case of intermediary organizations mandated to implement innovation policies provides a good illustration of this point. The contracts they sign with government agencies to act as policy implementers define mandates for time horizons of three to five years, thus providing an efficient mechanism to reduce costs that could derive from drastic changes in policies.

The measurement of the assets used in policy-tool design has an influence on the incentives of participants involved in the policy process. Whenever the assets used in policy design are difficult to measure, problems of adverse selection and moral hazard induce participants to behave opportunistically if it is likely to enhance their self-interest. On the basis of this argument, we can predict that (1) policy makers will have greater incentive than policy implementers and policy target groups to avoid selecting policy tools based on assets that are difficult to measure because such assets are less likely to contribute to maximizing votes; (2) policy implementers will tend to prefer policy tools based on assets that are difficult to measure because such tools more likely to facilitate maximization of financial resources for their agencies and maximization of margins of managerial discretion; and (3) policy target groups will tend to prefer policy tools based on assets that are difficult to measure because such tools are more likely to facilitate costs minimization or benefits maximization deriving from future changes in policies. Again, to take the case of the intermediary organizations mandated to implement innovation policies, their is a tendency to stress success based on indicators not easily amenable to measurement, such as increase in networking, knowledge transfer, and enhancement of manufacturing firms' learning skills, rather than on indicators like number of patents and number of jobs or firms created.

Frequency is the last important factor influencing policy tool choice. If the recourse to policy tools does not require frequent adjustment of asset combinations, problems of paralysis emerge when the status quo satisfies the interests of participants in the policy process. Based on this argument, we can predict that (1) policy makers will tend to prefer policy tools based on combinations of assets that can be adjusted and modified frequently in order to respond to changes in vote popularity; (2) policy implementers will tend to prefer policy tools based on assets that cannot be adjusted and modified frequently in order to ensure, in the long run, maximization of financial resources for their agencies as well as maximization of their margins of managerial discretion; (3) policy target groups will tend to prefer policy tools based on assets that cannot be adjusted and modified frequently in order to ensure, in the long run, minimization of costs or maximization of benefits deriving from future changes in policies. We have already pointed out above that intermediary organizations mandated to implement the new generation of innovation policies prefer to base their interventions on tools that are committed for a period of three to five years in advance.

## DISCUSSION AND CONCLUSION

The results of this chapter carry theoretical and practical implications for the students of policy-instrument choice. Let us first consider the theoretical points. How do the theoretical predictions derived in this chapter compare with the predictions of existing theories on the rational choice of policy instruments initiated by Trebilcock and others (1982)? By looking more closely than prior studies at the impact of the assets used in policy instrument design, we have been able to derive theoretical predictions that clearly differentiate the choices that policy makers can be expected to make from those that policy implementers and policy target groups can be expected to make. These predictions suggest that the context of instrument choice, especially the context of the interactive approach, is governed by incentives similar to those identified in the principal-agent theory. In the case of instrument choice, policy makers (as principal actors) are induced to choose the policy instruments that minimize opportunistic behaviour on the part of policy implementers and policy target groups (as agents). In this respect, our chapter extends a point developed recently by Salamon (2002, 12) on agency theory and policy instruments by more precisely predicting the conditions under which the assets used in policy-instrument design influence the choices made by the various categories of policy participants.

Furthermore, by focusing more closely than prior studies on the impact of uncertainty, we have been able to derive theoretical predictions that clearly distinguish between the incentives that encourage policy makers, policy implementers, and policy target groups to adopt opportunistic behaviour. Our chapter extends the work of Twight (1994) on transaction-cost manipulation by more precisely predicting the conditions under which the various categories of policy participants are induced to try to manipulate the perceptions of the other categories of policy participants.

Finally, in placing more emphasis than prior studies on the impact made by the frequency of adjustments and changes in policy-instrument asset combinations, our chapter sheds new light on the client-politics phenomena studied by Wilson (1989). According to Wilson, client politics occur when the benefits from using a given policy instrument are concentrated in the hands of a certain number of single-policy target groups, whereas the costs are spread across a large segment of the population or across the population as a whole. Our chapter extends the client-politics interpretation by predicting that even under conditions of client politics, policy makers have higher incentives than policy implementers and policy target groups to select policy instruments based on combinations of assets that can be adjusted and modified frequently.

The results of this chapter also carry significant practical implications. First, the chapter provides guiding principles regarding problems of redeployability, adverse selection, moral hazard, manipulation, and paralysis that could or should be minimized. Second, it shows that the choice of policy instruments cannot avoid dealing with the concrete attributes of the substance of the problems to be solved. In comparing the traditional and the new generation of policies fostering innovation in the manufacturing sector, the chapter has shown that the policy design of instruments must take into account both the variety of the particular needs and opportunities of the groups targeted by the policies and the larger context in which these groups operate. In studies on policy instruments, still often absent are a detailed discussion and knowledge of the specificities of the problem to be resolved and of the variety of situations characterizing the target groups.

Drawing on prior studies on the choice of policy instruments, this chapter has questioned the traditional deductive approach to policy-instrument choice to suggest that, in cases like innovation policies, there have been significant shifts regarding the units of analysis, structures implementing policies, control of resources, targets of government interventions, and actors targeted by policies. In this regard, four major shifts have clearly emerged:

1 The units of analysis are less often the program or agency and more often the policy instrument.
2 The structures mandated for implementation of policies and their associated instruments are less often traditional hierarchical government agencies and more often intermediary organizations operating like horizontal networks.
3 The target of government policies is less frequently related to increase of input factors and more frequently linked to enhancement of learning skills.
4 The actors targeted by government policies are less frequently individuals or isolated firms and more frequently groups, communities, regions, or industries.

These recent shifts concern not only the emergence of new policy instruments, but also and primarily the emergence of new forms of governance that tend to display five key features:

1 An increased tendency to use an interactive approach that emphasizes the creation of networks, clusters, partnerships, and horizontal cooperation generally
2 A focus on creating or building upon a consensus among actors targeted by policies by organizing activities that culminate in the formulation of community-based (industries, regions, etc.) strategies
3 The creation or strengthening of social values such as trust and mutuality to allow networks, clusters, and regional cooperatives for innovation to emerge (Landry, Lamari, and Amara 2002).
4 The creation or adjustment of programs to strengthen abilities to assimilate new information and knowledge at the level of the individual as well as collectively through interactions between actors targeted by policies and the other players in their shared environment
5 An increased tendency to perceive the community – defined in the broad sense – as a strategic location for introducing new forms of governance.

The paradigm shift from a rational, deductive approach to an interactive approach in matters of policy-instrument choice has been matched by the use of policy instruments targeting the improvement of intangible factors (skills instead of input production factors) and the emergence of forms of governance that are not limited to solving specific problems but that aim to change the social processes themselves. Clearly, such policy instruments (capacity building and learning instruments according to Schneider and Ingram 1990) will become more customized and likely more efficient, but the use of these new interactive policy instruments and their associated new forms of governance of communities will require new forms of accountability and evaluation based on strategic benchmarking exercises with the participation of policy makers, policy implementers, and actors targeted by policies. In short, there is a need to confront the ideas supporting these new interactive policy instruments and new forms of governance with the reality at both the theoretical and the empirical levels.

# 6

# Instrument Selection
# and Implementation
# in a Networked Context

HANS TH.A. BRESSERS AND
LAURENCE J. O'TOOLE, JR

The tools of government are not at the unencumbered disposal of formal policy makers. While instruments of governance may sometimes seem like so many arrows in a quiver, like options merely awaiting selection and application at appropriate strategic moments by public officials, this appearance is deceptive. This point holds, we argue in this chapter, for the selection of instruments, as they are likewise subject to constraints, and is even more important for those interested in having instruments actually make a useful contribution to achieving policy goals during implementation.

In the following, we point to some constraints on instrument selection stemming from the social and political context of their potential application. In so doing, we emphasize the multiplicity of instruments often operating in a policy setting and the networked character of many such implementation contexts. We do so because it seems clear that a careful recognition of such elements can increase the chances of successful policy action during implementation. Instrument selection certainly plays a role in such action, but we suggest that an appropriate way of anticipating and taking into account their likely impact in practice involves focusing on basic features of instruments that are likely to matter in shaping or reshaping ongoing processes of interaction among the interested parties. The chapter, therefore, offers both cautionary notes and also the outlines of a theoretical argument for how instrument selection can have productive impacts on implementation results.

## THE CIRCUMSTANCES OF INSTRUMENT SELECTION

The core perspective driving the analysis presented in this chapter can be simply stated: Instruments are best regarded not as initial shapers of behaviour in policy settings but as potential shifters of ongoing processes of policy action over time. Many implications flow from an effort to treat this notion seriously. One such initial point has to do with the link between the socio-political context of policy and the selection of instruments themselves. Instruments are usually intended to alter the status quo; accordingly, they carry political implications regarding changes in the distribution of benefits and costs via governance. These implications can impose constraints on what policy makers are able to decide.

Decades ago, Majone (1976) was one of the first to focus on this theme in connection with the relationship between the distribution of power and the selection of policy instruments. He argued that the selection of different instruments has little or no impact on the success or failure of a policy itself since instruments can be applied toward policy results only insofar as such an application is permitted by those holding the balance of power. Majone argued that even if it were possible to develop instruments that could be fully implemented despite powerful opposition, potent antagonists would prevent the selection of such during the process of policy formulation.

Majone's formulation may be seen as overly pessimistic regarding the potential impact of instrument selection since the implication is that selection is realistically confined to only those options that cannot seriously threaten the balance of power. But the balance of power is not fully static, and it is precisely through the tactical manipulation of power differences in different policy processes or at different times that a shift in the balance may be obtained. Policy processes and their outcomes can themselves change the conditions under which any subsequent processes develop – sometimes in substantial ways.

Recognizing this point, however, does not fully invalidate the perspective offered by analysts like Majone. The fact remains that it is first and foremost the extant circumstances that shape the outcome of a process. For instance, it is quite plausible that the greater the government's power in a policy setting, the more capable it will be of selecting instruments that give it – or its allies – sufficient leverage to implement the policy toward the desired objective. Similar reasoning could be applied to the distribution of information in a policy setting, the interests and objectives of the actors involved, and the level of interaction they have become accustomed to (Bressers 1998; Bressers and O'Toole 1998).

Discussions of cost effectiveness sometimes imply that this criterion does or should drive the choices made by policy makers. In the real world, however, this standard is but one of many that decision makers are required to consider. The correct formulation is not based on "good science" versus "bad or corrupting politics" but on the recognition that both are relevant and that each has a rationality of its own. Conceding this point does not imply that it makes no sense to explore the effects of different instrumental strategies on a target group[1] of (boundedly) rational actors. Rather, we emphasize that the groups targeted by policy are not the only relevant actors and that target groups may also be active during formulation. The behaviour of those implementing and/or formulating policy is also an important focus for analysis if we are to develop a viable theory of policy instruments (Bressers and Huitema 1999).

We begin, therefore, from the perspective that the selection of instruments is based – and indeed should be based – on the necessity of gaining and maintaining sufficient support from various parties in a policy setting. In earlier work, we developed this theme (for instance, Bressers and O'Toole 1998). In the present chapter, we move from this point to pursue more carefully a particular set of issues that can be framed by a simple question: Once selected, what is the "modus operandi" of policy instruments? How do they actually work in practice?

Addressing this matter in a fashion that is likely to lead to valid theoretical and practical advance requires consideration of a series of more specific queries that are sometimes acknowledged but seldom analyzed carefully by those interested in policy instruments and governance. For one thing, deciphering how instruments are likely to work in practice means treating seriously the reality that rather than being introduced into a tabula-rasa policy setting, such instruments operate alongside multiple instruments – often on the same or overlapping targets. It is crucial, therefore, that instruments be analyzed in their mutually reinforcing – or sometimes impeding – combinations. This topic is addressed in the next section. Another complication in practice is that oftentimes policy instruments are applied in settings where multiple actors are interdependent – in short, in networked contexts. How to consider some of the consequences of this feature during the implementation of policies is the topic of the second section below. Analyzing instruments in action requires, in turn, that we move away from ad hoc typologies, as the coverage later demonstrates. A subsequent section of the chapter, by considering the multiple "ingredients" of instruments, sketches a way of making progress along such lines. These several features of the coverage ground an argument for analyzing instruments as incentives to facilitate productive interaction processes. We outline a method for doing so and in the final section address some implications for the selection of instruments. We reason backward through the points and themes just mentioned to elicit some insights for effective instrumentation.

## INSTRUMENTATION STRATEGIES AS BLENDS OF INSTRUMENTS

In considering the needs of effective governance, analysts of policy instruments would do well to move away from a perspective that focuses on the separate and isolated instruments under consideration. Almost always, the influence of policy instruments is effectively a blend, or combination, of different instruments, sometimes enacted at different times and often for somewhat different purposes. Instruments are not parachuted onto an empty stage to debut a policy-relevant soliloquy. Newly chosen instruments must typically operate in settings where an array of them already function. The impact of any one is shaped heavily by how the full set works in concert.

This point is one on which analysts frequently remark and was emphasized early by implementation specialists adopting a "bottom-up" perspective (see Elmore 1979/80, 1985). Until fairly recently, however, systematic studies documenting the interactive effects of policy instruments have been lacking. Some such research has started to emerge, however, and this work provides empirical support for the sensible admonition to attend to the full set of instruments rather than only to individual ones.

Two environmental examples can be mentioned, one each from the Netherlands and the United States. In a Dutch study, van de Peppel and colleagues sought to explain air and water emissions reductions nationwide (van de Peppel, Klok, and Hoek 1998). A total of forty-three combinations of emitted substances and emitting target groups were included. Pollution reductions during the period 1980–95 seem to have depended almost completely on only two complex factors: the degree of societal awareness of the issue at stake and the added "intensity" of the *collective policy mix* involved. "Intensity" was measured according to the strength and scope of a complete inventory of environmental-policy instruments used in the country over a twenty-five-year period (a total of 251 relevant instruments were inventoried), with voluntary instruments (for instance) being scored as having less strength or intensity than legally binding requirements.

Of course, that the reduction in emissions can be fairly resoundingly accredited to these two factors – which accounted for more than 90 per cent of the observed variance – only initiates an effort to explain what may be happening in this setting. But the critical point is that the full complement of many instruments aggregated carefully and systematically must be considered in explaining a substantial portion of the policy outcomes.[2]

A second example is the reduction of toxic chemical releases across the states of the US. In a study examining the influence of different policy instruments adopted by the states on the extent of reductions, statistical analyses including relevant control variables demonstrated that while voluntary, informational instruments account for some reductions in states without regulatory programs, and while regulatory programs have some effectiveness absent informational instruments, the most sizable cutbacks occurred in those instances in which a combination of these different types of instruments was in place. More interestingly, the two types of instruments displayed interactive effects with respect to each other: Regulatory instruments have more influence when informational instruments are also present, and vice versa. The outcome is not simply the sum of their separable impacts (Yu et al. 1998).

In short, if we are to understand what instruments do in practice, we must take into account the broader context of instrumentation, in which different tools may reinforce or impede the intended effects of any single given instrument. This conclusion, in turn, has two implications: (1) Analysts interested in effective governance need to begin to grapple with the full social context within which instruments can be expected to shape action; and (2) attention to ongoing interactive processes is required rather than a simple and static kind of causality.

## THE CONFLUENCE OF INSTRUMENTS IN A NETWORKED CONTEXT

Policy instruments can be used in combination to influence the same or related phenomena. These sets of joint instruments are often called "policy mixes." Sometimes these address, or are selected to address, the same target-group behaviour. Different elements in the mix may influence in distinct fashions the way target groups think about their own behaviour and choices – for instance, by imposing legal requirements or providing financial incentives. More often, however, the various instruments in the mix address different points of action in the broader economic and ecological system. Alternatively, or in addition, they might structure arrangements at different levels of governance.

In this section, we provide more specifics about the ways that combinations of instruments might operate in policy settings. An important point that emerges from this analysis is that most circumstances in which a policy mix operates are also contexts in which networks of interdependent policy actors are also an important feature. Understanding how policy instruments work in practice, therefore, will require consideration of the networked character of much public action.

We can distinguish several joint forms of influence, or confluence, of which policy mixes are capable. Using the field of environmental policy as a specific setting in which a number of these might play out, we enumerate several:

1  *Increased intensity of policy intervention.* More than one instrument can be targeted simultaneously at the same target group to intensify a policy intervention. An example would be the announcement of a future (legal) obligation alongside the immediate establishment of a subsidy system to support certain behaviours now.

2  *Integration of multiple instruments into one interactive process between government and target groups.* More instruments can be targeted at the same process of interaction (for instance, technological innovation) but at different actors in the process (both research subsidies for information centres and support for demonstration projects in certain companies).

3  *Instruments and actions at different levels of governance.* Mutual influence of instruments applied at different levels of governance can reinforce or weaken their effects. In the Netherlands, for instance, the relationships between negotiated agreements are developed nationally between government and various industrial sectors, while issuing environmental permits is decentralized to individual companies. These different instruments and levels obviously carry implications for each other. In Canada and the United States, federal systems guarantee these sorts of intertwined arrangements in virtually all policy sectors.

4  *Competition and cooperation between different but interdependent policy fields.* Both competition and cooperation are possible among instruments from different but mutually dependent policy fields. Often other, or overlapping, sectors stimulate (for instance) patterns of production and consumption that influence the context in which particular instruments operate. Here, many illustrations would be possible, including the familiar links and sometimes tensions between economic-development policies and those aimed at enhancing the environment.

5  *Mutual strengthening or weakening of the effects of interventions at different points of action in the broader social and ecological system.* Again, an environmental example makes the point clear. Policies to shift the environmental behaviour of consumers might begin with

instruments to try to influence how consumers themselves think, but these can be enhanced or weakened by other instruments designed to influence the characteristics of products, the way these are sold in stores, and the images of them in the social environment more broadly.

The impact of multiple instruments directed at the same group of actors was a theme dealt with in the preceding section, but this more detailed sketch of the kinds of mixed-instrument circumstances that can arise shows some of the complexity operating during implementation. The first circumstance – increased intensity from multiple instruments – was covered to some extent in the preceding section. The other four possibilities also merit additional attention.

We begin with the second circumstance, the confluence of instruments in the policy-implementation process. The field of environmental policy provides a ready context. A particular source of tension is that arising between, on the one hand, the inherent flexibility exhibited by so-called "consensual instruments" (for instance, covenants in the Dutch context) and by economic instruments such as emissions trading and charges and, on the other hand, less flexible instruments like permits and similar regulatory requirements.

An example of this disjuncture on a small scale would be the frustration experienced in a proactive industrial firm that has worked hard to achieve a rather sustainable profile only to be confronted with detailed prescriptions on a single, fairly narrow issue. These kinds of tensions have not yet been resolved in the practical implementation process (for instance, see ECW 1996).

The third circumstance linked to the relationships between instruments is the confluence of instruments used at different levels in the governance system. Among policy researchers nowadays, it is fashionable to emphasize the theme of "multilevel governance." Federal-provincial (or -state) and national-local relations have often received considerable attention in part because of the patterns of subnational involvement in the implementation of national programs. More recently, the emergence of the European Union, along with a huge array of international and functionally specific agreements (see O'Toole and Hanf 2002), have been attracting considerable interest.

The Kyoto Protocol is a well-known version of the latter. For the former, an example combining European policy, national regulations, and subnational implementation challenges is illustrative. In some European countries, subnational levels of government have been expected to play significant roles in the implementation of national standards that have been in turn driven by European guidelines on air quality regarding such pollutants as sulphur dioxide, lead, and nitrogen oxides. One part of the explanation for disappointing implementation results subnationally has to do with differences at different levels. For instance, in the Netherlands, while European guidelines are based on ambient air-quality considerations, national law and established implementation practices have been more strongly emission-oriented (Booy Liewes et al. 1992). In this case, the fundamental underlying difference in perspective has made for an uneasy mix in the combination of instruments.

A fourth circumstance necessitating instrument mixes is the competition and cooperation between or among different policy fields. Policies frequently carry externalities for other efforts in related but distinct fields. In the United States, for instance, national agencies now provide data indicating – in regular reports required by the Governmental Performance and Results Act – that their missions overlap with the activities and objectives of many other agencies. Systematic analysis indicates that these links across fields, as well as units, are more the rule than the exception for new instruments and new programs (Hall and O'Toole 2000, 2004). Clearly, environmental policy offers a prime example. Most environmental topics are influenced at least as much by policies developed in other fields as by policies that are explicitly environmental. Environmental-policy instruments are sometimes used to mitigate environmental harm done by other kinds of instruments (Ligteringen 1998). In such cases, the best environmental policy might be simply to abandon the other environmentally unfriendly policies. Transportation-policy instruments, along with those in the fields of agriculture, industrial infrastructure, energy, and assorted other sectors, all carry important implications for sustainability. "Interpolicy cooperation" (Knoepfel 1995) is essential for an effective and efficient sustainability policy.

A fifth and final mixed-instrument circumstance is the confluence of instruments working at different points of action in an economy-ecology system. Multiple instruments are employed, for instance, to persuade people to use their cars less frequently. Some of these are directed toward the social environment – including indirect efforts, such as requirements that companies limit the number of parking spaces at their plants. Of course, the sets of instruments vary in their effectiveness. The point to be emphasized is that policy instruments that work at the different points of action in the system can be used to greatest effect only if the complete ecology of the instruments is taken into account. Doing so requires not only an examination of the full policy field, but also an effort to get beyond disciplinary or other forms of specialization – with economists emphasizing economic instruments, lawyers doing the same with regard to regulations, and social psychologists considering communicative instruments first and foremost.

Of the five circumstances of confluence sketched above, it is notable that the last four clearly imply a concept of the policy field as a networked context. By "networked" we mean that the policy-relevant actors operate not as autonomous or atomized units, nor merely as parts of a larger, straightforwardly hierarchical array, but in a matrix of interdependence.

The patterns of interdependence may stem from multiple instruments mobilized among actors engaged in an interaction process (the second circumstance), thus linking their relational patterns and subprocesses in causally complicated fashions. The networked action may be driven by the multilevel character of contemporary governance systems (the third circumstance), a phenomenon drawing increasing attention by analysts in North America (Lynn, Heinrich, and Hill 2001) as well as in Europe (Held 1996; Pierre and Peters 2000). The networked features of the setting may stem from the links between or among different but related policy fields (the fourth circumstance). This dimension may be encouraged by the very features of today's policy problems, which necessarily carry reverberations across multiple sectors and specialized communities. Consider, for instance, how a policy challenge like HIV-AIDS forces a consideration of such ostensibly discrete matters as health care, education, discrimination, homelessness, and scientific research. Finally, the networked patterns of interdependence typical of a developed and differentiated society and its associated ecology mean that multiple leverage points, instrument strategies, and interactions need to be considered to increase the odds of effective policy action during implementation (the fifth circumstance).

It is not surprising, therefore, that the theme of networks and policy action has become prominent on both sides of the Atlantic (Agranoff and McGuire 2003; Bogason and Toonen 1998; Bressers, O'Toole, and Richardson 1994; Mandell 2001; O'Toole 1997b; Provan and Milward 1995; Rhodes 1997). This work has documented the development of networked complexity, suggested a number of reasons why networks have assumed such salience, and offered partial theoretical characterizations of how to explain what happens when policy is executed in networked contexts.

The tempting possibility is to encourage the development of a field and perhaps theory of "network management" – a way of understanding how to shape concerted action in and through networks to deliver on the overall effectiveness of policy instruments. Some research has indeed been aimed at an understanding of network management, although the most careful work has been fairly clear that the idea of "management" connotes a more directive and muscular function than is likely to be possible in networked settings (see Kickert, Klijn, and Koppenjan 1997). Instead, "network management" involves such important but potentially multilateral tasks as facilitating exchange, identifying potential options for multiactor agreement, and helping to craft patterns of communication as well as multilevel and multiactor governance arrangements.

Still, heavy doses of caution are in order. Any attempt to alter the structure of a network requires, itself, direct interventions – often with "classic" instruments, albeit instruments aimed at intervention points in the system other than the ultimate targets. While such efforts clearly widen the scope for possible influence, they do not solve many of the lingering difficulties that are posed by such interventions.

Managerial efforts by public managers themselves, those ensconced in the matrix of actors involved in implementation, can be influential in helping to shape action in and through networks (see, for instance, O'Toole 1996, 1997a). But the very character of networks means that managers will have limited abilities to actually drive results. Furthermore, "management" of this sort may be undertaken simultaneously by several actors from distinct organizational units in the multiactor array. Networks are not subject to unilateral direction. As a result, although the managerial function can be exercised by actors within networks, and although this function can help shape what happens, managers themselves cannot be considered definitive shapers of what transpires when instruments are implemented in networks.

In short, then, the multiplicity and confluence of instruments in the real world not only makes their interaction complex, but also virtually guarantees that the context for converting them into streams of action will itself be complex – that is, networked. These are the sorts of environments in which management is clearly relevant, but management, too, cannot be expected to operate in a straightforwardly direct and instrumental fashion to achieve policy objectives.

## THE "MODUS OPERANDI" OF POLICY MIXES

As if this set of challenges were not enough, theorizing about how policy instruments work during implementation is further complicated because the most commonly used categories and typologies of instruments encourage conceptual confusion.

Take, for instance, the notion of "economic," or "market," instruments. This apparently straightforward label obscures the point that virtually *all* instruments involve some exchange of scarce resources. Likewise, the notion of "communicative" instruments obscures the reality that all instruments communicate relevant information to target groups. And referring to "judicial" or "rule-based" instruments draws attention away from the point that all instruments require a rule-based institutional framework.

The point can be illustrated by considering the instance of environmental subsidies and how these might have impacts on the behaviour of target groups. Subsidy schemes would conventionally be considered an economic-based or incentive-oriented instrument. Note, however, that subsidies can operate in considerably more complicated and nuanced ways, such that their effects include:

- Reducing costs for some behavioural alternatives – that is, the classic "economic" mechanism
- Creating essential financial opportunities for already-profitable alternatives that otherwise would exceed the investment capacities of some targeted companies
- Drawing attention to possible behavioural alternatives and thus potentially placing them on corporate agendas
- Signalling approval by authorities and thus reducing uncertainty about how a government is likely to respond to an environmentally oriented investment that might not fully meet standards
- Reducing technical uncertainty through advising on and supervising subsidized projects
- Stimulating a more positive attitude toward the environment
- Enhancing the legitimacy of accompanying environmental regulations (recall again that a confluence of instruments is likely to be operating)
- Improving relations between companies among the target groups, on the one hand, and environmental authorities, on the other
- Improving contacts with and activity levels of other organizations in the policy-relevant network – for instance, environmental-consulting companies.

This list contains a wide variety of interventions that can influence decisions made by members of the target groups. Some of them are "financial," or "economic"; others stress communication, or support for rules, or the activation of networking among and with the target groups. Empirical research illustrates the relative importance, sometimes dominance, of these noneconomic mechanisms (see, for example, Vermeulen 1992).

Further evidence supports the argument that instruments do not fit neatly into the conventional boxes. Systematic investigation shows that Dutch effluent charges do partially work via impacts on the cost-benefit calculations of polluters' decision makers. Approximately half of the impact, however, can be attributed less to a direct incentive-based causal channel than to the communicative modes of operation (Bressers and Lulofs 2004), such as: communication about the policy problem and possible solutions, a disruption of habitual behaviour (thus forcing the issue onto the agenda of firms), the encouragement of more legitimacy for environmental-rule enforcers (within both the companies and the government), and the activation of others in the network, like sectoral organizations and consulting firms. In the 1980s and 1990s the fees continued to rise, while the unit costs of pollution abatement did not grow nearly as much; yet the impact of the charges was cut in half during this period. Clearly, economic incentives alone cannot explain these results. Rather, the explanation lies in the loss of novelty and communicative salience of the instrument.

Another conventional categorization can also be critiqued. Distinguishing between so-called "incentives" and "directives" is often associated with a rather straightforward but ultimately misleading dichotomy. The former label is associated with target groups being able to choose whether to take advantage of (or "use") the opportunity provided by the instrument and also with an absence of an explicitly normative appeal. Directives, on the other hand, seem to refer to instruments that, having a normative injunction attached, lack this sort of freedom to choose. This separation, however, is a formalism. In practice, incentives can be more "compulsory" than directives. And some declared disincentives, like high alcohol or tobacco taxes, do carry normative overtones ("sin taxes").

Recognizing these elements is just the first step, however. If one's analysis also incorporates the degree of proportionality of a government reaction – positive or negative – to target group behaviour, a more basic set of instrument characteristics can be sketched (Bressers and Klok 1988). Several pure and mixed models can be visualized in this way, as Figure 6.1 suggests.

"Normative appeal" and "proportionality" are examples of the sort of characteristics that we regard as being more useful for analysis than the labels typically used in the literature about policy instruments (for a sample of instrument categorizations, see Gormley 1989; McDonnell and Elmore 1987; Salamon 2002; and Vedung 1998).

What kinds of core-instrument characteristics should be considered? We suggest that the selection criterion should be that the dimensions be those that actually make a difference in the processes through which instruments are developed and applied in practice. These include: (1) the process of instrument selection itself; (2) the activities of implementation, where the application of the instrument is executed (or blocked or

Figure 6.1
Proportionality of behaviour and response

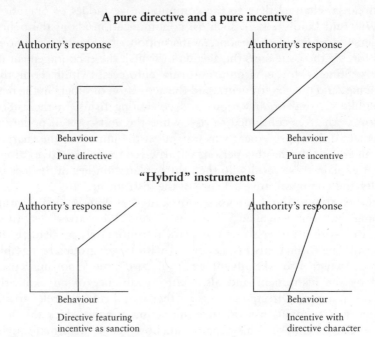

### A pure directive and a pure incentive

Authority's response

Behaviour

Pure directive

Authority's response

Behaviour

Pure incentive

### "Hybrid" instruments

Authority's response

Behaviour

Directive featuring
incentive as sanction

Authority's response

Behaviour

Incentive with
directive character

modified); and (3) the process through which society responds to the new realities created by the instrument(s) when applied.

Some of these kinds of characteristics can be sketched as follows (see also Bressers and O'Toole 1998):

- Whether and to what extent the instrument makes a *normative appeal* to the values and/or obedience of the target group. The expression of values may be viewed as very important when an instrument is selected, but sometimes it is explicitly avoided precisely because it would reduce possibilities for a pragmatic compromise. Similarly, the presence (or absence) of a normative appeal can be important during the processes of implementation and impact.
- *Proportionality* of target group behaviour and the amount of positive or negative governmental response to that behaviour (see Figure 6.1 and the next bulleted point).
- Whether on balance the instrument *provides or denies access to resources* desired by the target group and the degree to which this is the case (intensity of generosity or severity). Resources should be considered broadly here to include money (as with grants and other

subsidies and also with sanctions and taxes), rights (or the denial or withdrawal of them), information, and less obvious commodities like time and trust.

- *Differentiation*: the number of different parameters with which the behaviour of targets is measured and assessed and the number of different kinds of government responses. Some instruments, like a gasoline tax, are relatively simple in this sense, while others, like assessing the quality of environmental management systems, are considerably more differentiated.

- The amount of *information* needed to apply the instrument. This item is partially related to the preceding one but is somewhat distinct.

- How much discretion in application and/or *flexibility* does the instrument provide and – relatedly – how much incentive to adapt and "learn" on the part of target groups.

- The *resources provided for implementation itself*. The specification of an instrument is far from complete without the identification of its implementation structure and the identification – often the provision – of resources to bring the instrument to life during application. It must be determined, for instance, which organizations gain responsibilities, authority, and resources from the policy (aside from support for behavioural changes intended by the policy) and what the limitations are on these.

- *Interactive policy making*. At first blush it would seem sensible to regard the issue of whether an instrument is "unilaterally" formed by and in government or formed through a multilateral process involving government and stakeholders as a feature of the formulation process rather than as a characteristic of the instrument. In reality, however, there is often a strong connection between stakeholders' participation in policy formulation and their role during implementation (for evidence, see Bressers and de Bruijn 2003). So the boundaries among formulation, implementation, and impact are somewhat blurred. A result is that interactivity during policy making helps to explain or predict activities at later stages.

This set of characteristics does not make for a simple list of instrument possibilities. Indeed, the result is precisely the opposite. The array of potential combinations is very large. This feature, however, can be considered a strength. The idea is to identify elements that help to capture the richness and complexity of the arsenal of potential instruments rather than to place those instruments somewhat arbitrarily into a small number of boxes. Equipped with such a list, related to anticipated behavioural differences in the policy-oriented processes of interest, we can begin to develop a theory of instruments.

Developing a set of instrument dimensions does not constitute a full-blown theory, but it is a beginning. Further, for the reasons sketched in detail earlier, we would argue that it constitutes a theoretical improvement over the various lists of instrument types common in the research literature.

Using the set of instrument characteristics outlined above, one could characterize a certain instrument mix in a way that assists in analyzing policy formulation, implementation, and the efficacy of the instruments when applied to target groups.

The considerations worth taking into account in such analyses are the "five multiplicity aspects of governance" (Bressers and Kuks 2003) sketched below:

1  *Multiple levels of governance.* Which levels of governance dominate the policy discussion? What is the accepted role of government at various scales? Which other organizations are influential in the governance activities on these levels? Who decides or influences such issues? How is the interaction between various levels of governance organized?

2  *Multiple actors in the policy network.* How open is the policy arena? Open to whom and where, precisely? What role do experts play? How do the various governmental and other organizations relate to each other?

3  A *multiplicity of problem definitions and other policy beliefs.* What are the dominant maps of reality? To what degree do the actors accept uncertainty? Is the policy problem regarded as something individuals must deal with, or is it a problem for society in a collective sense? Where coordination is required with other fields of policy, what are the links accepted by the actors?

4  *Multiple other instruments – possibly even belonging to more than one relevant policy strategy.* Which (other) instruments belong to the relevant strategy or strategies? What are the target groups of the instruments, and what is the timing of their application? What are the characteristics of these instruments (see above)?

5  *Multiple responsibilities and resources for implementation.* Which organizations (including government organizations) are responsible for implementing the arrangements? What is the repertoire of standard reactions to challenges known to these organizations? What authority and other resources are made available to these organizations by the policy? With what restrictions?

All these questions can be important factors in determining the potential efficacy of a particular policy and can provide analysts with a view of the contextual factors relevant to the potential role of the instruments under consideration.

In particular, it is important to keep the often-networked character of policy action firmly in view. An advantage of a network perspective is that it can be used to direct attention to the larger structure of interdependence. Instead of assuming that influence takes place only through direct and observable interactions, whether as personal relationships or among representatives of institutional interests, a network approach – applied to portions of a policy process as varied as formulation and implementation – can investigate how the larger structure can have systematic effects on the behaviour of individual actors as well as on the content of decisions, policy responses, and implementation efforts. A network approach thus offers the chance to continue both interpersonal and structural explanations for policy-relevant events.

Of course, one must be cautious. To confirm the existence of networks of some kind may say no more than that networks operate in the setting! The degree of involvement and the goals, information, and power of the network actors often vary considerably from one process to another. Whenever this circumstance obtains, it is useful to analyze these processes separately, albeit not in isolation from the others in which the network actors are also engaged. This perspective, then, calls for a process-oriented theory built around the set of actors that interrelate in the context of efforts to shape behaviour via instruments. The following section sketches very briefly an approach to theorizing that begins to address this need.

## EXPLAINING EFFICACY WITH CONTEXTUAL-INTERACTION THEORY

Many studies of policy implementation set out not only to identify policy outputs, but also to explain them. These explanations vary from case to case, and the relevant scholarship has put forward a vast array of factors. A given policy may have run aground because "the municipalities responsible for implementation were not sufficiently motivated," or "there were staff shortages," or "the guidelines arrived late," or "the applicants did not understand the subsidy arrangements," or "there was insufficient support in society," and so forth. There are several disadvantages to such ad hoc explanations. First of all, although they may contain some degree of truth, they rarely tell the whole story. Typically, the identified factor exerts influence in combination with several others that, in and of themselves, need not adversely affect implementation. Relying on idiosyncratic explanations, therefore, tends to lead to or support recommendations that are more like proverbs than anything else (O'Toole 1986). We have thus been more systematic in explaining the processes of instrument selection and implementation. We summarize here the core notions undergirding a "contextual-interaction theory" as a device to help explain the implementation of policy instruments – both separately and in combined sets (for a detailed exposition, see Bressers 2004).

When developing implementation theory, it is important to avoid the trap of an implicitly top-down assumption. Target group actors, after all, are not in the business of responding to implemented policies but in the business of minding their own business. Often the incentives provided by policies are seen by such groups as merely a part (perhaps a small part) of the array of constraints and resources in their own environments of action – that is, possibly as something to reckon with but not as something vital or compelling from their perspective (see Elmore 1979/80). Contextual-interaction theory takes this point into account. On the one hand, it is open to considering all kinds of situational factors; on the other hand, it channels them all through (that is, considers their potential influence as shaping) a limited number of "core variables" that are used to build a deductive frame of analysis. The theory is completely neutral about whether the authorities or, instead, other actors in society take the active role in making use of the institutional and practical possibilities provided by policy schemes, which consist of one or more instruments and accompanying resources. In this way the approach tries to capture the best of both worlds.

Here, we have space to outline only the basic logic of the theory rather than the full set of relationships and specific propositions in the theoretical argument. For present purposes, the primary point is to indicate how some of the considerations sketched in this chapter, particularly about instruments and how they are likely to operate during implementation, can be accounted for in a theoretical logic.

The theory assumes that the policy-implementation process is not only about achieving implementation success, but also about attempts to prevent implementation altogether or perhaps to change the character of what is implemented. The process involves activities and interactions between the responsible authorities and other actors in society, such as members of the target groups. Often these same actors already maintain contact with each other in connection with other matters. Moreover, authorities and target groups often exert influence on each other before – sometimes long before – the policy that is to be implemented is introduced. The new policy does not replace this ongoing interactive process but adds a new contextual element. Therefore, to assess the possibility of the new instruments being applied and of this being done in a manner that is adequate to produce the anticipated action, it is first necessary to understand the factors determining the nature of the interactive process between authorities and other societal actors. One can then try to learn how these factors change upon the introduction of the new policy instruments – often in coevolution with changing network characteristics.

Thinking in terms of policy processes suggests emphasizing their character as patterns of social interaction. Doing so shifts the central focus from the semifinished "products" and ultimate end results of the policy-implementation process to the actors participating in the process itself. The basic assumption of the theory is thus that the course and outcomes of the processes depend not only on inputs (in this case, the characteristics of the policy instruments), but primarily on the characteristics of the actors involved, particularly their motivations, information, and relative power. All other factors that influence the process do so because, and insofar as, they influence the core characteristics of the actors involved. This point holds as well for the influence potentially achievable by policy instruments. The theory, therefore, allows for the influence of a multiplicity of possible factors but claims that theoretically their influence can be fully incorporated by assessing their impacts on the motivations, information, and power of the actors involved.

The complexity of implementation is thus rendered "manageable" by distinguishing two sets of independent variables: (1) "core circumstances" (factors that have a direct influence on the development of the processes) and (2) "external circumstances" (factors that have an indirect influence via their influence on the core circumstances). The characteristics of policy instruments can be counted among these external circumstances, as can all other contextual factors, including network relationships. The deductive and predictive elements of the theory (see Bressers 2004) are restricted to the relationship between core variables and dependent variables. The estimation of how the former are influenced by various external contextual variables is far more open and flexible.

The theory distinguishes two aspects of implementation processes. The first focuses on whether there will be any implementation at all. Some anticipated or envisaged implementation actions never really take off – for certain subsectors, at certain local sites, or sometimes even in general. The second aspect deals with the adequacy of the implementation. Since implementation can proceed at the price of substantially weakening the intended incentives for societal change (for example, fully exhausting the budget of a subsidy program without checking the behaviour of recipients), it makes sense to give special attention to this aspect as well. In fact, addressing the question "under what conditions will 'adequate' implementation occur?" opens the possibility of using the theory practically as an aid for adaptive implementation strategies.

The core concepts of motivation (values, interests, etc.), information (interpretation of reality, meaningful knowledge, etc.), and balance of power (resources, dependencies, etc.) are further specified in the theory, as are the various types of interaction. For each viable combination of motivation, information, and balance of power, a resulting type of interaction is hypothesized and a prediction can be generated regarding whether the instrument(s) will be implemented at all and, if so, to what extent their application can be labelled "adequate." Several tests and applications of the theory have been generated – on environmental subsidies and taxes, enforcement of license conditions, and negotiated agreements – and these have been shown to be supportive of the theory (see Bressers 2004). Further investigations are underway.

IMPLICATIONS FOR INSTRUMENT SELECTION

The arguments sketched in this chapter carry several implications for the selection of policy instruments. We can highlight only some of the broader points to be noted.

Instruments are not simply tools to be selected and applied with no eye toward the political and other constraints operating in the relevant social settings. It is seldom a question of selecting "the best" instrument for the task at hand via policy analysts whispering "truth" to those in formal positions of power. Rather, the ability to enact a particular kind of instrument is a function of the extant institutional and political arrangements. And determining the likely impacts of any given instrument requires taking into account the confluence of instruments operating in the context of interest.

The multiplicity of instruments and their resulting collective impact involve several dimensions, all of which deserve consideration for anticipating and perhaps improving the results of instrument selection in practice. The policy mix can intensify (or block) results, involve differentiated segments of those in the policy target groups, reverberate across multiple levels in the governance system, generate secondary effects in associated policy fields, and operate at different leverage points in the overall system. An implication is that policy action develops in and through a networked social context.

While it may be possible to shape policy action in such settings, the idea of managing the results of implementation – based on any standard, directive notion of managing – is misplaced. Neither instruments nor their managers control events, and even the most active public managers in such settings cannot be expected to concert action unilaterally on behalf of policy. The kind of management that may be possible is more akin to shaping indirectly, or even facilitating, multiactor processes.

These analytic points may seem to amount to a counsel of low expectations, suggesting in effect that everything is terribly complicated and that no one should expect to have much of a predictable impact. Yet this would be too simple, and too limited, a perspective. For while instruments themselves are not mere tools, they are much more fine-grained, varied, and variegated than conventional characterizations imply. There is not just one kind of "subsidy," but many. More fundamentally, elements of "subsidy" mix with elements of "exhortation" and with elements of "regulation" and so on – in great variety. Individual instruments can work through a range of causal processes, and common ways of characterizing instruments can obscure rather than reveal what some of these are likely to be. Only by focusing on the core dimensions of instrumentation, those likely to be important for shaping the results of policy in action, can a theoretically sound approach to understanding instruments and their impacts be developed.

A number of plausible dimensions have been sketched in this chapter, and they suggest an extensive set of possibilities. There are many, many ways, in other words, to help shape policy action via instruments – even if oftentimes no single instrument is likely to carry the day and even if network settings mean that policy action is multilaterally determined.

What is called for, then, is an orientation that begins with the on-the-ground processes of policy action involving key actors in the governance system as well as the putative targets of intervention. This argument suggests, ironically, that the wrong end of the system from which to approach the question of policy instrument selection is from the instruments and those who choose them. The choices made are, first of all, shaped by the networked pattern characteristic of the initial state from which policy-oriented change is sought. Even more fundamentally, any instrument must work its way through and be expected to perturb an existing set of processes involving actors in the policy system, such as implementers and targets of policy initiatives.

Like it or not, many of these actors have agendas that do not focus primarily, let alone exclusively, on any particular policy instrument. Nor do they begin or end their operations with the workings of such an instrument. Ongoing patterns of interaction, some extending well beyond the issues in question and some extending backward and forward in time beyond the period during which any instrument may operate, must be the starting point for analysis. Targets, and even implementers, may have little interest in effective implementation, or their actions may be driven primarily by factors entirely apart from any instrument, whether it be well or poorly chosen. Policy processes are ongoing, and patterns of interaction in governance systems are where instruments ultimately have their effect – or not.

One way of getting traction in explaining the results of instrument choice in action, a way grounded in these processes, is to adopt an approach such as contextual-interaction theory. This perspective, outlined very generally in this chapter, conceives of the drivers of implementation action not primarily as instruments per se – and, for that matter, not primarily through the nearly endless list of variables and circumstances that can be identified. Rather, the theory begins with the actors engaged in the processes of interaction and sees the key, or core, variables as consisting of their motivations, information, and relative power. All the particulars of a given case can be seen in terms of a set of elements that have their potential impacts via these core variables.

Instrument selection, therefore, can be made with the idea of affecting one or more of these core variables in an appropriate direction and of thus increasing the probability of achieving desired policy results through implementation processes as they unfold. Only in simple cases will the mere selection of a new instrument drive the results. The theoretical perspective requires one to consider the causal story implicit in any instrument choice and to test its plausibility against the ongoing processes and the core variables that shape such regular patterns of action.

A process-based theory, then, seems an apropos approach to assisting in the design and choice of policy instruments. One can increase the odds of efficacious selection by:

- Beginning with an assessment of the key relevant actors, their motivations, the amount and quality of information at their disposal, and the balance of power among them
- Mapping the ongoing processes that involve these actors in interaction
- Considering as a part of the assessment the set of instruments already in operation, including how these – individually and in combination – appear to influence the core variables and approximately how much
- Doing so by assessing the extant instruments in terms of the key dimensions of policy instruments that can be expected to shape behaviour in practice
- Attending to the relative efficacy of possible additional instruments, while also recognizing that network characteristics are likely to be important in determining which kinds of instruments, or instrument characteristics, can feasibly be selected in a given situation

- Designing and selecting any new instruments by taking into account the several relevant dimensions of instrumentation
- Bearing in mind in this analysis and selection that any given instrument can have multiple points of impact in the networked set of relevant actors and that these additional points of leverage may hold the prospect of strengthening – or, for that matter, weakening – the overall impact of any instrument on the core variables and thus on the policy-implementation process of interest.

These guidelines are rather general, and they surely do not serve as a cookbook for the complex and difficult challenges of choosing instruments for governance. Instead, they offer some direction and can alert decision makers to a number of the hazards that have been characteristic of instrumentation in many empirical cases. They also indicate some directions for improving the prospects of instrument choice that are both realistic and nuanced enough to address the complex circumstances operating in the world of networked governance.

Instruments can, after all, alter the pattern, and it is critical to consider carefully exactly which features of instruments can do so. A categorization of instrument characteristics developed from the context of ongoing processes should help in this kind of analysis.

How instruments can work to facilitate such processes by operating on and through the core variables involved in policy implementation is the central insight offered in this chapter, and contextual-interaction theory is one promising route. It offers the virtues of parsimony, clear links both to the processes that are at the core of policy action and to the instruments that are the focus of attention in this volume, and a method of incorporating the mixes of instruments and the pattern of interdependence that are hallmarks of contemporary public policy.

# 7

# Choosing among Forms
# of Public Action:
# A Question of Legitimacy

PIERRE ISSALYS

Should political decision makers contemplating specific types of public intervention – for example, a grant program, a tax incentive, a regulation containing a reference to technical standards, joint action by public and private stakeholders based on a contractual "partnership," delegation of authority to a self-regulating body, legislation formulating a program of public and private action, granting authority to waive statutory requirements, instituting criminal sanctions, and so forth – be concerned with the legitimacy of their choices? If so, in what way? In what terms should they pose the question of the legitimacy of their choices? And by what method might they attempt to answer these questions? This line of inquiry forms the subject of the present chapter.

At first glance, the theme of legitimacy, with its metapolitical connotations, seems fairly remote from the immediate and concrete concerns that arise as one considers choosing among instruments of public action. However, insofar as legitimacy resides in the acceptance both of an authority and of the rules laid out by this authority, it has obvious repercussions for the effectiveness and even for the efficiency of any mechanism of public intervention. One need only shift the angle of discussion slightly to the choice of the "legal forms" of public action, as opposed to the "instruments" of this action, for legitimacy to emerge as an unavoidable subject for examination.

In fact, recourse to the legal normative order – to which all of these "instruments" have at least an unavoidable, minimal connection – implies the question of the legitimacy of the norm, its axiological validity, its conformity to values of an ethical nature.[1] In its Reference re

Secession of Quebec,[2] the Supreme Court of Canada pointed out this "internal relationship,"[3] which is difficult to disentangle, between democracy, rule of law, and the order of values. On the one hand, the Court ascribed the legitimacy of the constitutional amendment of 1982 to the fact that it was effected in accordance with law (246); on the other hand, it noted the legitimacy of governments produced from political majorities within the different parliaments, federal and provincial, in that they express the will of the people (247). It then combined these two components of legitimacy – rule of law and democracy – thereby affirming in the tradition of English public law that the latter cannot exist without the former: "democratic institutions must rest, ultimately, on a legal foundation." But "there is more," the Court went on to add: Not only does the legitimacy of the political system require "an interaction between the rule of law and the democratic principle," but the legitimacy of the law "also rests on an appeal to moral values" (256).[4]

Given this relationship of close but fluid interdependence between democracy, law, and values, it does not seem so incongruous, at least for a legal scholar, to pose the question of legitimacy with respect to the (political) choice of a (legal) form of public action. The decisions contemplated by democratically designated political leaders to introduce new rules more or less directly guaranteed by legal sanction must be supported by claims to legitimacy. As the Supreme Court's analysis demonstrates, this claim cannot be limited either to these rules' conformity or material and formal compatibility with existing law or to their instrumental effectiveness relative to the will of the people's political representatives. Certainly, the requirements of legitimacy call for a justification of the decision in these two regards of legality and effectiveness; however, because legitimacy refers as well to the order of values, the choice among different possible configurations of norms or standards must also be justifiable in terms of values.

Naturally, in a pluralistic society, legal experts cannot proclaim themselves the guardians of all the values on which the legitimacy of legal norms is based. But when they intervene as advisors in the formulation or application of these norms, they are responsible for ensuring that this legitimacy itself is preserved.

"Preservation" implies that the lawyer does not confer legitimacy on the standard; rather, the standard receives its legitimacy from another source. The lawyer's task is instead to ensure that the conditions under which a legal standard is formulated and applied do not undermine the standard's legitimacy but, on the contrary, help to make it manifest. In this task, lawyers focus their attention on matters of procedure and form.

With respect to the legal form of a regulatory public action, lawyers advising political leaders will therefore want to facilitate, with the means offered by their expertise, the optimum justification of this legal form, thereby helping to strengthen the legitimation of the action itself. This – the legal expert's contribution to the legitimation of the legal forms of public action – is the context for the proposals that will follow. Such questioning of the manner in which the choice of a particular "tool" for carrying out a public intervention can be justified might help us to gain a better understanding of the conditions for the success of this intervention. Legitimacy is a matter of support; can one doubt the link that exists between the success of a public action and the support of those affected by it for its objectives and the methods it implements?

While it likely has a bearing on the success of any specific instance of public action, the linkage between support and legitimacy carries a broader significance. Any form of political authority must ultimately depend on this linkage for its own emergence and subsistence. The nucleus of political authority appears to be shaped as a virtuous circle: People give support to authority because they consider it legitimate, and authority derives legitimacy from the support it receives. Contemporary analysis of political institutions in terms of governance shows concern with this close linkage between support and legitimacy. Common to the various ways in which the concept of governance is understood, one can discern an attempt to describe or advocate new bases for the legitimacy of public action in the current context of diminishing "governability."[5] From the standpoint of governance studies, therefore, the legitimation requirements applicable to the choice of legal form for public action have relevance as a topic of investigation.

Such investigation will be approached in this chapter from what may seem, in the main, a relatively narrow point of view: that of public decision makers called upon to choose – in a concrete, one might say an everyday, context – a specific legal form for a projected public action. This angle of approach, however, is only superficially narrow and technical: Choosing a form for public action is in itself a political decision and therefore engages the issue of legitimacy.

First, this chapter analyzes the context within which the matter of choosing a form for a given public action stands to be considered by the legal expert: a context of proliferation and explosion. Such a characterization of context applies not only to the legal forms themselves, but also to the perspective from which choosing one of them can be legitimized. Second, one possibility for controlling this explosion will be examined, first by proposing a justification grid and then by indicating how this grid might be introduced in the process preliminary to a public intervention.

## THE CHALLENGE OF EXPLOSION

The task of designing a public initiative in today's environment is confronted straight off by two factors contributing to greater complexity and uncertainty. Both can be described by the image of an explosion. First, public decision makers and the counsel advising them must necessarily take note of the proliferation of legal forms of public action. This proliferation may seem to open up a wide spectrum of possibilities, but it is also a factor of legal uncertainty. In many cases, in fact, the classic categories of legal analysis do not afford one a grasp of certain practices. While allowed for or even mandated by formal enactments, these practices present some unorthodox characteristics, and their analysis can even lead one at times to cast doubt on their being considered a *public* action.

Second, there has been a proliferation of the perspectives from which we consider the legitimation of the forms of public action. The classical positivist perspective, which equates legitimacy with legality, remains predominant but no longer enjoys exclusive allegiance.[6] Other perspectives, seemingly beyond the expertise of legal scholars, have been proposed as more significant bases for legitimation. The legal perspective itself has changed: Notably, the concern with certain values has been added to the concern with formal correction in assessing the legitimacy of a form of public action.

### The Explosion of Legal Forms of Public Action

One might be tempted to describe the recent changes in the repertoire of legal forms of public action as a sort of "Big Bang." However, insofar as this image suggests a sudden transition from nothingness to existence, it is misleading. It seems more accurate to attribute the current impression of overabundance, overflow, and explosion to the gradual convergence and acceleration of three long-term trends: diversification, hybridization, and porosity.

#### DIVERSIFICATION
The first trend is fairly obvious: The legal forms of public action are diversifying. New modes of managing conduct are emerging in both practices and formal enactments. Some are unusual and lie outside the familiar range: We are seeing modes of sanction spreading through the legal order that are neither judicial nor disciplinary;[7] modes of producing norms that make rules appear relative, such as experimental legislation[8] or compliance agreements;[9] and modes of enforcement that dissolve the protective mission of public authorities, such as self-inspection.[10] Other

innovations consist rather in the use of more-or-less heretical variants of proven legal forms: for example, regulations setting qualitative goals[11] or the use of contractual forms in internal management relations within public administration.[12]

Whether this phenomenon of diversification is truly new is debatable. In many cases, what strikes us today as a bold advance has its precedents in the practices of other eras of creative interventionism. The real novelty lies not so much in the thing itself as in the way we look at it. For legal experts, what is most significantly new about this diversification of the forms of public action seems chiefly to be of a more comprehensive nature. The novelty resides mainly in the awareness that this diversification is not simply an episode – some would say, a fashion – in the evolution of our public law but a phenomenon that expresses a transformation in the very substance of public action. Therefore, analysis of the phenomenon and its consequences cannot perceive these consequences solely in terms of quantitative increase. Moreover, this renewal of the repertoire of the legal forms of public action should encourage lawyers to take a comprehensive view of them. To understand the phenomenon, Canadian legal science will need to carry out some inventory and synthesis work comparable to that recently directed by Lester Salamon in the field of political science in the American context.[13]

This sort of work is still to be done. The pioneering article by John Mark Keyes on "power tools" stands as an invitation to set upon such a course.[14] It gives a good idea of what is involved in approaching administrative law from the standpoint of diversification of the legal forms of public action. From this perspective, the law is viewed, as Pierre Lascoumes suggests, "less as a constraint than as a resource" – that is, more "as a system of potentialities from which are deployed specific activities for the mobilization of rules."[15]

Definition of the various "potentialities" offered by the expanded spectrum of legal forms of public action and their integration into a coherent "system" would therefore appear to be priority tasks for administrative law. Recent research on contracting-out public services,[16] on incentives,[17] and on the various modalities of self-regulation[18] illustrates such a dual effort of conceptualization and integration. However, the case of administrative rules and guidelines shows that the reception given the new techniques of public action is sometimes hesitant: After more than twenty years of contributions to the debate, courts and scholars are still divided between the three analytical frameworks at issue, founded respectively on exclusion from law, integration in the regime of statutory instruments, and institution of a specific regime.[19]

HYBRIDIZATION

The second trend, not as old as the previous one, is toward hybridization of the legal forms of public action. Within the general tendency of these forms to diversify, one can discern the emergence of techniques that combine in more-or-less original ways the characteristics of the classic forms of public law. The basic vocabulary used by public law to frame and define government action traditionally boils down to a few familiar institutions: legislation and its by-product, delegated legislation; the judgment of a court and its analogue, the tribunal or administrative decision; and contract, under its various guises (treaty, an administrative agreement, or a government contract). To each of these classic standard types, there corresponds a specific set of formal characteristics, procedures, and effects. It is even tempting, with respect to the three original concepts – legislation, judgment, and contract – to speak of archetypes, so rich are they in ethical, symbolic, and ideological representations and connotations.

An analysis of public law cannot, however, avoid the conclusion that the outlines of these traditional categories of public action are today frequently muddled. Novel notions are put into circulation to designate new practices that cannot be brought under the classic concepts.[20] For example, the notion of "negotiated rule making" refers to a regulation-contract hybrid: The apparently authoritarian imposition of imperative standards is in reality the product of genuine negotiation, more or less formalized, between the state apparatus and the persons affected, with or without the participation of third parties.[21] The notion of "contractual standard setting" is another hybrid of this type:[22] Here, the product of this form of action is ostensibly characterized as a contract between a plurality of "partners," but analysis reveals that these partners are not necessarily bound with equal intensity, or that the normative density of this "contract" is in reality very weak, or on the contrary that its content is part and parcel of some unilateral action by the government.[23] The rule or guideline laid down by the head officers of an administrative authority to structure the exercise of decision-making powers by their subordinates is the already-familiar hybrid of a regulation and a specific decision on an individual case.[24] Still other hybrids could be cited, with such strange designations as "active tolerance" (a hybrid of unilateral decision and negotiated commitment), "regulatory self-management" (a hybrid of command and control and contract for services), and "compliance agreement" (a hybrid of regulation making, including provision for regulatory offences, and negotiated commitment).[25]

Two predominant themes consistently emerge from this set of hybridization practices, which burst the traditional moulds of public

action. The first is the relative downgrading of legislation and regulations, the classic vectors of large-scale public action.[26] Both have often
become nothing more than elements of comprehensive machineries and
strategies, which simultaneously make use of other diverse and complementary techniques. When placed in this sort of relation to these techniques, legislation loses some of its self-sufficiency, preeminence, and
commanding role; in many respects, legislation now has a radical de-
pendence on these techniques to produce its effect. The long-observed
instrumentalization of statute law is presented here from another
perspective, perhaps less often noticed: Offered as an instrument, or
"tool," legislation is laid out like so many other tools on the work-
bench of the public "handyman." It is in this sense that the relative
downgrading of legislation becomes fully evident.

The second theme is the prominent display in all public action of
consensual processes. Often this display is precisely that and nothing
more: an appearance of consensualism, a contractual veneer. But sometimes it goes to the substance of things. Whether reality or appearance,
the theme of "contractualization" arises even at the heart of the functions most characteristic of classic state power, such as assistance to
persons in need, development of government policy, or definition of
tasks and deployment of resources within the state apparatus.[27]

Thus public action – lending itself to a mix of genres, inflecting the
missions associated with the classic techniques, and allowing for the
emergence of new, "indescribable" techniques – is hardly recognizable.
It is unrecognizable in the usual sense: Its physiognomy is altered to the
point that one is no longer sure of recognizing in it the features that define its public character. It is unrecognizable also in the sense that it becomes difficult to know, as these hybrid legal forms resist the analytical
grasp of the common categories. Beyond these uncertainties arises the
question of legitimacy.[28] Must one believe that this process of hybridization is entirely without consequence as to the legitimacy of the forms
of action it produces? Is it possible that, whatever the nature of the
public action contemplated, the use of any of these forms, classic or
new, "normal" or hybrid, can be made equally legitimate? This
question becomes all the more acute when one considers the third
"explosive" trend that can be observed in the repertoire of forms of
public action.

POROSITY
This final trend concerns the state legal order as a whole, and on that
basis it has repercussions for the legal forms of public action. State law
tends to establish new linkages with the normative networks external
to it or to intensify such linkages when they already exist. The demar-

cation between these systems of standards proves to be much more po-
rous than in the traditional, plainly self-sufficient representation of
state law. What is exploded this time is the border between "public"
and "private."

This is because the extension of state action to new substantive
spheres has multiplied the number of contacts with preexisting normative networks (in professional circles, trades, industries, religious de-
nominations, unions, scientific communities, moral or material interest
groups, etc.). Doubtless, many of these networks have been more or
less completely integrated with the state system of norms to the point
of losing much of their distinctiveness. The members of some of these
networks, in fact, actively pursue this integration, for they see it as an
opportunity to strengthen their network by giving it a twofold legitimacy.[29] In other cases, the state has confined itself to recognizing the
autonomy of certain normative networks on the condition that public
order and basic freedoms are preserved. A third series of instances, generally more recent, should be viewed in terms rather of interconnection
since state law is here linked to a preexisting normative network and
relies on the standards generated by it without altering their original
nature. The numerous cases of regulation by reference[30] and certain
mechanisms of "statutory self-regulation"[31] are examples of this form
of normative interconnection.

These practices of interconnection call into question many attributes
of our customary representation of state law.[32] The very notion of
"law" is no longer absolutely univocal: Standards whose origin and
legitimacy are external to the state are incorporated in the state normative order without losing their initial alien status. Hence a third
explosive effect: State law suffers a blow to its systemic coherence,
its self-sufficiency, its monocentric, self-generated, and self-referential
character. It is not a mortal blow, but it is substantial. That various
groups should thus gain access to the status of subjects actively producing standards that are incorporated in state law encourages aspirations
to autonomy on the part of substate communities making their own
claims to legitimacy. These aspirations do not lack for inspiring watch-
words: decentralization, subsidiarity, community-based management,
participative management, self-management, self-regulation, devolu-
tion of responsibility, empowerment, regulatory streamlining. They all
converge to the extent that they call into question the exclusive representation of state law as a unitary, hierarchical, and relatively self-
sufficient system.

Reflection on the legitimation of choices made from among the
forms of public action must therefore take account of this sort of
organized linkage between state law and external normative networks.

Perhaps this linkage, standing halfway between incorporation into state law and exclusion from it, ought to be described as a coordination in the literal sense of joint ordering. In such a set-up, the respective legitimacies should neither combat nor oust each other but be combined. This approach to the problem of legitimation does not seem to be self-evident: Thus far one-dimensional approaches have prevailed – and have therefore either ignored or confronted each other.

The same observation applies to the other two trends brought under the generic term of "explosion." Faced with the three phenomena of explosion – diversification, hybridization, and porosity – competing perspectives have developed to take on these transformations of public action and to propose the bases upon which their pursuit might be legitimized.

## The Explosion of Perspectives on Legitimation

The question of which criteria can or ought to dictate a choice between the various techniques available for public action generated a substantial amount of research in the early 1980s. At this time, two developments were lending this question greater visibility and acuteness. First, the diversification of the instruments of state action, described earlier, was entering a particularly intense phase. Second, the questioning of state intervention by neoconservative economic thinkers was prompting a critical and comparative reexamination of the forms of public action used thus far.

The research of this time partook either of public law and legislative science or of economic and political science. Rather predictably, legal scholars took a formalistic approach to the issue. This perspective was not in theory indefensible since the issue had to do with precisely the conditions justifying the use of a particular form of public action – as opposed to those justifying the substantive content of the action. From this standpoint, the choice must be dictated by the characteristics exclusively ascribed to each of the known legal forms, only one of which can be suitable for any one body of substantive content.

Just as predictably, economists and political scientists approached this issue of justification from an empirical angle. This perspective leads to validating either the choice of form of public action that seems the best adapted to the target goal, or the one that allows for the highest degree of technical effectiveness, or the one that is most timely given the circumstances of the action – that is, the current situation, its ideological interpretation, and the prevailing balance of power. Further, this empirical approach can – here a nod of recognition is directed at constitutional experts – ground itself in the sovereignty of Parliament or the need for executive freedom of action.

More recently, a third approach seems to have arisen to meet the challenge to the intelligibility and coherence of the law from the explosive tendencies manifested by the recent evolution of public action. Whether explicitly or not, this approach attempts to elude the alternative imposed by the competing propositions of formalism and empiricism. In other words, for purposes of legitimizing the forms of public action, it abandons the project of dividing that action up according to categories that make sense only under a monocentric, hierarchical, and self-sufficient conception of the law. But it also objects to the dissolution (or at least the incorporation) of the legal perspective in a dynamic dominated by technical imperatives or political contingency. It is thus led to seek out ways to articulate a justifying discourse of a legal nature, regarding the forms of public action, on the needs and concerns of political governance and its technical implementation. It thus proposes to effect this articulation with the help of values that can legitimize the forms of public action in terms that are at once allowable by lawyers, politicians, and technicians.

### THE FORMALISTIC APPROACH

In the early 1980s, several teams of Quebec legal scholars inquired into the basis upon which the localization of a general and impersonal rule ought to be determined. The problem was thus posed in relatively narrow terms since only public action with this type of content was taken into consideration. The range of possible choices was therefore restricted, given the practices of the time, to the Constitution, legislation, regulations, and administrative guidelines – the latter referring to documents issued by an administrative authority to provide guidance or directions in the form of rules having a general scope but not meant to have a legally binding effect. In essence, the core subject of this research work was the criteria for apportioning rules between statute and regulation.

The approach that emerges from this body of research is permeated with the classic representation of law as a unitary, self-centred, hierarchized, and self-sufficient system that is clearly set apart from other normative fields. This common view transcends the differences in the responses proposed in these various works to the central problem of justifying the use of regulations rather than statutes to set forth general and impersonal standards. The selection criteria advanced by the various authors are all based on the idea that to each of these two legal forms are attached specific characteristics that invite the attribution of its own field of action.

Some define the respective characteristics of statute and regulation in reference to a dual scale of transcendence and concreteness;[33] others refer instead to a quadruple scale based on the notions of generality,

hierarchy, accessibility, and mobility;[34] finally, others divide the substantive contents of rules up into categories, which are then attributed
to either the sphere of statutes, the sphere of regulations, or a mixed
sphere in accordance with an objective of providing citizens with information on their legal situation.[35]

All agree, however, that their grid for analyzing and classifying rules
renders but an imperfect account of actual practices. Observation of
these practices had in fact shown them that, while political leaders and
public administrators were not systematically insensitive to such
considerations on the optimum distribution of enacted rules, they felt
no qualms about deviating from them on grounds of effectiveness or
expediency.

### THE EMPIRICIST APPROACH

Such empirical considerations are precisely the basis for other research
that proposes a very different approach to the issue of which legal form
a public action should be given. This work focuses primarily on public
action involving state intervention in the economy, and in this sense its
angle of approach is relatively narrow. Nevertheless, it has framed the
issue of choice so as to include a fairly wide range of options, particularly those that appeared at the time as the principal alternatives to
conventional government regulation-making authority: state-owned
corporations, grant programs, tax incentives, regulation by an independent agency, and public inquiries.

Two types of response were proposed to the issue thus defined. Some
believe the choice of legal form depends on the view taken by political
leaders and public administrators of the technical effectiveness of the
various forms in terms of the objective aimed at and the costs they
entail. This apparent neutrality of the criterion for choice is, however,
nuanced by the premise that where all options are equally effective, the
first choice should go to the legal form that involves the lowest degree
of constraint for business operators.

Others, after finding that the technical effectiveness criterion presupposes that ends and means can be clearly distinguished – a distinction
that proves difficult to make in practice – and that it also fails to take
into account the potential effect of certain values, or of competing
goals of action, on the choice of instrument, suggest instead a criterion
based on political rationality.[36] According to this criterion, the choice
of a legal form for a state action is necessarily the result of four factors.
The first is the presence of a number of constraints inherent in the legal
system, particularly those arising from the Constitution and from international obligations. The second is the necessity for the government
parties to attract the votes of "swing" voters, generally "centrists,"

whose attitude frequently determines the outcome of elections. The third is the invincible yet uneven lack of information among the electorate – and even among political leaders themselves – who often have a poor grasp of complex issues. Finally, the fourth factor is the interdependence of the choices due either to their actual connection or to purely circumstantial links. In the final analysis, according to this theory, choices are dictated by electoral considerations, and their legitimacy is based on this political rationality.

What, in the formalist approach to the legitimation of the choices respecting the legal form of a public action, was simply a disillusioned concession to the primacy of realpolitik becomes, in the empiricist approach, the normal order of things. In this order, the influence of concerns for formal legal correction and values is only peripheral. Nor does the coherence of choices appear to be a significant consideration; on the contrary, incoherence is seen as the normal outcome of the process of choosing means for public action and as an indication that the various legal forms of such action are, at bottom, interchangeable.

### THE JUSTIFICATION APPROACH

Neither of these two approaches seems likely to provide a satisfactory solution – from the standpoint of the law – to the issue of how to justify the choice of a particular legal form for a given public action. With the empiricist approach, the legal system may lose all coherence and dissolve into a muddle of practices. The form of these practices is no longer legitimated, in this perspective, other than as the outcome contingent upon a combination of relevant facts, which are largely circumstantial. Beyond a point, the instrumentalization of law and its flexibility lead to its destruction; only a movement back to the normative basics of law[37] can prevent this outcome. The formalist approach is no more satisfactory, as legal forms are not actually – or are no longer – linked to a particular kind of content. Practice is more varied than supporters of formalism are willing to believe and thus frequently contradicts their expectations. A canonical understanding of a limited range of forms – an attitude that meets the caricatural definition of "classicism" – means renouncing any hope of reestablishing the coherence of practices.

Some legal scholars have therefore set about identifying, to legitimize the choice of a form of public action, criteria that would be more rigid than those suggested by the empiricist analysis but more sensitive to the flexibility of practices than those put forth by the formalist approach. Thus the third approach aims to strike a balance between rigidity and flexibility, satisfying both competing perspectives to a certain degree. Values are its foundation. Using values to guide and legitimize the choice allows the language of law to express perspectives foreign to it, such as those of the public administrator or of politics, and allows the logic of the law to assimilate such perspectives. In the presence of values justifying divergent solutions, the law performs its role in evaluating, balancing, and arbitrating – or, more accurately, in allowing for evaluation, balancing, and arbitration – and in expressing the result of this process. As for choosing a form for a public action, a debate on the relevance and the importance of certain values allows for identifying, by means of legal expertise, the grounds that warrant one option rather than another even if these grounds refer to orders of consideration foreign to the law.

Some recent research has identified ranges of values and applied these to certain legal forms of public action. Robert Baldwin, in an examination of the optimal justification for choosing between statute, regulation, or administrative rule, suggests basing the decision on a series of five criteria whose value content is clear: respect of the legislative mandate, accountability, fairness, expertise, and efficiency.[38] Margot Priest sets out a similar reasoning to establish and compare optimal conditions for justification of a series of legal forms associated with the concept of self-regulation. The criteria she lists in this regard partly reflect those of Robert Baldwin and are presented as values: effectiveness, efficiency, fairness, openness, and accountability.[39]

The analytical process of listing a series of guiding values is not new in legal writing, at least not in the field of public law. The lists by these two authors may even resemble attempts to update or to adapt well-known lists, several elements of which they, in fact, take up. However, the point of application of the process is no longer exactly the same. Until now the point was to assign objectives to public law or to some of its branches, objectives that were expected to be reflected permanently in the *content* of rules. Now the issue is that of requirements applicable to *producing* rules. The influence of these values is expected to occur at a specific and limited time in the process of producing the rule: the time when its legal form is decided.

This third approach, based on justification of choices using a specific range of values, is thus clearly different from the first two approaches. The implicit competition among the three models for rationalizing the choice of legal forms for public action effectively demonstrates the current fragmentation in perspectives on the law. It clearly shows the position of those who see positivist formalism as a central and vital attribute of the rule of law; the position of those who advocate a radical instrumentalization of law as a modifiable and versatile relay station for technical or political strategies; and finally, the position of those who believe that while law is, to some extent, unavailable, it is not thereby incapable of sharing values with other fields of human activity.

## PATHS TO REESTABLISHING COHERENCE

No attempt will be made here to draw, from the dual finding of explosion, conclusions that would exceed the scope of this finding. Although the finding seems valid with respect to the legal forms of public action, it could lead to wider analyses on changes occurring in public law.[40] In the remainder of this chapter, a narrower objective will be pursued: first, to outline, based on this finding, how to reformulate the issue of optimal legitimation of a choice of legal form for a public action and, second, to suggest practical terms for examining this issue in the process leading up to public intervention. Setting out this issue and solving it methodically are just as much a precondition of success for any such intervention as is, for example, prior definition of the problem that the intervention seeks to remedy.

In the final analysis, at stake in the process proposed herein is the coherence of the legal framework of public action. Postulating that a public intervention with a properly legitimated legal form has a better chance of success because it will, in all likelihood, be more accepted by those at whom it is aimed implies that there is both a plurality of forms and an unchanging standard of legitimacy. The purpose of the process is therefore to maintain, beyond the diversity of legal forms, a unifying principle of legitimacy.

### Framing the Issue of Legitimation

While the process of legitimating the choice of legal form for public action aims for coherence, its goal is not uniformity. On the contrary, the process stems from the fragmented reality of the practices described earlier. It is also inspired by the justification approach to legitimation in an attempt to answer both the need for intelligibility in the law expressed by the formalist approach and the need for adaptability in the law expressed by the empiricist approach.

#### ACCEPTING THE EXPLOSION IN FORMS OF PUBLIC ACTION

The issue of legitimation of choice can be effectively defined only if it takes into consideration all the forms of public action, with the characteristics they present today: growing diversity, frequent hybridization, and porosity of the state system of rules. Failing to do so would be tantamount to turning away from an entire segment of reality and to missing the issues that arise from the fragmentation phenomenon. Obstinately regarding only the conventional forms of public action while relegating the others to nonlaw would resemble formalism of the most dangerous kind.

A more promising formalist approach would be to create, for each such new form of public action, a specific regime integrated directly with conventional legality; the outcome of this could be a series of framework regimes. Such an undertaking may be possible for those forms that are sufficiently homogenous or if it is accepted that the framework will remain minimal. The outcome would largely be a reaffirmation of the state-centred model, restoring greater coherence to the legal framework of public action.

But by merely reiterating the conventional model of legality, this approach fails to provide a fully convincing solution to the issue of legitimating the choice of a particular legal form for a given public action. It runs the risk of finding, once again, that despite the premise that a certain type of content dictates the choice of a specific legal form, circumstances and contingencies often end up dictating the choice of a completely different form.

Thus the coherence of choices should not be sought through a formal congruence of some legal regime with a certain type of action. Instead, legitimation of the choice appears to reside in a relation of functional congruence with the task of a proposed public action. For a given action, the legal form enjoying the best justification is the one that can be shown to be the most adapted to the action's normative content and objectives. It will no longer be a matter of determining if the planned normative content falls within the "field of jurisdiction" assigned a priori to this or that legal form.

It can therefore be said that the perspective has been reversed. The legitimation of choice will no longer be based on an official, ideal list of accepted legal forms – even if this list is considerably expanded beyond its traditional scope – with each such form, a priori and specifically, assigned to a certain type of normative content. Legitimation will instead be based on the characteristic features of the situation at hand, from which a number of specific justification requirements will be drawn. It will thus be a *situated* justification, rather than a justification in reference to abstract models.

In its early steps, therefore, the approach proposed herein largely satisfies the empiricist perspective on legitimation. It recognizes the paramount influence exerted by the facts of the situation with respect to which a public action is contemplated. It even regards, at this initial stage, all the legal forms for public action as being on the same level to the point of being interchangeable. A priori, none is imperative and none is excluded. Legal forms will be differentiated only at a later stage.

## INTEGRATING THE PLURALITY OF PERSPECTIVES

To decide among the forms of public action, there must be criteria for concluding that one of them is more legitimate because it is better adapted to the characteristics of the situation at hand. The three perspectives on legitimation described above suggest their own: the formalism of legality, technical or political rationality, and the application of values. Competition between these perspectives on legitimation must not force us to decide among them. It suggests instead that the desired legitimacy of public action is in fact plural. None of these perspectives should, it seems, exclude the others. Each must be taken into consideration and put to debate when preparing to choose the form of a public action. The choice of that form will emerge from a critical examination of the recommended solutions based on each opposing perspective. The justification of this choice will thus be an *argued* justification.

The presence and overlap of several perspectives within public action itself is a reality familiar to anyone working in a public agency. An enlightening analysis of this kind of phenomenon is found in Jerry Mashaw's research on the decision-making process in the US Social Security Administration.[41] In his work he describes the interaction between the perspectives of bureaucracy, adjudication, and professional treatment in the course of the administrative decision-making process with respect to disability benefits. The first perspective, or model, is that of public administrators, whose concern is to best achieve the objectives assigned to them by their statutory mandates, making the most cost-effective uses of the means available to them for this purpose. The second is that of jurists, whose concern is the correct application of statutory rules in a spirit of justice – implying an element of moral judgment – and through a rule-bound procedure involving proof, debate, and principled decision. The third is that of the helping professions, which act on the basis of trust and expert judgment to improve the situation of individual clients and to contribute to the "remedial" objective of the statute.

The same type of analysis may apply to the process leading to the choice of a legal form for a given public action. This process also brings together a number of perspectives. Of course, it is not a matter of natural persons meeting and directly interacting on the premises of a social-security administration, as in the context observed by Jerry Mashaw. The process of interest here unfolds in a much broader theatre, has an altogether different purpose, and is likely to bring into play broad social categories and wide-ranging interests rather than just disciplinary cultures. Nevertheless, in either case, several perspectives on the justification of action must be accommodated through a type of relation that Mashaw describes in terms of "conflict and compromise."

Regarding the issue of which legal form is most justified for a particular public action, five competing perspectives can be discerned: those of the *political leader,* the *citizen,* the *jurist,* the *expert,* and the *administrator.*[42] To varying degrees, these perspectives will be involved in any intended public action regardless of the situation such action is meant to address. Each perspective brings expectations, a guiding principle, and a paramount value to the debate on the choice of a form of action. These expectations, principles, and values will be the basis for evaluating, in any given situation, the degree of justification for a particular legal form for the public action intended to address the situation at hand.

The political leader's perspective is grounded in the familiar tenets of representative democracy. It emphasizes the concept of collective self-government, according to which relations of authority can result only from a process of explicit auto-institution by the community.[43] Legal rules thus express the collective freedom of a society that governs itself through the mediation of its representatives. This value translates into a principle of public action, and ultimately, the impetus for this action belongs to the political authority. Any public action intended to address a situation, therefore, poses the following question: To what degree should Parliament itself, as the supreme political authority, conduct or control this action? The answer to this question will tend to justify a preference for certain forms of action.

The second perspective, that of the citizen, hinges on civic engagement. On the one hand, this value concerns the citizen as an addressee of public action who is directly affected by it but, especially and more broadly, as a member of the political community participating in defining the public interest and in exercising collective autonomy. On the other hand, civic engagement concerns the citizen on whom duties and powers are conferred in the context of public action, either as a public servant in the strict sense or as a private actor with a mandate to act in the public interest. The engagement of citizens in both capacities in managing the affairs of the political community[44] manifests itself, in particular, in the public space.[45] The public space is made up of all the settings for, and instances of, "public deliberation on the public good": exercise of civic participation, communication between political leaders and citizens, debate on the objectives and means of public action, accountability of the persons in charge of a public action (and thus invested with powers), and evaluation of the outcome of public action. The legitimacy of public action, therefore, partly arises from the fact that it takes place in a public space, the vitality of which it must consequently help to maintain. Civic engagement being a precondition and defining feature of a "free and democratic society," it follows that, as a matter of principle, public action must be subject to deliberation and critical examination by citizens. Any proposed public action accordingly raises the issue of the extent to which this particular action should be subject to such public deliberation and citizen review. Again, the answer to this question is relevant to the choice of a form of action for this project.

The third perspective, that of fairness, has long been present in the practice of choosing instruments for public action. Its influence is that exercised by jurists, who particularly support this value with respect to this type of decision. The concern for fairness obviously derives from the belief that justice is the founding value of collective life. Where the means of public action – rather than the action's objectives and substantive content – is concerned, the jurist's perspective focuses on procedure. Procedural justice, in the context of public action, leads to the principle that the action must have due regard for the persons, rights, and interests it affects. Given a proposal for public action, the fairness issue is as follows: What degree of individualization should the action present, and to what extent should it be subject to a rule-bound process designed to take into account persons, rights, and interests? Here again, the answer to the question will justify a preference for certain forms of action.

The fourth perspective, that of the expert, is even more familiar since from the early twentieth century it has had a growing influence on the choice of forms for public action. It favours knowledge, particularly scientific knowledge and technological expertise. It is hardly necessary to point out the obvious: The opinions of experts are a pervasive factor in political processes that determine and shape public action. Beyond this trite observation, one point deserves notice: The knowledge thus valued is essentially specialized knowledge. However, specialized knowledge is no longer exclusively associated with scholars and technicians: Increasingly, "field expertise" is a part of this knowledge – for example, that of businesspersons or entrepreneurs (who understand the practical conditions of their operations), users of a service (who understand the practical conditions of its provision), and even the poor or the marginalized (who understand the practical consequences of insecurity, deprivation, and isolation). Whatever the range of knowledge encompassed in this value, a single principle follows from it respecting public action: that a given action must be appropriate to reality or at least to the decision maker's understanding of reality. Consequently, any planned public right of action raises manifold issues: How, and to what extent, should the action be enlightened by the accumulation of, and confrontation between, which form(s) of expertise? Again, not all forms of public action will be equally suited to the answer.

The fifth perspective, that of the administrator, has also been highly present for a long time but has been particularly influential since the surge in neoconservatism of the past two decades. It favours the optimum use of resources available for public action. The premise that the resources of the state, the economy, and civil society are not unlimited leads to the principle that public action must pursue the objectives that the political authority assigns to it – objectives that are inevitably complex, wide-ranging, and concurrent and whose implementation therefore requires priorities and arbitration – by using these resources in the most effective way. This optimum can only be a balance of effectiveness, efficiency, and simplicity, synthesized by the concept of economy of means. Any proposal for public action involves determining, given the objective, the extent to which costs and the loss of public and private resources should be minimized and simplicity favoured in the methods of implementation. Again, the answer will dictate preference for certain forms of public action.

Thus a justification criterion may be formulated for each of these five perspectives (see Table 7.1). Each of the five criteria will lead to a preference – *subject to a weighting based on the preferences arising from the four other criteria* – for certain forms of public action. Accordingly, the political leader's perspective points to the criterion of *political control,* which leads to a preference for legal forms whose content Parliament directly or indirectly controls to a significant degree. The citizen's perspective leads to the criterion of *quality of the public space,* according to which the most justified form of action incorporates transparency requirements, procedures for public debate, and adequate opportunities for critical review. The *fairness* criterion, characteristic of the jurist's perspective, leads to a preference for forms of public action that lend themselves best to prior consideration of interests that may be affected, ideally in the context of a rule-bound process of publicity, consultation, possibly hearing from the parties concerned, and debate. The expert's perspective points to the criterion of *technical competence,* which leads to a preference for forms of action that allow for accumulation of and confrontation between specialized knowledge – not necessarily of a scientific nature – that may influence, even decisively, the content of the action. Finally, the public administrator's perspective introduces into the debate the criterion of *economy of means,* certainly the most complex, which leads to a preference for those forms of action that are the easiest and the least costly to use where such options are equally effective in terms of outcome.

Reformulated, the issue of justifying the choice can be put as follows: *Given the task to be accomplished through a public action* (situated justification), *which legal form is most justified* (argued justification) *based on these five criteria?* The answer in a given situation can result only from a balance between the five perspectives and their attendant preferred choices. Since in any case the nature of the task will require that a certain weight be given to most of the criteria, if not all, the final choice will necessarily be the product of a relation of "conflict

Table 7.1
Justifactory criteria for choosing a legal form for public action

| Perspectives | Criteria | Principles | Values | Forms |
|---|---|---|---|---|
| Political leader's perspective | Political control | The impetus of public action belongs to political authority. | Collective self-government | Forms that are directly or indirectly under Parliament's effective control |
| Citizen's perspective | Quality of public space | Public action should be subject to citizen deliberation and review. | Civic engagement | Forms that encourage participation, communication, deliberation, accountability, and evaluation in a public space |
| Lawyer's perspective | Fairness | Public action should respect the people, rights, and interests it affects. | Procedural justice | Forms displaying appropriate degrees of individualization and incorporating a rule-bound process |
| Expert's perspective | Technical competence | Public action should be appropriate to reality. | Knowledge, especially scientific | Forms that help to enlighten action by accumulating and confronting expertise |
| Administrator's perspective | Economy of means | Public action should pursue its objectives through the best use of the resources of the government, the economy, and civil society. | Optimal use of resources | Forms that minimize costs and drains on resources and that focus on simplicity |

Note: Each *perspective* calls into play a *criterion* based on a *principle* referring to a *value* that urges preference for certain *forms* of public action.

and compromise," to borrow Mashaw's expression. In other words, the legitimation of the choice will stem from the interaction between the facts and values associated with each perspective. The legitimacy of the choice is thus a product of the convergence of the modes of justification.[46]

It remains to be shown how this process of situated and argued justification can be introduced in the preparation of decisions about public intervention.

## Designing the Legitimation Procedure

The above has outlined the manner in which the question of choosing a proper form for a public action can be framed and the basis on which such a choice may be justified. What follows is a proposed method for implementing this justificatory approach, including a suggestion as to the point in the decision-making process leading to a public action at which this method should be applied.

### THE METHOD FOR JUSTIFYING A CHOICE OF FORM

The test, based on five criteria, for justifying the choice of a legal form for state regulatory intervention seems to need four stages:

1 analyzing the task in view
2 weighting the justificatory criteria
3 evaluating and shortlisting forms of action
4 choosing the form of action with the strongest overall justification

The first stage would focus on *defining the task* to be performed. The significance and priority of this operation follow logically from discarding the formalist approach in order to seek a justification that accommodates a specific situation's pragmatic requirements. For in its new formulation, the problem with locating rules becomes a matter of justifying the choice of a particular form of public action in view of the task this action sets out to perform through its normative element. Depending on its nature, this task brings into play some combination of restrictions, requirements, principles, and values. The choice of a form of action should reflect these features of the task.

The first step should be to analyze the proposed regulatory intervention and divide it up into discrete tasks. For example, a task might be described thus: obliging soft-drink distributors to collect their recyclable containers. As a second step in stage 1, the purposes of this public regulatory action, as well as the purpose of each specific task within it, should be brought into clear focus; the target group for the proposed rules should be identified. In the case just mentioned, for example, action is intended to prevent growth in the use of environmentally harmful materials; the addressees for these rules are all operators in the soft-drink production-and-distribution chain.

Stage 2 in this method involves *weighting the justificatory criteria* in relation to the proposed task. This weighting should take into account the purposes of the action and the persons for whom the rules are intended. As a first step, the relevance and weight of all five criteria, taken separately, should be gauged. For example, concerning soft-drink distributors' obligation to recover their recyclable containers, one should determine whether considerations stemming from the criterion of the quality of public space apply and, if so, what weight should be afforded these considerations. As a second step, one should gauge the relative weights of the criteria found to be relevant. This weighting will determine their influence on the choice of a form of state action for the proposed task. For instance, again concerning soft-drink distributors' recycling obligations, one should examine whether considerations stemming from the criterion of the quality of public space carry more weight than, say, those related to the criteria of fairness and economy of means. The validity of this weighting, crucial for subsequent stages, will largely depend on how strictly and precisely the nature of the task, the purpose of action, and the addressees of the rules have been defined during stage 1.

Stage 3 of the method is intended to *identify preferences* among the various forms of public action as indicated by the criteria. In order to do this, one has to be able to refer to a catalogue of forms containing a general assessment of each form from the standpoint of each of the five criteria. This prior assessment, performed without any reference to a specific task, could have only indicative and tentative value.[47] However, it would provide a broadly valid appraisal. It would afford a general indication of the types of situations in which a particular form of action would be strongly justified. It would allow for a tentative prediction that – if the task at hand required giving precedence, for example, to considerations of economy of means, political control, and technical competence – one would be justified in shaping public action as regulations coupled with noncriminal penalties. This prediction would be based on the general assessment, provided in the catalogue, of the compatibility of the various forms of action with each of the justificatory criteria.

Provided that such a catalogue is available, the initial step during stage 3 would consist of listing the forms of action generally seen as most fully justified by each of the relevant criteria taken separately. Assuming, for instance, that the criterion of quality of public space is deemed relevant with respect to a particular task, four of the "emergent" forms of public action would generally be viewed as enjoying the strongest justification: a structured process of negotiated regulations, a policy statement, outcome-based regulations, and contractual regulation.[48]

As the second step of stage 3, these lists would be compared in order to produce a synthetic, relatively short list of forms of action, from which the final selection would be made during the next stage. This short list would include forms figuring in the list of preferences derived from most, if not all, of the relevant criteria. Thus for a task in which, hypothetically, only the criteria of economy of means and political control would have been considered relevant, only two among the "emergent" forms of public action would make it to the short list: an informal process of negotiated regulations and a provision for non-criminal penalties. Since, in most situations, all criteria will have at least some relevance and since the preferences suggested by a majority of them should be enough to put a form of action on the short list, shortlisting should not excessively narrow the range of choice.

Stage 4 of the method would involve *choosing a form of action* from the short list. In order to allow further discrimination among the relatively limited range of possibilities offered by the short list, some hierarchy must be introduced among preferences. This can be done by referring to the relative weight attributed to the justificatory criteria at stage 2. The preponderance thus afforded to some criteria over others would now be reflected in forms of action preferred on the basis of these dominant criteria.

There is nothing mechanical about this final operation. Yet it cannot have a credible outcome unless the operations in earlier stages – analyzing the task, weighting the criteria, and evaluating and shortlisting forms of action – have been carefully conducted.

As this methodical process concludes (see Table 7.2), it is essential that an account of it be prepared so that the justificatory weight of its outcome can be understood. The recommended choice, supported by these justificatory criteria, would be provided in an advisory capacity. The actual choice, of course, is up to the political decision maker. To understand how, and at what point, the recommendation as to the choice of form, as well as the supporting justification, could factor into the decision, it is necessary to take a closer look at the way decisions are currently made.

THE MOMENT FOR JUSTIFYING A CHOICE OF FORM

This matter will be examined here on the assumption that the decision rests with Cabinet. For purposes of illustration, therefore, the implementation of this method of justifying choices will be considered in the

Table 7.2
Justifying the choice of a legal form for public action

| | |
|---|---|
| 1 | Define the task to be performed with the proposed rules: |
| A | Distinguish the tasks included in the proposed action |
| B | Specify the purposes of the proposed action and the addresses of potential rules. |
| 2 | Weigh the five justificatory criteria in relation to the task: |
| A | Appraise the relevance and weight of each criterion taken separately |
| B | Appraise the relative weight of the relevant criteria. |
| 3 | Identify the preferences indicated by the criteria: |
| A | Draw up a list of the most fully justified forms by each relevant criterion |
| B | By combining the lists, develop a range of options incorporating the forms with the strongest overall justification. |
| 4 | Choose a form of public action from this short list (3B) that reflects the relative weighing of the criteria (2B). |

context of decision making by the Executive Council of Quebec. The process leading to council decisions is structured by the Décret concernant l'organisation et le fonctionnement du Conseil exécutif (DOCE/ Cabinet Organization and Operations Order).[49]

This process has reflected for at least two decades a concern with impact assessment in advance of decisions.[50] As it now stands, the DOCE requires that memoranda drafted by ministers recommending decisions to the Executive Council canvass various potential solutions to the problem targeted by a proposed measure. A comparative appraisal of these solutions should bring out the pros and cons of each of them on a number of levels: impact on businesses, administrative and financial burdens on businesses, the relative impacts of these burdens according to the size of businesses, impacts on Quebec businesses compared to their competitors located in North American jurisdictions having significant trade links with Quebec, and finally, impacts on government finances and budgets and on intergovernmental relations. For a number of years, memoranda have also been required to mention any foreseeable impacts on regions and youth. Lastly, the recent Act to Combat Poverty and Social Exclusion requires mention of any direct and substantial impact by any legislative or regulatory proposal on the incomes of individuals and families in situations of poverty.[51]

These content requirements for Cabinet memoranda were buttressed and expanded by the 1996 addition of Section 31.1 and Schedule B to the DOCE. These texts call for an "impact study" prior to the drafting of the memorandum whenever a proposed measure would have a significant impact on business. The "significance" of this impact is determined by an annual cost threshold for private-sector businesses.[52] The study has to include an assessment of the likely impacts of the draft proposal.

In some respects, the impact-study requirements further specify the headings in the memorandum: minimizing the administrative load, adjusting these requirements to the size of companies, preserving the competitive position of Quebec business, anticipating more general impacts and costs to business. Other facets of the impact study, however, reflect a much more explicit concern with the form of public action. Thus the content requirements for the impact study involve:

- A comparative study both of solutions other than legislation or regulations (the examples given are information, education, or market-derived techniques) and of solutions in statutory form
- Consultation about potential solutions with concerned groups, including small business
- The establishment of a comparative cost-benefit trade-off for all proposed solutions
- A search for solutions that are outcomes-based rather than means-based – the former being presented as likely to minimize costs.

The perspective that emerges from these content requirements for the memorandum and impact study is very clear. Impact assessment is chiefly concerned with how measures affect the private sector of the economy and secondarily with their consequences for the public treasury. Several areas of concern that are or should be basic to government regulatory activity are virtually invisible from this standpoint – for example, social cohesion, enhanced equality, land-use planning, sustainable development, and environmental preservation.

With respect to the legal forms of public action, the DOCE in its present state suggests how a choice-justification process of the kind outlined above could be folded into this impact-assessment procedure. Two points are particularly suggestive. The first, mentioned above, is the presence among the impact-study content requirements of a mandate to consider the whole range of regulatory intervention strategies, from statutory enactments to the subtlest incentives. The second is that the memorandum and, to an even greater extent, the impact study are presented as supporting a demonstration or justification of the proposed measure.

The current process, therefore, contains a basis for progress in the form of an integrated, structured justification process for determining which form, or possibly forms (limited in number), would be optimal for the proposed public action, the substance of which would continue to be assessed and justified. Admittedly, form and substance tend to be closely connected and thus difficult to separate.[53] It would be going too far, however, to conclude that they cannot be justified separately. Both the final choice of the Executive Council and the recommendation addressed to it can and must reflect an overall rationale that combines both facets of a measure. Refusing to justify the choice of a form of action on the basis of specific, constant criteria is to accept that a part of the decision-making process and of the decision itself remains unaccounted for. It also means accepting an element of meaninglessness in the system of norms governing society.

The DOCE seems to be the logical place to introduce these requirements for justifying the choice of a form for public action. This process, proposed here as relying on five justificatory criteria that express the core values of a democratic legal order, would form a component of the impact study whenever this study is mandatory and, in any event, would be a heading in the memorandum submitted to the Executive Council. The DOCE should therefore set out the justificatory criteria and the method for their application.

Folding this preliminary justification process into the decision-making stream of Cabinet would tend to make the choice of a form for public action more thoughtful, more compatible with the substance of the action, and more consistent. If this operation is to have its full effect as a legitimation exercise, however, the relevant documents have to be publicly accessible. This is already happening in principle in Quebec with impact studies and the factual portions of memoranda to the Executive Council. Public access to supporting documentation dealing specifically with the choice of a form of public action is merely an application of the requirement of transparency in political decision making.[54]

## CONCLUSION

Government, it is said, is about making choices. The choice those in power have to make is primarily that of the ends of public action. But choosing also involves the means for this action. The people, parliamentarians, and ministers all contribute in their own ways to both choices.

Choices involve justifications. Proposing an option and preferring it over another involve finding reasons. Choosing involves defining and applying criteria and arguing for the conclusion to which these criteria lead. Choosing one action from all possible actions is truly to give meaning to action.

Both the form and content of an action must reflect this concern for meaning. The repertoire of forms available for public action is currently being broadened and transformed. This makes even more urgent the need to support public action by persuasive, reassuring, clarifying, and meaningful rationales. The bases for legitimation suggested thus far seem unable to meet this expectation.

As noted at the beginning of this chapter, attempts to develop new bases for legitimation are a feature of current discussions about political institutions in terms of governance. Given a tentative definition of governance as "a process for organizing and managing human societies through the acknowledgement and furtherance of diversity,"[55] the criteria and method suggested above could, at least to some extent, be said to reflect the spirit of governance.

Indeed, insofar as governance involves bringing together a variety of social actors, each of them asserting its own legitimacy, who seek to achieve coordinated action taking into account their respective objectives, values, and interests[56] through "discussion between orders of reasoning"[57] and a "combination of their own logic with that of others,"[58] the justification approach contemplated in this chapter can be characterized as a deployment of the concept of governance to deal with the issue of choosing the appropriate legal form for a specific public action. In relation to mainstream thinking about governance, this particular deployment of the concept may perhaps display some novelty in that it attempts to correct "asymmetries of influence"[59] by trying to integrate the citizen's and the jurist's perspectives and to broaden the expert's perspective on the issue.

From another angle, however, the justification approach developed above stands more clearly apart from mainstream understandings of governance. This is because the proposed approach accepts the distinction between ends and means in public action and concerns itself only with the latter. Both determining the ends of public action and, at the prior stage, identifying social realities as problematic are matters best left to political debate and decision. Naming and defining problems and setting ends and purposes for collective action are the object of government rather than governance. While the choice of legal means for action does, by contrast, carry a significant extrapolitical dimension, present in the specific perspectives of the administrator, the expert, and the jurist, it is also laden with political significance. The justification approach advocated above cannot therefore be subsumed under the technicist or depoliticizing view of governance. It should rather be characterized as a contribution to the development of an "open governance," giving full weight and effect to the logic of transparency.

Understood in these terms, the ideal of good governance may well reinforce the view that the time has come to reconsider the process leading to the deliberate choice of a form of public action. At stake is nothing less than the very intelligibility of democracy.[60]

# PART THREE
# From Instruments to Governance

# 8

# Instruments in Four: The Elements of Policy Design[1]

ARTHUR B. RINGELING

## INTRODUCTION

People rallied in The Hague, the Netherlands. It was the spring of 1934. Carrying flags and banners, they shouted: "Say yes to the plan!" The Western World was in the middle of the Great Depression. The plan encompassed an economic-recovery strategy. Two economists from the Netherlands – Herman de Man, a Belgian, and Jan Tinbergen, a future Nobel-prize winner – had developed a policy to get people back to work where the market, in that era, had failed. The message of the plan was that the Dutch government had to invest in public works and hire unemployed people. The designers as well as the people who marched were social democrats. But most interesting is that they marched for a government instrument: planning.

In this chapter, I try to make it clear that it is beneficial to develop different perspectives on governmental tools. My message is that these tools are highly political, stem from normative considerations, and are judged according to legal standards. Tools are anything but neutral; they are highly normative. Policy makers also have to determine whether what they want is permitted according to the law. So governmental tools are judged and can be judged from different perspectives. Different values can be used for their justification. Western European countries and the policies they have followed illustrate these different standards time and again.

For Europeans, it is important to make this statement because they are so familiar with Machiavelli's insight that the ends justify the means. In this chapter, I contradict his view. Political movements prefer particular instruments because of their political characteristics, because instruments are justified in their ideological view, and because they correspond with the rule of law (see Ringeling 1983, 1993; also Ringeling and van Nispen 1998).

For readers from the other side of the Atlantic, the message is important because they are educated in pragmatism, which gives rise to rationalistic policy making. Not only are policy instruments highly political, but they are also partly the components of the ideologies of political movements. Given these qualities of policy instruments, debates over government tools constitute an important part of the political and societal development of particular countries. Writing about government instruments is, in a certain sense, writing about political and administrative history.

This chapter first introduces a heuristic scheme that enables us to ask different questions about instruments, each question representing a different approach and different standards. The conceptual framework is further elaborated and illustrated using the results of a research project carried out, in six countries, on the implementation of measures of the European Union (EU). Europe is often considered a prime example of intensive governmental intervention. Differences between European states are stressed by pointing to different state traditions. For this reason, differences in instrument choice are used to illustrate how different standards for the selection of instruments are applied. Finally, conclusions are drawn from this analysis.

## CONCEPTUAL FRAMEWORK

Central to the phenomenon of policy instruments is the idea of fit, the basic notion being that the better the fit, the more effective the policy. Fit is a concept that is well known in policy sciences. Essentially, it comes down to correspondence in relationships. This correspondence can take different forms: a compromise between different actors, policy choices that look much the same, or a measure that is adequate when circumstances are taken into account. In the concept of fit, ideas about the rationalism of policy processes can be recognized. The concept can be found in ideas about contingency that are based on organizational theory and in network thinking and institutional theory in the policy sciences.

To apply the concept of fit, one looks at the characteristics of the policy, of the instruments of the private sector, and of governments. But fit can be interpreted in different ways. Hemerijck (2003) distinguished four kinds of questions about fit:

Table 8.1
Four types of policy-instrument fit

|  | Structural-formal | Cultural-normative |
|---|---|---|
| Logic of appropriateness | Feasibility (Does it suit?) | Acceptability (Is it normatively correct?) |
| Logic of consequence | Effectiveness (Does it work?) | Legality (Is it permitted?) |

Source: Adapted from A. Hemerijck 2003.

1 In terms of effectiveness, does it work?
2 In terms of feasibility, does it suit?
3 In terms of acceptability, is it normatively correct?
4 In terms of legality, is it permitted? (See Table 8.1.)

These four questions represent, to some extent, the development of the policy sciences. Originally, the pragmatic question dominated the field. Economists tried to calculate which measures were the most effective and efficient. Later, the context in which instruments were applied became more and more important. The question was a typical product of political scientists, as they paid attention to the behaviour of actors in a certain network. The acceptability or legitimacy question is a subject that has always inspired political philosophers. This picture has changed in recent decades (see Bobrow and Dryzek 1987, ch. 6). The question of legality of public policy is perhaps one of the oldest questions about public policy. But amazingly, for a long time it was almost fully absent from the policy sciences.

The different questions asked play, in one way or another, a role in policy research and in the theories that its practitioners have tried to develop. This is most clear for the question of effectiveness. Also, the question of feasibility has always been there, as has the question about the extent to which courses of action are permitted. The more we pay attention to the networks developing and implementing policies, the more important this question of legality becomes, as does the question of normative correctness.

This chapter illustrates its argument by making use of research conducted in the field of environmental policy. In an international project, I and my colleagues compared the way six European countries implemented two policy measures of the European Union. Both of these measures involved environmental policy. The first was the European directive on packaging. The second measure was a regulation on the international transport of hazardous waste. The countries compared were Belgium, France, Germany, Greece, the Netherlands, and Spain (Hafkamp et al. 1999).

A question that can be asked is what has to fit. The general answer is "choices." Without choices for policy makers or other actors, no attempt exists to reach a feasible policy. Now two other questions can be asked: choices of what and choices by whom? The "what" question can be answered by referring to policies and instruments. By policies we mean a combination of normative positions and goals to be reached and the policy theories behind these goals. To put it differently, a policy consists of problem analysis, problem definition, and possible solutions as well as strategies for reaching these solutions. A policy instrument provides the means to reach these goals. Both European and national governments may formulate instruments – that is, elements of policies that refer to specific means (legal, financial, procedural, etc.) to be applied in the implementation of a specific policy. "Who" might refer to, for instance, the European Union, national governments, or the business community or to other representatives of the private sector.

### DIFFERENT STATES

It is not unusual to look at the political–administrative developments in Europe as the systematic construction of the big state – a state that has a central position in societal development with little or no space for either private initiative or involvement in the market. This vision, however, is rather one-sided. There are different traditions in Western Europe concerning the state–societal relationship. Perhaps the formation of the big state is more adequate for France than for the United Kingdom. Perhaps it suits Sweden better than it suits the Netherlands. So there is at least diversity among the Western European countries. This diversity refers not only to the role of the public sector, but also to the relationships between the state and societal organizations.

Richard Stillman (1991), for example, made a distinction between concepts of the state: no state, bold state, pre-state, and pro-state. The concept of no state stands for a minimalist view of what the role of the public sector should be. The bold-state view represents an activist conception of the role of the state in societal development. The pre-state, or halfway state, represents a moderate view on the role of the state, whereas the pro-state concept stands for the state as a professional technocracy. All four conceptions can be found in Western Europe.

Perhaps the best example of the no-state tradition in the European context can be found in the United Kingdom. The picture changed when, in the 1920s, social democrats took over government for the first time. Societal conflicts were fought out in the companies and on the streets. Employers and unions opposed each other vehemently. In the United Kingdom, adversarial politics led to adversarial relationships in society as a whole. Under these circumstances, class conflict was more visible and more openly fought than in the other European countries. The Labour Party was closely connected to the unions, a phenomenon that was characteristic of the UK during the twentieth century. So the Labour Government tried to strengthen the position of the labourers. Regulation was, like in most countries, one of the instruments. But nationalization of big industries was another logical consequence of societal struggle.

After the Second World War, a system of social security and health service was created, Lord Beveridge being the intellectual author of this policy. In his thinking, the welfare state was a government affair. The provisions of social security were governmental tasks. By implementing this conception, the United Kingdom became more and more what Esping-Andersen (1990) called a "social-democratic" state. But the influence of Beveridge's philosophy was not limited to the United Kingdom. Most countries in Western Europe adopted his ideas. The institutionalization differed, however, from country to country.

To some extent, developments in France were comparable. But the no-state concept was absent. The dominant view was that the state had to take the lead in societal developments, a view once referred to as the "public management of society" (see van der Eyden 2003). Governance was based on professional–technocratic expertise. Special schools were created to build up the necessary knowledge and professional people: the "grandes écoles." Thus France has traits of both the bold-state and the pro-state conceptions. The important parties in France, from left to right, shared the idea of the centrality of the state. Their disputes concerned what the strong state should do and in what way rather than the notion of the strong state itself. Not surprisingly, the tool of direct government fits their conception most comfortably.

There is a third tradition in Western Europe in which state and society are intensively intertwined. Here, the welfare state is not a state affair alone. Societal organizations play an important role in its realization. The countries concerned were examples of the (neo)corporatist state. This model can be found in Belgium and Germany. The Netherlands can also be classified under this model even though it adopted to a high degree Beveridge's ideas about universal social rights as a basis for a generous welfare regime. But to an important extent, implementation of this philosophy was left to semipublic and private organizations, which delivered most of the state financial services.

In Stillman's terms, the Netherlands can be called a pre-state. Governmental and societal organizations share the burden of implementing tasks that are considered relevant by the state. In a number of Western European countries, activities that are characteristic of the modern welfare state are also implemented by private organizations, often called organizations of private initiative or semipublic organizations – also named quangos (quasi-autonomous nongovernmental organizations) or parastate organizations. This is not a development of recent years but one that is deeply embedded in the tradition of important political movements. Principles like "subsidiarity" and "sovereignty in one's own domain" have been essential for Catholic and Protestant politics in the past century.

This tradition can also be found in other parts of Western Europe, as Putnam has shown (1993). It concerns countries that have a less clear dividing line between forms of public and private organization. In the Anglo-Saxon world, organizations are either private or public. Among the European countries, by contrast, many of the societal organizations are hybrids. They are in part private, particularly with regard to their origin and legal status. But at the same time they fulfil public functions (see Anheier and Seibel 1990; Salamon 1989, 2002).

In general, the countries of this type were less active in economic than in social regulation. They are characterized by intensive relationships between governmental and societal organizations, business and industry included. More attention was paid to social policy than to the governance of market conditions. Subsidies, loan guarantees, and tax expenditures were more popular instruments than competition policy and the prevention of cartels. While regulations existed, they were not intensively enforced. This changed when the market regulations of the European Union became more important.

So the European countries have different state traditions. These traditions have consequences for the way they implement policies of the European Union. We may expect that different institutional setups will lead to different policy discussions in the countries concerned, to different instrument choices, and to different policy effects. The heuristic scheme based on the four questions can make us attentive to these differences. Clearly, there are more questions to ask about government tools.

## AN ORTHODOX PERSPECTIVE ON INSTRUMENTS AND THEIR CRITICS

It is possible to speak of an orthodox view of instruments when referring to the rational model. The choice of instruments in this view is a question of optimization – that is, selecting the best instruments given the policy goals. Policy debates often concentrate on this question. That economic instruments work better than regulation in the environmental field is frequently heard and fits the orthodox view (see Majone

1989, ch. 6), as does the idea that it is better to use voluntary agreements than top-down regulation when environmental policy has to become a success. The discussion centres on the effects of instruments from the point of view of policy intentions.

The design question is central in the policy sciences as well as in practice. Policy makers should choose those instruments that best serve their purposes. This is the core of the rational approach to instruments. Policy design is a result of insights as to what has worked and what has not (Hood 1984).

For a long time, design entailed putting goals, means, and time together. It can be considered a kind of planning. A lot of effort was put into these activities. Some public organizations compiled an intensive inventory of all their policy instruments. Others just asked for more instruments. It is possible that policy makers are frustrated by the fact that their instruments are not effective enough.

R.J. in 't Veld (1997) once mockingly formulated a law of policy accumulation: Whether a certain policy is successful or fails, the reaction of policy makers is always the same: more of it. When they reach their objectives, the policy can be considered a success. Everybody wants to share in a success. So the scope of the policy broadens; the target group is enlarged. More means are needed, and the policy sector will get more means because it is doing so well. And more policy includes more, and often more diverse, instruments. Wonderful examples of this mechanism can be found in the policy-sciences literature, particularly in the field of economic subsidies (see Hufen 1990).

If the choice of instruments were a question of optimization, all six European countries studied would have opted for the same instruments in implementing the European measures we studied. The intention of the European Union was to harmonize market conditions. And to some extent, it succeeded, although not as a result of all countries concerned choosing the same instruments for the policy. So other considerations than those derived from the direct relationship between policy goals and means must have played a role in these countries.

There are more problems when the instrumentation question is considered as an optimizing problem. From the moment the concept was keyed, this approach presumed that instruments had inherent characteristics. When applied, they would work in a specific way because of these characteristics. Regulation would lead to certain effects, and economic instruments would lead to others. But it turned out that the characteristics of instruments were not easy to specify.

Majone (1989) explained the reasons for this difficulty. He referred to the extensive discussion on what would work better in the environmental field: regulation or economic instruments. (This discussion can also be found in the Netherlands; see Wetenschappelijke Raad 1992.) Majone stated that the results do not point in a particular direction, so they make a choice possible. The reasons for this are many. First, there are countries that have reasonable results while working with permits and others that have reasonable results while working with effluent standards. Second, it turns out to be difficult to determine to what extent one instrument or another causes certain environmental effects. And third, the discussion is a theoretical one; the effects of instruments applied in practice are compared with the theoretical effects of instruments that do not exist in practice.

A fourth reason can be added. In practice, instruments can never be found in a pure form. So even if we have knowledge about the characteristics of policy instruments, their actual state is influenced by the fact that they always come in a mix. The policy mix is a result of the fact that, for economic instruments, there needs to be legislation of one type or another. The legality question is elaborated on below, but here it must be clear that governments cannot distribute subsidies or sell emission rights without a legal basis.

The design of an instrument is affected by a mix of instruments and by the political–administrative decision making associated with this mix.

## INSTRUMENTS IN A POLITICAL FRAMEWORK

The choices that the countries made can be explained by the national setting, particularly the political–administrative setting, which explains the process of policy formulation as well as the results of this process, including the choice of instruments. The question of which actor will be involved, and in what way, is answered differently from instrument to instrument. In the European context, the choice between a directive and a regulation can mean the difference between unanimity and a majority vote.

This insight is relatively new. In the history of public administration, there are all kinds of studies that illustrate the relationship between the political–administrative setting, on one side, and the choice and application of instruments, on the other. Selznicks' (1949) famous Tennessee Valley Authority (TVA) study is one that is worth mentioning. Economists have also come to this insight, but few considered its consequences. The preference of politicians for subsidies was explained by the special ties they could develop with the parts of industry at which the subsidies were targeted. So there are other reasons to choose particular instruments than finding an optimal relationship between policy goals and means, the political position of the policy makers being one of them.

Policy instruments, it can be concluded, have a political character. They are not neutral and thus will not be chosen or applied because, from an effectiveness point of view, they work best. From the point of view of variance in administrative settings, an extra step can be taken in analyzing policy-instrument choice in a political-administrative setting.

## GOVERNANCE MODELS AND INSTRUMENT CHOICE

In their activities in a variety of policy sectors, national governments follow certain governance models, but they do not follow a specific governance model all the time. However, a relationship between the problem configuration and the governance approaches used does exist. But besides this, a particular country seems to have a preference for a certain governance model. This has to do with the political–administrative structure and culture of a country. Studies on Western democratic countries demonstrate these differences in the ways policies are made and in the instruments chosen and used.

The often-used terminology is that of policy styles (Richardson 1982). I prefer the term "governance models." The first is considered mostly as a concept referring to a cultural phenomenon, whereas governance models include cultural as well as structural elements of a particular political–administrative setting. All kinds of different governance models can be distinguished. I have opted for the following four (see Peters 1996 for a somewhat different distinction):

1 command and control
2 governance along main policy lines
3 selective governance
4 facilitating governance

In the command-and-control model, the national government is the central player. It defines the problem and develops the solutions, and it does so in a rather autonomous way. So the central government is the policy designer. It orders other actors, public as well as private, to implement its policies. This model characterizes a government that uses direct regulation as the main instrument for environmental policy. Standards are set in national regulations. Other actors have to abide by these standards. In a lot of countries, this has been the usual model, and to some extent, it still is.

In the model of governance along main policy lines, the central government is still the important player. But it designs only the main lines of the policy, giving other actors the opportunity to specify the policy. In this model, there is a greater reliance on the self-governance capacity of the other actors. This model is characterized by setting framework laws and obligatory framework goals. Other policy actors can act within this framework according to the circumstances. Policy instruments can take the forms of general rule making on the national level and more detailed rule making by other governmental actors.

In the selective-governance model, central government intervenes only in certain crucial matters. These crucial matters change the course of events. But other actors have to apply the instruments that are offered in the selective intervention. Subsidies are a good example of this kind of governance. No other actor is obliged to make use of subsidies. The same is true of other economic instruments. Covenants can be a part of the strategy followed in this model, and other strategies will also fit.

In the facilitating model, the basic question for central government is how to enable the self-governance capacities of other actors. Essential for a facilitating strategy is that central governments understand the problems confronting other actors very well. Only then can they supply these actors with the necessary instruments. The relationship between the European Union and the member states can be put in these terms, as can the relationship between central and decentralized government within a country. Of course, there are differences in judicial relationships between the actors mentioned. But this model is crude enough to overlook them.

The countries we studied did not opt for or use the same governance model in everyday practice. In Germany, where the citizens are most worried about environmental issues, politicians made decisions on packaging-waste policy that were opposed by industry. They could do so because they were rather sure of their grass roots. In France, the government decided after consultation with leaders of industry that the German system was not the road to follow. So France opted for a policy that was very close to the already existing incineration system. The Netherlands, to give a third example, changed its policy style. In the 1970s and the beginning of the 1980s, the command-and-control style dominated. This style did not produce very good results. Then an approach evolved that was more in line with the policy style that had dominated this country in a variety of other policy fields: the consensual "older" style, allowing industry to find its own solutions for implementing a covenant that it had reached with the public authorities.

From our research, we also learned that there is no direct correspondence between the governance models that a specific government is following and the instruments applied. But a connection does exist between the governance models and the policy and instrument choices

made. Governance models tell us something about the arena, the relationships between different actors, which policy choices are feasible,
and which instrument options play a role. They can help us to better
understand why only certain possibilities were taken into consideration
in the policy processes studied. They also give us insight into why only
certain instruments are allowed from a political point of view. Choices
made in the context of these different governance models produce different results.

Is there a relationship between these governance models and the instruments that governing bodies select? Do some instruments fit a certain model much better then others? This point of view has been
defended. De Bruijn and ten Heuvelhof (1991) have made a distinction
between vertical and horizontal instruments. By vertical they mean a relationship between policy makers and a governed object that is higher or
lower in the hierarchy. In this relationship, traditional instruments, like
regulation, fit. Horizontal instruments fit in a relationship of equal partners – governmental representatives and representatives of industry – that
confer to reach agreements and make deals. Instruments in this category
are voluntary agreements, covenants, and information. The horizontal instruments fit governance models that rely, to a greater extent, on the self-
governance of the governed body. So vertical instruments are connected
to command and control and to governance along main policy lines. Horizontal instruments fit better in more horizontal governance models.

The reasoning seems to be plausible. But there are arguments against
this reasoning. The first is that instruments mostly come in a mix, as I
put forward earlier in this chapter. Policies for certain problems always
contain a lot of different instruments. This mix is even more impressive
when informal instruments are also taken into account. Regulation almost always constitutes a part of this mix. In the following paragraphs
I explain why.

The second argument is that instruments of the same type can have a
very different content. Here again, regulation serves as an example.
Not all regulation has the command-and-control structure. However, a
lot of laws, especially laws with the threat of negative sanctions, do
have this structure. But there is also a lot of regulation that attributes
certain rights to other actors or organizations, thereby enabling them
to realize specific policies.

## INSTRUMENTS ARE NORMATIVE

Earlier, I concluded that instruments are not just instrumental, or
phrased in another way, not just tools. They also have characteristics
related to a political–administrative situation. This situation can refer

to the institutional setting as well as to the negotiation process. Here, I want to add a third element to the political character of policy instruments. Instruments have a normative side, too (see Stone 1998). They can be goals in themselves, desirable to use when they are compared with other instruments. In the political history of Europe, these long-standing preferences can be connected with the most important political movements, which used some instruments more than others for ideological reasons.

The oldest is the liberal movement. The instrument that the members of this movement preferred was the law. The law meant freedom. This understanding of the law may seem a remarkable insight, but for the liberals of the late nineteenth century, the law was used as an instrument to curtail the power of the absolute sovereign, who, as a consequence, became less and less absolute. Rule making made clear, to some extent, what was permitted and what was not. This was the case for all citizens, whether they were in governing positions or not. But the abuse of power had to be blamed on the rulers, not on the ruled. The emphasis on regulation and on rights, more specifically on human and constitutional rights, was a logical consequence of this reasoning. So traditionally, liberals were rule makers, irrespective of their actual position.

Another, still influential, movement was the Christian Democrat movement. For Western European countries like Germany, Belgium, Italy, and to a lesser extent France, it was an important political movement. In these countries (neo)corporatism blossomed. In the Netherlands, this movement was politically pivotal. Its members participated in Dutch cabinets from 1918 until 1994 without interruption. Their instrument choice was very specific. The political philosophy of the Christian Democrats focused, among other things, on the relationship between the state and societal organizations. In their view, it was not necessary for the state to execute certain tasks itself. Preferably it did not. Services could also be delivered by societal organizations, particularly organizations with a certain religious character.

In the Netherlands, around the beginning of the twentieth century, a discussion took place concerning the financing of schools founded by religious groups. The principle decision in 1918 was to finance public and private schools in the same way. This decision, often called the pacification, became the model for a lot of other policy fields. In the fields of public housing, health organizations, and social welfare, the model of the educational field was followed. The Christian Democrats became the strongest defenders of this model. Their influence was so great that other political movements, like that of the social democrats, had to follow course. The Dutch system of pillarization was thus in place.

It may be clear that the system of pillarization could exist as long as the condition of financing private groups and organizations was secure. It was the Christian Democrat movement that designed instruments to channel public funds to private organizations. The system was further enlarged during the rise of the welfare state. For sociologists like van Doorn and Schuyt (1978), this development is reason to state that in the Dutch situation, one speaks of the welfare society instead of the welfare state.

The social democrats developed their preferences for policy instruments in a remarkable way. Initially, they were abhorred by the state and by the most important instrument of the liberal state, the law. The law was an instrument of oppression, used by the possessing ruling class. But things changed when representatives of this political movement became active in local government. The state was accepted as a temporary instrument for realizing socialist ideals; it would disappear afterward. The change became total, and the temporary character was dropped when general suffrage was realized. The state became an instrument for governance of societal relationships and for representative democracy, an instrument to obtain authoritative pronouncements about the course and the intensity of this governance.

With the acceptance of the state, the instruments of the state were accepted. Opposition to the use of the monopoly of violence took the social democrats the longest time to overcome. The law was also accepted as an instrument of governmental intervention – and not only accepted, but also increasingly used in a new way. In the past, the emphasis had been on the *codification* of already existing insights and practices – and on how unjust these practices were in the eyes of the social democrats. Now the law was used to change existing relationships, to create new and more just practices. The law became an instrument for *modification*. It became, in the view of the social democrats, the preeminent instrument for societal change.

Moreover, closely coupled with the law was the bureaucratic organization. Unlike the liberals and Christian Democrats, the social democrats were not great admirers of private initiative. Strong public organizations regulated by law were their alternative. In cases where other political movements did not accept this – for instance, because they had built up private organizations for the same purposes – the social democrats had to build up their own.

Finally, they were active in the development of new instruments. In the 1930s they constructed an instrument that became as popular as law. This instrument was, as we saw, planning. It was meant as an alternative to the blind, spilling forces of the market, the central instrument of capitalist society. In their view, planning should control societal conditions and relations. Planning was an instrument that created societal order as well as equilibrium between the society and the state. It was also an instrument for governing public activities on a day-by-day basis. The plan was the opposite of the market. Planning was the governing device. People marched for this instrument in the 1930s. And in building up the welfare state, planning turned out to be an important instrument in a number of European countries and in different policy fields.

The research done with my colleagues on the implementation of European environmental policy revealed many ways in which instruments are judged on normative grounds. In Germany the government forced industry to introduce the Duales System Deutschland, the local authorities' collection of garbage, on one side, and industry's separate collection of packaging waste, on the other. This policy's implementation was not just the result of the strong legitimization of politics with regard to the environmental issue. Behind this system, there was the normative insight that the polluters have to solve the problem. In France the public sector took on the responsibility after consulting the private sector and used public incinerators to solve the packaging-waste problem. This approach has everything to do with the normative idea of the state – that is, with the idea that societal relationships are the purview of a centralized state. Covenants like the ones used in the Netherlands underline the common responsibility of the public and the private sector with regard to the packaging problem. To put it another way, an instrument can constitute the expression of values and other normative conceptions that political actors hold.

It is also possible to choose instruments in environmental policy on considerations derived from other values like sustainability or societal efficiency. The German system of coping with packaging waste is not a cheap system, but it expresses the values held by a majority in Germany. The question can be asked about the extent to which the French system of incinerating packaging waste is contributing to sustainability. The "does it work" question is, however, not at stake here because both Germany's and France's approaches to the packaging-waste problem work to a certain degree. The judgment is put into terms of giving way to specific values. And these kinds of judgments take place in the heart of the public sector, where values and, more specifically, competing values are the business of the participants.

## BACK TO AN OLD QUESTION

Practitioners of the policy sciences almost forgot that governments are not free in the instruments they select. Only authoritarian states do not have to bother with this limitation. But the law binds a democratic *Rechtsstaat*. That was why the liberals of the nineteenth century were such active lawmakers. The term *Rechtsstaat* is German, but its significance is much wider than its role in this one country. It is a concept that is of importance in Europe as well as across the Atlantic. Above, I pointed out that nineteenth-century liberals were dedicated to limiting the power of the absolute sovereign by using regulation. The principle of legality was introduced, meaning that governments could not act without an adequate legal foundation in the law. This principle became the dominant focus of attention of the jurists, who specialized in public law, and also of their brethren in the law profession, whether in the courts or in the law firms. A whole industry is devoted to the question of whether certain actions of government are permitted or not.

So the possibilities available to policy makers in choosing between different instruments are to an important extent limited by considerations of legality. The amazing thing is that practitioners of the policy sciences seem to have forgotten this consideration when they developed ideas about optimal instrument choice. By studying public policy in a European context, we can easily observe important differences among nations. For instance, the member states have a different attitude toward legislation. The legislative tradition in Germany is much stronger than in the Netherlands. Indeed, it is not difficult to understand why *Rechtsstaat* is a German term.

But both countries cannot live easily with wide internal cleavages between regulation and practice. A correspondence between law and reality of 100 per cent is unattainable, but the correspondence should come as close to this as possible. In some southern countries of Europe, this attitude is less likely to be found. In these countries, a phenomenon like the implementation gap can be found more easily (see Majone et al. 1996) and is more widely accepted.

Looking at the two European measures that we studied, one can say that the choices of a directive in the packaging problem and of a regulation in the problem of transporting hazardous waste make sense from a juridical point of view. The directive was based on Article 100 of the European Treaty, aimed at harmonizing market circumstances. The regulation on transport of hazardous waste was a result of the obligations that the European Union itself had accepted after the Lomé Conference and the Basel Convention. So the choice of a regulation could be legally defended.

This point of view is also valuable at the level of the member states. They had to put the EU measures into their national systems of law (see Hanf and Soetendorp 1998). The directive on packaging waste gave them more leeway than the regulation on the transport of hazardous waste, which directly binds the member states. With the directive on packaging, two starkly different systems were developed with regard to packaging, and several countries took measures that were not in accordance with what other countries did.

But the leeway for the member states is clearly defined. Brussels was astonished at the road the Netherlands took when it decided to use a covenant (a voluntary agreement between the national government and the packaging industry) as a policy instrument. The European Union reacted by stating that the directive had to be implemented by Dutch law, not by a contract between the Dutch government and representatives of the packaging industry. The Dutch government was confronted with a dilemma. If it did not change its course, Brussels would possibly apply sanctions. If it did, it would demonstrate itself unreliable in the eyes of its negotiation partners. A few years later, the Netherlands solved the dilemma by putting the text of the first covenant into legislation, having already agreed with industry on a second one. The legislation constituted a formal "screen" of sorts. In Brussels, on the other side of the screen, they were still wondering whether what the Dutch had done was permitted. But the parties concerned were already active in looking for new ways to reduce the packaging problem. They tried to find, not behind but in front of the screen, answers to the question of feasibility.

So the question from the point of view of legality is what is permitted within the juridical framework. This is not the same as saying that jurists hold the same opinion about a certain question. But if they disagree, there are procedures to have their disputes decided. How the legality question is decided influences which policy instruments are used and how they are used. It also influences how the policy problems are formulated.

## INSTRUMENTS IN A COMPARATIVE FRAMEWORK

A number of conclusions flow from the developments and characteristics described above.

First, government instruments have to do with shaping society. People differ in their preferences for society and the way society should be treated by the state. That is what politics is about. Politicians differ in goals and in their preferences concerning the tools governments use. The choice of instruments is connected to the role the state plays in a society and the presence of direct and indirect ways of governance. For this reason, governmental tools are as highly disputed as policy aims.

Second, the toolbox approach to government instruments, or what is called the pragmatic view, has value but also serious shortcomings. The choices that policy makers face are limited for various reasons. Certainly, instruments are intended to be used as tools, but they are more than tools alone. They are political weapons and marching banners alike. They are normative in nature, irrespective of whether one follows a political strategy or, for instance, the philosophy of new public management.

Third, the notion that it is characteristic of Europe to have strong states and a dominance of direct governance is a misunderstanding. There are different traditions in this part of the world, the bold state not being the dominant pattern. Countries in Western Europe differ in the way the welfare state is institutionalized. As a result of the different state traditions and governance philosophies on this continent, indirect government can be seen all over Europe, some countries having more experience with this phenomenon than others. Indirect government is all but a new phenomenon in this region. It is embedded in a long-standing political (neocorporatist) ideology, to be found in particular among Christian Democrats.

Fourth, the different types of state also lead to differences in the selection of policy instruments. In the more social-democratic welfare states, bureaucracies were paired with public enterprises. In the more (neo)corporatist welfare states, government policy was implemented by private as well as public organizations. More horizontal tools are found to a larger extent in countries where more emphasis was placed on consensus building, where public and semipublic organizations were active in the public domain, and where a central position of the state was absent.

Fifth, there is a relationship between the governance model followed and the instruments applied. However, this does not mean that certain instruments are used in one model and that others are used in other models. Instruments have a great variety themselves. One law can differ much from another in structure, in context, and in effects. Subsidies can have a more-or-less compelling character. Instrument choice is influenced by the way a problem is formulated. It is interesting to see to what extent the opposite is true, how a problem's definition is a result of the kind of question asked with regard to instruments. In this approach, instruments are identified as the optimal choices not on the basis of given goals but as a result of the way problems are formulated.

Sixth, the instruments that the countries applied were harmonized less than the policies of the countries concerned. Instrument choices are the result of political ideology, of different governance visions, of legal traditions. Instruments have to fit within the political–administrative setting of a particular country.

Seventh, instrument choice is not constant. It changes over time as a result of the invention of new instruments, national and international developments, and the interventions of the supranational institutions. Some instruments become popular; others fall in disgrace. Fashion plays a role, as do policy routines. Thus instrument selection is far from a matter of simplistic rational choice.

Eighth, depending on the perspectives of policy makers concerning government instruments, differences in policy design will result. The choices of a policy analyst or policy maker asking whether a certain instrument might work or not will differ from those of the policy maker asking whether a certain instrument is normatively defendable. A policy analyst thinking in terms of what is politically feasible will make choices different from those of an analyst asking what is legally permitted. These policy analysts see different policy problems. The way they approach policy instruments influences their policy designs.

Ninth, in design, policy analysts and policy makers should not only ask whether a certain instrument works. They should also ask themselves three other questions: whether their instruments fit within a specific political–administrative context, whether the choice of a certain instrument can be defended normatively, and whether it is legally permitted to use a specific instrument. When they supplement their design with these other questions, they can reach a higher quality of policy making.

My tenth and last conclusion is that the different questions with regard to policy instruments should not be asked in isolation or in a manner excluding the other questions. In combination, the different approaches lead to a broader perspective on the choice and the application of policy instruments.

# 9

# The Swiss Army Knife Of Governance[1]

RODERICK A. MACDONALD

A SELF-REFLEXIVE PROLOGUE:
INSTRUMENT CHOICE AND DISCIPLINARY CHOICE

The organizers of the conference giving rise to this volume embarked on an audacious endeavour that might reasonably be characterized as a *beau risque* – a risk that those who have engaged in transdisciplinary research know all too well.[2] The risk is nicely framed by the metaphor of Babel: a failure of communication. Bringing together scholars and policy makers from different political states and from different disciplinary perspectives to address complex problems immediately engages two epistemological inquiries about integrating the various contributions: (1) Is there an Archimedean point from which the different texts may be judged, or must all disciplines be judged only through the lens of the others? And (2) is the object of the endeavour to recreate a single form of knowledge (a new discipline), or is it to provide a multidisciplinary conspectus for translation (a grammar, syntax, and dictionary) through which new knowledge may be generated and shared?

I raise these two questions not to argue that one approach rather than the other is to be preferred in all circumstances. What I wish to signal is that the design, organization, and execution of this volume presents exactly the same types of issues that confront scholars and policy makers on a daily basis. How does one design, organize, and execute a policy response to a complex problem?

Admittedly, in this prologue (indeed, by the very fact that I am choosing to write a prologue in order to address the concerns of coherence and integration attending to transdisciplinarity) I make clear my own answers to these questions. But let me first present the options. Integration can be achieved in several ways: by establishing a common set of themes; by framing a common set of concepts and definitions; by posing a common set of questions; by imposing a common set of analytical tools; by insisting on a common methodology; by requiring authors to attend to a common literature set; by implicitly adopting one disciplinary perspective (say, political science) as the default regime for all contributors; and so on.

Consistent with my general understanding of the intellectual endeavour at hand, I have chosen to address the issue of integration by adopting the same epistemology that informs my substantive arguments about instrument choice. My prologue develops this epistemology in two dimensions. To begin, I make several observations about transdisciplinary knowledge in a collection such as this. Then I provide an overview of the claims I make and how they may be read as against the other chapters herein.

Before embarking on this task, however, I should like to signal a key point. The editors of this collection have presented a masterful introduction to and summary of the overarching themes presented in this volume. They have drawn out the transversal ideas and clarified assumptions and future challenges, providing a rich orientation to the text.

## Integrated Knowledge or Disciplinary Choice?

In assembling this collection, the editors were confronted with a number of classical instrument-choice questions. I shall set these out (and answer them) as five theses.

First, what should be the driving objective? Is this a collection that has a particular instrumental purpose? Or is it meant primarily to increase our knowledge by opening up multiple lines of inquiry? *Thesis:* To assume that the collection has an a priori instrumental purpose is to assume (wrongly) that ends can be established in advance without attending to available means for their accomplishment.

Second, what should be the structuring framework? Is this a collection organized around the idea that it should focus on exploring a particular goal or end – say, what is better governance? Or a collection organized in a manner that focuses on means – say, what do different disciplines have to say about the means to achieve this? *Thesis:* The collection's working title – *From Instrument Choice to Governance: Future Directions for the Choice of Governing Instrument* (since compressed to *Designing Government: From Instruments to Governance*) – correctly intimates that both frameworks are in play.

Third, what should be the temporal focus? Is this a collection about what can be done now (or in the near future)? Or is it a collection about trajectories of knowledge: how and why ideas like instrument choice and governance have come to frame public policy debate today? *Thesis:* Human institutions and processes are culturally rooted, such that it is impossible to discern where one is and why certain options appear more plausible than others without knowing where one has been and why certain options (and certain ways of describing these options) seemed more plausible than others in the past.

Fourth, what should be the theoretical approach and research methodology? Is this a collection of empirical studies, analytical studies, conceptual studies, field studies, prescriptive studies? *Thesis:* Every type of research and every mode of scholarly inquiry can be understood as a tool of intellectual engagement – a governing instrument – and the choice of instrument cannot be fixed in advance by a metric that presumes a specified outcome.

Fifth, what are the sites of analysis? Is this a collection about processes and institutions? Or is it a collection about particular policy in defined fields? *Thesis:* Whether one seeks to understand the play of different policy instruments in different institutional settings (the state, the voluntary sector, the neighbourhood, the international community) or in different fields of endeavour (the environment, social welfare, consumer law, public health, education), the central question is how one stipulates the centripetal forces within these sites and locates the frontier between endogenous and exogenous variables.

Each of these questions (and their correlative thesis) is intimately connected to the others. Each would not have been posed in quite this manner at the outset of the project. Indeed, the initial letters that potential contributors received from the editors did not raise any of them in exactly this manner. Hence the fundamental epistemological point: What questions ultimately are raised, what disciplinary perspectives ultimately are engaged, what policy questions are put on the table for consideration cannot be decided in advance. The editors could not possibly have known what the title or the theme of the book would be until all the contributions had been received; nor could the editors have known how the various contributions could speak to each other or how they could be arranged in a table of contents until they were all submitted; and finally, the editors could not possibly have known what the lessons learned might be until the various disciplines, time frames, aims, modes, and sites were explored.

This, to my mind, is the most important feature and outcome of this collection. The process of imagining and realizing the work is a self-reflexive endeavour in which the enterprise of "instrument choice," "governance," and "policy formation" is pursued. So I conclude my reflections on the alternatives posed in the title to this subsection as follows. No discipline – be it law, political science, public administration, economics, sociology – has a monopoly on the vocabulary, concepts, and inquiries appropriate to studies of governance. Not only is their no Archimedean point outside disciplinary knowledge, but no discipline is entitled to claim ownership of the endeavour. If jurists are puzzled by the jargon of economics and political scientists, their task is to educate themselves; and the converse proposition is true as well. What is true of the various tools of governance is equally true of disciplinary perspectives.

## Instrument Choice and Governance

I turn now to my own contribution. Here, I should like to consider three main issues. What is the relationship of this contribution to the other contributions in the collection? What is the understanding of governance that underpins the analysis? What are the particular literature sets in law that can profitably inform discussions of governance? It should be apparent that this chapter lies at the frontiers of three fields of law and that it reaches across multiple literatures even within law. These I attempt to situate at the end of this preface.

Before embarking on this exercise, however, one point bears emphasis. As much as this chapter focuses on law and legal perspectives on instrument choice, it is also an examination of epistemology. The concern is not only to ask what the logic and limits of instrument-choice thinking in law might be, but also to ask what it means to frame inquiry into problems of governance in the language of "choice of governing instrument."

### INTELLECTUAL CONTEXTS
This chapter was conceived to address two presuppositions in the "instrument choice" literature that are, at best, dubious.

First, the standard account (whether in law, economics, political science, or sociology) is ahistorical. Scholars implicitly assume that the concerns at hand have always been expressed in the language of instrument choice. This chapter examines the broad sweep of public policy in liberal democracies over the past 150 years (with a focus on Canada since its Confederation in 1867). It aims to suggest that the conception one has of citizens and their capacities, of society and social differentiation, and of government (i.e., its role and place in society) shapes not only the policies one pursues, but also the means by which one pursues these policies and the vocabulary and conceptual structure by which the choices are described and characterized. "In-

strument choice" and "choice of governing instrument" are historically contingent terms for expressing these concerns.

I have chosen examples from Canada for a very simple reason. One
of my claims being that means cannot be divorced from ends, it follows
that one cannot adequately understand how choices about means are
made without grounding the question in particular contexts and particular times. Analytical tools and conceptual devices are culturally determined. It is simply inappropriate to assume that they can be projected
in some idealized form through time and space. Surely the lessons of
comparative law and colonialism are eloquent testimony to the point.

Second, the standard account of instrument choice rests on assumptions about the state that are strongly contested by non-mainstream
theorists in many intellectual domains – most notably, sociology, anthropology, and law. The post-1789 preoccupation with the state as
governing institution is beginning to subside. Nonstate actors and multilevel governance through overlapping legal and normative orders at
both the substate and suprastate levels are emerging as appropriate objects of study. As such, they and their processes, institutions, and actors
are being subjected to analysis through the lens of law in the same
manner as state instruments.

And there is a further point. Newer theoretical approaches reject the
primacy of the state as a governing institution; scholars in these traditions reject the phrases "nonstate," "substate," and "suprastate" as
describing the object of their investigations. These other normative and
regulatory sites are "informal" or "inchoate" alternatives to the state.
Indeed, the normative order of the state is simply one among many
regulatory sites. Hence to assume that the regulatory endeavours of the
state are qualitatively different from those of other sites of governance
is to misunderstand the special role of law as a process of social
ordering and to conflate the idea of law with one of its instantiations:
state law.

## A HYPOTHESIS OF GOVERNANCE

This chapter also adopts a particular understanding of governance. It
argues that governance is *the endeavour of identifying and managing
both aspiration and action in a manner that affirms and promotes human agency.* Let me make a number of observations about this understanding of governance.

To begin, no definition is true or false. The hypothesis of governance
that grounds this chapter derives from a particular philosophy of law,
and it is meant to foreground a particular set of questions. It is not, and
cannot, be true. More than this: Every author in this collection has at
least implicitly a working definition of what governance means.

There is a further point. The choice of a definition of governance is like the choice of governing instrument itself. Some definitions do some things better than others by highlighting some aspects of human experience better than others. To assume that there is one "best view" of governance is to assume that we can fix our goals in advance and in the abstract and that we can thus select our means to achieve those goals. In my view, it is the very divergence of conceptions of governance – contrast, for example, the views advanced in the chapters by Peters and Hoornbeeck, Toope and Rehaag, Trebilcock, and Webb – that make the central point about the inseverability of means and ends.

This said, I should like to set out the assumptions about human beings and their capacities that underlie the view of governance I take here, for these assumptions have clear policy implications. I assume that human beings are agents. Governance is not simply about telling them what to do. I assume that human beings are constantly discovering, pursuing, and modifying their ambitions and aspirations. Governance is not simply about telling human beings what their aims and aspirations should be. I assume that human beings act in concert with others in turning these ambitions into accomplishments. Governance is about providing facilities, processes, and institutions by which these common endeavours may be realized.

I acknowledge that this is an optimistic perspective. Others writing in this collection have a more pessimistic, even more deterministic, view of human beings. Many of them would have government act as concert master, organizing and orchestrating a range of policy instruments to frame the minutia of human action. It follows that the conception one adopts of what governance might mean is closely connected to the conception one has about what human beings are like and about what the project of the state entails. A definition of governance and its instruments cannot be decided in abstraction from an understanding of what goals one is seeking to achieve, and the goals one seeks to achieve cannot be decided in abstraction from the possibilities opened up by the range of instruments available for their achievement.

## LITERATURE SETS AS GOVERNING INSTRUMENTS

This chapter is obviously located in a specific disciplinary field: law. Consequently, its primary conceptual referents (and the literature that it typically cites) are those most familiar to jurists. But within law, the chapter sits at the intersection of three subfields: public and administrative law; legal-process thinking; and jurisprudence (or legal theory). I should, therefore, like to place these concepts and this literature in larger context. To do so properly, however, a caveat is in order.

As is the case with many disciplines familiar to faculties of arts, the universe of legal literature is highly fractured. Legal scholars in the US, for example, rarely read (let alone engage with) the domestic legal literature of other countries. For reasons relating to the general theory of "legal positivism" (about which I say more below) that pervades law faculties in Western democracies, conceptions of law and its concepts tend to be anchored in the politics of the nation state.

A primary consequence of this parochialism is that an international literature of law (as opposed to a literature of international law) has not really developed outside the domain of legal theory. A secondary consequence is that the conceptions of law that are held by scholars elsewhere in the academy (for example, in public administration, in political science, in economics) tend to be closely related to the perspectives of a national legal literature. In brief, the view that political scientists in the UK have of law is shaped by the dominant national legal literature of the UK., and so on. As it happens, some of the most catholic legal writing – incorporating ideas and theoretical approaches from France, Germany, the UK, and the US – is written and published in Canada. This inoculation from the curse of an exclusionary nationalistic legal literature has occurred, I believe, because of the coexistence of civil-law and common-law intellectual traditions.

Hence situating the literatures referred to in this chapter requires two developments. First, I try to identify and unpack the assumptions about law that are being contested in this chapter. Second, I attempt to locate some of the key sources referred to in the larger context of legal theory.

As to the first point, it is important to note that most non-North American legal thinking is grounded in the theory of legal positivism. On this view, law is nothing more than the explicit product of the political state and its institutions. Only the state makes law, and the paradigm form of law is legislation (or a code). Law is seen as a top-down projection of state authority, and there is a clear distinction between that which is law and that which is not law. Not surprisingly, public-choice theories in political-science and welfare-economics approaches implicitly adopt this state-centric conception of law.

"Legal positivism" is, however, more contested in North America, especially by scholars working in the "law and society" tradition. Non-state normative orders are conceived as legal systems; the enterprise of law is seen not as a top-down affair but as a joint project of law subject (in the state legal order, the citizen) and law maker (in the state legal order, Parliament), and the relationship between morals or values (the "ought") and legal rules (the "is") is seen as less sharp than in Europe. Broadly speaking, the "law and society" approach has been adopted in this chapter. As a consequence, many references and many assumptions about law will not necessarily be familiar to a European audience or even to an audience of economists and political scientists in North America. Of course, I should note that things are changing and that at least within "law and economics" circles a richer understanding of law – drawing on insights from sociology, psychology, and anthropology – is being advanced by scholars like Robert Ellickson and Eric Posner.[3]

My second point is to draw attention to developments in the legal literature that have largely escaped the notice of scholars in other disciplines. Indeed, I claim here that the concerns that burst onto the scene in the economics and political science literature only in the 1970s have been preoccupations in certain legal circles – largely by derivation from and elaboration upon the ideas of Max Weber and Talcott Parsons – since the Second World War.[4] For at least fifty years, a significant number of legal theorists have attempted to explore the forms and limits of different legal instruments and also to trace out the appropriate uses of institutions like legislation, adjudication, contract, voting, and so on. This tendency – the legal-process school – has not had much impact outside North America or outside the legal academy. It is a special burden of this chapter to show how "legal process" thinking of the type undertaken by Henry Hart and Albert Sacks in *The Legal Process: Basic Problems in the Making and Application of Law* (1958) has much to teach about problems of instrument choice.

Another literature set, again lasting about a half-century, can be described as the *eunomics* perspective on jurisprudence (or legal theory). Most legal philosophers follow the legal positivism of H.L.A. Hart or Hans Kelsen in elaborating their understanding of law.[5] This chapter takes as its organizing frame the work of Lon Fuller, a principal intellectual adversary of H.L.A. Hart. Fuller's major work is collected in a posthumous publication, *The Principles of Social Order* (1983), in which he carefully examines how different legal devices can be deployed to "subject human conduct to the governance of rules."[6]

So to conclude: This chapter draws its inspiration from two sets of legal literature not well known outside North America and not well known outside the legal academy. Yet these two literature sets are those that speak most eloquently to the themes and problems of governance addressed in this collection. It is a central goal of this chapter to introduce this literature (and its implications) to scholars in public administration and in economics and political science and also to legal scholars who have previously understood administrative law to embrace only the jurisdictional control of governmental activity by the courts. I believe that, more than any other frame of inquiry currently being pursued in the legal academy, these two perspectives reach across disciplinary boundaries, thereby challenging legal scholars to engage with the problems of instrument choice and governance that animate this collection.

## INTRODUCTION: SITUATING GOVERNANCE IN HISTORICAL CONTEXT

Governance is not simply about the instruments and tools of government. It is also about the substantive goals that states and other institutions pursue. For this reason, it is impossible to write about governance without anchoring the discussion in real problems experienced by real states at real moments in their histories. Given my own education and background, and in view of the context within which the conference occasioning this chapter was organized, I have quite naturally selected Canada as the primary empirical field in which to ground my comments. I have no doubt, however, that similar stories could be told about governance – about policy options and the means for their achievement – in other countries. Nonetheless, I leave it to the reader to make the necessary transpositions.

I should like to begin with a brief reflection on the idea of the polis. The polis (or political state) is not a natural necessity. The political state is a human creation. The modern, democratic, territorial political state is a relatively recent creation. The modern, democratic, territorial, social-welfare political state in its present form dates only from the middle of the twentieth century.

Of course, the polis has in some measure always been concerned with general issues of social welfare. Of course, the polis has always been territorial. Of course, the polis has always had elements of democratic enfranchisement. And, of course, while not a natural necessity, the polis has been a feature of human society almost from the moment human beings came to recognize the concept of society itself.

Modern political states sometimes claim their territorial and affective boundaries on the basis of language, culture, and ethnicity. Sometimes they claim boundaries for ideological reasons, such as "manifest destiny." Sometimes they do so for geographic and historical reasons and sometimes for economic reasons. None of these rationales has ever adequately explained Canada. Canada has been characterized as the "triumph of hope over experience."

This triumph has most assuredly been promoted by political institutions advancing political goals – in the guise of a governance agenda framed as a "national policy." Ever since the Rowell-Sirois Royal Commission of the 1930s, these governance concerns have actually been front and centre of policy debate in Canada.[7] This is not to say that matters of governance had not earlier been present in British North American politics. Twice previously there had been discrete national policies in Canada derived from the interweaving of a particular constellation of economic and social forces with political ideology. Specifically, the conflicts between Prime Ministers Sir John A. Macdonald and Alexander Mackenzie in the 1870s and 1880s about the first National Policy and about the building of the Pacific Railway were in large measure disagreements about the forms and limits of governance.[8] But there is something more intriguing about policy debate that explicitly frames itself as instrumental or technical and that is intensive rather than extensive.[9]

If the period from the 1940s through the 1980s was marked by a particular form of national policy known as "welfare-statism," one should recall that this was not unique to Canada. In this endeavour Canada was tracking developments (just as it tracked developments in the 1860s and 1870s) almost everywhere else in the North Atlantic world. Even in the United States, postwar welfare-statism existed, but it was primarily expressed through the indirect mechanism of massive defence spending by that country's federal government. Still the second National Policy in Canada, like policies pursued following the Beveridge Report in the UK or during the Fourth Republic in France, had substantive characteristics that privileged certain forms of government action, forms we recognize today in the epithet "the administrative state."

For the past fifty years, scholars in law and public administration have sought to understand the relationship between these substantive policies and the forms of government action they seem to call forth. Driven by the twin impulses of government programming to stave off the socialist threat[10] and the discovery by the US legal academy following Roosevelt's 1930s New Deal that practical politics could be theorized as expertise, the political ends pursued by democratic states have been taken as relatively unproblematic.[11] What is now known as the "legal process" approach to jurisprudence and legal theory was symptomatic of the idea that law could be cast as a mere instrument to be deployed to achieve predetermined social ends. The clarion call of the legal-process approach was to promote law as the enterprise of discovering and deploying processes of social ordering to promote ends accepted as valid by society.[12]

The architects of the process conception of law were professors at the Harvard Law School. For thirty years after the Second World War, one of these, Lon Fuller, pursued the idea of *eunomics*: the theory of "good and workable social arrangements."[13] In several essays – notably on contract, adjudication, mediation, custom, managerial direction, and legislation – he sought to explore the forms and limits, as well as the potential and perversions, of each of the key processes of social ordering found in democratic societies.[14] Fuller was not the only legal scholar at Harvard to puzzle about the principles and processes of social ordering. In 1958 Henry M. Hart and Albert Sacks published a set of teaching materials elaborating their belief that each legal institution – courts, legislatures, agencies – had a special competence for handling problems of social organization.[15] They argued that because institutional arrangements for the management of social tasks were not infinitely pliable, the task of the jurist was to ensure the appropriate allocation of tasks to these institutions in order to best achieve desired social purposes.[16]

Two decades later, driven by the challenge of the 1965 Civil Rights Act and by efficiency concerns arising from the "war on poverty," scholars of civil disputing at Harvard and elsewhere began to puzzle through problems of "access to justice" and institutional design. Their aim was to explore sites other than courts and modes other than adjudication for resolving conflict – that is, conciliation, negotiation, mediation, arbitration, etc. For enthusiasts of alternative dispute resolution (ADR), the central idea was that finding and deploying the right disputing process to manage conflict will inevitably produce socially preferred outcomes.[17]

In a similar vein, the criminal-law regime came under critical scrutiny. New procedural models, like "sentencing circles," and substantive conceptualizations, like "restorative justice," took their place beside traditional adversarial hearings and repressive sanctions.[18] At about the same time, public-law scholars took up the challenge of theorizing procedural fairness across a wide range of legal and social administrative settings.[19] Achieving effective and just governance in diverse agency processes and, more broadly, in diverse forms of business organization and diverse contexts of associational life emerged as a central concern of scholars in almost all public- and private-law domains.

This convergence of academic reconceptualizations of public regulatory law and the theoretical work on institutional design was paralleled in the late 1970s and early 1980s by a flourishing literature (inspired by "law and economics") that focused on the "choice of governing instrument."[20] In like manner, for thirty years students of public administration have been pursuing numerous new paradigms of governance as they puzzle over how best to organize collective action to address public problems.[21] More recently, this reflection has been reoriented and reinvigorated by the burgeoning set of institutions, procedures, and norms of international legal regulation.[22]

Yet this renewed interest in regulatory matters remains captured by the logic and the preoccupations of governance as developed during the period when countries were building the social-welfare state through intensive governmental programs.[23] Governments are still seeking to deploy traditional instruments in a universe increasingly constrained by globalization and new trade agreements and increasingly dominated by knowledge and intellectual property rather than by wealth in the form of tangibles (land and goods) and discrete services.

I shall add a final thought to this introduction. If there is to be a continuation of the national state as we have known it for 200 years, the animating logic will be found more in identity and symbol than in communications and transportation infrastructure (as in the late nineteenth century) or in social-welfare programs (as in the late twentieth century). To illustrate the point, I return to the Canadian example. If Canada is to survive as a "triumph of hope over experience," the programs needed to accomplish this will be found more in knowledge and culture – that is, in virtual citizens negotiating their way through multiple virtual communities of belief and belonging[24] – than in either renewed investment in communications and transportation infrastructure (the Information Superhighway, the twinning of the Trans-Canada Highway) or a reinvention of social-welfare programs (Medicare, pensions, millennium scholarships).

At the same time, human beings express their agency through their acts of self-governance and through their voluntary or coerced participation in governance structures that they share with others and that channel the occasions for exercising this human agency. Prescriptively, therefore, governance is taken to be the endeavour of identifying and managing both aspiration and action in a manner that affirms and promotes human agency. The shape and meaning of thinking about the "choice of governing instrument" as well as the mistakes to be avoided as Canada pursues this new symbolic state – its third National Policy – are the focus of this chapter.

## AN INSTRUMENT CHOICE RETROSPECTIVE (1977–2002): EFFICIENCY AND OTHER RECIPES

The above reflections bring me directly to the theme of "instrument choice." I begin with an obvious, but rarely expressly acknowledged, point. The whole idea of instrument choice is a historically contingent motif that reflects a certain conception of public policy. No one in the 1930s would have used such language to describe governmental actions of the previous half-century (in Canada, for example, the programs of Prime Ministers Macdonald, Sir Wilfrid Laurier, and Sir Robert Borden in pursuit of the first National Policy). By contrast, the expression does nicely capture the meaning and methods of welfare-statism.

The ideological challenge to welfare-statism (in Canada, the second national policy of the post-Second World War period) mounted by certain sectors of economic thinking beginning in the late 1970s had three key features. First, it was American, not indigenous to Canada. The colonization of Canadian universities in the 1960s figured prominently in legitimating the endeavour. Second, it was directed at particular forms of state building, not at state building as a political project itself. The role of government in creating national markets and the deployment of the state to sustain a capitalist economy were never targets of the "deregulatory agenda." Third, it presumed that there was a natural hierarchy of social-political values and a social-ordering process, within which welfare economics and markets stood on top. Efficiency became the trump value.

Reflection about "choice of governing instruments" as a particular, economically oriented subset of social-ordering theory may be periodized roughly into three time frames.[25] A first iteration (1977–85) – which is perhaps best reflected in the analysis set out in the important volume by Michael Trebilcock et al., *The Choice of Governing Instrument* (1982), on the one hand, and in several of the critical research studies published for the Macdonald Royal Commission on Canada's Economic Prospects,[26] on the other – was framed in terms of the meaning of regulation and the usefulness of an efficiency criterion in assessing different forms of governance.

During a second period (1988–95), these initial positions were developed and nuanced. The dimensions of legal scholarship during this period are best exemplified in the series of studies published in the *University of Toronto Law Journal* in 1990, prepared for the symposium "Law and Leviathan," sponsored by the Law Reform Commission of Canada. Much of the instrument-choice discussion at this conference focused on the idea of "smarter government" and the normative critique of such positions.[27] During this period the Canadian Institute for Advanced Research funded an interdisciplinary Law and Society Program that generated two collections of essays[28] meant to explore the legal challenges of contemporary regulatory management.

A third periodization (since 1995) may be understood as both more subtle and more overtly ideological in that its participants can recognize and articulate the theoretical underpinnings of positions being taken. Four central characteristics of this contemporary reflection are that (1) it purports to understand governance as a collaborative endeavour between state, citizen, and intermediaries; (2) it acknowledges that governance is not self-executing; (3) it recognizes that government often works best by indirection; and (4) it recognizes the large place that "social norms" play in effective regulatory governance.[29] Citizens, governments, and third-party intermediaries collaborate through different means, at different times, and in different sites to render democratically decided purposes into legitimated policy outcomes.[30]

It is the burden of this chapter's first part to provide a brief (intellectual?) history of "instrument choice" thinking, especially as this mode of thought engages fundamental concerns in legal theory and jurisprudence. My argument has two strands, the first being a claim that finds its origins in considerations about means. Here, I focus mostly on how legal theorists have understood the forms and limits of diverse processes of social ordering; my point is that "choice of governing instrument" rhetoric is at once an impoverished reflection of Hart and Sacks' "legal process" inquiries and an instrumentalized rendition of Fuller's *eunomics* insights.[31] The second strand is a claim that invokes ends. Only now, I believe, are theorists of government coming to see that the role of the state in creating and maintaining the conditions of citizenship through the development and application of public policy is contingent and that consequently the means available to pursue these goals are also contingent. Put otherwise, and again using Canada as the referent, only now are the substantive implications of Harold Innis and William Fowke's analyses of the second National Policy (that of the 1930s) being fully appreciated.[32] In developing the dialectic of means and ends in instrument-choice thinking, I rely on standard sources, using several superb texts, particularly by Michael Trebilcock, as touchstones.[33]

### First Thoughts (1977–85)

In retrospect, while trying to account for the pitfalls of historical revisionism, it would seem that the initial framing of "instrument choice" concerns involved a transposition of the jurisprudential insights of the "legal process" school about institutional design to the realm of public regulation. That is, the economic orientation seen in "instrument choice" literature is a rather late development in academic reflection about institutional design. That public administration and public-policy scholars were unaware of these earlier developments in legal theory says much about the way that a particular ideology of law had come to dominate other intellectual disciplines.[34] Whatever the cause, in the disciplinary transposition, three main ideas were engaged: (1) the relationship of means to ends in the elaboration of legal structures and institutions; (2) the meaning and scope of the regulatory-governance endeavour; and (3) the central purposes of regulation. Along all three of these dimensions, I believe, the "choice of governing instruments" perspective did not fully grasp the theoretical richness of the "principles of social ordering" thesis previously elaborated by legal scholars.

MEANS AND ENDS

From the beginning, it was acknowledged that means are inextricably bound with ends. This entails, contrary to early conceptions of instrument choice in the US administrative-law literature of the 1930s,[35] that there can never be, in any purely mechanical sense, a "best" regulatory instrument in any given situation. This is not an easy point for those bent on reform to grasp. Many of those who are proponents of alternative dispute resolution as an approach to organizing institutions of civil disputing adopt the slogan "make the forum fit the fuss."[36] But this is to misapprehend the extent to which the fuss is defined by the forum.[37] Social situations (including civil disputes) do not present themselves with ready-made labels.

The more elastic that ends are taken to be – that is, the more that they can be redefined and shaped – the less meaningful do rankings of instruments seem to become. Neither ends (the definition of the problem) nor means (the tool chosen to solve the problem) are necessary. A slight redefinition of either (i.e., reconceiving the problem or applying a different regulatory instrument) will change the rules of the game.[38]

This is the case because means shape the end, thereby making the end a moving target rather than simply a question of choosing the appropriate means for a given end. In describing his *eunomics* project, Fuller often spoke of "circles of interaction" between means and ends, holding that "a social end takes its 'character and colour' from the means by which it is realized."[39] More recently, even "law and economics scholars" have noted that goals are meaningless without institutions.[40]

THE SCOPE OF REGULATION

Initially, reflection on instrument choice was connected with two prior postulates about law. The first is that law is an official product of the political state as expressed in the rules (e.g., legislation, regulations, bylaws) and institutions (e.g., central agencies, administrative boards, regulatory tribunals) of government. The second is that regulation involves conscious policy intervention by imposing constraints upon markets. In other words, in this conception of things, problems of regulation or choice of governing instrument are centred on how the political sphere reacts to markets.

These postulates, of course, reflect a top-down paradigm, in which the entire process is an outgrowth of the state (whether the process is seen as a political one or as a working out of market forces). Of course, even in 1982 it was acknowledged that the model of political rationality does not fully capture what is at stake and that there is more behind choice of governing instrument than efficiency issues alone. Yet the paradigm persisted as a way of evaluating regulatory activity.[41]

By contrast, some critics of instrument-choice rhetoric contested both of these initial postulates. First of all, the problem of regulation was seen as much more broadly based, with a multiplicity of sites of governance, none necessarily privileged over the others.[42] Top-down views of regulation not only ignore a great deal of actual (although informal) regulatory behaviour, but also privilege and thus legitimate regulatory activity that looks like it is public action.

The second issue has to do with the modes of regulation. Regulation must be understood to embrace more than visible institutions. It includes tacit and implicit processes of social ordering, such as custom, practice, education, and "condign" power.[43] In this sense, once the regulatory endeavour is seen as a problem of social ordering, there is never any such thing as deregulation. Deregulation is simply the regulatory strategy chosen by the constructed markets of the "common law.". Like alternative dispute resolution, deregulation substitutes a different locus for the exercise of discretion and a different modality of social organization.

While "instrument choice" theorists today adopt a broader perspective and acknowledge public-private partnerships, franchises, operating agreements, product branding, and so on as regulatory strategies, they still have not abandoned the views that law is the product of the state and that all government regulation is an interference with a "naturally occurring market."

## Second Opinions (1988–95)

Following the initial conceptualization of the ambitions and strategies of "choice of governing instrument" analysis in the late 1970s and early 1980s, the next decade saw the development and nuancing of these positions. Again, two themes can be seen to have emerged in the literature. First, those who initially proposed instrument-choice analysis as a means of assessing state action solely on efficiency grounds began to incorporate into their perspectives the notion of public values. Second, the dynamic and shifting character of the policy process came to be recognized.

### PUBLIC VALUES AND GOVERNANCE

One of the catch phrases of the second generation of instrument-choice thinking was the notion of "smarter government," which holds that it is not enough to seek raw efficiency alone; rather, one must choose/design instruments in such a way that wider public values are promoted as well.[44] In this conception of the endeavour, economic incentives must be specifically deployed to promote these "community values" objectives. Efficiency still governs, but in certain cases a more costly alternative must be chosen in the name of higher good. The notion of "smarter government" thus responds to one of the initial critiques of instrument-choice analysis.

Here is a standard example of how public values can be accounted for within a "choice of governing instrument" framework. Private actors operating within markets may well optimize efficiency, but this can be deceiving because private actors are not subject to the same constraints as government – be these constraints imposed by obligations to human-rights and antidiscrimination, to bilingualism, to the promotion of cultural identity, and so on. As a consequence, there is a hidden community cost to privatization. During the late 1980s, the idea of public values as part of the regulatory calculus came to be a recurring theme, especially in the public-management literature.[45]

Yet once again, the attempt to recapture the problems with instrument-choice analysis by adopting a broader logic of efficiency missed the central challenge. Critics pointed out that this refinement nonetheless continued to rest on relatively controversial distinctions that legal scholars had essentially rejected. That is, even while some administrative law scholars continued to assert these dichotomies, in most other legal domains – property law, family law, contract law, tort law, criminal law, labour law, commercial law, corporate governance – they had been abandoned. Most notable among these contested dichotomies are the distinctions between state (i.e., public) and voluntary (i.e., private) associations; between law and politics; between legal rationality and political arbitrariness; between explicit (propositional) knowledge and tacit (inchoate) knowledge; and between external regulatory activity and internal agency management.[46]

## THE STRUCTURAL LOGIC OF THE POLICY PROCESS: WHERE LIES THE DEFAULT POSITION?

A second development in the literature flows from the recognition that all these factors interact and that they are changed in this interaction. A simple one-to-one mapping is not possible. Much of the literature on choice of governing instruments assumes that regulation is an activity that governments do for instrumental purposes. Law is perceived as a lever of action, its object being to change or control specific behaviour with prescriptions. On such a view, all social action is hypothesized as a market commodity. That is, the market metaphor is not deployed simply in relation to economic markets because the wealth that one seeks to maximize can embrace nonmonetary interests as well as money.

Once one adopts the market metaphor as a dominant logic, whatever content one gives to the market in question, the legitimate grounds for explicitly regulating human conduct are quite few. These could involve regulation to correct for market failures, regulation to ensure that a market can function according to its presumed postulates (for example, in the case of economic markets, providing for a stable currency, the enforcement of contracts, the protection of property, and so on), and possibly regulation to ensure that human beings have the capacity to function as market actors (for example, ensuring minimum levels of literacy and numeracy).[47] The problem is, of course, that once it is accepted that all human activity – from marriage, to reproduction, to religion – can be understood in terms of the market metaphor, then there is a second-order market for markets. At some point, it is necessary to make allocational decisions about which market shall predominate. Following the logic of instrument choice, one is driven to acknowledge not only that the very ideas of the state and government are just instruments, but also that there should be a market for government.

A contrasting response to the dynamic nature of the policy process is to adopt a contrasting default position. In recent memory the most sustained effort to extirpate the market from human interaction (and especially to extirpate the market from human economic interaction) was the failed project of Marxism. It is not necessary, however, to consign markets to the "dustbin of history" in order to combat the perverse consequences that flow from second-generation "instrument choice" thinking. Politics is meant to provide the forum by which collective decisions about the realm of markets are made, and regulatory governance is the vehicle by which these decisions are symbolized. In this conception, regulation (and deregulation) are not tools by which instrumental efficiency may be promoted over redistributional, social, or cultural goals; rather, regulatory governance is the symbolic construction of social solidarity through institutions recognizing and legitimating the identities by which people come to express who they are.

## Contemporary Trends (since 1995)

Over the past six years, as theorizing about neoliberalism and its impacts on the capacities of governments to govern has heightened, two other trends have emerged in the instrument-choice literature. It is now explicitly recognized that much in this field depends on one's perspective as either an optimist or a pessimist about the perfectibility of society. Moreover, all now see instrument choice and governance as dynamic.

## OPTIMISM VS PESSIMISM ABOUT
## HUMAN SELF-REGULATION

The question of regulatory governance can often be reduced to perspectives about the perfectibility of people and society: To what extent can (or should) people be trusted and left to their own devices? Conversely, to what extent should (or can) the state actively seek to manage the details of everyday life?

Many who explore "instrument choice" issues using the lens of public-choice theory have a moderately pessimistic view of human nature.[48] In the coauthored 1982 volume noted above, Michael Trebilcock also aligned himself with the pessimists, although in a 1990 essay with Prichard and Howse, Professor Trebilcock's position seems to have moderated.[49] Not surprisingly, therefore, in this most recent work, he arrives almost at a position of optimism on this score and thus assumes that indirect and third-party governance can be viable regulatory strategies.[50]

These perspectives translate into views about the capacity of people to conceive novel and self-directed solutions to social problems and to imagine the possibilities of social organization. Again, most "instrument choice" scholars adopt a "static pie" view of social life: Regulation is about distribution and redistribution of finite resources; as there is a closed class of instruments, each of which has associated costs, an "optimal" choice should be discoverable in any situation. By contrast, others who locate themselves as adherents to the "processes of social order" approach to governance believe that there is an almost infinite variety of instruments and social-ordering processes to choose from and that a more dynamic view of choice is called for: The end depends on how one chooses to get there, and how one chooses to get there depends on the end one has selected.[51]

## INSTRUMENT CHOICE AND GOVERNANCE AS DYNAMIC

Viewing governance as dynamic raises two lines of inquiry. The first leads to an exploration of the continuity of law and social life. The second emphasizes the importance of feedback loops in regulatory governance.

The modern literature of legal pluralism presents the strongest theoretical challenge to "instrument choice" thinking, for it hypothesizes the various modes and sites of regulatory governance as mutually constitutive and interdependent.[52] Consider the following. If one posits a particular governmental policy as deregulation, this is to assume that the primary site of regulation of human activity is the state and its instruments. Modern legal scholarship reverses this perspective. The state is a choice that people make as to the instrument they seek to deploy in their everyday regulatory endeavours. There is no disjuncture between law and social life nor between "legally binding" instruments (associated by public-choice theorists with the state alone) and other instruments that are believed not to have coercive outcomes. There is, in other words, no best or most efficient instrument that can be posited without taking into account the values promoted or advanced by the site of normative activity under consideration.[53]

As for feedback loops, the point is equally important. Many modern assessments from the field of public administration seek to define tools and to describe patterns of their use, how each tool is selected, and the management challenges inherent in each tool.[54] The idea that the choice of instrument is a path-dependent outcome of lexically ordered steps has been abandoned in favour of a dialogic model even by many law and economics scholars who work in the public-choice paradigm.[55] As far as I can discern, no theory of instrument choice today rests on the assumption that instruments do not shape ends and that certain ends cannot be pursued with certain instruments. Similarly, no choice of governing-instrument theory today presumes that the metric of evaluation can be applied along a single dimension – whether of efficiency or of other predetermined single ends.

### Back to the Future?

It is generally acknowledged that the first iterations of the "choice of governing instrument" thesis were ideologically loaded. Less accepted is the idea that the more nuanced, second-generation "choice of governing instrument" discourse in the late 1980s and early 1990s was also grounded in ideological considerations. Consider the position of those who expressed skepticism, even in regard to the moderate, thoughtful positions taken by Michael Trebilcock et al. in 1982. These critics focused on two core ideas.

First, they argued that deregulation was a misleading descriptor for a new regulation that was neither democratic (or enfranchising) nor just. The ideological point they advanced was that the state was not the enemy of citizens. Even though efficiency was acknowledged as only one of a number of intermediate ends that governments pursue, critics noted the persistence of the assumption that ends could be fixed in advance without regard to means. Second, they pointed out that a complex, modern society is shot through with multiple modes and sites of regulatory governance, generated by citizens themselves in their day-to-day interactions. The hyper-positivism of instrument-choice theory's focus on the state as the regulator of social action was seen as misguided. The role of the state was not to act as the top-down director of all manner of human action. Rather, the state was meant to facilitate the just achievement of individual and collective purposes in a manner that enhances human agency.

These are still live issues. Even though the "deregulatory and privatization" critique is now somewhat attenuated, the logic of "governing instruments" persists. So, for example, scholars today are being asked to consider governance in the globalized world order; and to focus on how governments can deploy their policy instruments more effectively in coopting private-sector actors into partnerships, joint ventures, and third-party governance strategies in order to recognize both social and economic interests; and to reflect on how better risk management in state action can be engendered.

To restate the central point of this intellectual history, it is the very logic of instrument-choice thinking that is problematic – rather than any particular outcomes that it may or may not mandate. To talk the language of "choice of governing instruments" is to talk the language of a divorce of means and ends, to reduce governance to mere instrumentalism, and to forget that society generates the state and not the other way around. Instrument-choice language simply begs a question to which I return in the conclusion to this chapter: Instrumental to what?

## A GOVERNANCE PROSPECTIVE (SINCE 2002): PLURAL MODES AND MULTIPLE SITES

In this part, I shall attempt to further the debates of the past two decades about instrument choice and the lessons of the past half-century about processes of social ordering through an extended allegory. I invite you to consider the Swiss Army Knife as an instantiation of the logic of plural modes and multiple sites of governance. In the discussion that follows, I develop at greater length nineteen theses about governance. For the moment I briefly note three general ideas.

Most importantly, we should remember that however much a Swiss Army Knife is an instrument or tool (or more accurately, an assemblage of instruments and tools), it is also more than that. The gadgets of the knife are hypotheses of action; they presuppose their own uses. They are also hypotheses about what human acts are valuable enough to warrant a tool; they lexically order the way in which human actions are judged. And they are hypotheses about the relationship between aspiration and action as mediated by human structures and institutions.

In addition, I want to note that the idea of the traditional Swiss Army Knife – whether made by Wenger or by Victorinox – does not exhaust the possibilities. For cognoscenti there is a "new kid on the block": a device made by the Leatherman Tool Group. The configuration of instruments at any given time is politically contingent. The very structure and labelling of tools – and our decision to call a Swiss Army Knife a knife (rather than a tool) or to call a kirpan a dangerous weapon rather than a ceremonial dagger – is not a decision about what an instrument is. It is a decision about ends and purposes.

Finally, a Swiss Army Knife is not idiot proof. As I note in the last thesis, there is a ghost in the machine. A human being. No amount of instruction, no amount of education in use, no amount of supervisory control can ever prevent a person intent on doing harm with a Swiss Army Knife from accomplishing his or her objectives.

## "Tool" Is Both a Noun and a Verb – a Means and an End

The central question of all institutional design, whether implicit or explicit, is *how are we to understand the relationship of means to ends in imagining and developing human institutions and processes of social ordering?* This question is necessarily prior to any reflection on "instrument choice" simply because the instruments wielded by the state are secondary. The initial means-ends question, deeply rooted in political theory, is "why the state?"

### THE STATE IS ALSO A TOOL

The political state is only one instrument, one institution among many, that people choose to let manage their lives in common. The state does not precede social life; nor does it precede law. Unless we begin with a metaphor of multiplicity, we cannot understand the range of options open to us in the governance of everyday life, let alone in the governance of the state and ultimately in the governance of the world.

The multiplicity metaphor does not imagine the state as primary, as the institution charged not only with making governance decisions, but also with allocating governance decisions among other actors. It is a perspective that sees the possibility of other social institutions – families, neighbourhoods, religious organizations, socio-ethnic groups, unions, cooperatives, communities of interest – also being primary normative sites.

The multiplicity metaphor also does not imagine the choice of governing instrument to be the direct consequence of goals being pursued. If contract is an instrument (a means), it is also an end (a consequence of a conception of human beings and human society); if delegated self-regulation (e.g., of a profession or of agricultural producers) is an instrument (a means), it is also an end (a consequence of a conception of local democratic decision-making).

THE SWISS ARMY KNIFE IS NOT JUST A TOOL
The allegory of the Swiss Army Knife frames the initial governance
consideration in two hypotheses:

1 I have to do X. Which tool (gadget, implement, instrument, device)
  on my Swiss Army Knife should I use?
2 I have a Swiss Army Knife. What can I do with it?

Question 1 initially appears to involve no more than finding an appropriate means to an end; the end is clear, but there are several means
available to achieve it. Viewed in this light, we can immediately see
how the end constrains the choice of means. Even if a Swiss Army
Knife were to have every conceivable gadget known to human society,
some of these would not be appropriate to the task at hand. If you are
seeking to whittle a block of wood into a toy boat, the corkscrew or
the reamer will likely be of little use.

Nonetheless, ends themselves are rarely given. Whatever you may
have wished to achieve in setting out to make a wooden toy boat, constraints on time, changes of desire, or discovering new possibilities of
action in the very act of construction may lead to an entirely different
appreciation of the possibilities for the corkscrew, the reamer, or the
can-opener. For example, a chance examination of a partially whittled
boat may suggest that a more satisfying project would be to carve a
beaver. In this endeavour, the corkscrew and the reamer may well reveal hidden utilities.

Question 2 initially appears to involve no more than finding an appropriate end attainable by the means available; the end is indetermi-
nate. It might well be possible to formulate a simple, generic end (for
example, whittling things), but there are also many other ends (even generic ends) possible with the tool in hand. Here, the means constrain
the choice of ends. With the typical Swiss Army Knife, you can fix your
eyeglasses, make a kite, whittle a toy boat, or carve a wooden beaver,
but you cannot change your sparkplugs, lever boulders out of a road,
or build a basement stud-wall.

Yet again, means are also rarely given in an unalterable form. Sometimes we can imagine a novel possibility for a gadget that presents itself
under a known or conventional label. Despite their names, the "hook
disgorger" or the "fish scaler" may turn out to be ideal woodworking
implements for roughing up the block in order to replicate the texture
of a beaver pelt. Sometimes a recasting of ends (or breaking them down
into smaller or intermediate ends) opens up possibilities for deployment of gadgets to accomplish previously unimaginable goals. No tool
on a Swiss Army Knife looks immediately helpful for constructing a

stud-wall. But when the task is described as ensuring that the wall is perfectly vertical, the key ring suddenly presents itself as an indispensable component of a plumb bob if the weight of the knife itself is being used to serve that end.

## The Swiss Army Knife of Governance

The company Victorinox manufactures several models of what it calls the "Original Swiss Army Knife," the largest of which – (the Swiss Champ) has thirty-four features (gadgets) and the most modest of which – (the Soldier) has twelve. (It may be noted in passing that even in the realm of the Swiss Army Knife, there is relatively little esteem visited upon the Soldier. On the other hand, as yet there is no top-of-the-line Swiss Diplomat model. Even in knife design, semiotic considerations go well beyond technology and gadget counting.) In most of the reflections below I have used the model name of a Victorinox Swiss Army Knife to identify a specific governance thesis.

### THE VICTORINOX SWISS CHAMP: TOO MANY TOOLS

"I want to immortalize my girlfriend and me by carving our initials in this tree. Should I use the large knife blade, the small knife blade, the reamer, or the corkscrew?"

*Problem:* Faced with a simple job, several tools (or perhaps several ways to use the same tool) might accomplish the job. There is not necessarily a best tool in a given situation. A variety of implements on the knife will work, some better than others, but there is no single tool designed specifically for this use. Moreover, different users might have preferences for one or the other tool, and these preferences might not be what the knife designer considers to be the best choice.

A related problem is that people's preferences might blind them to a more effective choice. A person might naturally think that the knife is the best choice. However, given the way the Swiss Army Knife folds, a knife tends to close unexpectedly when used to carve in trees, so the reamer or the corkscrew, which open perpendicular to the body of the knife, might work better to scratch in the writing (particularly if the tree has particularly rough or thick bark).

*Governance:* There is no best response to a given problem, particularly as the precise limitations of a given response cannot be known until it is implemented. Likewise, atavisms and deep ruts in our thinking tend to match particular obvious responses to particular problems (e.g., more police or stiffer penalties in response to a crime wave), when other less obvious solutions might actually prove to be more effective.

In particular, responses that seem to be politically necessary (e.g., the antiterrorism legislation in Bill C-36) may be the path of least resistance but are seldom the most effective since they tend to deal with the visible symptoms rather than the underlying disease.

### THE VICTORINOX HANDYMAN: OVERINCLUSIVENESS

"I just want a knife. Can't I get a model without all that other stuff?"

*Problem:* A multipurpose tool is, by design, very flexible, but flexibility may or may not be a relevant criterion for users. There are two aspects to this issue. First, you don't always know what you will need, so it doesn't make sense to limit yourself at the outset by rejecting all the other available implements. Second, if all you really want is a knife blade, you don't need to buy a Swiss Army Knife at all – look instead at other kinds of knives, such as pocketknives, penknives, or hunting knives. Although the Swiss Army Knife is flexible and highly varied, sometimes a different knife altogether is called for, whether a laguiole, a bayonet, or a stiletto, depending on whether you are planning to eat a steak, go to war, or mug people in an alley.

*Governance:* Conceptualizing the problem at the outset is important, and if there is a defined and specific end in mind, crafting the response to deal with that end is important. However, conceptualization in this way is a narrowing process, and there is a danger of closing off useful directions by designing a response solely for a particular end currently in view. Moreover, when governing through delegations, providing an *ex ante* menu of precise instruments rather than a general power may overly constrain the delegate.

### THE VICTORINOX MOUNTAINEER: WRONG TOOL

"My car broke down, and all I have is this lousy Swiss Army Knife!"

*Problem:* For certain jobs, a particular tool will be of no help at all. Sometimes it just won't work, and you've got to call someone else. In some cases the problem is the wrong tool for the job, but in other cases the problem is the wrong person. If you don't know how to fix a car, it doesn't matter whether you have a Swiss Army Knife or a full mechanic's set of tools.

*Governance:* Some problems are beyond the capabilities of the solution proposed. In such cases, an effective solution probably will involve both deploying a larger variety of tools as well as bringing in a different actor. For example, the problem of illegal drug use requires more than a quick-fix amendment to the Criminal Code or extra funding for police patrols. Government may not be the best actor to solve all aspects of this problem.

### THE VICTORINOX CLIMBER:
### INTENDED USE, UNFORESEEN PROBLEMS

"I tried to use the can-opener to open a tin of beans, and it slipped and cut my hand."

*Problem:* collateral damage from a poorly designed tool (or from using a less-than-optimal tool). Although a tool may be designed for a particular purpose, other design compromises can limit its effectiveness. The can-opener is designed not just to open cans, but also to fit into a small space, so can-opening tends to be somewhat awkward. Notice that this is not a problem of the user's lack of sufficient knowledge or adequate skill. Even when competence can be presumed, the tool itself carries the risk of unintended consequences. This is inherent in the separation of means and ends, for all means ultimately change ends. To put it most strongly, the more effective the means, the more radically will it have long-term implications in how we conceptualize our social ends.

*Governance:* Even when deployed within their design specifications, some regulatory solutions can have unforeseen negative consequences. Regulation is an interaction between the situation and the solution; thus the peculiarities of the situation can force the solution to behave in strange and unpredictable ways.

### THE VICTORINOX CAMPER:
### CREATIVE USE, UNFORESEEN PROBLEMS

"I tried to use the screwdriver to pry open a paint can, and it snapped off."

*Problem:* Sometime the actual use is beyond the capacity of the tool. Not all imagined uses of a tool are possible, given the tool's design limitations. A Swiss Army Knife needs to be small, and each implement needs to fold neatly into the casing. This limits the size, the shape, and the number of implements that are possible, and these design limitations limit the uses to which the implements can be put.

*Governance:* Regulatory solutions are not infinitely flexible, and efficiency and other problems can arise if a solution is asked to do too much. Some would say that the Criminal Code and the Income Tax Act are both already groaning under the weight of the multiple policy objectives that they are being asked to serve.

### THE VICTORINOX RANGER: DESIGN REDUNDANCIES

"Why are there always two knife blades, when they're not all that different in size?"

*Problem:* Remnants of vestigial uses can clutter an otherwise efficient tool. The large blade is generally seen as a multipurpose blade and is close to the length of the knife casing. The small blade began life as (and is still sometimes called) a penknife even though no one needs to trim pen nibs anymore. Given the small size of the Swiss Army Knife, the difference in size between the two blades is not great, so there is a large degree of overlap between the functions of these two blades. Yet design redundancies can produce novel approaches to use. I well recall that my father always kept his little blade razor sharp and only used it for what were (in his mind) well-defined purposes. The big blade was the all-purpose knife, good for cutting anything (and even spreading peanut butter).

*Governance:* Since explicit, legislative law reform tends to be incremental rather than revolutionary, new initiatives are constrained by the vestiges of existing regimes. Radical changes make legislators uncomfortable and often lead to outrage among citizens who are used to dealing with the familiar and who thus see innovation as a threat to stability. However, leaving these vestiges in place increases the possibility of duplication, which can lead to ambiguity and inefficiency, on the one hand, or to a further specification of more particular purposes, on the other.

## THE VICTORINOX TIMEKEEPER: SPECIFIC-USE TOOLS
"Thirty-two gadgets, and it still doesn't have the one I need!"

*Problem:* Greater specificity of intended use tends to cut off creative rethinking of uses. The smaller knives have a minimum of tools, although imaginative users can adapt them to a wide variety of uses. The larger knives have lots of specific-use tools (e.g., hook disgorgers, magnifying glasses, cigar cutters), suggesting a single use for each (although imaginative users can still find other uses even for specific-purpose implements). Moreover, when you get into highly specialized tools, might you not be better off getting the real thing? Is the hook disgorger on the Swiss Champ going to work well enough (and be used often enough) to warrant the extra thickness of the knife?

*Governance:* Microregulation tends to sell people short by denying the creative role that citizens can have in solving their own problems. Specific regulations (of the "do this, don't do that" variety) tend to promote a culture of legalism, in which rules are seen as rigid and inflexible, with the boundary between "law" and "not-law" (or "yes" and "no") roughly coterminous with the statute book rather than with people's moral intuition or common sense. Furthermore, excessive detail tends to make for unwieldy and unworkable regulation. It is worth comparing, in this respect, the general propositions of a classic civil code (e.g., the Code Napoléon and the Burgerlichesgesetzbuch) with the detailed quasi-regulatory provisions of the new Civil Code of Quebec.

THE VICTORINOX EXPLORER: DESIGN TRADE-OFFS
"Should I bring my Swiss Army Knife on the canoe trip or my tool-box?"

*Problem:* There are inevitable trade-offs in tool design, sometimes driven by use and sometimes by functionality. The knife does many things adequately and is both compact and lightweight. The toolbox does many things well but is a compendium of full-sized implements and is heavy. It also likely has many things in it that are completely unnecessary for any conceivable canoe trip (e.g., plumbing tools and an electrical circuit tester). A corded power drill with a full set of bits works much better than the reamer on a Swiss Army Knife but is useless in the bush. On a canoe trip, the Swiss Army Knife is a better choice. To assemble a bicycle, a toolbox is what you need.

*Governance:* The criterion used to evaluate a regulatory solution is important, and the criterion is closely related to the ends sought. The more complex the ends, the more difficult it is to weigh up alternatives. So, for example, a multifaceted program of criminal sanctions, public education, subsidies for mass transit, tax incentives, regulatory permits, and so on may be overkill if all you want to do is create no parking zones in front of schools.

THE VICTORINOX SOLDIER: CULTURAL LIMITS
"Why doesn't the US army carry Swiss Army Knives?"

*Problem:* Cultural factors influence the design of tools, their use, their nonuse, and even their characterization. Sometimes these cultural reasons are directly tied to images of the instrument in question. A kirpan is, and is not, a knife; a kirpan is not, and is, a weapon. Sometimes cultural reasons influencing the choice of an instrument or the manner of its deployment have little or nothing to do with the central characteristics or standard uses of the thing in question. In the abstract, both chopsticks and a fork are equally effective at conveying food to the mouth, although for cultural reasons the implement that one does not usually deploy is, at least initially, hard to use.

*Governance:* A Canadian-style health-care regime (regardless of the economic and administrative facts) raises the spectre of "socialized medicine" and is therefore unlikely to be adopted in the United States given its hostility toward anything smacking of socialism. So, too, the creation of Crown corporations. Yet the number and scope of "government-owned enterprises" in the US, especially on the periphery of the military, is substantial. Whatever these operations may be or do, they cannot be conceived as governmental business corporations. Another impact of cultural factors can be seen in the financing of university education and especially in the trade-offs between *ex post* tax-subsidized alumni donation programs and tax-subsidized *ex ante* tuition charges. Cultural predispositions limit at the outset the possible range or character of regulatory solutions available.

### THE VICTORINOX ANGLER: PRECONCEPTIONS OF USE

"Why does the Swiss Army Knife have a corkscrew? I never bring bottles of wine on my camping trips."

*Problem:* Preconceived notions of tool use, whether arising from labelling or prior experience, can limit flexibility in deployment. The point is both general and specific. To someone who remembers Swiss Army Knives only from boy-scout (or summer-camp) days, it may be hard to reconceptualize them as a handy household tool. More specifically, sometimes our preconceived notions of what something is used for can narrow the field of possible uses. The knife is useful in many situations other than camping, situations in which a corkscrew may well come in handy. Also, some people do bring corked (as opposed to decanted) wine on camping trips. This fact illustrates the converse of the idea that we can often (usually) find other uses for tools than the obvious ones. In some situations, our preconceptions about a tool's intended use actually prevent us from seeing other possible uses or other possible situations in which the tool might be used. The corkscrew is a key development in the modern pocketknife, for it shows us that ends are not simply servants of the means we employ but develop interactively and through a system of feedback loops. Camping as a cultural practice developed in response to many factors, which are not meaningfully limited by the range of tools in a Swiss Army Knife. That the knife has integrated a corkscrew suggests how the knife reflects changed social practices since corked wine would hardly have been the drink of choice of those who were initially the target consumer audience of the Swiss Army Knife.

*Governance:* Like anything else, regulation tends to follow well-worn paths. Criminal sanctions tend to be used for certain kinds of problems, tax incentives for others, deregulation for others, and so on. Sometimes a creative solution requires shifting categories.

### THE VICTORINOX SPARTAN:
### PRIMARY VS SECONDARY CHARACTERISTICS

"Should I buy my Swiss Army Knife in red plastic or in brushed aluminum?"

*Problem:* Decision making based on primary versus secondary characteristics tends to deflect from intelligent judgment. There are primary (essential) characteristics with which to judge tools (e.g., strength, durability, design) and secondary (external) characteristics that are often less important, like price and brand name. To judge solely based on one criterion to the exclusion of others is foolish. At the same time, however, with all other things being equal, there may be a reason to judge according to secondary as well as primary characteristics. Of course, in the very description of a characteristic as primary or secondary lies an important evaluative judgment: A feature is one or the other depending on why one is choosing the implement in question (e.g., actually using the knife on a canoe trip vs trying to impress other members of the trip).

*Governance:* Is efficiency an essential or a secondary characteristic of regulatory solutions? There will always be numerous criteria with which to judge a solution: efficiency, effectiveness, raw cost, political popularity, availability of trained personnel to implement it, etc. Determining which criteria are essential and which are secondary depends on the end sought. If the end is pure bang for the buck, then perhaps efficiency is essential. If the end is saving lives in emergency rooms, or getting the homeless permanently off the streets, then perhaps not.

THE VICTORINOX HUNTSMAN:
RELATIONS BETWEEN USES
"I used the hook disgorger on my Swiss Champ during my last fishing trip, and now there are fish guts all over the whole knife!"

*Problem:* A particular use can for various reasons negate or compromise other uses. Tools or practices pick up cultural meaning, which can in some situations close off certain uses to certain groups. One is probably not going to use one's Swiss Army Knife on a picnic to cut the brie after having used it to gut and scale fish the weekend before. Indeed, it is unlikely that one would ever use a Swiss Army Knife to cut brie (as opposed to cheddar) even on a camping trip.

*Governance:* A particular regulatory strategy might be effective and efficient but unpalatable to certain groups for other reasons. Sex education in schools, for example, can be effective in reducing unwanted pregnancies, but some religious or social groups may feel that moral reasoning should always trump public-health considerations. In any situation, finding the regulatory register is a precondition to imagining the entire range of possible regulatory responses. Often it is impossible to change registers (cutting brie) once patterns have been established (gutting fish). The inability of governments to deal intelligently with drugs as a matter of governance, economics, or public health flows directly from the "moral panic" campaigns of the 1930s that set a regulatory framework in the language of morality.

## THE VICTORINOX SWISS CHAMP
## OR THE WENGER HIGHLANDER: POLITICAL IDEOLOGY
"Should I buy one of the Victorinox or one of the Wenger models?"

*Problem:* Often we make choices for reasons external to all considerations of regulatory efficiency. The history of the Swiss Army Knife is instructive. In 1886 the Swiss Army decided to equip every soldier with a regulation knife. In the Swiss government's typical neutral fashion, contracts were issued for their Swiss Army Knives to both the Wenger steelworks, in the French-speaking Jura region, and to the Victorinox company, in the German-speaking Canton of Schwyz.[56] They are the exclusive producers of the Swiss Army Knife. By gentlemen's agreement, Wenger is proclaimed as the manufacturers of the "Genuine" Swiss Army Knife, and Victorinox uses "Original" Swiss Army Knife as its advertising tag line. While the designs of the knives are largely similar, there are many more models in the Victorinox catalogue, and the Wenger knives all seem to have only one blade, while Victorinox knives generally have two.

*Governance:* In all governance matters, ideology looms large. Sometimes this is merely labelling and can be traced to small-scale partisan ideology. One wonders, for example, whether the new Law Commission of Canada would have been reconstituted as the Law Reform Commission (to directly emphasize the policy disagreement with the previous government that abolished the agency) if there had not been another political party on the scene bearing the name "Reform." Frequently, ideological symbolism is more substantive. How much federal policy directed to the choice of governing instruments is shaped by the consideration that some forms of instrument – departmental management, departmental corporation, Crown corporation, land ownership, direct subsidy by cheque rather than by tax deduction (or even by electronic funds transfer) – make it easier to display the Canadian flag? And sometimes the ideology is fundamentally substantive. Only ideological zealots would privatize corporations that were initially created for ideological reasons (e.g., Ontario Hydro and Hydro Québec).

## THE WENGER CIGAR – CUTTER
## IN BRUSHED STAINLESS STEEL:
## ADMINISTRATIVE COST-BENEFIT ANALYSIS
"I wish they'd dispense with most of these gadgets and just produce an easy-to-use Swiss Ranger."

*Problem:* A number of gadgets on advanced models require a high degree of sophistication in order to be deployed properly and often demand a good sense of the purposes for which each tool was initially designed. Achieving this knowledge and sophistication may not be worth the time required to do so if the task at hand can be accomplished relatively effectively with another simpler instrument.

*Governance:* A particular governing instrument may require a regulatory infrastructure that is simply not justified given the purposes of the policy being advanced. One of the primary disadvantages of tort litigation as a regulatory strategy is the transaction costs associated with bringing a lawsuit. Especially where the idea is to shift a large number of small losses onto wrongdoers who are hard to identify, costs can be disproportionate. Even with procedural streamlining through class actions and with market-share liability presumptions, litigation may be cost-ineffective. A similar problem arises in respect of mass adjudications. While a full civil trial may result in a minor redistribution from some beneficiaries (who get too much) to others (who are short-changed), administrative compensation schemes (whether or not combined with no-fault regimes) can be administered far more cheaply than civil trials – resulting in a greater percentage of the total budgetary envelope actually finding its way into the hands of intended beneficiaries.

## THE WENGER TRAVELLER: DEPLOYMENT DIFFICULTY
"I read the instructions, and I just can't figure out how to make this darn thing work."

*Problem:* Every implement requires a certain knowledge and physical capacity in order to be used effectively. More than this, every implement requires a degree of judgment and maturity by users in order to avoid dangerous misdeployment. Of course, these difficulties decrease or multiply in proportion to the number of gadgets. But they are present even in the simplest devices. Some more complex Swiss Army Knives are inappropriate in the hands of an eight year old but generally safe in the hands of a teenager. Some more complex models have devices, like a wire stripper, hook disgorger, metal saw, and chisel, that require education for effective use. And no Swiss Army Knife is safe in the hands of anyone who thinks it can be used to pry a stuck plug out of a live electrical circuit.

*Governance:* A particular governing instrument may be appropriate in the hands of certain users or when deployed against a certain regulatory clientele but inappropriate in other circumstances. For example, the powers of arrest granted to peace officers under the Criminal Code and various police acts should not be given to security guards and private police forces. Or again, it is not clear that a regime of self-prescription or automatic renewals is optimal for potent medicines. This is especially the case where the regulatory targets (in this instance, the delegated power holder is the individual citizen, and the regulatory targets are licensed pharmacists) have the means and the desire to provide a check on those vested with self-regulatory authority.

THE WENGER PATRIOT:
THE POSSIBLE BECOMES THE NECESSARY
"Just hold on a second till I get my Swiss Army Knife awl; that's how we can unravel and retie the granny knot."

*Problem:* The great number of gadgets designed to achieve a wide range of purposes suggests the necessity of the Swiss Army Knife for whatever tasks it claims to be capable of performing. That is, the proliferation of implements invites people to look to the knife first to solve an issue rather than simply deploying other easily available mechanism – like fingers – to undertake a task. New uses come with each new implement. Need to rewire a lamp? – add a wirecutter. Need to tighten nuts? – add an adjustable crescent wrench. Need to repair tents or sails? – add a curved upholsterer's needle. And so on. These tools individually may be decent enough at their appointed tasks, but the knife as a whole gets so unwieldy that it becomes harder and harder to use it at all (consider, for example, the Income Tax Act). Finally, sometimes the "most appropriate" special-purpose gadget is more dangerous than it looks or than is necessary.

*Governance:* The extraordinary police powers of arrest without warrant granted by Bill C-36 have two immediate dangers. The first is that they implicitly suggest that regular police powers are not ever sufficient to deal with "suspected terrorism." That is, because these powers exist, they must be necessary and they must be deployed. Second, the proliferation of special-purpose tools destroys the reflection and judgment that are necessary in choosing between instruments or in choosing not to use a particular instrument. Rather than the holders of regulatory power asking themselves what kind of situation they confront, and how it should be managed, they now take the characterization of a particular situation (e.g., terrorism) that gives them the particular instrument they have deemed to be most efficient.

THE WENGER STANDARD ISSUE:
IF IT IS TOO COMPLEX IT WILL BE USED
FOR SOMETHING ELSE
"You know this thirty-four-gadget thing is just the perfect paperweight. Looks nice and is just the right size."

*Problem:* Almost any conceivable usage can be accommodated within the basic design of the Swiss Army Knife if the knife is simply made thicker and/or bigger each time. (There is a photo in old editions of the *Guinness Book of World Records* of the world-record pocketknife, which was about three feet high and bristling with blades like a porcupine.) One of the most popular Swiss Army Knife models is the Standard Issue. Interestingly, it appears that almost no Standard Issue models are given as gifts, whereas they are the largest selling model for personal purchase. It also appears that many of the Swiss Army Knives with lots of gadgets that are given as gifts are rarely used but languish on office desks or in dresser drawers as keepsakes. The remarkable success of the Nokia-brand cellphone is further confirmation of the virtue of simplicity.

*Governance:* Highly sophisticated regulatory analysis leads governments to create highly sophisticated regulatory instruments. This is especially the case in respect of "standards" regulation in drugs, food, toxic substances, and so on. But most often, in everyday social intercourse people do not think of orienting their conduct by reference to such a vast range of implements with highly specialized uses. Primary regulatory targets do respond to regulatory instruments that are tailor made to their concerns. The realm of tax deductions, credits, and rebates given to employers can often lead to micromanaged economic change. It is far less clear that the average taxpayer deploys them. The same is true of the detailed requirements for the storage and disposal of toxic chemicals. This is why the packaging and sale of such chemicals in quantities likely to be fully used in a first application is such an attractive regulatory strategy for the ordinary public.

### THE WENGER ESQUIRE: MULTIPLE REGULATORY SITES

"I had selected the knife I wanted from the brochure, but then I discovered that another company makes an almost identical product for a cheaper price."

*Problem:* Altogether Victorinox has about twenty models and Wenger has nine. But Wenger also has thirteen submodels of its Esquire model. Choosing the "absolutely right" model can, in the manner of constructing a meal from a genuine Chinese-food menu or a Caribbean vacation from among the array of tour and charter possibilities on the market, involve a considerable investment of time. At some point, the reality of choice becomes submerged in the paralysis of decision. There is, of course, another more important difficulty. There happens to be another company – the Leatherman Tool Group[57] – that makes a similar product to that of Victorinox and Wenger. Indeed, Leatherman enthusiasts claim that its implement far exceeds the Swiss Army Knife in practicality. No matter how one defines the relevant universe of choice, a slight recasting of the issue, usually by emphasizing functionality rather than "essential characteristics," opens an infinitely greater range of possibilities.

*Governance:* Typically, governance has been understood to be the affair of government. On such a view, the primary competition for governance (at least in federations) lies between the central and the provincial (or state) governments. This can cause considerable difficulty when different instruments are deployed. Whatever limitations may lie on governments when requesting legislatures to enact statutes, similar limitations do not apply when it comes to these governments' spending power. Moreover, while some constitutional limitations are still present in respect of taxation, to all intents and purposes both the provinces and the federal government can tax whatever of their residents they choose and in whatever manner. Still, some forms of regulation, especially when delegated to the private sector, may run afoul of constitutional limits. Can provinces create civil-status regimes in parallel to the federal regime of marriage? Could the Parliament of Canada create a Crown corporation to distribute alcohol and drugs? Functionality raises regulatory issues both in connection with the capacity of any government to legislate on such a basis and especially given the laundry list approach of Sections 91 and 92 of the Constitution Act 1867, whether certain regulatory instruments are constitutionally located in one jurisdiction or another. It also points to the possibility of multiple, overlapping sites of regulation, only some of which are under the direct management of the state. Whatever the Swiss government may do in splitting its concession between Victorinox and Wenger and whatever arrangements these companies may come to about dividing markets, attributing trade names, and sharing patents, none of these governance strategies will have any direct regulatory effect on the Leatherman Tool Group.

THE WENGER MINI-GRIP: THE GHOST IN THE MACHINE
"Can you believe it. You give a guy a Swiss Army Knife and he becomes a tire slasher."

*Problem:* No amount of instruction, no amount of education in use, no amount of supervisory control can ever prevent a person intent on doing harm with a Swiss Army Knife from accomplishing his or her objectives. There are few artefacts of modern society that cannot be deployed for nefarious purposes. A Swiss Army Knife is meant to facilitate the accomplishment of many human purposes, but slashing tires is not one of them – unless an abusive drunk is about to get into a car and drive off through a crowded sector of a city, or a robber inside a bank intends to use the car as an escape vehicle, and so on. Even acts that seem in one light to be morally beyond the contemplation of the implement designer, may in some cases be benign. But this is the exception.

*Governance:* As a matter of governance, certain tools enhance the agency of the user more than others; certain delegations formally escape obligatory governmental collateral norms. So for example, a privatized service will not necessarily fall under public-sector employment-equity guidelines, nor be required to respect federal policy on bilingualism, nor follow procurement norms of the federal contractor's program, nor follow basic labour standards of the delegating government. One presumes – in the same manner that one presumes owners of Swiss Army Knives will not become tire slashers – that the regulatory form will not undermine collateral regulatory objectives. Still, short of keeping the delegates of regulatory authority on short leashes (and even then, with no guarantee of success), agency-enhancing regulatory choices have typically had the effect of enhancing collateral policy risks.

## CONCLUSION:
## THE GOVERNANCE OF HUMAN AGENCY

I should now like to return to my primary substantive point – a point foreshadowed in the chapter's introduction. As much as it is worth contemplating the means by which we render public aspiration into accomplishment, it is even more important to be talking about what kind of society and state (or in Canada, what kind of national policy) we wish to achieve, what conception of human beings such an achievement presupposes, and what kinds of social, economic, and political institutions are most coherent with this vision of society and state.

It is certainly not my objective here to describe what type of society and state people should want in general. I am not even competent to answer an even narrower question: What should a third national policy for Canada look like? Nonetheless, on the basis of the considerations raised in the two core parts of this chapter, I do feel able to suggest what might be its general outlines. After doing so, I will raise four governance issues that I believe are at least as important as the subjects explicitly addressed in the final chapters of this collection – namely, the welfare state, the environment, occupational health and safety, and consumer protection.

The key feature of governance for the twenty-first century (and by implication the key feature of a new national policy for Canada) is to put citizens into the centre of the policy debate. As I have argued elsewhere, citizens are not merely law-abiding; they are law-creating.[58] What we have experienced as "identity politics" is nothing short of the claim that personal identity is an iterative endeavour between structures and agents, not the creation of structures alone. The invention of "international human rights" (in Canada, the equivalent being the

Charter of Rights and Freedoms) is important less for the impoverished and instrumental "rights discourse" that it promotes as a substitute for politics than for the symbolic aspiration to a "common humanity" (in Canada, Charter patriotism) that it has induced.

We should remember that the Swiss Army Knife was created to put a weapon or instrument in the hands of citizen-soldiers. The Swiss government asked: What equipment does the citizen-soldier need? Today democratic governments (in Canada and elsewhere) need to ask: What equipment and what resources does the citizen-regulator need?

This said, let me now turn to the central issues of governance that should be preoccupying scholars and policy analysts right now. The three I have selected are meant to highlight three themes that shape how identity is symbolically constructed in contemporary liberal democracies. I had initially included a fourth, equally as important – namely, foreign aid – but have left that aside in order to focus on domestic policy.

The first issue is the way we symbolize and seek to regulate "illegal" drugs. Today we treat this as a moral question to be decided by the criminal law. Surprisingly, just over a century ago (at the time when the Canadian government was elaborating its first National Policy and European states were promoting communications and transportation infrastructures) many Western democracies took a similar position on alcohol, gambling, and the sex trade. Today the first two of these are practically government monopolies. Might we not then ask whether there are not other ways of characterizing the consumption of recreational drugs? As a public health problem? As a problem of regulatory governance (like alcohol and gambling)? As a problem of resource expenditure? As a problem of corrupting citizens by forcing them into intercourse with organized crime? Even prior to thinking through these questions as a matter of instrument choice, we need to ask how we wish to symbolize drugs: Choosing between morality, health, and public-expenditure paradigms directly affects the range of instruments we see as plausible for achieving our regulatory purposes.

The second issue is the way we symbolize and seek to define close personal relationships of high affect. If the state should take an interest in the physical, emotional, and economic wellbeing of all citizens, why does it frame the introduction of significant social policy on same-sex unions as being dependent on its first defining marriage? Are not high-affect relationships of whatever sort equally important in terms of policy outcomes? More than this, on what basis should traditional moral prohibitions on who can marry (notably, but not exclusively, the opposite-sex requirement) be carried forward into the regulatory regime of the state? Aren't these definitional limitations best left to other sites of governance, such as religion? Again, even prior to thinking through the governance of marriage as a matter of instrument choice, we need to ask how to characterize the relationship that it ostensibly regulates.

The third issue is the way we understand the present "other" as a matter of history and policy. This issue arises for most countries in the domain of immigration and citizenship policy. On what basis do we decide who is to be "included" in our moral community? In most of the Americas and other white colonial states, such as Australia and New Zealand, there is a further dimension of "exclusion" that must be addressed. On what basis do we continue to think about aboriginal peoples as "wards of the state"? The lessons of the "residential schools" in Canada and the "stolen children" in Australia are not lessons about residential schools and aboriginal adoption. They are lessons about identity, agency, and community. Might it not be time to move beyond choosing the appropriate "governing instrument" as a vehicle of continued colonization?

The brilliant social historian, Carl Becker, famously claimed that the *philosophes* were not the heralds of the Enlightenment (as had usually been claimed in historical analyses) but were rather the last defenders of the Renaissance.[59] Those who speak the language of "instrument choice" are the *philosophes* of the welfare state. They now talk of increased social regulation as defining the new millennium. In fact, however, a failure to acknowledge the substantive foundations of the state to be imagined in the twenty-first century (i.e., to consider, in the case of Canada, what its new, and third, National Policy might be) means that they are simply "saving the appearances" of the past paradigm.

Much legal scholarship of the past quarter-century has focused on instrumental considerations – for example, how best to achieve compliance, or how to reduce the burden of government without losing policy control, or how to enhance regulatory efficiency by promoting so-called "smarter" government. Academic and policy reflection was so strongly influenced by "law and economics" analysis that issues of governance were conceived to involve little more than the selection of the optimally efficient "governing instrument" or "regulatory tool." While the idea of "governing instrument" does suggest the need for law in order to render public policy into prescriptions and programs, in this conception of the governance endeavour, there is an in-built presumption against certain forms of state action. This presumption was usually expressed in slogans like "deregulation," "privatization," and "smaller government" that imagine the possibility of a prepolitical societal *arcadia* where human beings and markets can operate free of the constraints of misguided, inefficient, redistributive "policy intervention."

Today, however, a broader understanding of the entailments of governance through law in a liberal democracy is emerging. Governance through law is a process of reciprocal construction of social interaction through which lawmaker and citizen constantly adjust their expectations of each other. At its margins, governance through law – especially in the form of the criminal law – involves establishing constraints on pathological action so as to make human agency possible. At its core, however, governance through law – whether in the form of rules of property, contracts and civil obligations, or processes of everyday administrative and regulatory law – involves creating mechanisms and incentives for largely self-directed human action. Descriptively, governance has been taken to be the iterative endeavour of identifying goals and objectives, designing policies, selecting processes and instruments, deciding upon particular programs, targeting sites and systems, and identifying actors by and through which human aspirations and actions may be rendered into achievements and accomplishments.

This said, the governance issue confronting governments today is how law and legal institutions should be deployed to achieve the symbolic governance of human agency in a manner that facilitates the just achievement of individual and collective human purposes. At the same time, human beings express their agency through their acts of self-governance and through their voluntary or coerced participation in governance structures that they share with others and that channel the occasions for exercising this human agency. Prescriptively, therefore, governance is taken to be the endeavour of identifying and managing both aspiration and action in a manner that affirms and promotes human agency.

# 10

# Sustainable Governance in the Twenty-First Century: Moving beyond Instrument Choice[1]

KERNAGHAN WEBB

## INTRODUCTION

The position taken in this chapter is that there is considerable value in moving beyond narrow investigations of which policy instrument governments should use to more broad and nuanced inquiries into how a range of societal actors can organize themselves to address problems of mutual concern. By changing the focus of inquiry in this manner, it is possible to more directly address some of the new realities of governing in the twenty-first century. These "new realities," which will be more fully explored in the body of the chapter, include:

- Factors that highlight some of the limits of the state, such as the increasing significance of international influences beyond the control of national and subnational governments, the continuous calls on government for "no new taxes," industry pressure to minimize regulatory burden and thereby enhance capacity to compete, and the rise in importance of technological issues
- Recognition that actors other than the state have both an interest in and a capacity to carry out governing functions, be they industry associations, nongovernmental organizations (NGOs), communities, or individual citizens.

To recognize some of the limits of the state and the importance of nonstate actors is not to suggest that state institutions will not remain the central actor in public policy or that conventional instruments of governing will not remain of central importance. But it is to suggest that governments can and should work more systematically with others to develop and implement sustainable approaches to governing – that is, governance approaches that, because they integrally involve other actors, have the potential to be more robust, responsive, efficient, effective, and flexible than conventional, state-imposed regulatory approaches. In the use of a diverse, multivariable approach to governing, the failure of any one approach does not necessarily mean an overall implementation failure but rather that another actor, instrument, institution, or process is in a position to "pick up the slack" or otherwise act as a check and balance concerning a particular behaviour. Illustrations of how this approach works in practice are provided later in the chapter, using the consumer- and environmental-protection contexts as examples.

In the sense that sustainable governance involves a combination of governmental and nongovernmental institutions, processes, instruments, and actors, it entails much more than simply a question of instrument choice. It also entails much more than a question of intelligent use of command-and-control regulations and financial-incentive instruments (although, clearly, intelligent use of such conventional approaches must remain an important preoccupation for governments).

Sustainable governance is a concept that attempts to recognize and draw on the largely untapped potential of the private sector, the third (voluntary) sector, and individual citizens to assist in governing in the public interest. It is a more collaborative and systematic approach to governing that focuses on developing – and putting in place the conditions for the development of – innovative institutions, instruments, and processes for use by a range of actors, often working in partnership with each other.

Although collaboration is a common feature of sustainable governance, so too is a certain amount of "creative tension," such as where one institution is established to act as a watchdog over the actions of others, or where industry and nongovernmental-association certification programs openly compete in the marketplace for public approval and customer buy-in, or where processes are created that facilitate the ability of citizens to challenge the actions of others. Thus sustainable governance recognizes and attempts to harness the value of both collaboration as well as rivalrous check-and-balance initiatives. As the examples of innovative approaches provided in the body of the chapter suggest, it would appear that many jurisdictions are "groping" their way toward more sustainable governance approaches but are not doing so consciously or systematically, with the result that the thinking and practice of policy implementation are not as advanced as they could be.

The objective of this chapter is to sketch out in a preliminary manner some key aspects of the sustainable-governance landscape. First, a brief description of some of the realities of governing in the twenty-first century is provided. Then an exploration of the concept of sustainable governance is undertaken. Following this, an examination of some of the key building blocks of sustainable governance is provided. Examples of government, private-sector, and third-sector institutional, rule-instrument, and process innovations are set out. Next, two Canadian policy contexts (consumer and environmental protection) in which a nascent sustainable-governance approach may be at play are described. The value of systematic as opposed to spontaneous approaches to governance innovation is explored. The corporate social responsibility phenomenon, and its relation to sustainable governance, is examined. The role of civil society in sustainable governance is discussed. Some caveats concerning the sustainable-governance concept are set out. Then conclusions are provided.

### Learning from our Mistakes: The Realities of Governing in the Twenty-First Century

There will always be breakdowns in public-policy implementation that can be characterized as the result of instrument-choice or public-policy "failures." It is difficult to extract a common theme or explanation underlying such varied public-policy breakdowns as the tragedies of the Walkerton water contamination and Westray mine collapse, the depletion of the East Coast cod-fishery stocks, the blood-contamination disasters in several jurisdictions, the outbreak of mad cow disease in the United Kingdom and Canada, or the Enron/WorldCom meltdown. The explanations are as diverse as the policy contexts within which such tragedies occur.

Typically, bodies that undertake inquiries into why these failures have occurred conclude by calling for more funding, more staff, more training, more inspections, more enforcement actions, higher standards, new laws, and more education and awareness. The sad fact is that there will rarely if ever be enough financial resources or inspectors available, enforcement actions undertaken, or sufficiently high standards in place to fully and properly address a given public-policy problem. Governments can't have an inspector on every street corner and in every establishment and operation. Enforcement agencies can't take every transgression to court. Governments will rarely have enough resources to do anything more than maintain minimally acceptable levels of implementation and enforcement. At the same time as the public wants rigorous and efficient administration and enforcement, they also want their taxes reduced. Moreover, they want a growing economy, which entails creating an environment that is attractive to businesses and business investment. Businesses want streamlined regulations that are not burdensome and that will give them a competitive advantage over, or a level playing field compared with, those operating in other jurisdictions. Political willpower for particular programs will vary from government to government and minister to minister; public interest in issues will wax and wane; and budgets and staff will increase and be cut back.[2]

As if these "realities of governing" in the twenty-first century weren't enough, they are joined by a host of other difficult challenges:

- Roller-coaster economies; the only thing of apparent certainty is that economies will rise and fall in ways that are not expected
- A growing but unpredictable influence of international factors (e.g., wars, terrorism, environmental problems, viruses, stock-market booms and crashes) on domestic affairs
- Strong economic interdependence, facilitated by trade agreements, which, in addition to increasing the influence of trade-partner economic developments on home jurisdictions, puts pressure on trade partners participating in the agreements to develop compatible regulatory approaches
- Alarmingly low levels of public trust in democratic institutions (matched by very low trust levels in corporations, particularly multinational corporations)[3]
- The introduction of new technologies at a rapid pace, with difficult-to-predict effects (e.g., reproductive technologies, genetically modified organisms, advances in telecommunications and computers); governments are struggling to maintain the knowledge/expertise base needed to keep abreast of technological developments that, on the one hand, offer the prospect of new opportunities and benefits for society and business while, on the other, possessing the potential to create significant problems
- A considerably more devolved, decentralized, and fragmented federal-provincial-municipal governing context than was in operation prior to the 1990s.

In short, the task of developing and implementing effective public-policy responses has become exceedingly challenging in the twenty-first century. We need to acknowledge the topsy-turvy, less-than-perfect world in which public policy takes place and devise approaches that operate effectively in these suboptimal conditions. In important ways, conventional command-and-control regulatory approaches are not well

suited to operate in conditions of wildly fluctuating budgets and priorities, and they are hard to adjust in midstream in order to address new
challenges. To put it another way, the "first-generation," resource-
intensive, top-down, state-centred approaches to regulation that were
largely put in place from the 1960s through the 1990s are particularly
vulnerable to failure in the conditions described above.[4]

The position taken here is that attention needs to be focused on devising public-policy approaches that are capable of effective operation
in the imperfect, difficult, and challenging circumstances we now face.
The suggestion being made is that multivariate, multiparty governance
approaches have a better likelihood of success in such choppy waters
because they harness the energies and experience of multiple parties
and perspectives and are therefore likely to be more robust, flexible, responsive, efficient, and effective. In a word, they are more likely be
*sustainable* in today's operating environment.

### Sustainable Governance:
### An Approach to Governing for the Twenty-First Century

The starting point for understanding how to respond to the realities of
governing in the twenty-first century is acknowledging that, while the
state has certain significant advantages in terms of governing when
compared with nonstate actors,[5] it doesn't have a monopoly on effective, efficient, and responsive governance approaches[6] – whether they
entail institutions, instruments, or processes.[7] Sustainable governance
recognizes and draws on the largely untapped potential of the private
sector, the third (voluntary) sector, and individual citizens to assist in
governing. As the examples discussed later in the chapter suggest, typically these nonstate actors are not eager to participate in governing out
of the goodness of their hearts. In the case of the private sector, their
motivations often revolve around maintaining or enhancing market
share. They are discovering that it can make good business sense to appropriately and expeditiously anticipate and address consumer, worker,
environmental, and community concerns through a variety of different
institutional, rule-instrument, and process innovations. In the case of
nongovernmental organizations, their interest in assuming governing
functions through certification programs, ombuds-schemes, and monitoring programs seems to stem from a lack of faith in government's
ability to perform these functions properly. In the case of individual
citizens or consumers, their motivations for challenging government
and private-sector actions or for boycotting certain companies may
also be largely ones of self-interest. Nevertheless, this motley array of
self-interested[8] nonstate actors can bring energies, perspectives, and

resources to the governance table that the state alone cannot bring to bear. In this sense, even if their motivations for addressing particular issues may differ, the private sector, NGOs, citizens, and consumers have in certain cases demonstrated a willingness to devise or support solutions in areas of mutual concern – solutions that have broad, public benefits. As noted above, sustainable governance puts emphasis on increased collaboration among actors[9] but also values a certain amount of creative tension among actors through the creation and support of rivalrous check-and-balance[10] techniques.[11]

Governance is a concept that, while not new, has recently gained prominence.[12] It represents a different and potentially promising way of looking at how we order ourselves. Governance has been defined as "the sum of the many ways individuals and institutions, public and private, manage their common affairs."[13] By involving the full range of public-sector, private, and civil-society organizations as well as citizens in public-interest governing,[14] the responsibilities, costs, and learning can be shared, and the ability to respond to new challenges or changing circumstances can be enhanced. Moreover, because these approaches characteristically involve more than one actor and often all three (government, industry, and civil society), they are likely to be more robust from the viewpoint of withstanding economic and fiscal downturns and shifting priorities.[15] It is for this reason that the governance strategy described here earns the name *sustainable* governance.

In the sense that sustainable governance is premised on the understanding that others than simply the state are capable of and willing to take on governing responsibilities, the concept of sustainable governance resonates in important respects, at the level of theory, with some of the work of Michel Foucault (in particular, his broad conception of government and governmentality) and Jürgen Habermas (in particular, his notion of "juridification").[16] For Foucault and those who have elaborated on his ideas, the concepts of government and governmentality are not limited to activities of the state and instead refer more generally to how entities (individuals and others) place themselves under the management, guidance, or control of others or seek to place others under their own sway. Looked at in this way, law is simply one of many forms of governance, and nonstate bodies – including the individual and entities between the individual and the state, such as the family, the community, industry associations, and NGOs – are all capable of creating or being subject to nonstate governance techniques. According to some writers who have explored Foucault's ideas, the notion of governmentality, when considered in light of modern liberal fixations with the proper limits of the state, generates an inclination to locate responsibility in actors other than the state. This phenomenon – referred to as "responsibilization" – takes place when actors accept and internalize an obligation.

The writings of Habermas are centrally concerned with the tendencies of law to engage in processes of "colonization of the life-world" (what he calls "juridification"), whereby informal means of structuring relations and activity are increasingly replaced by more formal, law-like approaches. While juridification can be positive, such as when notions of justice are imported into the resolution of disputes, it can also lead to increased bureaucratization and complexity, by which the individual is ultimately rendered less capable of protecting his or her own interests.

There appears to be implicit recognition in these interpretations of Foucault and Habermas that there are limits to the capability of the state and of the law and that, in view of these limits, there is a space for coexisting and sometimes competing forms of governance, including alternatives to law (this coexistence or competition has been referred to as "legal pluralism"). In light of these potential limitations, there also appears to be some acknowledgement that restraint in the use of law may be useful in some circumstances, as would be the development of legal approaches that increase the self-regulatory capacity of nonstate actors (this has been referred to as "reflexive law"). Building on the work of Habermas, Gunther Teubner describes the emerging strategy as follows: "The task of the law then is still to control power abuses, but the central problem becomes rather to design institutional mechanisms that mutually increase the power of members and leadership in private institutions."[17]

It is perhaps self-evident that there are potential dangers associated with devising systems and approaches that acknowledge or encourage nonstate actors to take on governance responsibilities and to internalize public-interest-oriented obligations. For example, there is the potential for the state to abdicate its legitimate responsibilities in favour of private bodies that are less accountable, transparent, and democratic. However, as discussed below, the notion of sustainable governance should in no way be understood as a call for or support of the idea of the state withdrawing from its legitimate governing responsibilities or as support for development of subpar governance approaches by nonstate parties. Rather, sustainable governance is based on recognition that bodies other than the state can take on certain governance responsibilities in a coordinated, accountable way that supplements the governance activities of the state. It is also based on recognition of the limitations of the state's conventional governance mechanisms. Sustainable governance is a structured and systematic approach to state and nonstate governing activities working in tandem, in the public interest, and in an accountable, transparent manner.

As noted above, an enhanced role for nonstate actors and approaches in no way takes away from the fact that, in most circumstances, conventional public-sector institutions, rule instruments, and processes of governing – approaches involving democratically elected legislative bodies, the courts, administrative tribunals, and government departments and agencies devoted to the administration of the justice system and to the implementation of regulatory regimes and other programs – will and should remain the central and most powerful components of governance in the public interest. Indeed, they are the formative foundation of such governance.[18]

However, an enhanced role for nonstate actors and approaches does suggest that conventional public-sector approaches, like all approaches, do have their share of weaknesses. Thus, for example, the processes of law development and administration and of court adjudication are slow, expensive, and formal and therefore difficult to adjust to changing circumstances.[19] Moreover, bureaucratic, centralized, "top-down" approaches to governing do not necessarily capture the full range of energies and actors that are available and could be harnessed in support of public-interest objectives. For these reasons, overreliance on conventional command-and-control regulations enforced by government departments and agencies can be problematic, leaving society vulnerable and not as effectively governed as it could otherwise be.

In light of these limitations, there is a space created for other institutions, rule instruments, and processes that can to some extent counter some of the weaknesses of the conventional approaches.[20] This is not to maintain that these nonstate approaches are without limitations. For example, industry and NGO-led approaches often experience difficulties addressing free riders (i.e., those who choose not to participate in a program) and have lower visibility and often lower credibility than public-sector approaches. There is also the possibility of less rigorous standards being developed and applied than those that would emerge from a conventional regulation-development process; there is often variable public accountability; and there is the potential for conflicts with regulatory approaches.[21] Some of these limitations of industry- and NGO-led approaches may be rectified or minimized through innovations introduced by the state.[22] In recognition of this sort of experience, it is maintained that the best approach to governing in the twenty-first century is a combination of conventional and innovative institutions, rule instruments, and processes that plays to the strengths of each while attempting to minimize and counter their weaknesses.

## THE BUILDING BLOCKS
## OF SUSTAINABLE GOVERNANCE

Institutional, rule-instrument, and process innovations are the three key building blocks of sustainable governance. Each of these is briefly described below, and examples are provided.

### Sustainable Governance: Institutional Innovations

INSTITUTIONS DEFINED

For the purposes of this chapter, institutions are organizational structures of government, industry, and nongovernmental organizations that carry out particular governance functions having an observable public-interest dimension. Innovative institutions take on such forms as public-sector, industry, or NGO ombudsmen, councils, associations, commissions, or commissioners. These institutions perform such functions as monitoring and reporting on the implementation of rule regimes, investigating and reporting on possible enforcement problems, and dispute resolution. They rely on drivers such as citizen-triggered petitioning powers, consumer complaints, peer pressure, and public opprobrium, and they typically operate against a backdrop of conventional state-based institutions, rule instruments, and processes.

INNOVATIVE GOVERNMENT INSTITUTIONS

Examples of innovative government institutions include the Ontario Commissioner for the Environment; the Commission for Environmental Cooperation (CEC), established as part of the North American Free Trade Agreement (NAFTA); and the federal Commissioner of the Environment and Sustainable Development, established as an offshoot of the Auditor General of Canada.[23] In the early 1990s, in apparent recognition of the need for some form of check and balance on its line ministries responsible for environmental protection (most notably, the Ministry of Environment and the Ministry of Natural Resources), the Government of Ontario established the Ontario Commissioner for the Environment. Among other things, the Commissioner oversees the administration of an online registry concerning environmental decisions and draft decisions of Ontario-government offices, which is accessible to all members of the public. In addition, citizens of Ontario are given the power to request an investigation or response concerning any potentially problematic environmental behaviour, and the Commissioner oversees and publishes the responses of the responsible ministries. The request for investigation and response provision has been used extensively by Ontario citizens and has led to enforcement actions being undertaken by government ministries. The Commissioner annually tables a published report (including the petitions and responses) in the Legislative Assembly. Arguably, the existence of such a check-and-balance institution, and the associated processes for citizen petitions, can act as a form of "distant early warning" device that may decrease the likelihood of environmental disasters such as that of Walkerton happening in the future. Under NAFTA a similar petitioning process is available for Canadian, American, and Mexican citizens concerned with possible instances of inadequate federal enforcement in any of the three jurisdictions (through the NAFTA CEC). More recently, the federal Commissioner of the Environment and Sustainable Development has also established a similar citizen-petitioning process. In the final analysis, these "watchdog" institutions have the power only to publicize and potentially shame parties into action; nevertheless, the information revealed through their activities can alert parties to problems and lead to regime improvements. It is noteworthy that citizen use of these institutions has been modest and responsible.

Another example of a government-led institutional innovation is the Ontario regulated-industry self-management model.[24] In the case of motor-vehicle sales, funeral sales, travel agents, and the safety of elevators, amusement devices, and pressure boilers, the Ontario Ministry of Consumer and Business Services has authorized through statutes and regulations the development of industry self-management councils, which are responsible for inspection and enforcement of rules pertaining to the industry sectors. Funding for the industry self-management is provided through fees from industry. The self-management councils include government and consumer/public-interest representatives. The councils are each accountable to the Ministry of Consumer and Business Services. Similar self-management approaches have been put in place in Alberta. Available evidence suggests that compliance rates have improved since the self-management councils were put in place, although there is potential for accountability and control problems now that considerable power and expertise have been "downloaded" to nonstate councils.

INDUSTRY INSTITUTIONAL INNOVATIONS

An example of a private-sector institutional innovation is the Canadian Banking Ombudsman[25] and its new partner organization, the Financial Services Ombudsnetwork. An elaborate banking-ombudsman system operates in Canada to resolve small-business and consumer complaints. It is entirely funded by industry, and it operates without any legislative basis. Consumer representatives sit on its board. Recently, it has evolved into a broader Financial Services Ombudsnetwork involving other financial

institutions. It, too, is entirely funded by industry. Because it is voluntary
and nongovernmental, the ombudsnetwork can operate in a seamless
way and cannot be tripped up by federal-provincial regulatory and jurisdictional issues. Although lacking a legislative foundation, the banking
ombudsman was developed "in the shadow of the law" in the sense that
the financial industry recognized that if they did not act, government
would impose a regime upon them. Government retains the authority to
put in place a regulatory response and will likely exercise this authority if
and when it concludes that the industry approach is not working. The
same can be said about the ombudsnetwork: It operates as a voluntary
network unless and until there is a reason for a regulatory response. That
the financial-services industry has chosen to "step up to the plate" and
provide a nonregulatory response and that federal and provincial governments have essentially allowed the financial sector to demonstrate its
capability to take on these functions instead of immediately developing a
conventional, government-funded and government-implemented regulatory response is evidence on both sides of sustainable-governance
thinking.

NGO INSTITUTIONAL INNOVATIONS
An example of an NGO institutional innovation is Oxfam Australia's
Mining Ombudsman.[26] In the 1990s the Australian Mining Council
(the Australian mining-industry association) developed a voluntary
code concerning environmental-management practices for its members,
to be applied to mining operations both in Australia and abroad. Community Aid Abroad (CAA), the Australian branch of Oxfam, a nongovernmental human-rights organization, had been critical of the code
from its introduction on a number of grounds, including its failure to
address possible human-rights aspects of Australian mining companies
operating in developing countries and its failure to put in place a dispute-resolution process open to communities that have concerns with
respect to the operation of mines. CAA decided to create the Mining
Ombudsman, which individuals and communities can turn to when
they have complaints regarding Australian mines. The Ombudsman
conducts fact-finding missions concerning complaints and then takes
well-founded complaints to the mining operators. Several mine companies have responded favourably to the actions of the Ombudsman,
leading to structured dialogues with affected communities and rectifi-
cation of certain issues.

An example of a community-based NGO institutional innovation is
the Riverkeepers organization.[27] Both Canadian and American communities have created Riverkeepers organizations, with the objective of
monitoring the quality of rivers in their respective areas and promoting

good practices. As community-based organizations, these entities work with the multiple governmental authorities and jurisdictions that are frequently involved in water quality (and the Riverkeepers are not impeded by the jurisdictional problems that may hamper governmental activity). Riverkeepers also work with local industries and individuals to develop best practices and to remove administrative impediments.

### Sustainable Governance: Rule-Instrument Innovations

Rule instruments are stipulations of objective criteria that are designed to influence or control behaviour and that allow for evaluation of whether an entity or an activity is or is not in compliance with the criteria. Innovative rule instruments include such techniques as performance- or results-based regulations, financial incentives based on performance to agreed-upon standards, procurement contracts premised on compliance with stipulated public-interest criteria, voluntary codes, good-neighbour agreements, accords, memoranda of understanding, and standards developed through the formal-standards system. Typically, these rule instruments harness community, market, NGO, and peer pressure to a much greater extent than do conventional rule instruments, although they also draw on conventional legal instruments, institutions, processes, and pressures.

GOVERNMENT RULE-INSTRUMENT INNOVATIONS
One example of an innovative government rule instrument is the new federal law to protect personal information.[28] In the early 1990s, as budgets and staff within government departments were being systematically cut back, there was little appetite for new consumer legislation of any kind in Canada. In recognition of this public mood, as well as of industry resistance to a new law, the federal Department of Industry (Industry Canada) spearheaded efforts to develop a market-driven voluntary code, not a law, pertaining to personal-information protection, involving other government departments and agencies from both the federal and provincial level, industry, and consumer organizations, and using the services of the Canadian Standards Association (CSA). Although the original intention was to use this code on a voluntary basis, upon its completion, a key industry player that had participated in its development requested that it become the basis for federal and provincial laws. A federal law has now been passed, the Personal Information Protection and Electronic Documents Act (PIPEDA), which draws expressly on the CSA code. PIPEDA has a distinctively "light" implementation approach. The rules are intended to be flexible and to allow organizations to adapt them to their own circumstances and to the

level of sensitivity of the personal information involved. It balances an individual's right to the privacy of personal information with the need of organizations to collect, use, or disclose personal information for legitimate business purposes. The Act designates the Privacy Commissioner of Canada as the ombudsman for complaints under the new law. The Commissioner seeks whenever possible to solve problems through voluntary compliance rather than heavy-handed enforcement. The Commissioner investigates complaints, conducts audits, and promotes awareness of and undertakes research about privacy matters. Rather than involving inspectors, as in conventional regulatory approaches, PIPEDA establishes a complaints-based system. Where the Privacy Commissioner has reasonable grounds to believe that an organization is contravening a provision of the Act, the Commissioner can audit the organization. Individuals can make complaints to the federal Privacy Commissioner, who has the power to investigate, report on, and publicize infractions. The Annual Report is a key information dissemination instrument for the Privacy Commissioner, wherein he or she can describe problems that the Commissioner has encountered and make suggestions for how firms can stay in compliance. Under certain specified conditions, unresolved complaints can be taken to the Federal Court, which can order offending organizations to correct practices, publish notices of rectifications, and pay damages.

To support its conventional command-and-control regulatory provisions in the Canadian Environmental Protection Act 1999 (CEPA 1999), Environment Canada now makes use of a number of innovative rule instruments that essentially facilitate the ability of Environment Canada to act in an expeditious manner in advance of formal regulatory instruments, usually with the cooperation of private-sector participants. Three such instruments are described here:

1 Environmental-performance agreements (EPAS).[29] Depending on the circumstances, Environment Canada can use environmental-performance agreements as a complement, a precursor, or an alternative to regulations in order to address toxic substances of concern. EPAS can be used for the reduction of pollution emissions, broad-based pollution-prevention planning, extended producer responsibility, and hazardous-waste management. A number of criteria concerning the capacity of participants and appropriateness are used before EPAS are developed. One agreement (referred to as a memorandum of understanding) has been developed between the minister of environment, the minister of industry, and the Automotive Parts Manufacturers' Association to seek voluntary, verifiable

reduction and/or elimination of the use, generation, or release of specified priority toxic substances.[30] The agreement does not and is not intended to establish legally binding obligations among the parties.

2 Environmental-protection alternative measures (EPAMS).[31] An EPAM is a negotiated agreement to return an alleged violator to compliance. Its purpose is to restore to compliance a person who has been charged and who is willing to take steps to return to compliance without undergoing a trial. The alleged offender must accept responsibility for the action that forms the basis of the offence. EPAMS can contain initiatives such as the development of effective pollution-prevention measures to reduce releases of toxic substances to regulated limits, the installation of better pollution-control technology, changes to production processes in order to ensure compliance with regulatory requirements, and clean-up of environmental damage. The EPAM must be completed within 180 days. If the EPAM discussions do not lead to a negotiated EPAM, the Attorney General has the right to proceed with the prosecution. The EPAM is registered with the court as a public document. In one case,[32] an EPAM required an offender to develop and implement a standard operation procedure and policy for the export and import of substances regulated under CEPA 1999; to develop a training program for this activity; to submit for publication an article or paid advertisement describing the facts of the case, issues relating to the environmental problem concerned, and the essential terms of the EPAM; and to make a payment of $30,000, in trust, to the Environmental Damages Fund for the storage and disposal of toxic substances in the possession of Environment Canada or for other work that would benefit the environment.

3 Pollution-prevention (P2) plans.[33] P2 plans can be required in respect of a substance specified on the List of Toxic Substances or through other provisions in CEPA 1999. Pollution prevention has been defined in CEPA 1999 as "the use of processes, practices, materials, products, substances or energy that avoid or minimize the creation of pollutants and waste and reduce the overall risk to the environment or human health." Typically, P2 plans include a statement from the CEO, the corporate or facility environmental policy, principles and commitments, the scope and objectives of the P2 plan, a baseline review, identification and evaluation of P2 options, an implementation plan, monitoring and reporting, and review and evaluation. Noncompliance with any of the requirements for pollution prevention stipulated under Section 56 of CEPA 1999 is an offence punishable by fines of up to $1 million or by imprisonment for up to three years.

Another example of a rule innovation is the Canada-Wide Standards (CWS) agreements developed by the Canadian Council of Ministers of the Environment.[34] The CWS agreements provide a national framework to address key issues in environmental protection and health-risk reduction that require common environmental standards across the country. Although the CWS agreements do not change the jurisdiction of governments or delegate authority, a key guiding principle is to avoid overlap and duplication of implementation activities. Each government has the flexibility to act in response to unique circumstances within its respective jurisdiction, yet each can work toward a common goal and timetable as well as provide public reporting on progress. In implementing CWS agreements, governments may take measures such as pollution-prevention planning, voluntary programs, codes of practice, guidelines, economic instruments, and regulations.

INDUSTRY RULE-INSTRUMENT INNOVATIONS
One example of an industry-led rule innovation is the Responsible Care Program of the Canadian Chemical Producers' Association (CCPA).[35] In the early 1980s, the CCPA, fearing a repeat of the Bhopal chemical-plant explosion on Canadian soil (and the negative repercussions of such a disaster for their sector) and wishing to forestall what they perceived as a possibly burdensome new Canadian Environmental Protection Act, developed the Responsible Care Program. Originally a simple set of principles, it has evolved to include a detailed 152-point code of behaviour; an advisory group including academics, environmental organizations, and community representatives; the monitoring of facilities by a combination of competitors, NGOs, and community representatives; and public reporting of results. Adherence to the Responsible Care Program has become a condition of membership in the CCPA. Both the federal government and the Ontario government have since entered into memoranda of understanding with the CCPA concerning its Responsible Care Program, and versions of Responsible Care now operate in over forty-five countries around the world. In a sense, an association of Canadian "branch-plant" chemical producers has influenced and altered the behaviour of the American and foreign chemical industry around the world. At a more subtle level, the Responsible Care Program marks the evolution of an industry association from a lobbying organization into a rule-making and self-policing body concerned with the behaviour of its members (which, at the same time, has also made it a more effective lobbying organization). Some critics have suggested that such programs are being used to impede the progress of new regulatory initiatives.

Another example of an industry rule-instrument innovation is the environmental-management systems (EMS) standards developed through the International Standards Organization (ISO), a nongovernmental organization with a private-sector focus. These EMS standards, called ISO 14001 standards, establish a structured approach to assessing an organization's environmental impacts; then, following a plan-do-check-act model, they describe a process for addressing and managing these impacts. Many firms pay to be "registered" for ISO 14001 assessments. In doing so, they are essentially undergoing private inspections at their own expense. The ISO 14001 standards not only assist firms in putting in place programs to meet regulated requirements and voluntary-code commitments, but also help firms to identify production improvements and energy-efficiency improvements within their operations. Achieving ISO standards also gives firms visibility for their environmental performance. Government-determined performance standards and regulations are foundation documents used in the implementation of environmental-management systems. ISO 14001 management-systems standards have been used by governments to address different forms of private-sector behaviour. It is perhaps self-evident that not all regulated actors are the same. Some are more than willing to exceed legal requirements. Some will meet legal requirements if pushed. Others will do everything possible to avoid compliance. In some jurisdictions,[36] governments have offered firms the possibility of expedited permit processes if they voluntarily choose to put in place an environmental-management system in compliance with ISO 14001 standards. Here, voluntary ISO 14001 standards are being employed by government as a reward or inducement in a manner that may be particularly attractive to "overachieving" firms that are willing to exceed regulatory requirements. In other cases, legislation provides that courts may take into account use of EMS systems in determining liability. Here, EMS systems seem to be employed by governments to address those firms that are generally law-abiding and simply need a nudge, or "another good reason" to reinforce their law-abiding behaviour. And finally, as part of sentencing, courts have imposed ISO 14001 registration on firms found not to be in compliance with the law. Here, ISO 14001 is being used to address laggards, and although the ISO 14001 standards were designed by nonstate actors for voluntary compliance, they have become decidedly nonvoluntary in these instances. These three examples show how a private, voluntary standard, as a supplement to a command-and-control regulatory scheme, can be used by governments and courts in different ways to address three different types of regulated actor.

An example of an industry rule-instrument innovation that was developed with significant government involvement is the Canadian Scanner Price Accuracy Code.[37] The code addresses the issue of the accuracy of supermarket bar-code scanners. An essential part of the

program is the requirement that, if a consumer finds a discrepancy between the price at the cash register and that on the product, he or she
gets the product for free (if it is priced at $10 or under; if it is more
than $10, the consumer gets $10 off the price of the product). The Canadian code was patterned on a similar code developed by the Australian supermarket-industry association. The Canadian code is operated
by the Canadian Association of Chain Drug Stores, the Canadian
Council of Grocery Distributors, the Canadian Federation of Independent Grocers, and the Retail Council of Canada. The Canadian Competition Bureau has endorsed the Code. Compliance rates have been
high, and complaints to government regulators are low in part because
the program creates incentives for both consumers and supermarkets to
be vigilant. The program supports regulatory provisions under the
Competition Act that prohibit misleading or deceptive marketing
practices but does so through nonregulatory, market mechanisms. The
program simultaneously harnesses consumers' self-interest in getting
products for free by being vigilant in checking their receipts[38] as well as
merchants' self-interest in not making any errors and thereby not having to give away products for free.

NGO RULE-INSTRUMENT INNOVATIONS

An example of an innovative NGO-led rule instrument is the Forest
Stewardship Council's program for sustainable-forestry certification
and labelling.[39] As efforts to negotiate a global forest-protection
convention sputtered in the early 1990s, several major international
environmental organizations (most notably, the Worldwide Fund for
Nature, WWF), working with retailers and others, spearheaded the development of the Forest Stewardship Council (FSC) and its certification
and labelling program for products from sustainably harvested and
managed forests. While initially facing much resistance from the forest-
extraction industry, and despite experiencing numerous start-up administrative difficulties, there are now more than 24 million hectares of
FSC-certified forests worldwide. In response to the FSC, forest producers have taken leadership roles in developing their own competing programs for voluntary sustainable forestry, in some cases using the
services of standards-development organizations, such as the Canadian
Standards Association. In addition to private-sector use of the programs, governments in Canada and the United States have begun efforts to have their regulatory forest-management regimes certified as
being in compliance with the FSC and with other forest-certification
programs. A separate spin-off Marine Stewardship Council has been
established for certified sustainable-fishery harvesting practices, and

now the WWF is considering developing a sustainable-mining steward-ship council and certification program.

Another example of an innovative NGO-led rule instrument is the good-neighbour agreement.[40] A good-neighbour agreement is a form of flexible accord between local communities or NGOs and businesses whose underlying philosophy is the mutual acknowledgment by a busi-ness and an independent community organization of the need to build a relationship responsive to the needs of each. Agreements are formally negotiated, although some remain voluntary and without legally bind-ing language, while others are incorporated as a condition of formal permitting processes and can be legally enforced. Although developed against a backdrop of legal instruments, these agreements typically do not involve government as a formal party, yet they work to further public-interest goals. At this point, good-neighbour agreements are largely an American phenomenon, although certain agreements on Ca-nadian aboriginals' community-resource extraction resemble the model of the good-neighbour agreement.

### Sustainable Governance: Process Innovations

Processes are techniques that facilitate the ability of parties to partici-pate in a meaningful and informed way in decision making that affects their interests. For the purposes of this chapter, those processes that have a public-interest dimension are of central importance. Process in-novations can take the form of (1) information-access programs that allow parties to better protect themselves and (2) approaches that fa-cilitate the ability of parties to access decision making on issues of concern to them, such as citizen-triggered investigation provisions concerning enforcement, private prosecutions, modernized class-action and contingency fees, and alternative dispute-resolution processes.

It is apparent that the process innovations discussed here operate un-der the tacit assumption that individuals and groups have both the desire and the capacity to engage in government and private-sector decision-making processes of concern to them. This assumption seems to be borne out in practice.

#### GOVERNMENT PROCESS INNOVATIONS
An example of an innovative government process (information-access) program is the National Pollutants Release Inventory (NPRI).[41] Follow-ing a similar model in place in the United States and drawing on the initiative of the Canadian Chemical Producers' Association to ensure reporting on national emissions reduction, Environment Canada has

developed a publicly accessible inventory of pollutants in use in Canada, pursuant to the Canadian Environmental Protection Act 1999. Firms are required to provide Environment Canada with a description of pollutants used in their operations and with the quantity of each. The NPRI allows individual citizens to determine which pollutants are used in their communities, in what quantities, and by whom. The NPRI may be of particular use in conjunction with programs such as Accel-. erated Reduction/Elimination of Toxics (ARET), a voluntary toxics-reduction initiative, since the NPRI ensures that information on the use of industry toxics is publicly available, thereby assisting communities and individuals in verifying whether progress is really being made in reducing toxics.[42]

Another example of a government process (information-access) innovation is the Consumer Gateway.[43] In the late 1990s, the Canadian Office of Consumer Affairs spearheaded the development of the Consumer Gateway as a single, central internet-based gateway to the information and services offered by Canada's governments, industry associations, and NGOs. Through a strategic partnership between more than 400 federal departments and agencies, provincial and territorial ministries, industry associations, and NGO partners, the Gateway allows Canadians to search for consumer information and services on the Internet, thus enabling them to better protect themselves. The Gateway has proven to be a particularly popular website destination for Canadians, attracting thousands of "hits" each month.

GOVERNMENT PROCESS INNOVATIONS
FOR ENHANCED CITIZEN ACCESS

The citizen-petitioning processes associated with the NAFTA CEC, the federal Commissioner of the Environment and Sustainable Development, and the Ontario Commissioner for the Environment were described above. While rightly framed as institutional innovations in the sense that new watchdog institutions have been created, they can also be characterized as good examples of administrative process innovations that enhance the ability of citizens to check up on and question government administrators.

Modernized class actions are another significant process innovation that enhances the ability of citizens to challenge those who negatively affect their interests. In recent years, both the federal and provincial governments have put in place new or revised provisions that facilitate the ability of citizens to file private-law representative (or class) actions to protect their interests through the courts. Six provincial jurisdictions have now put in place modernized class-action legislation. Without such legislation, there is frequently little motivation for individual citizens to go to courts to address problems affecting them, particularly where these problems are relatively small in cost or impact (e.g., individual consumers each possessing a defective household product or individual members of communities each inconvenienced by noise or odour caused by industrial activity). With class actions, these comparatively small problems can be aggregated and dealt with efficiently as a group of similarly affected individuals. Thus class actions enhance and expand the opportunity for citizens to protect their own rights instead of simply depending on government to act on their behalf. From an industry perspective, the possibility of class actions creates a stimulus for industry to proactively solve problems before they escalate to legal action and, thereby, to remain competitive with other jurisdictions, such as the United States, where industry is also open to class actions.

Another process innovation that has enhanced the ability of citizens to protect their interests is the creation of new private-law rights of action in both the consumer and environmental areas in stipulated incidents of illegal behaviour (e.g., Canadian Environmental Protection Act 1999, Ontario Environmental Bill of Rights Act, and the "civil damages" provision of the Competition Act).

Citizens can also file private prosecutions under the Fisheries Act and the Migratory Birds Convention Act, and if successful, they are entitled to one-half of the proceeds resulting from such actions.[44] As with modernized class-action legislation, these provisions enhance and expand the opportunity for individuals to protect their own rights without being dependent on governments to do so.

INDUSTRY PROCESS INNOVATIONS
FOR ENHANCED CITIZEN ACCESS

An example of an industry process innovation is the Canadian Automobile Motor Vehicle Arbitration Program (CAMVAP).[45] CAMVAP is a non-profit corporation with a board of directors that includes representatives of provincial and territorial governments, consumer organizations, and the automobile industry. CAMVAP is funded by automobile manufacturers, with fees based on market share and past CAMVAP case performance. CAMVAP arbitrates disputes that consumers have been unable to resolve directly with dealers. A consumer completes a CAMVAP claim form, and the manufacturer must reply within ten days. The consumer is then given a choice of three arbitrators who come from a variety of backgrounds but are not automobile experts. The consumer and dealer must agree to accept the decision of the arbitrator. More than 60 per cent of the arbitrators' rulings to date have been in the consumer's favour.

The Canadian Banking Ombudsman and the Financial Services Ombudsnetwork, described earlier, can also be characterized as institutional innovations with significant process aspects designed to enhance the ability of consumers to protect their interests without relying on government agencies to do so.

NGO PROCESS INNOVATIONS

The Mining Ombudsman, Riverkeepers, and good-neighbour agreements described earlier as institutional innovations all have significant components of citizen-access process innovation, permitting citizens to "converse" directly with firms and governments on issues of concern to them.

## DISTINGUISHING CHARACTERISTICS OF SUSTAINABLE-GOVERNANCE INNOVATIONS

The question might legitimately be asked as to how we can distinguish institutional, rule-instrument, and process innovations compatible with a sustainable-governance paradigm from any old run-of-the-mill institution, rule instrument, and process? Innovations that "fit" the sustainable-governance paradigm tend to:

- Work particularly well against a backdrop of conventional governance institutions, rule instruments, and processes[46]
- Recognize the value of multiple centres of authority and responsibility all targeted at the same policy context
- Frequently include elements of both policy development and policy implementation
- Often harness (or attempt to harness) citizen, consumer, community, NGO, and industry energies (not just fear of government-imposed legal liability) in order to address a particular policy problem
- Explicitly acknowledge the value of multiactor collaborations, particularly those that cross the public-, private-, and third-sector boundaries[47]
- Work under the assumption that a certain amount of rivalrous institutional, rule-instrument, and process friction is valuable as a check-and-balance mechanism and as a means to stimulate creative tension among initiatives and actors.

It should be pointed out that there is frequently overlap among institutional, rule-instrument, and process innovations. For example, the Responsible Care Program of the Canadian Chemical Producers' Association is on one level a rule-instrument innovation, but accompanying it is an institutional innovation as the Canadian Chemical Producers' Association moves from being a pure lobbying body to being an industry body with some degree of self-regulatory function. It also has process-innovation aspects given the involvement of communities, NGOs, and academics as part of an advisory panel; the use of community and NGO representatives and competitors in conformity verification reviews; and the public-reporting aspects of the program. Similarly, environmental commissions or commissioners at the federal, provincial, and NAFTA levels can be considered both institutional and process innovations.

It should also be pointed out that sustainable governance recognizes and acknowledges that evolution and change are part of the process of governance.[48] Thus, for example, the voluntary CSA standard pertaining to protection of personal information has evolved and become the basis for federal legislation. Similarly, voluntary systems standards for sustainable-forestry management developed outside of government have been subsequently implemented and applied by governments to Crown land as part of regulatory regimes (as has recently happened in New Brunswick). The Canadian Banking Ombudsman has evolved to become part of a larger Financial Services Ombudsnetwork. These sorts of examples demonstrate the considerable potential for evolution in the sustainable-governance model.

## MODELS OF PROTO-SUSTAINABLE GOVERNANCE: THE CONSUMER- AND ENVIRONMENTAL-PROTECTION CONTEXTS

Using the consumer- and environmental-protection contexts as examples, the two figures that follow are an attempt to illustrate that many individual innovations, when taken together, constitute models of proto-sustainable governance – so called because, while they display some of the characteristics of a mature sustainable-governance approach, such as a diversity of approaches and actors all directed at the same activity, they were not developed in a systematic and coordinated way and hence lack the sort of coherency and comprehensiveness that a mature sustainable-governance model would ideally exhibit.

### The Consumer-Protection Model of Proto-Sustainable Governance

There are a host of federal, provincial, and municipal command-and-control regulatory instruments that together form the foundation for consumer-protection efforts in Canada.

Included here are federal laws, such as the Competition Act, the Consumer Packaging and Labelling Act, the Hazardous Products Act, the Food and Drugs Act, and the Personal Information Protection and

Figure 10.1
Sustainable Governance: Consumer Protection in Canada

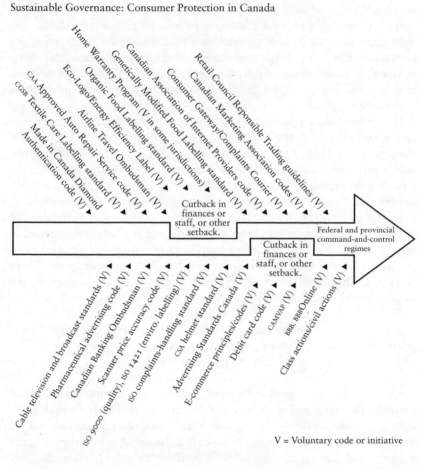

V = Voluntary code or initiative

Electronic Documents Act, as well as provincial laws, such as the Ontario Consumer Protection Act and the Alberta Fair Trading Act 1998.
In recognition of their pivotal role, these legal instruments represent the
main arrow in the centre of Figure 10.1.[49]

On both sides of the main arrow are a range of support institutions,
rule instruments, and processes, represented by smaller arrows.[50] Some
are initiatives where government plays a significant or lead role. For
example, the Air Travel Complaints Commissioner is a new institution
created by the federal government; the Environmental Choice Eco-
Logo product-labelling program is a rule-instrument innovation that
was initiated by the federal government; and modern class-action legislation, a process innovation, has been put in place by six of the ten
provinces.

In other cases, it is industry that has assumed the leadership role. For example, the Canadian Banking Ombudsman is an institutional innovation of the Canadian banking industry; the Code of Good Practice created by the Canadian Association of Internet Providers is a rule-instrument innovation for the internet industry; and the Canadian Automobile Motor Vehicle Arbitration Program (CAMVAP) is a process innovation funded and operated by the automobile industry (provincial-government and consumer-organization representatives sit on its board). In other cases, consumer organizations have played lead roles, such as the operation by the Quebec consumer organization SAC-Shawinigan of a merchant-certification program to ensure e-commerce consumer protection.

In many cases, government, industry, and consumer organizations are integrally involved. For example, the Canadian Code of Practice for Consumer Protection in E-Commerce is an innovative voluntary-code rule instrument involving federal, provincial, industry, and consumer organizations (brokered by Industry Canada's Office of Consumer Affairs), and the Consumer Gateway is a single-window internet portal for trustworthy consumer information from federal, provincial, and territorial governments as well as from consumer organizations and industry associations (developed and coordinated by Industry Canada's Office of Consumer Affairs). It is possible for small, nonlegislative "side arrow" initiatives to evolve into "main arrow" regulatory programs. For example, the voluntary CSA privacy code has become the basis for the federal Personal Information Protection and Electronic Documents Act and is also being used as the foundation for parallel provincial legislation (which is still in development at the time of writing).[51]

There is also potential for "small arrow" single-industry initiatives to evolve into bigger, multisector initiatives. For example, the Canadian Banking Ombudsman, an institution voluntarily created and funded by the Canadian Bankers Association in 1996–97, became a component of a broader Financial Services Ombudsnetwork in 2002, which provides single-window access to independent complaint-resolution services in the industries of banking, life and health insurance, general insurance, and securities and mutual funds. The Ombudsnetwork is voluntarily sustained and funded by the financial sectors involved.

Nonregulatory institutional, rule-instrument, and process innovations can potentially avoid some of the constitutional wrangling associated with conventional legislative instruments. For example, because the Financial Services Ombudsnetwork is a voluntary, industry-led institutional innovation it has neatly avoided some of the thorny constitutional division-of-powers issues that would have bedevilled a federal-provincial legislated approach even though it involves both federally and provincially regulated industries. Similarly, the CSA privacy code was a voluntary rule-instrument innovation developed outside the normal federal and provincial legislative arenas, with both federal and provincial input (as well as with the input of business and consumer organizations), and was intended to act as a national code to be used anywhere in Canada by any industry or government. As noted above, it has since become the basis for a federal law and is now being used as the basis for provincial laws. A joint federal-provincial initiative to introduce coordinated federal and legislated privacy laws would likely have bogged down in petty federal-provincial squabbling, as has happened with deliberations about whether to establish a national securities regulator.[52] The Canadian Automobile Motor Vehicle Arbitration Program (CAMVAP) is a process innovation funded and operated by the automobile industry that now operates across Canada, with Quebec finally joining the fold in 2002. A pan-Canadian legislated initiative to accomplish the same objective would face many obstacles that this voluntary initiative has avoided.

Nevertheless, with respect to all of these initiatives, the federal and provincial governments retain the right to impose a legislated regime if and when they choose. In this sense, these voluntary initiatives can be said to operate "in the shadow of the law"; indeed, the threat of government putting in place a law to accomplish the same objective is often a strong stimulus for industry action and helps to sustain continued diligence in the operation of these initiatives.[53]

To reduce the likelihood of insurance companies having to pay out compensation to their customers, the industry has put in place many process-oriented initiatives intended to stimulate more risk-prudent behaviour among their customers. Individual consumers know that their premiums will be reduced if they take driver-education programs; if they do not get into car accidents; if they adopt a healthy, smoke-free lifestyle; and if they install house alarms that meet insurance-company specifications. Insurance companies have also banded together to create the Insurance Institute for Highway Safety (IIHS), which in conjunction with an affiliated institute tests the safety of cars and publishes the results for use by consumers and insurers. The intended effect of this initiative is simultaneously to stimulate automobile manufacturers to make safer cars and to encourage consumers to purchase safer cars. The IIHS also regularly tables interventions before legislators in support of government initiatives that reduce the likelihood of accidents. By means of both insurance initiatives and consumer-information programs such as the Consumer Information Gateway, citizens are being encouraged to take on more risk-management responsibility for protecting their own interests, a phenomenon referred to in the literature as "prudentialism."[54]

Taken together, Figure 10.1 depicts what appears to be a thriving eco-system of institutional, rule-instrument, and process innovations, an ecosystem where the failure of or problems with any one initiative does not necessarily lead to an overall diminution of consumer protection be-cause, to some extent, the existence of one of the other innovations can potentially counter a particular initiative's problems or failure. Thus, for example, consumers having problems with automobiles that rust out prematurely have not one but several options from which to choose: They can turn to CAMVAP, complain to industry self-management bodies (such as the Ontario Motor Vehicle Industry Council) and to conven-tional government consumer agencies, or file legal actions using modern-ized class-action processes. The opportunities for effective consumer/ citizen resolution of any particular problem are enhanced through a mul-tipronged sustainable-governance approach, and the consumer/citizen is potentially less vulnerable to reductions in budgets when there are op-tions available other than simply going to an already burdened govern-ment consumer-protection agency. This having been said, it is clear that a fully and rigorously enforced regulatory regime is the optimal basis for sustainable-governance activities.

As is hopefully apparent, Figure 10.1 cannot fully and accurately de-pict the depth and diversity of interaction among actors, institutions, rule instruments, and processes that does take place. For example, it does not portray the dynamic relationship between, on the one hand, the Better Business Bureau (BBB) as a "frontline" business-led mechanism for ad-dressing consumer complaints and, on the other, government regulators, who frequently share information and work out coordinated responses with the BBB in order to address emerging problems. Nor does it portray nuances and problems associated with each of the initiatives.

Unanswered questions about the Canadian consumer-protection model of sustainable governance include whether:

- The range of initiatives are as effective as they could be
- There are mechanisms for "quality control" of industry- and NGO-led initiatives
- There is adequate coordination among initiatives
- There is adequate transparency and accountability associated with each of the initiatives
- Consumers are confused by or unsatisfied with the range of initiatives

- Government, business, and NGOs could be doing more and, if so, how and what
- There are gaps that need to be addressed.

Clearly, this is just a preliminary list of questions.

### The Environmental-Protection Model
### of Proto-Sustainable Governance

As with the consumer-protection model, federal, provincial, and municipal laws are again the dominant policy instrument used to protect the Canadian environment, and hence this approach is indicated by the "main arrow" in the centre of Figure 10.2 below.[55] Included here are such federal statutes as the Canadian Environmental Protection Act 1999 and the pollution-control provisions of the Fisheries Act as well as provincial legislation, such as the Ontario Environmental Protection Act and the British Columbia Waste Management Act. Supporting these command-and-control measures are intergovernmental (e.g., the NAFTA CEC), federal (e.g., the Commissioner of the Environment and Sustainable Development), and provincial (e.g., the Ontario Commissioner for the Environment) institutions and processes discussed above that facilitate citizen engagement concerning instances of alleged problematic enforcement as well as private prosecutions and private-law actions (including class actions). There are also a range of information-disclosure initiatives (e.g., the NPRI, discussed above), financial incentives (e.g., tax incentives), and voluntary codes and agreements pertaining to environmental and energy characteristics of products, reduction of toxic substances, reduction of harmful climate-change activity, sector-specific environmental management initiatives, and generic initiatives in environmental-management systems.

There are a wide number of ways that industry- or NGO-led initiatives can interact with and supplement regulatory command-and-control approaches (see, for example, earlier discussion of the interaction between, on the one hand, the industry-driven ISO 14001 standards for environmental-management systems and, on the other, judicial, legislative, and governmental activity supporting use of environmental-management systems as a complementary method of achieving regulatory objectives). It is also possible for there to be useful interaction among other initiatives. For example, use of the National Pollutants Release Inventory, an information-process innovation of the federal government in which businesses are required to disclose what chemicals they use and in what quantities, can assist in verifying the progress or failure of voluntary toxic-reduction pro-

Figure 10.2
Sustainable Governance: Environmental Protection in Canada

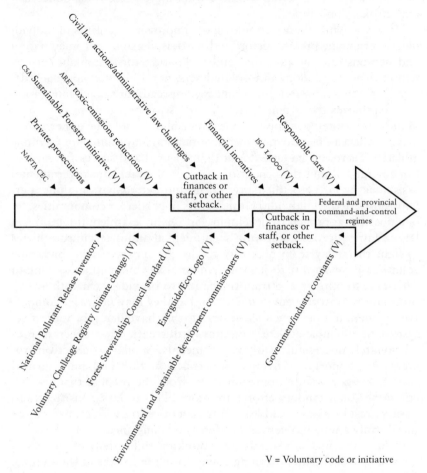

V = Voluntary code or initiative

grams.[56] As with the questions articulated above in the consumer-protection context concerning coordination and quality control of institutions, instruments, and processes, similar questions can be posed concerning the range of approaches and actors involved in the Canadian environmental-protection sustainable-governance model.

### Spontaneous vs Systematic: Does Anything More Need to Be Done?

In view of the existence of the examples of governing innovations provided above, an argument can be made that the best approach to encouraging sustainable governance is a hands-off, "let all flowers bloom" approach. After all, so the argument would go, if this approach has led to these innovations, what more needs to be done? If it ain't broke, don't fix it.

However, while these examples show impressive incidents of individual government, private-sector, and NGO leadership and imagination and demonstrate the potential and inclination for sustainable governance, they are random and isolated acts, not a planned approach designed to cultivate and encourage widespread, sustained innovation that maximizes the potential for all parties to contribute to governing in the public interest. Can more be done? Should more be done?

A parallel can be drawn to the identification and training of Olympic athletes. There can be little doubt that talented and successful athletes can emerge without the benefit of any sort of systematic governmental assistance by virtue of their raw talent and determination alone, perhaps supported by individual benefactors in particular communities. So one possible approach to developing an Olympic-athlete program is a laissez faire approach, allowing such talented and determined athletes to fight their way from obscurity to the top on their own. But some countries have set out to identify potential Olympic athletes from an early age, to nurture and train them, and to provide them with an appropriate competitive environment so that they may flourish. Comparatively small nations (such as Australia) that have developed effective, systematic Olympic-athlete programs of this nature have been disproportionately successful in obtaining medals. Similar to effective programs in support of Olympic athletes, a mature and fully formed sustainable-governance approach starts from the premise that systematic rather than random efforts are more likely to lead consistently to positive results and should lead to transferable knowledge that can be successfully applied to new and different circumstances.

Perhaps the most advanced recent thinking and activity on more systematic approaches to governing comes from the European Union (EU). Among other things, a recent white paper on governance calls for opening up the processes of government, for establishing partnership arrangements that go beyond minimum standards, and for greater use of co-regulatory instruments.[57] The European Union has also developed a legal framework for a voluntary environmental-management auditing program[58] and a network of national bodies to assist consumers in finding extrajudicial solutions to cross-border consumer disputes.[59]

Another innovative governance approach in place in the European Union is known as the "New Approach."[60] The New Approach is a legal technique that consists of defining mandatory essential product requirements through EU directives to ensure a high level of public protection while leaving the choice of technical solution up to interested parties (users, manufacturers, etc.), which must adhere to standards developed through recognized European-standards bodies. Because of its flexibility, the New Approach has proven to be a highly efficient technique for promoting industrial competitiveness, product innovation, and the free movement of goods across the EU. In the United Kingdom, the Office of Fair Trading has developed a new regime for review and approval of voluntary codes of practice pertaining to consumer matters.[61] The suggestion is not being made here that Canada, or indeed any other country, should adopt any of these European approaches. Each of these innovations is a product of the distinctive legal, political, social, and cultural environment in which it was originally conceived and developed. However, they do seem to demonstrate a more advanced and systematic approach to governance than is currently being used in Canada. It is worth emphasizing that sustainable governance will and should "play out" differently in different jurisdictions in keeping with the unique characteristics of each jurisdiction.

## AN ENHANCED ROLE
## FOR CANADIAN CIVIL SOCIETY

If the concept of sustainable governance is to succeed in Canada, civil society will need to play a key role in its success. As Susan Phillips has noted,

[b]y necessity, the process of governance is much more embedded in civil society institutions than was traditional government. Effective governance requires both a strong private and strong voluntary sector [that] ... includes not only those organizations providing direct services, but intermediary umbrella groups and those, either as independent interest groups or as part of social movements, that are dedicated primarily to advocacy activity ... In governance, the [voluntary] sector is necessary not only to deliver programmes that the state wishes to contract out or vacate, but to provide input into policy-making processes and to promote strong communities capable of helping themselves. Active citizenship, in which citizens engage in civic life through voluntary associations, supports governance by providing better input and monitoring of policy and, as a by-product of participation, by producing greater trust in other citizens and in government.[62]

In the fall of 2002, the Canadian Policy Research Network and its partner, Viewpoint Learning, invited a representative sample of Canadians to participate in one of ten day-long dialogue sessions on Canada's future and, looking ten years ahead, to create their own vision for "The

Kind of Canada We Want."[63] They were also asked to reflect on how this vision could be achieved and to indicate who should be responsible for making it happen. The resulting report suggested that Canadians are ready to revise the roles and responsibilities of governments, business, communities, and citizens themselves to suit the circumstances of the twenty-first century. According to the report, these updated roles and responsibilities "form a new unwritten social contract to shape Canada's future" (iv). Based directly on the executive summary of the report, three key points emerge:

1 Markets are no longer seen as separate from and even opposed to civil society. Instead, markets are now seen as an integral part of a working society, a part that serves public as well as private interests, with market values being integrated into Canadians' notions of civil society and social equity in a unique and compelling way. At the same time, citizens are pragmatic about the limitations of both markets and governments.

2 Citizens see themselves as more active participants in governance. Having moved toward greater self-reliance and beyond deference, they now demand a voice. Hidden beneath a thin crust of cynicism lies a keen desire for more active citizen involvement in public affairs. Citizens insist on greater accountability on the part of governments, business, and other institutions and are willing to assume greater responsibility and accountability themselves. They want to see more responsive governments that foster ongoing dialogue with and between citizens.

3 Canadians share a remarkably consistent set of values from coast to coast. This distinctive values base provides an essential foundation on which Canadians and their governments can build a different community north of the forty-ninth parallel, notwithstanding the growing economic integration of North America.

This report provides considerable support for the proposition that Canadian citizens have both an appetite for and a capacity to make significant contributions to government and private-sector decision making that affects their interests. In many ways, the dialogue sessions align with the various examples of citizen and NGO involvement in governance innovations discussed earlier in this chapter.

But at the same time, it is clear that much more needs to be done to create "the space" in which citizens can meaningfully play this greater governance role. Surveys show that fewer and fewer volunteers are doing more and more.[64] Surveys also show that Canadians are having difficulty coping with the complex choices made available to them. Incentives need to be put in place (and disincentives removed) so that Canadians can meaningfully understand the changes taking place around them and can have real opportunities to become more involved in decisions that affect them. At the end of the day, a new, more systematic participatory model for governance is possible, where governments, businesses, communities, and individuals all have important roles and responsibilities. This could be the basis for a uniquely Canadian approach to societal organization with competitive and social benefits for all concerned.

Approaches to enhancing citizen involvement in government and private-sector decision making that could be adopted include:

1 Government and private-sector recognition and encouragement of employees participating in volunteering activity. Several firms already systematically provide employees with a certain number of paid days per month for employees to engage in voluntary activity.[65]
2 More systematic and concerted efforts by governments and the private sector to provide "a seat at the table" for representatives of community or nongovernmental organizations in the operation of initiatives that affect the community. The inclusion of community and NGO representatives on the boards of (or on advisory committees to) logo/certification and code programs, ombudsprograms, and self-management initiatives are examples of how civil society could be more involved in governance institutions. By including citizen representatives in the formal decision-making processes of governance institutions, the level of public trust is likely to increase, and the quality of decision making might improve, while the representatives involved gain insights into the challenges and intricacies of governing in the twenty-first century.
3 More effort by governments and the private sector to systematically provide citizen voicing and action processes concerning policy development and implementation, building on the somewhat haphazard citizen petitioning, investigation, prosecution, and class-action initiatives already in place, which were discussed earlier in this chapter.
4 Reform of the regulatory regime applying to public interest organizations to ensure that these organizations can effectively and appropriately participate in public-policy decision making on a more-or-less even footing with other societal actors.[66] In important ways, enhancing the role for citizen participation in governing may be the key to rebuilding citizen trust in government and private-sector institutions.
5 As citizen groups take on greater public-interest responsibilities, they too will need to adopt more transparent, accountable, and accessible modes of governing, along with the government and private sectors.

## CORPORATE SOCIAL RESPONSIBILITY:
## THE PRIVATE-SECTOR CONTRIBUTION
## TO SUSTAINABLE GOVERNANCE?[67]

Corporate social responsibility (CSR)[68] is an evolving term that does not have a standard definition or a recognized set of specific criteria.[69] With the acknowledgment that businesses play a pivotal role in job and wealth creation in society, CSR is generally understood to be the way a company achieves a balance or integration of economic, environmental, and social objectives while at the same time addressing stakeholder expectations and sustaining or enhancing shareholder value. Insofar as sustainable development has been defined as *development that meets the needs of the present without compromising the ability of future generations to meet their own needs* and is generally understood as focusing on how to achieve the integration of economic, environmental, and social imperatives, CSR is frequently seen as the business contribution to sustainable development.

CSR applies to firms wherever they operate in the global economy. CSR commitments and activities typically address aspects of a firm's behaviour (including its policies and practices) with respect to such key elements as health and safety, environmental protection, human rights, labour relations, practices in human-resource management, corporate governance, community development (e.g., the broader social fabric within which firms operate), and others (e.g., reporting, supplier relations, consumer protection, competition, and bribery). These elements of CSR are frequently interconnected and interdependent.

The way businesses involve shareholders, employees, customers, suppliers, governments, nongovernmental organizations, international organizations, and other stakeholders is usually a key feature of the concept. While business compliance with laws and regulations on social, environmental, and economic imperatives set the minimum level of CSR performance, CSR is frequently understood as involving private-sector commitments and activities that extend beyond this foundation of compliance with laws (particularly where the legal frameworks are weak or not enforced). In this sense, CSR can be seen as a form of proactive political, economic, social, and environmental risk management, an effort to build a "social" licence to accompany the legal licence to operate that firms possess.

To date, private-sector CSR initiatives have taken many forms, including individual company codes and commitments, sectorwide programs, self-assessment tools, and voluntary reporting initiatives. In many ways, some of the programs and initiatives that have been described above (e.g., the Financial Services Ombudsnetwork, sustainable-forestry certification programs, ISO 14001 environmental-management standards, and the Responsible Care Program of the Canadian Chemical Producers' Association) can be seen as examples of CSR. Insofar as these initiatives acknowledge and attempt to breathe life into the notion that corporations need to recognize and balance social and environmental objectives with economic objectives, it should be apparent that CSR is a concept that resonates with sustainable governance. While the private sector quite rightly has the lead on many CSR initiatives, there is much that governments and NGOs can do to facilitate and encourage its development in a rigorous and effective manner.[70]

## SOME CAVEATS ABOUT THE SUSTAINABLE-GOVERNANCE CONCEPT

As stated above, a key theme and understanding underlying the concept of sustainable governance is the value of harnessing the energies, expertise, and advantages of multiple actors, instruments, institutions, and processes. Diversity, and even some degree of conflict, rivalry, and overlap among actors, institutions, instruments, and the like, creates a thriving (if somewhat chaotic and confusing), multivariate "ecosystem" of approaches addressing a particular policy issue or problem, with the effect that the failure of any one approach does not necessarily mean an overall implementation failure but rather that another actor, instrument, institution, or process is or could be in a position to "pick up the slack" or otherwise act as a check-and-balance concerning a particular behaviour.[71]

A dynamic of "mutually assured implementation" can occur when multiple actors, instruments, institutions, and processes are all brought to bear on the same activity. To put it another way, it takes a society to run a society.[72] It is time to move to a fully mature view of governing that recognizes and embraces the wide variety of interactions taking place and the complexity of the interrelations. It is also time to shed the artificial, mechanical, and frankly adolescent view that government has control over all the buttons and moves all the levers and therefore can structure society on its own. Sustainable governance should not be looked upon as a zero-sum game, in which the energy and resources spent on developing and implementing one initiative necessarily take away from the attention devoted to another initiative. A key value of sustainable governance is its ability to harness energies and expertise that are currently under-utilized, thereby increasing the total attention spent on addressing a particular problem while at the same time spreading costs.

Use of the sustainable governance approach is intended to assist policy makers in determining whether any particular policy context is as "robust" and responsive as it could be: That is, is the full range of actors, institutions, rule instruments, and processes in use? If not, why not? Where can adjustments and additions be made? What sort of interactions between actors, institutions, rule instruments, and processes are taking place? Could the system be better coordinated or more accountable and transparent? Where are the gaps? Is the operating environment as optimally conducive to governmental, private-sector, third-sector, and citizen action and innovation as possible? By mapping the range of instruments and actors employed in several particular contexts using the sustainable governance model, it may be possible to identify under-utilized or over-utilized approaches or actors as well as opportunities for better coordination.

The concept of sustainable governance should in no way be considered a call for the abandonment or even necessarily for a reduction in the use of conventional public-sector governing approaches. Rather, to practise sustainable governance is to acknowledge the limitations of such approaches and the need to draw on other approaches that are not as limited (although they have distinctive limitations of their own). Regardless of which innovation is used, all need to be assessed in terms of values such as accountability, transparency, credibility and legitimacy, cost effectiveness and efficiency, and fairness.

While it was probably the intention of the proponents of many of the innovative approaches to governing discussed in this chapter to devise more cost-effective approaches to governing, the result may not, in fact, necessarily be less costly, but it should be more sustainable. In this sense, any costs should be viewed as longer-term investments in better governing. To the extent that sustainable governance decreases the likelihood of another Walkerton-type environmental tragedy, the immediate investment may be well worth it. Likewise, to the extent that Canadian firms gain a competitive advantage through use of collaborative approaches (while other jurisdictions fight out issues in courts and through formal regulations), the investment may again be well worth it.

There may also be situations where particular sustainable-governance contexts turn out to be difficult to manage and even inflexible. Thus, for example, once in place, it may be difficult for government to change an industry-ombudsmen or voluntary-code scheme despite observable new trends in the marketplace that would seem to call for changed approaches.[73] This reflects the reality that sustainable governance is to some extent a less centralized approach to governing, where more than one "player" has governance responsibilities and powers.[74] Indeed, this very weakness is in other regards a strength. Because sustainable governance involves multiple responsibility centres and a sharing of power, it is difficult to control, but it is also less vulnerable to downturns.[75] In addition, it can be more responsive. For example, industry and NGOs may be able to respond more quickly and appropriately to certain technological advances (e.g., electronic commerce) than would conventional state-based approaches. Eventually, these "first-generation" instruments may come to be viewed as stop-gap measures to be superceded by more sophisticated regulatory approaches (this, arguably, was the trajectory of the Canadian privacy code, which has become the basis for a federal law). There is nothing wrong with this, nor is a move from voluntary private-sector or community-based approaches to governmental approaches a necessary or preferred path of evolution.

The challenge here is to devise framework approaches that empower a range of actors to assume governance responsibilities while at the same time creating and maintaining the overall framework within which this activity takes place, thereby maintaining quality control and the ability to intervene or to alter directions when necessary. In the more decentralized governance context that characterizes sustainable governance, law will continue to play a central role no matter which institution, instrument, or process is involved. Thus, for example, law can be used to maintain accountability over self-management regimes that are industry-run but government-structured, to stimulate firms to put in place management systems in order to meet due-diligence defences and thus avoid liability for strict-liability offences, to control anticompetitive behaviour, and to address misrepresentations concerning rule instruments.[76]

If the challenges of decentralized governing involving multiple centres of responsibility are acknowledged from the outset, there is a greater likelihood that appropriate responses can be "designed in" to the frameworks. For example, rivalrous check-and-balance initiatives and regular third-party reviews of programs and institutions offer opportunities for *in situ* and in-progress alterations to particular initiatives as necessary.

One of the greatest challenges associated with implementing the sustainable-governance concept may be attitudinal: accepting less-than-perfect operating conditions as a given; accepting the need for a sharing of power with diverse, less-than-perfect governance partners; and accepting that governance in the public interest is more like managing a complex, multivariate ecosystem full of unknowns and surprises than it is like operating a mechanical device with clear inputs and outputs.

## CONCLUSIONS

In conclusion, several points emerge concerning sustainable governance as a new approach to governing in the twenty-first century:

1 In view of the "suboptimal" realities of governing in the twenty-first century, governments need to do a better job of drawing on the full

range of state and nonstate institutions, rule instruments, processes, and actors that are available in support of the development and implementation of public policy. Governments need to recognize that they can play a greater role in encouraging nonstate actors to protect the environment, consumers, workers, communities, and the like and that, in fact, government sometimes creates disincentives and obstacles to performance through conventional regulatory approaches.

2 In adopting this new approach to governing, we move from single-provider (and hence vulnerable) regulatory approaches to multivariate, collaborative governance approaches and from fluctuating capabilities susceptible to a variety of "winds of change" to more sustainable, robust, effective, efficient, competitive, and innovative approaches to public-policy development and implementation. In the sense that sustainable governance involves a combination of governmental and nongovernmental institutions, processes, instruments, and actors, it entails much more than simply a question of instrument choice. It also entails much more than a question of the intelligent use of command-and-control regulations (although, clearly, intelligent use of regulations remains an important preoccupation for governments). While collaboration is a frequent hallmark of sustainable governance, so too is use of rivalrous initiatives, where one institution, rule instrument, or process is specifically designed as a check and balance on another. Sustainable governance will "play out" differently in different jurisdictions, reflecting the unique social, cultural, political, legal, and historical characteristics of each jurisdiction. In developing jurisdictions, where the legal and regulatory systems may be particularly weak, nonstate institutions and initiatives may need to play a particularly important role until the state's capacities can be brought up to speed.

3 While the Canadian context has been the focus of discussion here, it should be clear that the sustainable-governance concept should be equally relevant in other jurisdictions, although the specific manifestation of the concept will differ depending upon the circumstances.

4 There are many examples of innovative, collaborative approaches to governing that are used at the federal-government level, at the provincial level, and elsewhere. For a variety of cultural and historical reasons, Canada seems to possess a particularly receptive and positive environment for the development of innovative and collaborative approaches to governing. Innovations that "fit" the sustainable-governance paradigm tend to:

- Work particularly well against a backdrop of conventional governance institutions, rule instruments, and processes

- Recognize the value of multiple centres of authority and responsibility all targeted at the same policy context
- Frequently include elements of both policy development and policy implementation
- Often harness (or attempt to harness) citizen, consumer, community, NGO, and industry energies (not just fear of government-imposed legal liability) in order to address a particular policy problem
- Explicitly acknowledge the value of multiactor collaborations, particularly those that cross the public-, private-, and third-sector boundaries
- Work under the assumption that a certain amount of rivalrous institutional, rule-instrument, and process friction is valuable as a check-and-balance mechanism and as a means to stimulate creative tension among initiatives and actors.

5 While there are many examples of institutional, rule-instrument, and process innovations in Canada, these tend to be random and ad hoc rather than drawn together and used in a coordinated, coherent way, policy context by policy context. Sustainable governance is all about systematic, concerted efforts to draw on the full range of options available. Although far from perfect, and not necessarily appropriate for Canada, the various examples of sectorwide governance initiatives from the European Union discussed above provide useful illustrations of how sustainable governance could be undertaken.

6 Although sustainable governance may hold considerable promise as a more effective means of governing, this is not to downplay the significant challenges associated with its implementation. Systematically putting such a concept in place will involve a considerable investment of time and resources, will require acceptance of a greater degree of complexity associated with the use of multiple centres of authority, and will necessitate considerable efforts from governments, the private sector, and civil society to ensure maintenance of appropriate levels of accountability, transparency, fairness, and coordination.

7 Among other things, a strategy for implementation of the sustainable-governance model might include:

- Articulation of model sustainable-governance approaches
- Review of existing policy contexts at a macro level to determine what elements of sustainable governance are missing from current regimes and why
- Development and support of policy environments that stimulate sustainable governance

- Systematic support for an enhanced role for civil society
- Publication of case studies providing examples of nascent and promising sustainable governance (e.g., why have particular policy contexts proven to be more receptive to sustainable governance-type innovations?)
- Creation of multistakeholder learning and sharing forums on sustainable governance.

# From Welfare State to Social Union: Shifting Choices of Governing Instruments, Intervention Rationales, and Governance Rules in Canadian Social Policy

MICHAEL J. PRINCE

## INTRODUCTION

Consideration of policy tools helps us to understand the nature of social programs by giving us an appreciation for potential options in debating and designing policies of the Canadian state. In this chapter, the connection between governing instruments and rationales for government intervention is explored within the context of social policy, the Social Union Framework Agreement (SUFA) between the federal government and the provinces and territories, and the vastly improved budgetary circumstances of the federal government.

In focusing on the tools and rationales of public action, fiscal resources, and intergovernmental relations, my aim is to identify trends both in the instruments of social policy and in the ideas dominating their creation. The first section briefly describes what policy tools are and why it is particularly useful to look at them at the present time in social development. The section then lays out the repertoire of basic social-policy tools available to government. These tools are voluntary action, information and exhortation, direct public expenditures, tax expenditures, service provision, regulation, and taxation.

The second section outlines the reasons why certain government social interventions have been advanced and more or less accepted by governments and citizens over time, why social programs are needed, and why certain policy tools should be used. A review of intervention rationales is important because the language used (and not used) to talk about a problem or group of people can affect how the issues are constructed, which groups are either identified or ignored, and which solutions are either considered appropriate responses or likely to be left off the agenda. The third section examines the SUFA as a noteworthy recent development in Canadian federalism and social policy. A symbolic policy tool itself, the agreement can further be seen as a bundle of policy tools and rationales for government intervention.

The fourth and concluding section summarizes recent trends in the mix of social-policy tools and suggests some directions for Canada's social union. One such tool, the Social Union Framework Agreement, is both a substantive instrument (addressing the value content of policy decisions) and a procedural instrument (addressing decision processes and relationships among governments and societal actors). Within the context of intergovernmental relations, the SUFA is a politically negotiated statement of the norms of good governance for instrument choice and public action. A review of the SUFA reveals that it contains different rules for existing, versus new, Canada-wide social transfers and no rules for most other policy tools used by the federal government in social development. By itself, the agreement does not pose a great barrier to social-policy reforms by the federal government acting on its own or in partnership with provinces and territories.

The shifting choices of governing instruments and intervention rationales illustrate the transition in policy regimes from the welfare-state model of social security, which emerged and operated from the 1940s into the 1980s, to the more recent social-union model of socio-economic development. Rather than an either-or approach to instrument choice, these trends embrace a mix of expenditure-based instruments along with other substantive instruments. This mixed approach has long been the Canadian policy style in social spending and provision, exhibiting patterns of stability and change.

## REPERTOIRE OF SOCIAL-POLICY TOOLS

A core element of the design and content of all public policy is tools or governing instruments (Hood 1984; Doern and Phidd 1992; Pal 1997; Howlett and Ramesh 2003). In public management, policy instruments are often seen as administrative methods for implementing policy goals. Policy tools, however, are not value-neutral devices, nor just mechanical implements for implementing programs, a point made in chapters 3, 5, and 6, among others, in this volume. In politics, governing tools are also recognized to be methods for seeking compliance and changing or sustaining certain behaviours among citizens. In social policy, these tools are ends and means on several dimensions: They meet human and social needs through the redistribution of income, redress failures or gaps in economic markets, regulate the actions of individuals and groups, realize certain shared values, and grant official recognition to particular groups in the community (Richards 1997; Rice and Prince 2000).

Policy tools reflect and relate to the political culture and the style of governance as well as to economic, legal, constitutional, and social circumstances. Social-policy tools, and their availability, desirability, and efficacy, must be closely considered with respect to (1) community, political, and economic values, (2) general reasons of intervention and more specific program objectives, (3) perceived resource availability, and (4) the experiences and changing conditions of the diverse and diversified client groups. Debates over social issues and over the SUFA frequently focus on the policy means and instruments as well as on the purposes and goals. Certain policy tools are valued (or not) in themselves by particular groups and institutions in networked contexts. Social assistance versus workfare, universal versus selective programs, and tax points versus transfer payments for the provinces and territories are but a few of the arguments over design and implementation styles in Canadian social policy.

Consideration of social-policy tools is especially significant in the present period. The emergence of fiscal surpluses at federal and provincial levels in recent years has altered the social-policy toolkit with renewed possibilities for investments in services and spending programs as well as calls for tax relief (Prince 1998; Hale 2002). In addition, the SUFA, the 1999 agreement between the federal and the provincial and territorial governments, symbolizes some of the latest choices with respect to intergovernmental dialogue and processes concerning the exercise of the federal spending power in fundamental areas of social policy.

Considerable public and political attention has long been directed at the federal spending power – its use, legitimacy, and place within intergovernmental relations and social policy. Federal social-policy activities are not confined to only the areas of legislative jurisdiction of the federal domain. The Canadian Parliament may allocate funds to individuals, other governments, and nongovernmental organizations, with or without conditions attached, for any social purposes inside or outside its legislative jurisdiction.

The federal spending power has been central to the development and, at times, restraint of Canadians' social programs (Prince 1999a). As a policy tool, the spending power is certainly the most visible, most frequently used, most controversial, and likely most significant in addressing social issues and meeting human-development needs. As a statement on good governance, the SUFA seeks to ensure cooperation in identifying Canada-wide priorities and objectives as well as in improving both funding predictability and consultation and support prior to the introduction of any new federal initiatives in health care, postsecondary education, social assistance, and social services. Thus the legitimacy of the federal spending power is intended to rest on the norms of advance notice, joint planning, a degree of intergovernmental consensus on goals and priorities, respect for jurisdiction, and sustainable financing.

Yet the federal spending power is just one of the many social-policy tools in the government's repertoire of interventions. There is a fuller stock of policy tools available that modern governments are accustomed to and prepared to use when responding to needs and implementing social programs (Howlett and Ramesh 2003).

The welfare state – a somewhat misleading label of actual policy and administrative practice – has always contained multiple sites of authority, activity, and accountability. Governments have seven main policy tools with which to affect the material and social wellbeing of people and communities and to ensure compliance with policy decisions: (1) voluntary action, (2) information and exhortation, (3) direct public expenditures, (4) tax expenditures, (5) direct delivery and provision of services, (6) regulation, and (7) taxation. For each social policy tool, there are various possible applications and numerous actual examples. Some illustrations are presented in Table 11.1.

Acts of *charity and volunteerism* as well as efforts by community and family are seen as complements to, or even as substitutes for, governmental initiatives on certain economic and social matters. In contemporary visions of health care and health policy, for example, self-care, mutual aid, and livable communities are identified and put forward as health-promotion mechanisms. The 1990s witnessed a renaissance for social support both in public policy and in political rhetoric (Broadbent 1999), a distinguishing feature of the shift from the welfare-state model to the social-union model in Canada. This renaissance reminds us that nonstate actors and multilevel governance – topics explored more fully in chapters 8, 9, 13, and 15 – are classic features of social policy and administration (Rice and Prince 2000). The rediscovery of voluntarism and informal care is linked to the critical reevaluation of the welfare state, to economic and social changes shaping and shaking beliefs about needs and how best to meet them, and to a period of investigation and innovation in policy and practice. Voluntary action as a policy tool reflects a society-oriented conception of social care. A key theme in the prevailing discourse of community care points to the limits of

Table 11.1
Social-policy tools: Applications and examples

| Policy tools | Applications | Examples |
|---|---|---|
| Voluntary action | Mutual aid<br>Social and informal support<br>Charities and foundations | Self-help groups<br>Family care, food banks<br>United Way |
| Information and exhortation | Advisory councils<br>Consultations<br>Proclamations, speeches<br>Social marketing | National Council of Welfare<br>Social Security Review<br>Combat Racism<br>"Don't Drink and Drive" |
| Direct expenditures | Benefits to persons<br>Transfers to governments<br>Grants and contributions<br>to organizations | Canada Pension Plan<br>Canada Health and Social<br>Transfer<br>Multicultural and women's<br>groups |
| Tax expenditures | Personal-income provisions<br>Corporate-income provisions<br>Retail-tax provisions | Child Tax Benefit<br>Non-taxation of registered<br>charities<br>Government sales tax (GST)<br>credit |
| Service provision | Education<br>Employment<br>Health<br>Housing<br>Social Services | Schools<br>Job centres<br>Hospitals<br>Social housing<br>Daycare |
| Regulation | Civic<br>Economic<br>Social | Human rights<br>Occupational licensure<br>Consumer protection |
| Taxation | Consumption<br>Income<br>Payroll<br>Property<br>User Charges | GST<br>Personal and corporate<br>Employment-insurance premiums<br>School taxes<br>Tuition fees |

government in meeting needs and to the demand that its role be redefined. Linked with a reawakened interest in community approaches are the concepts of social capital and cohesion, partnerships and empowerment in relation to social networks and policy, and citizen engagement and consumer participation (Rice and Prince 2000).

*Moral suasion or exhortation* is frequently used in social programming since it involves a relatively low degree of state intervention, resources, and direct control. Community and government agencies employ exhortation to inform the general public or particular client groups about issues, to influence attitudes and actions of the public, and to induce support for or compliance with some policy direction. Methods of persuasion (telling and selling) include advertising, advisory bodies, consultations, conferences, proclamations, and speeches. Social marketing has emerged as an important application of this policy tool in recent decades (Stanbury and Fulton 1984). It involves efforts by public bodies to affect people's preferences and actions with respect to such matters as the use of alcohol, tobacco, and narcotics; fitness and eating habits; sexual behaviour regarding AIDS; and public health messages about Sudden Acute Respiratory Syndrome (SARS) and other communicable diseases. This instrument is also central to activities in community development and health, which typically involve gathering information about the assets and challenges of a locality (Glouberman et al. 2003) with a view to identifying possible interventions and to encouraging self-organization for tackling needs and issues.

When Canadians think about social policy, many equate it with *direct public expenditures* – that is, the allocation of tax dollars to programs, services, and benefits. This is certainly understandable given the visibility and scale of expenditures in the budgets of government, the direct link between cash benefits and citizens, and the prominence of spending issues and transfer-payment flows within Canada's system of fiscal federalism. The spending instrument comprises a large and complex system of expenditure designs and choices. It includes the provision of cash payments to (1) persons, on either an individual or a family basis; (2) transfers to other governments, including those of provinces, territories, and First Nations; and (3) nongovernmental organizations representing aboriginal people, minority official language groups, persons with disabilities, women, youth, and visible minorities. Transfers from the federal government to other levels of government take several forms, as do transfers to persons and nongovernmental organizations (Hobson and St Hilaire 1994).

Intergovernmental transfers in Canadian social policy have been of four main types. One kind has been cost-shared, conditional, and open-ended grants. The Canada Assistance Plan and the Vocational Rehabilitation for Disabled Persons (VRDP) program are examples that were eliminated in the mid-1990s by the government of Prime Minister Jean Chrétien. A second type is cost-shared, conditional, and closed-ended grants. The Employability Assistance for Persons with Disabilities program, the successor to the VRDP, and New Brunswick Works are examples. Block-funded and unconditional grants are a third kind, the programs for provincial equalization and territorial financing being the major examples. Block-funded and conditional grants are the fourth type, and examples include programs such as the Comprehensive Funding Arrangements for First Nations, the Canada Health and Social Transfer, and (as of April 2004) the latter's successors, the Canada Health Transfer and the Canada Social Transfer.

Along with direct expenditures, *tax expenditures* represent an important tool in the social-policy field. As special provisions in the tax laws, tax expenditures give preferences to selected individuals or groups in particular circumstances or who pursue particular courses of action. Tax expenditures can be in the form of exclusions of money income for tax purposes and exemptions and deductions that reduce assessed income in determining taxable income. Other types of tax expenditures are deferrals that delay the taxation of income and preferential tax rates, which reduce taxes by applying lower rates to part or all of a taxpayer's income. Increasingly more common in social policy since the 1970s are tax credits. These credits are subtracted from taxes normally computed and, if they are refundable tax credits, provide a cash rebate. In comparison with direct expenditures, tax expenditures of the same nominal amount are often worth more to individuals because most direct expenditures are taxable to the recipient. At the federal level, there are approximately seventy-five social-policy tax expenditures, most of them delivered through the system for taxing personal income (Government of Canada 2003). They pertain to culture and recreation, employment, education, children and families, health, housing, income support, pensions, and retirement. Over the past twenty-five years, provincial and territorial governments have also increased their use of tax expenditures to confer benefits and to address social-policy objectives.

*Direct delivery and provision of services* by government or public institutions (e.g., libraries, employment-counselling centres, schools, and hospitals) is another major instrument in the social-policy toolkit. Associated with this tool are public-sector payrolls and collective-bargaining systems, which are embedded with various values and policy issues. This tool is more significant at the levels of provincial and local government than at the federal level in Canada. This is apparent by the fact that only about 15 per cent of federal program expenditures is devoted to wages and salaries, while for the provinces about 60 per cent of all program spending is committed to financing labour-intensive services (Watson, Richards, and Brown 1994). Federal social-service delivery has traditionally centred on specific client groups, particularly on status Indians, Inuit, and more recently, Métis people, as well as on veterans and their dependants, on immigrants, and on refugees. In all these areas and others (e.g., social housing), the federal government has been withdrawing and or devolving responsibility for delivery and management of services to other governments and organizations. Thus part of the rethinking of government under the program review of the mid- to late-1990s resulted in a retooling of government (Paquet and Shepherd 1996). More recently, under Prime Minister Paul Martin, the federal government, for similar reasons of enhancing economies and efficiencies in the public service, has embarked on another program-review process.

A common thread running through most definitions of *regulation* as a policy tool is the idea of government intervening in the affairs of private-sector organizations and commercial processes. Economic regulation is about controlling the market activities of trade, competition, production, supply, and price. Even the concept of social regulation almost always refers solely to industrial and occupational activities and their effects, again related to market deficiencies. Thus social regulation comprises rules regarding workplace health and safety, consumer protection, environmental stewardship, and cultural content in popular media. A third type of regulation, ignored in the mainstream social-science literature, is "civic regulation" (Prince 1999b). Civic regulation refers to rule making by the state, or by agencies on its behalf, with respect to numerous aspects of human behaviour and needs, justice and public order, moral conduct and standards, intergovernmental relations, and human rights and civil liberties.

We all have a rendezvous with revenue. *Taxation,* of course, is a fundamental function of the state, and reports of the demise of taxation, as a core task of the body politic because of economic globalization, are greatly exaggerated. Modern governments derive their revenues from a variety of sources: income or production activity (personal and corporate taxes), consumption activity (general sales and excise taxes), and capital or wealth (property taxes). Each of these taxes prompts responses from the individuals and firms affected directly or indirectly by the measures. Thus each tax, the combination of all taxes together, and the interaction of taxes with transfers have allocative, redistributive, and political impacts that are critical to government-revenue systems (Trebilcock et al. 1982). Tax systems are generally called upon to perform three distinct functions:

1 Raise revenues to finance the operations of government, effectively collecting finances for use by all the other policy tools discussed above
2 Pursue a variety of economic and fiscal policy goals, such as stimulating private-sector consumption and spending during a recession, encouraging investment and saving, or promoting economic development and job creation in designated regions
3 Address social-policy goals such as alleviating low-income poverty, redistributing income across various groups, and modulating market-based inequalities, all in line with some notions of fairness and ability to pay.

Part of the critique of welfare states in recent decades holds that taxes are a "necessary evil" at best and have risen to excessively high levels. From this perspective, taxation is the public confiscation of private wealth. From another perspective, taxes are an essential tool for funding adequate cash benefits and high-quality services. Thus income taxes, health-care premiums, and school and property taxes, among others, are seen to represent private contributions to public wealth and social capital. The politics of taxation therefore revolve around the conflicts, choices, and compromises made between competing economic and social considerations, rival ideological beliefs, and varied public-policy objectives (Hale 2002).

## WHY SOCIAL POLICY?

A practical task for policy analysis is to explore the question of why governments might do something and approach problems in a certain way (Bardach 2000). Reasons for modern government intervention in social affairs may be grouped chronologically into two broad categories. The first category refers to the main reasons for government's social-policy role from the 1940s through the 1970s, generally the period of building a fairly comprehensive system of social programs in Canada – in short, a welfare state. The second category refers to reasons for public intervention that have emerged and been articulated more regularly in recent decades. This second category has not replaced the first set of reasons but rather has influenced and been influenced by those earlier reasons. Consequently, at the start of the twenty-first century, we have a complex array of aims and justifications for social-policy making that contribute to a partial shift at least from the welfare-state model to what, in Canada, political and bureaucratic elites now often call the social union.

### Classic Welfare-State Reasons for Government Intervention

Traditional reasons for the federal and provincial governments' social role were to address, promote, and maintain some degree of (1) social security and support; (2) economic stability and growth; (3) public order, justice, and safety; and (4) intergovernmental and interregional sharing (Armitage 1996; Manzer 1985).

*Social security and support* – at times called the "safety net" – are likely the most commonly recognized features of postwar social policy. The role of government here is to offer protection, through collective provision, against such risks and hazards as unemployment, sickness, disability, old age and retirement, premature death, and injury at work.

The aim of social policy is to achieve minimum standards of support in income, housing, hospital and medical care, employment services, and various community and personal services. Need for these programs and services is assumed to exist in certain cases (e.g., primary and second-ary education) but is tested by assessing means, income, or employabil-ity in other cases. The policy tools most associated with this reason for intervention remain direct expenditures in the form of universal bene-fits, social insurance, social assistance and income supplements, payroll taxes for contributing to social-insurance programs, and the direct pro-vision of services.

*Economic stability and growth* are strategic factors in social policy generally. From the standpoint of the economy as a whole, social-policy expenditures can aid in maintaining the flow of consumer pur-chasing power in a slowdown and can therefore assist in maintaining employment at higher levels than would otherwise occur. This is, of course, the thinking of Keynes and others. The task of government is to use a judicious mix of changes in taxation and in the level of total gov-ernment spending in order to stimulate consumption in goods and ser-vices when demand is deficient and to constrain demand when it is excessive in relation to the productive capacity of the economy.

Various policy tools are available with which governments can either stimulate their economies or deliberately restrain them. Automatic stabilizers include agriculture and farm subsidies, a graduated system for taxing personal income, unemployment insurance, and social-assistance payments. Discretionary tools include exhortation, tax mea-sures (e.g., cuts, freezes, and increases), job-creation schemes, housing construction, and public-sector wage controls. Another policy device for achieving a degree of personal economic stability is the indexation of certain benefits and tax brackets to rises in the cost of living or other indices. Economic and social regulations are also important policy tools. By improving the quality of labour, enhancing the mobility of workers, encouraging consumption or savings, and rewarding paid work, social-policy interventions can advance economic development and growth.

*Public order, justice, and safety* are often overlooked when thinking about social policy and the welfare state. Certainly, this reason for in-tervention relates to an earlier function of government: that of the "night watchman," or regulatory state. Yet it provides the framework of law and order that is essential for the pursuit of personal, market-oriented, and civic goals and public-policy activities within the Cana-dian community. Here, policies aim to reduce deviancy, prevent crime, and achieve a sense of safety, civility, and fairness in social relations. The related governing instruments encompass those public services and facilities concerned with corrections, policing, and the courts as well as regulatory tools, including civic regulations and disciplinary rules (Prince 1999b).

*Intergovernmental and interregional sharing* is central to Canada's system of federalism and social policy. Fiscal arrangements between the federal and the provincial and territorial governments, related to this fourth reason for government intervention, give concrete meaning to the term "social union," the latest phrase to describe this aim and achievement of policy and governance. Intergovernmental grants address (1) fiscal gaps between the expenditure responsibilities and the taxation powers of provinces/territories; (2) fiscal equity in terms of equalizing capacities of governments; and (3) interjurisdictional spillovers or externalities in the social benefits and costs of particular economic or social interventions (Boadway 1992). The aim for the federal spending power is to alleviate the wide disparity of wealth and tax-raising capacity among provincial/territorial governments and to adapt public policy to changing circumstances and values. Intergovernmental grants may well enhance social cohesion or national unity by offering comparable benefits and services across the country and by raising the visibility of the federal government with citizens.

Over time, each of these rationales has changed in different ways with respect to political meaning and public attention. The trend for each approach has been to expand in scope, although this trend was constrained somewhat in the 1980s and 1990s due to government restraint efforts. Each of these justifications for social policy remains relevant today and arguably even more essential and vital than in earlier decades because of new risks and opportunities facing the Canadian economy and society (Rice and Prince 2000).

### Contemporary Reasons for Government Intervention

Alongside these traditional rationales, newer reasons have arisen that justify new and altered government roles in social policy. These contemporary rationales are (1) investment, development, and adjustment; (2) compensation and reconciliation; (3) equity and diversity; and (4) Canadian citizenship and social rights.

The *investment, development, and adjustment* justification for government intervention implies investing in people in order to support their developmental needs and to assist them in adjusting to changes in the economy and their own lives. With some exceptions, the concepts of adjustment and investment were traditionally used infrequently to justify social-policy interventions.[1] In the current era, however, talk of human-resource investment and labour adjustment – oriented more

toward micro and supply-side economics than toward Keynesian demand management – is a major part of social-policy discourse in Canada and other countries of the Organization for Economic Cooperation
and Development (OECD).

Behind each policy tool and reason for government intervention is a
theory of action – that is, a logic of how resource inputs and program
activities are related to certain desired and intended outcomes. In the
case of social investment, the commitment of funds and services is
believed to support personal and community development as well as
labour-market adjustments of various kinds, resulting in the prevention
of certain problems and in the advancement of citizen participation in
economic and social affairs.

Notions of adjustment and investment have entered into program areas previously justified by concepts of social security and human need.
This language is apparent in the fields of education, training, child
daycare, welfare, and employment insurance. Investing in people and
helping them adjust to change can involve broadening access to em-
ployment-development services, literacy programs, and higher learning.
It can mean helping people to complete high school and to obtain ap-
prenticeship opportunities. Another motive for investing in people is to
tackle the problem of earnings and income polarization among Canadians. Investment also concerns the social capital, or capacity and
infrastructure, of our cities and communities. Resources necessary to
sustaining either formal or informal support networks and agencies or
the physical locales of schools, hospitals, housing, libraries, and other
public facilities can all be regarded as societal investments.

The federal policy blueprint *Canada's Innovation Strategy*, released
in 2002, comprises two documents, *Achieving Excellence: Investing in
People, Knowledge and Opportunity* and *Knowledge Matters: Skills
and Learning for Canadians*. The document *Achieving Excellence* considers knowledge to be a strategic national asset that can strengthen the
role of science and research in building an innovative economy. The
companion document, *Knowledge Matters*, examines policy options
for strengthening education and training in Canada in order to provide
greater opportunities for all to participate in and benefit from the new
economy (Government of Canada 2002).

Demographic and labour-market research shows that by 2020, Canada could be short a million workers due to the retirement of the large
cohort of middle-aged workers currently in the labour force. Moreover,
half of those who will comprise the workforce in the year 2015 are already working and will require continuous upgrading of skills if they
are to thrive in the new economy. In just a few years, fully 70 per cent
of the new jobs created in Canada's economy will require some form

of postsecondary education (Stewart 2002). Accordingly, *Knowledge Matters* sets out national goals, milestones, and targets for improving the skills and learning of children and youth, students, adult workers and learners, and immigrants. With Canada already having one of the highest college and university participation rates in the world, potential for enrolment growth is paramount among less advantaged individuals and groups. These include low- to moderate-income families, aboriginal youth, persons with disabilities, people who did not complete high school (about 12 per cent in Canada), and high-school graduates with inadequate literacy skills (approximately one-quarter of graduates in Canada).

*Compensation and reconciliation* as rationales for public intervention are now also finding relatively more use as arguments for social-policy development. Historically, restitution was part of sentencing and punishment practices in the criminal-justice system (Manzer 1985), and forms of compensation were apparent in a few social programs such as workers' compensation schemes, orphans' benefits, and veterans' disability and survivor pensions. Since the 1980s, the concept of compensation has been constitutionally rooted in the Canadian Charter of Rights and Freedoms, permitting affirmative-action programs to ameliorate conditions of disadvantaged individuals and groups, such as the federal employment-equity laws of 1985 and 1996.

The last decade alone abounds with examples of compensation and reconciliation claims in Canadian politics and policy responses, with claimants having included the following:

- Individuals, health-care workers, local economies, and provincial and federal health budgets seeking redress of the impacts of Sudden Acute Respiratory Syndrome (SARS)
- People born with thalidomide-induced physical defects
- Persons wrongly convicted and jailed
- People who contracted hepatitis-C through tainted blood
- Groups of workers in the public and private sectors seeking redress of pay inequity
- Haemophiliac and transfusion patients infected with the AIDS virus
- People with mental disabilities sterilized without their permission
- Aboriginal men and women sexually and physically abused at residential schools
- Victims of crimes seeking the right to prepare and read impact statements in the courts.

Charter politics shape some claims, but many are rooted in the personal and social costs of past policy decisions and practices. In certain cases, public authorities and other societal institutions, such as churches, are identified as responsible for costs that result in various forms of personal and cultural harm and loss. These costs and issues are not as abnormal or marginal as is often thought by students or practitioners of social policy. Other claims for compensation, such as those arising from SARS, are related in part to globalization and international travel (thus reminding us of the continued presence of contagious and communicable diseases) and in part to the politics of fiscal federalism (Levy and Fischetti 2003). Such serious outbreaks illustrate that public-health measures are a "merit good" that, while undersupported by some individuals for various reasons (Trebilcock et al. 1982, 66), has significant externalities, justifying government action through any number of policy tools.

In choosing governing instruments for social policy, it is well to remember that a number of individuals and groups in Canadian society are pressing to have their respective pasts publicly acknowledged and attended to by social policy in the present. Compensation and reconciliation are about accepting and assuming responsibility for the consequences of past policies or practices. They can also be efforts to correct mistakes and normalize relations between a group and government. They involve, in part, the policy tool of exhortation and symbolic reassurance and often, in part, expenditures, services, and legislation.

Promoting and recognizing *equity and diversity* is another prominent rationale for contemporary social policy in Canada. Perhaps this is most apparent at the federal level with respect to aboriginal peoples through land claims, treaty negotiations, and governance initiatives. To be sure, "technological innovation and the internationalization of markets have changed the political calculus by introducing new constellations of interests into the policy-making process" (Trebilcock 2002, 30–1). As well, shifting immigration patterns, constitutional developments, and the politicization of previously marginalized social groups have introduced new interests into policy processes in Canada (Rice and Prince 2000). Fairness and inclusion, seen in relation to a large set of social and cultural categories, now go beyond the territorial and political categories of governments and regions and beyond the material category of income groups, although these remain profoundly important in our politics and policy making. Government intervenes in society and the economy to modify the living and working relationships within and among such categories as gender, race, ethnicity, language, new immigrants, disability, generations (e.g., baby-boomers, generation-Xers), and sexual orientation. Some of these categories are recognized as "special client groups" in policy while others are not. Many find mention in the Canadian Charter of Rights and Freedoms.

A challenge for developing a new vision for government social policy is to decide how best to increase the opportunities, status, and well-being of diverse individuals and groups; how best to achieve inclusion while respecting difference at the same time; what values are widely shared among Canadians; and what roles do (and can) social programs play in strengthening cohesion. In our increasingly globalizing economy and pluralized society, this challenge has become a central task of statecraft in Canada.

The legal concept of citizenship is a relatively recent one in Canada's history. It received statutory recognition in 1947 and constitutional status only in 1982 with the entrenchment of the Charter. As a consequence, *citizenship and social rights* have become a major rationale for contemporary social-policy debate and development. Citizenship is about membership and participation in a political community. It is about the terms and conditions and about the rights and duties under which members have agreed to live with one another and in relation to the state.

Terms and conditions of social citizenship are rarely absolute and undemanding but rather entail trade-offs and the balancing of various values. Consider the example of mobility rights. Section 6 of the Charter deals with mobility rights (i.e., the right of every citizen or permanent resident of Canada to international movement and interprovincial movement and to the pursuit of a livelihood in any province). However, Section 6(4) qualifies the mobility right of pursuing a livelihood in any province. This subsection permits "any law, program or activity that has as its object the amelioration in a province of conditions of individuals in that province who are socially or economically disadvantaged if the rate of employment in that province is below the rate of employment in Canada." Provincial governments may introduce preferential employment practices favouring local trades or specific occupations if the province's unemployment rate is higher than the national average (Hogg 2000).

Section 15(1) of the Charter, which deals with equality rights, states that every individual is equal before and under the law and has the right to equal protection and equal benefit of the law without discrimination. Section 15(2) adds, however, that "Subsection (1) does not preclude any law, program, or activity that has as its object the amelioration of conditions of disadvantages of individuals or groups including those that are disadvantaged because of race, national or ethnic origin, colour, religion, sex, or mental or physical disability." Thus the first subsection provides for the universal application of every law, while the second subsection immediately qualifies this provision by validating affirmative-action and equity programs, what some social-policy analysts call "positive discrimination" on behalf of the underprivileged.

Under Canadian federalism, citizenship is also about how governments have agreed to work together and relate to their residents. This is clearly evident in the Social Union Framework Agreement, reached in 1999 between the federal government, the provinces (except Quebec), and the territories.

## THE SOCIAL UNION FRAMEWORK AGREEMENT

The SUFA is an interesting mixture of policy-tool characteristics. An administrative agreement among first ministers, the accord is an exercise in exhortation and symbolism. Governments at both the federal and provincial/territorial levels retain considerable discretion in interpreting, observing, and implementing the various parts of the agreement. It contains a series of nonjusticiable commitments – that is, public pledges by government leaders that have no legal status and thus are nonenforceable in the courts. Since it concerns intergovernmental relations, the SUFA conveys the promise of a high level of state provision of social policy and the state's significant presence in Canadians' lives. The immediate aim of the agreement was to restore and stabilize federal funding for social programs, particularly in health care and postsecondary education. The framework has been the subject of much scholarly analysis and debate (Gagnon and Segal 2000; McIntosh 2002). My interest here is to examine the expression of intervention rationales and policy instruments in the agreement.

The SUFA addresses several elements of citizenship and several policy instruments. The most obvious perhaps is exhortation. The following are among the values and initiatives to which the accord commits the governments:

- The equality, rights, and dignity of all Canadians
- Full and active participation of all Canadians in Canada's social and economic life
- Opportunities for Canadians to have meaningful input respecting social policies and programs
- A full review of the agreement and its implementation
- The mobility right of Canadians to pursue opportunities anywhere in Canada
- Access for all Canadians, wherever they live or move in Canada, to essential services
- Social programs and services of reasonably comparable quality nationwide

- Appropriate mechanisms by which citizens can appeal unfair administrative practices and lodge complaints about access and service.

Another prominent feature of the agreement is its emphasis on citizen engagement, or participatory citizenship, in policy processes. The agreement includes stated commitments to ensuring that effective mechanisms are in place not only for informing Canadians of decision processes (e.g., accountability and transparency features), but also for involving Canadians in developing social priorities and in reviewing the performance and outcomes of social programs. A good deal of the agreement deals with information as a governing tool – that is, the monitoring of programs, the sharing of results with other governments and the public, joint planning, consultation, and the provision of reciprocal notice on intended policy reforms.

Both classic and contemporary rationales for social policy are given expression in the SUFA. Social assistance and interregional sharing are the traditional themes, while the modern reasons given emphasize pan-Canadian citizenship, investment in labour mobility, and to a lesser extent, equity and diversity. Different rationales for social intervention appear to correspond to the stated interests of the different levels of government in reaching agreement on the social accord. For the federal government, the priority rationales were those respecting labour mobility and citizenship. For the provinces and territories, of priority were those rationales respecting stable and adequate federal funding through equalization and other social transfers, process matters of notice and dispute resolution, and the recognition of diversity and equity objectives. Absent from the text of the agreement are the rationales of macroeconomic development, public order, and compensation/restitution. Their nonappearance perhaps reflects the decline of Keynesianism as a policy paradigm, the tendency to overlook issues of justice and public order as social policy, and the fact that issues of compensation, almost by definition, involve irregular policy processes and decisions. The agreement is full of references to mobility, legal, and equality rights as well as to aboriginal and treaty rights. These statements, along with a pledge to provide citizens with appropriate appeal mechanisms, underscore the legislative and regulatory tools of governing and governance.

The agreement also affirms equalization[2] and the five principles of Medicare[3] as vital elements to Canadian federalism and social policy. In this regard, given that these are statements of substance and thus, in essence, policy blueprints of fundamental importance to national unity and social wellbeing, the SUFA is about more than merely process. In the case of equalization, for instance, the rationale is to promote equal opportunities and to reduce disparities by making payments that ensure provincial and territorial governments sufficient revenues with which to provide reasonably comparable levels of public services at reasonably comparable levels of taxation.

### Legitimacies, Commitments, and Silences

What potentially is the influence of the SUFA on major changes in federal transfer payments? Divergent views exist in the literature on the implications of the SUFA for social-policy making. Sherri Torjman of the Caledon Institute on Social Policy is wary of the SUFA's hidden consequences and suggests that "new federal-provincial relationships inadvertently could end up impeding progress on disability issues" (Torjman 2001, 152). Her concern is that the emphasis on collaboration may make it more difficult for the federal government to exercise strong leadership and to take definitive action. David Cameron and Fraser Valentine are more optimistic, noting that to the extent that the SUFA encourages a more collaborative approach to intergovernmental relations and social-policy making, "it could establish some principles aimed at national coordination in these areas" (Cameron and Valentine 2001, 31).

The agreement validates the federal spending power by signalling its political recognition and acceptance by the signatory provinces and territories. The historical importance of the spending power is noted, and its underlying value is tied to the pursuit of national objectives. In addition to granting *legitimacy* to the federal spending power, the SUFA contains some *limits* on and some important *silences* about when and how the spending power might be used. Put another way, the SUFA speaks about some of the policy tools and rationales discussed earlier but not about others. The relation of the SUFA to the federal spending power and to particular policy tools is outlined in Table 11.2.

With respect to the "renewal [of] or significant funding changes" to *existing* social transfers to provinces/territories, the federal government commits to consulting with these governments "at least one year prior." The agreement contains a restriction on *new* Canada-wide intergovernmental transfers initiated by the federal government in the areas of health care, postsecondary education, social assistance, and social services, whether these transfers are block-funded or cost-shared. The limitation on this function is not especially onerous. The federal government agrees to "work collaboratively with all provincial and territorial governments to identify Canada-wide priorities and objectives" and will "not introduce such new initiatives without the agreement of a majority of [that is, six] provincial governments."[4]

Table 11.2
Policy tools and the Social Union Framework Agreement's commitments
to the federal spending power

| Policy tools | Commitments to existing transfers | Commitments to new transfers |
|---|---|---|
| Intergovernmental financing | Federal government will consult at least one year prior to renewal of transfers or on significant funding changes | Federal government will work with provinces and territories to get agreement on priorities and objectives and will not introduce a new transfer without agreement of at least six provinces |
| Income benefits and tax-expenditure benefits | Silent | Federal government will give at least three months notice to provinces and territories and consult |
| Transfer to organizations: Infrastructure and capacity building | Silent | Federal government will give at least three months notice and consult on any new social transfers to organizations |
| Regulations: Developing rules and defining rights | Silent | Silent |
| Service provision | Silent | Implicit commitment perhaps to give at least three months notice and to consult |

To receive their share of funding for new social initiatives, *all* provincial and territorial governments would need to meet or commit to meeting the agreed Canada-wide objectives and need to respect an agreed accountability framework. The agreement states that "Each provincial and territorial government will determine the detailed program design and mix best suited to its own needs and circumstances to meet the agreed objectives. A provincial-territorial government which, because of its existing programming, does not require the total transfer to fulfill the agreed objectives would be able to reinvest any funds not required for those objectives in the same or a related priority area."[5] The accord is silent on initiatives that are less than Canada-wide, such as bilateral or regional intergovernmental agreements.

The SUFA does not include rules or commitments regarding either (1) *existing* direct transfers to individuals through income-benefit programs or through the system for taxing personal income or (2) *existing* direct transfers to organizations for capacity building or for research and innovation purposes. With respect to *new* transfers to individuals and families or to organizations, the agreement does commit the federal government to giving at least three months notice and to offering to consult with provinces and territories. This section of the SUFA reflects the long-standing position taken by the federal government that it should have the right to initiate transfer programs to individuals and organizations, when only federal funds are involved, without the requirement of formal approval by other governments. Hence the SUFA has different governance rules for existing and new transfers and no rules for most of the other policy roles played by the federal government in social development. By itself, the agreement appears not to pose great barriers to social initiatives by the federal government acting on its own or in partnership with provinces and territories.

That the SUFA is a rather soft set of governance rules for intergovernmental relations is revealed by the continued implementation, over the last five years, of federal social-policy initiatives in areas of provincial jurisdiction with little or no prior consultation and by the move toward earmarked transfers for early-childhood development and health care under the Canada Health and Social Transfer (CHST).[6] At the same time, however, scope for policy and program diversity and discretion by provincial and territorial governments is quite evident in recent federal-provincial-territorial agreements on early learning and childcare. As a result, in all likelihood we will see more social-policy divergence across jurisdictions in Canada over the next several years.

CONCLUSIONS: SHIFTING POLICY REGIMES

Instrument choices for welfare states are multiple and diverse, yielding various blends of social policy, provision, and governance. There are seven main policy tools in the provinces' and federal government's repertoire for addressing public needs and implementing social programs. These tools are voluntary action, information and exhortation, direct public expenditures, tax expenditures, service provision, regulation, and taxation. The same policy tool can be used for a remarkable variety of economic and social purposes. Each tool has several possible applications, and each application in turn has a number of prototypes. In exercising social policy, spending and taxation are not the only "traditional" instruments. What are sometimes called the "newer instruments" and sources of governance, such as social regulation and a reliance on civil-society agencies, are in fact (to varying degrees and in various guises) longstanding elements of provision in European and North American welfare states.

How governments choose policy instruments is shaped by when and why they undertake public action. Process, context, and rationale all must be considered. "Policy analysts have to know which way the wind is blowing," Leslie Pal has remarked, "or instruments that they may recommend for good policy reasons may turn out to have little or no legitimacy among the wider public" (Pal 1997, 103) – and, one could add, little credibility among politicians, bureaucrats, interest groups, and journalists. Since Pal wrote this, the fiscal fortunes of the federal government have dramatically improved, and there has been a shift from fiscal-deficit politics to fiscal-dividend politics.

Budgetary surpluses obviously strengthen the ability of client groups to call for the reinstatement of program cuts and the allocation of new resources. Fiscal prudence continues to be an *idée fix*, with concern shifting from deficit reduction and controlling the debt to deficit avoidance and reducing the debt. At the same time, however, budget surpluses increase public expectations and raise questions for national debate. Easing the fiscal constraints on the federal government widens the policy agenda and the array of policy instruments available. By means of intense concentration on deficit reduction and expenditure controls, the federal government, and many provinces, have regained a capacity to respond to issues with direct expenditures, service provision, tax expenditures, and tax cuts. Paul Martin, when federal finance minister, urged voluntary-sector organizations and charities to submit ideas on job creation and social-services partnerships or else risk not getting a share of the fiscal surplus (Prince 1998).

The belief that the federal government can and should be an active agent of social change, offering new blueprints of reform, is gaining greater currency again. This potential activism is apparent in the SUFA, which both structures and strengthens the federal spending power for future initiatives. This is probably the most controversial part of the agreement (Clarkson and Lewis 1999; Gagnon and Segal 2000; McIntosh 2002). A paradox, for some provinces at least, was that to regulate the federal spending power, they had to recognize its existence. The agreement endorses a positive view of the federal spending power, a governing instrument only loosely conditioned by formal commitments to joint planning and collaboration, advance notice and consultation, and dispute avoidance and resolution. The relative autonomy of the federal state, it seems, is maintained.

Along with continuities, some discernible changes in the mix of policy tools in Canadian social policy have taken place in recent decades (Rice and Prince 2000; Battle and Torjman 2001). Families are still the dominant source of care giving and income redistribution, and there has been a renewed emphasis on community and informal helping.

Reliance on social marketing and other forms of information collection and dissemination has expanded, facilitated greatly by the Internet and other new technologies. The social-expenditure tool has been not simply restrained by all recent governments, but also restructured toward being more targeted than universal in the provision of income security and more "active" than "passive" in labour-market programming. There has also been a shift away from open-ended, cost-shared intergovernmental transfers in favour of closed-ended transfers to provinces and territories. For some First Nations governments, transfers are gradually becoming more multiyear, with relatively fewer program conditions being attached (Abele and Prince 2002). Reliance on tax expenditures as a social-policy tool has grown substantially over the last decade, particularly for families with children, postsecondary students, and persons with disabilities and their family care givers. With respect to service provision, the federal government has been actively exploring alternative delivery approaches. The administration of federal programs for social-housing and labour-market development have been devolved to most provinces and territories, and education and health programs continue to be transferred to First Nations communities. In the field of regulation, while certain industries have seen economic deregulation, some reregulation has taken place, and social regulation and civic regulation have most likely expanded (Doern et al. 1999). On the tax side, surcharges have been eliminated and rates lowered, and in a dramatic move announced in the February 2000 budget, tax brackets were reindexed in full to the inflation rate, greatly reducing the "politics of stealth" in federal social policy (Prince 1999a).

Policy tools, apart from being implementation devices, are value-laden approaches to governance. Neither the choice between different tools nor the pursuit of good governance is merely a technical or managerial concern but an issue of major political significance. Social programs and policy regimes are social constructions, and the meaning of good governance is not self-evident or straightforward. The beliefs and interests of client groups are at stake along with broader ideas about the roles of the state and other institutions in the economy and society. Rethinking and reforming policy invariably involves retooling government (Richards 1997). Aims of the classic welfare-state era, together with more recently articulated policy objectives, provide an elaborate array of shifting and contested reasons for social intervention. In the end, policy means have political meanings.

# 12

# Risk Management and Governance

BRIDGET HUTTER[1]

In recent decades we have witnessed a move from government to governance. In the regulatory area this move has embraced a broad mix of state and nonstate sources of regulation and the use of various instruments that combine incentives and sanctions and appeal to varying deterrence and social-responsibility motivations among the regulated. Good governance has come to refer to coordinated, "joined-up" approaches to policy making, to a recognition that both governments and business are involved in the allocation of finite resources, and to a need for regulatory regimes and agencies to be regarded as legitimate. Such a climate has in some instances fostered the growing alignment of regulation and risk. Both in the academic literature and in the worlds of business and government, risk has become a new lens through which to view the world, and in some parts of the world and in some domains, its relevance has been heightened by a shift in regulatory design toward the cooption of corporate risk-management systems (Hutter 2001; Power 1999).

This chapter will focus on one manifestation of the increasing alignment of risk and regulation, namely the growing prominence of risk-based regulation. The term "risk-based regulation" is used here to refer to the growing prominence of a particular framework for governance and thus comprises more than a loose connection between two concepts; indeed, it denotes a much more systematic and all-embracing approach to governance and instrument choice. I will first consider the emergence and development of risk-based regulation, discussing examples derived from the British experience. Brief attention will be paid to the evidence of its growing popularity elsewhere before moving on to a consideration of why the approach appears to have gained currency at all and the related issue of its merits and limitations.

## RISK-BASED REGULATION

The notion of risk-based regulation emerged during the 1980s and 1990s, when regulatory discussions in a number of countries incorporated an imperative to adopt risk-based strategies. The extent to which such strategies have actually been adopted does, as I will show, undoubtedly vary. But in the most intense cases, this movement was more than a call for the ad hoc adoption of risk-management tools by regulators, representing in its more extreme versions an entire perspective, or framework, for governance. Indeed, in the most pronounced examples, risk-based regulation has emerged as a relatively new and very particular type of risk-regulation regime.[2]

This risk-based regime comprises a system in which there is an overall commitment to a risk-based philosophy. This "philosophy" conceives of risks as manageable and controllable (Bernstein 1996) and, perhaps partly in recognition of this risk-based regulation, is characterized by an anticipatory approach that considers the prevention of risks not yet fully realized. This philosophy is also premised on a holistic, coordinated approach to risk management that conceptualizes risks as interrelated to each other and as having potential consequences for broader economic, natural, social, and political environments.[3] The complexities involved may well lead to an emphasis upon output-based, as opposed to prescriptive, regulation.

This philosophy is translated into practice through a greater emphasis upon technical *risk-based tools*, emerging out of economics (cost-benefit approaches) and science (risk-assessment techniques). Hood et al. (2001) refer to this shift in emphasis as a move to a "cost-benefit analysis culture" – that is, a move away from informal, qualitatively based standard setting toward a more calculative, formalized approach. In such a regime, this shift is typically evident in both standard setting and enforcement, both of which involve the use of multiple tools and sources of regulation. The necessity to coordinate these tools and regulation sources, especially in the ethos of integration, is reflected in the institutional geography of the regime.

Integrated and more holistic approaches to regulating risks involve a number of institutional features. One is the coexistence and coordination of public and private sources of regulation – a move captured in the term "governance." Another is the emergence of superregulatory organizations – that is, large, centralized agencies responsible for a domain of risk management across all relevant sectors. These agencies represent a move from sector-related regulation to domain-related regulation, from particular inspectorates to umbrella agencies that take a broader and more integrative view of risk management, that coordinate across and between sectors, and that facilitate the cross-fertilization and sharing of knowledge. Changes in institutional geography also involve a move from generalist institutional structures for regulation toward institutional machinery characterized by Hood et al. (2001) as "risk bureaucracies" employing specialists in risk management.

While we do not have data that can verify the extent to which regulatory systems have bought into the more extreme versions of risk-based regulation, we can consider the emergence of ideas about risk-based regulation by analyzing regulatory agencies' websites and written documentation. Agencies' websites reflect the ways they wish to portray themselves. Often this may be an ideal portrayal that does not match up with what they actually do, but for the purposes of assessing the extent to which a particular rhetoric about risk-based regulation has been adopted, such data sources do offer opportunities for conducting some preliminary appraisals. I will first consider two cases where there does appear to be a strong commitment to at least the rhetoric of risk-based regulation, namely financial and occupational health-and-safety regulation in Britain.

## OCCUPATIONAL HEALTH AND SAFETY: THE HEALTH AND SAFETY EXECUTIVE

The Health and Safety Executive (HSE), the regulatory agency responsible for occupational health and safety in Britain, was one of the earliest and most prominent examples of a regulatory agency's adopting a risk-based approach to regulation. During its first decade (1974–84), the HSE's encounters with risk were developed very much on a piecemeal basis.[4] The institutional geography of the superagency was in place, and to the extent that the Health and Safety at Work etc. Act 1974 had taken effect, a single organization had been established. But in practice it took some time before the various constituent inspectorates making up the agency were even located in one place. Differences between the constituent inspectorates were often substantial, ranging from their degree of specialization and technical expertise to their individual traditions and organizational cultures (Hutter and Manning 1990). And these differences were reflected in their approaches to work. For example, in the area of enforcement, individual inspectorates adhered very much to their own inspection programs and traditions (Hutter 1997, ch. 5). Indeed, the role of technical knowledge and models varied between inspectorates. Whereas technical expertise was crucial to the work of three inspectorates (i.e., the Mines and Quarries, Nuclear Installations, and Industrial Air Pollution Inspectorates), it was of less significance to the more generalist Factory and Agriculture Inspectorates (Hutter and Manning 1990). Formalized risk models were not at this stage prominent in regulatory design.

During the mid to late 1980s things started to change, and the HSE developed a more systematic risk-based approach to its work. In 1988 it published a landmark document, *The Tolerability of Risk from Nuclear Power Stations.* This document was mainly a consequence of the Sizewell B Inquiry, in which the agency was challenged to define its regulatory position with reference to the building of a nuclear-power station. In the document, the HSE attempted for the first time to outline its approach and philosophy for regulating industrial risks.[5] The report explained the agency's approach to determining what levels of risk are tolerable,[6] as illustrated in Figure 12.1.

The risk assessments took account of (1) plant reliability and risk of plant failures, (2) quality of the plant and its operational procedures, (3) individual risk, and (4) societal risk. As with many risk-based tools, one of the fundamental building blocks of this approach is cost-benefit analysis; thus, in assessing the extra costs of safety measures, "the principle of reasonable practicability (ALARP) applies in such a way that the higher or more unacceptable a risk is, the more, proportionately, employers are expected to spend to reduce it ... Where the risks are less significant, the less, proportionately, it is worth spending to reduce them and at the lower end of the zone it may not be worth spending anything at all" (UK HSE 1988, 10).

This risk-based approach to regulation was innovative and in many respects bold for its time given that the language of risk was not commonplace in either government or regulation. While the approach was developed with specific reference to the nuclear industry, its appeal partially lay in its applicability to other sectors and to cross-sector work.

The HSE's 1988 report was highly influential and had enduring authority over occupational health-and-safety regulation in Britain. This was exemplified in 2001 when the HSE published *Reducing Risks, Protecting People,* in which it outlined its decision-making process as a regulator of risks and stressed the agency's commitment to risk-based approaches to regulation. In this document the HSE set out a framework for reaching decisions about the acceptability of risks that was directly derived from the 1988 document.[7]

Figure 12.1
The UK Health and Safety Executive's approach to determining tolerable levels
of industrial risk

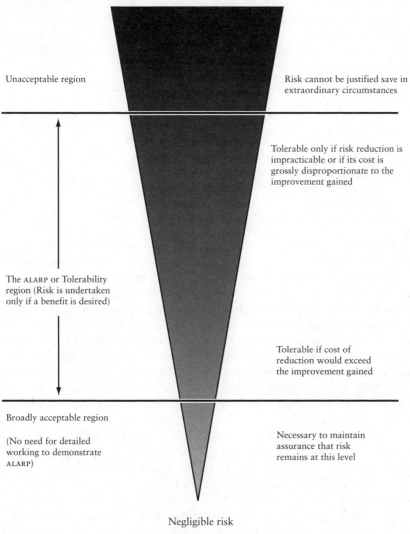

Unacceptable region

Risk cannot be justified save in
extraordinary circumstances

Tolerable only if risk reduction is
impracticable or if its cost is
grossly disproportionate to the
improvement gained

The ALARP or Tolerability
region (Risk is undertaken
only if a benefit is desired)

Tolerable if cost of
reduction would exceed
the improvement gained

Broadly acceptable region

(No need for detailed
working to demonstrate
ALARP)

Necessary to maintain
assurance that risk
remains at this level

Negligible risk

*Source:* UK HSE 1992, 8.

Figure 12.2
The UK Health and Safety Executive's framework for the tolerability of risk

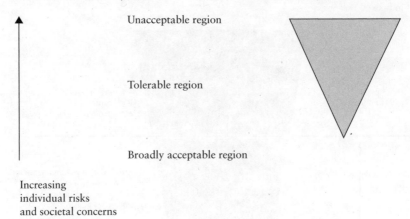

Unacceptable region

Tolerable region

Broadly acceptable region

Increasing
individual risks
and societal concerns

*Source:* UK HSE 2001, 42.

The model is particularly interesting, as it encompasses both quanti-tative and qualitative indicators. Moreover, it actively acknowledges the dynamic and situated nature of risk acceptability, noting that ex-pectations change over time and across space (UK HSE 2001, 43). Yet for some commentators, the 2001 document represents a much diluted version of its 1980s predecessor, suggesting perhaps a step back from the systematic and analytical robustness of the late 1980s.[8] Cited as ev-idence of this retreat are a decline in the principle of proportionality be-ing scaled to risk and an increase in the ratio of analysis to political discretion as apparently signalled by the removal of specified and quantified limits for acceptable and unacceptable risks identified in the 2001 document.

Within broad frameworks such as these, the HSE employs a num-ber of other risk-based tools. In the 1990s these included, for exam-ple, total quality management (TQM) and safety cases (Dalton 1998). The safety-case approach to health and safety was advocated by the Cullen Inquiry into the Piper Alpha explosion in 1988 (UK Depart-ment of Energy 1990). Since then it has been promoted by the HSE as a major tool of inspection and self-regulation; however, in practice it does not appear to have been adopted across sectors, its presence being most noticeable in the offshore-oil and railway indus-tries.[9] Indeed, this does beg the question of how much the HSE has managed to build on its cross-sectoral mission. Its published mate-rial suggests some movement, with the majority – but not all – of its directorates being cross-sectoral. But within these bodies there are often sectoral divisions. One indication of a cross-sectoral, risk-based initiative is the creation in 1996 of the UK Interdepartmental Liaison Group on Risk Assessment (ILGRA), which was set up so that senior policy makers could consider "more efficient and effective ways for regulating and managing risks" (UK ILGRA 1998, 2). However, this initiative was short-lived, and ILGRA has since become part of a pan-government risk-steering group (UK Cabinet Office, 2002).

The HSE has promoted risk-based regulation for some twenty years, starting with a period of rapid development in the mid to late 1980s and a levelling-off since then. Its publications, at least, indicate a commitment to risk-based regulation, but they also indicate that a more in-depth study of what actually happens may reveal that this commitment is more partial than the publicity may suggest. In my next example, that of the financial area, an apparently risk-based approach to regulation was adopted within a short space of time, following the creation of a new superregulatory body for financial regulation in Britain.

## THE FINANCIAL SERVICES AUTHORITY

The Financial Services Authority (FSA) was created as part of a massive reorganization of financial regulation in Britain, announced on 20 May 1997 by Gordon Brown, the new Labour government's Chancellor of the Exchequer. The reforms sought to simplify a complex regulatory system that involved nine regulatory agencies collectively employing over 2000 staff and regulating many thousand authorized firms and registered individuals. This new superagency brought into its embrace different regulatory bodies with different regulatory traditions and additional regulatory duties, most notably consumer education. And its task was to implement new cross-sector, integrated legislation – in contrast to the previous system, which had been characterized by functional, statute-based regulation.[10]

The emergent FSA took shape before the enactment of the Financial Services and Markets Act 2000. In June 1998 the Securities and Investment Board (SIB) changed its name to the FSA, and a new Banking Act transferred banking supervision from the Bank of England to the new FSA.[11] In 1998 the organization consolidated its operations, occupying a single building in London's Docklands. It also acted very quickly to effect a cross-sector agency, creating a single management and organizational structure in June 1998 and, within the limits of the existing legislation, trying to create functions that operate on an integrated basis.

Almost immediately after the new agency was set up, it signalled its intention to adopt a "new" risk-based approach that would be integrative, proactive, and transparent. In its document *A New Regulator for the New Millennium,* the FSA explains that its operating framework "is founded on a risk-based approach to the regulation of all financial businesses" (UK FSA 2000, 5). In a later document, the FSA repeats its "intention to move to a new risk-based regulatory approach" and to set a timetable for doing so (UK FSA 2001, 1). It has also noted a change in emphasis: "It will be apparent that in future a greater proportion of the FSA's activities are likely to be directed at the industry or consumers in general, rather than the supervision of the individual institutions" (UK FSA 2000, 25). It has further explained that implementation would involve "developing a single risk-based approach for use across all sectors, markets and firms which the FSA will regulate" (ibid., 33). Interestingly, one aim of the risk-based approach is to maintain a balance between risk and regulation: "Achieving a 'zero-failure' regime is impossible and would in any case be undesirable. Any such regime would be excessively burdensome for regulated firms and would not accord with the statutory objectives and principles. It would be likely to damage the economy as a whole and would be uneconomic from a cost-benefit point of view; it would stifle innovation and competition; and it would be inconsistent with the respective responsibilities of firms' management and of consumers for their own action" (ibid., 6–7).

The FSA's discussion of its risk-based approach is interesting, for it applies to its own operations the model it advocates for others, thus simultaneously attempting to be transparent in its own operations and offering an ideal typical example for others to follow. Figure 12.3 sets out the FSA's new operating framework, Figure 12.4 explains how it would apply to firm-specific risks, and Figure 12.5 sets out the main steps in the risk-assessment process.

The FSA's approach incorporates existing risk-assessment procedures developed by some of its predecessor bodies. For example, the banking supervisors at the Bank of England had developed an approach premised on Risk Assessment, Tools of Supervision and Evaluation (RATE), and the Securities and Futures Authority had developed a broadly similar approach premised on Financial Stability, Quality of Systems, and Internal Control Quality of Business Supervisory Complexity, Quality of Personnel, and Management (FIBSPAM).

Figure 12.3
The UK Financial Services Authority's new operating framework

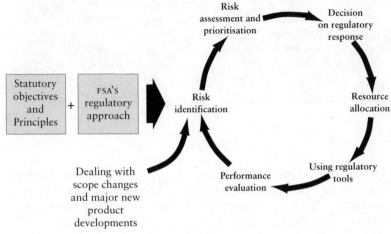

*Source:* UK FSA 2000, 14.

Figure 12.4
The UK Financial Services Authority's risk assessment and prioritization: firm-specific

*Source:* UK FSA 2000, 16.

Figure 12.5
The UK Financial Services Authority's risk-assessment process

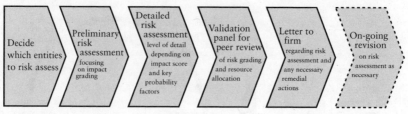

*Source:* UK FSA 2000, 18.

The approach is presented as quantitative: "It involves scoring the risk against a number of probability and impact factors. The probability factors relate to the likelihood of the event happening and the impact factors indicate the scale and significance of the problem were it to occur. A combination of the probability and impact factors gives a measure of the overall risk posed to the FSA's objectives. This will be used to prioritise risks, inform decisions on the regulatory response and, together with an assessment of the costs and benefits of using alternative regulatory tools, help determine resource allocation" (UK FSA 2000, 15). More generally, its uses are seen to centre on determining probability and impact factors, deciding on regulatory responses and the development of regulatory tools, and most important, informing allocative decisions in deploying limited resources.

The FSA started work in June 1998 and had its new framework in place for the organization's operation under the new legislation in December 2001. On the evidence of recent documents, it remains fully committed to developing its risk-based approach to regulation (UK FSA 2001, 2002). As with the HSE, the FSA's website and written publications appear to suggest that these agencies have at least a wish to convey the message that they have bought into the idea of risk-based regulation. The extent to which this reflects any change in behaviour is of course a topic for future research. Clearly, notions of precisely what a risk-based approach means will vary between, and even within, these agencies and others purporting to adopt similar strategies. But there is a shared rhetoric about reconceptualizing the regulatory task in terms of risk, a commitment to choosing risk-based instruments, and an institutional geography oriented toward holistic anticipatory approaches to regulation.

OTHER COUNTRIES[12]

British agencies are not alone in their adoption of risk-based approaches to regulation; parallels can be found in a number of advanced industrial societies, especially Australia, Canada, and the United States. Precise approaches to risk management may vary, but the rhetoric in each country shares a number of the key features of risk-based regulation. The adoption of an entire risk perspective is one such characteristic. In some cases the shift to risk-reduction/management strategies is self-conscious and is characterized as a transition from ad hoc, reactive styles of regulation to more systematized, integrated, transparent, and scientific strategies of risk management. Australia's environmental, financial, and occupational health-and-safety regulators have incorporated elements of risk theory and management into their online publications and strategic plans. The Australian environmental agency explains that its risk-management approach has evolved from "a prescriptive regulatory approach" into more "sophisticated, performance-based approaches" (Commonwealth of Australia 1999a). The Canadian government explains the transition in terms of its modernization program (Government of Canada 2001b), and the Environmental Protection Agency (EPA) in the United States explicitly announced its transformation from a "reactive agency" into one that is more proactive and preventative (US EPA 1990).[13]

Important components of the move to risk-based regulation are formalization and systematization. Again these are themes that appear in, for example, the US EPA literature. In announcing its transformation from a reactive into a proactive agency in 1990, the US EPA explained that "This reactive mode although understandable when seen in its historical context, has limited the efficiency and effectiveness of EPA's environmental protection efforts" (US EPA 1990). The Australian mining series on environmental-risk management (Commonwealth of Australia 1999a) is equally explicit: "Just as risk management has been an inherent form of mining activities over the years, so has some implicit form of risk assessment. What is new is the formalisation of risk assessment and management processes, the increased and increasing emphasis on environment protection and management and regulatory requirements being developed for [environmental-risk management] ERM." Likewise, the Canadian Office of the Superintendent of Financial Institutions "is focussing its efforts on evaluating an institution's material risks and the quality of its risk management practices, rather than applying a functional approach when conducting on-site reviews" (Government of Canada OSFI).

Systematization is related in a number of these regimes to a greater emphasis upon the employment of risk-based tools. Some of these tools are economics-based, and others are science-based. Science-based tools are more prevalent in the occupational health-and-safety area, often as risk assessments. Economics-based tools are especially prominent in environmental and financial regulation.[14] These tools are employed, first, to derive a more holistic conception of the risks generated by economic life and, second, to facilitate a more integrative approach to the management of these risks. The US EPA, for instance, refers to "new" understandings of the environment as an "interrelated whole," which demands that "society's environmental protection efforts should be integrated as well" (US EPA 1990). Canadian documents particularly stress the importance of integrative approaches to management (see also Government of Canada 2001b).

But the move to risk-based regulation is not universal. Commitment to this approach varies within countries and across domains. For example, environmental regulation in Britain is characterized by a partial buy-in to some aspects of risk-based regulation rather than by a full commitment to the approach. In some countries there is little evidence of a self-conscious move to risk-based approaches or, indeed, to a strong commitment to risk-based philosophies. France is one European country that has taken on a more holistic conception of risk-based regulation.[15] But in few other European countries is there strong evidence of the entire risk-based approach set out earlier. For example, while some Scandinavian countries display elements that fit the approach, they do not – on the evidence of their websites at least – appear to adopt the new conceptualizations of risk and risk-based philosophies. Rather, any references to risk and risk-based approaches are more ad hoc and piecemeal. It is possible that in some cases we need to look for a proxy to the word risk; for instance, notions of sustainable development and the precautionary principle may be relevant.[16] Germany is a case in point. German agencies' websites rarely use the language of risk, yet there is evidence of a move – for example, in environmental and occupational health-and-safety regulation – to develop more systematic quality targets and evaluation techniques (German Berufsgenossenschaften 2002). Moreover, the precautionary principle is prominently on the agenda in German regulation. But while this principle has affinities with risk-based regulation, it does not on its own constitute evidence of such regulation. Further research is of course required to map out where the approach has and has not been taken up, and undoubtedly this research should extend from the desk-based research reported here to incorporate interview data. But working with what we have for the moment, I shall consider in more depth those cases where risk-based regulation is in evidence in institutional publications.

Where we do find a commitment to risk-based approaches, the timing is interesting. An analysis of British documentation for the three domains of environmental protection, financial regulation, and occupational health-and-safety regulation suggests that the early 1990s represents the peak period in the incorporation of risk approaches into regulatory legislation. The growing popularity of risk-based regulation in France and the US seems to have occurred during approximately the same period, namely from the late 1980s through the 1990s, whereas in Australia and Canada the adoption of this approach has occurred much more recently, namely from the late 1990s into the early twenty-first century. It is thus opportune to consider why risk-based regulation has emerged and been developed in a number of key regulatory arenas.

## ACCOUNTING FOR THE EMERGENCE OF RISK-BASED REGULATION

Explanations for the emergence of risk-based regulation will vary to some extent between nations and policy domains. But generally, there are two main clusters of explanations. The first set relates to wider government and regulatory trends that came to the fore in the 1980s and 1990s and that were arguably highly conducive to the emergence and development of risk-based philosophies. The second set focuses much more on changing economic and social conditions.

A key attraction of risk-based regulation is its potential role in legitimating regulation, particularly in an environment where government is less direct and less visible (Howlett 1999). Risk-based tools are seen as efficient instruments for making policy choices and aiding in decision making. They are regarded as particularly helpful in resolving any "conflict" between differing interest groups when determining appropriate levels of risk management. This is because they are apparently objective, transparent, and well tested and well trusted by the business community. The importance of these factors is underscored in the British case when we consider the period during which risk-based regulation gained in popularity. The 1980s and 1990s witnessed a so-called "regulatory crisis" in a number of advanced industrial societies, which overlapped with the emergence of what some term the "regulatory state." There was a strong deregulatory rhetoric, centring on alleged overregulation, legalism, inflexibility, and an alleged absence of attention being paid to the costs of regulation. During this period Britain witnessed waves of deregulatory initiatives concerned with the costs of compliance, the overregulation of business, and institutional reforms to control this overregulation.[17]

This climate is associated with a number of governmental changes, and especially relevant here is the set of changes often termed "new public management" (NPM).[18] Of particular relevance are four of the seven doctrinal components of NPM identified by Hood (1991, 4–5): namely, (1) "explicit standards and measures of performance"; (2) a "stress on private sector styles of management practice"; (3) "hands-on professional management" in the public sector; and (4) a "stress on greater discipline and parsimony in resource use." Three themes to emerge from these doctrines are significant to fostering an environment in which risk-based regulation could be encouraged and flourish: first, the call for tighter control both of costs within government and, in accordance with the deregulatory rhetoric of the time, of costs imposed by government on business; second, the emphasis upon accountability and the need for public agencies, such as regulators, to account for their demands and to be transparent; and, three, the emphasis upon adopting private-sector styles of management. Such a climate arguably created and sustained an environment favourable to adopting approaches that incorporated cost-benefit analysis and that were apparently "objective" and apparently "transparent." Risk-based approaches appear to satisfy these criteria and have the added bonus of originating with the business sector. This environment was further encouraged and developed from the mid-1990s onward, a period that has witnessed what some commentators refer to as the rise of the regulatory state, during which the "virtues" of private business, transparency, and accountability have again been extolled.[19]

These changes are discussed by Salamon (2002) as fostering "third-party government" and as signalling the move from hierarchically based to network-based regulation and the adoption of new indirect tools of government. More broadly, these new collaborative arrangements represent a move from government to governance. In essence, we have seen a strengthening of the imperatives favouring increased accountability and a renewed call to adopt business practices. Most important for this chapter's discussion, the process has involved increased systematization of governmental approaches to regulation, a change that was itself a furtherance of the broader governmental call to "modernize" government by running the administration as a business (Hood and Jones 1996; Power 1997). In essence, this systematization has been effected by reframing the deregulatory rhetoric and repackaging ideas prominent in the period of so-called "regulatory crisis."

The virtues of these changes are cited by official regulatory websites to explain the move to risk-based regulation, particularly in sectors where the need for greater transparency has been emphasized. Such explanations are prominent in Canadian documents linking risk-based regulation to a more general modernization of public administration and, more specifically, in the government's Integrated Risk Management Framework (Government of Canada 2001b). The Australian Mining website also reiterates the virtues of risk-based management, adding a further observation that such an approach is encouraged by the popularity of performance-based regulation and also by the European trend to hold managers, directors, and workers more accountable for accidents (Commonwealth of Australia 1999a). Australian and Canadian financial regulatory reforms are explained with reference to accountability and sustaining public confidence (Government of Canada 1996; Commonwealth of Australia APLA). Thus the use of risk-based models may be regarded as a means of "objectively" demonstrating that reasonable steps were taken to reduce and manage risks.

In many respects, therefore, the merits of risk-based regulation centre on the risk-management strategies of regulatory agencies and governments as they manage their own political and legal risks and respond to potential assaults on their legitimacy with apparently increased accountability and transparency. Arguably, such a response is especially necessary where broader governance structures operate and where government delegates to itself or coopts other sources of regulation for inclusion in its broad embrace. The approach also plays an important role in financial-risk management, as it simultaneously aids and legitimates governmental and agency decisions about the deployment of limited resources (see, in particular, the discussion of the FSA above). Moreover, the hope is that risk-based regulation will help to reduce the political element in key regulatory decisions about what constitutes an acceptable risk. Determining what is an acceptable risk or acceptable cost is difficult and negotiated, and it raises a host of issues. For example, from whose point of view should one view risk, cost, and benefit? We need to decide how to choose between competing analyses and how much weight to give to public fears and complacency. None of these elements are fixed, being dependent upon time, place, and perspective; thus they necessitate shifting calculations. One of the expected benefits of risk-based regulation is that it can minimize and distance the political element of the decision.

The second set of explanations for the popularity of risk-based regulation focus much more on changing economic and social conditions. Many official publications on risk policy present the move to risk-based regulation as a *natural* response to changing social and economic conditions. These include changes in the nature of work (US Department of Labor 1998); the evolution of scientific knowledge (see, e.g., Commonwealth of Australia 1999b); rapid technological changes, which are also held responsible for creating new risks (Government of

Canada 2001a); and changing financial markets (see Commonwealth of Australia APRA; Government of Canada OSFI). Change also derives from altering attitudes to risk. For example, various environmental regulatory sites refer to changes stimulated by public demands for higher standards (Government of Denmark 1998; Government of the Netherlands 2002).

Several countries attribute their national approaches to international pressures for the regulation of these risks (Government of Finland 2002; Lindholm 2002). But whether these international bodies are encouraging risk-based regulation is unclear. In many cases there is little evidence that they are doing more than introducing elements of a risk-based approach rather than a whole new philosophical approach to regulation. Documents produced by the Organization for Economic Cooperation and Development (OECD) do not make reference to risk-based perspectives. Rather, they reveal support for approaches and tools associated with such a perspective and only on an ad hoc basis, such as in implementing integrative and proactive strategies.[20] European Union (EU) documents make scant reference to risk-based regulation. But a search of the relevant websites does provide evidence of EU encouragement to move to more systematic approaches to regulation although there is evidence of EU policy moving from ad hoc legislation to a more strategic and integrated framework for managing risks, including advocating risk-based tools such as risk-assessment techniques.[21]

Risk-based approaches are also promoted by the G10 Central Bank Governors' Basle Committee. The development of the second Basel Accord, which began in 1998, has focused on providing a more risk-sensitive calibration of credit risks in particular and has sought to provide encouragement and incentives (in the form of lower regulatory-capital requirements) for good risk management in banks (Basel Committee 2003).

The appeal of risk-based regulation thus appears to be twofold. First, it aids in the allocative decisions of governments and regulatory agencies. And second, it serves as a framework for fostering accountability and legitimation in the public interest. Yet there are significant limitations to the approach that also warrant discussion.

## THE LIMITATIONS OF RISK-BASED APPROACHES

The main criticisms of risk-based regulation focus largely on the detail of risk-based tools/techniques rather than on any direct and fundamental questioning of the merits or otherwise of the overall philosophy of the approach. Many of the limitations of risk-based techniques are acknowledged by the agencies adopting them,[22] the main criticisms centring on the simplification inherent in the tools and the dangers of their misuse. As a European Environment Agency report explains, "There in no credible way of reducing the pros and cons of alternative courses of action to a single figure, economic or otherwise, not least because of the problem of comparing incommensurables and because the pros and cons are unlikely to be spread evenly across all interest groups" (EEA 2001, 168).

But while this document urges caution in the use of these techniques, it adds that there are "constructive ways of dealing with these complications" (ibid.). Academic criticisms of these approaches are less benign. Some commentators argue that many of these techniques are simply unable to achieve their goals, while others reject the proposition that regulation should involve balancing public protection against costs. Various tools have attracted criticism. For example, Froud et al. (1998) found cost-benefit analyses and compliance-cost assessments (CCAs), both of which form the basis of much risk-based regulation, to be lacking. They argue, for instance, that CCAs in practice embrace a variety of methods that, due to the unreliability of the information presented, cannot offer the authoritative information upon which to either appraise the law-making process or protect it from the influence of particular interest groups. Quantitative risk techniques (QRAs) have been the subject of a great deal of academic criticism. For instance, the mathematical basis of the QRAs is disputed, especially where there are small numbers involved or where there are no reliable data from which to work (Cohen 1996; Toft 1996). Recent experiences in Britain with the railway industry highlight the difficulties. Unease with the risk-management techniques used by the railway industry was apparent in two major accident inquiries. The Southall Inquiry into one of these accidents is blunt in its criticism, stating that "risk assessment procedures have been shown to produce variable results, which are seldom rigorous and sometimes questionable" (Uff 2000, 208).

The key point of these criticisms must be to drive home the message that these methods, like all methods, are partial. Accordingly, they should be used with awareness of their limitations. Questions about the interpretation of the results generated by risk-based techniques are especially important.

Indeed, the difficulties surrounding interpretation are the focus of a second main set of criticisms of risk-based techniques. Particular attention is paid to the role of values in the interpretation of the data generated by risk-based tools (Hood and Jones 1996),[23] and doubt is cast upon how objective risk-based regulation can really be. For example, the HSE's consideration of individual risks and societal concerns (see above) is based on criteria that is essentially qualitative and thus arguably immeasurable. Similarly, the apparently "objective" probability factors incorporated in the FSA's approach to risk are subjective, and no developed measures are presently available that would produce an objective quantity. Thus the scope for broad interpretation is wider than may be implied by the use of apparently objective modelling techniques.

The status of scientific and other forms of expert knowledge is also increasingly contested, as the public and the media are less willing to accept the legitimacy of any authority and are skeptical that there is always sufficient reliable evidence upon which to base a dependable analysis. It was partially in the hope that public trust in regulatory models could be increased that apparently open, transparent, risk-based regulation was introduced. Indeed, this is one rationale for the adoption of the precautionary principle, a fact explained by the European Environment Agency: "Society's growing commitment to the precautionary principle is essentially a response to a growing tension between two aspects of science: its growing innovative powers were increasingly outrunning its capacity to anticipate the consequences" (EEA 2001, 185). However, research evidence demonstrates that risk-based tools may be differentially interpreted according to cultural and other factors. The precautionary principle, for example, means different things in different countries (EEA 2001, 1; Wiener and Rogers 2002). Similarly, Radaelli's examination of the introduction of Regulatory Impact Analysis (RIA) in nine countries and the European Union found that RIA is a form of benchmarking that has become a "standard policy instrument in most countries" (Radaelli 2002, 11). But although there are some similarities across nations, he found that the use of RIA and the intentions for its application varied in each nation. There are also variations in the impact of trends between domains within the same country. Hood et al. (2001, 151), for example, found that accounts of pressures on risk-regulation regimes to be more open were possibly overgeneralized. Rather, they discerned differences in the degree of openness demanded between areas and over time.

Interested parties can of course exploit these uncertainties and points of contestability regarding the more technical aspects of risk-based regulation. Indeed, the very tools used by state regulators may be used to challenge their decision making and authority (Hutter 2001, ch. 11). Certainly, there is a danger that too much faith can be placed in the success of risk-based tools and audits (Power 1997). Depending upon circumstances, audits and cost-benefit analyses can become as much a form of mystification as an analytical tool. Indeed, one US study into the safety performance of the American railroads found a counterintuitive negative correlation between safety performance and audits and inspections (Bailey and Peterson 1989).

The usefulness of risk-based approaches is of course partly depen-dant upon the skills of regulators. A survey by the UK National Audit Office (NAO) found variable levels of qualification among civil ser-vants, especially in their understandings of how to implement risk-management approaches (UK NAO 2000). Hood and Rothstein (2000), in an appendix to the NAO Report, accede that there are potential ben-efits of using business risk-management practices in government, but they are also sensitive to its limitations and dangers. The merit of the approach, argue these authors, is that such practices can encourage sys-tematic debate about the contradictory pressures on regulators. But the dangers lie in the mechanistic and tokenistic application of these prac-tices, in their potential to undermine other public-sector values, and in the real possibility that they may be used to augment blame-prevention strategies.

However robust the tools used in risk-based regulation, much de-pends at the end of the day on the political will to act. The European Environment Agency publication *Late Lessons from Early Warnings* offers prescient reading. Based upon a detailed examination of twelve case studies, it notes that in many cases adequate information about potential hazards did not result in action, as it was either not used or ignored. And most worrying, "It is also true that in some of the case studies, early warnings – and even 'loud and late' warnings – were ef-fectively ignored by decision-makers because of short-term economic and political interactions" (EEA 2001, 168). So the best regulatory ap-proach possible is limited in its effects if there is no political resolve to act on sound information. This said, we should continually strive for the best regulatory framework and perhaps build into it a more proac-tive capacity to influence governments. Risk-based approaches do have the potential to serve as templates for good governance but only if they are used realistically – that is, with an appreciation of their limitations. Achieving this throughout the policy-making and implementation pro-cess is no mean feat. Hopefully, a more systematic and comparative ex-amination of the ways risk-based ideas have spread across domains and across nations would give us a clearer picture of where risk-based governance strategies and tools of government are most effective, where they are challenged, and the prospects for employing them in international arenas.[24]

# 13

# Globalization
# and Instrument Choice:
# The Role of International Law

STEPHEN J. TOOPE AND SEAN REHAAG

First we must offer a confession: We are scholars of international law. This means that we are most imperfect political scientists. Our methodologies are suspect because our profession is devoted not merely to describing how things are, but also to imagining how they might be if the nations of the world actually acted in accordance with their oft-stated respect for an international rule of law.[1] We must also emphasize, by way of preface, that our discussion will focus primarily upon the ways international norms are coming to shape Canadian law and politics and, therefore, to shape the parameters of "instrument choice" in the creation of government policy. However, the processes we describe are certainly not limited to Canada. One of the undertheorized aspects of globalization is the increased interpenetration of international and domestic law that it has occasioned in most states.

Of course, "law" is very much a part of the rhetoric of contemporary international relations. Ronald Reagan used to refer to "outlaw states" (perhaps hearkening back to his days on the sets of Hollywood "B" Westerns). More recently, we have been told that across a range of issue areas – and notably in the area of trade – we are witnessing the "legalization" of international politics. In an influential special issue of the flagship of the American international-relations academy, the journal *International Organization*, leading theorists opined that global politics display an increasing tendency to legalization, defined as a specific set of characteristics that institutions may possess: obligation (binding rules), precision (specificity of obligation), and delegation (whereby decision-making functions are accorded to third parties).[2]

Obviously, if this description is true, the implications for domestic politics and national decision making are enormous: International legal institutions will shape the parameters that determine which policy options are available domestically. Various possibilities are simply "off the table," and instrument choice, in the original and narrow sense of the term,[3] may be significantly constrained.[4]

One of our international law colleagues, Harold Koh, views the possibility of such constraint in a very positive light: as a useful means by which progressively minded public-law litigants can seek to change what they view as objectionable domestic-policy choices, such as resort to the death penalty in the United States.[5] While Koh's optimistic understanding of the progressive nature of the content of international norms must be questioned,[6] what is most interesting in his analysis is that he views challenges brought by public-law litigants as the primary mechanism through which international legal norms acquire their real-world legal effects. By "effects," he means "enforcement" – or at least the potential for enforcement – in domestic courts.[7] Notice here that Koh, who offers an otherwise sophisticated account of how international legal norms emerge from transnational interactions and discourses on the proper interpretation of these interactions, ultimately falls back on a narrow understanding of law surprisingly compatible with the one driving the "legalization" literature. In the end, law derives its effects through enforcement in dispute-resolution forums that either look like or in fact are domestic courts.[8]

We argue, however, that such a narrow understanding of how legal norms have real-world effects implies both too much and too little for the role of international legal norms in shaping domestic policy and law[9] – "too much" because in the areas where highly "legalized" norms ought to have the greatest bite, they often fail to constrain in practice;[10] and "too little" because the legalization of world politics is actually a broader and more pervasive phenomenon than is captured by the elements of obligation, precision, and delegation.

Our argument can be summarized in four points, which we will elaborate briefly, offering specific examples. First, international law is best seen as functioning through processes of both compulsion (especially when implemented through domestic-court action) *and* persuasion that are not dependent upon formal mechanisms of enforcement. In this context, customary norms are just as powerful as explicit texts (treaties) in shaping the behaviour of states and other international actors – and these norms are constructed through discursive processes of persuasion. Second, the Canadian government will discover more and more that its freedom of action is limited by increasingly dense international obligations, both explicit and implicit. Third, the self-understanding of the

Canadian legal system has not yet adjusted appropriately to changes in global normative evolution that are actually affecting the development of Canadian law and policy. Fourth, a much better integration is needed of Canadian-government agencies engaged in global normative development and departments charged with the crafting of national policy. Indeed, the two are now inseparable, and this evolution must be reflected both structurally and substantively in the government-policy community.

What does our understanding of international law's influence mean for the precise themes of this volume? We will show that a more robust – and we believe more accurate – view of international legal normativity calls into question the very idea of "instrument *choice.*" More and more, Canadians will find that their policy choices are shaped, or at least guided, by international regimes containing specific obligations. Moreover, forces outside the borders of the nation-state will often directly affect the appropriate instruments for the implementation of policy. The real choices will relate to the correlation of national-policy aspirations with international normative evolution.

## HOW DOES INTERNATIONAL LAW WORK?

Our central, and admittedly controversial, assertion is that states can now be bound by obligations that they do not explicitly assume.[11] Despite the growing importance of international treaty regimes throughout the twentieth century (especially in the areas of trade, the environment, and human rights), explicit treaties have not displaced the traditional role of customary international law.[12] The resilience, and indeed prominence, of customary international law is significant because it shows that international law can emerge through discursive processes and can become binding on all states regardless of particular state objections.

The claim that international law can develop by consensus and can come to bind even objecting states may seem surprising to some, especially to those familiar with the doctrine of the "persistent objector" in customary international law. Historically, the principle that sovereign states could only be bound by obligations to which they had consented was often viewed as the foundational norm of international law.[13] However, given the remarkable proliferation of states in the past two centuries, to insist on the affirmative consent of every single state before a practice could "crystallize" into a customary international norm became, for obvious reasons, unworkable. On the other hand, any standard less than unanimous affirmative consent could mean that a state might find itself bound by a norm to which it would not have assented but which "crystallized" without – or, indeed, despite – its input.[14] To address this tension, the doctrine of the "persistent objector" allowed states to opt out of any developing norm to which they objected, without such objections being fatal to the crystallization of the norm: The international norm would emerge, but the objecting state would not be bound.[15]

The validity of the persistent-objector doctrine has been questioned for some time on both practical[16] and theoretical[17] grounds, and the doctrine has become increasingly difficult to reconcile with various categories of international law that are of growing importance. Consider, for instance, *erga omnes* obligations, which no state may unilaterally disavow because such obligations are owed not simply to other individual states through treaty or custom but rather to the "international community as a whole."[18] The paradigmatic example of an *erga omnes* obligation is the obligation incumbent on all states to prevent genocide. Such an obligation derives not only from affirmations of state consent manifest in various provisions in international treaties,[19] but also from the simple fact that the prevention of genocide, acknowledged to be one of the gravest international wrongs imaginable, must fall within the category of obligations owed generally if such a category is to have any salience.[20]

A more recent and more fundamental challenge to the persistent-objector doctrine comes from international lawyers who question consent-based theories of law generally. Bruno Simma, now a member of the International Court of Justice, argues that international law as a whole is subject to increasing endeavours to "soften the edge of consent." He focuses upon consensus-based decision making in intergovernmental forums and suggests that a "community consciousness" can displace individual consent in the formation of specific norms.[21] Jutta Brunnée pushes the argument a step further in positing that consent's role in international law is best analyzed within a framework of legitimation rather than of formal validity.[22] In other words, the "softening" of consent means that we need to persuade states to consent to a norm because that will lend greater legitimacy and effectiveness to the norm. But an absence of individual consent does not preclude the existence or application of a norm (its binding quality). This theoretical perspective is bolstered by a number of studies demonstrating that, empirically, international legal norms not only emerge without the consent of some of the most powerful international actors, but indeed, come to bind these powerful actors despite active and vociferous objections.[23]

Canadian scholars are particularly well situated to see at work the process through which states may find themselves bound by obligations to which they have not consented because Canada, as a state historically committed to multilateralism, is often actively involved in the development of international legal norms that other powerful states find unpalatable – and its efforts have proven surprisingly successful. For instance, despite the persistent objection of the United States,[24] Canada's claim to a special regime for the protection of the arctic environment[25] has come to be accepted in customary law.[26] In a similar vein, the claim to an expanded territorial sea was solidified in customary law even before the United Nations' Law of the Sea Convention 1982,[27] again despite the long-time refusal of the United States to endorse the idea.[28] On the human-rights front, Canada consistently invokes human-rights obligations contained in customary law to open up discussions with states such as China that have not ratified all the major multilateral human-rights conventions.[29]

Eventually, however, the evolution of customary law will also come to challenge Canada. Consider the growing recognition of the right to self-determination of aboriginal peoples.[30] How will this affect Canadian policy and law in the future?[31] The same questions could be asked about the controversial implications of customary law in disputes regarding both past and present border-control policies.[32] Or, to pick up one of the themes of this volume, what might be the effects of the increasing consensus around the need to address issues of climate change?[33] It is arguable that the fuss around the Kyoto Protocol will turn out to have been a diversion if the great stream of customary international environmental law further advances the "precautionary principle"[34] and the principle of "intergenerational equity."[35] Canada, like other industrialized states, may discover that it has no real choice in cutting greenhouse gas emissions, at least no choice compatible with international law.

## LIMITATIONS ON CANADIAN FREEDOM IN POLICY DEVELOPMENT

Given the entirely appropriate focus upon trade and investment in many of the contributions to this volume, we will look at the increasing limits placed upon Canadian freedom of policy in an entirely different issue area: that of human rights. Today, we are witnessing a flourishing of international engagement with economic, social, and cultural rights and their increasing institutionalization in an international regime.[36] Because of initiatives such as the United Nations' human-development index, the appointment of special rapporteurs on violence against women as well as on other culturally and socially charged issues, and the regular reports of the Committee on Economic, Social, and Cultural rights, the density of international obligations in this field is growing even though the Convention on Economic, Social and

Cultural Rights[37] is itself notoriously aspirational rather than tightly normative. These developments have already caused Canada deep embarrassment. The social and economic policies of the governments of Ontario and Alberta have been singled out for international censure,[38] as have the incidence of child poverty in Canada as a whole[39] and the state of the First Nations within our borders.[40] This pattern will not soon change and is likely to be repeated in the years to come.

Our point is not that current international scrutiny directly constrains policy options, but rather that the discursive interactions flowing from such scrutiny are likely to shape them. However, if the norms of customary human-rights law become stricter, as they seem to be doing in relation both to aboriginal peoples and children, to take but two examples, then Canada will find itself in a position where it will be breaching international law if it does not improve its performance. Indeed, Canadian litigants have already begun to attack governmental domestic-policy choices for such breaches. And courts have, albeit reluctantly, responded.[41]

To summarize our argument thus far: Canada, along with all other states, will find more and more that it is facing a number of increasingly dense sets of international legal obligations, to which it may find itself bound even in the absence of specific consent and which will inevitably play a role in domestic policy choice. As we will now see, however, even choices regarding the manner in which these obligations are to be met are strongly influenced – and may even be predetermined – by international legal discourse.

## THE INTERPLAY BETWEEN CANADIAN LAW AND INTERNATIONAL LAW

It seems to surprise legal and policy elites to discover that the Canadian legal system is in a state of confusion as concerns its attitude toward international law. This is a complex topic and one in which there is a growing interest. We can but sketch out the problems here.[42]

Traditionally, the starting proposition of the relationship between domestic and international law is that international treaties are not directly applicable in Canada but require "transformation."[43] Beneath the surface of this straightforward proposition, however, lies an array of twists and turns that make the domestic application of treaties complex territory to navigate. Canadian courts struggle to determine not only when international norms require implementation through legislation but also whether such implementation has actually occurred. Here, the narrow instrument-choice problem discussed by Trebilcock et al. in 1982 is directly engaged.[44]

One particularly convoluted challenge with which courts are struggling concerns the common-law principle that "Parliament is not presumed to legislate in breach of a treaty or in a manner inconsistent with the comity of nations and the established rules of international law."[45] In the case law, it remains unclear when this principle comes into play and how it relates to the implementation requirement. There is concern that too wide an application of the presumption would undermine the requirement that international treaties must be transformed in order to apply domestically in Canada.[46] At the same time, perhaps due to this concern, there is a worrying trend in recent decisions toward viewing all international norms, regardless of whether they are binding on Canada, through the lens of a highly restricted reading of the common-law principle.[47] As a result, courts sometimes appear to assert that *all* international legal norms are merely potentially persuasive considerations that may help to inform a contextual approach to domestic statutory interpretation and judicial review but that are not, strictly speaking, legally binding on Canadian courts.[48]

Another recurring difficulty is that it is often remarkably unclear what exactly constitutes transformation.[49] In a narrow sense, transformation is an explicit legislative act through which Parliament or a provincial legislature adopts the treaty obligation and implements it within Canadian law. However, in practice, there are many ways in which such implementation can be accomplished. Obviously, a treaty may be incorporated directly by reproducing all or part of its text within a statute, either in its body or as a schedule. Alternatively, a preambular statement may indicate that a given piece of legislation is passed to fulfil specific treaty commitments.[50] Less direct still is the common Canadian practice of "inferred implementation" through the enactment of new legislation or through the amendment of existing legislation.[51] Whether inferred implementation constitutes actual "transformation" is a difficult question and one that places considerable pressure on our courts to sort out the status of the treaty commitment.

Even greater difficulties arise when transformation is said to occur as a result of prior statutory, common-law, or even administrative-policy conformity with the new treaty obligation. Whether intentionally or through mere sloppiness, Parliament has often left the status of Canadian treaties, especially human-rights obligations, unclear. Whatever the case may be, lingering uncertainties about domestic implementation have not prevented the Canadian government from ratifying international human-rights treaties on the basis of prior domestic-law conformity.[52] Indeed, the government frequently reports to international-treaty bodies that it has already implemented the treaty in question and therefore has met its international commitments. For example, in its reports to the Human

Rights Committee under the International Covenant on Civil and Political Rights (ICCPR),[53] Canada has claimed implementation mainly through the Charter of Rights and Freedoms and related constitutional jurisprudence, complemented by various amendments to existing statutes.[54] In such cases, from the standpoint of Canadian domestic law, is the treaty implemented? We believe that the most persuasive view is that any of the above variations can, in principle, transform treaty obligations into domestic law, but this is an admittedly controversial proposition,[55] one that courts accept only intermittently.[56]

The status of customary international law within Canadian law is, if anything, even more ambiguous. Senior Canadian courts have vacillated on the application of customary international law in Canada. In some decisions, customary law seems to be treated as part of the law of Canada and thus as directly applicable, although this is rarely stated explicitly.[57] Other decisions would appear to point in the opposite direction or remain unclear.[58] We believe that the best view is the one that predominated in Canada until a divided and ultimately confusing judgment in the 1940s muddied the waters.[59] Until this decision, customary international norms were viewed as directly applicable in Canadian domestic law,[60] as they still are today in the United States[61] and the United Kingdom.[62] A recent, and most welcome, decision of the Ontario Court of Appeal may help to clarify the status of customary international law within the Canadian legal system. In *Bouzari*, the Court held unanimously, *per* Goudge JA., that "customary rules of international law are directly incorporated into Canadian domestic law unless explicitly ousted by contrary legislation."[63] This is the clearest recent statement of a senior Canadian court; it is hoped that the Supreme Court will soon follow suit in an appropriate case.

Of course, as the *Bouzari* citation suggests, even if customary international law operates of its own force, this does not preclude the lawful domestic authorities from legislating contrary to custom. We are not suggesting that international law should apply in Canada without regard for the laws and policies of the duly elected governments of Canada and the provinces. Our point is that customary law should be presumed to apply unless altered, explicitly or implicitly. This conclusion would have significant implications for instrument choice. Canadian policy makers, notably politicians, would have to consider evolutions in customary international law that might have direct effects within Canada. If Canadian policy makers wished to diverge from those international standards, specific action would be required.

More broadly, the uncertainties that we have described mean that it is often unclear which instruments the Canadian government should choose in order to implement its international-treaty or customary obligations. Even more surprisingly, it is not clear whether any instrument is needed at all. Explicit legislation is often, but not always, required. It is, of course, important to keep in mind that Canada is bound to international legal norms whether or not it has explicitly incorporated them. But the extent to which obligations that are not transformed through explicit legislative incorporation have effects within domestic law remains uncertain – and ought to be clarified by Canadian courts.

## BETTER INTEGRATION OF INTERNATIONAL AND DOMESTIC LAW AND POLICY

Increasingly, international obligations and domestic law are closely linked. This reality has not yet fully penetrated the Canadian legal and political imagination. As the discussion around the Kyoto Protocol has revealed so clearly, when Canada makes express international commitments, they often imply significant effects internally. But the issue is broader and deeper, for as we have seen, even customary-law rules that are not expressly accepted by Canada can be binding on Canada. They may have automatic internal legal effects; they at the very least require domestic-law action. If customary international legal norms do have automatic domestic effects in Canada, as we believe is the most persuasive view, then both policy makers and those who study decision-making processes need to pay significantly more attention to international legal discourses than is currently the case.

To give just one current example of the potentially profound impact of international legal norms on Canadian policy choices, consider the effects of human-rights laws upon the choices of the Canadian governments regarding deportation and extradition, an area that is particularly fascinating because absolute discretion over border control has historically been viewed as a fundamental feature of state sovereignty.[64] The recent spate of dramatic court decisions overturning executive decisions in this area demonstrates how Canada's international obligations can force reinterpretations of domestic statutes and settled common- or civil-law principles, trumping the domestic policy and instrument choices that underlie this previously settled law.[65] If international norms can have such profound effects on an area of law in which courts have repeatedly asserted that the executive is deserving of a large degree of deference,[66] policy makers must take more notice of international-law developments that may come to alter (or perhaps even to control) other domestic policy calculations.

Such attention is even more important once we realize that domestic decisions and actions increasingly have an impact upon the evolution of international norms. The decision of the Supreme Court of Canada in the *Quebec Secession Reference* is a prime example of this trend.[67] One could make a similar argument about the potential international effects of the fact that an increasing number of state governments and courts have overturned resort to the death penalty.[68] There appears to be a growing mutual interpenetration of the domestic and international systems.

This reality of interconnection has significant implications for Canadians interested in policy and policy instruments. There is no such thing any longer as a purely "domestic" or "national" policy divorced from international influences, constraints, and effects. So policy makers across Canada must pay due attention to international normative developments. Similarly, those who negotiate Canada's positions in international forums must be enormously sensitive to the potential effects on domestic law of changing international rules. For a long while now, the federal Cabinet has been presented with analyses of the potential effects of the Canadian Charter of Rights and Freedoms upon particular legislative or regulatory initiatives.[69] The time has come to provide for a similar international-law filter for at least some major policy and legislative proposals.

To allow an international-law policy filter to operate effectively, the federal government (and often the provinces) will have to do a better job of encouraging regular contact between the formally international and formally national institutions of the bureaucracy. For example, the division between the Department of Foreign Affairs and International Trade (DFAIT), which negotiates treaties, and the Department of Justice, which implements them within the fields of federal legislative jurisdiction, only makes sense if constant communication and a sharing of viewpoints within the bureaucracy is structurally assured. This implies regular interdepartmental policy discussions, shared training on trends in international law, and joint delegations to some negotiating sessions. The model of the joint trade-law section of the DFAIT and the Department of Justice may need to be replicated in other fields.[70] These observations connect us to Roderick Macdonald's central point in his contribution to this volume: The real question is not "instrument choice" at all but rather how to ensure that Canadians create legitimate and effective processes that can develop and articulate the policy aspirations that will help them to shape the obligations that they as a society actually want to assume and act upon.[71]

To this end, pressure must be placed upon Canadian courts, particularly upon the Supreme Court of Canada, for greater clarity regarding the relations between domestic and international law. Policy makers, at both the domestic and international levels, cannot decide how Canadian aspirations can best relate to international legal discourses until the legal effects of international law are clear. We need to know when a legal obligation that is internationally binding on Canada will have domestic legal effects. We need to know which instruments can be held to implement international commitments, whether conventional or customary. We have suggested that Canada may find itself bound by norms that develop through international interactions and discussions rather than through actual or even implied state consent. We have, moreover, suggested that regulations and even policies not rendered into formal legal instruments may in fact "implement" international law within Canada and that full-scale legislative intervention is not necessarily required. If this is the case, then it is high time, in the face of what will be the ever-increasing volume and scope of international law, that Canada get its house in order on these significant questions.

# 14

# Reconfiguring Environmental Regulation[1]

## NEIL GUNNINGHAM

RECONFIGURING ENVIRONMENTAL REGULATION

This chapter reviews the changing role of the regulatory state and the evolution of a number of next-generation policy instruments intended to overcome, or at least to mitigate, the considerable problems associated with previous policy initiatives and with traditional forms of regulation in particular. The goal is, in the words of the US Environmental Protection Agency (US EPA 2000, 1), "to adapt, improve and expand the diversity of our environmental strategies" and to address the circumstances not only of laggards but also of leaders.

Over the last two decades, policy reform has taken place in what is, in many respects, a hostile political and economic environment. The 1980s and '90s saw a resurgence of free-market ideology that, assisted by the economic and political collapse of the former Soviet Union, enabled neoliberalism to triumph almost unchallenged for most of this period and beyond. And while public opposition precluded the sort of wholesale deregulation that occurred in some other areas of social regulation, environmental regulatory budgets were substantially cut in almost all jurisdictions. This trend shows little sign of changing under the lower taxation regimes that now characterize the large majority of economically advanced states, irrespective of the party in power.

During the same period, governments have also experienced considerable pressure from industry to reduce the economic burden of complying with environmental regulation. Although, on most calculations, the costs of compliance are relatively modest,[2] industrial lobby groups have argued strongly, and often successfully, that the imposition of such regulation would put industry at a competitive disadvantage. In an era of globalization, in which capital flight to low-tax, low-regulation regimes is increasingly plausible (although far less often demonstrated), governments have listened particularly closely to industry concerns and have frequently responded sympathetically. Thus the confluence of economic and political pressures has often precluded the application of direct regulation.

But while government regulators have been losing both their power and their resources, others have begun to fill the regulatory space that governments previously occupied. For example, environmental non-governmental organizations (NGOs), aided by advanced techniques for information gathering (from digital cameras to satellite imaging) have become increasingly sophisticated at communicating their message (via global television, international newspapers, and the Internet) and in using the media (and sometimes the courts) to amplify the impact of their direct-action campaigns. They have sought not only to shape public opinion, to lobby governments, and to pressure industry directly, but also to influence consumers and markets through indirect strategies, such as orchestrating consumer boycotts or advocating a preference for green products. Indeed, they have commonly bypassed governments altogether where they perceived them to be overly sympathetic to industry or incapable of effective action.

At the same time, a variety of commercial third parties have also begun to take a considerable interest in environmental issues. Banks and insurance companies seek to minimize their financial risk by scrutinizing more closely the environmental credentials of their clients (Schmidheiny and Zorraquin 1996). And financial markets themselves have become responsive to good or bad environmental news, rewarding environmental leaders with a share-price increase and discounting the share price of laggards (Lanoie et al. 1997). So, too, is supply-chain pressure increasingly important, with a substantial number of companies seeking accreditation under the standards for environmental management established by the International Standards Organization (ISO 14001) – not because regulators require it or because they believe it necessary but rather because their trading partners insist upon it.

As part of this reshaping of the regulatory landscape, a number of environmental stakeholders have to some extent departed from their traditional roles. Some business groups, such as the World Business Council for Sustainable Development, have become proactive, arguing that business is part of the solution rather than merely the problem, and have sought to develop a variety of voluntary initiatives through which business seeks to shape its own environmental destiny. Environmental NGOs, frustrated with their limited impact on governments, or with the ineffectiveness of government in protecting the environment, have redirected their attention toward corporations through strategies ranging from confrontation to partnership. And government policy makers, constrained by diminishing resources and having noted the increasing power of NGOs and financial markets, as well as the potential for industry self-management, have become increasingly enamoured with the possibilities of "steering not rowing" in policy design.

What has evolved is not a retreat of the regulatory state and a return to free markets but rather a regulatory reconfiguration. Nevertheless, a continuing government role is evident in the US EPA's Reinventing Environmental Regulation Program, negotiated agreements in Western Europe, a plethora of informational regulation initiatives, various forms of industry self-management, and a variety of enterprises (commonly using supply-chain and financial-market pressure) built around harnessing third parties as surrogate regulators. Even in relation to problems that the state is ill-equipped to address directly, it almost invariably retains a supporting role, underpinning alternative solutions and providing a backdrop without which other, more flexible options would lack credibility (and stepping in where they fail). That is, in almost all circumstances, the state is still involved in engineering solutions to environmental problems rather than trusting the market, unaided, to provide them.

This reconfiguration is still in progress, and the next-generation instruments that have emerged are very diverse. Some seek out and nurture win-win solutions, some seek to replace conflict with cooperation between major stakeholders, and others seek to mitigate power imbalances and to increase transparency and accountability, as is the case with informational regulation. Many, in stark contrast to the first generation of command-and-control instruments, seek to encourage and reward enterprises for going beyond compliance with existing regulation. But neither the precise direction of this reconfiguration nor its results are yet known. Much work remains to be done in mapping progress, in identifying what works, what doesn't, and why, and in providing a better understanding of how to match types of instruments, and institutions, with particular environmental problems. In the following sections, I provide a broader perspective on this regulatory reconfiguration. First, I examine it through a variety of different lenses and in terms of a number of different conceptual frameworks. Second, I reflect on some broader lessons for the future of regulatory reform.

## CONCEPTUALIZING REGULATORY
## RECONFIGURATION

Below, I examine five different frameworks, or lenses, through which one might better understand regulatory reconfiguration. None of these lenses offers (or necessarily purports to offer) a complete prescription for what the next generation of policy instruments should involve. However, as I will show, individually and collectively, they enrich our understanding of specific policy instruments and what they might achieve. They also provide insights into the challenges facing regulatory reconfiguration and how they might be resolved.

### Reflexive Regulation

The literature on reflexive law[3] recognizes that the capacity of the regulatory state to deal with increasingly complex social issues has declined dramatically. As Teubner and others (Teubner 1983; Teubner et al. 1994) have argued, there is a limit to the possibility of adding more and more specific prescriptions without this resulting in counterproductive regulatory overload. Traditional command-and-control regulation (a form of "material law")[4] is seen as unresponsive to the demands of the enterprise and unable to generate sufficient knowledge to function efficiently. To give a concrete example, one cause of the Three-Mile Island nuclear accident and near meltdown was that operators simply followed rules, without any capacity for strategic thinking; thus, as events unfolded that were not covered by a rule, they had no capacity to read the situation and respond appropriately.[5]

In contrast, reflexive regulation, which uses *indirect* means to achieve broad social goals, has, according to its proponents, a much greater capacity to come to terms with increasingly complex social arrangements. This is because it "focuses on enhancing the self-referential capacities of social systems and institutions outside the legal system, rather than direct intervention of the legal system itself through its agencies, highly detailed statutes, or delegation of greater powers to the courts ... [It] aims to establish self-reflective processes within businesses to encourage creative, critical, and continual thinking about how to minimise ... harms and maximise ... benefits" (Orts 1995, 1232). Put differently, reflexive regulation is procedure-oriented rather than directly focused on a prescribed goal and seeks to design self-regulating social systems by establishing norms of organization and procedure (Fiorino 1999).

Such a strategy can also be viewed as a form of "meta risk management" whereby government, rather than regulating directly, risk-manages the risk management of individual enterprises.[6] This is what happens under the "safety case" regime, instituted on North Sea oil rigs following the Cullen (1990) enquiry into the Piper Alpha disaster, in which 167 lives were lost. This involves what is in effect a safety-management system being developed by the rig operator and submitted to the regulator for scrutiny and approval. Similarly, the safety regime established for the nuclear-power industry, post Three-Mile Island, ceased to be primarily about government inspectors checking compliance with rules and more about encouraging the industry to put in place safety-management systems, which were then scrutinized by regulators and, in this case, by the industry association in the form of the Institute of Nuclear Power Operations (Braithwaite and Drahos 2000; Rees 1994).

A number of the second-generation instruments could be readily interpreted as examples of reflexive law, whose goal, rather than regulating prescriptively, is to encourage organizations to establish processes of internal self-regulation in order to monitor, control, and replace economic activities injurious to the environment.[7] Take the use of environmental-management systems (EMSs), which form the principal component of regulatory-flexibility initiatives and some forms of negotiated agreement. Such systems seek by law to stimulate modes of self-organization within the firm in such a way as to encourage internal self-critical reflection about its environmental performance. They establish processes and procedures that encourage self-reflexive learning and thinking about reducing environmental impact rather than seeking to influence behaviour directly by proscribing certain activities. Similar mechanisms are being devised to suit the circumstances of small and medium-sized enterprises (SMEs). These include not only "slimmed-down" EMSs, but also self-inspection, self-audits, and checklists.

In part, informational regulation can also be viewed in these terms (although it is much else besides). For example, requiring facilities to track and report their emissions – as under the Toxic Release Inventory (TRI) – not only empowers community groups and enables markets to make more informed judgments, but also leads to a degree of self-reflection on how things might be done differently. Dow Chemicals is among those firms who freely acknowledge that they had not previously measured their wastes and as a result had no idea how much they were discharging. Once they did so, they realized that there was a business opportunity to make pollution prevention pay – through reuse, recycling, the substitution of different substances, and the use of fewer chemicals (Gunningham and Cornwall 1994b). Thus a strategy that did not require firms to do anything other than estimate discharges and disclose them had a variety of broader consequences, including internal organizational change (and corporate shaming), which in turn resulted in substantially improved environmental performance for many companies.

On close inspection, a number of other strategies also contain elements of reflexive regulation. Industry self-management initiatives certainly fall within this category to the extent that they deliberately build in a variety of mechanisms to generate internal compliance and self-organization. Even economic incentives, on one view, have reflexive elements, although whether their designers would have viewed them in these terms is debatable. Nevertheless, Fiorino (1999, 450) argues that marketable permits, such as those used in US programs for emissions trading and for acid-rain-allowance trading, "induce reflection by specifying a goal and allowing firms to decide how to achieve it, given their circumstances." However, he also notes that because they are implemented in the context of technology requirements, such permits involve a combination of substantive and reflexive law.

### Regulatory Pluralism

Traditionally, regulation was thought of as a bipartite process involving government and business, with the former acting as regulator and the latter as regulatee. However, a substantial body of empirical research reveals that the there is a plurality of regulatory forms, that numerous actors influence the behaviour of regulated groups in a variety of complex and subtle ways (Rees 1988, 7), and that mechanisms of informal social control often prove more important than formal ones (Gunningham 1991). In the case of the environment, the regulatory-pluralism perspective suggests that we should focus our attention on the influence of international-standards organizations, trading partners and the supply chain, commercial institutions and financial markets, peer pressure and self-regulation through industry associations, internal environmental-management systems and culture, and myriad forms of civil society.

These insights have led some policy makers to investigate how public agencies may harness institutions and resources residing *outside* the public sector in order to further policy objectives in specific, concrete situations. This approach can be seen as part of the broader transition in the role of governments internationally – from "rowing the boat to steering it" (Osborne and Gaebler 1992) – as governments increasingly choose not to regulate directly but to "regulate at a distance" by acting as facilitators of self- and co-regulation (Grabosky 1995). Thus for regulatory pluralists, environmental policy making involves government harnessing the capacities of markets, civil society, and other institutions to accomplish its policy goals more effectively, with greater social acceptance, and at less cost to the state (Gunningham et al. 1999a). And since parties and instruments interact with each other and with state regulation in a variety of ways, careful regulatory design will be necessary to ensure that pluralistic policy instruments are mutually reinforcing rather than duplicative or, worse, conflicting (Gunningham and Grabosky 1998, ch. 6).

A substantial number of next-generation instruments are pluralistic in conception. Some, such as the regulatory-flexibility programs established under the Clinton-Gore Reinventing Environmental Regulation initiative (Clinton and Gore, Jr 1995), were directly inspired by one version of regulatory pluralism – and, in particular, by Osborne and Gaebler's (1992) concept of "steering not rowing." Seeking to embed environmental values and processes within the corporate culture in such a way that it becomes self-regulating, and relying upon oversight from local communities and perhaps third-party auditors in order to supplement or even to replace direct regulation, is a quintessential pluralist strategy.

Many informational regulation initiatives can also be understood in pluralist terms. Providing communities and financial markets with greater information about corporate environmental performance effectively empowers both of these groups. Communities and environmental NGOs respond by using this information to shame bad corporate performers, while the same information apparently influences share prices, thereby indirectly punishing bad performers and rewarding environmental leaders (Lanoie et al. 1997). In particular, the powerful impact of the TRI as a surrogate regulatory tool is well documented (Fung and O'Rourke 2000).

## Environmental Partnerships

Environmental partnerships came of age in the 1990s when parts of industry, government, and NGOs recognized that conflict and confrontation were not necessarily the best means of achieving either the best economic or environmental results. Governments sought alternatives to direct regulation, and business enterprises, dissatisfied with the cost and inflexibility of command-and-control regulation and sometimes seeking win-win outcomes, sought more flexible and less confrontational alternatives. NGOs, too, began to see virtue in "green alliances" with environmentally proactive enterprises. Sometimes these partnerships involve agreements between business and NGOs, or between governments and business, or even between business and business along the supply chain. On other occasions, they may embrace governments, NGOs, business, *and* a range of other third parties, which, as we have seen, hold out the promise of acting as surrogate regulators and performing many of the functions that government regulation is no longer ready, willing, and able to perform.

According to their proponents, environmental partnerships provide an additional policy option that steers a middle course between the two extremes of traditional regulation, on the one hand, and self-regulation and voluntarism, on the other. In doing so, partnerships take advantage of the respective attributes of these extremes while compensating for their particular weaknesses (Long and Arnold 1994). Environmental partnerships also provide opportunities to replace adversarialism with cooperation and, in doing so, may provide benefits for all sides. For example, through "green alliances" business may obtain the political goodwill and credibility that NGOs bring to the partnership, while in return, environmental groups gain commitments to improved environmental practices on the part of their business partner. In industry-government partnerships, governments can offer resources, expertise, regulatory relief, and external legitimacy in return for improved industry environmental performance. Government can also play a broader role in encouraging, facilitating, rewarding, and shaping a variety of partnership forms.

In Europe negotiated agreements between government and individual companies or industry sectors have rapidly become one of the principle instruments of environmental-management policy at a national level. The goal here is often to fill in the gaps not covered by regulations, to encourage companies to go beyond compliance, or even to find a more politically acceptable alternative to regulation. Public voluntary programs also fit the partnership model, with government offering technical support and public relations benefits in return for industry commitments to improved environmental performance. In the United States such programs have also become an important component of the Reinventing Environmental Regulation initiative (Clinton and Gore, Jr 1995), under which government seeks to replace the typically adversarial relationship that has existed between business and government in the US with a more cooperative approach based on trust and reciprocity.

## CIVIL REGULATION
## AND PARTICIPATORY GOVERNANCE

As defined by Murphy and Bendall (1998, 8), "civil regulation is where organisations of civil society,[8] such as NGOs, set the standards for business behaviour. Enterprises then choose to adopt or not to adopt those standards." Those who advocate a greater role for civil regulation argue that the regulatory state is starved of resources, lacking in political will, and incapable of reaching the many businesses that can now operate outside national territorial boundaries. The goal of civil regulation[9] is to fill the vacuum left by the contracting state and to compensate for "the deficit of democratic governance that we face as a result of economic globalisation" (Bendell 2000, 241). As a result, there is considerable overlap between this perspective and some aspects of regulatory pluralism, discussed above.

Under civil regulation, the various manifestations of civil society act in a variety of ways to influence corporations, consumers, and markets, often bypassing the state and rejecting political lobbying in favour of what they believe to be far more effective strategies. Sometimes NGOs take direct action, usually targeted at large reputation-sensitive companies. Greenpeace's campaign against Shell's attempted deep-sea disposal of the *Brent Spar* oil rig is one example. Sometimes they boycott products or producers deemed to be environmentally harmful, as with the effective boycott of Norwegian fish products organized by Greenpeace in protest against Norway's resumption of whaling. Market campaigning, focusing on highly visible branded retailers, is a particularly favoured strategy.[10] Less common are campaigns that seek to provide a market premium for "environmentally preferred" produce due largely to the unwillingness of consumers to support such a strategy. More recently certification programs such as that of the Forest Stewardship Council are "transforming traditional power relationships in the global arena. Linking together diverse and often antagonistic actors from the local, national and international levels ... to govern firm behavior in a global space that has eluded the control of states and international organizations" (Gereffi et al. 2001).[11]

However, the evolving role of civil regulation has not taken place entirely divorced from state intervention. On the contrary, either in response to pressure from the institutions of civil society or in recognition of the limits of state regulation, governments are gradually providing greater roles for communities, environmental NGOs, and the public more generally. Thus a number of next-generation policy instruments are geared to empower various institutions of civil society to play a more effective role in shaping business behaviour. In effect, they facilitate civil regulation (and regulatory pluralism). These include public participation provisions under the various US Reinventing Environmental Regulation initiatives, Community Right to Know (CRTK) legislation, some second-generation voluntary agreements that contemplate a significant role for third parties, and some forms of environmental partnership in which the public, or public-interest groups, are major players.

Arguably, the most powerful forms of civil regulation are those in which environmental NGOs or communities have the capacity to threaten the social-licence and reputation capital of large corporations.

Sometimes they do so independently of government, but more commonly government and next-generation instruments play a crucial facilitative role.

## ECOLOGICAL MODERNIZATION
## AND THE "GREEN GOLD" HYPOTHESIS

Another emerging paradigm is what has become known as ecological modernization.[12] In contrast to many analyses suggesting that a radical reorientation of our current economic and social arrangements will be necessary to avert ecological disaster,[13] ecological modernization suggests that ecologically sound capitalism is not only possible, but worth working toward.[14] This good-news message may indeed be a substantial part of the attraction of the ecological-modernization approach. Beyond the goal of introducing ecological imperatives within the framework of capitalism, the main tenets of this perspective are difficult to encapsulate since writings under the banner of ecological modernization are diverse and draw from a number of different schools of thought.[15]

For present purposes, I focus on its core, which emphasizes how strategies such as eco-efficiency can facilitate environmental improvements in the private sector (particularly in relation to manufacturing) by simultaneously increasing efficiency and minimizing pollution and waste (Buttel 2000, 59). This will require switching to the use of cleaner, more efficient, and less resource-intensive technologies, shifting from energy and resource-intensive industries to those that are value- and knowledge-intensive, incorporating anticipatory planning processes, and furthering the "organisational internalisation of ecological responsibility" (Cohen 1997, 109).

However, this is not to suggest that markets unaided, or past environmental policy, will provide the appropriate messages and incentives to enable industry to achieve these goals. On the contrary, such an outcome requires action on a number of fronts, and government regulation in particular will need to promote innovation in environmental technology. In terms of public-policy prescriptions, Mol (one of the most influential proponents of this perspective) suggests two directions that should be pursued. First, state environmental policy must focus not on prescription but rather on prevention and participatory, decentralized decision making, which "creates favourable conditions and contexts for environmentally sound practices and behaviour on the part of producers and consumers" (Mol 1995, 46). The second option includes a transfer of responsibilities, incentives, and tasks from the state to the market, which provides the flexibility and incentives to enable more efficient and effective outcomes. Under this approach, "the state provides the conditions and stimulates social 'self-regulation,' either via economic mechanisms and dynamics or via the public sphere of citizen groups, environmental NGOs and consumer organisations" (ibid., 47).

In these respects, the ecological-modernization literature has resonance with a number of other perspectives described in this chapter, especially those favouring civil regulation, regulatory pluralism, and to some extent, reflexive regulation. However, on one fundamental issue, ecological modernization departs substantially from these other perspectives, namely in its assumption that following the precepts of ecological modernization will result in a "dissolution of the conflict between economic progress and responsible environmental management because it will be possible to achieve both objectives simultaneously" (Cohen 1997, 109).

In arguing that the business community could successfully combine the objectives of environmental protection and economic growth, ecological modernization resonates with the views of a variety of business strategists, environmental commentators, and corporations that subscribe to what has become known as the "green gold" hypothesis. This group argues that by preventing pollution and thereby directly cutting costs and avoiding waste, by more effective risk management, by gaining an increasing share of expanding "green markets" or price premiums within them, and by developing the environmental technology to compete effectively in the global environmental market, businesses can achieve win-win outcomes, gaining economically from environmental improvements (Smart 1992; Schmidheiny 1992).

Of particular influence have been the views of Porter (1990), who has argued that in a highly regulated world, innovative companies can acquire competitive advantages or cut costs by developing novel methods of reducing environmental problems. Notwithstanding some differences of emphasis, a common refrain has been that going beyond compliance was both good for business and good for the environment.[16] However, both Porter and the ecological-modernization theorists acknowledge that there may be more scope for win-win outcomes in some sectors and circumstances than in others (Porter 1998; Baylis et al. 1998).

A number of next-generation instruments might facilitate win-win outcomes. For example, instruments that harness market forces in order to encourage rather than inhibit commercial drive and innovation (including many economic instruments and performance standards)[17] meet with approval. Various other flexible and arguably cost-efficient mechanisms for curbing environmental degradation, such as self-regulation, information-based strategies, the use of liability rules, and other financial instruments, are consistent with Mol's two directions, summarized above. Government's role includes nudging firms toward cleaner production, heightening their awareness of environmental issues, providing them with financial incentives (which at the margin may be crucial), and encouraging the reordering of corporate priorities in order to reap the benefits of improved environmental performance.

The question of whether, in a particular set of circumstances, there are opportunities for win-win outcomes is both highly contentious and important because in the absence of such opportunities, it cannot be assumed that organizations will voluntarily become greener or that they have any incentive to pursue beyond compliance environmental strategies in the absence of external pressure to do so. As regards the latter issue, Reinhardt (2000) has demonstrated that it makes sense to pursue policies beyond compliance if they increase the enterprise's expected value or if they appropriately manage business risk, but in a substantial number of circumstances, they do neither.

## REGULATORY REFORM:
## THE NEVER-ENDING JOURNEY

While each of the perspectives described above provides insights concerning how best to approach the task of regulatory reconfiguration, there are considerable disparities between them, and none provides unproblematic or comprehensive answers as to what next-generation environmental regulation should involve. Nevertheless, both the commonalities and the differences between these perspectives provide insights into how best to approach the journey ahead.

In terms of the commonalities, there is general agreement that returning to the policies of the past is not an option. A common theme is that traditional regulation is not suited to meet many contemporary policy needs (although, as I emphasize below, it still has a role to play); indeed, it was partly in response to the perceived shortcomings of the regulatory status quo that each of these conceptual frameworks evolved. As Fiorino (1999, 464) puts it, "underlying each strand in the literature is the belief that the increased complexity, dynamism, diversity, and interdependence of contemporary society makes old policy technologies and patterns of governance obsolete."

There is also recognition that regulated enterprises have a diversity of motivations and that it cannot be assumed (as in some versions of command-and-control regulation) that deterrence is the principal weapon available to regulators and policy makers. Notwithstanding differences of emphasis, there is a shared awareness of the complexity of motivational forces influencing environmental behaviour and of the need to develop instruments and strategies that take this complexity into account. As a result, each of these perspectives, to a greater or lesser extent, recognizes the importance of such broader motivational drivers as the effects of negative publicity, informal sanctions and shaming, incentives provided by various third parties, the significance for private enterprise of maintaining legitimacy, and the necessity to maintain cooperation and trust.[18]

Again, some instruments and approaches are common to almost all of these perspectives. For example, informational regulation is important to reflexive regulation, civil regulation, and regulatory pluralism, is supportive of environmental partnerships, and is at least consistent with the goals of ecological modernization. Similarly, process-based strategies, such as EMSs, are central to reflexive regulation, many environmental partnerships, ecological modernization, and, as a form of industry self-management, some variants of regulatory pluralism. And none of these perspectives would deny that there is a role for public-interest groups, although their role is regarded as more central to environmental partnerships, regulatory pluralism, and civil regulation than to reflexive regulation or ecological modernization.

And in contrast to traditional forms of environmental regulation, each of the perspectives I have examined sees virtue in engaging with environmental leaders and in encouraging or rewarding their further improvement rather than focusing only on bringing laggards up to compliance. This is perhaps most obvious in the case of environmental partnerships (which often only the best firms are willing to join), but regulatory pluralism and civil regulation also reward environmental leaders (for example, in terms of reputation, or market advantage, or share price premium) and seek to shame laggards or otherwise provide them with negative incentives. Reflexive regulation, while less explicit, builds in processes that often lead to continuous improvement, while ecological modernization, with its emphasis on win-win outcomes and cleaner production, also seeks to encourage best practice rather than merely minimum standards and compliance.

However, when it comes to identifying where the focus of regulatory reconfiguration should be, there is much less agreement, with very different policy prescriptions flowing from different perspectives. In terms of reflexive regulation, the perceived solution is to establish regulatory structures that strengthen the capability of individual institutions or enterprises for internal reflection and self-control. For regulatory pluralism, the solution is a plethora of instruments that enable the state to steer, not row, and to harness the capacities of second and third parties in order to more effectively fill the space vacated by the contracting regulatory state. From a civil-regulation perspective, the state's principal role is to provide mechanisms that will empower the institutions of civil society to make corporations more accountable. A partnership perspective would seek out opportunities to build reciprocal gains from cooperation, with the state playing an additional role as facilitator. For ecological modernization, the aspiration is to create incentives that will facilitate industry's movement toward sustainability using new technologies and techniques of production, with economic and environmental considerations being mutually reinforcing.

My own perspective is that each of the above frameworks has something valuable to offer and that none of them is "right" or "wrong" in the abstract. Rather, they make differing contributions depending upon the nature and context of the environmental-policy issue to be addressed. For example, ecological modernization has most to offer where industry can demonstrably benefit economically from environmental improvements (the so called win-win scenario),[19] but it is far less persuasive in the variety of contexts where this is not the case.[20] Civil regulation has considerable power when it comes to changing the behaviour of large reputation-sensitive companies, which are vulnerable not only to shaming, but also to market forces and consumer pressure, but it has far less to offer when dealing with the environmental excesses of many SMEs and firms that are not vulnerable to such pressures. Reflexive regulation is demonstrably effective in dealing with complex and sophisticated environmental issues, such as regulating major-hazard facilities,[21] but it may be redundant when it comes to more traditional challenges.[22] Environmental partnerships have attractions where both partners can see common ground and mutual benefits from constructive engagement[23] but not where there are irreconcilable philosophical differences between stakeholders (Poncelet 1999, forthcoming).

## A Case Study: Regulating Agricultural Nonpoint-Source Pollution

Nonpoint-source pollution is one of the most serious water-quality problems confronting many jurisdictions, and agriculture is the most substantial contributing factor. Controlling such pollution presents a very considerable policy challenge because, by definition, pollution from diffuse sources cannot be readily identified and measured as it leaves a landholder's property. Moreover, it is caused by a diversity of practices and land uses, it enters the water system in a number of different ways, and its impact is mitigated by weather conditions, soil type, and a variety of other factors, not all of which are fully understood. Against this backdrop, how should environmental law and policy address nonpoint-source pollution from agriculture? For present purposes, three main policy categories can be identified: (1) farm-management practices, (2) landscape changes, and (3) land-use patterns.

Perhaps because of its complexity and political sensitivity, policy makers have chosen to address this issue largely through voluntarism and other forms of exhortation. However, while politically acceptable, such approaches have been manifestly unsuccessful in achieving change. Elsewhere, it has been argued that what is required is not only the establishment of credible pollution targets, time frames, and assessment criteria, but also the development of a range of policy instruments that are demonstrably effective and that deliver acceptable trade-offs in terms of efficiency, equity, and political acceptability.

This implies matching the type of standard with the context in which it is to be applied and developing a blend of positive and negative incentives, underpinned by coercive mechanisms in some circumstances. There is value in applying a *range* of policy instruments under each of the three broad categories (i.e., farm-management practices, landscape changes, and land-use patterns) in order to engage with different facets of the problem. There are particular virtues in the use of process-based standards under the first of these categories (e.g., environmental-management systems, farm-management plans, Best Management Practices), specification standards under the second (e.g., buffer zones by waterways fifty metres wide, limits on fertilizer application), and broad-scale planning and development-control strategies under the third.

Managing the inevitable trade-offs between cost effectiveness, equity, and political acceptability raises a particular challenge, which might be addressed through a phased approach, engaging a diversity of mechanisms to deal with different aspects of this complex environmental challenge. In the first instance, this approach relies on a complementary package of measures based on positive inducements (e.g., subsidies and auctioned grants) in recognition of the political and cultural difficulties in achieving the desired change and of imposing it on a resistant and politically powerful rural constituency. Ultimately, however, if these measures demonstrably fail to meet agreed performance outcomes at the catchment and subcatchment levels, then a more interventionist mix of measures is demonstrably justified, including the use of negative incentives and direct regulation (Gunningham and Sinclair 2004).

## Case Assessment

In the box above, I give an example of a particular, complex, contemporary environmental challenge, nonpoint-source pollution from agriculture, and a short analysis of the policy options that might best be applied in addressing the challenge. But how does this analysis match with each of the frameworks that has been examined above?

Initially, it may appear that reflexive and meta-regulation have little to offer. Nonpoint-source pollution, after all, is not concentrated in a major-hazard facility that needs to be controlled; rather, numerous small and unsophisticated farmers are the problem. However, controlling this group is also complex. Just as "regulating by rules" is beyond the practical reach of government in dealing with highly complex organizations, so, too, does this limitation affect government when dealing with a multitude of small enterprises spread over a large land mass. Encouraging or requiring these enterprises to adopt some type of management standard, such as an environmental farm plan, and then requiring them to self-audit and send the results (e.g., a two-page checklist) to the regulator is at least one practicable option, even though the scope for government oversight (for the "regulation of self-regulation") remains limited.

Is there scope for environmental partnerships and civil regulation? Certainly, at the catchment level, the task of identifying appropriate pollution targets and allocating responsibility for achieving them will have far greater legitimacy if it is done in some collaborative fashion with a diverse group of stakeholders. That is, collaborative governance has much greater potential than command and control, and experience with integrated catchment management, in countries such as Australia, strongly supports this conclusion. But having set the targets and having sought to allocate responsibilities in broad terms, deliberation and persuasion may still not be enough to persuade those upstream to incur considerable costs for the perceived benefit of those downstream.

For this reason, a diverse range of policy instruments will likely need to be invoked, capable not only of encouraging and rewarding those who have some inclination to "do the right thing," but also of penalizing those who do not. Steering a middle course between the often competing demands of equity, efficiency, and political acceptability may well require both the harnessing of a range of instruments and their carefully sequenced use. And even though in these circumstances the state will still need to play an important role (albeit with some steering as well as rowing), there is only limited scope to leave the rowing to third parties, such as industry associations. Nevertheless, the general principles of regulatory pluralism manifestly have an important role to play.

Much less so, in this particular context, can the precepts of ecological modernization make a practical policy contribution. This is because there is a considerable gap between the perceived self-interest of the rural landholders, who are primarily responsible for agricultural non-point-source pollution, and the public interest in reducing it. Certainly, there is some scope for more targeted fertilizer and pesticide use that would both save money and have environmental benefits. But such "win-win" solutions are relatively rare in this context. For example, there are upfront capital and/or labour costs associated with installing fencing, ongoing costs in reducing feral animals and pests, losses of productive capacity in converting farmed land for nonfarming uses, and so on. Perhaps ecological modernization's most valuable insight in this context is its recognition of the need for sustainable farming practices over the long term rather than its provision of any short-term policy solutions.

The limitations of each of the major policy innovations and of the conceptual frameworks that drive next-generation regulation, as well as their context-specific nature as illustrated above, lead to a plea for pragmatism and regulatory pluralism. None of the policy instruments or perspectives I have examined work well in relation to all sectors, contexts, or enterprise types.[24] Each has weaknesses as well as strengths, and none can be applied as an effective stand-alone approach across the environmental spectrum. In part, such a conclusion suggests the value of designing complementary combinations of instruments, such that the weaknesses of each are compensated for by the strengths of others while avoiding combinations of instruments deemed to be counterproductive or at least duplicative. Indeed, this is the central message of my previous collaborative work embedded within the pluralist perspective (Gunningham and Sinclair 1999b, 1999c). From this perspective, no particular instrument or approach is privileged, whether it be reflexive regulation, civil regulation, or the tenets of ecological modernization. Rather, the goal is to accomplish substantive compliance with regulatory goals by any viable means, using whatever regulatory or quasi-regulatory tools might be available, including any or all of the next-generation instruments. As Parker (2000, 45) points out, "the objective is to steer corporate conduct towards public policy objectives in the most effective and efficient way, without interfering too greatly with corporate autonomy and profit, rather than fruitless expenditure of government and business resources on traditional styles of regulation that ignore the effects of indigenous regulatory orderings."

However, even in circumstances where a particular perspective (or combination of perspectives) and one set of policy tools seem well suited to a particular problem, there may still be a substantial gap between theory and practice. Indeed, some of the policies at the very heart of next-generation regulation are largely untested, and their efficacy is uncertain. This is certainly the case with environmental-management systems, which play an important role under a number of the frameworks reviewed above. There is only very limited evidence available of how they work in practice (mainly in relation to major-hazard facilities), and there remains a risk that they will produce the trappings of self-reflection and internal control without achieving more than business as usual. Moreover, it has proved very difficult to develop incentives sufficient to persuade substantial numbers of organizations to participate in an EMS-based alternative regulatory track. And we know even less about whether or to what extent a "slimmed-down" version of this approach might be applied to SMEs.

Some second-generation agreements are much better designed, but we still have incomplete evidence as to whether, or under what circumstances, they will be successful. Indeed, there still remain considerable risks of wrong turns and of reenacting the mistakes of previous decades.[25] Much the same can be said for many environmental partnerships (Gunningham and Sinclair 2001). Even informational regulation, generally hailed as a success story, has been challenged by its critics as not demonstrably achieving many of its objectives, at least in some jurisdictions (Antweiler and Harrison 1999). The limitations of our current experience is even greater in the case of SMEs, for which the empirical picture remains extremely unclear.

Thus much of our knowledge about policy instruments and, in particular, about what works and when is tentative, contingent, and uncertain. This suggests the virtue of adaptive learning and the merits of treating policies as experiments from which we can learn and which, in turn, can help shape the next generation of instruments. From this perspective, following Fiorino (1999, 468), it is important to ask "how may mechanisms that promote policy-learning ... be strengthened? To what extent do policy-making institutions provide mechanisms for learning from experience and altering behavior based on that experience?" This might imply, for example, monitoring, post-implementation evaluation, revision mechanisms, and "building reliable feedback mechanisms into policy-making, strengthening learning networks, creating conditions that would lead to more trust and more productive dialogue and building enough flexibility into the policy system so that it is possible to respond to lessons drawn from one's own experience or that of others" (ibid.).

In particular, adaptive learning is heavily dependent on the depth and accuracy of an agency's statistical database and of other information sources. Only with adequate data collection and interpretation can one know how effective or otherwise a particular regulatory strategy has been. There will be a need to establish databases that provide more accurate profiles of individual firms, hazards, and industries.[26]

Environmental-information systems have the potential to play a key role here. Work in this area is still in its embryonic stage, but recent initiatives (Rapp et al. 2000) suggest that it is developing quite rapidly. Of particular note is the Finnish compliance-monitoring system (VAHTI), which comprises a database for the input and storage of information on the environmental permits of industries and their discharges into water, emissions into air, and solid wastes.[27]

Finally, I return to the role of direct state regulation under a next-generation approach. I do so because it is important not to lose sight of the residual but nevertheless important role that command-and-control regulation can and should continue to play in environmental policy. Only the state can impose criminal sanctions and the full weight of the law, and only the state, under statute, may enter private property to conduct inspections, take samples, and gather evidence of illegality more generally. While, as advocates of civil regulation, reflexive regulation, and regulatory pluralism would argue, there may be some circumstances where far more can be achieved by various other forms of state and nonstate action, this is certainly not the case across the board.

For example, there remain situations where SMEs, in particular, need the highly specific and concrete guidance that specification standards can provide. And in the case of large industries, such as pulp and paper, the most important changes in environmental performance have been achieved through mandated technological change (Gunningham, Thornton, and Kagan 2003). It should likewise not be forgotten that, according to various surveys, the single most important motivator of improved environmental performance is regulation (Henriques and Sadorsky 1995; ENDS Report 1997). The more general conclusion, as the US EPA (2000, 4) has recognized, is that "in some cases, nationwide laws and regulations will continue to be the best way to reduce risk. But in others, tailored strategies that involve market based approaches, partnerships, or performance incentives may offer better results at lower costs."

The broader point is that many less interventionist strategies are far more likely to succeed if they are underpinned by direct regulation. For example, under reflexive regulation, some enterprises may be tempted to develop "paper systems" and tokenistic responses that "independent" third-party auditors may fail to detect (O'Rourke 2000). However, the threat of sanctions if these enterprises fail to deliver on performance targets set by the state will substantially reduce the risk of free riding. Again, there is evidence that information-based strategies cannot necessarily replace traditional regulation and enforcement practices but rather that the two instruments work best when they are used in a complementary combination (Foulon et al. 1999). So, too, as I have showed, can the fear of regulation or its enforcement be used to good effect in the case of small business in order to complement other more innovative approaches.

Once again, what we are witnessing is not the demise of the regulatory state but a regulatory reconfiguration, in which command and control retains a place, albeit no longer at centre stage, as a complement to a range of next-generation policies. This reconfiguration, however, remains a work in progress. Certainly, our knowledge of what works and why is much greater than it was a decade ago. Notwithstanding the considerable promise of the new generation of environmental-policy tools, the road to regulatory reform is long and tortuous, and the journey is far from over.

# Conclusion:
# The Future of Instruments Research

## B. GUY PETERS

The research presented in this volume, along with the scholarly work contained in other recent publications on policy instruments (see especially Salamon 2002; Peters and van Nispen 1998), indicates the significance of the progress that has been made in understanding the nature and importance of instruments in the policy process. Although much of this development has been done in an academic context, the practical application of this work has not been lost on government; indeed, this book and the conference that provided its basis are a consequence of the concern of government officials about the need to understand instruments in order better to understand how to govern.

Instruments have been always been used in governing; what has changed is that we now understand that instruments can, and should, be considered independently of other aspects of the design of policies (see Linder and Peters 1984). Rather than being inherently intertwined in the policies that they deliver, instruments do have some autonomous effects of their own and can independently impact the policies for which they are chosen. These effects can determine the success or failure of a program in reaching its policy goals as well as the *political* success or failure of a program.[1] Understanding the independent influence of instrument choice is important because policies that appear to be failures because they have chosen goals that are not achievable through collective action may, in fact, be quite feasible and even popular if they were attempted utilizing different instruments.

Therefore, both academic analysts and practical policy makers need to think consciously about the strengths and weaknesses of each instrument and need to attempt to understand instruments not only in the abstract, but also in the contexts of the particular political, social, and economic situations within which they will be put into operation. Individuals and organizations tend to have commitments – intellectual as well as practical – to particular instruments (see Linder and Peters 1998) and tend to adopt these instruments whenever faced with the need to design a new program, regardless of the goals or the environmental conditions.[2] While this "path dependency" in instrument selection is very human, and although an individual commitment to an instrument may be reinforced by membership in organizations, such dependency may produce suboptimal decisions for a program.

Even though the instruments research has made substantial progress and has enjoyed something of a revival in recent years, there are still a number of issues remaining if this literature is to fulfil its potential. The instruments approach, as is true of many aspects of the policy-studies literature, is an area in which there is nothing so practical as a good theory. That is, while experience and habit may provide useful rules of thumb for the selection of instruments, having a more comprehensive conceptualization of instruments and their correspondence to the environment will provide more general assistance in making decisions about program design. At the same time, these attempts at conceptualization must be linked with empirical research on the consequences of instrument choice if the type of progress that is needed is to be achieved.

## DEVELOPING THE INSTRUMENTS APPROACH

What will follow here is a set of observations about what needs to be done in order to further develop the instruments approach and to make the research more usable for practitioners and academics. These observations constitute a research agenda that to some extent reflects the papers and discussions arising from the conference as well as my own observations on developments in the instruments literature. The first premise motivating this research agenda is that we have a reasonably good understanding of how individual instruments perform in a functional, technical manner. The literature, such as that collected in Lester Salamon's *The Handbook of Policy Instruments* (2000) or in studies of individual instruments (Steuerle et al. 2000; Howard 1997), demonstrates a substantial understanding of individual instruments and their technical effects. The second premise is that, although this level of understanding is certainly important, it can serve only as a beginning for a more complete comprehension that will involve more dimensions of analysis: not only the technical, but also the political, ethical, and managerial.

## THE POLITICS OF INSTRUMENTS

A first point to be made about the selection of policy instruments is that the selection is being done in a political setting. The foundation of the instruments approach was largely in economics (Kirschen 1964), and a good deal of the available literature continues to emphasize the technical economic and legal attributes of these tools. As I will point out below, these technical attributes of instruments are important, but it is likewise crucial always to remember that the decisions about tools are being made for the purpose of governing and that governing is a political process.

The political importance of policy instruments arises both in their capacity to build political coalitions and in their capacity to implement policies in a manner that maximizes the legitimacy of the policy and of government more generally (see Issalys ch. 7 herein). First, in order to be successful, policy instruments have to be acceptable to a political coalition sufficient to justify the adoption of the policy. The need to create political coalitions around a policy choice – substantive or instruments-based – is an obvious point but one that may be forgotten if an analyst perceives solutions to policy problems from a more technical perspective. A scholar may be quite capable of demonstrating that a particular tool could produce a desired outcome with minimum distortions in the economy and perhaps even with minimum administrative costs. As laudable as these features may be for an instrument, they do not ensure that the instrument will be acceptable to the political actors needed to adopt the program.

Take, for example, the provision of financial aid to university students in the United States. Probably the simplest way to deliver this aid would be to give students grants directly. However, politically, there appears to be a majority that favours loans over grants given that this tool could save public money and also could be a means of forcing individual responsibility on the students. Then, after the decision for a loan-based program is made, the simplest alternative might be to give the money to the universities and have them administer the loan programs on behalf of their students. This option, however, would not include one influential industry that stands to gain from the loan program: banking. Therefore, the largest program that has developed for student aid is one of guaranteed student loans through private lenders. While this involves several more administrative steps and more actors than is necessary, it is capable of benefiting not only students and universities, but also banking interests.

Legitimacy is the second dimension of the political relevance of instrument choice. Some instruments are simply more legitimate in different countries than they are in others, and any attempt to ignore this cultural and political context will reduce the probability of the program's being successful. For example, a good deal of the Canadian literature (Woodside 1986; see also Howlett 1991) on policy instruments emphasizes that, everything else being equal, instruments that are less intrusive are more acceptable politically than are instruments that are visible to the public and that make it clear to the public that costs and benefits are being created. Again, these instruments are often not the most effective in achieving public purposes, depending as they often do upon the initiative of individual citizens to be effective.

Again, context is important for understanding the legitimacy of different types of policy instruments. For example, the political culture of the United States tends to favour, perhaps even more than that of Canada, unobtrusive policy instruments. However, policies that are directed to the poor may have to be more intrusive and may have to exercise more control over the recipients if they are to be acceptable to much of the public. The welfare reform of 1996, for example, reduced some controls over the poor but substituted what have become in many ways even more direct controls over the lives of the recipients of benefits. Thus the acceptability of instruments is shaped not only by national cultures, but also by the image associated with particular policies and particular target groups of clients.

The political importance of instruments is most evident when we think about these tools in the broader context of governance. As governments come to place less reliance on regulatory instruments, or at least on regulatory instruments alone, and begin to involve the third sector in the delivery of public services, the political support for instruments will also change. In many industrialized democracies, the legitimacy of organizations in the third sector is as great as or greater than that of governments, as is the legitimacy of the public sector itself. Further, providing policies through partnerships or quasi-public arrangements may be perceived as less intrusive than mechanisms that depend entirely upon the authority of government.

## MULTIPLE CRITERIA

The above points illustrate a more general point about instrument choice, namely that there are a range of criteria that need to be considered when making a choice. My own inclination as a political scientist is to begin with the political considerations inherent in making the selection of an instrument, but as noted this has not been the dominant approach to selection. Each academic discipline will assume the primacy of its approach and its criteria, but in reality the exercise is one of balancing a wide range of concerns and values. Policy instruments have economic, administrative, and even ethical dimensions in addition to the political dimension emphasized above, and selection therefore involves means of assessing the relative importance of these different concerns.

It is easy to say that it is necessary to balance a range of concerns when making the selection of policy instruments. It is substantially more difficult to make the required trade-offs in practice. Again, there may be technical aids for making, or at least improving, such decisions. For example, the decision maker may begin with the premise that one criterion or another is primary, and then if the alternative instruments are equal on this primary criterion, proceed to second- or third-order considerations.[3] Alternatively, decisions could be made by developing some weighting of the multiple criteria that are relevant for the decision on instruments and then adding together the scores of alternative instruments. This approach implies a great deal of knowledge and a well-developed sense of priorities and may not be practical in the majority of cases.

In the end, most decision makers are capable only of recognizing that there are numerous dimensions of instruments that should be considered when deciding between alternatives. Above, I made the more general point about the necessity of conscious deliberation when selecting instruments. As this deliberation is carried into the process of making choices based on multiple criteria, the process may involve no more than simply recognizing the multiplicity of the criteria and the trade-offs that are involved. This process may be enhanced by making it more transparent so that habit and familiarity do not return to dominate decisions in the guise of a highly subjective weighting scheme. In the final analysis, the use of multiple criteria for assessing policy instruments may come down to the exercise of good judgment.

## MULTIPLE INSTRUMENTS

In addition to the multiple criteria for consideration, there are multiple instruments that should be considered (see Macdonald ch. 9 herein). One of the important points made in several of the papers in this volume is that decision makers, and analysts, need to consider mixes of instruments rather than the single, lonely instrument when designing programs. Most of our thinking about the selection of instruments has been focused on the idea that we should think about choosing the one best instrument for achieving the purpose at hand. In reality, most efforts at program delivery involve multiple instruments and indeed combine their effects with other policies and other instruments in order to achieve their purposes.

The emphasis on a single instrument corresponds nicely with the tendency to regard redundancy in public programs as wasteful and more streamlined mechanisms for delivering services as inherently desirable (but see Landau 1969; Bendor 1985). It may well be, however, that thinking about mixes of instruments is not only a political and programmatic reality, but also a virtue when attempting to achieve public purposes. The needs of potential clients of programs may be varied as well, such that governments could be well-advised to select different ways of reaching these clients. In the case of assistance for higher education, for example, some potential students may require more aid than could be reasonably provided through student loans; the student would be burdened with so much debt for so long that the consequences would be highly undesirable or would prevent the student from ever taking up the program of study. Therefore, without a mixture of instruments, delivering this service effectively would be less likely, if not impossible.

Once one has decided that a mixture of instruments may be the most important means of addressing public-policy issues, deciding what will comprise this mixture is substantially more difficult. The above example is rather clear, given the alternative approaches to addressing the financial needs of students seeking to attend universities, but most options for inclusion in effective policy mixes are less clearly defined. This is especially true when seeking to combine instruments that utilize very different types of underlying instruments to achieve their purposes. For example, the several methods discussed for addressing the financial needs of students all depend upon using public money (or the guarantee of public money) to achieve their purposes, but there may be options for mixing the "treasure"-based instrument with other forms of control, especially controls over the providers, to achieve the policy goals.

One might argue that instruments utilizing different underlying mechanisms to achieve their purposes might be the most effective for achieving policy goals. While different versions of the same fundamental instrument may help considerably in achieving the goals of the programs, the more extensive the range of instruments involved in attaining the policy goals, the more incoherent the government is likely to be. The administrative literature tends to focus on eliminating redundancy and multiple provision of the same service. There may be, however, a good deal of rationality in redundancy (Landau 1969) in that different types of instruments may address the needs of different types of potential clients that might be missed by a more linear conception of governing.

We can extend the above example of providing opportunities for students in higher education to think about extending the mix even further. For example, rather than providing funds to students directly or insuring bank loans to those students, the issue might be dealt with by regulations. For example, universities might be mandated to maintain low tuition fees or to provide scholarships to students from socio-economically deprived backgrounds. This strategy might address the financial needs of potential students.

## LINKING INSTRUMENTS AND ORGANIZATIONS

Policy instruments are highly dependent on institutional capacities for their implementation. Even those instruments that permit the individual beneficiaries to make the decisions about whether to use them depend upon one or more organizations for effective implementation. For example, although individuals make decisions about whether to claim tax preferences (tax expenditures), the taxing authority must monitor the take-up of this benefit and provide some credible threat of monitoring and enforcement if the instrument is to be used as intended (Sparrow 1994). Even more obviously, governments rarely go seeking individuals to apply for social benefits. Instruments such as regulation and subsidies are even more dependent upon public organizations for their success in producing the desired economic and social consequences.

As well as the basic structural issues involved in the implementation of programs through public organizations, there are other considerations in developing and implementing policies. First, as governments involve the for-profit and the not-for-profit sectors in delivering public services, the emerging structures are moving away from the "single lonely organization" (see Hjern and Porter 1981) and toward more complex structures for employing instruments; thus there is a need to consider the design of these structures. On the one hand, if these structures are to be inclusive and to provide nongovernmental organizations some capacity to influence the outcomes of the process, then decision making becomes difficult. If, on the other hand, the same authoritative decision making is to remain in place, then these structures may be meaningless and may be incapable of effectively delivering complex programs. That is, organizations outside the public sector may not be willing to be used by government without some real influence on the outcomes of the process.

Second, there is a need to consider the political dimension of policy instruments not only in the context of mass politics, as discussed above, but also in terms of another dimension of politics: that involving the role of organizational actors. Organizations have commitments to instruments as well as to the policies that are delivered through these instruments. These commitments may be a function of an organization's experiences and the familiarity that it has with certain instruments, or they may be a function of the staffing of the organization. Organizations staffed by lawyers, for example, are more likely to use regulation and other legal instruments than are those staffed by economists or public administrators.

Finally, organizations can use instruments as a political strategy to "capture" programs, thereby increasing budgets and staffing. For whatever reasons, however, organizations are not neutral about instrument choice and will be engaged in a variety of political actions to influence selections.

### HOW CAN WE LEARN?

One of the difficulties for instrument research, and for many other areas of policy research, is that instruments pose important problems for research. In the best of all worlds, we might experiment with a range of instruments as means of reaching a policy goal and use the resulting evidence to guide the final selection of a program. Rarely do governments have the options to perform such experiments and instead must rely on quasi-experimental results to guide decision making (Cook and Campbell 1979).[4] In the relatively few cases in which large-scale experiments on policy and policy instruments have been possible, as in the New Jersey Income Experiments, they have produced a great deal of useful information about the impacts of program choice.[5]

The absence of strong experimental evidence is a general problem for policy analysis given that the public rarely want to be experimented upon and that their behaviour might be different if they were aware that the intervention was indeed an experiment. For example, among the few experiments that have been done on policy instruments, some of those involving vouchers for education suggested that potential providers of educational services were reluctant to enter the market as long as the program was discussed as an experiment (Loomis 2000). Why should these potential providers invest their time and energy in a program to which government is not really committed? Likewise, why should parents risk disturbing their children's education when there is no certainty that the program will continue?

The obvious source of quasi-experimental evidence about policy instruments is our experience with other political systems. For many policy areas, there have been a range of attempts to provide the services and to reach the same goals through alternative means. These attempts thus comprise a natural laboratory for the implementation of programs and should provide us a means of understanding what instruments can be successful. Within the United States, Brandeis's famous comment on the

US's being the laboratory of democracy was but one indication of the utility of collecting evidence from multiple locations, and there is an international literature on the importance of learning about policy interventions from other geographical areas (Rose 1992; Dolowitz 1998).

As valuable as this evidence may be, its use can be problematic. As noted above, much of the existing literature on policy instruments assumes that the instruments are in essence technical instruments that are largely independent of the context within which they are being employed. This assumption is almost certainly incorrect, and the political, social, and economic circumstances within which an instrument is being used are of great relevance to the success of the instrument. For example, over the past decade or more the United Kingdom has been moving toward greater financing of higher education by the consumers of the service, much as students (or parents) pay high tuition in the United States (Brown 2002). British policy makers appear to have assumed that this form of financing is consistent with broad participation of students in higher education. Using this instrument successfully, however, depends both on middle and working class parents beginning to save for higher education practically from the birth of a child as well as on universities having substantial, independently financed scholarship programs to help the most needy students. Neither of these conditions exists in the United Kingdom, and hence there might be little reason to expect the instrument to be successful.

The above example is only one of any number of examples of attempts on the part of governments to learn from experience in which borrowing program elements has been less than successful once they are transplanted. Therefore, there appears to be a need to think more systematically about the mechanisms through which successful learning can be conducted and about the manner in which the environmental factors having an impact on the utility of an instrument can be assessed.[6] From this perspective, the analysis of policy instruments may move away from strict technical analysis of the economic or administrative criteria to consider policy instruments in the context of comparative policy studies more generally (see Ringeling ch. 8 herein). The agenda of the conference from which this book emerged was to think broadly about instruments, their utility, and their applicability in a wide range of circumstances.

## GOVERNANCE AND POLICY INSTRUMENTS

Finally, we need to remember throughout the analysis of contemporary policy instruments that the purpose of thinking about policy instruments is to improve the state's capacity to govern and thereby to improve the quality of life for citizens within a political system. At one point in our collective political and administrative histories, a discussion of the state's capacity to govern would have involved an almost exclusive role for the public sector (see Dror 2001). As already noted in a number of places in this book, government is increasingly involved in complex and multiorganizational structures for the delivery of programs. There is some tendency to think of instrument choice in terms of rather simple principal-agent terms, with delegation from one principal (the legislature or the minister) to a public agent, which uses an instrument to produce action. The contemporary world of policy implementation and governance, however, is a good deal more complex.

Further, policy instruments are, as also noted throughout this volume, increasingly moving away from regulatory and other "command and control" instruments depending directly upon the formal authority of government and toward softer, less direct forms of intervention into the social system. Even when law and regulation remain the principal instruments for intervention, they are increasingly implemented in the form of "soft law," such as compacts or voluntary agreements or other negotiated settlements with the private sector, rather than by means of hierarchical imposition (Héritier 2002; Mörth 2003).

Both of the above shifts in policy making are transforming the nature of government and governing, and the conventional analysis of instruments has been broadened along with the instruments themselves. Put somewhat differently, there are now multiple principals that charge individuals and organizations with implementing programs.

As "governance" has become one of the more important manners of conceptualizing the tasks of policy making and steering society (see Pierre and Peters 2000; Lynn 2001), scholars and practitioners interested in how instruments are being used must begin to consider more carefully the general question of using not only multiple instruments, but also a mixture of public- and private-sector instruments. Indeed, as the "soft law" example mentioned above indicates, the conventional distinction between public and private instruments may become increasingly difficult to maintain. Regulations emerging from processes of creating "soft law" may have the force of law, but they are the product of delegation of some amount of authority and discretion to non-public actors.

At the extreme, the public sector may delegate a good deal of its potential regulatory authority to the private sector and even to individuals. The clearest example of this is using individuals to monitor the actions of service providers or even of governments. Governments may, for example, provide opportunities for individuals to use the courts and tort actions to monitor the performance of important service providers, such as the medical profession, rather than investing in public regulation (Schuck 2002; Komesar 1994). At the extreme, the European Union relies heavily upon individuals to monitor the extent to which individual national administrations deviate from European rules and to use the court system to ensure compliance (Pollack 2003).

With the emergence of these less formal means of instrumentation as a standard mechanism for coping with public problems, the mixture of public and private instruments implies a new range of interactions and significant managerial challenges for the public sector (Kettl 2002). Not only do bundles of instruments have to be designed that will in principle work, and work in harmony, but they must be managed within a more complex political environment. In this environment, bargaining shapes the manner in which the instruments are utilized, just as do the actual instruments selected (Sorenson and Torfing 2002). Further, these mixed instruments that involve the private sector require developing the means for managing multiple relationships among actors that may have conflicting goals and commitments to services (Peters 2000a; Frederickson 1997).

## CONCLUSION

The tools, or instruments, approach to public policy can add a great deal to the analysis of public policy. On the one hand, instruments can be used as the foundation for understanding policy in general, and the argument might be made that the instrument selected may be the most important element of the choices made about policy. This strong argument is especially applicable if we examine the underlying foundations of action contained within the tools and the dynamics of instruments for coping with social problems (Hood 1986). A less extreme version of the argument is that instruments are a crucial element of the design of a program, and of governance, but not necessarily the only – or even the most central – element in governing. In either version of the argument, developing the instruments literature can improve the academic and practical dimensions of policy studies.

If the instruments approach is to reach its potential, then some of the issues raised in this volume will have to be addressed. When taken together, these points add up to the need to cope with the real, and increasing, complexity of policy. Policy making and implementation have always been complex, but globalization and the increasing involvement of societal actors have made these tasks all the more difficult. Perhaps the most significant challenge to the conventional understanding of the use of instruments is the need to involve nonofficial actors in the delivery of services, thereby broadening the simple principal-agent model implied in much of the literature to include multiple agents and multiple principals.

# Notes and References

INTRODUCTION

1 The editors are grateful to Laura Chapman and Donald Lemaire, who were champions of this project in its early phases, and to Jean-Pierre Voyer for his support. We also thank Michael Trebilcock, who provided valuable comments on this introductory chapter. Any mistakes, of course, are those of the editors.

2 M.J. Trebilcock, et al., *The Choice of Governing Instrument* (Ottawa: Minister of Supply and Services Canada, 1982).

3 See H. Lasswell, "Key Symbols, Signs and Icons," in L. Bryson, L. Finkelstein, R.M. MacIver, and Richard McKean, eds, *Symbols and Values: An Initial Study*, 77–94 (New York: Harper Brothers, 1954); M. Edelman, *The Symbolic Uses of Politics* (Chicago: University of Illinois Press, 1964); T.J. Lowi, "Four Systems of Policy, Politics and Choice," *Public Administration Review* 32, no. 4 (1972): 298–310; L.M. Salamon, "Rethinking Public Management: Third-Party Government and the Changing Forms of Government Action," *Public Policy* 29, no. 3 (1981): 255–75; and L.M. Salamon, ed., *The Tools of Government: A Guide to the New Governance* (New York: Oxford University Press, 2002).

4 Thanks to Roderick Macdonald for this formulation of the assumptions guiding instrument choice.

5 Bridget Hutter offers a useful description of good governance in her chapter, "Risk and Regulation": "Good governance has come to refer to coordinated, "joined-up" approaches to policy making, to a recognition that both governments and business are involved in the allocation of finite

resources, and to a need for regulatory regimes and agencies to be regarded as legitimate." For a discussion on the consequences of a superfi-
cial approach to efficiency, and its impact on governance, see for example,
Janice Gross Stein, *The Cult of Efficiency* (Toronto: House of Anansi
Press, 2001).

6  The Walkerton Inquiry investigated the contamination of water tables in
rural Southern Ontario, which had resulted in several deaths and widespread illness. The judge presiding over the inquiry blamed not only human
error and negligence, but also poor structuring of the relationship between
the responsible ministry, health officials, and laboratories, as well as inadequate reporting systems. See D. O'Connor, *Report of the Walkerton Inquiry,* parts 1 and 2 (Toronto: Queen's Printer for Ontario, 2002); available
at http: //www.attorneygeneral.jus.gov.on.ca/english/about/pubs/walkerton/
part1; and at http: //www.attorneygeneral.jus.gov.on.ca/english/about/pubs/
walkerton/part2.

7  S. Wood, "Green Revolution or Greenwash? Voluntary Environmental
Standards, Public Law, and Private Authority in Canada," in Law Commis-
sion of Canada, ed., *New Perspectives on the Public-Private Divide*
(Vancouver: University of British Columbia Press, 2003), 123–65 at 144.
See also, J. Freeman, "Collaborative Governance in the Administrative
State," UCLA *Law Review* 45, no. 1 (1997): 1–98.

8  See also M. Minow, *Partners Not Rivals: Privatization and Public Good*
(Boston: Beacon Press, 2002); Pearl Eliadis and Margaret M. Hill, "Instrument Choice in Global Democracies," *Policy Research Initiative Horizons*
6: http: //policyresearch.gc.ca/page.asp?pagenm=v6n1_art_15.

9  OECD Reviews of Regulatory Reform: Regulatory Reform in Canada:
Government Capacity to Produce High Quality Regulation (2002),
www.oecd.org/dataoecd/47/42/1960472.pdf.

10  Press release, "Prime Minister Names Members of External Advisory Committee on Smart Regulation," www.smartregulation.gc.ca/en/04/pr-02.asp.
It is worth noting that the drafting of the OECD reports occurs in close consultation with policy makers in the Privy Council Office, at least as regards
Canadian reports.

11  D. Zussman, "Let's Protect Canadians without Strangling Them," Ottawa
Citizen, 26 August 2002, A13.

12  Canada, External Advisory Committee on Smart Regulation, Final
Report, *Smart Regulation: A Regulatory Strategy for Canada* (2004),
http: //www.smartregulation.qc.ca.

13  D. Waldo, *The Administrative State: A Study of the Political Theory
of the American Public Administration* (New York: Ronald Press,
1948).

14  Pierre Lascoumes, "Normes juridiques et mise en oeuvre des politiques
publiques," *L'Année sociologique* 40 (1990): 43–71 [translation].

CHAPTER ONE

1 From "Tools as Art: The Hechinger Collection," an exhibit at the National Building Museum, Washington, DC, 2002–04.

2 See Watson 2002 and Sherwood 1990. For one of the most interesting and sophisticated analyses that has been undertaken, however, see Sanford et al. 1995 for a comparison of the roles that two seminal pieces on policy making – *America in Ruins* (1981) and *Silent Spring* (1962) – have played in their respective fields of infrastructure and environment policy. More recently, see also the Great Books Revisited Series launched in *Canadian Public Administration* in 2003.

3 From the standpoint both of Frederick Taylor and his fellow followers of scientific management and of other, more recent proponents of "government by the efficient," this was not unproblematic. As Mosher (1982) helpfully reminds us, however, duality – pursuing efficiency alongside democratic goals – is a standard characteristic of government action.

4 For an introduction to some of this literature, see, for example, Pal 1997. See also Kingdon 1997.

5 See Sherwood 1990.

6 It is interesting to speculate about the degree to which this dual resonance could be attributed to the explicit policy relevance of *The Choice of Governing Instrument* and to the hybrid interests of the authors. The late Doug Hartle, for instance, had known a distinguished career both as an academic and in Ottawa (e.g., as former director of research for the Carter Commission) by the time he was involved in the Regulation Reference. He is also reported to have famously said something along the lines of: "There's much more to public policy than maximizing a social-welfare function." On the role of practitioners in the development of public administration, see Bellavita 1990, and on the changing nature of the relationship between theoretical and practitioner knowledge, see Schmidt 1993 and Hummel 1991.

7 Seeing regulation as a tool of government stands in contrast to portrayals of regulation, in the broadest sense, as governing or, in a much narrower sense, delegating legislation.

8 See, for example, Dwivedi 1982.

9 This is the basic approach developed in Hill 1994.

10 On the basic point, see Hill 1998 and 1999.

11 See, for instance, the various studies from this period by the Law Commission of Canada and the Institute for Research on Public Policy.

12 See Doern and Wilks 1997; and Doern et al. 1999.

13 Doern et al. are in no way unique in reducing the centrality of self-interest in work inspired by the original instrument-choice approach. See, for example, Waldo 1968, which views nonrational action as the important factor in public administration.

14 For more fulsome discussion of the issues presented in this and the following paragraph, see Hill 1998 and 1999.
15 See also Privy Council Office 2000.
16 For example, the regulatory impact-analysis statement in the case of regulatory initiatives and the expenditure-management system in the case of program and policy decisions with spending implications.
17 See Treasury Board Secretariat of Canada 1998.

## References

Allison, Graham T. 1971. *Essence of Decision: Explaining the Cuban Missile
   Crisis*. Boston: Little, Brown.
Bellavita, Christopher. 1990. "The Role of Practitioners in the Intellectual De-
   velopment of Public Administration." In Christopher Bellavita, ed., *How
   Public Organizations Work: Learning from Experience*. New York: Praeger.
Bemelmans-Vidac, Marie-Louise, Ray C. Rist, and Evert Vedung, eds. 1998.
   *Carrots, Sticks and Sermons: Policy Instruments and Their Evaluation*. New
   Brunswick, NJ: Transaction Publishers.
Coleman, William D., and Grace Skogstad. 1990. *Policy Communities and
   Public Policy in Canada: A Structural Approach*. Mississauga, ON: Copp
   Clark Pitman.
Doern, G. Bruce, and S. Wilks, eds. 1997. *UK-North American Regulatory In-
   stitutions: Models and Issues for Reform*. Oxford: Oxford University Press.
– Margaret M. Hill, Michael J. Prince, and Richard J. Schultz, eds. 1999.
   *Changing the Rules: Canadian Regulatory Regimes and Institutions*.
   Toronto: University of Toronto Press.
Dwivedi, O.P. 1982. *The Administrative State in Canada*. Toronto: University
   of Toronto Press.
Economic Council of Canada. 1981. *Reforming Regulation*. Ottawa: Minister
   of Supply and Services.
Economic Council of Canada. 1979. *Responsible Regulation*. Ottawa: Minis-
   ter of Supply and Services.
Greenberg, George D., Jeffrey A. Miller, Lawrence B. Mohr, and Bruce C. Vla-
   deck. 1977. "Developing Public Policy Theory: Perspectives from Empirical
   Research." *APSR* 71: 1532–43.
Harter, Philip J., and George C. Eads. 1985. "Policy Instruments, Institutions,
   and Objectives: An Analytical Framework for Assessing Alternatives to Regulation." *Administration Law Review* 37, no. 3: 221–58.
Hill, Margaret M. 1994. "The Choice of Mode for Regulation: A Case Study
   of the Federal Pesticide Registration Review, 1988–1992." PhD thesis, Carleton University.
– 1997. "The Theory and Practice of Regulation in Canada and the United
   States: Opportunities for Regulatory Learning in the U.K." In G. Bruce

Doern and S. Wilks, eds, *UK-North American Regulatory Institutions: Models and Issues for Reform*. Oxford: Oxford University Press.

– May 1998. "A Historical Perspective on Regulatory Reform: Institutions and Ideas after the Regulation Reference." Ottawa: Treasury Board Secretariat.

– 1999. "Managing the Regulatory State: From 'Up,' to 'In and Down,' to 'Out and Across.'" In G. Bruce Doern, Margaret M. Hill, Michael J. Prince, and Richard J. Schultz, eds, *Changing the Rules: Canadian Regulatory Regimes and Institutions*. Toronto: University of Toronto Press.

Hood, Christopher C. 1986. *The Tools of Government*. Chatham, NJ: Chatham House Press.

Howlett, Michael. 1991. "Policy Instruments, Policy Styles, and Policy Implementation: National Approaches to Theories of Instrument Choice." *Policy Studies Journal* 19, no. 2 (Spring): 1–21.

Hummel, Ralph P. 1991. "Stories Managers Tell: Why They Are as Valid as Science." *Public Administration Revue* 51, no. 1: 31–41.

Kingdon, John W. 1997. *Agendas, Alternatives and Public Policies*. 2nd ed. Boston: Little, Brown.

Linder, Stephen H., and B. Guy Peters. 1989. "Instruments of Government: Perceptions and Contexts." *Journal of Public Policy* 9, no. 1: 35–58.

Mosher, Frederick C. 1982. *Democracy and the Public Service*. 2nd ed. New York: Oxford University Press.

Organization for Economic Cooperation and Development, Public Management Committee. November 2001. "Government Capacity to Produce High Quality Regulation in Canada." Paris.

Pal, Leslie A. 1997. *Beyond Policy Analysis: Public Issue Management in Turbulent Times*. Scarborough: ITP Nelson.

Peters, B. Guy, and Frans K.M. van Nispen, eds. 1998. *Public Policy Instruments: Evaluating the Tools of Public Administration*. Northampton, MA: Edward Elgar.

Privy Council Office. April 2000. "Report on Law-making and Governance: A Summary of Discussions Held by the Deputy Ministers' Challenge Team on Law-Making and Governance." Ottawa.

Salamon, Lester M. 1981. "Rethinking Public Management: Third-Party Government and the Changing Forms of Government Action." *Public Policy* 29, no. 3 (Summer): 255–75.

– ed. 2002. *The Tools of Government: A Guide to the New Governance*. New York: Oxford University Press.

Sanford, Kristen L., Joel A. Tarr, and Sue McNeil. 1995. "Crisis Perception and Policy Outcomes: Comparison between Environmental and Infrastructure Crises." *Journal of Infrastructure Systems,* no. 1 (December): 195–203.

Schmidt, Mary R. 1993. "Grout: Alternative Kinds of Knowledge and Why They Are Ignored." *Public Administration Revue* 53, no. 6: 525–30.

Sherwood, Frank P. 1990. "The Half-Century's Great Books in Public Admin-istration." *Public Administration Revue* 50, no. 2: 249–63.

Smith, Arthur J.R. 1997. "The Contribution of the Economic Council of Canada to Business Economics in Canada." *Canadian Business Economics*, no. 6 (Winter/Spring): 117–20.

Stigler, George J. 1971. "The Theory of Economic Regulation." *Bell Journal of Economics and Management Science* 2 (Spring): 3–21.

Taylor, Joshua C. 1981. *Learning to Look: A Handbook for the Visual Arts.* 2nd ed. Chicago: University of Chicago Press.

Treasury Board Secretariat of Canada. March 1998. "Retooling the Law-Making Process: Symposium Summary and Analysis." Ottawa.

Waldo, Dwight. 1968. "Public Administration in a Time of Revolution." *Public Administration Revue* 28: 362–8.

Watson, William. 2002. "The Books that Made the Wonks." *Policy Options* 23 (January/February): 3–4.

Wilson, James Q. 1981. "Policy Intellectuals and Public Policy." *Public Interest* 64 (Summer): 31–46.

CHAPTER TWO

1 For early works that sharply display the contrasting approaches taken to the subject in the two disciplines, see E.S. Kirschen et al., *Economic Policy in Our Time* (Chicago: Rand McNally, 1964); and Murray Edelman, *The Symbolic Uses of Politics* (Chicago: University of Illinois Press, 1964).

2 Welfare economists argue that numerous market failures exist that legiti-mize extensive government regulatory activities, while neoclassicists tend to restrict such "failures" to the provision of pure public goods. On the con-cept of market failures, see Francis M. Bator, "The Anatomy of Market Failure," *Quarterly Journal of Economics* 72, no. 3 (1958): 351–79; and Richard O. Zerbe and Howard E. McCurdy, "The Failure of Market Fail-ure," *Journal of Policy Analysis and Management* 18, no. 4 (1999): 558–78. On the concept's application to instrument choices, see Stephen Breyer, "Analyzing Regulatory Failure: Mismatches, Less Restrictive Alternatives, and Reform," *Harvard Law Review* 92, no. 3 (1979): 549–609; and Rich-ard Zeckhauser and Elmer Schaefer, "Public Policy and Normative Eco-nomic Theory," in R.A. Bauer and K.J. Gergen, eds, *The Study of Policy Formation,* 27–102 (New York: Free Press, 1968).

3 On the aims and ambitions of these studies, see Lester M. Salamon, "Re-thinking Public Management: Third-Party Government and the Changing Forms of Government Action," *Public Policy* 29, no. 3 (1981): 255–75; and George I. Balch, "The Stick, the Carrot, and Other Strategies: A Theo-retical Analysis of Governmental Intervention," *Law and Policy Quarterly* 2, no. 1 (1980): 35–60.

4 John Markoff and Veronica Montecinos, "The Ubiquitous Rise of Econo-mists," *Journal of Public Policy* 13, no. 1 (1993): 37–68.

5 See Theodore J. Lowi, "Distribution, Regulation, Redistribution: The Func-tions of Government," in R.B. Ripley, ed., *Public Policies and Their Politics: Techniques of Government Control,* 27–40 (New York: W.W. Norton, 1966); and James Q. Wilson, "The Politics of Regulation," in J.W. McKie, ed., *Social Responsibility and the Business Predicament,* 135–68 (Washing-ton, DC: Brookings Institution, 1974). Many of these insights were ex-tended by "public-choice" economists working in the area. See Michael Trebilcock and Douglas G. Hartle, "The Choice of Governing Instrument," *International Review of Law and Economics* 2 (1982): 29–46.

6 Charles Wolf, Jr, *Markets or Governments: Choosing between Imperfect Alternatives* (Cambridge: MIT Press, 1988); Charles Wolf, Jr, "Markets and Non-Market Failures: Comparison and Assessment," *Journal of Public Pol-icy* 7, no. 1 (1987): 43–70; and Julian Le Grand, "The Theory of Govern-ment Failure," *British Journal of Political Science* 21, no. 4 (1991): 423–42.

7 See, for example, Christopher Hood, "Using Bureaucracy Sparingly," *Pub-lic Administration* 61, no. 2 (1983): 197–208; and G. Bruce Doern and Ri-chard W. Phidd, *Canadian Public Policy: Ideas, Structure, Process* (Toronto: Nelson, 1988).

8 See K. Woodside, "Policy Instruments and the Study of Public Policy," *Ca-nadian Journal of Political Science,* 19, no. 4 (1986): 775–93.

9 See, for example, Hans Bressers and Pieter-Jan Klok, "Fundamentals for a Theory of Policy Instruments," *International Journal of Social Economics* 15, nos 3–4 (1988): 22–41; and Christopher Hood, *The Tools of Govern-ment* (Chatham, NJ: Chatham House, 1986).

10 See Frans K.M. van Nispen and Arthur B. Ringeling, "On Instruments and Instrumentality: A Critical Assessment," in B.G. Peters and F.K.M. van Nispen, eds, *Public Policy Instruments: Evaluating the Tools of Public Ad-ministration,* 204–17 (New York: Edward Elgar, 1998); and Johans A. de Bruijn and Hans A.M. Hufen, "The Traditional Approach to Policy Instru-ments," in Peters and van Nispen, eds, *Public Policy Instruments,* 11–32. See also Hans Th.A. Bressers and Laurence J. O'Toole, "The Selection of Policy Instruments: A Network-based Perspective," *Journal of Public Policy* 18, no. 3 (1998): 213–39.

11 See B. Dan Wood and John Bohte, "Political Transaction Costs and the Politics of Administrative Design," *Journal of Politics* 66, no. 1 (2004): 176–202.

12 See P.N. Grabosky, "Green Markets: Environmental Regulation by the Pri-vate Sector," *Law and Policy* 16, no. 4 (1994): 419–48; and Neil Gunning-ham and Mike D. Young, "Toward Optimal Environmental Policy: The Case of Biodiversity Conservation," *Ecology Law Quarterly* 24 (1997): 243–98.

13 Peter Neil Grabosky and Darren Sinclair, *Smart Regulation: Designing Environmental Policy* (Oxford: Clarendon Press, 1998); Neil Gunningham
   and Darren Sinclair, "Regulatory Pluralism: Designing Policy Mixes for Environmental Protection," *Law and Policy* 21, no. 1 (1999): 49–76; and
   Gunningham and Young, "Toward Optimal Environmental Policy."

14 On the range of available instruments, see Lester M. Salamon, ed., *The
   Tools of Government: A Guide to the New Governance* (New York:
   Oxford University Press, 2002). (Washington, DC: Urban Institute, 1989);
   and Marie-Louise Bemelmans-Videc, Ray C. Rist, and Evert Vedung, eds,
   *Carrots, Sticks and Sermons: Policy Instruments and Their Evaluation*
   (New Brunswick, NJ: Transaction Publishers, 1998).

15 For early works, see Robert A. Dahl and Charles E. Lindblom, *Politics,
   Economics and Welfare: Planning and Politico-Economic Systems Resolved
   into Basic Social Processes* (New York: Harper and Row, 1953); Kirschen
   et al., *Economic Policy in Our Time*; Edelman, *The Symbolic Uses of Politics*; and Lowi, "Distribution, Regulation, Redistribution."

16 See Harold Lasswell, "Key Symbols, Signs and Icons," in Lymon Bryson et
   al., eds, *Symbols and Values: An Initial Study*, 77–94 (New York: Harper,
   1954); and Harold D. Lasswell, *A Pre-View of Policy Sciences* (New York:
   American Elsevier, 1971). See also the discussion of "symbolic" outputs in
   works such as Doern and Phidd, *Canadian Public Policy*; and G.B. Doern
   and V.S. Wilson, "Conclusions and Observations," in G.B. Doern and V.S.
   Wilson, eds, *Issues in Canadian Public Policy*, 337–45 (Toronto: Macmillan, 1974).

17 On the aims and ambitions of these studies, see Salamon, "Rethinking Public Management."

18 See Woodside, "Policy Instruments and the Study of Public Policy."

19 On "traditional" substantive policy tools, see Salamon, ed., *Beyond Privatization*; Bemelmans-Videc, Rist, and Vedung, eds, *Carrots, Sticks and Sermons*; and Peters and van Nispen, eds, *Public Policy Instruments*.

20 See Gjalt Hippes, "New instruments for Environmental Policy: A Perspective," *International Journal of Social Economics* 15, nos 3–4 (1988): 42–51;
   and Michael J. Trebilcock, "Regulating Service Quality in Professional Markets," in D.N. Dewees, ed., *The Regulation of Quality: Products, Services,
   Workplaces, and the Environment*, 83–108 (Toronto: Butterworths, 1983).

21 See, for example, the taxonomies developed in the 1980s by A. Tupper and
   G.B. Doern, "Public Corporations and Public Policy in Canada," in A. Tup-
   per and G.B. Doern, eds, *Public Corporations and Public Policy in Canada*,
   1–50 (Montreal: Institute for Research on Public Policy, 1981); and Hood,
   *The Tools of Government*. On this process of model building, see Evert Ve-
   dung, "Policy Instruments: Typologies and Theories," in Bemelmans-Videc,
   Rist, and Vedung, eds, *Carrots, Sticks and Sermons*, 21–58; and Michael
   Howlett, "Policy Instruments, Policy Styles, and Policy Implementation:

National Approaches to Theories of Instrument Choice," *Policy Studies Journal* 19, no. 2 (1991): 1–21.

22 For an overview of the application of this literature to privatization, see M. Howlett and M. Ramesh, "Patterns of Policy Instrument Choice: Policy Styles, Policy Learning and the Privatization Experience," *Policy Studies Review* 12, no. 1 (1993): 3–24.

23 While some links exist between this new emphasis in implementation studies and New Public Management (NPM) ideas, NPM has not generated a useable model of instrument choice. Related work on "heresthetics" and "collibration" by Riker and Dunsire provides only a very general introduction to the subject, and neither author directly addresses instruments nor systematically moves toward theory construction. On problems with New Public Management theory, see Christopher Hood, "Contemporary Public Management: A New Global Paradigm?" *Public Policy and Administration* 10, no. 2 (1995): 104–17; Christopher Hood, "A Public Management for All Seasons?" *Public Administration* 69, no. 1 (Spring 1991): 3–19; and Patrick Dunleavy and Christopher Hood, "From Old Public Administration to New Public Management," *Public Money and Management* 14, no. 3 (1994): 9–16. On heresthetics, see William H. Riker, *The Art of Political Manipulation* (New Haven: Yale University Press, 1986); and William H. Riker, "Political Theory and the Art of Heresthetics," in Ada W. Finifter, ed., *Political Science: The State of the Discipline,* 47–67 (Washington, DC: American Political Science Association, 1983). On collibration, see Andrew Dunsire, *Manipulating Social Tensions: Collibration as an Alternative Mode of Government Intervention* (Koln: Max Plank Institut, 1993); Andrew Dunsire, "A Cybernetic View of Guidance, Control and Evaluation in the Public Sector," in Franz-Xavier Kaufman, Giandomenico Majone, and Vincent Ostrom, eds, *Guidance, Control, and Evaluation in the Public Sector,* 327–46 (Berlin: Walter de Gruyter, 1986); and Andrew Dunsire, "Modes of Governance," in J. Kooiman, ed., *Modern Governance,* 21–34 (London: Sage, 1993).

24 For an encyclopedic overview of these instruments, see Lester M. Salamon, ed., *The Tools of Government: A Guide to the New Governance* (New York: Oxford University Press, 2002).

25 Hood, *The Tools of Government.* For an earlier, similar model, see Charles W. Anderson, *Statecraft: An Introduction to Political Choice and Judgement* (New York: John Wiley and Sons, 1977).

26 Réjean Landry, Frédéric Varone, and Malcolm L. Goggin, "The Determinants of Policy Design: The State of the Theoretical Literature" (Chicago: Midwest Political Science Association, 1998).

27 Bressers and Klok, "Fundamentals for a Theory of Policy Instruments."

28 Anne L. Schneider and Helen Ingram, "Behavioural Assumptions of Policy Tools," *Journal of Politics* 52, no. 2 (1990): 511–29 at 513–14. See also

Anne L. Schneider and Helen Ingram, "Policy Design: Elements, Premises and Strategies," in Stuart S. Nagel, ed., *Policy Theory and Policy Evaluation: Concepts, Knowledge, Causes and Norms*, 77–102 (New York: Greenwood, 1990).

29 Schneider and Ingram adopted much of their terminology from the work of Elmore and his colleagues. McDonnell and Elmore, for example, used a four-fold classification of instruments, although unlike Hood, they classified instruments not according to the resources used, but according to the end desired. For these latter two authors, instruments could be categorized as "Mandates," "Inducements," "Capacity-building," or "System-changing." See Lorraine M. McDonnell and Richard F. Elmore, *Alternative Policy Instruments* (Santa Monica: Center for Policy Research in Education, 1987). See also Richard F. Elmore, "Organizational Models of Social Program Implementation," *Public Policy* 26, no. 2 (1978): 185–228; and Richard F. Elmore, "Instruments and Strategy in Public Policy," *Policy Studies Review* 7, no. 1 (1987): 174–86.

30 See, for example, Janet A. Weiss and Mary Tschirhart, "Public Information Campaigns as Policy Instruments," *Journal of Policy Analysis and Management* 13, no. 1 (1994): 82–119; Robert Bellehumeur, "Review: An Instrument of Change," *Optimum* 27, no. 1 (1997): 37–42; Richard A. Chapman, "Commissions in Policy-Making," in Richard A. Chapman, ed., *The Role of Commissions in Policy-Making*, 174–88 (London: George Allen and Unwin, 1973); R.E. Wraith and G.B. Lamb, *Public Inquiries as an Instrument of Government* (London: George Allen and Unwin, 1971); B. Guy Peters, "Government Reorganization: A Theoretical Analysis," *International Political Science Review* 13, no. 2 (1992): 199–218; and Kenneth Kernaghan, "Judicial Review of Administration Action," in Kenneth Kernaghan, ed., *Public Administration in Canada: Selected Readings*, 358–73 (Toronto: Methuen, 1985).

31 See Simon J. Bulmer, "The Governance of the European Union: A New Institutionalist Approach," *Journal of Public Policy* 13, no. 4 (1993): 351–80; Kathryn Harrison, "Retreat from Regulation: The Evolution of the Canadian Environmental Regulatory Regime," in G. Bruce Doern et al., eds, *Changing the Rules: Canadian Regulatory Regimes and Institutions*, 122–42 (Toronto: University of Toronto Press, 1999); and G. Bruce Doern and Stephen Wilks, eds, *Changing Regulatory Institutions in Britain and North America* (Toronto: University of Toronto Press, 1998).

32 On public-sector interest-group patronage in Canada, see Leslie A. Pal, *Interests of State: The Politics of Language, Multiculturalism, and Feminism in Canada* (Montreal and Kingston: McGill-Queen's University Press, 1993); Sandra Burt, "Canadian Women's Groups in the 1980s: Organizational Development and Policy Influence," *Canadian Public Policy* 16, no. 1 (1990): 17–28; Peter Finkle et al., *Federal Government Relations with Interest*

*Groups: A Reconsideration* (Ottawa: Privy Council Office, 1994); and Susan D. Phillips, "How Ottawa Blends: Shifting Government Relationships with Interest Groups," in Frances Abele, ed., *How Ottawa Spends, 1991–92: The Politics of Fragmentation,* 183–228 (Ottawa: Carleton University Press, 1991). On private-sector patronage in the US, see Anthony Nownes and Grant Neeley, "Toward an Explanation for Public Interest Group Formation and Proliferation: 'Seed Money,' Disturbances, Entrepreneurship, and Patronage," *Policy Studies Journal* 24, no. 1 (1996): 74–92; and Richard C. Lowry, "Foundation Patronage toward Citizen Groups and Think Tanks: Who Gets Grants?" *Journal of Politics* 81, no. 3 (1999): 758–76.

33 See William T. Gormley, *Taming the Bureaucracy: Muscles, Prayers and Other Strategies* (Princeton: Princeton University Press, 1989). On the Canadian case, see Jane Jenson, "Commissioning Ideas: Representation and Royal Commissions," in Susan D. Phillips, ed., *How Ottawa Spends, 1994–95: Making Change,* 39–69 (Ottawa: Carleton University Press, 1994); Alan C. Cairns, "Reflections on Commission Research," in Christie Innis, John A. Yogis, and A. Paul Pross, eds, *Commissions of Inquiry,* 87–110 (Toronto: Carswell, 1990); and Liora Salter and Debra Slaco, *Public Inquiries in Canada* (Ottawa: Science Council of Canada, 1981).

34 Saward, for example, uses such a "resource-based" schema, although not explicitly. See Michael Saward, *Co-optive Politics and State Legitimacy* (Aldershot: Dartmouth, 1992), 27, 150, 153.

35 See Claus Mueller, *The Politics of Communication: A Study in the Political Sociology of Language, Socialization and Legitimation* (New York: Oxford University Press, 1973).

36 A path-breaking effort in this process was the work of G. Bruce Doern and his collaborators in the 1970s and 1980s. See G. Bruce Doern and Peter Aucoin, eds, *The Structures of Policy-Making in Canada* (Toronto: Macmillan, 1971); G.B. Doern and V.S. Wilson, eds., *Issues in Canadian Public Policy* (Toronto: Macmillan, 1974); and Tupper and Doern, "Public Corporations and Public Policy in Canada."

37 M. Howlett and M. Ramesh, *Studying Public Policy: Policy Cycles and Policy Subsystems* (Toronto: Oxford University Press, 1995). On the origin of the criterion of state involvement, see Nicolas Baxter-Moore, "Policy Implementation and the Role of the State: A Revised Approach to the Study of Policy Instruments," in Robert J. Jackson, Doreen Jackson, and Nicolas Baxter-Moore, ed., *Contemporary Canadian Politics: Readings and Notes,* 336–55 (Scarborough, ON: Prentice-Hall, 1987).

38 See Erik-Hans Klijn, "Analyzing and Managing Policy Processes in Complex Networks: A Theoretical Examination of the Concept Policy Network and Its Problems," *Administration and Society* 28, no. 1 (1996): 90–119; Johan A. de Bruijn and Ernst F. ten Heuvelhof, "Policy Networks and Governance," in David L. Weimer, ed., *Institutional Design,* 161–79 (Boston:

Kluwer Academic Publishers, 1995); and J.A. de Bruijn and E.F. ten Heuvelhof, "Instruments for Network Management," in W.J.M. Kickert, E-H. Klijn, and J.F.M. Koppenjan, eds, *Managing Complex Networks: Strategies for the Public Sector*, 119–36 (London: Sage, 1997). On the manipulation of networks, see Robert K. Leik, "New Directions for Network Exchange Theory: Strategic Manipulation of Network Linkages," *Social Networks* 14 (1992): 309–23.

39 de Bruijn and ten Heuvelhof, "Policy Networks and Governance"; and J.A. de Bruijn and E.F. ten Heuvelhof, "Policy Instruments for Steering Autopoietic Actors," in Roeland in 't Veld et al., eds, *Autopoiesis and Configuration Theory: New Approaches to Societal Steering*, 161–70 (Dordrecht: Kluwer, 1991). See also E.H. Klijn and G.R. Teisman, "Effective Policymaking in a Multi-Actor Setting: Networks and Steering," in Roeland in 't Veld et al., eds, *Autopoiesis and Configuration Theory*, 99–111; and B. Guy Peters, *Managing Horizontal Government: The Politics of Coordination* (Ottawa: Canadian Centre for Management Development, 1998).

40 On this latter point and the role played by government agencies in this process, see Martin J. Smith, David Marsh, and David Richards, "Central Government Departments and the Policy Process," *Public Administration* 71 (1993): 567–94; and Donald J. Savoie, *Governing from the Centre: The Concentration of Power in Canadian Politics* (Toronto: University of Toronto Press, 1999).

41 See Lester M. Salamon and Michael S. Lund, "The Tools Approach: Basic Analytics," in Salamon, ed., *Beyond Privatization*, 23–50.

42 See David Beetham, *The Legitimation of Power* (London: Macmillan, 1991); and Mark C. Suchman, "Managing Legitimacy: Strategic and Institutional Approaches," *Academy of Management Review* 20, no. 3 (1995): 571–610.

43 See Sandford F. Borins, "World War Two Crown Corporations: Their Wartime Role and Peacetime Privatization," *Canadian Public Administration* 25, no. 3 (1982): 380–404; and A.R. Vining and R. Botterell, "An Overview of the Origins, Growth, Size, and Functions of Provincial Crown Corporations," in J.R.S. Pritchard, ed., *Crown Corporations: The Calculus of Instrument Choice*, 303–68 (Toronto: Butterworths, 1983).

44 Peter J. May, "Mandate Design and Implementation: Enhancing Implementation Efforts and Shaping Regulatory Styles," *Journal of Policy Analysis and Management* 12, no. 4 (1993): 634–63; and Keith Hawkins and John M. Thomas, eds, *Making Regulatory Policy* (Pittsburgh: University of Pittsburgh Press, 1989).

45 See Doern and Wilson, "Conclusions and Observations"; and G. Bruce Doern, "The Concept of Regulation and Regulatory Reform," in Doern and Wilson, eds, *Issues in Canadian Public Policy*, 8–35. More generally, see Howlett, "Policy Instruments, Policy Styles."

46 See Robert B. Gibson, ed., *Voluntary Initiatives: The New Politics of Corporate Greening* (Peterborough, ON: Broadview Press, 1999); and Paul Grabosky, "Counterproductive Regulation," *International Journal of the Sociology of Law* 23 (1995): 347–69. See also M.J. Trebilcock, C.J. Tuohy, and A.D. Wolfson, *Professional Regulation: A Staff Study of Accountancy, Architecture, Engineering, and Law in Ontario Prepared for the Professional Organizations Committee* (Toronto: Ministry of the Attorney General, 1979); and C.J. Tuohy and A.D. Wolfson, "Self-Regulation: Who Qualifies?" in P. Slayton and M.J. Trebilcock, eds, *The Professions and Public Policy*, 111–22 (Toronto: University of Toronto Press, 1978).

47 See, for example, A.P.G. de Moor, *Perverse Incentives: Hundreds of Billions of Dollars in Subsidies Now Harm the Economy, the Environment, Equity and Trade* (San Jose: Earth Council, 1997); and Norman Myers and Jennifer Kent, *Perverse Subsidies: How Tax Dollars Can Undercut the Environment and the Economy* (Washington, DC: Island Press, 2001).

48 M. Minogue, "Governance-Based Analysis of Regulation," *Annals of Public and Cooperative Economics* 73, no. 4 (2002): 649–66.

49 Robert A. Kagan and Lee Axelrad, "Adversarial Legalism: An International Perspective," in P.S. Nivola, ed., *Comparative Disadvantages? Social Regulations and the Global Economy*, 146–202 (Washington, DC: Brookings Institution, 1997); and Robert A. Kagan, "Should Europe Worry about Adversarial Legalism?" *Oxford Journal of Legal Studies* 17, no. 2 (1997): 165–83.

50 See Robert A. Kagan, "Adversarial Legalism and American Government," *Journal of Policy Analysis and Management* 10, no. 3 (1991): 369–406.

51 See Stephen H. Linder and B. Guy Peters, "Instruments of Government: Perceptions and Contexts," *Journal of Public Policy* 9, no. 1 (1989): 35–58; Bressers and O'Toole, "The Selection of Policy Instruments"; and Schneider and Ingram, "Behavioural Assumptions of Policy Tools," 513–14.

52 For examples of each type of instrument choice, see Steven K. Vogel, *Freer Markets, More Rules: Regulatory Reform in Advanced Industrial Countries* (Ithaca, NY: Cornell University Press, 1996); Marc Allen Eisner, "Economic Regulatory Policies: Regulation and Deregulation in Historical Context," in D.H. Rosenbloom and R.D. Schwartz, eds, *Handbook of Regulation and Administrative Law*, 91–116 (New York: Marcel Dekker, 1994); Allan Tupper, "The State in Business," *Canadian Public Administration* 22, no. 1 (1979): 124–50; Jeanne Kirk Laux and Maureen Appel Molot, *State Capitalism: Public Enterprise in Canada* (Ithaca, NY: Cornell University Press, 1988); and Michael Hall and Keith Banting, "The Nonprofit Sector in Canada: An Introduction," in Keith Banting, ed., *The Nonprofit Sector in Canada: Roles and Relationships*, 1–28 (Montreal: McGill-Queen's University Press, 2000).

53 See M. Stephen Weatherford, "Political Economy and Political Legitimacy: The Link between Economic Policy and Political Trust," in Harold D.

Clarke, Marianne C. Stewart, and Gary Zuk, eds, *Economic Decline and Political Change: Canada, Great Britain, the United States,* 225–51 (Pittsburgh: University of Pittsburgh Press, 1989). See also B. Guy Peters and Jon Pierre, "Citizens versus the New Public Manager: The Problem of Mutual Empowerment," *Administration and Society* 32, no. 1 (2000): 9–28; and Suchman, "Managing Legitimacy." More generally, see Beetham, *The Legitimation of Power;* and Peter G. Stillman, "The Concept of Legitimacy," *Polity* 7, no. 1 (1974): 32–56.

54 On this tendency, see Renate Mayntz, "Legitimacy and the Directive Capacity of the Political System," in Leon N. Lindberg et al., eds, *Stress and Contradiction in Modern Capitalism,* 261–74 (Lexington: Lexington Books, 1975); and Jurgen Habermas, *Legitimation Crisis* (Boston: Beacon Press, 1975). For empirical examples, see Sven Jentoft, "Legitimacy and Disappointment in Fisheries Management," *Marine Policy* 24 (2000): 141–8; and Sudhir Chella Rajan, "Legitimacy in Environmental Policy: The Regulation of Automobile Pollution in California," *International Journal of Environmental Studies* 42 (1992): 243–58. Examples in Canada include William D. Coleman, "Monetary Policy, Accountability and Legitimacy: A Review of the Issues in Canada," *Canadian Journal of Political Science* 24, no. 4 (1991): 711–34; Michael Howlett, "The Round Table Experience: Representation and Legitimacy in Canadian Environmental Policy Making," *Queen's Quarterly* 97, no. 4 (1990): 580–601; and Alan B. Simmons and Kieran Keohane, "Canadian Immigration Policy: State Strategies and the Quest for Legitimacy," *Canadian Review of Sociology and Anthropology* 29, no. 4 (1992): 421–52.

55 Arco Timmermans et al., "The Design of Policy Instruments: Perspectives and Concepts" (Chicago: Midwest Political Science Association, 1998); and Paul A. Sabatier and Neil Pelkey, "Incorporating Multiple Actors and Guidance Instruments into Models of Regulatory Policymaking: An Advocacy Coalition Framework," *Administration and Society* 19, no. 2 (1987): 236–63.

56 See May, "Mandate Design and Implementation"; Peter J. May and John W. Handmer, "Regulatory Policy Design: Co-operative versus Deterrent Mandates," *Australian Journal of Public Administration* 51, no. 1 (1992): 45–53; and Peter J. May, "Coercive versus Cooperative Policies: Comparing Intergovernmental Mandate Performance," *Journal of Policy Analysis and Management* 15, no. 2 (1996): 171–206.

57 See Bridget M. Hutter, "Variations in Regulatory Enforcement Styles," *Law and Policy* 11, no. 2 (1989): 153–74.

58 On this distinction and its consequences, see Jurgen Habermas, "What Does a Legitimation Crisis Mean Today? Legitimation Problems in Late Capitalism," *Social Research* 40, no. 4 (1973): 643–67; Richard M. Merelman, "Learning and Legitimacy," *American Political Science Review* 60,

no. 3 (1966): 548–61; William C. McWilliams, "On Political Illegitimacy," *Public Policy* 19, no. 3 (1971): 444–54; and John H. Schaar, *Legitimacy in the Modern State* (New Brunswick, NJ: Transaction Publishers, 1981).

59 See Suchman, "Managing Legitimacy." For empirical examples, see Adrienne Heritier, "Policy-Making by Subterfuge: Interest Accommodation, Innovation and Substitute Democratic Legitimation in Europe: Perspectives from Distinctive Policy Areas," *Journal of European Public Policy* 4, no. 2 (1997): 171–89; and Adrienne Heritier, "Elements of Democratic Legitimation in Europe: An Alternative Perspective," *Journal of European Public Policy* 6, no. 2 (1999): 269–82.

60 Saward, *Co-optive Politics and State Legitimacy;* and R.A.W. Rhodes, "From Marketisation to Diplomacy: It's the Mix That Matters," *Australian Journal of Public Administration* 56, no. 2 (1997): 40–54.

61 See David C. King and Jack L. Walker, "An Ecology of Interest Groups in America," in Jack L. Walker, ed., *Mobilizing Interest Groups in America: Patrons, Professions and Social Movements,* 57–73 (Ann Arbor: University of Michigan Press, 1991); and William P. Browne, "Issue Niches and the Limits of Interest Group Influence," in Allan J. Cigler and Burdett A. Loomis, eds, *Interest Group Politics,* 345–70 (Washington, DC: CQ Press, 1991). On Canada, see Pal, *Interests of State;* and Burt, "Canadian Women's Groups in the 1980s."

62 See Christopher Hood, "The Hidden Public Sector: The 'Quangocratization' of the World?" in Kaufman, Majone, and Ostrom, eds, *Guidance, Control, and Evaluation in the Public Sector,* 183–207; and Christopher Hood, "Keeping the Centre Small: Explanation of Agency Type," *Political Studies* 36, no. 1 (1988): 30–46. More generally, see David S. Brown, "The Management of Advisory Committees: An Assignment for the '70s," *Public Administration Review* 32 (1972): 334–42; Thomas B. Smith, "Advisory Committees in the Public Policy Process," *International Review of Administrative Sciences* 43, no. 2 (1977): 153–66; and Leon Dion, "The Politics of Consultation," *Government and Opposition* 8, no. 3 (1973): 332–53.

63 Generally, see D. Osborne and E. Gaebler, *Reinventing Government* (Reading: Addison-Wesley, 1992). On the impact of this thinking on instrument-choice analysis, see Lester M. Salamon, "The New Governance and the Tools of Public Action: An Introduction," *Fordham Urban Law Journal* 28, no. 5 (2001): 1611–74; and John Mark Keyes, "Power Tools: The Form and Function of Legal Instruments for Government Action," *Canadian Journal of Administrative Law and Practice* 10 (1996): 133–74.

64 Darren Sinclair, "Self-Regulation versus Command and Control? Beyond False Dichotomies," *Law and Policy* 19, no. 4 (1997): 529–59.

65 Neil Gunningham and Darren Sinclair, *Leaders and Laggards: Next Generation Environmental Regulation* (Sheffield: Greenleaf, 2002).

66 Bressers and O'Toole, "The Selection of Policy Instruments"; and Hans Th.A. Bressers, "The Choice of Policy Instruments in Policy Networks," in Peters and van Nispen, eds, *Public Policy Instruments,* 85–105.

67 Howlett and Ramesh, *Studying Public Policy.*

68 See de Bruijn and ten Heuvelhof, "Policy Instruments for Steering Autopoietic Actors"; de Bruijn and ten Heuvelhof, "Instruments for Network Management"; and de Bruijn and ten Heuvelhof, "Policy Networks and Governance."

69 On this distinction, see Mueller, *The Politics of Communication*; and Mayntz, "Legitimacy and the Directive Capacity of the Political System."

70 See Jos C.N. Raadschelders, *Handbook of Administrative History* (New Brunswick, NJ: Transaction Publishers, 1998). See also Jos C.N. Raadschelders, "Administrative History of the United States: Development and State of the Art," *Administration and Society* 32, no. 5 (2000): 499–528; and Marc Allen Eisner, "Discovering Patterns in Regulatory History: Continuity, Change and Regulatory Regimes," *Journal of Policy History* 6, no. 2 (1994): 157–87. More generally, see Lowi, "Distribution, Regulation, Redistribution."

71 On the paradox of restricted state autonomy despite high state capacity in the era of globalization, see Philip G. Cerny, "International Finance and the Erosion of State Policy Capacity," in Philip Gummett, ed., *Globalization and Public Policy,* 83–104 (Cheltenham: Edward Elgar, 1996).

72 See Gerhard Lehmbruch, "The Organization of Society, Administrative Strategies, and Policy Networks," in Roland M. Czada and Adrienne Windhoff-Heritier, eds, *Political Choice: Institutions, Rules, and the Limits of Rationality,* 121–55 (Boulder, CO: Westview, 1991); and Renate Mayntz, "Modernization and the Logic of Interorganizational Networks," in J. Child, M. Crozier, and R. Mayntz, eds, *Societal Change between Market and Organization,* 3–18 (Aldershot: Avebury, 1993).

73 On recent European experiences, for example, see Thad E. Hall and Laurence J. O'Toole, "Structures for Policy Implementation: An Analysis of National Legislation, 1965–1966 and 1993–1994," *Administration and Society* 31, no. 6 (2000): 667–86; Beate Kohler-Koch, "Catching up with Change: The Transformation of Governance in the European Union," *Journal of European Public Policy* 3, no. 3 (1996): 359–80; and Roine Johansson and Klas Borell, "Central Steering and Local Networks: Old-Age Care in Sweden," *Public Administration* 77, no. 3 (1999): 585–98.

74 For instances of the innovative use of procedural policy instruments in Canada, for example, in recent years, see Katherine A. Graham and Susan D. Phillips, "Citizen Engagement: Beyond the Customer Revolution," *Canadian Public Administration* 40, no. 2 (1997): 225–73; Kenneth Kernaghan, "Partnership and Public Administration: Conceptual and Practical Considerations," *Canadian Public Administration* 36, no. 1 (1993): 57–76; Susan Delacourt and Donald G. Lenihan, eds, *Collaborative Government: Is*

*There a Canadian Way?* (Toronto: Institute of Public Administration of
Canada, 2000); and Janice Gross Stein et al., "Citizen Engagement in Con-
flict Resolution: Lessons for Canada in International Experience," in David
Cameron, ed., *The Referendum Papers: Essays on Secession and National
Unity,* 144–98 (Toronto: University of Toronto Press, 1999).

75 See Michael Howlett, "Beyond Legalism? Policy Ideas, Implementation
Styles and Emulation-Based Convergence in Canadian and U.S. Environ-
mental Policy," *Journal of Public Policy* 20, no. 3 (2000): 305–29; and
Eisner, "Economic Regulatory Policies."

76 For examples of some of the more sophisticated recent uses of substantive
policy instruments, see Gibson, ed., *Voluntary Initiatives;* and David L.
Weimer, "Claiming Races, Broiler Contracts, Heresthetics, and Habits:
Ten Concepts for Policy Design," *Policy Sciences* 25 (1992): 135–59.

77 See Jan Kooiman, "Governance and Governability: Using Complexity,
Dynamics and Diversity," in Kooiman, ed., *Modern Governance,* 35–50;
B. Guy Peters and Jon Pierre, "Governance without Government?
Rethinking Public Administration," *Journal of Public Administration
Research and Theory* 8, no. 2 (1998): 223–44; E.H. Klijn and J.F.M. Kop-
penjan, "Politicians and Interactive Decision Making: Institutional Spoil-
sports or Playmakers," *Public Administration* 78, no. 2 (2000): 365–87;
and Lawrence C. Walters, James Aydelotte, and Jessica Miller, "Putting
More Public in Policy Analysis," *Public Administration Review* 60, no. 4
(2000): 349–59.

78 Holly Doremus, "A Policy Portfolio Approach to Biodiversity Protection
on Private Lands," *Environmental Science and Policy* 6 (2003): 217–32;
and Thomas Sterner, *Policy Instruments for Environmental and Natural
Resource Management* (Washington, DC: Resources for the Future, 2002),
esp. 212–18.

79 See Stephen H. Linder and B. Guy Peters, "Policy Formulation and the
Challenge of Conscious Design," *Evaluation and Program Planning*
13 (1990): 303–11; and Anne Larson Schneider and Helen Ingram, *Policy
Design for Democracy* (Lawrence: University Press of Kansas, 1997).

80 Kooiman, "Governance and Governability"; and Lehmbruch, "The Organization of Society."

CHAPTER THREE

1 See also Michael Trebilcock and Douglas G. Hartle, "The Choice of Governing Instrument," *International Review of Law and Economics* 2 (1982):
29–46.

2 See, for example, Dennis Mueller, *Public Choice II* (Cambridge University
Press, 1989); Michael Trebilcock, J.R.S. Prichard, Douglas Hartle, and Don
Dewees, *The Choice of Governing Instrument* (Minister of Supply and

Services Canada, 1982); Andrei Schleifer and Robert Vishny, *The Grabbing Hand* (Cambridge, MA: Harvard University Press, 1998).

3 Trebilcock et al., *The Choice of Governing Instrument*, 103.

4 Ibid.

5 For recent insightful critiques of public-choice theory, see Albert Breton, *Competitive Governments: An Economic Theory of Politics and Public Finance* (New York: Cambridge University Press, 1996); Donald Wittman, *The Myth of Democratic Failure: Why Political Institutions are Efficient* (Chicago: University of Chicago Press, 1995); Steven Croley, "Theories of Regulation: Incorporating the Administrative Process," *Columbia Law Revue* 98 (1998): 1–168; Daniel Farber and Philip Frickey, *Law and Public Choice* (Chicago: University of Chicago Press, 1991); Jerry Mashaw, "The Economics of Politics and the Understanding of Public Law," *Kent Law Review* 65 (1990): 123–60; Daniel Farber, "Democracy and Disgust: Reflections on Public Choice," *Kent Law Review* 65 (1989): 161–76.

6 See Croley, "Theories of Regulation."

7 Ibid., 5.

8 Ibid., 6, 7.

9 See George Stigler, "Law or Economics?" *Journal of Law and Economics* 35 (1992): 455–68; Gary Becker, "A Theory of Competition among Pressure Groups," *Quarterly Journal of Economics* 98 (1983): 371–400.

10 See, for example, Frances Fukuyama, *The End of History and the Last Man* (New York: Free Press, 1992).

11 See, for example, Noam Chomsky, *Profits over People: Neoliberalism and Global Order* (New York: Seven Stories Press, 1999).

12 Barbara Geddes, "Challenging the Conventional Wisdom," *Journal of Democracy* 5 (1994): 104–18 at 117.

13 Fazil Mihlar, "The Cost of Regulation in Canada," 1998 edition, Fraser Institute Occasional Paper, no. 12, 1998.

14 See David Moss, *When All Else Fails: Government as the Ultimate Risk Manager* (Cambridge, MA: Harvard University Press, 2002); Nicholas Barr, "Economic Theory and the Welfare State: A Survey and Interpretation," *Journal of Economic Literature* 30, no. 2 (1992): 741–803; Nicholas Barr, *The Economics of the Welfare State*, 3rd ed. (Cambridge, MA: Harvard University Press, 1998); Joseph Heath, *The Efficient Society* (Toronto: Penguin Books, 2001).

15 See David Henderson, *The Changing Fortunes of Economic Liberalism: Yesterday, Today and Tomorrow* (London: Institute of Economic Affairs, 1998); Robert Howse, Robert Prichard, and Michael Trebilcock, "Smaller or Smarter Government?" *University of Toronto Law Journal* 40 (1990): 498–541; Michael J. Trebilcock, "Lurching around Chicago: The Positive Challenge of Explaining the Recent Regulatory Reform Agenda," in Richard M. Bird, Michael J. Trebilcock, and Thomas A. Wilson, eds,

*Rationality in the Public Policy: Retrospect and Prospect, a Tribute to Douglas Hartle* (Toronto: Canadian Tax Foundation, 1999).

16 See William Meggenson and Jeffrey Netter, "From State to Market: A Survey of Empirical Studies of Privatization," *Journal of Economic Literature* 39 (2001): 321–89.

17 Lester Salamon, ed., *The Tools of Government: A Guide to the New Governance* (New York: Oxford University Press, 2002), ch. 1; see also Jody Freeman, "The Private Role in Public Governance," *New York University Law Review* 75 (2000): 543–675.

18 "Sectoral Studies," vol. 1 of "OECD Report on Regulatory Reform" (Paris, 1997).

19 For an insightful review of alternative explanations of regulated-industries reforms in the US, see Joseph D. Kearney and Thomas W. Merrill, "The Great Transformation of Regulated Industries Law," *Columbia Law Review* 98 (1998): 1323–1409 at 1383–1403.

20 Cited at note 5.

21 See, for example, C. Winston, "Economic Deregulation," *Journal of Economic Literature* 31 (1993): 1263–89; R. Crandall and J. Ellig, "Economic Deregulation and Customer Choice" (Washington, DC: George Mason University, Centre for Market Processes, 1997).

22 I recognize that in some sectors, such as airlines, the rents from price-and-entry controls may have been largely dissipated through nonprice forms of competition, rendering incumbent interests less committed to resisting reforms. However, this argument seems to have less obvious application to other sectors that have been deregulated (e.g., railways, trucking, natural gas). Moreover, in other sectors, such as agriculture, rents tend to be capitalized in asset, quota, or licence values, rendering deregulation politically intractable because of large out-of-pocket transitional losses; see Gordon Tullock, "The Transitional Gains Trap," *Bell Journal of Economics* 6, no. 2 (1975): 671–8.

23 J.M. Keynes, *The General Theory of Employment, Interest and Money* (London: Macmillan, 1936), 384.

24 Steven Kelman, *Making Public Policy: A Hopeful View of American Government* (New York: Basic Books, 1987).

25 Joseph Schumpeter, *Capitalism, Socialism and Democracy* (Cambridge, MA: Harvard University Press, 1975), 87.

26 See Henderson, *The Changing Fortunes of Economic Liberalism;* Jeremy Fraiberg and Michael Trebilcock, "Risk Regulation: Technocratic Tools for Regulatory Reform," *McGill Law Journal* 43 (1998): 835–87.

27 See Trebilcock, "Lurching around Chicago."

28 See R. Kent Weaver and Bert A. Rockman, eds, *Do Institutions Matter?* (Washington, DC: Brookings Institution, 1993); Michael M. Atkinson, ed., *Governing Canada: Institutions and Public Policy* (Toronto: Harcourt

Brace, 1983); Laurent Dobuzinskis, Michael Howlett, and David Laycock, eds, *Policy Studies in Canada: The State of the Art* (Toronto: University of Toronto Press, 1996).

29 Atkinson, ed., *Governing Canada*, ch. 1.

30 Cited in Dobuzinskis et al., eds, 321.

31 Croley, "Theories of Regulation."

32 See Richard Schultz, "Paradigm Lost: Explaining the Canadian Politics of Deregulation," in C.E.S. Franks et al., eds, *Canada's Century: Governance in a Maturing Society* (McGill-Queen's University Press, 1995); more generally, see Albert Hirschman, *Exit, Voice and Loyalty* (Cambridge, MA: Harvard University Press, 1970).

33 Michael Trebilcock and Robert Howse, "Trade Liberalization and Regulatory Diversity: Reconciling Competitive Markets with Competitive Politics," *European Journal of Law and Economics* 6 (1998): 5–37.

34 Anthony Downs, *An Economic Theory of Democracy* (New York: Harper, 1957); Mancur Olson, *The Logic of Collective Action* (New York: Schoken, 1965).

35 See Michael Trebilcock and Robert Howse, *The Regulation of International Trade,* 2nd ed. (London: Routledge, 1999), 15–17.

## CHAPTER FOUR

1 This emphasis, in turn, mirrors the distinction between the consequentialist approach to institutional choices and an approach in which these choices are based upon routine and symbols.

2 Although particularly well stated and argued, some aspects of the Schon and Rein argument are not entirely novel. For example, there is a strong link to the social-constructionist approach in sociology (Best 1989). Also, Lowi's (1972) and Wilson's (1980) seminal discussions of public policy tend to have some of the same aspects of defining the problem in terms of winners and losers and even in terms of the arenas within which the problem is addressed.

3 This argument is not dissimilar to the historical institutionalist arguments (Thelen, Steinmo, and Longstreth 1992; King 1995).

4 This problem has been referred to as "brass plaque institutionalism," meaning that institutions are defined by the brass plaques on their buildings.

5 This discussion draws on an earlier paper by William T. Gormley, Jr, and B. Guy Peters. See Gormley and Peters 1987.

6 As has been noted (Hogwood and Peters 1983), few problems in government of any consequence are ever really solved. Still, there are marked differences in the extent to which they are likely to require reconsideration.

7 As has been noted, when discussing policy failures there is an important difference between the political and the programmatic elements of policy problems. See Bovens, 't Hart, and Peters 1998.

8 This assessment leaves aside some religious groups who do not believe in immunizations as well as some medical evidence about the risk-vs-benefit ratios of some of the standard shots children receive.

9 This need for adjustment may be thought of as a chronic problem, but the choice of the basic technology or technologies used may be made on a more discrete basis. That is, after the choice to have a Federal Reserve and to use money supply as a major economic instrument, the rest is simply a matter of playing with the one instrument rather than of selecting multiple instruments in independent decisions.

10 For a discussion of these terms in relationship to policy failure, see Bovens, 't Hart, and Peters 1998, 2001.

11 This reality represents, of course, Lindblom's (1980) rather famous point about "partisan analysis" being used in selling programs to different constituencies.

12 One of the ironies of contemporary political life is that the problem-solving capacity of government is consistently being denigrated even as more and more issues are apparently being defined as public issues.

13 This danger is in part the reason that governments create new organizations to address large-scale problems – for example, the Office of Economic Opportunity (OEO) in the United States as a vehicle for creating and implementing programs for the "war on poverty" or even the current efforts in the United States to develop a Department of Homeland Security.

14 The central role of agricultural products in North American Free Trade Agreement (NAFTA) deliberations are indicative of the expansion of this policy issue.

## References

Alm, Alvin. 1992. "Tools to Protect the Environment: A Need for New Approaches. *EPA Journal* (Office of Communication, Education, and Public Affairs) 18, no. 2, Washington, DC: US Environmental Protection Agency.

Bagchus, R. 1998. "The Trade-off between Appropriateness and Fit of Policy Instruments." In B.G. Peters and F.K.M. van Nispen, eds, *Public Policy Instruments: Evaluating the Tools of Public Administration*. Cheltenham: Edward Elgar.

Bardach, E. 1980. "Implementation and the Study of Implements." Paper presented at the Annual Meeting of the American Political Science Association, Washington, DC.

Baumgartner, F.R., and B.D. Jones. 1993. *Agendas and Instability in American Politics*. Chicago: University of Chicago Press.

Best, J. 1989. *Images of Issues*. Chicago: Aldine de Gruyter.

Bonser, C.F., E.B. McGregor, and C.V. Oster. 1996. *Policy Choices and Public Action*. Upper Saddle River, NJ: Prentice-Hall.

Bovens, M.A.P., P. 't Hart, and B.G. Peters. 1998. "The Study of Policy Disasters." In P. Gray, ed., *Public Policy Disasters in Western Europe*. London: Routledge.

– P. 't Hart, and B.G. Peters. 2001. *Policy Success and Failure*. 2 vols. Cheltenham: Edward Elgar.

Buchanan, J.M. 1987. *Public Finance in the Democratic Process*. Chapel Hill, NC: University of North Carolina Press.

Cobb, R.W., and C.D. Elder. 1983. *Participation in American Politics: The Dynamics of Agenda-Building*. Baltimore: Johns Hopkins University Press.

Dunn, W.N. 1994. *Public Policy Analysis: An Introduction*. 2nd ed. Englewood Cliffs, NJ: Prentice-Hall.

Eagle, S.J. 1996. *Regulatory Takings*. Charlotteville, VA: Michie.

Elster, J. 1998. *Deliberative Democracy*. Cambridge, UK: Cambridge University Press.

Epstein, R.A. 1985. *Takings*. Cambridge, MA: Harvard University Press.

Gormley, W.T. 1986. "Regulatory Issue Networks in a Federal System." *Polity* 18, no. 4 (Summer).

– and B.G. Peters. 1987. *Characteristics of Policy Problems*. Unpublished paper. University of Pittsburgh.

Gray, P. 1998. *Public Policy Disasters in Europe*. London: Routledge.

Hisschemoller, M., and B. Hoppe. 1995. "Coping with Intractable Controversies: The Case for Problem Structuring in Policy Design and Analysis." *Knowledge and Policy* 8: 40–60.

Hogwood, B.W., and B.G. Peters. 1983. *Policy Dynamics*. Brighton: Wheatsheaf.

– and B.G. Peters. 1985. *The Pathology of Public Policy*. Oxford: Oxford University Press.

Hood, C. 1986. *The Tools of Government*. Chatham, NJ: Chatham House.

Howlett, M. 1991. "Policy Instruments, Policy Styles and Policy Implementation: National Approaches to Theories of Instrument Choice." *Policy Studies Journal* 19: 1–21.

Ingram, H., and A.L. Schneider. 1997. *Policy Design for Democracy*. Lawrence: University Press of Kansas.

in 't Veld, R. 1991. "Autopoesis, Configuration and Steering: Impossibility Theory or Dynamic Steering Theory." In R. in 't Veld et al., eds, *Autopoesis and Configuration Theory*. Dordrecht: Kluwer.

Jones, C.O. 1982. *Congress: People, Place and Policy*. Homewood, IL: Irwin.

Kettl, Donald. 1999. "Environmental Policy: The Next Generation." In *La Follette Policy Report* 9, no. 2, University of Wisconsin.

King, D.S. 1995. *Actively Seeking Work*. Chicago: University of Chicago Press.

Kingdon, J. 1994. *Agendas, Alternatives and Public Policies*. 2nd ed. New York: Harper Collins.

Lindblom, C.E. 1980. *The Policy-Making Process*. 2nd ed. Englewood-Cliffs, NJ: Prentice-Hall.

Linder, S.H., and B.G. Peters. 1984. "From Social Theory to Policy Design." *Journal of Public Policy* 4: 237–59.

– and B.G. Peters. 1989. "Instruments of Government: Perceptions and Contexts." *Journal of Public Policy* 9: 35–58.

– and B.G. Peters. 1998. "The Study of Policy Instruments: Four Schools of Thought." In B.G. Peters and F.K.M. van Nispen, eds, *Public Policy Instruments: Evaluating the Tools of Public Administration*. Cheltenham: Edward Elgar.

– and B.G. Peters. 1990. "An Institutional Approach to the Theory of Policy-making: The Role of Conscious Choice in Policy Formulation." *The Journal of Theoretical Politics* 2: 59–83.

Lowi, T.J. 1972. "Four Systems of Policy, Politics and Choice." *Public Administration Review* 32: 298–310.

May, Peter. 2002. "Social Regulation." In Lester, Salamon, ed., *The Tools of Government: A Guide to the New Governance*, Editor, Lester Salamon. Oxford, UK: Oxford University Press.

Mucciaroni, G. 1990. "Public Choice and the Politics of Comprehensive Tax Reform." *Governance* 3: 1–32.

Nelson, B.J. 1984. *Making an Issue of Child Abuse: Political Agenda Setting for Social Problems*. Chicago: University of Chicago Press.

Nelson, R.R. 1978. *The Moon and the Ghetto*. New York: W.W. Norton.

Olsen, J.P. 1987. *Organized Democracy*. Oslo: Universitetsforlaget.

Perrow, C. 1970. *Organizational Analysis: A Sociological Perspective*. Belmont, CA: Wadsworth.

– 1990. *The AIDS Disaster*. New Haven: Yale University Press.

Peters, B.G. 2000. "The Politics of Policy Instruments." In L.M. Salamon, ed., *The Handbook of Policy Instruments*. New York: Oxford University Press.

– and F.K.M. van Nispen, eds. 1998. *Public Policy Instruments: Evaluating the Tools of Public Administration*. Cheltenham: Edward Elgar.

Petersillia, J., and J. Lane. 1998. *Criminal Justice Policy*. Cheltenham: Edward Elgar.

Petracca, M.P. 1992. "Issue Definitions, Agenda-Building and Policymaking." *Policy Currents* 2, no. 1: 4.

Poulton, E.C. 1994. *Behavioral Decision Theory*. Cambridge, UK: Cambridge University Press.

Rettig, R. 1977. *Cancer Crusade*. Princeton: Princeton University Press.

Ringeling, A., and F.K.M. van Nispen. 1998. "On Instruments and Instrumentality: A Critical Assessment." In B.G. Peters and F.K.M. van Nispen, eds, *Public Policy Instruments: Evaluating the Tools of Public Administration*. Cheltenham: Edward Elgar.

Ringquist, Evan. 1993. *Environmental Protection at the State Level*. Armonk, NY: ME Sharpe.

Rochefort, D.A., and R.W. Cobb. 1994. *The Politics of Problem Definition*. Lawrence: University Press of Kansas.

Rushefsky, M. 1986. *Making Cancer Policy*. Albany: State University of New York Press.

Salamon, L.M., ed. 2000. *The Tools of Government: A Guide to the New Governance*. Oxford, UK: Oxford University Press.

– and M. Lund. 1989. *Beyond Privatization: The Tools of Public Policy*. Washington, DC: Urban Institute.

Scharpf, F.W. 1988. "Joint Decision Trap." *Public Administration* 46: 239–79.

Schon, D.A., and M. Rein. 1994. *Frame Reflection: Solving Intractable Policy Controversies*. New York: Basic Books.

Schulman, P. 1980. *Large-Scale Policymaking*. New York: Elsevier.

Silberman, Bernard. 1993. *Cages of Reason: The Rise of the Rational State in France, Japan, the United States, and Great Britain*. Chicago, IL: University of Chicago Press.

Tatalovich, R., and B. Daynes. 1997. *Social Regulatory Policy*. 2nd ed. Boulder, CO: Westview.

Thelen, K., S. Steinmo, and F. Longstreth. 1992. *Structuring Politics: Historical Institutionalism in Comparative Politics*. Cambridge, UK: Cambridge University Press.

Thompson, J.D., and A. Tuden. 1959. *Strategy, Structure and Process in Organizational Design, in Comparative Studies in Administration*. Pittsburgh: University of Pittsburgh Administrative Studies Center.

Timmermans, A., C. Rothmayr, U. Serduelt, and F. Varone. 1998. "The Design of Policy Instruments: Perspectives and Contexts." Paper presented at the Annual Meeting of the Midwest Political Science Association, Chicago, 23–25 April.

Wildavsky, B. 1998. "Looming Liabilities." *National Journal* 17 (January): 102–5.

Wilson, J.Q. 1980. *The Politics of Regulation*. New York: Basic Books.

CHAPTER FIVE

Acs, Z., ed. 2000. *Regional Innovation, Knowledge and Global Change*. New York: Pinter.

Alexander, E.R. 1979. "The Design of Alternatives in Organizational Contexts: A Pilot Study." *Administrative Science Quarterly* 24: 382–404.

– 1982. "Design in the Decision-Making Process." *Policy Sciences* 14: 279–92.

Amable, B., et al. 1997. *Les systèmes d'innovation à l'ère de la globalisation.* Paris: Economica.

Atkinson, M.M., and M.A. Chandler. 1983. "Strategies for Policy Analysis." In M.M. Atkinson and M.A. Chandler, eds, *The Politics of Canadian Public Policy,* 3–19. Toronto: University of Toronto Press.

– and R.A. Nigol. 1989. "Selecting Policy Instruments: Neo-institutional and Rational Choice Interpretations of Automobile Insurance in Ontario." *Canadian Journal of Political Science* 22, no. 1: 107–35.

Baxter-Moore, N. 1987. "Policy Implementation and the Role of the State: A Revisited Approach to the Study of Policy Instruments." In R.J. Jackson et al., eds, *Contemporary Canadian Politics,* 336–55. Scarborough: Prentice Hall.

Bemelans-Videc, M-L., et al., eds. 1998. *Carrots, Sticks and Sermons: Policy Instruments and Their Evaluation.* New Brunswick, NJ: Transaction Publishers.

Bennett, C.J., and M. Howlett. 1992. "The Lessons of Learning: Reconciling Theories of Policy Learning and Policy Change." *Policy Sciences* 25: 275–94.

Braczyk, H.J., et al., eds. 1998. *Regional Innovation Systems: The Role of Governance in a Globalized World.* London: UCL Press.

Bressers, H.Th.A. 1998. "The Choice of Policy Instruments in Policy Networks." In B.G. Peters and F.K.M. van Nispen, eds, *Public Policy Instruments: Evaluating the Tools of Public Administration,* 85–105. Cheltenham: Edward Elgar.

Brousseau, E. 1993. *L'économie des contrats.* Paris: Presses Universitaires de France.

Bryson, J.M., and P. Smith Ring. 1990. "A Transaction-based Approach to Policy Intervention." *Policy Sciences* 23: 205–29.

Cohen, W.M., and D.A. Levinthal. 1990. "Absorptive Capacity: A New Perspective on Learning and Innovation." *Administrative Science Quarterly* 35: 1288–1352.

Cooke, P., et al., eds. 2000. *The Governance of Innovation in Europe: Regional Perspectives on Global Competitiveness.* New York: Pinter.

Dahl, R.A., and Ch. Lindblom. 1953. *Politics, Economics and Welfare.* New York: Harper and Row.

de la Mothe, J., and G. Paquet, eds. 1998. *Local and Regional Systems of Innovation.* Amsterdam, Kluwer.

– 2000. "Regional Innovation: In Search of An Enabling Strategy." In Z.J. Acs, ed., *Regional Innovation, Knowledge, and Global Change,* 37–49. London: Pinter.

Doern, B.G., and R.W. Phidd. 1992. *Canadian Public Policy: Ideas, Structure, Process.* Toronto: Methuen.

Dogson, M. 1991. *The Management of Technological Learning: Lessons from a Biotechnology Company.* Berlin: Walter and Gruyter.

Dosi, G. 1982. "Technological Paradigms and Technological Trajectories." *Research Policy* 11, no. 3: 147–62.

Edquist, D., ed. 1997. *Systems of Innovation. Technologies, Institutions and Organizations.* London: Pinter.

– and I. Hommen. 1999. "Systems of Innovation: Theory and Policy for the Demand Side." *Technology in Society* 21: 63–79.

Elmore, R.F. 1987. "Instruments and Strategy in Public Policy." *Policy Studies Review* 7, no. 1: 174–86.

Foray, D. 2000a. "Characterizing the Knowledge Base: Available and Missing Indicators." In Organization for Economic Cooperation and Development, *Knowledge Management in the Learning Society,* 239–55. Paris: OECD.

– 2000b. *L'économie de la Connaissance.* Paris: Editions la découverte.

Foss, P., ed. 1995. *Economic Approaches to Organizations and Institutions.* Brookfield: Dartmouth Publishing.

Hall, P.A., and R.C.R. Taylor. 1996. "Political Science and the Three New Institutionalisms." *Political Studies* 44, no. 5: 936–57.

Heidenheimer, A.J., et al. 1990. *Comparative Public Policy.* New York: St Martin's Press.

Hood, C.C. 1984. *The Tools of Government.* London: MacMillan.

Holbrook, J.A., and D.A. Wolfe, eds. 2000. *Innovation, Institution, and Territory: Regional Innovation Systems in Canada.* Montreal and Kingston: McGill-Queen's University Press.

Howard, J.L., and W.T. Stanbury. 1984. "Measuring Leviathan: The Size, Scope and Growth of Governments in Canada." In G. Lermer, ed., *Probing Leviathan: An Investigation of Government in the Economy,* 93–110. Vancouver: Fraser Institute.

Howlett, M. 1991. "Policy Instruments, Policy Styles, and Policy Implementation: National Approaches to Theories of Instrument Choice." *Policy Studies Journal* 19, no. 2: 1–21.

– and M. Ramesh. 1993. "Patterns of Policy Instrument Choice: Policy Style, Policy Learning and the Privatization Experience." *Policy Studies Review* 12, nos 1–2: 3–24.

– and M. Ramesh. 1995. *Studying Public Policy. Policy Cycles and Policy Subsystems.* Toronto: Oxford University Press.

Jensen, M., and W. Melking. 1976. "Theory of the Firm: Managerial Behavior, Agency Costs, and Ownership Structure." *Journal of Financial Economics* 3: 305–60.

Johnson, B. 1995. "Institutional Learning." In G-A. Lundvall, ed., *National Systems of Innovation,* 23–44. London: Pinter.

Kaufmann, F-X., and B. Rosewitz. 1983. "Typisierung und Klassifikation politischer Massnahmen." In Renate Mayntz, ed., *Implementation politischer Programme II, Ansätze zur Theoriebildung,* 25–49. Opladen: Westdeutscher Verlag.

Kingdon, J.W. 1984. *Agendas, Alternatives and Public Policies.* New York: Harper Collins.

Kirschen, E.S., et al. 1964. *Economic Policy in Our Time.* Amsterdam: North Holland.

Kline, S.J., and N. Rosenberg. 1986. "An Overview of Innovation." In R. Landau and N. Rosenberg, eds, *The Positive Sum Strategy: Harnessing Technology for Economic Growth,* 275–306. Washington, DC: National Academy Press.

Koenig, K., and N. Dose, eds. 1993. *Instrumente und Formen staatlichen Handelns.* Köln: Carl Heymanns Verlag.

Lakatos, I. 1970. "Falsification and the Methodology of Scientific Research Programs." In I. Lakatos and A. Musgrave, eds, *Criticism and the Growth of Knowledge,* 91–196. Cambridge: Cambridge University Press.

Landry, R. 1996. "Rational Choice and Policy Studies." In L. Dobuzinskis, M. Howlet, and D. Laycock, eds, *Policy Studies in Canada: The State of the Art,* 170–92. Toronto: University of Toronto Press.

– and N. Amara. 1998. "The Chaudière-Appalaches System of Industrial Innovation." In J. de la Mothe and G. Paquet, eds, *Local and Regional Systems of Innovation,* 257–76. Amsterdam: Kluwer.

– M. Lamari, and N. Amara. 2002. "Does Social Capital Determine Innovation? To What Extent?" *Technological Forecasting and Social Change* 69: 681–701.

Laudan, L. 1981. "A Problem Solving Approach to Scientific Progress." In I. Hacking, ed., *Scientific Revolution,* 144–55. Oxford: Oxford University Press.

Lengrand, L., and I. Chatrie. 1999. *Business Networks and the Knowledge-Driven Economy.* Brussels: European Commission.

Linder, S.H., and B.G. Peters. 1984. "From Social Theory to Policy Design." *Journal of Public Policy* 4, no. 3: 237–59.

– and G.B. Peters. 1989. "Instruments of Government: Perceptions and Contexts." *Journal of Public Policy* 9, no. 1: 35–58.

– and G.B. Peters. 1990. "The Design of Instruments for Public Policy." In S.S. Nagel, ed., *Policy Theory and Policy Evaluation: Concepts, Knowledge, Causes, and Norms,* 103–19. New York: Greenwood Press.

Lowi, T.J. 1966. "Distribution, Regulation, Redistribution: The Functions of Governement." In B. Ripley, ed., *Public Policies and Their Politics: Techniques of Government Control,* 27–40. New York: W.W. Norton.

– 1972. "Four Systems of Policy, Politics and Choice." *Public Administration Review* 32, no. 4: 298–310.

Lundvall, G-A. 1985. *Product Innovation and User-Producer Interaction.* Aalborg: Aalborg University Press.

– 1992. "Explaining Interfirm Cooperation: The Limits of Transaction Cost Approach." In G. Grabher, ed., *The Embedded Firm: On the Socioeconomics of Industrial Networks,* 52–64. London: Routledge.

McDonnell, L.M., and R.F. Elmore. 1987. *Alternative Policy Instruments.* Santa Monica: Center for Policy Research in Education.

Maillat, D. 1995. *Systèmes territoriaux de production, milieux innovateurs et politiques régionales.* Unpublished. Neuchâtel, Switzerland: University of Neuchâtel.

Majone, G. 1976. "Choice among Policy Instruments for Pollution Control." *Policy Analysis* 2, no. 4: 589–613.

Malerba, F. 1992. "Learning by Firms and Incremental Technical Change." *The Economic Journal* 102: 845–59.

May, P.J. 1992. "Policy Learning and Failure." *Journal of Public Policy* 12, no. 4: 331–54.

Milgrom, P., and J. Roberts. 1992. *Economics Organization and Management.* Englewood Cliffs, NJ: Prentice Hall.

Miller, T.C. 1984. "Conclusion: A Design Science." In T.C. Miller, ed., *Public Sector Performance: A Conceptual Turning Point,* 251–68. Baltimore and London: Johns Hopkins University Press.

Nauwelaers, C., and R. Wintjes. 2000. "SME Policies and the Regional Dimension of Innovation: Towards a New Paradigm for Innovation Policy?" Working paper. Maastricht, Netherlands: MERIT and University of Maastricht.

Niosi, J. 1993. "National Systems of Innovation in Search of a Workable Concept." *Technology in Society* 15: 207–27.

Norgaard, A. 1996. "Rediscovering Reasonable Rationality in Institutional Analysis." *European Journal of Political Research* 29, no. 1: 31–57.

Peters, B.G., and F.K.M. van Nispen, eds. 1998. *Public Policy Instruments: Evaluating the Tools of Public Administration.* Cheltenham: Edward Elgar.

Peterson, T. 1995. "Principal-Agent Relationship in Organizations." In P. Foss, ed., *Economic Approaches to Organizations and Institutions,* 187–212. Brookfield: Darthmouth Publishing.

Porter, M. 1999. "Clusters and the New Economics of Competition." *Harvard Business Review* (December): 77–90.

– 2000. "Location, Competition and Economic Development: Local Clusters in a Global Economy." *Economic Development Quarterly* 14, no. 1: 15–34.

Ripley, B. 1966. *Public Policies and Their Politics.* New York: W.W. Norton.

Rochefort, D.A., and R.W. Cobb. 1994. *The Politics of Problem Definition.* Lawrence: University Press of Kansas.

Rose, R. 1993. *Lesson-drawing in Public Policy: A Guide to Learning across Time and Space.* Chatham, NJ: Chatham House.

– and Ph.L. Davies. 1994. *Inheritance in Public Policy: Change without Choice in Britain.* New Haven and London: Yale University Press.

Sabatier, P.A., and N. Pelkey. 1987. "Incorporating Multiple Actors and Guidance Instruments into Models of Regulatory Policymaking: An Advocacy Coalition Framework." *Administration and Society* 19, no. 2: 236–63.

Salamon, L.M. 1981. "Rethinking Public Management: Third-Party Government and the Changing Forms of Government Action." *Public Policy* 29, no. 3: 257–75.

– 1989. "The Changing Tools of Government Action: An Overview." In L.M. Salamon, ed., *Beyond Privatization: The Tools of Government Action,* 1–21. Washington, DC: Urban Institute Press.

– ed. 2002. *The Tools of Government: A Guide to the New Governance.* Oxford: Oxford University Press.

Schneider, A., and H. Ingram. 1988. "Systematically Pinching Ideas: A Comparative Approach to Policy Design." *Journal of Public Policy* 8, no. 1: 61–80.

– and H. Ingram. 1990. "Behavioral Propositions of Policy Tools." *Journal of Politics* 52, no. 2: 510–29.

Schön, D.A., and M. Rein. 1994. *Frame Reflection: Toward the Resolution of Intractable Policy Controversies.* New York: Basic Books.

Storper, M. 1997. *The Regional World: Territorial Development in a Global Economy.* New York: Guilford Press.

Timmermans, A., et al. 1998. "The Design of Policy Instruments: Perspectives and Concepts." Paper presented at the 56th Annual Meeting of the Midwest Political Science Association.

Trebilcock, M.J. 1994. *Can Government Be Reinvented?* Toronto: University of Toronto.

– et al. 1982. *The Choice of Governing Instrument.* Ottawa: Minister of Supply and Services Canada.

Twight, Ch. 1994. "Political Transaction-Cost Manipulation: An Integrating Theory." *Journal of Theoretical Politics* 6, no. 2: 189–216.

Varone, F. 1998. *Le choix des instruments de politiques publiques.* Bern: Velag Paul Haupt.

Vedung, E. 1998. "Policy Instruments: Typologies and Theories." In M-L. Bemelans-Videc et al., eds, *Carrots, Sticks and Sermons: Policy Instruments and Their Evaluation,* 21–58. New Brunswick, NJ: Transaction Publishers.

Weimer, D.L. 1993. "The Current State of Design Craft: Borrowing, Tinkering, and Problem Solving." *Public Administration Review* 53, no. 2: 110–20.

– and A.R. Vining. 1992. *Policy Analysis: Concept and Practice.* 2nd ed. Englewood Cliffs, NJ: Prentice Hall.

Williamson, O.E. 1975. *Market and Hierarchies: Analysis and Antitrust Implication.* New York: Free Press.

– 1985. *The Economic Institutions of Capitalism.* New York: Free Press.

Wilson, J.Q. 1989. *Bureaucracy: What Governement Agencies Do and Why They Do It.* New York: Basic Books.

Woodside, K. 1986. "Policy Instruments and the Study of Public Policy." *Canadian Journal of Political Science* 19, no. 4: 775–79.

CHAPTER SIX

1 We use the concept of target group straightforwardly to designate those individuals or organizations, including corporations, whose actions are intended to be shaped by policy instruments.

2 Public awareness seemed to have contributed an equally large amount to explaining the reduction in emissions. It may be the case that the quality of environmental-policy implementation changes under the influence of public awareness or that it becomes more effective under the pressure of increasing public exposure of the polluting target groups.

*References*

Agranoff, R., and M. McGuire. 2003. *Collaborative Public Management: New Strategies for Local Governments.* Washington, DC: Georgetown University Press.

Bogason, P., and T.A.J. Toonen. 1998. "Comparing Networks." Symposium in *Public Administration* 76, no. 2: 205–407.

Booy Liewes, M.M.T., J.J. Ligteringen, and J.Th.A. Bressers. 1992. *Evaluatie Besluiten Luchtkwaliteit* [Evaluation of EU decrees on air quality]. Leidschendam, Netherlands: Ministry of VROM.

Bressers, J.Th.A. 1998. "The Choice of Policy Instruments in Policy Networks." In B. Guy Peters and F.K.M. van Nispen, eds, *Public Policy Instruments: Evaluating the Tools of Public Administration,* 85–105. Chaltenham: Edward Elgar.

– 2004. "Understanding the Implementation of Instruments: How to Know What Works, Where, When and How." In W. Lafferty, ed., *Governance for Sustainable Development,* forthcoming. Cheltenham: Edward Elgar.

– and P.-J. Klok. 1988. "Fundamentals for a Theory of Policy Instruments." *International Journal of Social Economics* 15, nos 3–4: 22–41.

– L.J. O'Toole, Jr, and J. Richardson. 1994. "Networks as Models of Analysis: Water Policy in Comparative Perspective." *Environmental Politics* 3, no. 4 (Winter): 1–23.

– and L.J. O'Toole, Jr. 1998. "The Selection of Policy Instruments: A Network-Based Perspective." *Journal of Public Policy* 18, no. 3: 213–39.

– and D. Huitema. 1999. "Economic Instruments for Environmental Protection: Can We Trust the 'Magic Carpet'?" *International Political Science Review* 20, no. 2: 175–96.

– and S.M.M. Kuks. 2003. "What Does 'Governance' Mean? From Conception to Elaboration." In H.Th.A. Bressers and W.A. Rosenbaum, eds, *Achieving Sustainable Development: The Challenge of Governance Across Social Scales*, 65–88. Westport, CT: Praeger.

– and T. de Bruijn. 2003. "The Use of Covenants in Target Group Policy: Evaluating a Dutch Environmental Policy Innovation." Paper presented at the conference "Greening of Industry," San Francisco, October.

– and K.R.D. Lulofs. 2004. "Fees in Dutch Water Quality Management: How Effective Are They in Reducing Pollution?" In W. Harrington and R.D. Morgenstern, eds, *Effectiveness and Efficiency of Environmental Regulation*, forthcoming. Baltimore: Resources for the Future.

ECW (Evaluatie Commissie Wet Milieubeheer/Evaluation Commission, Law on Environmental Governance). 1996. *Vergunnen met Beleid: Advies over de Milieuvergunning in Bedrijf* [Licensing with policy: Advice about environmental permitting in business]. The Hague, Netherlands: Ministry of VROM.

Elmore, R.F. 1979/80. "Backward Mapping: Implementation Research and Policy Decisions." *Political Science Quarterly* 94, no. 4 (Winter): 601–16.

– 1985. "Forward and Backward Mapping: Reversible Logic in the Analysis of Public Policy." In K. Hanf and T.A.J. Toonen, eds, *Policy Implementation in Federal and Unitary Systems*, 33–70. Dordrecht, Netherlands: Martinus Nijhoff.

Gormley, W.T., Jr. 1989. *Taming the Bureaucracy: Muscles, Prayers, and Other Strategies*. Princeton, NJ: Princeton University Press.

Hall, T.E., and L.J. O'Toole, Jr. 2000. "Structures for Policy Implementation: An Analysis of National Legislation, 1965–66 and 1993–94." *Administration and Society* 31, no. 6 (January): 667–86.

– and L.J. O'Toole, Jr. 2004. "Shaping Formal Networks through the Regulatory Process." *Administration and Society* 36, no. 2 (May): 1–22.

Held, D. 1996. *Democracy and the Global Order: From the Modern State to Cosmopolitan Governance*. Cambridge, UK: Polity Press.

Kickert, W.J.M., E.-H. Klijn, and J.F.M. Koppenjan, eds. 1997. *Managing Complex Networks: Strategies for the Public Sector*. London: Sage.

Knoepfel, P. 1995. "New Institutional Arrangements for a New Generation of Environmental Policy Instruments: Intra- and Inter-policy Co-operation." In B. Dente, ed., *Environmental Policy in Search of New Instruments*, 197–222. Dordrecht, Netherlands: Kluwer, 197–222.

Ligteringen, J.J. 1998. "The Effects of Public Policies on Household Metabolism." In *Green Households? Domestic Consumers, Environment, and Sustainability*, 212–35. London: Earthscan.

Lynn, L.E., Jr, C.J. Heinrich, and C.J. Hill. 2001. *Improving Governance: A New Logic for Empirical Research*. Washington, DC: Georgetown University Press.

Majone, G. 1976. "Choice among Policy Instruments for Pollution Control." *Policy Analysis* 2 (Fall): 589–613.

Mandell, M., ed. 2001. *Getting Results through Collaboration: Networks and Network Structures for Public Policy and Management.* Westport, CT: Quorum Books.

McDonnell, L.M., and R.F. Elmore. 1987. "Getting the Job Done: Alternative Policy Instruments." *Educational Evaluation and Policy Analysis* 9: 133–52.

O'Toole, L.J., Jr. 1986. "Policy Recommendations for Multi-Actor Implementation: An Assessment of the Field." *Journal of Public Policy* 6, no. 2: 181–210.

– 1996. "Rational Choice and the Public Management of Interorganizational Networks." In D.F. Kettl and H.B. Milward, eds, *The State of Public Management,* 241–63. Baltimore: Johns Hopkins University Press.

– 1997a. "Implementing Public Innovations in Network Settings." *Administration and Society* 29, no. 2: 115–38.

– 1997b. "Treating Networks Seriously: Practical and Research-Based Agendas in Public Administration." *Public Administration Review* 57, no. 1 (January-February): 45–52.

– and K.I. Hanf. 2002. "American Public Administration and Impacts of International Governance." *Public Administration Review* 62, special issue (September): 158–69.

Pierre, J., and B.G. Peters. 2000. *Governance, Politics, and the State.* London: Macmillan.

Provan, K.G., and H.B. Milward. 1995. "A Preliminary Theory of Interorganizational Network Effectiveness: A Comparative Study of Four Community Mental Health Systems." *Administrative Science Quarterly* 40: 1–33.

Rhodes, R.A.W. 1997. *Understanding Governance: Policy Networks, Reflexivity, and Accountability.* Buckingham, UK: Open University Press.

Salamon, L.M., ed. 2002. *The Tools of Government: A Guide to the New Governance.* New York: Oxford University Press.

van de Peppel, R.A., P.-J. Klok, and D. Hoek. 1998. "Effecten van Milieubeleid" [Effects of environmental policy]. *Beleidswetenschap* [Policy science] 12, no. 2: 103–19.

Vedung, E. 1998. "Policy Instruments: Typologies and Theories." In M.-L. Bemelmans-Videc, R.C. Rist, and E. Vedung, eds, *Carrots, Sticks, and Sermons: Policy Instruments and Their Evaluation.* New Brunswick, NJ: Transaction Publishers, 21–58.

Vermeulen, W. 1992. *De Vervuiler Betaald* [The polluter paid]. Utrecht: Jan van Arkel.

Yu, C., L.J. O'Toole, Jr, J. Cooley, G. Cowie, S. Crow, and S. Herbert. 1998. "Policy Instruments for Reducing Toxic Wastes: The Effectiveness of State Information and Enforcement Actions." *Evaluation Review* 22, no. 5: 571–89.

CHAPTER SEVEN

1 François Ost and Michel Van de Kerchove, *Jalons pour une théorie critique du droit* (Brussels: Publications des Facultés universitaires Saint-Louis, 1987), 270–1.
2 [1998] 2 SCR 217.
3 Jürgen Habermas, "Law and Morality," in S.M. McMurrin, ed., *The Tanner Lectures on Human Values*, vol. 8 (Salt Lake City: University of Utah Press, 1988).
4 The Court did not consider it necessary, in this case, to develop the consequences of this appeal to moral values for the permanence of judgments of legitimacy. Since the Court sees itself as sensitive, in its interpretation of the Canadian Charter of Rights and Freedoms, to changing practices and values in contemporary society, it would probably agree that legitimacy is today "a complex and precarious construction, in constant transformation"; see Raymond Polin, "Analyse philosophique de l'idée de légitimité," in Collective, *L'idée de légitimité*, 17–28 (Paris: Presses universitaires de France, 1967), 27 [translation]. On this theme, see the rather sombre analysis by Simone Goyard-Fabre, "De la légitimité du Pouvoir," *McGill Law Journal* 35 (1989): 1–18 at 16.
5 Vincent Simoulin, "La gouvernance et l'action publique: Le succès d'une forme simmélienne," *Droit et Société* 54 (2003): 307–28 at 317.
6 Olivier Corten, "La persistance de l'argument légaliste: Éléments pour une typologie contemporaine des registres de légitimité dans une société libérale," *Droit et Société* 50 (2002): 185–203.
7 Highway Safety Code, RSQ c. C-24.2, ss. 76, 110–17, and 186 (demerit points); Employment Insurance Act, SC 1996, c. 23 and amendments, s. 7.1 (increase in number of hours of insurable employment); Act Respecting Income Support, Employment Assistance and Social Solidarity, RSQ c. S-32.001, s. 56–57 (reduction of benefit).
8 Act Respecting the Practice of Midwifery within the Framework of Pilot Projects, RSQ c. P-16.1; Employment Insurance Act, s. 109–110.
9 Environment Quality Act, RSQ c. Q-2, s. 31.10–31.31 (depollution attestation); Forest Act, RSQ c. F-4.1, s. 25.3 (special forest-management standards).
10 Act Respecting Petroleum Products and Equipment, RSQ c. P-29.1, ss. 8 (mandatory self-inspection) and 57 (private inspection programs).
11 Regulation Respecting Occupational Health and Safety, O.C.885–2001, (2001) 133 GOQ II 3888, s. 5.
12 Public Administration Act, RSQ c. A-6.01, s. 12–18 (performance and accountability agreement); Act Respecting Health Services and Social Services, RSQ c. S-4.2, ss. 182.1–182.7, 385.1–358.9 (management and accountability agreement).

13 Lester Salamon, ed., *The Tools of Government: A Guide to the New Governance* (Oxford: Oxford University Press, 2002).

14 John Mark Keyes, "Power Tools: The Form and Function of Legal Instruments for Government Action," *Canadian Journal of Administrative Law and Practice* 10 (1997): 133–74.

15 Pierre Lascoumes, "Normes juridiques et mise en oeuvre des politiques publiques," *L'Année sociologique* 40 (1990): 43–71 [translation].

16 Yves Derome, "Le contrat de gestion privée d'un service public," *Cahiers de droit* 36 (1995): 323–78.

17 Robert Howse, "Retrenchment, Reform or Revolution? The Shift to Incentives and the Future of the Regulatory State," *Alberta Law Review* 31 (1993): 455–92; Kernaghan Webb, "Thumbs, Fingers and Pushing on String: Legal Accountability in the Use of Federal Financial Incentives," *Alberta Law Review* 31 (1993): 501–35.

18 Margot Priest, "The Privatization of Regulation: Five Models of Self-Regulation," *Ottawa Law Review* 29 (1998): 233–302.

19 France Houle, *Les règles administratives et le droit public* (Cowansville: Éditions Yvon Blais, 2001).

20 Louis Borgeat and Isabelle Giroux, "Droit et administration publique: Entre tradition et postmodernité," *Canadian Public Administration* 40 (1997): 307–27; Daniel Mockle, "Gouverner sans le droit: Fonction normative et nouveaux modes de régulation," *Cahiers de droit* 43 (2002): 143–211.

21 Paule Halley, "Le droit, l'environnement et la déréglementation au Québec," in Collective, *Développements récents en droit de l'environnement 1997*, 343–80 (Cowansville: Éditions Yvon Blais, 1997).

22 Pierre Issalys, *Répartir les normes: Le choix entre les formes d'action étatique* (Quebec City: Société de l'assurance automobile du Québec, 2001), 210–20.

23 Pierre Vigneault, "L'approche contractuelle: L'expérience des mutuelles de prévention à la Commission de la santé et de la sécurité du travail," in Collective, *Actes de la XIII<sup>e</sup> Conférence des juristes de l'État*, 127–46 (Cowansville: Éditions Yvon Blais, 1998).

24 Suzanne Comtois, "Les directives: Un compromis entre le droit traditionnel et le règne de la discrétion," in Collective, *Droit contemporain*, 804–21 (Cowansville: Éditions Yvon Blais, 1994).

25 Issalys, *Répartir les normes*, 146–7, 124–9, 189–203.

26 Daniel Mockle, "Crise et transformation du modèle légicentrique," in Josiane Boulad-Ayoub, Bjarne Melkevik, and Pierre Robert, eds, *L'amour des lois*, 17–52 (Quebec City and Paris: Presses de l'Université Laval and L'Harmattan, 1996).

27 Françoise Saint-Martin, "L'utilisation des contrats comme mode de participation des parties privées à la détermination de normes," in Collective,

*Actes de la XVᵉ Conférence des juristes de l'État,* 61–114 (Cowansville: Éditions Yvon Blais, 2002).

28 François Dépelteau and Paule Halley, "Les effets et la légitimité d'une régulation néo-libérale," in Guy Giroux, ed., *L'État, la société civile et l'économie,* 105–44 (Quebec City and Paris: Presses de l'Université Laval and L'Harmattan, 2001).

29 These other normative orders are also orders of legitimate domination with their own capacity for legitimation; see Michel Coutu, "Légitimité du droit et transformation de la culture juridique," in Bjarne Melkevik, ed., *Transformation de la culture juridique québécoise,* 67–82 (Quebec City: Presses de l'Université Laval, 1998), 80.

30 Regulation Respecting the Reduction of Pollution from Agricultural Sources, O.C. 742–97, (1997) 129 GOQ II 2607, ss. 11, 17; Regulation Respecting Reserved Designations, (1997) 129 GOQ II 5043, ss. 1, 2, 4, 5.

31 Act Respecting Reserved Designations, RSQ c. A-20.02; Act Respecting the Agence nationale d'encadrement du secteur financier, SQ 2002, c. 45, s. 59–91; Canadian Payments Association Act, RSC (1985), c. C-21, ss. 4, 5, 18.

32 Jody Freeman, "Private Parties, Public Functions and the New Administrative Law," *Administrative Law Review* 52 (2000): 813–58.

33 Jean Alarie and Guy Boisvert, "Les critères de répartition des normes entre la loi et le règlement," *Cahiers de droit* 21 (1980): 567–78.

34 Michel Sparer and Wallace Schwab, *Rédaction des lois: Rendez-vous du droit et de la culture* (Quebec City: Éditeur officiel du Québec, 1980), 81–98.

35 Patrice Garant and Pierre Issalys, *Loi et règlement* (Quebec City: Laboratoire de recherche sur la justice administrative, 1981).

36 Michael Trebilcock, Robert Prichard, Doug Hartle, and Donald Dewees, *The Choice of Governing Instrument* (Ottawa: Minister of Supply and Services Canada, 1982).

37 Marie-Anne Frison-Roche, *Droit, finance, autorité: Les modes de régulation juridique propres aux autorités de marchés financiers* (Paris: Université Paris-Dauphine, 1999), 36.

38 Robert Baldwin, *Rules and Government* (Oxford: Clarendon Press, 1995), 33 ff.

39 Priest, "The Privatization of Regulation," 274 ff.

40 Borgeat and Giroux, "Droit et administration publique"; Charles-Albert Morand, *Le droit néo-moderne des politiques publiques* (Paris: Librairie générale de droit et de jurisprudence, 1999); Mockle, "Gouverner sans le droit."

41 Jerry Mashaw, "Conflict and Compromise among Models of Administrative Justice," *Duke Law Journal* (1981): 181–212.

42 Issalys, *Répartir les normes,* 23–33.

43 Philippe Gérard, *Droit et démocratie: Réflexions sur la légitimité du droit dans la société démocratique* (Bruxelles: Publications des Facultés universitaires Saint-Louis, 1995), 118.

44 See Lorne Sossin's stimulating reflection on the topic of engagement in administrative action in: "Redistributing Democracy: An Inquiry into Authority, Discretion and the Possibility of Engagement in the Welfare State," *Ottawa Law Review* 26 (1994): 1–46; "Democratic Admistration," in Christopher Dunn, ed., *The Handbook of Canadian Public Administration*, 77–99 (Don Mills: Oxford University Press, 2002); and "An Intimate Approach to Fairness, Impartiality and Reasonableness in Administrative Law," *Queen's Law Journal* 28 (2002): 809–58.

45 Jürgen Habermas, *Between Facts and Norms* (Cambridge, MA: MIT Press, 1996), esp. 359–73; on the development of this concept by Habermas and its relation to public action, see Ricky G. Richard, "Les fondements de l'espace public chez Habermas: De la critique à l'intercompréhension," *Globe* 6 (1995) 25–45; and Jean-Paul Bari, "Nouveaux instruments de mise en oeuvre des politiques et espace public," *Annuaire suisse de science politique* 33 (1993): 295–320.

46 Nicolas Tenzer, *Philosophie politique* (Paris: Presses universitaires de France, 1994), 178.

47 For an attempt at this assessment of certain forms of public action, see Issalys, *Répartir les normes*, chs 2 and 3.

48 Ibid., 68, 101, 221–2, 243.

49 D. 140–96, (1996) GOQ II 1518 and amendments.

50 See the 1981 Order in Council of the same title: D. 1900–81, (1981) 113 GOQ II 3489; and Raoul Barbe, *La réglementation* (Montreal: Wilson and Lafleur/Sorej, 1983), 262–81. On regulatory impact assessments, see François Lacasse, "Des savoirs vraiment utilisés: Les enjeux de l'évaluation prévisionnelle des lois et règlements," in Collective, *Évaluation prévisionnelle de l'impact des lois et des règlements*, 72–97 (Paris: OECD, 1997); Stéphane Braconnier, "La technique de l'étude d'impact et le renouveau de l'action étatique," *Revue du droit public* 114 (1998): 817–43; and Fazil Mihlar, "The Federal Government and the 'RIAS' Process: Origins, Need, and Non-compliance," in Bruce Doern, Margaret Hill, Michael Prince, and Richard Schultz, eds, *Changing the Rules: Canadian Regulatory Regimes and Institutions*, 277–92 (Toronto: University of Toronto Press, 1999).

51 SQ 2002, c. 61, art. 20.

52 Assessment of measures that impact on businesses below the threshold is carried out in the simplified form of an "impact statement."

53 Trebilcock et al., *The Choice of Governing Instrument*, 24; Frans van Nispen and Arthur Ringeling, "On Instruments and Instrumentality: A Critical Assessment," in B. Guy Peters and Frans van Nispen, eds, *Public*

*Policy Instruments: Evaluating the Tools of Public Administration,* 204–217 (Cheltenham: Edward Elgar, 1998), 210–11.

54 Kenneth Woodside, "The Acceptability and Visibility of Policy Instruments," in Peters and van Nispen, eds, *Public Policy Instruments,* 162–81: "Policy instruments should be seen as a necessary part of any institutional explanation of the politics of a public policy" (179).

55 Philippe Moreau Defarges, *La gouvernance* (Paris: Presses universitaires de France, 2003), 6.

56 Jean-Pierre Gaudin, *Pourquoi la gouvernance?* (Paris: Presses de Sciences po, 2002), 43.

57 Defarges, *La gouvernance,* 71.

58 Catherine Baron, "La gouvernance: Débats autour d'un concept polysémique," *Droit et Société* 54 (2003): 329–51 at 337.

59 Simoulin, "La gouvernance et l'action publique," 323.

60 Patrice Duran, *Penser l'action publique* (Paris: Librairie générale de droit et de jurisprudence, 1999), 111.

## CHAPTER EIGHT

1 Josta de Hoog edited this chapter, for which I am very grateful. However, I am responsible for any possible mistakes.

## References

Anheier, H.K., and W. Seibel, eds. 1990. *The Third Sector: Comparative Studies of Nonprofit Organizations.* Berlin and New York: De Gruyter.

Bobrow, D.B., and J.S. Dryzek. 1987. *Policy Analysis by Design.* Pittsburgh: University of Pittsburgh Press.

de Bruijn, J.A., and E.F. ten Heuvelhof. 1991. *Sturingsinstrumenten voor de overheid* [Governance instruments for the government]. Leiden: Stenfert Kroese.

Esping-Andersen, G. 1990. *The Three Worlds of Welfare Capitalism.* Cambridge: Polity Press in association with Basil Blackwell.

Hafkamp, W.A., M. Hozee, and A.B. Ringeling, eds. 1999. *The Effectiveness of Instruments for Environmental Policies in the Field of Industry.* Rotterdam: Erasmus University Rotterdam.

Hanf, K., and B. Soetendorp, eds. 1998. *Adapting to European Integration.* London: Longman.

Hemerijck, A. 2003. "Vier beleidsvragen" [Four policy questions]. In Victor Bekkers and Arthur Ringeling, eds, *Vragen over beleid* [Questions about policies]. Utrecht: Lemma.

Hood, C.C. 1984. *The Tools of Government.* London: MacMillan.

Hufen, J.A.M. 1990. "Instrumenten in het technologiebeleid" [Instruments in technology policy]. PhD thesis, Leiden University.

in 't Veld, R.J. 1997. *Noorderlicht, over scheiding en samenballing* [Nothern-light: About separation and concentration]. Den Haag: VUGA.

Klok, P.J. 1989. *Convenanten als instrument van milieubeleid* [Covenants as in-struments of environmental policy]. Enschede: Twente University Press.

Koopmans, T. 1978. *Vergelijkend publiekrecht* [Comparative public law]. De-venter: Kluwer.

Liefferink, J.D., ed. 1997. *European Environmental Policy*. Manchester: Manchester University Press.

Ligteringen, J.J. 1999. *The Feasibility of Dutch Environmental Policy Instru-ments*. Enschede: Twente University Press.

Lijphart, A. 1968. *The Politics of Accommodation*. Berkeley: University of Cal-ifornia Press.

Majone G. 1989. *Evidence, Argument and Persuasion in the Policy Process*. New Haven and London: Yale University Press.

– et al. 1996. *Regulating Europe*. London and New York: Routledge.

Peters, Guy B. 1996. *The Future of Governing: Four Emerging Models*. Lawrence: University Press of Kansas.

– and F.K.M. van Nispen, eds. 1998. *Public Policy Instruments:. Evaluating the Tools of Public Administration*. Cheltenham: Edward Elgar.

Putnam, R.D. 1993. *Making Democracy Work*. Princeton: Princeton University Press.

Richardson, J. 1982. *Policy Styles in Western Europe*. Boston: Allen and Unwin.

Ringeling, A.B. 1983. *De instrumenten van het beleid* [The instruments of gov-ernment policy]. Inaugural lecture, Erasmus University Rotterdam. Alphen aan den Rijn: Samsom.

– 1993. *Het imago van de overheid* [The image of government]. 's-Gravenhage: VUGA.

– and F.K.M. van Nispen. 1998. "On Instruments and Instrumentality: A Crit-ical Assessment." In B.G. Peters and F.K.M. van Nispen, eds, *Public Policy Instruments: Evaluating the Tools of Public Administration*. Cheltenham: Edward Elgar.

Salamon, L.M., ed. 1989. *Beyond Privatization: The Tools of Government Ac-tion*. Washington, DC: Urban Institute Press.

– ed. 2002. *The Tools of Government: A Guide to the New Governance*. New York: Oxford University Press.

Selznick, P. 1949. *TVA and the Grass Roots: A Study in the Sociology of Formal Organization*. Berkeley: University of California Press.

Stillman, R.J. 1991. *Preface to Public Administration*. New York: St Martin's Press.

Stone, Deborah. 1998. *The Policy Paradox: The Art of Political Decision Mak-ing*. New York and London: Norton.

van der Eyden, Ton. 2003. *Public Management of Society: Rediscovering French Institutional Engineering in the European Context*. Amsterdam: IOS Press.

van Doorn, J.A.A., and C.J.M. Schuyt. 1978. *De stagnerende verzorgingsstaat* [The stagnating welfare state]. Meppel and Amsterdam: Boom.

Visser, J., and A. Hemerijck. 1997. *A Dutch Miracle*. Amsterdam: Amsterdam University Press.

Wetenschappelijke Raad voor het Regeringsbeleid (Scientific Council for Governmental Policy). 1992. *Milieubeleid* [Environmental policy] 41.

### CHAPTER NINE

1 This chapter, first prepared for delivery at the opening plenary session of the research conference occasioning this volume, was revised for publication in October 2002. Apart from minor editing, it has not been recast to incorporate themes and ideas addressed in the scholarly and policy literature since then.

    I am most grateful to my research assistant, Eric Reiter, for his superb development of the Swiss Army Knife allegory. Most of the chapter's second part derives from his research notes. Simon Chamberland has also provided excellent research assistance throughout this project. My colleagues at McGill – Richard Janda, Nicholas Kasirer, Desmond Manderson, and Shauna van Praagh – closely reviewed and critiqued an earlier version of the manuscript, as did Professor R.D. Wolfe at the School of Policy Studies, Queen's University, and Nathalie DesRosiers, president of the Law Commission of Canada. I am much in their debt. The usual caveat applies.

2 For an outstanding effort to plumb the promise and perils of transdisciplinarity, see Somerville and Rapport 2000.

3 See Ellickson 1991 and Posner 2000.

4 See Parsons and Shils 1962 and Weber 1986.

5 See Hart 1994 and Kelsen 1967.

6 Fuller 1969, 106.

7 See *Royal Commission of Inquiry into Dominion-Provincial Relations* (1937). For contemporary critical commentary, see Innis 1940; for reflections a generation later also incorporating an assessment of Quebec's *Report of the Royal Commission on Constitutional Problems* (the Tremblay Report; 1957), see Smiley 1962.

8 See Creighton 1937 for the argument that a national policy cannot be simply the policy of the national government and that no national government can have only one policy over a period of many years. In fact, Creighton maintains that a national policy is a policy for building a nation and that, in rough form, the first National Policy predates Confederation. Indeed, he

argues that Canada was an instrument of the policy, not the other way around. That is, the national policy as a project of Montreal elites was conceived at least as early as 1840, and Confederation was simply one more instrument for its pursuit. The importance of this observation – that the state itself can be seen as a tool of governance – to my claims later in this paper about the interconnection of means and ends cannot be understated.

9 See, for example, Smiley 1975; the Symposium "Canada's National Policies" 1993; and Courchene 1997.

10 See notably Fowke 1952.

11 See Duxbury 1995, ch. 4.

12 A good intellectual history of the legal-process approach is presented in Roach 1997.

13 The first iteration of this idea was set out in chapter 6 of Fuller 1949. Fuller was the Carter Professor of General Jurisprudence at Harvard from the mid-1940s to the mid-1970s. While not well known outside North American legal circles, he is generally acknowledged to have been the most significant figure in US legal philosophy during the twentieth century. For an intellectual biography, see Summers 1984.

14 Fuller's several essays on the *eunomics* theme were collected in a posthumous volume (1983).

15 See Hart and Sacks 1958. For an interpretation of the legal process school, see Eskridge and Frickey 1994b.

16 For many followers of Hart and Sacks, and contrary to the *eunomics* ideas advanced by Fuller, the logic of legal process also compelled the search for nonpolitical "neutral principles" to constrain judicial activity. See, for example, Peller 1988. Compare Winston 1999.

17 The path-breaking work on models of civil disputing was Goldberg, Green, and Sander 1973.

18 See Packer 1968. The literature on restorative justice is extensive. For an overview, see Cragg 1992.

19 See Chayes 1976. A thoughtful summary of contemporary theorizing of procedural fairness may be found in Bayles 1990.

20 An extended review of this literature in Canada is presented in Macdonald 1985, especially at footnotes 2–13.

21 See, for an iteration of these themes, Hood 1986 and Salamon 1989.

22 See, for an illuminating discussion, Wolfe 2002.

23 The program pursued during this period in Canada, to recall, was known as the second National Policy. Recently, some scholars have argued, in my view unpersuasively, that a third National Policy of "post-embedded-liberalism *compensatory liberalism*" has been on the policy agenda for two decades. See, for one such endeavour, Eden and Appel Molot 1993.

24 On the legal framework implied by such a conception of the state, see Janda and Downes 1998.

25 For a slightly different periodization, see Hill 1996.

26 Bernier and Lajoie 1986; see especially volumes 46 and 48.

27 The lead paper on this theme was Howse, Prichard, and Trebilcock 1990.

28 Friedland 1989 and 1990.

29 Salamon 2002c.

30 Of course, the "tools of government" model remains statist. The assumption is that governments can often usefully conscript private actors into the regulatory endeavour, not that truly democratic collaboration may involve deference to nongovernmental mechanisms of governance. For discussion of "regulatory absence" as a legitimate policy option, see van Praagh 1996. I have attempted to apply this type of analysis in a recent paper analyzing legal-policy options that was prepared for the Senate Committee on Illegal Drugs; see Macdonald 2002a.

31 The parallels between the theoretical concerns of this collection (and, more generally, modern instrument-choice thinking such as that animating Salamon 2002c) and the institutional design preoccupations of the Harvard legal-process approach are striking. See, for example, Eskridge and Frickey 1994a as well as the several essays published in Witteveen and van der Burg 1999.

32 See Innis 1946 and 1956. In addition to the famous article by Fowke (1952), see Fowke 1957. For a modern proposal, see Courchene 1997.

33 In addition to those coauthored essays already cited, see Trebilcock 1994 and 2001.

34 This is not the place to rehearse the nefarious effects of "state legal positivism" as dominant ideology within faculties of law and other university departments. For an overview, see Cotterrell 1989.

35 A fine overview of regulatory history is presented in McCraw 1984, which is comprised of biographical studies of Charles Francis Adams, Louis D. Brandeis, James Landes, and Alfred Kahn.

36 The slogan was coined in Goldberg, Green, and Sander 1973.

37 For an elaboration of the point, see the papers collected in Ontario Law Reform Commission 1995.

38 See, for an elaboration of this idea, Peters 2002.

39 Fuller 2001c, 69.

40 See, for example, Komesar 1994, 274: "Reform is not ... [just] ... the embracing of goals. Reform is ... [also] ... the designation of the means of achieving them."

41 For classical presentations, which show the power of the paradigm even over those committed to "reregulation" rather than "deregulation," see (from a business-school perspective) McCraw 1981 and (from a law-faculty perspective) Breyer 1982.

42 Macdonald 1985.

43 On condign power, see Galbraith 1983.

44 See Howse, Prichard, and Trebilcock 1990.

45 Smith and Ingram 2002.

46 The point is trite and hardly merits a note. Yet it is difficult to find the underlying theoretical point stated in broad compass. For a now classical statement, see de Sousa Santos 1995. An early allegorical attempt to show the bearing of a rejection of these dichotomies on questions of public governance was attempted in Macdonald 1990.

47 Charles Lindblom (1977) was one of the first to frame the point in such a manner. For his further reflections, see Lindblom 1993.

48 See, for example, Farber and Frickey 1991.

49 For an excellent study reflecting the policy outcomes that would flow if law and economics scholars adopted a stance of moderate pessimism, see Ellickson 1991.

50 See, for an elaboration of a strongly optimistic perspective, Fuller 2001a.

51 See Hart and Sacks 1958.

52 This is not the occasion to give a full-blown presentation of contemporary theories of legal pluralism. For two recent studies, see Tamanaha 2001 and Melissaris 2004.

53 I have tried to explore this point in Macdonald 2002b.

54 See notably, Salamon 2002a and 2002b.

55 See, for example, Elster 1992 and Posner 2000.

56 Wenger, www.wengerasi.com; Victorinox, www.victorinox.com.

57 Leatherman Tool Group, www.leatherman.com.

58 For an extended development of this idea, see Kleinhans and Macdonald 1997.

59 See Becker 1932.

## References

Bayles, M.D. 1990. *Procedural Justice: Allocating to Individuals*. Dordrecht: Kluwer.

Becker, Carl. 1932. *The Heavenly City of the 18th Century Philosophers*. New Haven: Yale University Press.

Bernier, I., and A. Lajoie, coordinators, 1986. *Law, Society and the Economy*. Vols 46–51 of the collected research studies for the Royal Commission on the Economic Union and Development Prospects for Canada. Toronto: University of Toronto Press.

Breyer, S. 1982. *Regulation and Its Reform*. Cambridge, MA: Harvard University Press.

Chayes, A. 1976. "The Role of the Judge in Public Law Litigation." *Harvard Law Review* 89: 1281–1316.

Cotterrell, R. 1989. *The Politics of Jurisprudence*. London: Butterworths.

Courchene, T.J. 1997. "Proposals for a New National Policy." In Tom Kent, ed., *In Pursuit of the Public Good*, 65–92. Montreal and Kingston: McGill-Queen's University Press.

Cragg, W. 1992. *The practice of Punishment: Towards a Theory of Restorative Justice*. New York: Routledge.

Creighton, Donald. 1937. *The Empire of the St. Lawrence*. Reprint, Toronto: MacMillan, 1956.

de Sousa Santos, Boaventura. 1995. *Toward a New Common Sense: Law, Science and Politics in the Paradigmatic Transition*. New York: Routledge.

Duxbury, N. 1995. *Patterns of American Jurisprudence*. Oxford: Clarendon.

Eden, L., and M. Appel Molot. 1993. "Canada's National Policies: Reflections on 125 Years." *Canadian Public Policy* 19 (September): 232–51.

Ellickson, Robert C. 1991. *Order without Law: How Neighbours Settle Disputes*. Cambridge, MA: Harvard University Press.

Elster, Jon. 1992. *Local Justice: How Institutions Allocate Scarce Goods and Necessary Burdens*. New York: Russell Sage Foundation.

Eskridge, William N., Jr, and Philip P. Frickey. 1994a. "A Historical and Critical Introduction to *The Legal Process*." In Henry M. Hart, Jr, and Albert M. Sacks, *The Legal Process: Basic Problems in the Making and Application of Law*, rev. and ed. W.N. Eskridge, Jr, and P.P. Frickey, li–cxxxix. Westbury, NY: Foundation Press.

– and Philip P. Frickey. 1994b. "The Making of *The Legal Process*." *Harvard Law Review* 107: 2031–55.

Farber, Daniel A., and Philip P. Frickey. 1991. *Law and Public Choice: A Critical Introduction*. Chicago: University of Chicago Press.

Fowke, V. 1952. "The National Policy: Old and New." Reprinted in W.T. Easterbrook and M.H. Watkins, eds, *Approaches to Canadian Economic History: A Selection of Essays*, 237–58. Toronto: McClelland and Stewart, 1988.

– 1957. *The National Policy and the Wheat Economy*. Toronto: University of Toronto Press.

Friedland, M.L., ed. 1989. *Sanctions and Rewards in the Legal System: A Multidisciplinary Approach*. Toronto: University of Toronto Press.

– ed. 1990. *Securing Compliance: Seven Case Studies*. Toronto: University of Toronto Press.

Fuller, Lon L. 1949. *The Problems of Jurisprudence*. Temporary edition. Brooklyn: Foundation Press.

– 1969. *The Morality of Law*. Rev. ed. New Haven: Yale University Press.

– 1983. *The Principles of Social Order: Selected Essays of Lon L. Fuller*. Edited by K.I. Winston. 1st ed., Durham: Duke University Press; 2nd rev. ed., Oxford: Hart, 2001.

– 2001a. "The Case Against Freedom." In Kenneth I. Winston, ed., *The Principles of Social Order: Selected Essays of Lon L. Fuller*, rev. ed., 315–27. Oxford: Hart.

– 2001b. "The Lawyer as an Architect of Social Structures." In Kenneth I. Winston, ed., *The Principles of Social Order: Selected Essays of Lon L. Fuller*, rev. ed., 285–91. Oxford: Hart.

– 2001c. "Means and Ends." In Kenneth I. Winston, ed., *The Principles of Social Order: Selected Essays of Lon L. Fuller*, rev. ed., 61–78. Oxford: Hart.

Galbraith, J.K. 1983. *Anatomy of Power*. Boston: Houghton Mifflin Company.

Goldberg, Stephen B., E.D. Green, and Frank E.A. Sander. 1973. *Dispute Resolution*. 2nd. ed., Boston: Little Brown, 1985.

– Frank E.A. Sander, and Nancy H. Rogers. 1992. *Dispute Resolution: Negotiation, Mediation, and Other Processes*. 2nd ed. Boston: Little Brown.

Hart, Henry M., Jr, and Albert M. Sacks. 1958. *The Legal Process: Basic Problems in the Making and Application of Law*. Unpublished tentative edition. Revised and edited by W.N. Eskridge and P.P. Frickey, Westbury, NY: Foundation Press, 1994.

Hart, Herbert Lionel Adolphus. 1994. The Concept of Law. 2nd ed. Oxford: Clarendon Press.

Hill, M. 1996. *A Historical Perspective on Regulatory Reform: Institutions and Ideas after the Regulatory Reference*. Ottawa: Treasury Board Secretariat.

Hood, C. 1986. *The Tools of Government*. Chatham, NJ: Chatham House.

Howse, Robert, J.R.S. Prichard, and Michael J. Trebilcock. 1990. "Smaller or Smarter Government?" *University of Toronto Law Journal* 40: 498–541.

Innis, H. 1940. "Rowell-Sirois Report." *Canadian Journal of Economics and Political Science* 6: 562–73.

– 1946. *Political Economy and the Modern State*. Toronto: Ryerson.

– 1956. *Essays in Canadian Economic History*. Ed. Mary Q. Innis. Toronto: University of Toronto Press.

Janda, R., and D. Downes. 1998. "Virtual Citizenship." *Canadian Journal of Law and Society* 13, no. 2: 27–64.

Kelsen, Hans. 1967. *The Pure Theory of Law*. Berkeley: University of California Press.

Kleinhans, Martha-Marie, and Roderick A. Macdonald. 1997. "What Is a Critical Legal Pluralism?" *Canadian Journal of Law and Society* 12, no. 1: 25–46.

Komesar, Neil K. 1994. *Imperfect Alternatives: Choosing Institutions in Law, Economics, and Public Policy*. Chicago: University of Chicago Press.

Lindblom, Charles. 1977. *Politics and Markets*. New York: Basic Books.

– 1993. *The Policy-Making Process*. 3rd ed. Englewood Cliffs: Prentice Hall.

Macdonald, Roderick A. 1985. "Understanding Regulation by Regulations." In Ivan Bernier and Andrée Lajoie, eds, *Regulations, Crown Corporations and Administrative Tribunals*, 81–154. Toronto: University of Toronto Press.

– 1990. "Office Politics" *University of Toronto Law Journal* 40: 419–76.

– 1995. "Prospects for Civil Justice." In Ontario Law Reform Commission, *Study Paper on Prospects for Civil Justice*, 1–178. Toronto: Ontario Law Reform Commission.

– 2002a. *The Governance of Human Agency.* Unpublished.

– 2002b. *Lessons of Everyday Law.* Montreal and Kingston: McGill-Queen's University Press.

McCraw, T. 1981. *Regulation in Perspective: Historical Essays.* Cambridge, MA: Harvard University Press.

– 1984. *Prophets of Regulation.* Cambridge, MA: Harvard University Press.

Melissaris, E. 2004. "The More the Merrier? A New Take on Legal Pluralism." *Social and Legal Studies* 13: 57–79.

Ontario Law Reform Commission. 1995. *Study Paper on Prospects for Civil Justice.* Toronto: Ontario Law Reform Commission.

Packer, H. 1968. *The Limits of the Criminal Sanction.* Stanford: Stanford University Press.

Parsons, Talcott, and Edward A. Shils, eds. 1962. *Toward a General Theory of Action.* Rev. ed. New York: Harper.

Peller, G. 1988. "Neutral Principles in the 1950s." *Michigan Journal of Law Reform* 21: 561–622.

Peters, B. Guy. 2002. "The Politics of Tool Choice." In Lester M. Salamon, ed., with the special assistance of Odus V. Elliott, *The Tools of Government: A Guide to the New Governance,* 552–64. New York: Oxford University Press.

Posner, Eric A. 2000. *Law and Social Norms.* Cambridge, MA: Harvard University Press.

Roach, K. 1997. "What's New and Old About the Legal Process." *University of Toronto Law Journal* 47: 363–94.

Salamon, Lester M. 2002a. "The New Governance and the Tools of Public Action: An Introduction." In Lester M. Salamon, ed., with the special assistance of Odus V. Elliott, *The Tools of Government: A Guide to the New Governance,* 1–47. New York: Oxford University Press.

– 2002b. "The Tools Approach and the New Governance: Conclusion and Implications." In Lester M. Salamon, ed., with the special assistance of Odus V. Elliott, *The Tools of Government: A Guide to the New Governance,* 600–11. New York: Oxford University Press.

– ed. 1989. *Beyond Privatization: The Tools of Government.* Washington, DC: Urban Institute Press.

– ed. 2002c. *The Tools of Government: A Guide to the New Governance.* Oxford: Oxford University Press.

Smiley, D.V. 1962. "The Rowell-Sirois Report, Provincial Authority and Post-War Canadian Federalism." *Canadian Journal of Economics and Political Science* 28: 54–69.

– 1975. "Canada and the Quest for a National Policy." *Canadian Journal of Political Science* 8: 40–62.

Smith, Steven Rathgeb, and Helen Ingram. 2002. "Policy Tools and Democracy." In Lester M. Salamon, ed., with the special assistance of Odus V.

Elliott, *The Tools of Government: A Guide to the New Governance*, 565–84. New York: Oxford University Press.

Somerville, M., and D. Rapport, eds. 2000. *Transdisciplinarity: reCreating Integrated Knowledge*. Oxford: EOLSS Publishers.

Summers, R.S. 1984. *Lon L. Fuller*. Palo Alto: Stanford University Press.

Symposium: "Canada's National Policies: Reflections on 125 Years." 1993. *Canadian Public Policy* 19, nos 232–339.

Tamanaha, B.Z. 2001. *A General Jurisprudence of Law and Society*. New York: Oxford University Press.

Teachout, Peter R. 1999. "'Uncreated Conscience': The Civilizing Force of Fuller's Jurisprudence." In Willem J. Witteveen and Wibren van der Burg, eds, *Rediscovering Fuller: Essays on Implicit Law and Institutional Design*, 229–54. Amsterdam: Amsterdam University Press.

Trebilcock, Michael J. 1994. *The Prospects for Re-inventing Government*. Toronto: C.D. Howe Institute.

– 2001. "Journeys Across the Divides." Unpublished.

– Douglas G. Hartle, J.R.S. Prichard, and Donald N. Dewees. 1982. *The Choice of Governing Instrument*. Ottawa: Minister of Supply and Services Canada.

van Praagh, S. 1996. "The Chutzpah of Chassidim." *Canadian Journal of Law and Society* 11: 193–215.

Weber, Max. 1986. *Economy and Society*. Ed. G. Roth and C. Wittich. Trans. E. Fischoff. Berkeley: University of California Press.

Westerman, Pauline. 1999. "Means and Ends." In Willem J. Witteveen and Wibren van der Burg, eds, *Rediscovering Fuller: Essays on Implicit Law and Institutional Design*, 145–68. Amsterdam: Amsterdam University Press.

Winston, K.I. 1999. "Three Models of Law." In Willem J. Witteveen and Wibren van der Burg, eds, *Rediscovering Fuller: Essays on Implicit Law and Institutional Design*, 21–77. Amsterdam: Amsterdam University Press.

Witteveen, Willem J., and Wibren van der Burg, eds. 1999. *Rediscovering Fuller: Essays on Implicit Law and Institutional Design*. Amsterdam: Amsterdam University Press.

Wolfe, R.D. 2002. "See You in Geneva? Democracy, the Rule of Law and the WTO." Unpublished.

## Recent Governance Debates in Legal Periodicals

Cooter, Robert. 2000. "Do Good Laws Make Good Citizens? An Economic Analysis of Internalized Norms." *Virginia Law Revue* 86: 1577–1601.

Dau-Schmidt, Kenneth G. 1997. "Economics and Sociology: The Prospects for an Interdisciplinary Discourse on Law." *Wisconsin Law Review, no.* 3: 389–419.

Ellickson, Robert C. 1998. "Law and Economics Discovers Social Norms." *Journal of Legal Studies* 27: 537–52.

– 2001. "The Market for Social Norms." *American Law and Economics Review* 3: 1–49.

Heimer, Carol A., and Arthur L. Stinchcombe. 1997. "Elements of the Cooperative Solution: Law, Economics, and the Other Social Sciences." *Wisconsin Law Review, no.* 3: 421–32.

Posner, Eric A. 1998. "Symbols, Signals, and Social Norms in Politics and the Law." *Journal of Legal Studies* 27: 765–98.

– 2001. "Law and the Emotions." *Georgia Law Journal* 89: 1977–2012.

– 2002. "The Signalling Model of Social Norms: Further Thoughts." *University of Richmond Law Review* 36: 465–80.

Posner, Richard A. 1998. "Social Norms, Social Meaning, and Economic Analysis of Law: A Comment." *Journal of Legal Studies* 27: 553–65.

Rachlinski, Jeffrey J. 2000. "The Limits of Social Norms." *Chicago-Kent Law Review* 74: 1537–67.

Scott, Elizabeth S. 2000. "Social Norms and the Legal Regulation of Marriage." *Virginia Law Review* 86: 1901–70.

Symposium: "Getting Beyond Cynicism: New Theories of the Regulatory State." 2002. *Cornell Law Review* 87, nos 267–696.

Symposium: "Law and Society & Law and Economics: Common Ground, Irreconcilable Differences, New Directions." 1997. *Wisconsin Law Review* 375–637.

Symposium: "Law, Economics, and Norms." 1996. *University of Pennsylvania Law Review* 144, nos 1,643–2,339.

Symposium: "The Legal Construction of Norms." 2000. *Virginia Law Review* 86, nos 1,577–2,021.

Symposium: "New Forms of Governance: Ceding Public Power to Private Actors."2002. *UCLA Law Review* 49, nos 1, 687–1,824.

Symposium: "Social Norms, Social Meaning, and the Economic Analysis of Law." 1998. *Journal of Legal Studies* 27, nos 537–823.

van der Burg, Wibren. 2001. "The Expressive and Communicative Functions of Law, Especially with Regard to Moral Issues." *Law and Philosophy* 20: 31–59.

CHAPTER TEN

1 I would like to express my appreciation to a number of people who provided me with their thoughts on the sustainable-governance concept: David J. Bell, of the York Centre for Sustainability; Kathy Brock, of the School of Public Policy, Queen's University; John Chibuk, of Strategic Policy, Industry Canada; Cary Coglianese, of the John F. Kennedy School of Government, Harvard University; Bruce Doern, Les Pal, and Susan Phillips, of the School of Public Policy and Administration, Carleton University; David Hecnar, of Alcan Incorporated; Derek Ireland, of Chreod Associates; Michael Jenkin, of

the Office of Consumer Affairs, Industry Canada; Michael Kane, of the
United States Environmental Protection Agency; Gernot Kofler, of the Competition Bureau, Industry Canada; Richard Paton and Brian Wastle, of the
Canadian Chemical Producers' Association; Paul Pross, Professor Emeritus of
the School of Public Administration, Dalhousie University; Tom Rotherham,
of the International Institute for Sustainable Development; Bella Wilson, of
the United Kingdom's Department for International Development; and
Stepan Wood, of Osgoode Hall Law School, York University. The opinions
expressed are those of the author and not those of any institution with which
he has an affiliation. The original articulation of the sustainable-governance
concept is contained in Kernaghan Webb, "Sustainable Governance: A Public
Policy Perspective on Corporate Social Responsibility and the Global Marketplace," paper presented at the *Canada@theworld.ca* Policy Research Initiative Conference, November 2000, Ottawa. More recent and developed
discussions are included in Kernaghan Webb, *Sustainable Governance: Developing an Approach for Canada* (forthcoming); and Kernaghan Webb, ed.,
*Voluntary Codes: Private Governance, the Public Interest and Innovation*
(Carleton Research Unit for Innovation, Science and the Environment, 2004).

2  For example, see the chart tracking fluctuating federal-government budgets
and Environment Canada's budget in particular, prepared by the Commissioner of the Environment and Sustainable Development, as presented at
page 3 of the Commissioner's 2002 report, "The Commissioner's Perspective,
2002: The Decade after Rio," www.oag-bvg.gc.ca/domino/oag-bvg.nsf/html/
environment.html. Similar charts could be prepared for consumer protection,
worker protection, health and safety, and other policy contexts at both the
federal and provincial levels.

3  A global public-opinion survey released in November 2002, based on poll-
ing data of 36,000 citizens in forty-seven countries (including Canada)
gathered between July and September 2002, indicates that, around the
world, the principal democratic institution in each country (e.g., Parliament, Congress, etc.) is the least trusted of the seventeen institutions tested,
including global companies. For more information, see www.environicsin-
ternational.com/default.asp?sp-gim.asp?article=Trust_Survey.pdf.

4  In a similar vein, the then-OECD head of the Program on Regulatory Reform, Scott Jacobs, has stated that the effectiveness of traditional national
institutions and policy tools has diminished and that "second-generation"
regulatory reforms are needed through better institutions and policy tools,
market incentives, and cooperation with civil society. Scott Jacobs, "The
Second Generation of Regulatory Reforms," paper prepared for delivery at
the International Monetary Fund Conference on Second Generation Reforms, 8–9 November 1999.

5  For example, only the state has the legitimate authority to deprive someone
of his or her physical liberty in support of public-policy aims.

6 A similar point is made by Bryne Purchase in "The Political Economy of Voluntary Codes," in Webb, ed., *Voluntary Codes*, 77–96.

7 These terms are defined in the next section.

8 This is not to suggest that nonself-interested behaviour (e.g., based on notions of ethics and civic duty) cannot also play important roles in driving such initiatives but rather to signal that even base, self-interested motivations can be harnessed for the purposes of public-interest governance.

9 While collaborations and partnerships are common features of sustainable governance, it is wrong to assume that government is always a direct partner in these collaborations. For example, industry associations have developed environmental, social, or consumer programs, working with civil society organizations, without having government representatives at the table (see examples below). Similarly, NGOs have developed voluntary initiatives, such as ombudsman programs, certification programs, and good-neighbour agreements without any government participation (see examples below). While there may be the looming threat of law or an indirect legal dimension to some of this activity, sustainable governance does not assume that government is a necessary partner for direct collaboration. But government can put in place conditions that increase the likelihood of collaborative industry-NGO governance innovations being developed.

10 In his discussion of "destablization rights," Roberto Unger seems to be referring to a similar concept to the notion of "built-in" institutional, instrumental, and process checks and balances referred to here. According to Unger, the introduction of "destablization rights" is intended to empower the disadvantaged, to undermine the status quo, and to advance processes of social change. Roberto Unger, "The Critical Studies Movement," *Harvard Law Review* 96 (1982): 561–675.

11 In acknowledging the importance of creative tension and rivalrous initiatives as part of a system-wide approach to governing involving multiple government, industry, NGO, and citizen actors, sustainable governance differs from the "horizontal governance" concept, which seems premised exclusively on the notion of collaboration across organizational boundaries. See, for example, the Canadian Centre for Management Development's discussion of horizontal management at www.ccmd-ccg.gc.ca.

12 Recently, American scholars such as Lester Salamon have articulated the concept of "the new governance," which in many ways is similar to what is described here. See, for example, Lester Salamon, "The New Governance and the Tools of Public Action: An Introduction," *Fordham Urban Law Journal* 28, no. 5 (June 2001): 1611–74. Where "the new governance" would appear to differ from sustainable governance is in its failure to separate institutions from rule instruments and processes (Salamon collapses these into a single concept: "tools"), its lack of recognition of the fact that sustainable governance in the public interest can take place by private

actors with no direct government involvement (he speaks of "public" or "public-private" but not purely "private" approaches), and in its apparent failure to recognize the value of rivalrous initiatives. Canadian work on governance also appears to concentrate more on collaborative horizontal approaches; see, for example, Gilles Paquet, "Tectonic Changes in Canadian Governance," in Leslie A. Pal, ed., *How Ottawa Spends, 1999–2000: Shape Shifting: Canadian Governance Toward the 21st Century* (Toronto: Oxford University Press, 1999), 75–111.

13 Commission on Global Governance, *Our Global Neighbourhood* (Oxford: Oxford University Press, 1995), 2. It perhaps goes without saying that the governance of central interest in this chapter is governance that has public-interest dimensions. This means that a wide range of private-sector and civil-society governance activity is of no direct relevance to this chapter. It is possible for miniature-train aficionados to band together and create a club with a governance structure and, potentially, rule instruments and processes designed to support the aims of the miniature-train enthusiasts, but this sort of governance has little relevance to the discussion here. Similarly, there are institutions for the development of technical standards designed to enhance private-sector commercial activity (e.g., standards concerning screws and fasteners used in machinery) that, while highly useful to the private sector, usually have little or no public-interest dimension. Hence, while important, these sorts of institutions, rule instruments, and processes with no overt public-interest aspects are not the subject of discussion here.

14 Public-interest governing takes place whenever any entity purports to put in place approaches that have or could have a significant public-interest component. Thus industry initiatives such as Responsible Care or the Canadian Banking Ombudsman and NGO initiatives such as the Forest Stewardship Council's certification programs, Oxfam Australia's Mining Ombudsman, or community-group-led Riverkeeper or good-neighbour agreements (all discussed below) are examples of public-interest governing even though they were not initiated, developed, or implemented by the public sector.

15 While collaborative approaches with multiple actors can be more robust, flexible, and cost-effective, it is also possible for them to be difficult to manage, quite rigid, and expensive. This is discussed in greater detail later in the chapter.

16 The following description of the relevant thinking of Foucault and Habermas draws substantially on A. Hunt, "Legal Governance and Social Relations: Empowering Agents and the Limits of Law," in M. MacNeill, N. Sargent, and P. Swan, eds, *Law, Regulation, and Governance* (Don Mills, ON: Oxford University Press, 2002), 54–77. See also Stepan Wood, *Green Revolution or Greenwash? Voluntary Environmental Standards, Public Law and Private Authority in Canada* (Ottawa: Law Commission of Canada, 2002).

17 G. Teubner, "After Legal Instrumentalism? Strategic Models of Post-Regulatory Law," *International Journal of the Sociology of Law* 12 (1984): 375–400, at 394.

18 One need only look at jurisdictions where one or more of these aspects are deficient to see how easily governance in the public interest can falter. Thus, for example, in developing countries where public-sector institutions are weak and/or corrupt, it is difficult for individuals and organizations to feel secure about and to plan for the future and difficult for societies to thrive and improve their quality of life. A culture of trust and integrity concerning public institutions may be missing (this culture of trust and integrity is often taken for granted in Canada). Nevertheless, even in developing countries where public institutions are weak and/or corrupt, private-sector, NGO, and citizen-based institutions, rule instruments, and processes can play integral roles in capacity building, which can help to stimulate the development of effective public-sector institutions, instruments, and processes. Sustainable governance is an approach to governing that is equally relevant to developed and developing countries, although the precise combination of institutions, rule instruments, processes, and actors may vary considerably from one jurisdiction to another.

19 See, for example, itemizations of limitations in Kernaghan Webb, "Understanding the Voluntary Codes Phenomenon," in Webb, ed., *Voluntary Codes*, 3–32. A Canadian example of cost and time issues associated with regulations is the process of amending the Metal Mining Effluent Regulations that began in 1990 and only reached fruition in late 2002, that involved dozens of studies and consultations with hundreds of stakeholders, that cost in excess of $1 million to develop, and that is estimated to necessitate an expenditure of $2 million annually to enforce. See the *Canada Gazette* for the "Regulatory Impact Assessment Statement" associated with the regulations: www.ec.gc.ca/nopp/docs/regs/mmer/mmer.pdf.

20 Thus, for example, industry-funded consumer ombudsmen, councils, and programs can act as frontline resolvers of consumer disputes, with governments and the courts acting as last-resort mechanisms. Similarly, the implementation of environmental-management systems within firms, subject to third-party audits, can usefully supplement government's inspection capacity.

21 For a comparison of the strengths and weaknesses of voluntary approaches and conventional regulatory approaches, see Kernaghan Webb and Andrew Morrison, "Voluntary Approaches, the Environment and the Law: A Canadian Perspective," in C. Carraro and F. Leveque, eds, *Voluntary Approaches in Environmental Policy* (London: Kluwer Academic, 1999), 229–59.

22 For example, voluntary toxics-reduction programs may be made more effective through the creation of government-mandated toxics-release disclosure programs (as discussed in greater detail below); legal actions for

misrepresentations can help to ensure that firms keep their voluntary code commitments; and regulatory prosecutions or tort actions can lead to judicial recognition of voluntary codes as evidence of industry-wide standards for reasonable care. For discussion of these latter two points, see Kernaghan Webb and Andrew Morrison, "Voluntary Codes and the Law: Untangling the 'Tangled Web,'" in Webb, ed., *Voluntary Codes*, 97–174.

23 For information regarding the Ontario Environmental Commissioner and its investigation process, see www.eco.on.ca. For information regarding the citizen-petitioning process of the federal Commissioner of the Environment and Sustainable Development, see www.oag-bvg.gc.ca/domino/oag-bvg.nsf/html/environment.html. For information regarding the citizen-petitioning process of the NAFTA Commission for Environmental Cooperation, see www.cec.org.

24 See, for example, discussion of the Ontario self-management model in M. Winfield, "Public Safety in Private Hands: A Study of Ontario's Technical Standards and Safety Authority," *Journal of Canadian Public Administration* 45, no. 1 (Spring 2002): 24–51.

25 For more detailed discussion of the Canadian Banking Ombudsman, see David Clarke and Kernaghan Webb, *Market-driven Consumer Redress Case Studies and Legal Issues* (Office of Consumer Affairs, Industry Canada, 2002), http://strategis.ic.gc.ca/pics/ca/redress_case_studies_eng.pdf.

26 For more detailed discussion of this initiative, see Kernaghan Webb, "Voluntary Codes and the Mining Industry: Digging out the Legal Implications," in E. Basteda, ed., *Mining and the Law* (University of Dundee, forthcoming).

27 For more information on Canadian Riverkeepers, see www.ottawariverkeeper.ca and www.elements.nb.ca/theme/rivers/michel/michel.htm.

28 For more detailed discussion of the Canadian privacy code and the Personal Information Protection and Electronic Documents Act, see Colin Bennett, "Privacy Self-Regulation in a Global Economy: A Race to the Top, the Bottom or Somewhere Else?" in Webb, ed., *Voluntary Codes*, 227–48.

29 The following discussion is derived from Environment Canada, *Environmental Performance Agreements*, www.ec.gc.ca/epa-epe/pol/en/framewk7.cfm.

30 This agreement is available at http://strategis.ic.gc.ca/epic/internet/inauto-auto.nsf/vwGeneratedInterE/am01504e.html.

31 Information derived from Environment Canada, *The New CEPA and Environmental Protection Alternative Measures (EPAMs)*, www.ec.gc.ca/CEPARegistry/gene_info/fs_12_e.pdf.

32 See the case concerning Sherritt International Corporation at www.ec.gc.ca/CEPARegistry/enforcement/sherritt_agree.cfm.

33 Information derived from Environment Canada, *Pollution Prevention Handbook*, www.ec.gc.ca/NOPP/DOCS/P2P/hbook/En/index.cfm.

34 Information derived from the website of the Canadian Council of Ministers of the Environment: www.ccme.ca.

35 For more detailed discussion of the Responsible Care Program, see John Moffet, François Bregha, and Mary Jane Middelkoop, "Responsible Care: A Case Study of a Voluntary Environmental Initiative," in Webb, ed., *Voluntary Codes*, 177–208.

36 The discussion here is derived from Webb and Morrison, "Voluntary Codes and the Law."

37 For discussion of the Australian code, see N. Gunningham, "Codes of Practice: The Australian Experience," in Webb, ed., *Voluntary Codes*, 317–34. For a copy of the Canadian Scanner Price Accuracy Code, go to http://strategis.ic.gc.ca/SSG/cto2379e.html.

38 Although many consumers may be "too busy" to check their receipts, the author can point to seniors such as his father who have both the time and the inclination to carefully scrutinize such receipts. The comparatively small number of vigilant consumers act as unpaid inspectors whose activities, although motivated only by concern for their own welfare, can nevertheless benefit a wide number of nonvigilant consumers (and reduce the need for government-agency intervention at the same time).

39 For more detailed discussion of this program, see Gregory Rhone, David Clarke, and Kernaghan Webb, "Two Voluntary Approaches to Sustainable Forestry Practices," in Webb, ed., *Voluntary Codes*, 249–72.

40 See the discussion at www.rccproject.org/clw2001_panel1.pdf.

41 For more information, see www.ec.gc.ca/pdb/npri.

42 This point was made by Werner Antweiller and Kathryn Harrison, "Toxic Release Inventories and Green Consumerism: Empirical Evidence from Canada," *Canadian Journal of Economics* 36, no. 2, (May 2003): 495–520 at 495.

43 To visit the Consumer Gateway, go to http://consumerinformation.ca/cgi-bin/main.cgi?Language=E.

44 For more discussion concerning use of this provision, see Kernaghan Webb, "Taking Matters into Their Own Hands: The Role of Citizens in Canadian Pollution Control Enforcement," *McGill Law Journal* 36 (1991): 770–830; the abstract is available at http://journal.law.mcgill.ca/abs/363webb.htm.

45 For more detailed discussion of this initiative, see Clarke and Webb, *Market-driven Consumer Redress*.

46 Thus, for example, the environmental commissions or commissioners that have been established assume the existence of a command-and-control environmental-protection infrastructure. By the same token, however, the sustainable-governance model also works in jurisdictions where the existing

institutional, rule-instrument, and process infrastructure is minimal (e.g., in developing countries), although it works differently.

47 However, collaborations or partnerships are not a necessary condition of sustainable-governance innovations, and where such collaborations do occur, they may not involve government as a direct party.

48 Indeed, the very notion of sustainability is based on the need to recognize that there is a time element in governance, that conditions change, and that those governance systems that have a capacity to respond to change will likely be the most robust and effective.

49 The indentations on either side of the large arrow are intended to represent the occasional budget setbacks or other setbacks that occur with regulatory programs. The indentations do not relate to any particular cutback or setback; in other words, the specific location of each indentation on its side of the main arrow is not significant. The abbreviation CGSB refers to the Canadian General Standards Board, and BBB refers to the Better Business Bureau.

50 The small arrows are not placed in any particular order on either side of the main arrow. In other words, no attempt should be made to interpret the placement of any of the small arrows as particularly significant in relation to the main arrow or to the other small arrows. Simply put, they represent supplementary or secondary institutions, rule instruments, and processes. There are many more secondary institutions, rule instruments, and processes that could be included; the initiatives that have been identified should be considered a more-or-less representative sampling of what is currently in operation. An attempt has been made to characterize each of the small arrows as institutions, rule instruments, or processes and to note which actors played particularly significant roles in their development or implementation. But both the resulting characterizations and the role ascriptions are somewhat arbitrary.

51 For example, see draft Ontario privacy legislation, as discussed at www.cbs.gov.on.ca/mcbs/english/57PUWP.htm.

52 Nevertheless, this has not stopped some provinces from threatening to challenge the constitutionality of the federal privacy legislation based on the CSA privacy code. However, these possible challenges relate not so much to the substantive obligations contained in the code as to the scope of coverage of the federal law.

53 For discussion of the "shadow of the law" phenomenon in the context of environmental protection, see Kernaghan Webb, "Voluntary Environmental Initiatives and the Law: Exploring the Potential for a Constructive Partnership," in R. Gibson, ed., *Voluntary Initiatives: the New Politics of Corporate Greening* (Peterborough: Broadview Press, 1999), 32–50.

54 See P. O'Malley, "Risk, Power and Crime Prevention," *Economy and Society* 21 (1992): 252–75.

55 As was noted with respect to the consumer-protection initiatives included in Figure 10.1 above, the indentations on the side of the main arrow are not intended to relate to any particular cutback or setback, and the small arrows are not placed in any particular order. There are many more institutions, rule instruments, and processes that could be included; thus Figure 10.2 is an attempt to portray only a representative sampling of what is currently in operation. As noted with respect to the consumer-protection context, the characterization of initiatives as institutions, rule instruments, or processes is somewhat arbitrary, as is the ascription of who among government, industry, or NGOs played lead roles.

56 This point is discussed in Antweiller and Harrison, "Toxic Release Inventories."

57 Commission of the European Communities, *European Governance: A White Paper* (Brussels: 2001).

58 More information concerning the Eco-Management and Audit Scheme can be found at http://europa.eu.int/comm/environment/emas/index_en.htm.

59 More information concerning this network, referred to as EEJ-net, can be found at www.eejnet.org.

60 More information concerning the New Approach can be found at www.newapproach.org.

61 More information concerning the UK Office of Fair Trading's regime for Consumer Codes of Practice can be found at www.oft.gov.uk/Business/Codes/default.htm.

62 Susan Phillips, "More than Stakeholders: Reforming State-Voluntary Relations," *Journal of Canadian Studies* 35 (2000–2001): 182–201, at 183–4.

63 The following is taken directly from M. MacKinnon, J. Maxwell, S. Rosell, and N. Saxena, *Citizens' Dialogue on Canada's Future: A 21st Century Social Contract* (Ottawa: Canadian Policy Research Networks and Viewpoint Leaning, 2003).

64 See surveys prepared for the Voluntary Sector Initiative involving the Canadian Centre for Philanthropy at www.vsi-isbc.ca.

65 See, for example, discussion of Suncor's approach to encouraging volunteering by its employees, described in a case study at www.volunteer-calgary.ab.ca/CWVC/case_studies/suncor.html.

66 See, for example, the discussion in A. Paul Pross and Kernaghan Webb, "Embedded Regulation: Advocacy and the Federal Regulation of Public Interest Groups," in K. Brock, ed., *Delicate Dances: Partnerships between the Nonprofit, Public, and Private Sectors* (Montreal and Kingston: McGill-Queen's University Press, 2003), 63–122.

67 For more information, see the ISO Consumer Policy Committee's report, *The Desirability and Feasibility of ISO CSR Standards*, http://europa.eu.int/comm/employment_social/soc-dial/csr/isoreport.pdf.

68 Corporate social responsibility is also known as corporate sustainability, corporate responsibility, corporate accountability, corporate citizenship, corporate sustainable development, and so on. At this point, corporate social responsibility, corporate responsibility, and corporate sustainability appear to be the most prevalent terms used to describe the concept.

69 The following definition draws on work prepared by a federal interdepartmental committee tasked with exploring how CSR relates to federal activities. It reflects a synthesis of other definitions from institutions such as the Organization for Economic Cooperation and Development (OECD), World Business Council for Sustainable Development, Business for Social Responsibility, European Union, Conference Board of Canada, and Canadian Business for Social Responsibility. The definition should be taken as an evolving concept that will change in the future as the concept is examined and developed in different domestic and international contexts.

70 For example, government could require firms to report on their CSR activities (and thereby enhance the ability of consumers, communities, investors, lenders, governments, and others to make informed decisions concerning a firm) or put in place financial incentives to encourage CSR activities. NGOs can play significant roles in development, implementation, and monitoring of CSR initiatives.

71 Some might argue that it is inefficient to target more than one institution, rule instrument, or process at the same activity and to thereby potentially create unconstructive interinitiative rivalries. While there is this potential, there is also the likelihood of creative tension, which is the hallmark of innovation. Elsewhere, the author has argued that, while harmonization and coordination of federal-provincial activity on environmental enforcement (which sees the federal government cede lead authority to the provinces in some circumstances) is laudable, the federal government nevertheless should not relinquish its capacity to engage in enforcement actions whenever it feels necessary. See Kernaghan Webb, "Gorillas in the Closet? The Impact of Intergovernmental Relations on Enforcement of Environmental Standards, Using the *Fisheries Act* as a Case Study," in P. Fafard and K. Harrison, eds, *Managing the Environmental Union: Intergovernmental Relations and Environment Policy* (Montreal and Kingston: McGill-Queen's University Press and Queen's University Institute of Intergovernmental Relations, 2000), 163–206.

72 Yes, this is a variation on the aphorism that "it takes a village to raise a child." My apologies to all concerned.

73 However, see the examples given above of the voluntary privacy code evolving into law and of the Canadian Banking Ombudsman evolving to become part of the Financial Ombudsnetwork, both over very short periods. Moreover, it is difficult to imagine that it would be easier to adjust such initiatives if they were laws.

74 Commentators refer to the increased likelihood of "principal-agent" problems when functions are delegated from one body to another. See, for example, Salamon, "The New Governance."

75 In this regard, sustainable governance is not unlike the claims made about the Internet – i.e., that it is uncentralized and hence less vulnerable to full-system shutdown.

76 As discussed in Kernaghan Webb, "Government, Private Regulation and the Role of the Market," in MacNeill, Sargent, and Swan, eds, *Law, Regulation, and Governance*, 240–63.

## CHAPTER ELEVEN

1 The Marsh report of 1943, *Social Security in Canada,* stated that "The social insurances, and even some straightforward disbursements like children's allowances, are investments in morale and health, in greater family stability, and from both material and psychological viewpoints, in human productive efficiency" (273). Echoing Marsh, the Canadian Opportunity Plan (being the 1960s Canadian version of the "war on poverty") spoke of achieving the fullest realization of our human resources. Interestingly, the federal budget of 1998 also unveiled a Canadian Opportunities Strategy, with an emphasis on postsecondary education and learning (Prince 1999a).

2 Under Section 36 of the Constitution Act of 1982, which lies outside of the Canadian Charter of Rights and Freedoms, the federal government and the provincial governments are committed to "promoting equal opportunities for the well-being of Canadians"; "furthering economic development to reduce disparity in opportunities"; and "providing essential public services of reasonable quality to all Canadians." In addition, the section states that the federal government and Parliament are committed to the principle of making equalization payments to ensure that provincial governments have sufficient revenues to provide reasonably comparable levels of public services at reasonably comparable levels of taxation. This constitutional guarantee of equalization codifies a practice that dates from the 1950s. Each year the federal government makes equalization payments to most of the provinces, the so-called "have-not" provinces in Canadian political language, totalling several billions of dollars. These payments help to ensure that provinces with tax-raising capacities below a defined national average do not have substantially lower levels of public services or far higher levels of taxation than residents in wealthier provinces.

3 The five principles set out in the Canada Health Act 1984 are accessibility, comprehensiveness, portability, public administration, and universality. For further discussion see Rice and Prince 2000.

4 Unlike the Canada Pension Plan and other amending formulas, the SUFA provision does not contain a population threshold along with the number

of provinces that must agree to a new federal initiative supported by inter-governmental transfers. This illustrates another important silence on governance in the agreement.

5 In theory, these sections represent an opting-in mechanism for any of the one to four provincial governments that might not initially support a new Canada-wide social-policy initiative. Any such government could make a choice to receive the available funding if it committed to meeting the agreed objectives and to respecting the agreed accountability framework. For example, the Quebec government did not sign the multi-lateral framework on the Employability Assistance for Persons with Disabilities (EAPD) but did sign a bilateral agreement with the federal government.

6 Examples of federal unilateralism in social policy of late include the Millennium Scholarships Fund, the national homelessness initiative, and the Canadian Innovation Fund. See Noel 2001 for further analysis.

## References

Abele, Frances, and Michael J. Prince. 2002. "Alternative Futures: Aboriginal Peoples and Canadian Federalism." In Herman Bakvis and Grace Skogstad, eds, *Canadian Federalism in the Millennium: Performance, Effectiveness and Legitimacy*, 220–37. Toronto: Oxford University Press.

Armitage, Andrew. 1996. *Social Welfare in Canada Revisited: Facing Up to the Future*. 3rd ed. Toronto: Oxford University Press.

Bardach, Eugene. 2000. *A Practical Guide for Policy Analysis*. New York: Chatham House Seven Bridges Press.

Battle, Ken, and Sherri Torjman. 2001. *The Post-Welfare State in Canada: Income-Testing and Inclusion*. Ottawa: Caledon Institute of Social Policy.

Boadway, Robin. 1992 *The Constitutional Division of Powers: An Economic Perspective*. Ottawa: Minister of Supply and Services.

Broadbent, Edward. 1999. *Building on Strength: Improving Governance and Accountability in Canada's Volunteer Sector*. Ottawa: Panel on Accountability and Governance in the Voluntary Sector.

Cameron, David, and Fraser Valentine. 2001. "Comparing Policy-Making in Federal Systems: The Case of Disability Policy Programs: An Introduction." In D. Cameron and F. Valentine, eds, *Disability and Federalism: Comparing Different Approaches to Full Participation*, 1–44. Montreal and Kingston: McGill-Queen's University Press.

Clarkson, Stephen, and Timothy Lewis. 1999. "The Contested State: Canada in the Post-Cold-War, Post-Keynesian, Post-Fordist, Post-Nationalist Era." In Leslie A. Pal, ed., *How Ottawa Spends, 1999–2000: Shape Shifting: Canadian Governance Toward the 21st Century*, 293–340. Toronto: Oxford University Press.

Doern, G. Bruce, and Richard Phidd. 1992. *Canadian Public Policy: Ideas, Structure, Process*. 2nd ed. Toronto: Nelson.

– Margaret M. Hill, Michael J. Prince, and Richard J. Schultz, eds. 1999. *Changing the Rules: Canadian Regulatory Regimes and Institutions*. Toronto: University of Toronto Press.

Gagnon, Alain-G., and Hugh Segal, eds. 2000. *The Canadian Social Union without Quebec: Eight Critical Analyses*. Montreal: Institute for Research on Public Policy.

Glouberman, Sholom, Phillipa Campsie, Michael Gernar, and Glen Miller. 2003. *A Toolbox for Improving Health in Cities: A Discussion Paper*. Ottawa: Caledon Institute of Social Policy.

Government of Canada. 2002. *Knowledge Matters: Skills and Learning for Canadians*. Doc. 2 of *Canada's Innovation Strategy*. Hull: Human Resources Development Canada.

– 2003. *Tax Expenditures 2003*. Ottawa: Department of Finance.

Hale, Geoffrey. 2002. *The Politics of Taxation in Canada*. Peterborough: Broadview Press.

Hobson, Paul A.R., and France St Hilaire. 1994. *Reforming Federal-Provincial Fiscal Arrangements: Towards Sustainable Federalism*. Halifax: Institute for Research on Public Policy.

Hogg, Peter. 2000. *Constitutional Law of Canada*. Toronto: Carswell.

Hood, Christopher. 1984. *The Tools of Government*. London: Macmillan.

Howlett, Michael, and M. Ramesh. 2003. *Studying Public Policy: Policy Cycles and Policy Subsystems*. 2nd ed. Toronto: Oxford University Press.

Levy, Elinor, and Mark Fischetti. 2003. *The New Killer Diseases: How the Alarming Evolution of Mutant Germs Threatens Us All*. New York: Crown.

Manzer, Ronald. 1985. *Public Policies and Political Development in Canada*. Toronto: University of Toronto Press.

Marsh, Leonard. 1943. *Social Security in Canada*. Ottawa: King's Printer.

McIntosh, Tom, ed. 2002. *Building the Social Union: Perspectives, Directions and Challenges*. Regina: Canadian Plains Research Centre and the Saskatchewan Institute of Public Policy.

Noel, Alain. 2001. "Power and Purpose in Intergovernmental Relations." *Policy Matters*. Vol. 2, no. 6. Montreal: Institute for Research on Public Policy.

Pal, Leslie A. 1997. *Beyond Policy Analysis: Public Issue Management in Turbulent Times*. Toronto: ITP Nelson.

Paquet, Gilles, and Robert Shepherd. 1996. "The Program Review Process: A Deconstruction." In Gene Swimmer, ed., *How Ottawa Spends, 1996–97: Life Under the Knife*, 39–72. Ottawa: Carleton University Press.

Prince, Michael J. 1998. "New Mandate, New Money, New Politics: Federal Budgeting in the Post-Deficit Era." In Leslie A. Pal, ed., *How Ottawa Spends, 1998–99: Balancing Act: The Post-Deficit Era*, 31–55. Toronto: Oxford University Press.

- 1999a. "From Health and Welfare to Stealth and Farewell." In Leslie A. Pal, ed., *How Ottawa Spends, 1999–2000: Shape Shifting: Canadian Governance Toward the 21st Century*, 151–96. Toronto: Oxford University Press.
- 1999b. "Civic Regulation: Regulating Citizenship, Morality, Social Order, and the Welfare State." In G. Bruce Doern, Margaret M. Hill, Michael J. Prince, and Richard J. Schultz, eds, *Changing the Rules: Canadian Regulatory Regimes and Institutions*, 201–27. Toronto: University of Toronto Press.

Rice, James J., and Michael J. Prince. 2000. *Changing Politics of Canadian Social Policy*. Toronto: University of Toronto Press.

Richards, John. 1997. *Retooling the Welfare State: What's Right, What's Wrong, What's to Be Done*. Toronto: C.D. Howe Institute.

Schneider, A., and H. Ingram. 1993. "Social Construction of Target Populations: Implications for Politics and Policy." *American Political Science Review* 87 (June): 334–47.

Stanbury, William T., and Jane Fulton. 1984. "Suasion as a Governing Instrument." In Allan M. Maslove, ed., *How Ottawa Spends, 1984: The New Agenda*, 282–324. Toronto: Lorimer.

Stewart, Hon. Jane, Minister of Human Resources Development Canada. 2002. News Conference to announce the publication of *Knowledge Matters: Skills and Learning for Canadians*. Doc. 2 of *Canada's Innovation Strategy*. February 12.

Torjman, Sherri. 2001. "Canada's Federal Regime and Persons with Disabilities." In D. Cameron and F. Valentine, eds, *Disability and Federalism: Comparing Different Approaches to Full Participation*, 151–96. Montreal and Kingston: McGill-Queen's University Press.

Trebilcock, Michael J. 2002. "The Choice of Governing Instrument: A Retrospective." Paper presented at the conference "Instrument Choice in Global Democracies." Montreal: Faculty of Law, McGill University.
- R.S. Prichard, D.G. Hartle, and D.N. Dewees. 1982. *The Choice of Governing Instrument*. Ottawa: Minister of Supply and Services Canada.

Watson, William G., John Richards, and David M. Brown. 1994. *The Case for Change: Reinventing the Welfare State*. Toronto: C.D. Howe Institute.

## CHAPTER TWELVE

1 Peacock Professor of Risk Management and co-director of the Economic and Social Science Research Council (ESRC) Centre for Analysis of Risk and Regulation, London School of Economics and Political Science. I am indebted to Sarah Amsler for her assistance in collecting data for this chapter and also to Gwynne Hawkins and Jim Ottaway. Michael Spackman and Martin Lodge provided very helpful comments on the chapter, for which I am very grateful.

2 Hood et al.'s notion of a risk-regulation regime refers to "the overall way risk is regulated in a particular policy domain" and, more particularly, to "the complex of institutional geography, rules, practice, animating ideas that are associated with the regulation of a particular risk or hazard" (2001, 8–9). A particularly important aspect of public-administration regimes is that they are control systems.

3 An important example here is changing conceptions of the environment. There is now a greater appreciation that environmental problems are interrelated, more far-reaching, and more long-term than previously understood. So the ideal risk-based regime would lead to a more holistic approach to managing environmental risks and ensure that pollution control in one area takes into account the effects of potential pollution displacement to other mediums and localities.

4 For example, their investigation into petrochemical activity on Canvey Island adopted risk assessments (UK HSE 1978).

5 Risk was taken to refer to "the chance that something adverse will happen" (UK HSE 1988, 2).

6 "Tolerability" does not mean "acceptability" but refers to a willingness to live with a risk both in order to secure certain benefits and in the confidence that it is being properly controlled. Tolerating a risk means that we do not regard it as negligible or as something we might ignore but rather as something we need to keep under review and reduce still further if and as we can. For a risk to be "acceptable," by comparison, means that for purposes of life or work, we are prepared to assume the risk pretty well as it is (UK HSE 1988).

7 The triangle in Figure 12.2 represents increasing levels of risk (measured by individual risk and societal concerns). The top area represents the *unacceptable zone,* the smaller area at the bottom represents the *broadly acceptable zone,* and the area in between is the *tolerable region.*

8 Michael Spackman, as expressed in private correspondence.

9 This approach requires companies to carry out formal safety assessments of serious hazards and risks in the workplace and to explain how these are being managed. The assessments include consideration of safety policy, risk assessment, safety-management systems, safety standards, accident investigation, the design of premises and plant, and provision for audit.

10 For example, the Banking Act 1987 was the responsibility of the Bank of England, which supervised banks. The Financial Services Act 1986 was enforced under the "umbrella" of the Securities and Investment Board (SIB), which comprised three Self-Regulating Organizations (SROs): the Securities and Futures Authority (SFA), which supervised securities and derivatives firms; the Investment Management Regulatory Organisation (IMRO), which supervised fund managers; and the Personal Investment Authority (PIA), which supervised life companies and investment advisers.

11 Until the Financial Services and Markets Act came into force on 1 December 2001, the FSA operated under the previous legislation.

12 The data are derived from agency websites. The limitations of these data are fully acknowledged, as is the tentative status of the findings. It is believed that these data are valuable in light of the absence of other data on the subject. In due course, more systematic and direct forms of data collection are recommended.

13 The shift is not always straightforward and may be contested, as is indicated for instance by US Congressional hearings about occupational and environmental risks (see, e.g., US Congressional Testimony 1995, 1999).

14 Financial regulators in Australia and Canada describe a variety of risk-based approaches and strategies involving assessment, measurement, rating schemes, and differential strategies based on different degrees of risk.

15 For example, France's Ministry of the Environment has a Department for the Prevention of Pollution and Risks (www.environment.gou.fr/english/prevent.htm), whose primary responsibility is to "prevent risks arising in connection with both human activity ... and natural events." Likewise, France's occupational health-and-safety regulation stresses the importance of risk management (www.sante-securite.travail.gouv.fr/Anglais.html).

16 There are many definitions of the precautionary principle (see below), but most have in common the idea that where there appears to be a real risk to human and environmental health, precautionary measures may be instituted in advance of scientific evidence of the potential harm. This allows for intervention in situations of uncertainty and ignorance and also raises questions about the levels of scientific proof required before intervening.

17 Froud et al. (1998) report that the failure of the 1985 movement to effect cultural change led to the relaunch of the deregulatory initiative in 1992, which culminated in 1994 with the Deregulation and Contracting Out Act and the establishment of a Deregulation Task Office. A further relaunch took place in 1995. Similar measures were taken across Europe, dating from the mid-1980s and with a similar emphasis on costs (Majone 1990). Meanwhile, President Ronald Reagan's United States had a parallel rhetoric of "regulatory relief" entailing reducing government intervention in economic life (Breyer and Sunstein 1999).

18 Some scholars dispute the relevance of the term NPM. See, for example, Rhodes 1997.

19 For discussion of the regulatory state, see Braithwaite 1999, Osborne and Gaebeler 1992, and Scott 2000.

20 A search of OECD environmental policies did not reveal any references to risk. Neither did a search of the OECD websites for risk-based criteria for waste management, yet OECD control systems were more risk-oriented. The evidence thus suggests an ad hoc, rather than conscious, change in overall perspective.

21 This is most evident in European Union environmental policies, which appear to be largely driven by the development of an integrated framework on sustainable development (EU 1998).

22 For example, the US Occupational Safety and Health Administration (OSHA) does not claim that its approach to preventing injury at work is foolproof and even notes that its measurements of the external factors that could affect its success are subject to reevaluation and revision (US Department of Labor 1998). A UK National Audit Office report entitled *Supporting Innovation: Managing Risk in Government Departments* outlines nine different risk-management tools that could be used to manage risks in government departments and, in each case, identifies the disadvantages of the risk-management tools it discusses (UK NAO 2000).

23 A more extreme position negates the whole attempt to produce an objective measure of risk, arguing that all assessments are inherently subjective (Slovic 1992).

24 Also needed is research that coordinates the website data used in this chapter with other forms of data and that moves onto the important task of investigating in detail the extent to which the rhetoric and ideas about risk-based approaches translate into action.

## References

Bailey, C.W., and D. Petersen. 1989. "Using Safety Surveys to Assess Safety System Effectiveness." *Professional Safety* 2: 22–6.

Basel Committee on Banking Supervision. 2003. *Overview of the New Basel Capital Accord*. www.bis.org/bcbs/cp3ov.pdf.

Bernstein, P. 1996. *Against the Gods: The Remarkable Story of Risk*. New York: John Wiley and Sons.

Braithwaite, J. 1999. "Accountability and Governance under the New Regulatory State." *Australian Journal of Public Administration* 58, no. 1: 90–3.

Breyer, S.G., and C.R. Sunstein. 1998. *Administrative Law and Regulatory Policy: Problems, Text, and Cases*. New York: Aspen Law and Business.

Brown, G. 1997. Commons speech. *Hansard* 294, cols 507–24 (20 May).

Cohen, A. 1996. "Quantitative Risk Assessment and Decisions about Risk." In C. Hood and D. Jones, eds, *Accident and Design*, 87–98. London: University College of London Press.

Dalton, A. 1998. *Safety, Health and Environmental Hazards in the Workplace*. London: Continuum Publishing Group.

European Environment Agency (EEA). 2001. *Late Lessons from Early Warnings: The Precautionary Principle 1896–2000*. Environmental issue report no. 22. Copenhagen. http://reports.eea.eu.int/environmental_issue_report_2001_22/en.

European Union (EU). 1998. *Fifth European Community Environment Programme*. http://europa.eu.int/scadplus/printversion/en/lvb/I28062.htm.

Froud, J., et al. 1998. *Controlling the Regulator*. London: Macmillan.

Hood, C. 1991. "A Public Management for All Seasons." *Public Administration* 69: 3–19.

– and H. Rothstein. 2000. "Business Risk Management in Government: Pitfalls and Possibilities." In United Kingdom, National Audit Office (NAO), *Supporting Innovation: Managing Risk in Government Departments*, Appendix 2. London: HMSO. www.nao.gov.uk/publications/nao_reports/9900864.pdf.

– et al. 2001. *The Government of Risk*. Oxford: Oxford University Press.

– and D. Jones, eds. 1996. *Accident and Design*. London: University College of London Press.

Howlett, M. 1999. "Complex Network Management and the Paradox of Modern Governance: A Taxonomy and Model of Procedural Policy Instrument Choice." Paper presented to the Annual Meeting of the Canadian Political Science Association, University of Sherbrooke.

Hutter, B.M. 1997. *Compliance: Regulation and Environment*. Oxford: Clarendon Press.

– 2001. *Regulation and Risk: Occupational Health and Safety on the Railways*. Oxford: Oxford University Press.

– and P.K. Manning. 1990. "The Contexts of Regulation: Impact on the Health and Safety Inspectorate in Britain." *Law and Policy* 12, no. 2: 103–36.

Lindholm, A. 2002. "Finland in EU Environmental Policy." *The Finnish Environment* Institute (SYKE) Paper 551: www.environment.fi/download.asp?contentid=14545&lan=EN.

Majone, G. 1990. *Deregulation or Reregulation? Regulatory Reform in Europe and in the United States*. London, Pinter.

Osborne, D., and T. Gaebler. 1992. *Reinventing Government: How the Entrepreneurial Spirit Is Transforming the Public Sector*. Reading, MA: Addison-Wesley.

Power, M. 1997. *The Audit Society: Rituals of Verification*. Oxford: Clarendon Press.

– 1999. "The New Risk Management." Inaugural lecture of the P.D. Leake Professor of Accounting and Finance, London School of Economics and Political Science.

Radaelli, C. 2002. "Regulatory Impact Assessment in Comparative Perspective." Paper delivered at the ESRC Future of Governance/CARR Workshop, London School of Economics and Political Science.

Rhodes, R.A.W. 1997. *Understanding Governance: Policy Networks, Governance, Reflexivity and Accountability*. Buckingham, UK: Open University Press.

Salamon, L. 2002. "The New Governance and the Tools of Public Action." In L. Salamon, ed., *The Tools of Government: A Guide to the New Governance*, 1–47. New York: Oxford University Press.

Scott, C. 2000. "Accountability in the Regulatory State." *Journal of Law and Society* 27, no. 1: 38–60.

Slovic, P. 1992. "Perception of Risk: Reflections on the Psychometric Paradigm." In S. Krimsky and D. Golding, eds, *The Social Theories of Risk,* 117–52. Westport, CT: Praeger.

Toft, B. 1996. "Limits to Mathematical Modelling of Disasters." In C. Hood and D. Jones, eds, *Accident and Design,* 99–110. London: University College of London Press.

Uff, J. 2000. *The Southall Accident Inquiry Report.* London, UK: Health and Safety Commission.

Wiener, J., and M. Rogers. 2002. "Comparing Precaution in the United States and Europe." *Journal of Risk Research* (forthcoming): www.env.duke.edu/solutions/documents/pp-eu_us_jrr_2002_03_25.pdf.

## Government Website Information and Publications

Commonwealth of Australia, Australian Prudential Regulatory Authority (APRA). www.apra.gov.au/AboutAPRA.

– Environment Australia. 1999a. *Best Practice Environment in Mining.* In the Environmental Risk Management Series. www.ea.gov.au/industry/sustainable/mining/booklets/erm/index.html.

– Environmental Protection Agency. 1999b. *Environmental Best Practice: Environmental Management in Mining.* www.ea.gov.au/industry/sustainable/mining/booklets/erm/index.html.

German Berufsgenossenschaften. August 2002. www.hvbg.de/e/pages/arbeit.htm.

German Federal Environment Agency, Department of Environment and Health. August 2002. www.umweltbundesamt.de/uba-info-e/e-fach2.htm.

Government of Canada, Office of the Superintendent of Financial Institutions (OSFI). www.osfi-bsif.gc.ca/eng/how/index.asp.

– Department of Finance. 1996. *Canadian Office of the Superintendent of Financial Institutions 1996 Annual Report.* Ottawa: Canadian Government Publishing Directorate. www.fin.gc.ca/afr/1996/afr96e.pdf.

– 2001a. *A Canadian Perspective on the Precautionary Approach/Principle.* Ottawa: Canadian Government Publishing Directorate. www.pcobcp.gc.ca/raoicssrdc/docs/precaution/Discussion/discussion_e.htm.

– Treasury Board of Canada. 2001b. *Integrated Risk Management Framework.* Ottawa: Canadian Government Publishing Directorate. www.tbssct.gc.ca/pubs_pol/dcgpubs/RiskManagement/rmf-cgro11_e.html.

Government of Denmark, Ministry of Environment. 1998. *The Danish Environmental Protection Agency in the Year 2002: Visions and Perspectives for a Developing Agency.* Copenhagen: Danish Environmental Protection Agency. www.mst.dk/homepage.

Government of Finland, Ministry of the Environment. 2002. *Economic Instruments in Finnish Environmental Policy.* Helsinki: Finnish Environmental Administration.
www.vyh.fi/eng/environ/econinst/econotax.htm.

Government of France, Ministry of Environment. 2001. *Report to the Minister of Regional Planning and the Environment.* www.environment.gouv.fr/english/prevent.htm.

– Department for the Prevention of Pollution and Risks. August 2002. www.environnement.gouv.fr/english/prevent.htm.

– Department for Workplace Health and Safety. August 2002. www.santesecurite.travail.gouv.fr/anglais.html.

– Ministry of Environment. August 2002. www.environnement.gouv.fr.

Government of the Netherlands, Ministry of Agriculture, Nature Management, and Fisheries. August 2002. www.minlnv.nl/international/.

United Kingdom, Cabinet Office. 1999. *Modernizing Government.* London: HMSO. www.cabinet-office.gov.uk/moderngov/download/modgov.pdf.

– Cabinet Office. 2002. *Risk: Improving Government's Capability to Handle Risk and Uncertainty.* London: Cabinet Office.

– Department of Energy. 1990. *The Public Inquiry into the Piper Alpha Disaster.* Report by the Hon. Lord Cullen. London: HMSO.

– Financial Services Authority (FSA). 2000. A *New Regulator for the New Millennium.* London: HMSO. www.fsa.gov.uk/pubs/policy/p29.pdf.

– Financial Services Authority (FSA). 2001. *Plan and Budget 2001/00.* London: HMSO. www.fsa.gov.uk/pubs/plan/pb2000_01.pdf.

– Financial Services Authority (FSA). 2002. *Annual Report 2001/02.* London: HMSO. www.fsa.gov.uk/pubs/annual/aroo_01.pdf.

– Health and Safety Commission. 1998. *Annual Report and Accounts 1997/1998.* London: HSE Books.

– Health and Safety Executive (HSE). 1978. *Canvey: An Investigation of Potential Hazards from Operations in the Canvey Island/Thurrock Area.* London: HMSO.

– Health and Safety Executive (HSE). 1988. *The Tolerability of Risk from Nuclear Power Stations.* Rev. ed, London: HMSO, 1992.

– Health and Safety Executive (HSE). 2001. *Reducing Risks, Protecting People.* London: HMSO.

– Interdepartmental Liaison Group on Risk Assessment (ILGRA). 1998. *Risk Assessment and Risk Management: Improving Policy and Practices within Government Departments: Second Report Prepared by the Interdepartmental Liaison Group on Risk Assessment.* London: www.hse.gov.uk/dst/ilgra/minrpt2.htm.

– National Audit Office (NAO). 2000. *Supporting Innovation: Managing Risk in Government Departments.* London: HMSO. www.nao.gov.uk/publications/nao_reports/9900864.pdf.

United States, Congressional Testimony. 3 February 1995. Statement of Joseph A. Dear, Assistant Secretary of Labor for Occupational Safety and Health, for the Hearing of the House Science Committee on Risk Assessment and Title III of H.R. 9. www.osha.gov/pls/oshaweb/owadisp.show_document?p_table=TESTIMONIES&p_id=72&p_text_version=FALSE.

– Congressional Testimony. 4 March 1999. Statement of Charles N. Jeffers, Assistant Secretary for Occupational Safety and Health, US Department of Labor, before the Subcommittee on Employment, Safety, and Training of the Health, Education, Labor, and Pensions Committee, United States Senate. www.osha.gov/pls/oshaweb/owadisp.show_document?p_table=TESTIMONIES&p_id=98&p_text_version=FALSE.

– Department of Labor, Occupational Safety and Health Administration. 1998. Revised OSHA Strategic Plan, FY 1997–FY 2002. "The Changing Workforce and Workplace." www.osha.gov/oshinfo/strategic/toc.html.

– Environmental Protection Agency (EPA), Science Advisory Board. 26 September 1990. "Reducing Risk: Setting Priorities and Strategies for Environmental Protection." EPA press release. www.epa.gov/history/topics/risk/01.htm.

CHAPTER THIRTEEN

1 We adopt the terminology of the rule of law as shorthand for a complex set of ideas relating to both procedural and substantive commitments. We acknowledge that there is no universally accepted manner in which the substantive content of the rule of law can be defined; this content will inevitably depend upon cultural constructs and value preferences. However, the idea is invoked so consistently in domestic and international discourse that it cannot be avoided. For us, "the rule of law" signals a commitment to guiding self-directed human behaviour with reference to rules rather than managing human beings by fiat and reflects the priority of publicly known laws over individual or sectoral interests. Any sophisticated understanding of the rule of law must also include equality of treatment for all subjects of the law, without favours to political, economic, or social elites. While we are intentionally leaving the precise contours of the "rule of law" vague here in the hopes of avoiding some of the deep controversies the term generates, to our minds, interactional legal scholarship that builds on the work of Lon Fuller offers the most persuasive and nuanced understanding of the uses (and misuses) of the term. See J. Brunnée and S. Toope, "International Law and Constructivism: Towards an Interactional Theory of International Law," *Columbia Journal of Transnational Law* 39, no. 11 (2000): 19–74 at 43–64; G. Postema, "Implicit Law," in W. Witteveen and W. van der Burg, eds, *Rediscovering Fuller: Essays on Implicit Law and Institutional Design* (Amsterdam: University of Amsterdam Press, 1999), 255–78; L. Fuller, *Anatomy of the Law* (New York: Mentor Books, 1968).

2 K. Abbott et al., "The Concept of Legalization," *International Organizations* 54, no. 3 (2000): 401–20.

3 On the narrow view of "choice of governing instrument," see R. Macdonald, "The Swiss Army Knife of Governance," ch. 9 herein. See also note 44 below and accompanying text.

4 For an example of an argument that explicitly adopts such an understanding of "legalization" and concludes that instrument choice has indeed been empirically constrained in the context of the so-called "War Against Terror," see D. Jinks, "Legalization of World Politics and the Future of U.S. Human Rights Policy," *St Louis Law Journal* 46, no. 2 (2002): 357–76. Jinks notes that "An increasingly precise body of universally-applicable human rights standards developed through various global associational processes will increasingly constrain the policy options of nation-states. Democratic polities will be governed, in part, by exogenously-defined legal norms" (359).

5 H. Koh, "Paying 'Decent Respect' to World Opinion on the Death Penalty," *University of California Davis Law Review* 35, no. 5 (2002): 1085–1131.

6 For examples of very different challenges that could be raised, see P. Trimble, "Human Rights and Foreign Policy," *St Louis University Law Journal* 46, no. 2 (2002): 465–75, which critiques Koh's liberal approach from a realist perspective for failing to adequately address important domestic political concerns, such as military and economic security; and R. Teitel, "The Future of Human Rights Discourse," *St Louis University Law Journal* 46, no. 2 (2002): 449–61 at 460, which critiques Koh's liberal approach from the opposite end of the political spectrum for masking the role of international law in preserving inequalities in the status quo of economic globalization.

7 See generally, H. Koh, "Bringing International Law Home," *Houston Law Review* 35, no. 3 (1998): 623–81; H. Koh, "Transnational Legal Processes," *Nebraska Law Review* 75, no. 1 (1996): 181–207; and H. Koh, "Why Do Nations Obey International Law?" *Yale Law Journal* 106, no. 8 (1997): 2599–659.

8 This narrow understanding of how law has effects is predicated on the view of "law as constraint" that Pierre Issalys critiques in chapter 7 herein: "From this perspective, the law is viewed, as Pierre Lascoumes suggests, 'less as a constraint than as a resource' – that is, more 'as a system of potentialities from which are deployed specific activities for the mobilization of rules.'"

9 For a detailed critique of the "legalization" literature, see M. Finnemore and S. Toope, "Alternatives to 'Legalization': Richer Views of Law and Politics," *International Organization* 55, no. 3 (2001): 743–58; and J. Brunnée, "Review: Legalization and World Politics. Edited by Judith L. Goldstein, Miles Kahler, Robert O. Keohane, and Anne-Marie Slaughter.

Cambridge, MA: MIT Press, 2001," *Perspectives in Politics* 1, no. 1 (American Political Science Association, 2003): 231. But see, by comparison, J. Goldstein et al., "Response to Finnemore and Toope," *International Organization* 55, no. 3 (2001): 759–60.

10 See E. Lutz and K. Sikkink, "International Human Rights Law and Practice in Latin America," *International Organization* 54, no. 3 (2000): 633–60, which evaluates the effectiveness of norms displaying varying degrees of "legalization," finding that some of the most highly "legalized" norms, particularly the prohibition against torture, have empirically had less of a constraining effect than other less "legalized" norms, such as the principle of democratic governance.

11 For a more detailed discussion, see S. Toope, "Powerful but Unpersuasive? The Role of the United States of America in the Evolution of Customary International Law," in M. Byers and G. Nolte, eds, *United States Hegemony and the Foundations of International Law* (Cambridge: Cambridge University Press, 2003), 287–316.

12 A customary international norm is a binding rule created through the coalescence of state practice (actions, reactions, and failures to act), matched with a so-called *opinio juris* – that is, a belief that the practice is required by law; see I. Brownlie, *Principles of Public International Law*, 5th ed. (New York: Clarendon, 1998), 4–7. Customary international norms continue to predominate in many areas of international law, including state responsibility, legal personality, territory, and the use of force; see Finnemore and Toope, "Alternatives to 'Legalization,'" 746.

13 For a typical statement to this effect, see American Law Institute, *Restatement of the Law (Third), Foreign Relations Law of the United States* (Philadelphia: American Law Institute, 1987): "Modern international law is rooted in acceptance by states which constitute the system. Specific rules of law also depend on state acceptance. Particular agreements create binding obligations for the particular parties, but general law depends on general acceptance. Law cannot be made by the majority for all" (part 1, ch. 1).

14 Such a possibility is rendered much more likely by the fact that the exact moment at which a state practice crystallizes into a customary international law is notoriously difficult to identify. Consider, for instance, the following statement made in a recent and unanimous Supreme Court of Canada decision: "This is the difficulty in interpreting international law; it is often impossible to pinpoint when a norm is generally accepted and [even] to identify who makes up the international community." *Suresh v. Canada (Minister of Citizenship and Immigration)*, [2002] 1 S.C.R. 3 at 38 [*Suresh*].

15 Brownlie, *Principles of Public International Law*, 10; M. Byers, "Custom, Power, and the Power of Customary International Law from an Interdisciplinary Perspective," *Michigan Journal of International Law* 17, no. 1 (1995): 109–80: "Persistent objection is the term used to describe the

option each state has to oppose the development of a new rule of customary international law and to continue opposing that rule once it comes into existence" (163). For a judicial examination of persistent objection, see *Fisheries Case (U.K. v. Nor.)* (Dec. 18), [1951] I.C.J. Rep. 116 at 131, which holds that the UK had not sufficiently objected to the formation of a customary norm to qualify as a persistent objector.

16 See Byers, "Custom," 163–4, which argues that nonobjecting states, state agencies, national courts, and even international courts are reluctant to recognize persistent objection; J. Charney, "The Persistent Objector Rule and the Development of Customary International Law," *British Year Book of International Law* 56, no. 1 (1985): 1–24, which argues that the invocation of the persistent-objection exception is seldom empirically effective and that the exception itself is falling into disuse.

17 See M. Koskenniemi, "The Normative Force of Habit: International Custom and Social Theory," *Finnish Year Book of International Law* 1, no. 1 (1990): 77–153 at 136, which notes that, in most cases, so-called persistent objectors do not in fact object to being bound by a particular customary norm but rather dispute the validity of the claim that a state practice has in fact crystallized into a customary norm.

18 *Case Concerning the Barcelona Traction, Light and Power Company (Belgium v. Spain), Second Phase,* [1970] I.C.J. Rep. 3 at para. 33.

19 See for instance, Convention on the Prevention and Punishment of the Crime of Genocide, 9 December 1948, 78 U.N.T.S. 277, Art. 1 (entered into force 12 January 1951), wherein the contracting parties "confirm that genocide, whether committed in time of peace or in time of war, is a crime under international law which they undertake to prevent and punish."

20 For a fuller discussion, see S. Toope, "Does International Law Impose a Duty on the United Nations to Prevent Genocide?" *McGill Law Journal* 46, no. 1 (2000): 187–95; and O. Schachter, *International Law in Theory and Practice* (Boston: M. Nijhoff Publishers, 1991), 200.

21 B. Simma, "From Bilateralism to Community Interest," *Recueil des Cours* 250, no. 6 (1994): 217–384 at 225–7.

22 J. Brunnée, "COPing with Consent: Lawmaking under Multilateral Environmental Agreements," *Leiden Journal of International Law* 15, no. 1 (2002): 1–52.

23 Toope, "Powerful but Unpersuasive?"

24 T. Szulc, "US Rejects Canadians' Claim to Wide Rights in Arctic Seas," *New York Times*, 10 April 1970, A13; and T. Wills, "U.S. Won't Accept Canadian Claims over Arctic Waters," *(Toronto) Globe and Mail*, 10 April 1970, A1. The Canadian claims were also attacked by several influential members of the American international legal community. See, for example, R. Bidler, "The Canadian Arctic Waters Pollution Prevention Act: New Stresses on the Law of the Sea," Michigan Law Review 69, no. 1 (1970):

1–54 at 25–6; L. Henkin, "Arctic Anti-Pollution: Does Canada Make or Break International Law?" *American Journal of International Law* 65, no. 1 (1971): 131–6 at 134–5.

25 In 1970 the Canadian Parliament passed the Arctic Waters Pollution Prevention Act, R.S.C. 1985, c. A-12 as am. (1970), which amounted to a unilateral – and at the time clearly illegal – extension of Canadian maritime jurisdiction 100 miles into the arctic high seas, ostensibly for the purposes of environmental protection.

26 Despite US objections, a generalized right of coastal states to exercise broad pollution-prevention jurisdiction had been established by the time that states concluded the United Nations' Law of the Sea Convention, UN Conference on the Law of the Sea, Official Records, vol. 17, reprinted in *International Legal Materials* 21, no. 6 (1982): 1261–1354. See generally, A. Gotlieb and C. Dalfen, "National Jurisdiction and International Responsibility: New Canadian Approaches to International Law," *American Journal of International Law* 67, no. 2 (1973): 229–58 at 258; and R. Macdonald et al., "The Canadian Initiative to Establish a Maritime Zone for Environmental Protection," *University of Toronto Law Journal* 21, no. 1 (1971): 247–51 at 250–1.

27 United Nations' Law of the Sea Convention, UN Conference on the Law of the Sea, Official Records, vol. 17.

28 In the early 1970s Canada followed the twentieth-century trend of coastal states expanding their territorial seas from the three-mile limit insisted upon by the United States to the twelve-mile limit. See generally, M. Byers, *Custom, Power and the Power of Rules: International Relations and Customary International Law* (Cambridge: Cambridge University Press, 1999), 114–20. The United States formally objected to this move, as they had to similar extensions by other states; see United States of America, "United States Statement on Canadian Fisheries Closing Lines Announcement," *International Legal Materials* 10, no. 2 (1971): 441. However, their objections did not prevent a customary norm for broader territorial seas from emerging, and ultimately this new norm was codified in the UN's Law of the Sea Convention. See generally, Toope, "Powerful but Unpersuasive?" 309–13; H. Arruda, "The Extension of the United States Territorial Sea: Reasons and Effects," *Connecticut Journal of International Law* 4, no. 3 (1989): 697–727 at 704–5; and S.A. Swarztrauber, *The Three-Mile Limit of Territorial Seas* (Annapolis: Naval Institute Press, 1972), 230–1.

29 In the 1990s the Canadian and Chinese governments instituted a formal bilateral human-rights dialogue in which customary-law norms were routinely raised by Canadian participants.

30 For arguments that the right to self-determination has crystallized into an operable norm of customary international law, see S. Anaya, "Indigenous Rights Norms in Contemporary International Law," *Arizona Journal of In-*

*ternational and Comparative Law* 8, no. 2 (1991): 1–39; W. Bradford,
" 'With a Very Great Blame on Our Hearts': Reparations, Reconciliation,
and an American Indian Plea for Justice," *American Indian Law Revue* 27,
no. 1 (2002): 1–175; T. Franck, "The Emerging Right to Democratic Governance," *American Journal of International Law* 86, no. 1 (1992): 46–91;
F. MacKay, "Universal Rights or a Universe unto Itself? Indigenous Peoples'
Human Rights and the World Bank's Draft Operational Policy 4.10 on Indigenous Peoples," *American University International Law Review* 17,
no. 3 (2002): 527–624; and S. Wiessner, "The Rights and Status of Indigenous Peoples: A Global Comparative and International Legal Analysis,"
*Harvard Human Rights Journal* 12, no. 1 (1999): 57–128.

31 Indeed, Canadian courts have already begun to grapple with this question
in the present. See, for instance, *Delgamuukw v. British Columbia,* [1993]
41 A.C.W.S. (3d) 234 (CA) at 397, wherein the British Columbia Court of
Appeal struggled with the issue of the relation between the common law
and customary international law in relation to First Nations peoples. On
appeal, the Supreme Court of Canada did not directly address this issue; see
*Delgamuukw v. British Columbia,* [1997] 3 S.C.R. 1010.

32 *Mack v. Canada (Attorney General)* (2002), 60 O.R. (3d) 737 (Ont. CA) at
746–50 [*Mack*], wherein plaintiffs argued that racial discrimination in pre-
Second World War Canadian immigration policies violated then existing
customary international law; *Suresh*, Supra note 14, at 57–8, which assesses
whether deporting an alleged terrorist to a country where he or she may
face torture would violate a potential peremptory customary international
norm against "refoulement," the forcible return of someone to the country
from which they claim to be fleeing persecution.

33 N. Gunningham, "Reconfiguring Environmental Regulation," ch. 14
herein.

34 The precautionary principle finds one of its articulations in the Rio Declaration on Environment and Development, UN Conference on Environment
and Development, UN Doc. A/CONF.151/5, reprinted in *International Legal Materials* 31, no. 4 (1992): 874–80. Principle 15 of the Rio Declaration
reads: "Where there are threats of serious or irreversible damage, lack of
full scientific certainty shall not be used as a reason for postponing cost-effective measures to prevent environmental degradation" (879). D. Freestone and E. Hey note that the precautionary principle, in one form or
another, is present "in virtually every recently adopted policy document related to the protection and preservation of the environment"; see D. Freestone and E. Hey, "Origins and Development of the Precautionary
Principle," in D. Freestone and E. Hey, eds, *The Precautionary Principle
and International Law: The Challenge of Implementation* (Boston: Kluwer,
1996), 3–15 at 3. For a discussion of the precautionary principle in judicial
settings, see *114957 Canada Ltée (Spraytech, Société D'Arrosage) v. Hud-*

son (Town), [2001] 2 S.C.R. 241 at 267; and *Southern Bluefin Tuna Cases (N.Z. v. Japan; Austl. v. Japan)* (order of ITLOS, 27 August 1999), www.worldbank.org/icsid/bluefintuna/award080400.pdf.

35 See *Case Concerning the Gabcikovo-Nagymaros Project (Hung. v. Slovk.)*, [1997] I.C.J. Rep. 7 at 88–9 (Separate Opinion of Judge Weeramantry), which holds that principles of intergenerational justice are emerging as international norms. See also V. Lowe, "Sustainable Development and Unsustainable Arguments," in A. Boyle and D. Freestone, eds, *International Law and Sustainable Development: Past Achievements and Future Challenges* (Oxford: Oxford University Press, 1999), 19–39 at 19, which argues that intergenerational equity is too broad to be properly called a norm but that it is a meta-principle that now has a place in judicial reasoning.

36 See generally, P. Alston, "Peoples' Rights: Their Rise and Fall," in P. Alston, ed., *Peoples' Rights* (Oxford: Oxford University Press, 2001), 259–94.

37 Convention on Economic, Social and Cultural Rights, 19 December 1966, Can. T.S. 1976 No. 46.

38 UN Committee on Economic, Social and Cultural Rights, *Consideration of Reports Submitted by States Parties under Articles 16 and 17 of the Covenant*, UN ESCOR, 20th Sess., UN Doc. E/C.12/1/Add.31 (1998). At paragraph 27, "The Committee expresses its grave concern at learning that the Government of Ontario proceeded with its announced 21.6% cuts to social assistance in spite of claims that it would force large numbers of people from their homes."

39 Ibid.: "The Committee is concerned at the crisis level of homelessness among youth and young families [in Canada]" (para. 35).

40 Ibid.: "[T]he Committee views with concern the direct connection between Aboriginal economic marginalization and the ongoing dispossession of Aboriginal people from their lands [in Canada]" (para. 18).

41 See, for instance, *Baker v. Canada (Minister of Citizenship and Immigration)*, [1999] 2 S.C.R. 817 [*Baker*], which overturns a decision by Canadian immigration officials to deport a permanent resident with several children based partially on international norms regarding the interests and needs of children even though these norms had not been explicitly incorporated into Canadian law through legislation.

42 For a more comprehensive analysis, see J. Brunnée and S. Toope, "A Hesitant Embrace: The Application of International Law by Canadian Courts," *Canadian Year Book of International Law* 1 (2002): 3–60.

43 Broadly speaking, "transformation" means the mechanism through which an international treaty obligation is made binding within a domestic system of law. See generally, R. Macdonald, "The Relationship between International Law and Domestic Law in Canada," in R. Macdonald, G. Morris, and D. Johnston, eds, *Canadian Perspectives on International Law and Organization* (Toronto: University of Toronto Press, 1974), 88–136. For a

typical judicial articulation of this principle, see *Francis v. The Queen,*
[1956] S.C.R. 618, which states that "treaty provisions affecting matters
within the scope of municipal law, that is, which purport to change existing
law or restrict the future action of the legislature ... in the absence of a constitutional provision declaring the treaty itself to be law of the state ... must
be supplemented by statutory action" (626).

44 M. Trebilcock et al., *The Choice of Governing Instrument* (Ottawa: Minister of Supply and Services Canada, 1982), wherein it is stated that "We
need to understand the constraints under which policy makers (especially
politicians) choose instruments of intervention, so that recommendations
for reform designed to effect a different matching of objectives and instruments either recognize or change those constraints" (101).

45 *Daniels v. White and The Queen,* [1968] S.C.R. 517 at 541. For a recent restatement of the vitality of this doctrine, see *Schreiber v. Canada (Attorney
General),* [2002] 3 S.C.R. 269 at para. 50 [*Schreiber*]. See also R. Sullivan,
*Driedger on the Construction of Statutes,* 3rd ed. (Markham, ON: Butterworths, 1994), 330.

46 See *Baker,* Supra note 41, at para. 80 (Iacobucci and Cory JJ. express this
concern in their concurring judgment). But see D. Dyzenhaus et al., "The
Principle of Legality in Administrative Law: Internationalisation as Consti-
tutionalisation," *Oxford University Commonwealth Law Journal* 1, no. 5
(2001): 5–34, which contests these commonly expressed concerns regarding
the legitimacy of reference to international norms in the judicial review of
the exercise of executive authority.

47 Brunnée and Toope, "A Hesitant Embrace."

48 Ibid. See also *Re Reference by Governor in Council concerning Certain
Questions relating to Secession of Quebec from Canada* (1998), 161
D.L.R. (4th) 385 at 433 [*Secession Reference*], wherein the Court appears
to state that all international norms, ranging from customary law to treaties ratified by Canada and declarations of intergovernmental organizations and assemblies, operate as mere "considerations" rather than as
binding law.

49 In *Pfizer v. Canada,* [1999] 4 F.C. 441 (T.D.), the Federal Court held that
referential incorporation of the World Trade Organization (WTO) Agreement (cast as approval of the treaty) did not constitute "transformation."
However, in *R. v. Crown Zellerbach Canada Ltd,* [1988] 1 S.C.R. 401, the
Supreme Court relied on mere statutory references to an international
treaty in order to interpret the "purposes" of an Act that did not expressly
seek to transform the treaty.

50 See *R. v. Hydro-Québec,* [1997] 3 S.C.R. 213, wherein the Court gives in-
terpretive weight to a preambular statement in environmental legislation
that makes reference to Canada's international environmental obligations.

51 See Sullivan, *Driedger on the Construction of Statutes,* 330.

52 See, for example, Canada, Senate Standing Committee on Human Rights, *Promises to Keep: Implementing Canada's Human Rights Obligations* (Ottawa: Standing Committee on Human Rights, 2001), which acknowledges that the practice of ratification on the basis of prior conformity has rendered the application in Canada of international human-rights norms uncertain.

53 International Covenant on Civil and Political Rights, 19 December 1966, 999 U.N.T.S. 171 (entered into force 23 March 1976).

54 Human Rights Committee, *Consideration of reports submitted by states under Article 40 of the Covenant: Fourth periodic report of States parties due in 1995: Canada,* UN CCPROR, 1995, UN Doc. CCPR/C/103/Add.5; see Office of the United Nations High Commissioner for Human Rights at www.unhchr.ch/tbs/doc.nsf/(Symbol)/CCPR.C.135.En?Opendocument.

55 See, for example, P. Hogg, *Constitutional Law of Canada,* 4th ed. (Scarborough: Thomson, Carswell, 1997), §11.4(a), which states that "Canada's constitutional law ... does not recognize a treaty as part of the internal ... law of Canada. Accordingly, a treaty which requires a change in the internal law of Canada can only be implemented by the enactment of a statute which makes the required change in the law."

56 See *Ahani v. Canada* (2002), 58 O.R. (3d) 197 (CA), wherein the Court held that because the International Covenant on Civil and Political Rights and its Optional Protocol had not been implemented in Canada through specific legislation, individuals did not enjoy any direct legal entitlements in Canada flowing from these instruments; and *Baker,* Supra note 41, wherein the majority and concurring judgments diverged only on the question of whether treaties that had not been implemented through direct and specific legislation could play any role whatsoever in the domestic legal system.

57 See, for example, *Saint John (City) v. Fraser-Brace Overseas Corp.,* [1958] S.C.R. 263, wherein the Court seems to favour [author] direct incorporation; *Schreiber,* Supra note 45, at paras 48 to 50, which suggests that customary law is relevant to the interpretation of domestic law and that *jus cogens* norms not only oust ordinary customary norms but are directly applicable within domestic law; and *Mack,* Supra note 32, at 750, which treats all customary law as directly applicable unless ousted by contrary domestic legislation.

58 See *Congo v. Venne,* [1971] S.C.R. 997, wherein changes to customary law were held not to operate automatically within Canadian law; *Reference Re Mining and Other Natural Resources of the Continental Shelf,* (1983) 41 Nfld. & P.E.I.R. 271 (Nfld. C.A.), wherein the Court implicitly required transformation of customary law.

59 *Reference re Powers of Ottawa (City) & Rockcliffe Park (Village) to Levy Rates on Foreign Legations and High Commissioners Residences,* [1943] S.C.R. 208 [*Re Foreign Legations*].

60 See Macdonald, "The Relationship," 109.

61 *The Paquette Habana* (1900), 175 U.S. 688, being the seminal case wherein the Court stated that "International law is part of our law, and must be ascertained and administered by the Courts of Justice of appropriate jurisdiction, as often as questions of right depending upon it are fully presented for their determination. For this purpose, where there is no treaty and no controlling executive or legislative act or judicial decision, resort must be had to the customs and usages of civilized nations" (700). It must be noted, however, that this doctrine has been severely curtailed in subsequent case law.

62 *Trendtex Trading Corp. v. Nigeria (Central Bank)*, [1977] 1 Q.B. 529 (C.A.), wherein Lord Denning famously held that, where appropriate, customary international law operates directly within the domestic legal system to affect the obligations of the state and of private entities.

63 *Bouzari v. Islamic Republic of Iran* (30 June 2004), Docket: C38295 (Ont. C.A.) at para 65.

64 See *Ekiu v. United States* (1892), 142 U.S. 651, wherein the US Supreme Court stated: "It is an accepted maxim of international law, that every sovereign nation has the power, as inherent in sovereignty, and essential to self-preservation, to forbid the entrance of foreigners within its dominions, or to admit them only in such cases and upon such conditions as it may see fit to prescribe" (659); and E. de Vattel, *The Law of Nations*, ed. J. Chitty (Philadelphia: T. and J.W. Johnson, 1853), 169–70: "The sovereign may forbid the entrance of his territory either to foreigners in general, or in particular cases, or to certain persons, or for certain particular purposes, according as he may think it advantageous to the state. There is nothing in all this that does not flow from the rights of domain and sovereignty." It is worth noting that that this view continues to hold much sway. Indeed, both of the above two references have been cited with approval in a recent Supreme Court decision: *Mitchell v. M.N.R.,* [2001] 1 S.C.R. 911 at 990.

65 Consider, to name only two controversial Supreme Court decisions in this area: *United States v. Burns*, [2001] 1 S.C.R. 283 [*Burns*], wherein the Court refused, partly on the basis that developing international norms regarding the illegitimacy of the death penalty should shape judicial interpretations of "fundamental justice" in Section 7 Charter cases, to uphold the extradition of an individual to the United States in a capital case in the absence of assurances that the United States would not seek to exercise the death penalty; and *Baker,* Supra note 41, which overturns a decision by Canadian immigration officials to deport a permanent resident with several children based partially on international norms regarding the importance of the interests and needs of children even though these norms had not been explicitly incorporated into Canadian law through legislation.

66 See *Baker*, Supra note 41: "Considerable deference should be accorded im-migration officers exercising their powers" (857); *Burns*, Supra note 65: "The customary deference to the Minister's extradition decisions is rooted in the recognition of Canada's strong interest in international law enforce-ment activities" (312); *Kindler v. Canada (Minister of Justice)*, [1991] 2 S.C.R. 779: "[T]he court must be 'extremely circumspect' to avoid undue interference with an area [i.e., extradition] where the executive is well placed to make these sorts of decisions" (849); and *Suresh*, Supra note 14: "The threshold finding of whether Suresh faces a substantial risk of torture [if he is deported] ... attracts deference by the reviewing court to the Minis-ter's decision" (28).

67 *Secession Reference,* Supra note 48. For an investigation into the interna-tional effects of the *Secession Reference*, see M. Walters, "Nationalism and the Pathology of Legal Systems: Considering the *Quebec Secession Refer-ence* and its lessons for the United Kingdom," *Modern Law Review* 62, no. 3 (1999): 371–96, which notes that the *Secession Reference* has served to develop a normative framework whereby governments are reminded that "their conduct in relation to secessionist claims should be governed by basic unwritten legal rules and principles relating to democracy, the rule of law, and respect for national identities and minority rights" (396).

68 For an attempt to increase the international effects of such norms, see Koh, "Paying 'Decent Respect.' "

69 For a discussion of the role of these types of analyses in contributing to a rich constitutional interaction between courts and the legislatures that helps both to develop the sophisticated substantive content of the Charter and to enhance its perceived legitimacy, see J. Hibert, *Charter Conflicts: What Is Parliament's Role?* (Montreal and Kingston: McGill-Queen's University Press, 2002). But for a very different – although to our minds somewhat court-centric – understanding of these analyses as legislative attempts to "charter-proof" legislation and hence to effectively preclude interbranch constitutional "dialogue," see K. Roach, "The Dangers of a Charter-Proof and Crime-Based Response to Terrorism," in R. Daniels et al., eds, *The Se-curity of Freedom: Essays on Canada's Anti-Terrorism Bill* (Toronto, Uni-versity of Toronto Press, 2001), 131–50.

70 See the description of the "Trade Law Division" of the Department of Jus-tice and its joint mandate with DFAIT at www.infosource.gc.ca/Info_1/pdf/iso49e00.pdf.

71 Macdonald, "The Swiss Army Knife of Governance." Our interactional view of the rule of law leads us to agree with Macdonald when he states that "Prescriptively ... governance is taken to be the endeavour of identi-fying and managing both aspiration and action in a manner that affirms and promotes human agency". See our discussion of the rule of law at note 1.

CHAPTER FOURTEEN

1   Part of this chapter was first published in Gunningham and Sinclair 2002. Other parts are drawn from an ongoing research project on Regulatory Design for Urban Water Quality, supported by the Australian Research Council.

2   These costs are between 1 and 2 per cent of gross domestic product.

3   Reflexive law, in Teubner's (1983) terminology, is a form of law using indirect means to achieve broad social goals, being a distinct shift from the previous approach (material law), which has broad goals but uses specific direct means to achieve these goals. Material law, according to Teubner, has largely failed because the complexity of modern society cannot be matched by a legal system of comparable complexity capable of harnessing direct, goal-seeking law in order to accommodate social goals.

4   As defined in note 3 above.

5   For an excellent analysis of the alternative and much more reflexive regime that evolved in the aftermath of Three-Mile Island, see Rees 1994.

6   This concept is further developed in Parker 1999a and 1999b and in Braithwaite and Williams 2001.

7   For a development of this concept, see Orts 1995.

8   Civil society is conventionally defined as involving "citizens acting collectively in a public sphere to express their interests, passions, and ides, exchange information, achieve mutual goals, make demands on the state, and hold public officials accountable. Civil society is an intermediary entity, standing between the private sphere and the state" (Diamond 1996).

9   The term is used *not* to imply the use of civil rather than criminal law but as a variant of "civil society."

10  For example, a highly successful Greenpeace campaign has been largely responsible for sensitizing European consumers (particularly in Germany and the UK) to the clear-felling of old-growth forests. This has had a profound impact upon North American companies exporting to these markets, who are increasingly being pressured by European buyers to provide evidence that the timber they supply has come from sustainably harvested sources.

11  See also Gamble and Ku 2000.

12  For an overview of the literature on ecological modernization, see Mol and Sonnenfeld 2000. See also "Ecological Modernization: Citizenship and Ecological Modernization in the Information Society," *Futures* 33, special issue (April/May 2000).

13  See for example Commoner 1972 and O'Connor 1996.

14  For a more nuanced statement of this position, see Mol and Sonnenfeld 2000.

15  For an excellent overview see Buttel 2000.

16  See generally Gunningham 1994a.

17 For example, Porter and van der Linde's (1995) argument is that a well-designed regulatory system can foster innovation by concentrating on outcomes (i.e., performance standards) rather than on techniques (i.e., specification- or technology-based standards). This is because performance standards free up an enterprise to respond to a regulator's requirement in the way that best suits the enterprise.

18 For an excellent summary of the recent literature on these issues, see Parker 2000.

19 For example, there may be considerable win-win opportunities in relation to SMEs (there is much low-hanging fruit of which to take advantage), and an important contribution can be made by mechanisms that seek out cleaner production and eco-efficiency opportunities.

20 The evidence suggests that the range of circumstances where it is possible for enterprises to benefit both the environment and their own economic bottom line (even with certain policy interventions) is more limited than many ecological-modernization theorists and their fellow travellers have claimed. Many of the best essays on this debate, couched mainly in terms of Porter's 1990 "green gold" hypothesis, are contained in *Harvard Business Review on Business and the Environment* 2000. See also Newton and Harte 1997; Howes et al. 1997, 86; and Reinhardt 2000.

21 Such facilities are extremely complex and demonstrably beyond the reach of rule-based regulation. Policy makers have relied instead on the use of risk- and environmental-management systems and on internal self-control, with apparent success. After the Three Mile Island near meltdown, the nuclear-safety regime in the US shifted from rule-based regulation to a new paradigm, which Braithwaite and Drahos (2000) characterize as regulatory scrutiny of risk-management systems and shaming within the community of nuclear-power companies that failed to improve their systems. Within a decade safety-related automatic shut-downs of nuclear plants (SCRAMS) fell seven fold. See also Rees 1994.

22 For example, the most effective means of dealing with highly hazardous pesticides may be simply to ban their use. Again, reflexive regulation can only play a minor role in curbing the environmental excesses of small and medium-sized enterprises, perhaps in terms of simplified EMSs.

23 Environmental partnerships are much more likely to flourish in situations where there is a genuine commonality of interest between the environment and economic interests. Where this commonality does not exist, these partnerships may only be credible when underpinned by the threat of direct intervention if the partnership fails to achieve specified public-interest objectives.

24 Indeed, apart from regulatory pluralism (which almost by definition is catholic in its approach), each has only a limited sphere in which it is likely to be effective.

25 For example, it has been pointed out that voluntary approaches, "while enjoying a resurgence ... in fact represent the dominant approach throughout
history. Self-regulation was the norm prior to the 1970s, and its failure was
the reason we started regulating in the first place" (Andrews 1998, 179).

26 Note that the US EPA's Office of Enforcement and Compliance Assurance,
through its National Performance Measures Strategy, is developing a measurement framework of outputs, outcomes, and environmental indicators;
see http://es.epa.gov/oeca/perfmeas.

27 The main value of the database is derived from its use as a tool for regulators. By enabling them to estimate the level of compliance, the database assists regulators in focusing their resources on areas where intervention is
most needed, thereby facilitating better processing and monitoring of permits. In the future, the database will be accessible to the public and will
therefore also facilitate CRTK. In the European Union the value of such systems is likely to be increased by a number of current initiatives. In particular, the European Commission has determined that member states must
identify installations/discharges falling within the scope of the Integrated
Pollution Prevention and Control Directive, collect information on emis-
sions/discharges from these installations/facilities, and report all necessary
information to the Commission; see, in particular, Hietamaki 2000a and
2000b and Koski 2000.

## References

Andrews, R.N.L. 1998. "Environmental Regulation and Business 'Self Regulation.'" *Policy Sciences* 31: 177–97.

Antweiler, W., and K. Harrison. 1999. *Environmental Regulation vs Environmental Information: A View from Canada's National Pollutant Release
Inventory.* Washington, DC: Association for Public Policy Analysis and Management.

Baylis, R., L. Cornnell, and A. Flynn. 1998. "Sector Variation and Ecological
Modernization: Towards an Analysis at the Level of the Firm." *Business
Strategy and the Environment* 7: 150–61.

Bendell, J. 2000. "Civil Regulation: A New Form of Democratic Governance
for the Global Economy." In J. Bendall, ed., *Terms of Endearment: Business,
NGOs and Sustainable Development,* 239–54. London, UK: Greenleaf.

Braithwaite, J., and P. Drahos. 2000. *Global Business Regulation.* Cambridge,
UK: Cambridge University Press.

– and R. Williams. 2001. *Meta Risk Management and Tax System Integrity.*
Canberra: Centre for Tax System Integrity.

British Columbia Ministry of Environment, Land and Parks, Environment and
Resource Management Pollution Prevention Compendium. www.env.gov.bc.ca/
epd/cpr/regs/pcrsprat.html.

Buttel, F.H. 2000. "Ecological Modernization as Social Theory." *Geoforum* 31: 57–65.

Clinton, W.J., and A. Gore, Jr. 1995. *Reinventing Environmental Regulation.* Washington, DC: White House.

Cohen, M.J. 1997. "Risk Society and Ecological Modernisation." *Futures* 29, no. 2: 105–19.

Commoner, B. 1972. *The Closing Circle: Nature, Man and Technology.* New York: Bantam Books.

Cullen, Lord, chairman. 1990. *Piper Alpha Inquiry.* London, UK: HMSO.

Diamond, L. 1996. "Towards Democratic Consolidation." In L. Diamond and M. Platter, eds, *The Global Resurgence of Democracy.* Baltimore, MD: Johns Hopkins University Press.

"Ecological Modernization: Citizenship and Ecological Modernization in the Information Society." 2000. *Futures* 33, nos 3–4, special issue (April/May).

ENDS Report. 1997. "DoE Rediscovered Business Benefits of Environmental Policy." *ENDS Report* 226: 24.

Fiorino, D. 1999. "Rethinking Environmental Regulation: Perspectives from Law and Governance." *Harvard Environmental Law Review* 23, no. 2: 441–69.

Foulon, J., P. Lanouie, and B. Laplante. 1999. *Incentives for Pollution Control: Regulation and (?) or (?) Information.* Policy research working paper. Washington, DC: World Bank.

Fung, A., and D. O'Rourke. 2000. "Reinventing Environmental Regulation from the Grassroots Up: Explaining and Expanding the Success of the Toxics Release Inventory." *Environmental Management* 25, no. 2 (February): 115–27.

Gamble, J.K., and C. Ku. 2000. "International Law: New Actors and New Technologies: Center Stage for NGOs?" *Law and Policy in International Business* 31: 221–62.

Gereffi, G., R. Garcia-Johnson, and E. Sass. 2001. "The NGO-Industry Complex." *Foreign Policy* (July/August): www.foreignpolicy.Council of Ministers/_issue julyaug_2001/gereffi.html.

Grabosky, P. 1995. "Using Non-Government Resources to Foster Regulatory Compliance." *Law and Policy* 17, no. 3: 256–81.

Gunningham, N. 1991. "Private Ordering, Self-Regulation and Futures Markets: A Comparative Study of Informal Social Control." *Law and Policy* 13, no. 4: 297–326.

– 1994a. "Beyond Compliance: Management of Environmental Risk." In B. Boer, R. Fowler, and N. Gunningham, eds, *Environmental Outlook: Law and Policy,* 254–82. Sydney: Federation Press.

– and A. Cornwall. 1994b. "Legislating the Right to Know." *Environmental Law and Planning Journal* 11, no. 4: 274–88.

– and P. Grabosky. 1998. *Smart Regulation: Designing Environmental Policy.* Oxford, UK: Oxford University Press.

– P. Grabosky, and M. Phillipson. 1999a. "Harnessing Third Parties as Surrogate Regulators: Achieving Environmental Outcomes by Alternative Means." *Business Strategy and the Environment* 8, no. 4: 211–29.
– and D. Sinclair. 1999b. "Integrative Regulation: A Principle-Based Approach to Environmental Policy." *Law and Social Inquiry* 24, no. 4: 853–96.
– and D. Sinclair. 1999c. "Regulatory Pluralism: Designing Environmental Policy Mixes." *Law and Policy* 21, no. 1: 49–76.
– and D. Sinclair. 2001. *Environmental Partnerships: Combining Commercial Advantage and Sustainability in the Agriculture Sector*. Canberra, Australia: Rural Industries Research and Development Corporation.
– and D. Sinclair. 2002. *Leaders and Laggards: Next Generation Environmental Regulation*. Sheffield, UK: Greenleaf.
– R. Kagan, and D. Thornton. 2003. *Shades of Green: Business, Regulation and Environment*. Stanford, CA: Stanford University Press.
– and D. Sinclair. 2004. "Curbing Non-Point Source Pollution: Lessons from the Swan Canning." *Environment and Planning Law Journal* 21: 181–99.
– and D Sinclair. Forthcoming. "Regulating Non-Point Source Pollution from Agriculture." *Environmental and Planning Law Journal*.
Hart, S.L. 1997. "Strategies for a Sustainable World." *Harvard Business Review* 75, no. 1 (January/February): 66–76.
*Harvard Business Review on Business and the Environment*. 2000. New York: Harvard Business School Press.
Henriques, I. and P. Sadorsky. 1995. *The Determinants of an Environmentally Responsive Firm: An Empirical Approach*. Toronto: Faculty of Administrative Studies, York University.
Hietamake, M. 2000a. "Why to Build EIS." In M. Rapp and W. Hafner, eds, *IMPEL 2000 Conference on Environmental Compliance and Enforcement, Villach, Austria, 11–13 October 2000: Final Report*, 71–2. European Union, Environment Directorate, http://europa.eu.int/comm/environment/impel/conference_report.pdf.
– 2000b. "Needs and Plans to Further Develop EIS." In M. Rapp and W. Hafner, eds, *IMPEL 2000 Conference on Environmental Compliance and Enforcement, Villach, Austria, 11–13 October 2000: Final Report*, 76–7. European Union, Environment Directorate, http://europa.eu.int/comm/environment/impel/conference_report.pdf.
Howes, R.J., J. Skea, and B. Whelan. 1997. *Clean and Competitive? Environmental Performance in Industry*. London: Earthscan Publications.
Koch, C., and K. Nielsen. 1996. *Working Environment Regulation: How Reflexive, How Political? A Scandinavian Case*. Working paper. Lyngby, Denmark: Technical University of Denmark.
Koski, O. 2000. "Presentation on the Finnish VAHTI-System: Database, Emission, Discharge, Waste, Air and Water Quality Monitoring." In M. Rapp and W. Hafner, eds, *IMPEL 2000 Conference on Environmental Compliance*

*and Enforcement, Villach, Austria, 11–13 October 2000: Final Report,* 74–8. European Union, Environment Directorate, http://europa.eu.int/ comm/environment/impel/conference_report.pdf.

Lanoie, P., B. Laplante, and M. Roy. 1997. *Can Capital Markets Create Incentives for Pollution Control?* Washington, DC: Policy Research Department, World Bank.

Long, F.J., and M.B. Arnold. 1994. *The Power of Environmental Partnerships.* Fort Worth: Dryden Press.

Mol, A.P.J. 1995. *The Refinement of Production.* Utrecht: Van Arkel.

– and D.A. Sonnerfeld. 2000 "Ecological Modernisation around the World: An Introduction." *Environmental Politics* 9, no. 1 (Spring): 3–14.

Murphy, D., and J. Bendell. 1997. *In the Company of Partners.* Bristol, UK: Policy Press.

– and J. Bendell. 1998. "Editorial." *Greener Management International* (Winter): 8.

Newton, T., and G. Harte. 1997. "Green Business: Technicist Kitsch?" *Journal of Management Studies* 23, no. 1: 75–98.

O'Conner, J. 1996. "The Second Contradiction of Capitalism." In T. Benton, ed., *The Greening of Marxism.* New York: Guilford.

O'Rourke, D. 2000. *Monitoring the Monitors: A Critique of Pricewaterhouse-Coopers (PWC) Labor Monitoring.* Massachusetts: Department of Urban Studies and Planning, Massachusetts Institute of Technology.

Orts, W.E. 1995. "Reflexive Environmental Law." *Northwestern University Law Review* 89, no. 4: 1227–1340.

Osborne, D., and T. Gaebler. 1992. *Reinventing Government: How the Entrepreneurial Spirit Is Transforming the Public Sector.* Boston: Addison-Wesley.

Parker, C. 1999a. "Evaluating Regulatory Compliance: Best Practice and Standards." *Trade Practices Law Journal* 7, no. 2: 62–73.

– 1999b. *Just Lawyers.* Oxford, UK: Oxford University Press.

– 2000. "Summary of the Scholarly Literature on Regulatory Compliance." Annex to *Reducing the Risk of Policy Failure: Challenges for Regulatory Compliance.* Working paper 77. Paris: Organization for Economic Cooperation and Development (OECD).

Poncelet, E. 1999. "In Search of the 'Win-Win': Possibilities and Limitations of Multi-Stakeholder Environmental Partnerships." Paper presented at the conference "Greening of Industry," University of North Carolina at Chapel Hill.

– Forthcoming. "A Kiss Here and a Kiss There: Conflict and Collaboration in Environmental Partnerships." *Environmental Management.*

Porter, M. 1990. *The Competitive Advantage of Nations.* London: Macmillan.

– 1998. "How Competitive Forces Shape Strategy." In H. Mintzberg, J.B. Quinn, and S. Goshal, *The Strategy Process,* 60–9. Bath, UK: Prentice Hall.

– and C. van der Linde. 1995. "Green and Competitive: Ending the Stalemate." *Harvard Business Review* 73, no. 5 (September/October): 120–34.

Rapp, M., G. Wolschner, and W. Hafner, eds. 2000. *European Union Network on the Implementation and Enforcement of Environmental Law Conference on Environmental Compliance and Enforcement*. Final report. Villach, Austria: Klagenfurt, Flatschacherstrasse 70.

Rees, J.V. 1988. *Reforming the Workplace: A Study of Self-Regulation in Occupational Safety*. Philadelphia: University of Pennsylvania Press.

– 1994. *Hostages of Each Other: The Transformation of Nuclear Safety since Three Mile Island*. Chicago: University of Chicago Press.

Reinhardt, R. 2000. *Down to Earth*. Massachusetts: Harvard Business School Press.

Schmidheiny, S. 1992. *Changing Courses*. Massachusetts: MIT Press.

– and F. Zorraquin. 1996. *Financing Change: The Financial Community, Eco-Efficiency and Sustainable Development*. Massachusetts: MIT Press.

Smart, B., ed. 1992. *Beyond Compliance: A New Industry View of the Environment*. Washington, DC: World Resources Institute.

Teubner, G. 1983. "Substantive and Reflexive Elements in Modern Law." *Law and Society Review* 17: 239–85.

– L. Farmer, and D. Murphy, eds. 1994. *Environmental Law and Ecological Responsibility: The Concept and Practice of Ecological Self-organization*. Chichester, UK: Wiley.

United States Environmental Protection Agency (EPA). 2000. *A Decade of Progress: Innovation at the Environmental Protection Agency*. EPA Innovation Annual Report. Washington DC: EPA.

## CONCLUSION

1 For a discussion of the independence of these forms of success and failure, see Bovens, 't Hart, and Peters 2000. See also Peters 2002 on the political impact of instrument choice.

2 The desire of the Department of Justice in Canada to move beyond its traditional commitment to legal instruments and regulation was part of the motivation for the conference giving rise to this book, indicating its desire to develop a broader repertoire of tools for government action.

3 This approach is referred to as "lexicographic preferencing" in decision theory.

4 In reality most policy choices have an element of experimentation (Campbell 1969; Dunn 1998), and given the relatively poor level of knowledge we have about most policy areas, even with the spate of interest in "evidence-based" policy making, we are arguably well advised to consider most of our interventions into complex social and economic processes to be in essence experimental efforts.

5 This experiment involved altering the amount and type of benefits given to a large number of social-welfare recipients. The purpose was to

find a mix of benefits and work incentives that would maximize the incomes of these recipients.

6 The Future Governance Program in the United Kingdom, funded by the Economic and Social Research Council, is an attempt to institutionalize the process of learning about which policy instruments are effective. The scholarly success of the program appears substantial, but the question remains of how well the learning can be brought to bear on governance.

## References

Bendor, J. 1985. *Parallel Systems: Redundancy in Government.* Berkeley: University of California Press.

Bovens, M.A.P., P. 't Hart, and B.G. Peters. 2000. *Success and Failure in Public Governance.* Cheltenham: Edward Elgar.

Brown, N. 2002. "Loans for Student Support in Higher Education: The UK Experience." In M. Fletcher, ed., *Loans for Lifetime Learning.* London: Learning and Skills Development Agency.

Campbell, D.T. 1969. "Reforms as Experiments." *The American Psychologist* 24: 409–29.

Cook, T.D., and D.T. Campbell. 1979. *Quasi-Experimentation: Design and Analysis for Field Situations.* Chicago: Rand-McNally.

Dolowitz, D. 1998. *Learning from America: Policy Transfer and the Development of British Workfare State.* Portland, OR: Sussex Academic Press.

Dror, Y. 2001. *The Capacity to Govern.* London: Frank Cass.

Dunn, W.N. 1998. *The Experimenting Society.* New Brunswick, NJ: Transaction Books.

Frederickson, H.G. 1997. *The Spirit of Public Administration.* San Francisco: Jossey-Bass.

Héritier, A. 2002. "New Modes of Governance in Europe: Policy-Making Without Legislating?" In A. Héritier, ed., *Common Goods: Reinventing European and International Governance.* London: Rowman and Littlefield.

Hjern, B., and D.O. Porter. 1981. "Implementation Structures: A New Unit of Administrative Analysis." *Organisation Studies* 2: 211–24.

Hood, C. 1986. *The Tools of Government.* Chatham, NJ: Chatham House.

Howard, C. 1997. *The Hidden Welfare State: Tax Expenditures in the United States.* Princeton, NJ: Princeton University Press.

Howlett, M. 1991. "Policy Instruments, Policy Styles and Policy Implementation: National Approaches to Theories of Instrument Choice." *Policy Studies Journal* 19: 1–21.

Kettl, D. 2002. "Managing Indirect Government." In L.M. Salamon, ed., *The Tools of Government.* New York: Oxford University Press.

Kirschen, E.S. 1964. *Economic Policy in Our Time.* Amsterdam: North-Holland.

Komesar, N.K. 1994. *Imperfect Alternatives: Choosing Institutions in Law, Economics and Public Policy*. Chicago: University of Chicago Press.

Landau, M. 1969. "Redundancy, Rationality and the Problem of Duplication and Overlap." *Public Administration Review* 29: 346–58.

Linder, S.H., and B.G. Peters. 1984. "From Social Theory to Policy Design." *Journal of Public Policy* 4: 237–59.

– and B.G. Peters. 1998. "Contingency and Choice in the Study of Policy Instruments." In B.G. Peters and F.K.M. van Nispen, eds, *Public Policy Instruments: Evaluating the Tools of Public Administration*. Cheltenham: Edward Elgar.

Loomis, B. 2000. "The Politics of Vouchers." In C.E. Steuerle et al., *Vouchers and the Provision of Public Services*. Washington, DC: Brookings Institution.

Lynn, L.E. 2001. "The Myth of the Bureaucratic Paradigm: What Traditional Public Administration Really Stood For." *Public Administration Review* 61: 144–60.

Mörth, U. 2003. *Soft Law in Governance and Regulation: An Interdisciplinary Approach*. Cheltenham: Edward Elgar.

Peters, B.G. 2000a. "Linking Policy Instruments and Management." *Journal of Public Administration Research and Theory* 10: 35–84.

– 2000b. "The Politics of Policy Instruments." In L.M. Salamon, ed., *The Handbook of Policy Instruments*. New York: Oxford University Press.

– and K.M.F. van Nispen. 1998. *Public Policy Instruments: Evaluating the Tools of Public Administration*. Cheltenham: Edward Elgar.

Pierre, J., and B.G. Peters. 2000. *Governance, Public Policy and the State*. Basingstoke: Palgrave.

Pollack, M. 2003. *The Engines of European Integration: Delegation, Agency and Agenda Setting in the EU*. Oxford: Oxford University Press.

Rose, R. 1992. *Lesson Drawing in Public Policy*. Chatham, NJ: Chatham House.

Salamon, L.M., ed. 2000. *The Handbook of Policy Instruments*. New York: Oxford University Press.

– ed. 2002. *The Tools of Government*. New York: Oxford University Press.

Schuck, P. 2002. "Tort Liability." In L.M. Salamon, ed., *The Tools of Government*. New York: Oxford University Press.

Steuerle, C.E., et al. 2000. *Vouchers and the Provision of Public Services*. Washington, DC: Brookings Institution.

Sorenson, E., and J. Torfing. 2002. "Network Politics, Political Capital and Democracy." *International Journal of Public Administration* 26: 609–34.

Sparrow, M.K. 1994. *Imposing Duties*. New York: Praeger.

Woodside, K. 1986. "Policy Instruments and the Study of Public Policy." *Canadian Journal of Political Science* 19: 775–9.

# Index